11/85

MEMORY
AND
THE BRAIN

In this world some sow and others reap.
Nor can we reap the fruit of our own labors;
what we gather is chiefly the result of the toil of others.
While we reap the harvest of their sowing,
let us be content to sow in our turn that others
who come after us may have their gathering.

Alban Goodier

MEMORY
AND
THE BRAIN

Magda B. Arnold

 LAWRENCE ERLBAUM ASSOCIATES, PUBLISHERS
1984   Hillsdale, New Jersey   London

Lawrence Erlbaum Associates, Inc., Publishers
365 Broadway
Hillsdale, New Jersey 07642

Library of Congress Cataloging in Publication Data

Arnold, Magda B.
  Memory and the brain.

  Bibliography: p.
  Includes indexes.
  1. Memory. 2. Brain—Localization of functions.
3. Neural circuitry. 4. Memory, Disorders of.
5. Neuropsychology—Philosophy. I. Title. [DNLM:
1. Brain—Physiology. 2. Memory—Physiology. 3. Neural
pathways. WL 102 A757m]
QP406.A74 1984   153.1'2   83-25455
ISBN 0-89859-290-9

Printed in the United States of America
10 9 8 7 6 5 4 3 2 1

CONTENTS

PREFACE

In this book I attempt to do two things. First, I try to identify the psychological operations we must perform to perceive something, recall or recognize it, grasp its meaning and respond to it. Second, I try to trace and identify the brain structures and pathways that make such psychological operations possible.

Memory is not an isolated process. It depends on perception, is influenced by emotion and imagination and embedded in the whole sequence from perception to action. Without memory, there can be no perception as we experience it, no learning, no motivated action. We cannot discover how memory is registered and recalled unless we know where it occurs in this sequence. To discover where memory fits in, we must analyze the total psychological sequence and identify the individual links. What I try to do in this book is to outline the brain structures and pathways that mediate each link in the chain and sketch their operations during psychological activities. That is the sum and substance of my theory of brain function. I hope to show that it is supported by a great deal of experimental and clinical evidence.

This theory was first published in my book "Emotion and Personality" (1960). It had been formulated on the basis of neuropsychological research published before 1958. During the first few years, all my attempts to trace a connected brain circuit that would mediate psychological activities from perception to action proved unsuccessful. Every new research report disproved one or the other hypothesis. But once I had worked out the present theory, everything fell into place and every new research report supported it. The functions I ascribe to various brain structures (e.g., association cortex, limbic cortex, amygdala) are the only ones that will fit. Mine is a closely knit theory. If any one of the main links were changed, it would no longer fit the evidence.

The research germane to my theory spans a period of over forty years. I have included older as well as more recent findings because it is important to show that through the years, research results have supported all the links in my theory. In the late Sixties, when I was Director of the experimental laboratory at Loyola University of Chicago, we explored some of the crucial structures in my theory (anterior insula, anterior thalamic nuclei, cingulum). Reports of these investigations are mentioned throughout the book. In the last twenty years, research in the brain sciences has exploded. Obviously, I can refer only to some examples, but I have tried to include research in fields that have begun to flourish only comparatively recently (split-brain, neurotransmitters, etc.). Since this book is not intended as a historical introduction to neuropsychology, nor as a review of current research in the field, I have made no effort to be strictly up-to-date. A theory does not depend on the latest research. If it is adequate and has the support of years of research by widely scattered experimenters, it will not be replaced in a year or so.

The theory is complicated, but so is the brain. Difficult as it is, the attempt of finding definite pathways to relay neural excitation from one structure to the next, strictly correlated with the sequence of psychological functions, can provide a check and perhaps a corrective for too exuberant psychological theorizing. It is all too easy to offer any number of hypotheses for the way memory functions if we do not have to identify the pathways in the brain that might mediate these functions. Computer models of memory processing, as Tulving (1979) remarks, "may provide a sense of accomplishment to their creators" but such "correspondence models do not bring us any understanding of memory or its phenomena."

It is my conviction that the best guide to a theory of brain function is subjective experience. The only way we have been able to locate sensory and motor areas in the brain is to depend on the reports of patients after brain damage or brain stimulation. Since subjective experience must be our guide, I propose to use subjective terms. Such a description of subjective experience is not "introspection," either in the sense of Titchener or of Freud. Titchener focused on subjective feelings and sensations and would allow no other experiences; and Freud centered on personal experiences of traumatic situations. Both types of introspection could be (and were) contaminated by theoretical bias and faulty recollection.

The description of subjective experience I propose to use is often called a phenomenological analysis. We focus on a given activity and try to discover what must happen before this result is achieved (e.g., a learned discrimination, a habit, a skill). The subjective experience of one observer is used as a clue, to be checked by the experience of every other observer using the same kind of analysis. Sensory experience is rightly considered a hallucination unless other observers confirm it; and a phenomenological analysis is unacceptable unless other observers agree.

Experiential terms help to fit each activity into the sequence from perception to action. But they have other advantages as well. Unlike objective terms, they are understood immediately because they are part of our linguistic heritage and do not have to be specially defined. A theory couched in objective terms forces the reader to learn new terms and new distinctions. Such terms not only burden the reader but very quickly go out of fashion. I try to use common English terms as far as possible to enable the reader to follow the argument. Of course, the technical terms employed in neurophysiology are necessary in any discussion of brain structures and pathways. To call the hippocampus "seahorse" or the thalamus "chamber" would not profit the reader. But I hope to avoid scientific jargon even in discussing technical matters and do my best to be intelligible to anyone who has a basic knowledge of the brain.

It is very easy to become so enamored of the terms used in one's own field that clarity suffers. As one example among many, consider Bertrand Russell's criticism of Watson's theory of language as a verbal habit, and the paraphrase couched in present-day objective terms. Says Russell:

> . . . when we recount a past incident in words we never used before . . . it is not the actual words that we repeat but only their meaning . . . thus my recollection is certainly not a definite verbal habit. (1927, p. 73–75.)

Anderson and Bower (1974) comment that

> in current terms, Russell was arguing that habits defined over surface strings of verbal units . . . will not suffice to account for paraphrastic descriptions of witnessed events. (p. 35.)

Only psychologists working in the field of memory would understand Anderson and Bower's translation at first glance. Other psychologists, let alone professionals in other fields and the lay reader, would have serious difficulties in grasping the paraphrase, but none in understanding Russell's point.

In the first, psychological, part of this book, the reader will miss many topics usually treated in a book on memory. But my aim is simply to discuss the psychological aspects of memory that can throw light on the brain structures and pathways that mediate memory registration and retrieval. I do not describe how we encode what we perceive, nor am I concerned with different strategies of encoding or remembering, or how to prevent forgetting. I try to answer the following questions:

Chapter 1. What is the role of perception in memory?
    2. Is attention necessary for memory?
    3. Is reinforcement or reward involved in memory?
    4. Is memory unitary or modality-specific?
    5. Is memory processed in definite steps or stages?
    6. Are memories replayed or reconstructed?
    7. What is the difference between recall and recognition?
    8. Possible models of memory
    9. What would be an adequate theory of memory?

In the second, neurophysiological part of this book, I want to show that each of the psychological activities discussed in the first part can be assigned to areas and pathways in the brain that mediate them (chapter 10). Many of these have been explored for their association with memory for a good many years, but have never been connected into continuous circuits activated in sequence. I attempt such connections in the later chapters, which form an extended statement of my theory of brain function.

In chapters 11–16, I review the evidence that seems to support my view of the cortical areas in which impressions are registered, and of the circuits that reactivate such registered memories. Chapter 17 deals with the diffuse thalamic system in connection with attention and the appraisal system, while chapter 18 discusses damage to the appraisal system and the affective memory circuit. Chapter 19 reviews clinical and experimental reports on split-brain patients and animals, which have given us much-needed information on the way memory functions. The extensive literature on hippocampus and amygdala tends to support my suggestion that the hippocampus is the main relay station in the action and memory circuits (chapters 20–22), and the amygdala, the relay station in the imagination circuit (chapter 23). These circuits depend on different neurotransmitter systems, which also are involved in brain self-stimulation and psychiatric illness (chapters 24, 25). Finally, chapters 26–28 describe the descending and ascending links of the action circuit that connects the sensory areas with the motor cortex, and mediates the initiation and execution of action; and of the associated motor memory circuit.

MEMORY
AND
THE BRAIN

PSYCHOLOGICAL ASPECTS

1 Perception

Only recently have psychologists begun again to speak of direct perception as the basis of knowledge and a "valid and reliable source of information" (Turvey & Shaw, 1979). Unless we trust our perception, we cannot come to veridical conclusions about the world. As Turvey and Shaw point out, if we do not perceive what is really out there, all knowledge, necessarily based on perception, is suspect and no amount of reasoning or inference can make it valid. If perception is not veridical, it is inconceivable that animals could have successfully coped with their environment and evolved in it. While vision alone may deceive us, neither human beings nor animals depend on the information derived from a single sense.

PERCEPTUAL INTEGRATION

It is generally agreed that sensory experience depends on selective attention. The very word "stimulus" indicates that not everything in the environment will prompt a reaction. In any psychological experiment, conditions are so arranged that the subject will respond to the stimulus selected by the experimenter. In animal experiments, the animal usually has to be "shaped" before it will attend to the selected stimulus and give the desired response. To select and attend to one thing, it must be perceptible to our sense organs. It also must be sufficiently defined to stand out from its background.

Whatever the type of energy that impinges on the organism, whether electromagnetic, mechanical, or chemical, the sensory experience depends on the specific receptor organs stimulated. A single object may be experienced via different senses. We see a man playing the violin, hear the sound, can touch the violin and feel its vibrations. We know without any process of reasoning that the sound comes from the man playing the violin.

Individual senses cannot convey such integrated experience. All the sense of sight can do is mediate visual experience; the sense of hearing, auditory experience. Yet we see *things,* not patches of color, hear *melodies,* not single tones following one another. We touch an object and form a notion of its shape, rather than having discrete touch sensations. Sensory experience is integrated before we become aware of it. Such an integration of experience must be some kind of sensory function because it is unperceived, preattentive, as direct as all sensory experience.

A phrase coined by William James has it that the infant experiences the world as a "buzzing, blooming confusion." If James meant, as some of his successors did, that the infant's world has no articulation, that objects must be established by moving toward them and manipulating them (Schilder, 1950), it is curious that he never explained how the child would ever manage to find the objects toward which to move. A visual field without any articulation, without up or down or side-by-side would make it impossible to single out anything for attention or manipulation. More than that, there is no reason in the world why the sense of touch, in manipulating something, should convey the notion of an object separated from other objects if the sense of vision cannot do so.

Much more likely, James meant that the infant's world has as yet no meaning, that the infant sees things but does not know what they will do to him or how he can cope with them. For such knowledge, he has to touch and manipulate them and find out how they will affect him. The memory of such experiences will then gradually make the world meaningful to him.

The integration and articulation of the environment into separate objects must necessarily occur before we experience anything. It must be a sensory function, completing the experience of seeing, hearing, touching; we could call it the function of an integrative sense, mediated, like sensory experience, by the cerebral cortex. In recent years, some "preattentive" perceptual integration has been postulated by theorists. So Johansson (1979) pointed out that seeing movement when a spot of light is directed successively at neighboring positions, presupposes an integration that is an immediate sense experience without any cognitive inference. And Allport (1979) assumes a preattentive visual integration. In the nature of the case, the existence of such an integrative sensory function must be inferred; it cannot be directly demonstrated because any conscious experience already contains the result of such integration. However, such integration can be prevented, either experimentally or as the result of brain lesions.

Thus Allport (1979) points out that conscious perception of a tachistoscopic array as words rather than as rows of squiggles is limited by the rate at which this perceptual integration can operate. And Faust (1955) has reported that patients experience a disintegration of form after occipital lesions. When such a patient looks at something for a short time, its form disappears; it may return if he looks away for a while. Usually, this disintegration of the visual field has been explained as abnormally quick fatigue of the visual apparatus after brain lesions. But if that were so, such disintegration should also be experienced without brain lesions when long periods of reading or close visual work result in fatigue. But normally, while increased visual fatigue may produce blurring or flimmering, it never results in a disintegration of the total visual field. According to Faust, this disintegration failed to occur if letters or words were shown on a tachistoscope where each item is shown separately. Only when the patient tried to read a page of print did he seem incapable of coping with the task. Faust calls this impairment "spatial blindness" and says, "Characteristic for spatial blindness is the 'loss' of things seen, together with a continual seeking with the eyes, while the transition from one thing to the other becomes extremely difficult."[1] From Faust's careful description it seems clear that this is a perceptual defect resulting in the impairment of visual integration, after damage to the primary visual cortex. In addition, the registration and recall of perceptual experience seems to be deficient as well. Faust points out that these patients are also unable to order things in imagination into a visual space. To imagine things in some side-by-side order, we need a visual memory schema. If it is missing, visual imagination cannot organize visual memory images.

VISUAL SPACE

Since Faust and other workers in this field often speak of "spatial ability," it might be profitable to ask just what is implied in space perception. How do we see space? Is space, as Kant has it, a "condition of sensibility" that necessarily precedes all sensory knowledge? Or is it a special way of seeing, as Faust seems to imply?

Our notion of visual space implies that there is a certain order among the things that surround us, that they are spread out before our eyes. There is good reason to assume that depth perception is innate: the "visual cliff" is avoided by infants of many species before any learning can have occurred. This innate perception of distance seems to give us the first awareness that some things are near and others farther away. Similarly, there is a primitive knowledge (before any concepts are formed) that something is located to one side or another, in front or behind us, a knowledge that is acquired not only by sight but by hearing, touch, even smell, and is tested by every attempt to reach or avoid the things so experi-

---

[1] Charakteristisch für die Ortsblindheit ist das 'Verlieren' von gesehenen Objekten zusammen mit einem ständigen Suchen der Augen, wobei der Uebergang von Objekt zu Objekt ausserordentlich erschwert ist.

enced. Not every sensory modality can give us a precise notion of the location of things around us. We know that something we touch is close at hand, but we do not know exactly how far something is that we see or hear. But various cues (relative size, relative clearness, etc.) allow us to learn how to estimate distance more accurately. We *innately* perceive things ordered side-by-side and in depth; but the *accurate* perception of distance demands experience and memory.

When a man lacks sight, it is much more difficult for him to achieve a correct notion of the direction and distance of things in relation to himself, but it is possible with the help of movement and touch. People born blind are able to find their way around the house, around the neighborhood, and even around their district, with remarkable confidence. This surely means that they have formed a notion of the way things are arranged around them. They must have a map of their environment so that they can use spatial concepts without difficulty. Of course, their space is not a picture of things spread out around them but a structure of objects in various directions and at various distances from themselves, measured by the time it takes to walk to them.

Their space perception differs from that of the sighted, as shown by reports of people born blind who later gained their sight through an operation. When such a patient first opens his eyes, he seems to think that the things he sees are touching his eyes, and often covers them with his hand, afraid his eyes will be hurt. Senden (1932), who has collected many reports of such patients, emphasizes the difference in their space perception compared to the sighted. But he draws the unjustifiable conclusion that only vision can provide us with the notion of space. It is true that a man born blind has no perception of *visual* space; but it does not follow, as Senden claims, that the notion of space is inherent only in vision and can be formed from no other sense. If it were, a person born blind would not be able to move in space with confidence while blind, but should have normal space perception as soon as his vision was restored. Actually, some patients who have regained their sight find the effort required to move with eyes open too exhausting and never learn to use their newly acquired sense of sight for their daily tasks. What seems to have happened is that while blind they formed memory images of their environment on the basis of motion and touch. Because they have no visual memory of objects and their position around them, they are unable to recognize anything by sight or to move among the things they see.

Senden reports, for instance, that such patients did not recognize simple objects on seeing them. They could distinguish a circle from a square but could not say which was a circle and which a square. But when they traced the outline of both, they immediately knew their name, and ever after could recognize these two figures, no matter what size or color they were, or of what material they were made. Apparently, when blind, the patients had learned to recognize circle and square on the basis of tactual and particularly motor memory. Since the shape traced manually and so registered and remembered as a motor memory image had no connection with any visual memory image, merely seeing the two figures did not suggest the outlines the patients had traced and remembered. Once they had both *seen and traced* the two figures, and so connected the two experiences, they were able to recognize circle and square on seeing them.

It is curious how often we are misled by our linguistic habits. Because visual, tactual, motor, and conceptual memory normally work together, we speak of "memory" and assume that it is a single function, no matter what sense modality has produced it. When we are told that on gaining sight a man born blind cannot recognize a circle or a square although he can see that they are different, we assume that his difficulty cannot be a memory deficit because he still remembers the concept "circle" and "square" formed on the basis of motor and tactual experience.

Thus Senden assumes that the defect must be a "lack of space perception" supposedly inherent in vision. But once we entertain the notion that memory depends on various sense modalities that normally act in unison, it becomes plausible that visual memory requires the registration of visual impressions and their connection with memory traces from other modalities. We must see something and find out what it is called before we can recognize it by sight alone and repeat its name.

When sight can be used normally, together with all other senses, it will dominate our experience, not because of some mysterious "spatial" property of vision but simply because visual memory can be checked by moving about, in a way tactual memory cannot. Without sight, a person's notion of space is based on touch, hearing, and movement. The blind do not move, as Senden suggests, by calculating the distance and direction; if they did, they would never be able to move with assurance even among familiar things. They are guided by the memory of the steps they have taken in walking toward something, or the movements they have made in reaching for something or tracing its outline. Such motor and tactual memory is not as efficient as visual memory. Using sight, a man can recognize landmarks before he comes to them and so can change his direction, if necessary, without retracing his steps. A person born blind certainly acquires a concept of space: he knows in which direction to move, and approximately for how long, before he can touch a particular piece of furniture. But because this spatial map is not a visual image, such a person will be intolerably confused on gaining sight until he has tried to move among the things he sees and by manipulating them has connected his tactual and motor memory with the visual images. This takes time and effort. It is not surprising that many people on gaining their sight as adults lose patience and prefer the familiar non-visual way—just as many people who become blind never manage to acquire a scheme based on touch and movement.

In short, Senden's explanation that space is an inherent characteristic of vision comes from first mistaking the visually ordered *images* of things for the *concept* of space, and next concluding that people born blind who have no such images cannot have a concept of space. They do have such a concept, but in their sightless days they had to derive it from touch, hearing, and moving, without the help of the visual perception of things arranged side-by-side, in front or behind them, which is the most important basis of the concept of space for the sighted.

CONSCIOUSNESS, MEMORY AND PERCEPTION

Every perceptual experience presupposes awareness; and awareness is impossible without memory. Our awareness includes not only the present moment but a stretch of time immediately before, what William James called the "specious present." To be conscious means that we are aware of what goes on around us, that we sense, think, feel, can move and talk, that we can remember our immediate as well as our distant past, and reflect on our experiences. As Gasson says:

> what is *conscious* must indicate some psychological experience, something lived through of which we know; a *knowing* or a *wanting* or a *doing* or *happening* in us of which we have direct knowledge and which we refer to ourselves. Such psychological experience, moreover, in itself or in its content, must be fully *available* to us here and now for the needs of the present moment. (1954, p. 209. Original emphases.)

Accordingly, unconscious in its simplest sense means the absence of the activities of knowing, wanting, doing, remembering, and reflecting. A disturbance of consciousness is an interference with these activities, or their temporary loss.

Of course, some of these activities may not be observable. A person may not be able to move or to talk, yet he may be fully aware of what goes on around him. But to be conscious at all, he must be able to perceive and evaluate what he perceives. To be fully conscious, he must be aware of the external world and of his own experience, present and past, and must be able to use what he knows.

Consciousness, like memory, has been a step-child of psychological science during the last few decades. But unlike memory, it has not as yet made a comeback. Early in this century, when psychology had barely been accepted as an experimental science, Watson had insisted that consciousness is not a fit object for scientific research; that science has to restrict itself to the investigation of phenomena accessible to public observation and measurement. Whatever the methodological reasons for such an ostrich policy, psychologists have followed it for many a long year. This neglect of consciousness has impoverished experimental psychology and has deprived clinical psychology and psychiatry of help in an area crucial for understanding mental disorders as well as the effects of brain injury. Only recently, with the advent of cognitive psychology, have theorists come to realize that there is an important gap in their scientific domain. As Norman (1979) says: "the phenomenon of consciousness is so fundamental to our mental lives that it seems strange that experimental psychologists have ignored it so conclusively." (p. 142.)

While the functioning of at least some afferent sensory pathways is necessary for consciousness, the normal functioning of the sensory system is not sufficient. Experimental subjects may not even "see" a word presented tachistoscopically when it is "masked" by an inappropriate word that follows immediately afterward. According to Allport (1979), conscious awareness depends on a preattentive processing of visual impressions. An unconscious patient may receive sensory impressions (as shown by electrical potentials recorded from the sensory cortex) yet be unable to react to them in any way. In contrast, a person may move and even speak, yet be unable to reflect on what he is doing or remember his actions afterwards—for instance, in "temporal automatisms" (Penfield, 1952).

Full consciousness necessarily includes a person's ability to remember what is happening or what he is doing, and also to remember who he is, where he is, and what he is about to do. So-called "clouding of consciousness" is characterized by confusion: The patient does not know where he is, what year or season it is, or who are the people around him. Although this state has been defined differently by different psychiatrists, there is agreement on the main symptoms. The patient is confused, incoherent, inattentive, misidentifies things and people; in short, is unable to grasp the real situation. As a result, the patient is disinclined to move, is indifferent and apathetic. Even after this condition has cleared up again, the patient often cannot remember what happened to him or what he did during this period. Such clouding of consciousness occurs in delirium or shortly afterwards, in widespread brain lesions, immediately after electroshock and concussion, and in acute psychosis. It seems clear that brain function has been disturbed in such cases and has brought about an interference with the spontaneous continuous recall needed for remembering what is happening and what we are doing in our daily life. Delirium, brain damage, electroshock, and concussion, represent such an obvious interference with normal brain function that we may well ask ourselves whether psychosis might not also have the same effect.

THE SENSE OF IDENTITY

We acquire a sense of identity in the most literal sense of the term by having a spontaneous continuing recall of what is happening and what we are doing. When we discuss something with a friend, we remember what we have said: the last sentence, the idea behind it, the other's reply. It may happen that a person contradicts himself as the argument goes on, but he usually does remember his previous opinion once his attention is drawn to it. We remember what we have done a moment ago, an hour ago, the day before. We continue being aware of what we are doing or what we are saying. It is this continuous memory, embracing not only our own actions but also the actions of others with whom we are dealing, that makes available all our experience for use as occasion demands.

It is the psychological basis of full awareness, so that each one of us knows who he or she is, where we live, where we are at present, and how we got here, what we are doing and what we intend to do. We know our name, our family, our job, our belongings. This kind of continuous recall requires conceptual memory as well as sensory and motor memory. It also requires the evaluation of our situation and our recognition of familiar things.

When we are fully conscious, we perceive and interpret what we see around us, what is said to us and what we experience through all of our senses; and we necessarily make such interpretations on the basis of memory. Without memory, full consciousness is not possible. "Clouding" of consciousness means that such spontaneous and all but unnoticeable recall is interrupted. A patient is confused because he cannot remember where he is, what time it is, with whom he is speaking, or even who he is. He suffers from a disturbance of memory. His thinking is incoherent and contradictory because he cannot keep in mind what he has said before, or what conclusions he has drawn. He is inattentive because he cannot judge what is and what is not important, a judgment that is based on memory. He is apathetic because nothing makes sense to him and he is unable to react to this incomprehensible world; the basic difficulty again is a memory disturbance. Today, the connection between perception and memory is increasingly recognized (Murdock, 1979; Turvey & Shaw, 1979).

Obviously, neither awareness nor perception is the simple phenomenon it has sometimes been made to appear. If perception were no more than the reception of a stimulus, and had no connection with anything else, it might be left aside in the interest of scientific purity—as it actually is in the strict behavioristic system. If consciousness were no more than an inferred "mental state," the scientist could easily insist that his concern is with what he can observe and not with doubtful inferences. But perception contains the memory of earlier encounters, and consciousness is the very precondition of perception. A psychology of perception must necessarily include both an exploration of memory and of consciousness.

When we try to identify the processes used in perception, we find that we must be aware of a situation, attend to it, and identify it by recalling similar situations. Often, when memory fails, we imagine what must have happened to fill the gaps. We can recall and imagine something seen or heard, even smelled, tasted or touched. We may need the help of visual images to form a memory image of what it feels like to touch velvet, what a good steak tastes like, or to re-experience the fragrance of a rose. Still, these memories are not pure visual images; they are also touch, taste, and olfactory images. We could call this type of recall *modality-specific memory*.

In addition, we evaluate perceptual experiences. We appraise the situation as good or bad for us, as beneficial or harmful, to be approached or avoided. This appraisal also draws upon memory, both on the recall of specific similar instances, but also on past appraisals. What we have found pleasant in the past, we will find pleasant when we meet something similar. We could call this immediate positive or negative reaction to something *affective memory*. This type of memory is immediate, spontaneous, and non-deliberate, while modality-specific memory may be recalled spontaneously or deliberately. Ordinarily, affective memory accompanies modality-specific recall. But it may happen that we instantly (we often say, "instinctively") like or dislike something or someone without any conscious memory of having had such an encounter before.

As soon as we experience something as good or bad, we feel an *impulse* either to approach or avoid it. If we have appraised it as indifferent, we leave it aside. If we have no habitual way of dealing with the situation, we make a guess what to expect from it. This requires *imagining* possible situations and possible ways of dealing with them. The choice of what we judge the best alternative leads to a particular response.

To give an intelligible account of memory disturbances, particularly memory disturbances after brain lesions, we must know something about the way in which the brain mediates memory. Since perception involves different activities in a specific sequence, we have to look for structures and pathways that mediate each of these activities, one after the other, rather than looking for particular "memory centers."

2 Attention

To become aware of sensory experience apparently requires more than the activity of the different sense modalities. It requires a turning toward the source of such experience: it requires attention.

According to William James, everyone knows what attention is: "It is the taking possession by the mind, in clear and vivid form, of one out of . . . several simultaneously possible objects or trains of thought." (1890, p. 403.) But how do we pay attention, what is this "taking possession by the mind"? Is it a cognitive process? Most psychologists would unhesitatingly answer that it is. However, our experience speaks against this interpretation.

Take, for example, seeing, hearing, or touching: these are cognitive processes. They mediate knowledge and do so directly, immediately. We see as soon as we open our eyes, provided there is enough light; we hear whenever there is a sound, provided we are awake and our attention is not otherwise engaged. In contrast, attention is *directed* here or there, and can be withdrawn from something in front of our eyes and directed toward something imagined or remembered. Attention can increase the intensity of a sense experience: if we expect a sound, attention can lower the threshold of hearing. When directed elsewhere, attention may altogether prevent perception. Attention is a condition of cognition just as light is a condition of sight. A man engrossed in a book may not be aware that somebody is asking him a question. That he hears is shown by the fact that calling his name will attract his attention, although the questioner may not have raised his voice. Cognitive functions do not act in this manner. Sight, hearing, touch, smell, taste, simply mediate experience, they do not change it. They neither increase nor decrease the intensity of experience. Sensory receptors receive stimulation and relay it to sensory areas in the brain, even when the stimulus is not attended to. Sensory stimulation produces potential changes in cortical sensory areas even during sleep or light anesthesia.

Attention makes reflective knowledge or awareness possible; but is attention itself a cognitive function? This problem is usually not talked about. Recent experiments and theories of attention (Norman, 1968, 1969; Kahneman, 1973) treat the effect of attention on sensory experience at great length, but never raise the question whether attention itself is cognitive in nature. As a result, theorists often conceive of the sensory system as a single communication channel with a selective filter (attention) that is part of the system and filters out irrelevant sensory impressions (Broadbent, 1958; Bower, 1967). This filter, they postulate, can be tuned to any one of several inputs. Only information passed by the filter can be further processed and remembered.

Such a model seems to fit experiments on selective listening in which the subject is asked to repeat aloud what he hears in one ear while a different (irrelevant) message is fed to the other ear. In these experiments, the subject can switch attention at will from one message to the other, even when the voices in the two channels are identical. In fact, Spieth et al. (1954) found that such selective listening was possible when the voices were heard over loudspeakers placed only ten to twenty degrees apart. The subjects could also follow a voice coming through a low-pass filter, rather than one sent through a high-pass filter. Finally, Egan et al. (1954) found that the subjects can attend either to intensity or to frequency of sounds. In short, it is possible to attend to one of two simultaneous sequences of sounds different in quality, location, intensity, and frequency.

However, when the irrelevant (unattended) message contains the subject's name, he begins to attend to it (Moray, 1959); also, he switches from one ear to the other when the message in that ear becomes relevant, for instance, when the message in the non-attending ear continues the passage read to the attending ear (Treisman, 1960, 1964a,b). This switching in the middle of the message is difficult to explain on the basis of a filter theory. How can relevant stimuli on unattended channels capture attention? This problem is discussed by Craik and Jacoby (1979). For instance, several subjects recognized the rejected message if it was identical with the message they attended to. In fact, some bilingual subjects recognized such identity although the unattended message was in another language (Treisman, 1964a,b). Treisman tried to explain this phenomenon by postulating several levels of processing, and insisted that the level reached depends not only on the physical characteristic of the stimulus but on current expectations in the analyzing system. Broadbent (1971) later accepted this modification of his filter theory. But neither the original theory nor Treisman's modification can explain how attention can be directed toward meaningful material when the filter is only equipped to deal with the physical features of the stimulus. It can hardly have biases and expectations that go beyond these characteristics.

Norman (1968, 1969) has faced the difficulty of explaining a switch of attention on the basis of a filter model. He claims that a model that can account for such changed filters needs a more complicated system. According to him,

> "all signals arriving at sensory receptors pass through a stage of analysis performed by the early physiological processes. Then, the parameters extracted from the processes are used to determine where the representation of the sensory signal is stored. Thus . . . all sensory signals excite their stored representation in memory. Now, at the same time, we assume that an analysis of previous signals is going on. This establishes a class of events deemed to be pertinent to the ongoing analysis. The set of pertinent items also excite their representation in memory. The item most highly excited by the combination of sensory and pertinent inputs is selected for further analysis." (Norman, 1969, p. 33)

The difficulty with this description is that we are not certain what Norman is speaking about. Is he referring to a neural network, a computer model, a flow diagram, or a set of human activities? Often, Norman speaks explicitly of human mental processes, particularly in his later articles (Norman, 1979). But he also describes processes that operate on knowledge structures in an almost mechanical way. When he speaks of "the item most highly excited by the combination of sensory and pertinent inputs," which is selected for further analysis (and presumably attended to), we begin to wonder whether he is perhaps alluding to the neural network. In such a network, the most intense excitation wins out. But the human being may pay attention not to the lecturer's loud voice and erudite discourse but to a fleeting distraction—and who is to decide whether the distracting thought is more intense? Norman's notion of attention as the algebraic sum of excitation from perception and memory analyses does not explain why a subject should recognize a message read to the non-attending ear as identical with the message to which he has been paying attention all along, particularly when the two messages are in different languages. Nor does it explain why a memory analysis should establish a pertinent item in the first place—unless it is the human being who decides what is relevant and directs his recall accordingly.

Both Norman's and Broadbent's models depend on the presence of memory traces, some of which are excited by the sensory input. But can we assume that there will always be stored memories to select an item for attention? Supposing a subject is instructed to press a button every time he sees a shade of red in the tachistoscope. No matter how many shades are shown, the subject has no difficulty in judging them correctly as red and pressing the button. The notion that there must be a memory trace for every type and intensity of sensory experience leads, as Norman says in another connection, "to a staggering amount of complexity in the neural network required to do the task. Moreover, it is not clear that any finite network could ever suffice, for there are truly an infinite number of ways we can see well-known objects" (1969, p. 40). Norman's solution is to suggest that stimulus-analyzing mechanisms recognize patterns, and recognize them by rules: "a set of rather general purpose operations examine the set of features extracted by the basic physiological analyzers and classify patterns, more by synthesizing them anew than by any other procedure" (p. 40). But if attention is merely the effect of various operations, as Norman says, the model does not explain how the subject decides that a given color is a shade of red. If he is instructed to look for "red," so that the instructions make this color pertinent, how does the expectation so aroused excite the trace for that particular shade? The concept "red" has no particular shade, hence there can be no memory trace for any given shade. Even if we assume, as some theorists do, that a concept is the generalized image of a class of objects, that is, a generalized shade of red, how can a particular shade excite the trace of such a generalized memory image? Again, it is the human being and not a stimulus-analyzing mechanism that forms concepts and recognizes a given shade of red as belonging to the class of "red."

Neisser (1967), a cognitive psychologist, also insists that attention "is simply an allotment of analyzing mechanisms to a limited region of the field. To pay attention to a figure is to make certain analyses of, or certain constructions in, the corresponding part of the icon." (p. 89.) For Neisser, focal attention can function only after "preattentive" global processes have already segregated the figural units involved. He insists that even a mechanical recognition system would have to have such a feature for separating certain units and selecting one after another for further processing.

Neisser's "preattentive processes" have an obvious similarity with the integrative sense discussed in chapter 1; so do Norman's stimulus-analyzing mechanisms. Without the ability to see a well-articulated scene, or to distinguish patterns of sound, it would be impossible to direct attention to any part of the visual field, or to begin listening to discover the drift of a conversation or the theme of a musical composition.

Like Norman, Neisser seems to consider attention simply as the result of certain preconscious operations. When he says that attention is "the allotment of analyzing mechanisms," who or what makes the allotment? Neisser disagrees with psychoanalytic writers who regard attention as the manifestation of a single process, an allocation of energy; but his own formulation shows little improvement. Whether attention is a process of allocating energy, or the allotment of analyzing mechanisms, we have no clue how this allotment is done, just as we do not know how the allocation of energy can result in attention.

It is more than doubtful that the same preattentive or preconscious process that segregates the manifold of sensory impressions into distinguishable units could also select a given unit for further processing. The preattentive global process that results in crude percepts cannot direct what is to be done next. Another function is needed that will allot mechanisms, allocate energy, and direct the memory search. And when we ask with Neisser: Who does the searching, the allotting? Is there a little man in the head, a homunculus? Neisser answers:

As recently as a generation ago, processes of control had to be thought of as homunculi, because man was the only known model of the executive agent. Today, the stored-program computer has provided us with an alternative possibility, in the form of the executive routine. This is a concept which may be of considerable use to psychology. (1967, p. 295.)

Of course, Neisser admits that the executive routines must be programmed into the computer from the beginning and would not allow a change of direction in midstream, yet this is a common phenomenon in human experience. In man, he thinks, such executive functions are acquired through experience—a case of learning like any other.

But learning is not the explanation. We do not learn attention, we merely learn to what we should attend, just as we do not learn to see, we merely learn to interpret what we see. It is odd that psychologists should be willing to accept "executive routines" that somehow (nobody knows how) direct man's behavior, when they are unwilling to agree that the human being directs his own behavior, yet that is a fact of everybody's direct experience. The very notion of a "little man in the head" could gain credence only because psychologists were convinced that psychological activities, like the movements of physical bodies, must be explained objectively, without appealing to any human agency. Yet a human being sees, pays attention to what he sees, appraises it, thinks about it, chooses to react to it in some way. He sometimes throws a ball or digs a ditch. We do not assume that a little man in the head pulls strings to make us see, make us dig ditches or throw a ball—why should we need a homunculus to attend to something, to remember, to think?

To insist that human behavior is the result of learned executive routines is to indulge in a double analogy, from man to machine and from machine to man. Executive routines are instructions directing computer searches, on the analogy of a human being directing himself or others to investigate a particular area of interest. Instead of assuming that the human being uses executive routines, it is much simpler and closer to human experience to assume that we use various functions to deal with the world around us. When we do that, the only problem left is to identify the functions needed in a particular activity.

There has never been any difficulty about obvious sensory functions. Seeing, hearing, smelling, touching, and tasting have always been accepted as something we do—except for early behaviorists who admitted responses to stimuli, but not the perception of stimuli. But the notion of an integrative sense that enables us to see objects rather than colored patches has found few adherents until it surfaced comparatively recently in the guise of global preattentive processes (Neisser, 1967). Yet it is obvious that the visual sense itself can only mediate color. However, special cell columns in the visual cortex have been found to respond to vertical, horizontal, and oblique lines, and to movement (Hubel & Wiesel, 1962). Hence it is the visual cortex with its six layers that seems to mediate visual form and movement. It is a reasonable inference that the feltwork of the sensory cortex mediates sensory integration and articulates the visual field in such a way that we can focus on any part of it.

The primary function of attention is not that of analyzing or integrating sensory impressions, but of focusing other functions on the area of interest. We turn toward the object of attention, look, listen, and try to discover what we can about it. In other words, attention is a desire to see, hear, taste, smell, touch, think about, and so to know something as best we may. Attention requires some kind of intuitive or deliberate, unconscious or conscious judgment that something is worth knowing or investigating. Attention can be voluntary or involuntary. Involuntary attention is based on an intuitive, unwitting appraisal: a sudden loud sound, a bright color in a dull landscape, a whiff of perfume, or an unpleasant smell, all of these can alert us and draw our attention. Voluntary attention, on the other hand, is based on a person's conscious, deliberate judgment that this particular thing is something worth knowing about. If an experimental subject is instructed to press a button every time he sees a shade of red, he attends to the visual array. He wants to know it so that he can respond to it. As long as this desire lasts, he will be "set" to notice and report the shade that fits the concept. He may see other colors but will not react to them and may not even remember them.

Posner (1973) allows for both preconscious and conscious perceptual processing in his model of attention. A single-channel central processing capacity represents conscious attention, and is followed by rehearsal and the choice of response. Conscious attention is made possible by two stages of perceptual processing: the encoding of the stimulus, and a comparison of the stimulus with the contents of long-term memory. In his experiments, Posner showed a target stimulus (a digit or letter) to the subject, and later an array of similar stimuli with the instruction to locate the target stimulus. According to Posner, this search and comparison is preconscious. He comments that "both the target and non-target items are subject to a memory search process but only the target item gives rise to the phenomenological experience of jumping out at the subject." (p. 41.) But there is considerable doubt that this experience of the stimulus jumping out at the subject is the result of a comparison of each array stimulus with the remembered target stimulus. Indeed, research findings seem to be against such an assumption. For instance, Sternberg (1975) had his subjects commit a set of stimuli (letters, digits, figures) to memory; he called this the "positive set." He then showed a single test stimulus and asked his subjects to press one switch if the test stimulus was a member of the positive set, another if it was not. Sternberg found that the reaction time was so short that the subjects must have made about thirty comparisons per second, a rate considerably faster than the rate of subvocal speech which might have to be used for such comparisons. Sternberg also reported that the subjects were not aware of any search or comparison. Apparently the test stimulus simply felt familiar.

This is a prime example of an assumption based on a computer analogy: because the computer can locate the test stimulus only by search and comparison, the human being must do so, too. But the human being can *recognize* the test stimulus if he has seen it before (or memorized it, in Sternberg's experiment), that is, he can find it *familiar*. Recognition has always been considered different from recall. It is inaccessible to analysis, accounts for the target stimulus "jumping out" at the subject and is far faster than recall and comparison could ever be. In chapter 5, I discuss the difference between recall and recognition at greater length. Here, I will merely point out that recognition attracts attention (the stimulus "jumps out").

Shevrin and Dickman (1980) reviewed several different theories of attention and perception, all of which assume preconscious processing. A few of them also assume that such processing is qualitatively different from conscious attention. These authors suggested, on the basis of the available body of experimental research, that an initial preconscious stage of cognition is psychological (not physiological), affects conscious experience and may differ from conscious cognition in its principles of operation; conscious cognition is a later stage.

I would like to suggest that this preconscious cognition is an intuitive appraisal of something as familiar, or as good to know better because unfamiliar; this arouses a desire to turn toward it, look, listen, and investigate it. In the case of familiar objects, their recognition brings about a desire to do something about it, whether to report the occurrence or respond to it as usual. Hence attention is an appetitive and not a cognitive function. We want to turn toward the object, look, and listen. This immediately solves the problem of selective attention: all appetition implies a choice of goal, whether we want a new hat, a meal, to travel to Europe, or to look at a new car. If we attend to something, we select out of many possible things one we want to know better, whether we want to listen to a recording, watch an eclipse, or report on shades of red, locate a target stimulus, or identify the test stimulus in the positive set.

Involuntary attention, then, is the same impulse to look and listen, but based on the completely unconscious intuitive appraisal that this is unfamiliar, and should be investigated. Voluntary attention is based on a deliberate, conscious appraisal. In both cases, we have an impulse to focus on the selected object. But in voluntary attention, we *want* to look, in involuntary attention, we feel an *urge* to look.

3 Reinforcement, Reward: Appraisal and Affective Memory

In the last chapter, I have argued that attention is a necessary condition for perceiving and remembering, and that attention is initiated by an appraisal that this is good to know. Perception, aided by memory, eventually leads to action. But before we can approach anything or even want to do so, we must appraise it as good for us in some way: good to know, which leads to attention; good to have, which results in wanting and approaching it. We must also appraise a possible action as "good to do" and want to do it. No memory experiment will succeed unless the subject wants to learn, remember what he has learned, and wants to report it. Although modern cognitive psychologists are apt to disregard motivation in connection with memory experiments, the subjects must be motivated to do what the experimenter asks them to do. Given the docility of the usual subjects, psychology students, all the motivation they need is to know that participating in the experiment is required for a passing grade.

In animals, a psyiological state or drive (hunger, thirst) is assumed to impel the animal toward something (food, water) that will satisfy the drive. But both human beings and animals must be motivated to learn what the experimenter expects them to learn. Learning has usually been ascribed to the "law of effect" (Thorndike, 1931), or the reinforcement of the correct response. In other words, the subject must be reinforced by each correct response to go on learning. Thorndike assumed that the correct response strengthens the stimulus-response association directly and automatically. He rejected the view that reinforcement merely determines the choice of response after correct recall. Later views of reinforcement have been divided between these two views (Atkinson & Wickens, 1971). One view sees reinforcement as influencing the registration of memory (learning), the other, as determining the retrieval (performance).

Some theorists are beginning to doubt that reinforcement theory, developed from animal research, can apply to human learning (Estes, 1971). In answer, Voss (1971) points out that the real priority is to develop a satisfactory theory of human learning, and a theory of animal learning will take care of itself. He says: "Thus, even if one adheres to the continuity position, it does not necessarily follow that a reinforcement framework should be adopted for understanding reward and punishment in human learning; instead, it also would be possible that development of some other view may be fruitful, and even applicable to animal behavior" (p. 39).

Despite the vast research effort devoted to this problem for many years, none of the available reinforcement theories spells out just how reward or reinforcement produces its effect. True, the learner is rewarded and the response (or the association between learned items) is reinforced. But how does the reward promote learning, or how is the response reinforced? I propose to review briefly the more important motivational theories to discover whether any of the mechanisms proposed explains the function of reinforcement and could aid in the quest of identifying the pathways that mediate its effects.

REINFORCEMENT THEORIES

In an extensive review, Tapp (1969) classifies reinforcement theories, according to the main factor stressed, as motivational theories, stimulus theories and response theories. I follow him in this ordering.

Among *motivational theories,* Tapp points out, the drive-reduction theory has found considerable experimental support. According to this theory, the drive spurs the animal to learn a task; successful performance reduces the drive. But the theory cannot explain why "animals will learn a task . . . to taste a non-nutritive sweet substance . . . press bars to turn on lights or receive a puff of a novel odor . . . run mazes . . . to explore an empty goal box. . . . (or why) they will work to receive electric shocks or injections of minute amounts of chemicals into certain parts of their brain." (p. 390). None of these performances can reduce a physiological drive. The only way these experimental findings could be incorporated into the drive-reduction theory would be to postulate a new drive for every new reward, which, as Tapp says, would be rather uncomfortable.

The newer *arousal theories* (Berlyne, 1967) hold that a stimulus or a need that moves the animal from an optimal state of arousal induces drive or tension; and anything that reduces this state again to an optimal level is reinforcing. Such theories avoid the paradox fatal to drive reduction theories that organisms sometimes seek arousal, and not drive reduction. But the concept of arousal, taken from the reported EEG arousal on stimulation of the brainstem reticular system, has little definition and suffers from lack of agreement as to what constitutes arousal. In addition, Berlyne's argument states that a reward is reinforcing when it can induce an optimal level of arousal. And the arousal potential of the reward is a function of the arousal level of the subject (his need). But how does the optimal (or near optimal) level of arousal reinforce?

Stimulus theories recognize that both internal (drive or need) and external (sensory) stimuli influence behavior. They propose that a stimulus of any kind will reinforce a response if the response immediately follows upon the stimulus. But it can be objected that many stimuli are followed by responses and not all responses are reinforced. Accordingly, some attribute of the stimulus is needed that will enable it to reinforce the response. One possibility is to say that responses that are reinforced *change* the learning situation so that incompatible responses are no longer likely (Guthrie, 1959). Estes (1950), like Guthrie, recognizes that reward or reinforcement facilitates response after information about reward has been acquired. But, as Tapp says, what is there about the reward that gives it the capacity to facilitate S-R association?

Other theorists have suggested that a response-produced *change in stimulation* is reinforcing (Kish, 1966). But while it is true that every reinforcement has an element of stimulus change, there are many instances where the response producing the change is not reinforced. Tapp also points out that repeated response-produced changes lose their ability to reinforce the response.

The advantage of stimulus theories of reinforcement is the ease with which they can "explain" the reinforcement of responses that are not connected with conventional drive or need states. However, they do not explain why there should be such a difference in the effectiveness of reinforcement between drive-connected stimuli and all others. Tapp (1969) himself suggests that:

> Innate preference hierarchies may produce the more long range effects of reinforcing stimuli. In the short run the animal may react to any stimulus that is deviant (novel) from its expectant level of stimulation. This stimulus is evaluated, and long-range behaviors are initiated in terms of the results of the evaluation process. The ease with which evaluation will occur will depend on the modality of stimulation, the neural organization of that modality with reflexive response systems, and the previous experiences of the animal with the stimulus (p. 399).

It is rather obvious that Tapp's explanation falls outside any stimulus theory of reinforcement. No S-R system can tolerate an evaluation of the stimulus. Such an evaluation is necessarily an activity of the person, not determined by the stimulus. Indeed, as Tapp says, it is the evaluation that determines the response, hence the evaluation that leads to reinforcement.

On a less sophisticated and more orthodox level, theorists may assert that some stimuli are preferred and lead to approach, others are disliked and lead to withdrawal; and some of the preferences and aversions are genetic in nature. This is the *hedonic stimulus theory* of reinforcement. But this theory does not explain how preferred stimuli induce approach and disliked stimuli lead to withdrawal.

Also, as Tapp asks: "How are the informational attributes of stimuli related to preferences for these stimuli, and vice versa?"

Among *response theories,* some emphasize the effects of the consummatory response. As Tapp says, these theories refer to "the satisfying state of affairs which accompanies the achievement of a goal." (p. 403.) Since this satisfying state cannot be observed, the consummatory response itself is the only usable measure. According to one theorist (Sheffield, 1966a, b), stimuli excite the animal and sensitize the activation mechanism for the appropriate consummatory response. Learning occurs when the response-produced cues (sensory feedback) associated with the instrumental behavior (CS) become conditioned to the reward stimuli (UCS). Tapp points out that it is difficult to say just when reinforcement occurs—and, I might add, just what it does. To treat it as a conditioned reflex in which the instrumental activity is the conditioned and the reward the unconditioned stimulus is simply evading the issue altogether. Why is the consummatory response rewarding? And how does the reward affect the instrumental response to the stimulus?

At any rate, such theories cannot accommodate empirical evidence showing that animals can learn without consummatory response. Miller and Kessen (1952) reported that rats learned a T-maze for a milk reward delivered directly into their stomach. And Epstein (1960) found that hungry (or thirsty) rats will press a lever for a reward of milk (or water) injected directly into the stomach. Injection of glucose into the blood stream can reward choice behavior (Clark et al., 1961).

A variant of the response theory is Thorndike's "confirming reaction." When a reward is given, it initiates the "overhead control mechanism" that confirms (stamps in) the S-R association. Underlying all the response theories is the belief that a reward initiates some central neural event that confirms and somehow facilitates the response to the stimulus. While a number of experimental reports make it likely that a reward initiates some central neural event, such an event cannot recognize a reward and still less confirm it. It is the individual who recognizes and confirms. Lorenz (1969) puts the problem in more objective terms when he asks: "How do the modifiable parts of the behavior get the information necessary to fulfill tissue needs" (p. 54). The answer is, of course, that behavior cannot receive any information, nor can it change itself; only the individual can recognize a reward and adjust his behavior accordingly.

Later reinforcement theorists have not been able to solve this problem or suggest a mechanism by which reinforcement affects learning. Atkinson and Wickens (1971), who offer one of the best worked out theories of memory, suggest that reinforcement modulates the information flow in both components of memory, storage (acquisition) and retrieval. This theory illustrates the shift in point of view in recent years from reinforcement as a mechanism of *reward* to reinforcement as a mechanism of *information processing.* Since Atkinson and Wickens have derived their theory from verbal learning experiments, they suggest that reinforcement is essentially applied to *verbal reports* of memories acquired and recalled. Reinforcement is supposed to strengthen these responses as well as the connections between the paired associates learned before. Atkinson and Wickens, like other theorists, have no suggestion as to how that strengthening could be done. Carroll (1971) suggests that Stein's (1968) discussion of brain functions that mediate punishment and reward might explain the way in which reinforcement affects storage and recall. Unfortunately, neither Stein nor other neurophysiologists studying the brain reward system have specified the circuits over which reward or punishment affects either memory or behavior.

APPRAISAL

Obviously, these circuits cannot be identified unless we can form some notion of how reinforcement fits into the sequence from perception to action. Atkinson and Wickens say that reinforcement "modulates" the information flow in memory acquisition and retrieval; but how does it do so? Lorenz (1969) implies that the reward must be perceived in some way and that perception must then initiate a change of behavior.

In my theory, appraisal is part of perception. When the reward is perceived and appraised, an action impulse is initiated that eventually leads to action. Both appraisal and action impulses are mediated by special brain structures and pathways, discussed in Part II of this volume.

The Appraisal of Objects and Bodily States

The appraisal that something is "good for me here and now" is necessary for approach. When we appraise something as bad, we feel an impulse to avoid it. But if we appraise something as indifferent, neither good nor bad, we leave it aside, because it requires no action. Such appraisals of good or bad, beneficial or harmful, complete sense experience and are necessary for normal awareness. Since such appraisals are immediate, intuitive, or unwitting, we do not experience them, we merely experience the resulting impulse toward or away from the object we have appraised. Everything we encounter requires such an appraisal if we are to pay attention to it or respond in some other way. Like other sensory functions, sensory appraisal is unlearned, spontaneous. Indeed, if we could not make such appraisals from the beginning of life, how could we ever learn to do so? Similarly, if we could not see with eyes open, how could we learn to do so?

Even the infant knows what is good for him: warm milk, gentle handling, being carried or rocked—and he shows his enjoyment by stopping his crying and smiling instead. He knows what is bad for him: being hungry, wet, uncomfortable, unattended—and he shows his distress by wailing. In time, as the child's experience grows, he discovers a great many other things that are pleasant or unpleasant, beneficial or harmful, and acts accordingly. Such intuitive appraisals, like all sensory experiences, must be mediated by a particular neural system. I have called it the appraisal system and discuss it in detail in a later chapter (chapter 17; see also Arnold, 1960, vol. 2).

Sensory appraisal is different from other sensory functions because it indicates not the quality of things around us, but their *effect* on us. We appraise this effect as good or bad. On the level of somatosensory experience, what is bad or harmful is experienced as pain. What is good or beneficial is experienced as pleasure. This appraisal is unconscious, immediate, and results in the experience of pain or pleasure and the impulse to seek alleviation or continuation.

In an earlier work (1960) I have suggested that the so-called pain fibers mediate not only pain but pleasure; or rather, that the system of fibers (the appraisal system) which includes pain fibers also includes pleasure fibers. This peripheral system connects with areas in the brain that mediate pleasure or pain, often called the brain reward system. Since pleasure/pain are reactions to somatic sensations, early theorists have called them *feelings*. For the same reason, some philosophers have called the appraisal sense an "internal sense" like memory or imagination, assuming that such feelings could not be mediated by known peripheral fibers.

When peripheral fibers were identified which produced pain on stimulation, physiologists decided that pain is a somatic sensation like touch or muscle strain. Pleasure was disregarded or reduced to sexual pleasure and often described as "sexual sensation." But pain and pleasure are different from sensations. They are opposites in all gradations, down to mild pleasantness or unpleasantness. Sensations like sight, hearing, or touch are different from each other and have no opposites. Any sensation may be either pleasant or unpleasant, pleasurable or painful; no sensation is thus intimately connected with other sensations in different modalities. Sensory functions stand on their own, while pleasure or pain are always reactions to some sensory experience. It is usually assumed that pain results when pain fibers are excited together with visual, auditory, or olfactory fibers; but in many cases, we experience unpleasantness rather than pain. A glaring light, a sharp blow, a piercing sound, or a pungent smell may be actually painful; but we do not experience a painful taste. It is perhaps more consistent to assume that sensory experiences also excite fibers of a peripheral appraisal system that mediates all gradations of pain and pleasure. This system is discussed in more detail in chapter 17. Here, it is sufficient to note that pleasure and pain are reactions to experience, based on sensory appraisal. Hence they are feelings rather than sensations.

We do not experience intuitive *appraisals,* either the primitive appraisal of somatic sensations resulting in pleasure or pain, or the appraisal of things and people. That is, we are not reflectively aware that we are making a judgment of good or bad, beneficial or harmful. We only experience the *action impulse* that flows from it. On the level of somatic sensations, we experience pleasure with its readiness to enjoy, or pain with the impulse to ease it. On the level of object relations, we are attracted to anything we have appraised as good, repelled from anything we have appraised as bad.

Animals also appraise what they encounter and have an impulse to approach or withdraw. This applies to drive states as well as to performing a task to earn the taste of saccharin, receive a puff of a novel odor, or explore an empty goal box. It applies to seeking stimulation or exercise when rested, seeking rest when tired. Depending on the present bodily state, a given object may be found suitable or unsuitable, liked or disliked, approached or avoided.

Not only objects can be appraised as good and liked; bodily experiences can be appraised also. When milk is injected directly into the stomach of a hungry animal, it stills hunger pangs and abolishes discomfort. Animals will work for such relief; but they will work better if they are given food (Miller & Kessen, 1952). Chewing is pleasant, and so is the taste of food. Eating means having a triple pleasure: the pleasure of chewing, tasting, and satiation.

This explanation also holds for rewarding brain stimulation. When the "pleasure centers" are stimulated, the animal relaxes and experiences pleasure. It will press a lever to obtain such stimulation over and over. The reward is more direct than food. Food has to be chewed to enjoy the taste, and swallowed before the animal can experience the pleasure of satiation. When the brain is stimulated, pleasure is experienced immediately, directly, without intervening activity, without any waiting. There is no limit to such pleasure, hence the animal can go on pressing the bar for brain-stimulation until it can press no longer. Eating has to stop as soon as the stomach is filled. No wonder that animals press the bar continuously for long periods of time.

The Appraisal of Action

After appraising something as good or bad for us, we also have to estimate what we can do about it. Some things are good to eat, others are pleasant to look at, still others are nice to stroke or pet. In contrast, some things are annoying and disliked. We feel urged to strike at them, obliterate them in some way, or get away from them. Others are dangerous, and we feel a desire to escape before they can hurt us. Every situation requires an estimate of its effect on us, but also a gauging of the action required to approach or avoid it. The first appraisal leads to a positive or negative attitude toward the object; the second, to an impulse to act on it in a particular way. It is the whole appraisal complex, the thing-appraised-as-good-for-a-particular-action, that produces the inclination to a particular action and arouses a specific action tendency.

An action tendency is felt either as a simple intention or, if it is strong, as an emotion. However, in human beings, the judgment that produces an impulse to action is both intuitive and deliberate, based on both concrete and abstract values; and there is a possibility that the two might conflict. A boy may like to eat more than is good for him; but he also wants to make the baseball team and knows he has no chance as long as he is overweight. In this case, his intuitive appraisal of what to do conflicts with his deliberate judgement. He would like to have another helping but for reasons entirely irrelevant to his liking for food, he manfully declines the offer. This decision presupposes repeated rounds of appraisal. In each, he considers the situation from a different aspect until he cuts short his deliberation. The last appraisal of action, following his judgment that making the team is more important in the long run, leads to action. What is important to remember is that the sequence from perception to action is not like a chain in which one link follows upon the other, but more like a network in which each relay leads to several branching loops until one of these leads to the final step, the action.

This is not only a logical or psychological sequence but a temporal one as well. True, it may be so quick that action seems to follow immediately on perception or on a sudden thought. But that only happens when there is no deliberation, either because there is a sudden emergency that leads to panic action, or because similar situations in the past have evoked a decision that has become habitual. The longer the boy follows his resolution and declines second helpings, the easier will be the decision at mealtime, and the less time he will take over it; until it becomes automatic and needs no further thought.

Appraisal of Success or Failure

The appraisal of something as good for a particular action accounts for engaging in the action. But the appraisal that this action was successful, in addition to the appraisal that the object obtained is good to have, accounts for the decision to repeat the performance, to learn the task. Such an appraisal theory can dispense with the notion of reinforcement and all its problems. Successful performance is appraised as good, which induces an impulse to repeat the response and earn the reward.

In short, every appraisal gives rise to an impulse to action. What is intuitively appraised as good, attracts; what is appraised as bad, repels. The appraisal that something is good to know leads to attention; that it is good to have, results in desire; that it is good to remember, in recall. It is even possible to want to imagine something and become lost in fantasy.

AFFECTIVE MEMORY

There are only a few things we can immediately appraise as good or bad for us: a gentle touch, a pinprick, a blow, a taste, something hot or cold. All these sensations are experienced via the somesthetic system and affect us directly. We react to them with a range of feelings, from pleasure to pain. A sharp tone or a penetrating odor is immediately felt as unpleasant because it affects fibers of the appraisal system in addition to auditory or olfactory receptors. In contrast, anything we see or hear, but that is not near enough to touch us, we appraise as good or bad only because we have experienced its effects in the past, we have heard or read about it. A fire in the fireplace on a cold winter night is enjoyable; seeing a blazing fire on a hot summer night is annoying. We appraise it at sight, long before feeling the heat, because we relive the feelings we had on similar occasions.

We relive our feelings, we do not remember them. We experience a renewed liking or dislike, an immediate negative or positive attitude. This "affective memory," as we could call it, is experienced as a here-and-now emotional impulse, not as a remembered attitude. It accounts for the "instinctive" likes and dislikes we have all experienced, for the fact that once we like or dislike something, we continue to do so unless a contrary experience intervenes.

Freud thought that repression accounts for inexplicable likes or dislikes, for apparently groundless emotions. Traumatic experiences, he said, are forgotten, "repressed," but the emotion they caused goes underground until a chance occurrence allows it to resurface. However, it does sometimes happen that a traumatic experience has never been forgotten, yet the emotion is experienced in situations that have some resemblance to the original trauma, but by themselves would never arouse such strong reactions. In such a case, a person may remember the traumatic experience but does not connect it with today's emotion. Nor does he know that the emotion that distresses him today is the result of an experience long past. He is at a loss to account for the strength of his emotion but has no way to connect it with the emotion he felt long ago. His original experience has not been "repressed" because it has not been forgotten. Repression cannot account for such emotional revival but affective memory can: If today's situation has revived a past appraisal, and perhaps many of them, it will be far more intense than today's situation warrants.

The notion of affective memory can explain the difference between the time it takes an animal to learn active as compared to passive avoidance. In passive avoidance, the animal is shocked as soon as his mouth touches food. It only takes one or two trials before he will stop approaching the dish. In active avoidance, the animal sees a light or hears a buzzer and shortly afterwards is shocked where he stands. He can escape the shock by crossing into the safe compartment, or avoid it altogether by crossing as soon as buzzer or light is turned on. But it will take him many trials and much pain before he will learn to do that. It is sometimes said that passive avoidance is "emotional conditioning," which is fast, while ordinary conditioning is slow. But emotion is involved in both cases, the shock is equally painful. But in passive avoidance, the "good" food is suddenly felt as "bad, painful" and avoided after one or two tries. In active avoidance, the home compartment is at first appraised as "good, no pain" and after a few shocks, as "bad, threatens pain." But the light or buzzer has never hurt, so the animal does not see it as a threat. It takes some time before the animal learns that the negative cue announces pain.

Perception includes interpretation; and part of the interpretation is the intuitive appraisal that this is "good or bad for me." In human beings, this unconscious appraisal is supplemented by a deliberate value judgment, just as sense knowledge is supplemented by conceptual knowledge. Sense experience starts a process of spontaneous recall that helps us identify what we see, hear, or experience in some other way. In addition, we relive the favorable or unfavorable attitude this situation or its like has aroused in the past. This attitude may support our simultaneous deliberate judgment of present circumstances, or it may run counter to it. Such feelings are incipient action tendencies. The stronger they are, the more will they urge to action. They make action easy if they support our deliberate decision but may produce a painful conflict if our rational judgment goes against them.

Ordinarily, affective memory accompanies deliberate recall. When we recall a stay in the mountains or at the seashore, the feelings of ease and the enjoyment of a perfect vacation are revived with it. When we remember an embarrassing incident, we flush at the memory. But affective memory is independent of sensory memory. It can plague us with troublesome emotions unless we manage to realize from where they come.

4 Types of Modality-Specific Memory: Sensory, Motor, Conceptual

In the last chapter I tried to show that sensory experience is completed by an appraisal that results in an impulse to approach the "good" and avoid the "bad" object. This appraisal is registered and revived on encountering a similar situation. Such affective memory is unconscious, the repetition of past unwitting intuitive appraisals which results in newly experiencing an earlier favorable or unfavorable reaction. In contrast, what we usually mean by remembering is the intended or spontaneous recall of something seen, heard, or otherwise sensed. We usually assume that memory is a unitary function. We intend to recall a play or a conversation, and we remember the people involved, their talk, and their actions. We recall the whole scene complete with sights, sounds, and movements. Accordingly, we assume that recall is a single function no matter what modalities are involved. Yet we recall memories in different modalities, and these memory images are as different as the sensory modalities on which they are based.

Some memory images are easy to recall, but some cannot be recalled at all. The memory of a fragrance, a taste, a touch, is evanescent, almost impossible to recapture. Yet it appears unbidden when something else calls it to mind. Often, such memory images are taken for sensations. For instance, when a person is placed blindfolded before an electric heater and is asked to report as soon as he feels the heat coming on, he reports sooner or later feeling the heat, although the current was never turned on. The sensation of heat he reports is a memory image, recalled by his expectation. Similar experiments have succeeded with visual, auditory, and olfactory images.

MODALITY-SPECIFIC MEMORY

Memory seems to be modality-specific just like sensory experience itself. Just as some people have excellent eyesight but indifferent hearing, so there are people who have excellent visual and indifferent auditory memory. They may be able to report exactly what they have seen, but be unable to remember or recognize the simplest melody. Indeed, there seems to be differentiation even within a given modality: An individual may, after some training, be able to repeat a conversation verbatim, but not be able to reproduce a simple melody. There are people who have to see a name written or printed before they can remember it. There are others who remember a lecture better than something they have read.

Occasionally, we hear of someone who not only has an exceptional visual imagination but combines it with simultaneous images in other sensory modalities (smell, touch, hearing, even taste). Luria's (1968) fascinating report on such a man has been recently published in this country. This man was able to remember almost anything indefinitely, provided the material was given to him slowly enough so that he could form images, almost act out a scenario in imagination, complete with sounds, scents, and touches. In doing so, he not only registered sensory impressions in various modalities, he also rehearsed or recalled them. This report demonstrates that not the sensory experience but the sensory image is registered and retained. When a memory is anchored in various modalities, it can be remembered much more readily. Even people not distinguished by a faithful memory can remember something they want to by forming visual and auditory images. By repeating a man's name when he is introduced, by observing and immediately rehearsing any distinguishing marks—his face, voice, shape, dress, movements—it is possible to train oneself to remember names and the persons to whom they belong.

Visual and Auditory Memory

Many experiments have confirmed that visual and auditory memory images do exist. Neisser (1967) has suggested the term "iconic memory" for visual and "echoic memory" for auditory memory. These terms have been used in recent years by most experimenters. Sperling (1960, 1963) found that eight letters, flashed briefly on a tachistoscope screen, could be perceived at the rate of about 10 milliseconds per character; but they could be named (reported) only at the rate of about six per second. Indeed, the subjects claimed that for a brief time after the display was turned off, all the letters were clearly available but faded rapidly during the process of identifying and reporting them.

The necessity for auditory memory (Neisser's echoic memory) is perhaps even more compelling than for visual memory. While a scene or an array of letters can be seen all at once, auditory patterns require some time for completion. During that time, earlier parts of the speech or musical pattern must be held in mind to comprehend the sentence or recognize the melody. Guttman and Julesz (1963) found that subjects could recognize that a section of a random broadband noise was repeated. They described the periodic repetition as the sound of a motor boat, at a repetition rate between one and four times a second. At faster repetition rates, they heard the sound as a low tone. As Crowder (1976) points out, it is quite remarkable that the men were able to hold the segments in memory for as long as a second because "detecting repetition of white noise segments is like recognizing two patches of waves while one is sailing across the ocean" (p. 46). Various other methods have been used to demonstrate echoic memory. Apparently, auditory presentation produces better retention than visual presentation.

Motor Memory

There is one memory modality that is more often denied than acknowledged, and that is motor memory. Motor memory accounts for the fact that complicated movements become smooth, well-coordinated, and unroll almost automatically after they have been well practiced. It used to be said that learning "stamps in" such movements. Even today, when this term is no longer in favor, learning theorists say that movements are "reinforced," and so learned. This term, like the older analogy, implies that engrams have been strengthened and connections reinforced until the newly learned pattern becomes automatic.

Most theorists take for granted that it is kinesthetic and proprioceptive memory that accounts for learning motor skills. But a careful analysis does not support this notion. Kinesthesis is the sensation of moving, a somatosensory experience. To assume that motor learning depends on the memory of the sensations experienced in muscles, tendons, and limbs during practice would make any motor skill a well-nigh incredible performance. Instead of hitting the golf ball and learning by the success or failure of the stroke how to aim and hit more effectively, we would have to try and reproduce the kinesthetic and proprioceptive sensations induced by our movement. But until the ball is hit, we do not know what sensations we will experience. According to such a theory, practice would have to facilitate kinesthetic sensations instead of facilitating movements.

We do not recall seeing, hearing, or smelling. We only recall *what* we have seen, heard, smelled, or tasted. Indeed, we remember best what we have seen or heard, because a landscape or a melody is highly structured and well differentiated. To recall something smelled, tasted, or touched, we usually have to visualize it: the perfume of a rose or carnation, the taste of coffee or roast beef, the touch of velvet or sandpaper. To recall or recognize the way a movement has felt is impossible because we cannot recall moving, just as we cannot recall seeing or hearing. We can, of course, imagine movements we have made in the past, like swinging a golf club or hitting a tennis ball. But such images cannot bring back the sensations that had accompanied the actual movement. Neither can we recognize these kinesthetic sensations when we become aware of them during a similar movement, just as we do not recognize that looking now arouses the same sensations as looking yesterday. A golf stroke feels "right"; it does not feel familiar. While we cannot remember moving, just as we do not remember seeing or hearing, we do remember the aim of movement, the fact that we have played tennis or golf, or that we have turned the key and locked the house door. But these memories are usually visual rather than motor memories. We see ourselves playing, we visualize the golf course, the caddy, our partner, our score. We remember hitting the golf or tennis ball. We learn a motor skill by improving our aim and increasing our speed.

Vision and sometimes hearing serve to correct our aim. Consider, for instance, the finger movements involved in piano playing. The pianist has learned long motor sequences that keep recurring in different combinations. After years of practice, the pianist has a considerable repertoire of music that is played from memory, and can go through complicated sequences of finger movements that last many minutes. The pianist pays no attention to the position of fingers or hand; in fact, such attention is apt to interrupt the smooth flow of his play. Still less does he pay attention to kinesthetic sensations. The pianist does not recall previous finger movements nor try to reinstate earlier kinesthetic or proprioceptive sensations. He intends to play a piece of music and, if well practiced, the fingers obey.

The curious notion that motor learning depends on the memory of sensations we can neither recall nor recognize surely stems from the conviction—never voiced yet present—that we cannot be aware of anything except sensations; that we are not aware of movements until after the fact, when we sense the changes in position. This notion seems to be a remnant of Titchener's dictum that mental contents can only be sensations and feelings. Titchener's theories have gone out of fashion, but some of his dicta persist. Indeed, it seems that the notion that motor learning depends on kinesthetic memory has become an article of faith only a heretic would doubt.

Fortunately, some heretics have raised their voices in recent years. To quote a recent critic (Taub & Berman, 1968):

> It would hardly be an exaggeration to say that proprioceptive hypotheses have been used as a sort of glue to hold a number of learning theories together on what appeared to be empirical grounds, in the face of apparently contradictory evidence . . . . When proprioception is invoked as an explanatory device in situations where its relevance has not received specific demonstration, it begins to assume a mythological character, notwithstanding its undeniable existence. (p. 189)

Surely our awareness of movement is primarily the knowledge that we intend to move, and the experience of doing what we intend to do, reaching what we intend to reach. The awareness that I am moving my arm is quite different from the experience I have when someone else moves it. When I move it, even with my eyes closed, my awareness of the intention to move and of doing it is so strong that the kinesthetic sensations are barely conscious. When someone else moves it and I cannot see the movement, these sensations are the only evidence I have that the arm is moving. Without such sensations (e.g., in *Tabes dorsalis*) the patient can move and is aware of moving, although his gait changes because he can no longer check his movements on the basis of somesthetic sensations.

The kinesthetic feedback postulated by cyberneticists (Wiener, 1961) to explain the improvement in aiming is far too slow to account for the lightning speed and accuracy of the quick draw expert or the newly revived "quick kill" technique of aiming in which the weapon is used as an extension of the arm in pointing. This technique gives the only assurance of hitting a moving target before being hit by the enemy. Pointing is made more accurate by repeated drawing, that is, by motor memory, and not by any kind of feedback, kinesthetic or visual, both of which would retard the draw.

Obviously, feedback is used to improve the aim of automatic tracking mechanisms. A tracking torpedo needs a computer to calculate the speed and direction of missile and target to aim at the point at which the two will intersect. The lightning speed of the computer is equal to this task. Human mental processes would never finish the calculation in time. The computer is not aware of movement, but the human being is; and every time he practices a skilled movement, he increases his speed and accuracy.

The notion that a motor skill is based on kinesthetic memory seems to depend on the assumption that skilled movement is impossible without kinesthetic and proprioceptive feedback. Evidence for this assumption came from a report by Mott and Sherrington (1895) that monkeys do not use a limb after its sensory nerve supply has been cut, although they still use it in reflex or emotional responses. This report seems to imply that normal somatosensory experience is necessary for movement, and particularly, for motor learning. However, recent findings have thrown doubt on this inference. According to Knapp et al. (1958, 1963), when the intact limb was restrained, monkeys did use the deafferented arm and hand to press a lever that stopped an electric shock. They did that even when they could not see their arm. After the operation, there was some retention deficit, but the animals quickly relearned. But when the same monkeys were allowed to move around, they did not use the deafferented arm.

In contrast, when the sensory nerves were cut in both arms, the monkeys not only learned to use either arm in pressing the lever but also learned to use both arms freely outside the learning situation. Within a period from two to six months, they began to walk normally, with both palms on the floor. They could climb quickly, were able to pick up small objects and in every respect resembled intact monkeys, even when blindfolded. Hence Taub and Berman (1968) stated that there is:

the possibility that behavior can be learned and performed in the absence of all topographic feedback from either movement or its associated neural events, either peripheral or central. This implies that "neural traces" can be laid down . . . entirely on the basis of centrifugal impulses without requiring the return of centripetal impulses from the normally resulting motor and neutral activity to, as it were, stamp them in . . . the neurons of a motor center do not have to be told that they have fired, they know. (p. 189)

Of course, it is not the neurons that know they have fired, it is the person or the animal who knows he has moved.

When one limb is deafferented, the monkey is not aware of the limb and its position in space. The monkey may have an impulse to move, for instance, to reach for a banana, but he will do so with the arm he can locate. But in expressing anger, the monkey acts out his emotion without regard to the condition of his limbs. With both arms deafferented, or with the intact arm restrained, the monkey will try moving even though he cannot feel the deafferented arm. It takes time before the animal with both arms deafferented achieves normal movement, not because proprioceptive or kinesthetic sensations are necessary for movement, but because the animal has to learn to move although he cannot sense his limbs. Normally, there is an unbroken sequence of conscious activities, from the intention to move, the appraisal that movement is suitable, the movement and its attendant sensations, to the realization that the goal is reached. With both arms deafferented, the monkey must learn to carry out his intention even without being able to locate his arm, and wait for the result of his movement to find out whether he made the correct move.

Any movement is appraised as pleasant or unpleasant. A smooth, coordinated movement feels pleasant—hence the pleasure of dancing, skiing, skating. A movement that reaches its goal is also appraised as successful. A monkey with arms deafferented can no longer appraise moving them as pleasant or unpleasant. Since he does not sense their movement, he has no way of gauging the way this movement will affect him. But although he has lost the possibility of appraising the sensory effect of movement, he has retained the capability of appraising the success of movement (when he has avoided the shock, or grasped the banana) and so can correct his aim and learn even a complex motor response.

If learning a motor skill depends on motor memory, it would seem reasonable to expect that movements are registered in the brain as motor engrams and are revived during practice. There have been many experimental findings that support such a conclusion. For instance, rats that have learned a motor maze can perform it either running or swimming; they can do it even when they are partly paralyzed or forced to drag themselves along. What is preserved is the movement pattern, its direction and aim, not the felt pattern of muscular contractions or any other type of kinesthetic feedback. As Taub and Berman (1968) say, the neural traces are laid down entirely on the basis of centrifugal impulses.

Hence motor learning seems to depend on the cortical registration of movements and movement impulses, in strict analogy with sensory discrimination learning, which depends on the cortical registration of sensory impressions. Every movement would have to be registered, retained, and reactivated in similar future movements. As the motor pattern is repeated, it becomes an effortless, almost automatic performance. Indeed, thinking about a learned sequence often disturbs recall. A singer may recall the words of a song perfectly in singing but may fail if he is asked to say them. A speech or a poem may be reproduced perfectly from beginning to end, but the speaker may be unable to recite the second verse without reciting the first.

With motor memory now taking its rightful place within modality-specific memory, and affective memory (together with immediate appraisal) supplying the motivation of learning, the only type of memory still to be discussed is conceptual memory, which builds on both modality-specific and affective memory.

CONCEPTUAL MEMORY

Like conceptual knowledge, conceptual memory cuts across all memory modalities. We not only remember something seen, heard, touched, or otherwise experienced, we also know what it is, what it is called, its use, origin, and meaning. This is the kind of memory that distinguishes human beings from animals. It makes thinking possible because it allows us to recall concepts at will so that we can use them in interpreting things around us as they are in their relations to each other and to ourselves. Conceptual memory supplements both modality-specific and affective memory. Sensory memory allows us to recall what we have experienced; conceptual memory allows us to recall the knowledge we have gained and draw on it in interpreting what we experience here and now. Affective memory helps us to relive our positive or negative attitudes toward concrete individual things; conceptual memory allows us to recall past value judgments. In fact, our revived likes and dislikes are based on past value judgments as much as on affective memory, or rather, affective memory incorporates past value judgments.

That conceptual memory supplements modality-specific memory can be shown by experimental results. Miller (1956), for instance, found that the immediate memory span (about 7 items) can be increased by organizing the items into groups (chunking). For instance, in learning radio-telegraphic code, each dit and dah is at first remembered separately. Soon these sounds are organized into letters, that is, into bigger chunks. Then the operator hears not separate letters but whole words, and finally whole phrases, so that he is able to remember more and more items, in bigger and bigger chunks. Sidney Smith (1954) trained himself to organize binary digits in such a way that he recoded from a base-two arithmetic to a base-four arithmetic: 00 is recoded as 0.01, while 1.10 is recoded as 2, and 11 is recoded as 3. In this way, eighteen binary digits are recoded into chunks of two, that is, nine in all. This is within the span of immediate memory, which is eight for decimal and nine for binary digits (see Table 4.1). When the eighteen

TABLE 4.1
Ways of Recoding Sequences of Binary Digits

Binary Digits (Bits)	1	0	1	0	0	0	1	0	0	1	1	1	0	0	1	1	1	0
2:1 Chunks	10		10		00		10		01		11		00		11		10	
Recoding	2		2		0		2		1		3		0		3		2	
3:1 Chunks	101			000			100			111			001			110		
Recoding	5			0			4			7			1			6		
4:1 Chunks	1010				0010				0111				0011				10	
Recoding	10				2				7				3					
5:1 Chunks	10100					01001					11001					110		
Recoding	20					9					25							

From: G. A. Miller (1956).

items are regrouped into chunks of three, and given a new name between 0 and 7, we obtain 6 chunks, which is well within the span of immediate memory. The original 18 digits can also be recoded in chunks of 4 and 5 digits, resulting in 4 and 3 chunks respectively. Smith found that in doing so he could eventually remember and repeat 40 binary digits.

The same feats of memory are possible by using various systems of mnemonic (cf. Loisette, 1896; Weinland, 1957). Essentially, these consist in organizing the material, grouping it into meaningful structures, forming unique or bizarre associations, and visualizing them. Of these transformations, everyone except visualization depends on conceptual memory. Without concepts, there cannot be any ordering into categories, no meaningful structures, no associations, whether unique or bizarre. In the same way as concepts enable us to achieve human conceptual knowledge that vastly transcends concrete sensory knowledge, so conceptual memory enables us to transcend sensory and motor memory by organizing it and building upon it.

Remembering the time of day, the day of the week, or the year of the calendar are examples of the way in which conceptual memory is combined with modality-specific memory. The division into hours, days, months, and years obviously depends on concepts and conceptual memory. No animal counts hours, days, or years. Clock time or calendar time depends on high order abstractions and arbitrary but conventional classification. But once these concepts are formed and remembered, the remembering of actual dates depends mainly on speech (motor) memory, and the remembered number (year) recalls the appropriate event.

When a memory deficit occurs, as for instance in Korsakoff psychosis, in which one of the symptoms is the patient's inability to tell which day or year it is, or in what year certain important historical events happened, or even events the patient has lived through, this is not a deficit in a special "time sense" but a deficit in remembering numbers, dates, or days of the week. Recalling numbers means a memory task almost as difficult as recalling nonsense syllables because they have no connection with any other visual, auditory or even conceptual memory. To remember historical dates means to link up the event to be remembered with the year it happened. The more often such numbers are used, the more easily they will be recalled, not only because repetition facilitates recall but also because visual, auditory, and speech memory are active at the same time. For this reason, ages of parents and children in a family are easier to remember than, say, the age at which a given President started his term of office. The only way most of us have of remembering the age of a public figure, or the year of an important event, is by a process of reasoning in which we start from things we know and can date, and connect them with other events, until we finally arrive at the number we are looking for. The Korsakoff patient cannot remember dates of recent events and often cannot remember his own age or the age of his children; but to conclude from this that his basic defect is his inability to perceive the "flow of time" so that his experience is no longer "impregnated with a temporal sign," as one theorist says, is not to explain the defect but merely to replace the mystery with an empty phrase. What are these "temporal signs?" Whence do they come, how are they registered?

The very fact that intellectual functioning is apparently not disturbed in Korsakoff patients so that they can reason from data given to them and come to correct conclusions is a sign that we are dealing with a memory disturbance and not with an interference with conceptualization or reasoning. As we have seen, the difficulty is that memory is not a unitary function and thus may be mediated by widely differing brain structures and pathways. It is conceivable that the brain lesions that undoubtedly exist in Korsakoff psychosis may involve some of these structures more than others, which may account for the differing symptomatology.

To sum up: I have suggested that there are two main types of memory: *affective memory*, which retains earlier appraisals of good/bad, and *modality-specific memory*, which retains impressions of sensory experience, movements and movement impulses. Both types of memory have a conceptual dimension. While concepts are not bound to a particular modality or a particular brain site, they do need sensory and motor memory. Children born blind and deaf can be taught to speak, read Braille and use concepts; but concepts include the sound, sight or touch of letters, words and sentences, and must be expressed in speech or writing. Similarly, value judgments are based on sensory appraisals and are retained with the help of affective memory.

While the strategies employed in using conceptual (semantic) memory are of great importance for anyone wanting to explore or improve human memory, they are irrelevant for my purposes. My aim in this book is to explore the neural mediation of memory. This aim will be served by discussing modality-specific and affective memory, and their neural substrate. It should be understood, however, that human beings employ semantic memory together with modality-specific memory, and value judgments together with affective memory.

5
Memory Registration, Retention, Recall

> *The rapidity with which permanent mnemonic traces can be created . . . suggests that the distinction often made between short-term and long-term memory is not applicable to the mnemonic process itself but rather to some aspect in the effective retrieval of the trace. This is further indicated by such phenomena as transient global amnesia or the gradual clearing of retrograde amnesia that follows cerebral concussion. Obviously, in these instances the memory trace is not destroyed; it is simply inaccessible, as may be so-called short-term memory after similar traumatic occurrences.*
>
> Doty, (1979) p. 56

It is usually assumed that memory progresses in three stages: from registration to retention, and finally retrieval. Only the retrieval stage can be directly investigated; registration and retention can only be checked by recall or recognition tests. When they fail, we have to infer on the basis of indirect evidence whether the material has been registered but cannot be either recognized or recalled, whether it has never been registered, or, lastly, whether it has been registered but not retained.

REGISTRATION

When a sensory impression is registered as a memory, what is it that is registered and preserved? Is it the sensory impression itself, that is, the neural change produced by sensory experience, or is it a separate memory trace? If it is the sensory experience or its neural trace that is preserved, it is reasonable to expect that these traces are preserved in the primary sensory cortex. However, damage to these areas seems to block only immediate sensory experience but leaves earlier memories intact. For instance, damage to the visual cortex does not prevent the patient from remembering earlier visual experiences, or from visualizing things and people. In contrast, when the visual association areas are badly damaged but the primary visual areas are intact, he finds it difficult if not impossible to remember, recognize, or imagine something seen before.

Hence, the trace that is preserved çannot be that of the primary sensation but must be a trace of its image. Every sense experience is accompanied by an image: If we look at something and then quickly close our eyes, we see the image of the object, although the sensation itself has disappeared. When we hear something, a tune, a word, a noise, we can still hear it as an image although the sound has stopped. It is almost as if the original sights and sounds lingered as a positive after-image. This image seems to be produced together with the sensation although we do not advert to it until the sensation has ceased. It must be simultaneous because we sense no gap between cessation of the sensation and becoming aware of the image, nor do we need to recall it—it is there as soon as we attend to it.

It is unfortunate that the term "image" is derived from visual experience. Such psychological traces of sensory experience seem to occur in all modalities. We have a lingering image of something just heard, touched, tasted, or smelled after the stimulus is gone. We also have a distinct impression of a movement just made. All these psychological traces could be called "images" of the original impressions.

Since these images are modality-specific like sensations, the various memory modalities may also be mediated by brain structures that are separate for each modality. Many research reports indicate that such modality-specific memories may be registered in the association cortex close to the neighboring primary sensory or motor cortex of the same modality. So damage to area 17 (the primary visual cortex) results in the inability to see pattern and movement, but visual memories are untouched. But with the visual association areas 18 and 19 destroyed, and intact area 17, a monkey can catch a gnat in midair, but he cannot learn a visual discrimination. He can see, but can no longer remember what he has seen. A patient with damage to the visual association area can pick up a pin, but he does not recognize it as a pin until he holds it in his hand. I discuss the evidence of association cortex as memory areas in Part II, chapter 12.

RETENTION

Once a memory is registered, it is retained and can be recalled. Any memory test we care to apply tests primarily recall or recognition and only by inference registration and retention. Registration is the beginning of retention; and retention is said to consist in the "storage" of memories. The professional literature has spoken for almost a century of "memory storage" and so created the image of a storehouse in which memories are packed away. But memories cannot be stored like bales or even filed away on filing cards. If they were, we could never recover them quickly enough to be of much use. There have been psychologists who have tried to change the storehouse image. Bartlett (1932) has talked about an active process of remembering instead of memory as a storehouse. And Ulric Neisser (1967) has insisted that memory is *used* for the needs of the present, it is not replayed in unchanged form. But the memory store seems to be one of the notions that stubbornly resists change.

Since memory images occur together with sensations, their traces seem to be registered in the brain over a receptor pathway, with one branch going to the primary sensory cortex, the other to the neighboring association cortex (see chapter 12). Such memories cannot be registered as images or words. They can be preserved only as a pattern of cell changes, laid down by neural impulses, and must be capable of being reactivated by other neural impulses reaching the same area. We could call such registered sense impressions potential memories, dispositions that can be revived, made actual, during retrieval. Instead of a storehouse, the more appropriate image would be a constellation of memory dispositions.

RECALL

The process by which recall is achieved has not received sufficient attention, either from psychologists or neurologists. Psychologists have concentrated on what is recalled, while neurologists and biochemists have spent a great deal of time studying the way in which memory traces might be registered; but the neural mechanism of recall and recognition has never been seriously investigated. Yet it seems obvious that memory traces must be reactivated over a neural pathway we might attempt to identify.

Psychologically speaking, recall seems to function strictly by association. Something we see, hear, or think about recalls something else associated with it. Several modalities might be involved in such associations. For instance, something touched in the dark will immediately recall visual images of several things that could provide this particular touch sensation, as an overstuffed chair, a bed, drapes, and the like. It is by means of such spontaneous recall that we identify the things we encounter.

Human beings can also recall deliberately what they have experienced. We may recall personal experiences in the form of visual and auditory images. We may also recall impersonal conceptual knowledge, as is required, for instance, in examinations. Finally, we may recall actions, either by reporting them or by repeating them, in learning a skill.

Spontaneous or implicit recall, though almost unnoticed, is the most frequently occurring type. Such recall is almost impossible to investigate experimentally because we only pay indirect attention to it. Such implicit recall is at the root of our sense of identity, of our awareness of self and others as continuing beings. It is the source of our whole orientation in space and time. (see chapter 2.)

Deliberate recall is the only type of recall investigated in psychological experiments. Only incidentally is it a direct recall of visual or auditory images; rather, it is a report of such images or, more likely, some performance that is based on recall. In reporting what he has seen (e.g., a series of letters or digits on the tachistoscope) the subject recalls the visual image; but in reporting on it, he forms a speech and auditory memory trace. When he is asked to reproduce a design from memory, he draws on his visual image; but in drawing the design, he also forms a motor memory trace. In any further reproductions of the design, he will now have a stronger visual image (based on the design shown him, and his own drawing) and can also draw on the memory of his movements in reproducing the design. In recalling words, letters or digits for a second time, he can now draw upon visual, auditory and speech memory. Every reported recall makes it easier to refocus on the remembered word, and so facilitates access. The more memory modalities (motor: speech, drawing, writing; visual: sight of word or design; hearing: sound of word or melody) are used in recall, the stronger the probability that recall will be perfect.

Deliberate recall is possible only in a few memory modalities: we can recall a picture, a scene, a spoken phrase, or a melody. But we cannot easily form a memory image of a smell, a taste, or a touch we have known, we merely remember that we have tasted caviar, smelled the scent of a gardenia, or touched sandpaper. We usually have to visualize these things to help us imagine the taste, scent, or touch, and even then these images are faint and fleeting. But we have no difficulty in recognizing scent, taste, or touch when we experience them again.

Movements also can be recalled by remembering the situation in which they have occurred. For instance, in trying to remember whether we have locked the house door, we may recall searching for the key, see ourselves turning it in the lock and trying the door to see whether it has caught. But ordinarily, motor memory is revived spontaneously in repeating the learned movement. In learning a skill, the revival of past motor memory traces helps to make the desired movements smooth, fast, and fluid, until they become almost automatic.

Speech memory also is a type of motor memory. Whether we memorize word or digit lists, or learn lists of paired associates, we recall not only the sight and sound of the words, but their articulation as well. We experience at first hand just how important such speech memory is when we try to learn a foreign language later in life. Because we have no motor memory traces available for the articulation of the foreign language sounds, we find ourselves almost unable to form the vowels and consonants as they are pronounced in that language. Despite our best efforts, we may never lose a heavy accent because native pronunciation habits keep intruding.

IMMEDIATE VERSUS LONG-TERM MEMORY

The fact that it is possible to repeat immediately something heard just before, or to recall a number of objects seen briefly, or to reproduce immediately a diagram seen for a moment, has been discussed in the past under "attention span" and more recently, under "immediate" or "primary" memory. Early in the history of experimental psychology, immediate memory or attention span was defined as the number of discrete units that can be recalled in the original order after one presentation (Jacobs, 1887).

Immediate memory has also been called "very short-term memory" (Atkinson et al., 1967), "primary memory" (James, 1892), "perceptual trace" (Adams, 1967), "preperceptual stimulus trace" (Broadbent, 1967), "perceptual image" (Bower, 1967), and "icon" (Neisser, 1967). It seems to be accessible to recall for anywhere between three to four seconds (Melton, 1967).

Despite the variety of terms used, there is substantial agreement that immediate memory exists, as Broadbent (1967) puts it, as a "kind of afterglow, like an after-image, which dies very rapidly, within a second or so." (p. 64.) There is also agreement that the time during which this "afterglow" continues is very short. Averbach and Sperling (1960) showed that a large number of items flashed on a screen, followed by a marker (which required a report on this item), made it possible to retrieve almost any item shown. But in the time it took to report the wanted item, the rest of the items had disappeared. Also, the subject found it more difficult to retrieve the item marked if the time between the flash card and the marker was increased, even when the interval remained less than a second.

Besides immediate memory, psychologists distinguish short-term, intermediate, and long-term memory. They disagree on the time difference between short-term and intermediate memory, and between intermediate memory and long-term memory. Some experiments testing recall repeatedly over a day or two, or over several weeks, are considered studies in long-term memory. Other theorists would consider them studies in intermediate memory and would reserve the "long-term" label for memories that can be recalled over a period of months and years.

Crowder (1976) reviewed the voluminous research published in recent years concerning the difference between primary memory (immediate, short-term) and secondary (long-term) memory. I discuss only those factors important for my purpose, namely, the factors that might help to identify the pathways in the brain that serve memory registration and recall.

Since the terms short-term and intermediate memory are so fluid in their meaning, I use Crowder's term "secondary memory" for both. He uses "primary memory" in William James' sense as immediate memory, not needing recall but present as the continuation of perception. I follow him in this usage as well.

The first question demanding an answer is this: Are primary and secondary memory two stages of one process or do they represent two different processes? If they are stages of one continuous process, how does it progress from one stage to the next? If two different processes, do they use two different memory stores? If they do, how are memories transferred from the primary store to the secondary memory store? In either case, the fleeting nature of immediate memory and its connection with secondary memory will have to be explained.

With a few exceptions (Melton, 1963; Postman, 1964), most psychologists have accepted the notion of different memory systems. In a careful review, Postman came to the conclusion that the data do not seem to justify "the formulation of special explanatory principles which apply to only a circumscribed range of phenomena, delimited . . . along the temporal dimension" (Postman, 1964, p. 193–4). In his view, it is always the same memory, stored in the same way, but lasting different periods of time. Unfortunately, neither Melton nor Postman suggest an alternative explanation of the data on which the distinction between short-term and long-term storage has been based. Memory as a continuous process is appealing because it would not require two storage systems or a special transfer mechanism that maintains the connection between the two. However, such a concept does require some statement how this memory process progresses from one stage to the next.

DECAY, DISPLACEMENT AND INTERFERENCE THEORIES

The fleeting nature of immediate (primary) memory has been explained as decay by disuse. But there is no way to establish that such decay occurs in the memory traces in the brain—and any other meaning can only be an analogy that cloaks our ignorance. Theorists have also suggested that immediate memories may be displaced by other memories; or that later interpolation of other tasks (and memories) may interfere with earlier memories (retroactive interference); or that earlier memories may intrude upon later memories (proactive interference). All these theories try to explain how it is that primary memory may be lost before it can become secondary memory.

Interference theories in particular would have to explain how interpolated tasks can cause the loss of earlier memories. Many experiments have established that the more difficult the interpolated task, the worse the recall of the learned material (Posner & Rossman, 1965; Crowder, 1967). Apparently, retention is better if the first five or ten seconds after learning are occupied with an easy rather than a difficult interpolated task (Dillon & Reid, 1969). Crowder (1976) suggests on the basis of these experiments, that "rehearsal does not simply maintain items 'in' the primary memory, but rather that rehearsal 'is' primary memory" (p. 196). Be that as it may, rehearsal seems to be needed to make the transition from primary to secondary memory, unless the original memory is part of a strong emotional experience.

Proactive interference has been particularly resistant to explanation. Why should recall be disturbed by earlier memories? One answer has been the extinction hypothesis of interference: When reinforcement of a learned performance no longer occurs, the rate of performance declines. For instance, when a rat is rewarded with a food pellet every time it presses the bar in a Skinner box, it will press the bar at a fast rate until it is sated. But when the bar press is no longer rewarded by a food pellet, the rate of bar pressing gradually decreases, although the rat is still hungry. The curve of bar pressing during learning and extinction is quite similar to the memory decrement in proactive interference. For instance, when a list of paired associates is learned in such a way that the subject responds to one member of the pair (A) with the other member (C), he will soon be able to respond without mistake. Next, he has to learn another list in which the response to A is not C but B. This corresponds to an extinction for learning the A-C pairs. After a rest period, the earlier A-C memories tend to recover so that some A-C responses occur instead of the correct A-B responses. The curve for the A-B responses, which gradually increase with relearning, and for the A-C responses which gradually fall off, is quite similar to part of the learning curve for A-B and the extinction curve for A-C.

This sounds like an ingenious explanation. Unfortunately, to explain such interference as "extinction" describes only what happens and not why or how it happens. In fact, it explains only part of what happens. If the earlier list is extinguished, why does the earlier learning recover after a rest period? Why does the cue elicit a word that was paired with the cue in the earlier list but does not appear in the later list? The answer seems to be that the learner does not recall the list to which his response belongs. The words themselves, either in the earlier or in the later list, are well known to all subjects. What the learner has to do is to recognize the cue as belonging to the last list he has learned. If instead he recalls a word that is also familiar but belongs to the earlier list, he has exchanged a word that should be more familiar with one that is less familiar, because it had been learned earlier. The words in the earlier list are not extinguished. They are gradually replaced by words that become more familiar as they are repeated and learned in the more recent experiment.

Retroactive interference does not seem to come from working on an interpolated task per se but from shifting attention from one memory task to another.

Perhaps an experiment will clarify the problem. In a study that has become a classic, Peterson and Peterson (1959) showed a card with a three-consonant syllable (a trigram) to their subjects and asked them to remember it. Immediately afterwards, they told their subjects a three-digit number and asked them to subtract three from that number and go on counting backwards by threes out loud. After three seconds, recall of the trigram was tested and proved to be 80%. When the interval was increased, the percentage correct rapidly decreased. Eighteen seconds after the original presentation, it approached zero.

This experiment illustrates what "response interference" really means, namely, a second operation of remembering. Counting backwards by threes is a rather demanding task because the original number has to be kept in mind during each subtraction and the result must be remembered again. During this time, the subject could pay no attention to the trigram because the subtraction was paced by a metronome at a brisk rate. In this experiment we are not dealing with a simple decay of a memory trace but a replacement of one memory operation by another. Something similar happens when I go to cut the lawn and a neighbor stops me with a question. By the time I have answered, I may have forgotten what I was going to do. In both cases, attention has shifted from one task to another. Instead of remembering the trigram, the subjects in the Petersons' experiment were engaged in another memory task.

Crowder (1976) thought that attention alone was involved in retroactive interference. He suggested that mental arithmetic, when interpolated before the retention test, interferes with retention because both tasks converge on the same attention channel. The fact that interference is more severe when the two tasks employ the same modality (visual memory is less impaired by verbal distractor tasks than verbal memory) implied to him that at some level there must also be multiple attention channels (p. 156). Multiple attention channels may exist; but in that case, it should be more difficult to switch attention from one channel to another than to switch attention from one task to another within the same attention channel. The situation is different when we specify modality-specific memory so that each modality is recalled *via a different branch of the recall circuit*. To select the correct response when two sets of verbal memories are involved is more difficult than to recall the verbal memory set when the interpolated task engages visual memory. Of course, attention is involved as well. If the experiment is arranged in such a way that the subject must pay exclusive attention to the interpolated task instead of being able to switch attention to the trigram occasionally, he is soon unable to recall the trigram.

Research has certainly shown that interpolated activities do interfere with recall; but the interference theory merely describes what is happening rather than giving an explanation. The best guess has been that interpolated tasks interfere with recall because they prevent rehearsal so that primary memory fails to consolidate.

CONSOLIDATION THEORY

The consolidation theory has a long history. Müller and Pilzecker (1900) suggested that neural activity perseverates for some time after learning. When perseveration is prevented by interpolated activities, memories cannot consolidate and soon disappear. The fact that retention is improved if the learner is allowed to sleep before he is tested for retention seems to support this notion (Ekstrand, 1967). However, it is unlikely that perseveration would last longer than a few minutes. Yet McGeoch (1942) found that retroactive interference occurs if the learner is given an interpolated word list to learn, six weeks after the original word list.

Hebb's (1961) dual-trace consolidation theory is a quasi-neurological explanation of short-term and long-term memory that assumes a two-stage process: an early and relatively brief stage during which the memory trace is maintained by some type of reverberative process in neuronal networks, and a later consolidation stage characterized by a structural modification of neurons. This modification may be a change in nucleotide sequences or base rations in RNA, or a modification of perineural glia cells (Chorover, 1965). But the actual chemical or structural change has never been identified.

Consolidation time may vary from several minutes (Pearlman et al., 1961; Thompson & Dean, 1955), to several hours (Bureš et al., 1962) or days (Russell, 1958). According to Chorover, under certain conditions, such consolidation may be completed within a few seconds after learning. Apparently, the time at which consolidation becomes complete depends entirely on the conditions of the experiment.

There is no evidence that primary (immediate) memory is mediated by reverberating circuits. Also, neither Hebb nor other theorists have spelled out how consolidation is achieved. It is certain that rehearsal has something to do with converting primary memory into secondary memory. But again, we do not know how rehearsal maintains primary memory and helps to convert it into secondary memory.

There is no difference in the prediction of recall, no matter whether decay, interference, or consolidation theory is used. Whether a trace decays, suffers interference, or fails to consolidate, there will always be a slowly decreasing memory curve for old learning and a slowly rising curve for new learning. Both interference and consolidation theory can account for proactive and retroactive inhibition of recall, the one by postulating interference, the other by assuming that only part of the memory traces had achieved consolidation. There is a little more difficulty for the decay theory in explaining proactive inhibition: Why should a decaying trace interfere with later traces? Even this difficulty has been explained by "overwriting," so that the last items are still legible when the first items of the new memory task are presented. But "overwriting" is merely another doubtful analogy.

Most of the experiments done to prove or disprove a particular theory can be explained just as well when the other two theories are used. But there are a few experiments that seem to have confounded most theorists. Hebb (1961), for instance, wanted to test his notion that immediate memory is based on reverberating neural activity and should disappear if consolidation of these traces is disrupted by incompatible tasks. He called out 24 nine-digit numbers at the rate of one digit per second, and asked his subjects to repeat each nine-digit number immediately after its presentation. The third nine-digit number heard and repeated by the subject recurred after every three intervening numbers, seven times in all. Contrary to expectations based on his interference theory, Hebb found that the repeated presentation and repetition did improve recall. There undoubtedly was intervening activity: Indeed, the same nine digits had been used throughout the series in different combinations. But apparently it did not interfere with recall. Melton (1963) replicated the experiment, but used consonants instead of digits. Working with two sets (set A was B, D, G, J, L, N, Q, S, Z; set B was C, F, H, M, P, R, T, V, Z), Melton projected different sequences of set A on a screen. Every fourth presentation consisted of a sequence from set B in one experiment, from set A in the other. These intervening sets were repeated seven more times, always in the same order. After each of the repetitive sets, the subjects were asked to write down what they remembered. Again, the recall of the critical sets was considerably better at the end of the series than in the beginning. When the same set (A) was used for the repetitive combination, there was moderate improvement. But when a different set (B) was used for the repetitive series, there was pronounced improvement of recall from the beginning to the end of the session. It seems, then, that recall is improved in this type of experiment whether digits or consonants are used, whether the various combinations are called out or shown on the screen.

ACCESS THEORY OF RECALL

These results cannot be explained by the interference theory, nor can they be explained by trace decay or trace consolidation. They can be explained, however, if we assume that memory is retained indefinitely, but access to it can be lost. Access can be established and maintained by rehearsal and recall. In both experiments described above, access was maintained by repeated rehearsals: The visual or auditory presentations were always repeated, either orally or in writing. Apparently, competing activities do not materially interfere as long as rehearsal is also possible.

That some rehearsal is necessary if something is to be remembered despite intervening activity is shown by another experiment, superficially similar, that did not result in learning. In this experiment, Bower (1967) used what has been called the "missing digit span" method. Eight out of nine digits (from 1 to 9) were called out to the subject in random order; he had to report the missing ninth digit. This proved to be fairly easy for most subjects who averaged between 60-70% correct. One particular digit (e.g., 6) was then left out eight times in a series of 24 sets, that is, every third set. In the intervening sets, other digits were missing, but none of them was missing more than twice in the whole series. Instead of improving in their report that digit 6 was missing, the subjects' performance deteriorated markedly toward the end of the 24 sets. This was true even when the critical set was repeated in the same order. It could be argued that the subjects should have recognized the critical combination and realized that the same digit was missing. This seems to have been prevented by the instructions which did not call for recognition but solely for spotting the missing digit. In the whole experiment, there was no set to remember anything—hence nothing was learned. If more time had been allowed, it is likely that at least some people might have realized that certain combinations recurred; also, if the digit combinations had been projected instead of being called out, there might have been a better chance of recognizing the critical combination.

None of the hypotheses discussed earlier can explain the lack of learning in this situation. But it can be explained on the assumption that rehearsal (of either image or response) is a necessary and sufficient condition for maintaining access to the original experience. In this experiment, the missing digit was never recalled or rehearsed although it was reported missing repeatedly. Each time a combination of digits was scanned, the lack of this digit was newly discovered. The sets called out were recalled and scanned; but the missing digit was judged missing—it was never recalled as a memory. For this reason, the repeated presentation of the critical combination did not result in improvement.

If rehearsal serves to maintain access to the memory image, as I have suggested, the absence of rehearsal and the switching of attention to another memory operation is sure to make it difficult if not impossible to recall the original experience after such interference. Such a hypothesis can dispense with the notion that there are several different memory stores. What happens in long-term memory is that access to the memory image has been facilitated through so many rehearsals in various modalities that it can no longer be lost. Indeed, memory may never be lost, but it may easily become inaccessible.

Tulving and Pearlstone (1966) have also made a distinction between memories that are available but not accessible, and memories that are both available and accessible. They presented words ordered into categories to several hundred high school students by announcing the category first (e.g., parts of clothing) and then calling out the words in that category (e.g., belt, coat, shoe). In the free-recall retention test, one group of students was given two minutes to recall as many items as they could. In the cued-recall condition, another group of students was allowed two minutes after a category was called out, to recall as many words as they could in that category. The second group recalled many more words in each category than the students who were not given the category cues. The authors concluded that both groups must have acquired and retained the same amount of information because they were treated alike up to the retention test. But cued recall made it easy to gain access to the stored information.

The access theory of recall makes it unnecessary to postulate two different memory systems, one primary, one secondary, or to show how immediate memory turns into long-term memory. If access to immediate memory is established and maintained, such memories will be rehearsed, reported, and recalled repeatedly. This will produce auditory and speech (verbal) memory traces in addition to what may have been an exclusively visual memory. Moreover, the original sensory impressions are ordered, arranged into categories, and have become material for thought. Conceptual memory, anchored to verbal (speech), visual, and auditory memory, can be maintained indefinitely because it is used continuously. A person's vocabulary is enlarged throughout his life but never lost, except through severe brain injury.

Rehearsal seems to establish access to memory by facilitating particular neural pathways. If we assume, as we must, that memories are registered in the cortex in the course of perception, it would seem reasonable to suppose that they must be revived by a circuit that reactivates the registered engrams.[1] Rehearsal seems to facilitate conduction over this recall circuit. Until the recall pattern is firmly established, head trauma, electroconvulsive shock (ECS), or drugs may interfere with synaptic conduction just as a magnet in the vicinity of a recording tape can interfere with the proper alignment of electrons and so "wipe" the tape.

It has been found, for instance, that animals can no longer perform a learned task if ECS is applied shortly after training. Three hours after learning, ECS no longer interfered with memory and the performance remained intact (Thompson & Dean, 1955; McGaugh, 1965). Patients also show such loss of recent memory after ECS, head injury, or severe concussion. Usually, this loss starts some hours or days before the head injury. Apparently, the continuous recall of immediate memory stops at the moment of injury, which scrambles the recall circuit; hence the most recent recall patterns are affected most. When the effects of trauma wear off, the previously established neural access pattern is again ready for conduction and recall is once more possible. The lost memory is usually recovered, except for a short period just before the injury. Apparently, it takes a few seconds before access is securely established by continuous recall. I give evidence supporting the suggested neural recall circuits in Part II of this volume.

---

[1]After a series of experiments in which he recorded electrical potentials from many brain structures, John (1967) concluded that learning decisively alters the wave pattern in sensory cortex, thalamus, and midbrain. Such altered wave patterns have two components: One is the result of the cue stimulation, the other seems to represent the read-out from memory.

FORGETTING: LOST ACCESS OR LOST MEMORY?

The notion that forgetting means a loss of access rather than loss of memory has recently been challenged. Loftus and Loftus (1980) mention the evidence on which such a theory rests and find it wanting: Penfield's (1969) brain stimulation studies, which reported vivid memory "flashbacks," found such retrievals in only three percent of their attempts at brain stimulation, and even these were "reconstructions or inferences rather than memories." Loftus and Loftus point out that hypnosis and psychoanalytic free association do not reliably recover childhood memories, as has often been claimed; they also refer to recent reports that people may lie under hypnosis. While admitting that spontaneous or prompted memory recovery may happen, these authors insist that such instances do not prove that all memories are potentially recoverable.

These objections apply only on the assumption that memory retrieval means playing back a videotape of the original situation. Such an assumption completely disregards the vagaries of the retrieval process; and even more so, the way memories are registered and preserved (the coding process). Much research has been done on coding and recoding (see Melton & Martin, 1972; Crowder, 1976). We can take it as established that what is registered and preserved is what an individual has seen as relevant and has abstracted from the wealth of details contained in the situation. How such coding is done, pictorially, semantically, or in any other way, is not relevant for our purposes. The point is that these idiosyncratically coded memories are available but need not be used in the way they have been laid down.

Since imagination always accompanies recall, nothing prevents a man from recalling not so much what actually happened but what he either wishes or fears might have happened. It is easy for a person to convince himself that what he would like to have happened did actually happen. Recall is not isolated from our wishes and desires. A lie may become a belief and so be reported under hypnosis or in free association.

In addition, the methods of testing memory as used by Loftus and Loftus lack subtlety. For instance, they showed a series of film slides depicting successive stages in an auto accident. The car was a red Datsun traveling along a side street toward an intersection; on turning, it knocked down a pedestrian. The sign at the intersection was a stop sign for half the group, and a yield sign for the other half. After a filler activity, the subjects were asked: "Did another car pass the red Datsun while it was stopped at the stop (yield) sign?" Half the group were asked the "stop sign" question, the other half the "yield sign" question. This information was wrong half the time. When the question was misleading, recall was disturbed. In one condition, over 80% of the group who were asked the misleading question "recognized" the wrong slide when two slides were shown, one with the stop sign, the other with the yield sign. The author's comment: "If recognition were assumed to be a relatively passive process of matching stimuli to specific locations in a content-addressable storage system, one would expect that a representation of the actual and true scene would result in a match and that an alteration would fail to match. This does not occur.' (p. 417.)

The answer is, of course, that recognition is no such process. It is a feeling of familiarity that comes when we see again what we have seen before. In the Loftus' experiment, the stop or yield sign was inconspicuous because attention was centered on the accident. It would take a highly observant and critical person to concentrate on the sign and immediately ascribe blame either to the driver or to the pedestrian. If the group had been warned to observe the sign, recall and recognition would probably have been more accurate. The misinformation contained in the question was also remembered and had the advantage of being free of the emotional connotations of seeing the accident. Recognition is accurate only if an object has been in the center of attention or has been experienced repeatedly.

Even hypnosis does not make up for lack of attention. Loftus and Loftus mention an experiment reported by Putnam (1979) in which a similar videotape of an accident was shown. The subjects were then hypnotized and told that under hypnosis they would see the entire accident again but would be able to zoom in on details. Putnam found that these subjects made more errors under hypnosis than they made without it. He concluded that hypnosis does not reduce retrieval difficulties. In fact, the subjects appear to be "more suggestible in the hynpotic state and are, therefore, more easily influenced by the leading questions." (Loftus & Loftus, 1980, p. 444.) This is exactly what we would expect if recall, as I am suggesting, is influenced by the emotional (or suggestible) state during recall. After all, the subject uncritically accepts every suggestion of the hypnotist, why not his intentional misinformation? Such suggestibility was particularly obvious when the leading question mentioned that the major character's hair was blond when it was actually black in the film. One hypnotized subject who had remembered blond hair according to the misinformation, said, when shown the videotape again: "It's really strange because I still have the blond girl's face in my mind and it doesn't correspond to her (pointing to the dark woman on the videotape) . . . it was really weird." (p. 444.) Apparently, the misinformation contained in the question had induced an image and it was that image he reported instead of the memory image of the scene he had been shown. The later fantasy image was more familiar than the earlier memory image because it was in the focus of attention while the black-haired woman he actually saw in the picture had not been.

The report that people can lie under hypnosis does not prove that they can no longer remember what really happened. If a person has had a compelling reason to falsify his account of what has happened or what he has done and has maintained his lie, he will do so even under hypnosis or pentothal. Hypnosis does not compel accurate recollection. It does no more than free the individual from distractions so that he can accurately focus on the area the questioner suggests. But if he has substituted a lie for the truth, he will recollect the lie, not what really happened. On the other hand, when the hypnotized person has no reason to lie, he will recall an episode more accurately under hypnosis than he could normally. I myself have listened to a man under hypnosis reproduce the TAT stories he had given several weeks before. His recollection corresponded word by word to the protocol I had in my hands. He had recounted the stories originally, hence they had been in the center of his attention and could now be reproduced word perfect.

6 Imagination and Recall

Imagination complements memory and even substitutes for it when recall fails (Bartlett, 1932). The study of imagination has suffered eclipse for many years, perhaps because it cannot be studied by objective methods. And any method that even faintly resembles introspection has long been discarded as "mentalistic."

IMAGES AND IMAGINATION

On the face of it, images are no more "mentalistic" than concepts or meanings. Yet behavioristically trained psychologists have long found themselves able to accommodate language and even meaning in their system, despite the fact that both depend on concepts. For meaning, it was easy enough to find a behavioral definition (e.g., meaningfulness is the number of associates produced by a given word); but images that can only be produced in private and are not directly communicable proved to be intractable and so were exiled. However, in the last few years the increasing interest in the way memory is encoded has led to a resurgence of interest in images; but imagination as an image-making function is still disregarded.

Among clinical psychologists and psychiatrists this topic has never lost its appeal. Disorders of imagination, like delusions and hallucinations, had to be considered and treated, if possible. Indeed, normal imagination itself was found to be important. Freud insisted that the first psychological activity of the infant consists of wish-fulfilling fantasy images. He called fantasy the oldest form of thought, primary process thinking, which slowly is replaced by logical thinking as the childs is growing up. However, even the adult has wishfulfilling fantasies when his wishes are not immediately gratified. Such fantasy is expressed in day-dreams, night dreams, and stories, all of which Freud considered wish fulfillments.

In clinical psychology, fantasy products have long been investigated to discover the mainspring of a patient's actions. Freud's notion of the wish-fulfillment function of fantasy has not always been accepted. Some scoring methods of so-called "projective" techniques are based on the conviction that imagination is used to plan action and so can give us valuable hints as to the habitual attitudes of a person (Arnold, 1962). If Paivio (1971) claims that images were disregarded for so long by experimental psychologists because they fulfilled no useful function, he must have thought of Freud's notion of imagination. Paivio attributes the recent resurgence of interest in images to the "discovery" that images do play a role in remembering. This merely illustrates the quaint conceit of experimental psychologists who believe that nothing exists except what they have demonstrated in the laboratory. Mnemonic systems based on the visualization of figures, words, and objects to be remembered have existed from antiquity; but not until recently have psychologists taken notice.

Perhaps the first psychologist who assigned an important role to imagination was Bartlett (1932), who showed that memory is always complemented and often supplanted by imagination. Imagination steps in where memory fails. In the extreme case of Korsakoff psychosis, the patient "confabulates," that is, he uses imagination exclusively because he has lost the ability to recall his experiences in their proper sequence and context. Instead of using both recall and imagination, as normal people do, his attempt to remember can no longer reactivate memories but only succeeds in forming images that draw on past experience but out of proper sequence and context. He believes he is doing what he has always done and does not realize that one part of the combined recall-imagination function is no longer available.

RECALL AND IMAGINATION

When we try to imagine something, we have to draw on the same memory material we use when we recall something. Whether we recall or imagine it, there must be some deposit of experience that we can use. The difference between recall and imagination is that recall is constrained to the reproduction of the original experience in its temporal sequence and spatial context while imagination is free to roam and can recombine such memories regardless of time, place, or logical context.

Imagination can be used deliberately, in telling a story or painting an abstract picture. We set the goal and allow our imagination to produce what it may. Far more frequently, it is used spontaneously, in anticipating future occurrences and planning future action. Animals also use imagination for action. No matter how often a lion has hunted, today's hunting is never a repetition of yesterday's. Every new situation brings its own dangers and challenges. He has to adapt his strategy to the changes as they occur so that he can counter and even forestall the evasive maneuvers of his prey.

Experimental psychologists have theorized that rats form "hypotheses" in the maze. What are these hypotheses but images of the right and wrong turn? Curiously enough, psychologists are willing to grant rats the ability to form hypotheses (which surely require abstract thinking) but unwilling to admit that they have imagination—which requires nothing but sensory images of concretely experienced things.

Modality-Specific Images.   That human beings can imagine in various modalities needs no proof. There are individual differences in imagining. Some people can imagine speech or musical patterns much more readily than they can visualize something. Others are mainly visualizers and can recall a melody only with difficulty. In a recent survey, McKellar (1965) found that 97% of 500 British adults reported visual imagery, 92% auditory imagery. Over half the group reported various images, including images of movement, touch, taste, smell, and temperature. All those surveyed had some imagery. It seems reasonable to assume that sporadic reports of people who possess no imagery are based on a misunderstanding. They may think that images must be clear and enduring before they can be reported, and so disregard the fleeting, fugitive images that serve them in their daily life.

Visual and Auditory Images.   Visual and auditory imagery, according to McKellar's report, are the two most frequent modalities. The chances are that every reader has experienced both. There are reports of prodigious feats of auditory imagery. Mozart apparently was able to hear whole symphonies in imagination; and Arnold Schoenberg mentioned that he heard his String Quartet No. 2 as a finished work in imagination and simply wrote it down as he heard it. Granted these are feats possible only to musical genius; but all of us can hear in imagination the praise we think we deserve or the words of love we have waited for in vain. Olfactory and tactual images are a little more difficult to produce. Most of us have to imagine a rose before we can imagine its perfume, or visualize velvet before we can imagine what it feels like to touch it. But tactual and temperature images can be demonstrated: If we tell a blindfolded subject he will be touched with a feather and ask him to report the exact moment when he feels the touch, he will do so sooner or later, although the feather does not come near him. Or he will report the moment at which he feels the warmth of an electric heater, although the current has never been turned on. Even taste images can be demonstrated: When a subject is told that out of several glasses with water one contains a trace of salt or quinine and is asked to report the glass in which he notices the taste, he will do so although none of the water is contaminated with salt or quinine.

In recent years, some of these images have been demonstrated experimentally. Posner et al. (1969) showed single letters printed on flash cards and asked their subjects at the second presentation to report whether the letter has the same name. They found that the letters were identified faster as having the same name if they had the same shape (e.g. B and B versus B and b). However, when the delay between the first and the second presentation was 2 seconds or more, the difference in rate of recognition disappeared. These investigators assumed that the subjects had a visual image of the first presentation that made recognition easy if the letter presented the second time had the same visual shape. Later, the same effect was obtained when the first presentation was made orally. If the letter B, for instance, was pronounced one half to one second before the same letter was shown on a flash card, recognition was just as fast as when both were shown visually. A shorter delay prevented recognition. Hence these experimenters assumed that the subject generates a visual image on hearing the first letter which then is matched with the visual shape.

Phillips (1958) used a more sophisticated design. His subjects learned five names (nonsense syllables) to five gray patches varying in brightness; then the experimenters conditioned the galvanic skin reflex (GSR) to the word for the lightest gray. When the subject's GSR to the other nonsense syllables was tested, it showed a smooth generalization gradient to these words. The closer the gray patch was in brightness to the lightest gray, the more pronounced the GSR to its name. These results show clearly that there must have been a visual image of the lightest gray that determined the reaction to the other shades.

Kinesthetic Images. Kinesthetic imagery seems to be responsible for Natadze's (1960) results. He asked his subjects to imagine a metal ball being hefted in each hand, and to imagine that the left-hand ball was considerably heavier. When they were tested with two actual balls equal in weight, and were asked to judge which was heavier, they reported the right one as heavier.

Motor Imagination. There is not only sensory imagination but motor imagination. Motor images can be easily demonstrated, but they usually are not recognized as such. When a subject is asked to watch a Chevreuil pendulum or when, standing with eyes closed, he is told "you are falling forward, falling, falling," it is usually assumed that the movement of the pendulum or his own movement is the result of "suggestion"; but it is rarely realized that suggestion acts by creating the expectation of movement—in other words, the subject *imagines* the movement. Motor imagination is involved every time we imagine the clever retort we should have made or the excuses we ought to have given. We do not imagine hearing the words, we imagine ourselves speaking them—and speech is a motor performance, a movement of the speech musculature.

Richardson (1963) has shown that imaginal practice improved some skills (basketball shooting, mirror tracing); and Start and Richardson (1965) found greater improvements in subjects with vivid but well-controlled imagery. Beattie (1949) found that practicing dart throwing in imagination for ten minutes daily was as effective as actual practice for 15 minutes a day. When ten minutes were taken for imaginary practice and an additional five minutes for actual practice, performance four weeks later was far better than after fifteen minutes actual daily practice for that length of time. It should be emphasized that we are dealing here with motor imagination that has resulted in motor learning. Usually, it has been assumed that motor learning is the result of kinesthetic memory, i.e., the remembered sensations produced by movement (see Chapter 5). Now it is true that Jacobson (1932) found that motor imagination resulted in minimum innervation of the muscles used. But since the subject is usually quite unaware of these effects, it is most unlikely that sensations from such minimal innervation could be used for learning. Rather, imagining a movement seems to result in motor memory traces much as actual movement does. When repeated, the movement is facilitated.

Memory Images and Fantasy Images   What distinguishes memory images from fantasy images is not necessarily their greater clarity; it is the feeling of familiarity we have when we remember something. We recognize the images of some objects and so know that they are memory images. Of course, we do not know how we produce fantasy images or how we recall memories, just as we do not know how we manage to draw a logical conclusion from given premises. But we do know that we can produce images and use them. In recalling and reproducing a drawing or map, we may be certain about parts of it and uncertain about others. We recognize the general outline, but are unsure about the details. Of course, in reproducing a drawing from memory, the outlines we draw obscure the visual image—just as the words we recall from a list shown before obscure the sensory image of the rest of the words. But in reproducing the map of Africa, for instance, we are able to fill in the contours because we know roughly what it ought to look like. This is the imaginative supplementation of memory Bartlett demonstrated; his results show that there are no definite boundary lines between recall and imagination. When the drawing is finished, we may decide that it is adequate—or, that it is hopelessly inadequate. In other words, we either recognize the drawing or we do not.

Imagination is often used as a basis for recognition. For instance, it is sometimes difficult to understand the words of a song, particularly if sung by a choir. Despite the closest attention, we may be unable to make out more than a word or two. But if we know the song or read the words while they are sung, we have no difficulty at all in following. This cannot be explained as an excitation of words in memory storage. Since the sound pattern is a musical pattern instead of an ordinary speech pattern it is difficult to see how it could excite a speech pattern in memory storage. When we know the words of the song, we can recognize them as familiar because we can imagine their speech sound pattern. We know the sounds as they are spoken and recognize the same pattern when the words are sung.

In a later chaper, we shall see that recall is actually mediated by a brain circuit different from that mediating imagination. This explains why the Korsakoff patient can still confabulate even when he can no longer recall his experiences.

Voluntary and Involuntary Imagination.   Imagination, like recall, can be voluntary or involuntary. It is involuntary in dreams; during sleep, normal recall seems to be impossible, which may explain why the dreamer never questions the veridity of his dream experiences, just as the Korsakoff patient never doubts the veridity of his confabulations. Such sensory impressions as can still be experienced during sleep (differences of light and darkness, sounds, touches) are woven into his dream instead of being correctly identified.

VISUAL IMAGERY AND VERBAL MEMORY

In recent years, much research has explored the role of visual imagery in verbal memory. It has been known since ancient times that using visual images to remember words and sentences improves recall. In the last few decades, experimental research has shown that words which elicit vivid images are learned faster than abstract words; that people learn paired-associate words more quickly if these words arouse spontaneous visual images; and that instructing people to imagine situations that include the objects to be memorized results in faster learning of paired-associate nouns (Anderson & Bower, 1974).

Theorists are divided as to how the influence of imagery is to be explained. Bugelski (1970) suggests that the verbal material is converted to mental pictures that are stored in memory, and are revived and described in retention tests. Anderson and Bower called this the "radical imagery" hypothesis. Their own "conceptual-propositional" hypothesis states that knowledge, whether derived from verbal instructions or from visual impressions and images, is always couched in abstract propositions about objects and their relations to other objects. Imagery helps retention because it contains a rich set of spatial determinants that can bind concepts together. Finally, Paivio (1969, 1971) advocated a "dual-coding" hypothesis. He suggested that there are two storage systems, the verbal and the imaginal; the verbal system processes information sequences while the imaginal system works on simulaneous arrays of information. Paivio assumed that in using images to memorize concrete words, a person establishes one memory trace in the verbal-associative store, another in the imagery store. Abstract words, encoded only in the verbal-associative store, are not rememberd as easily because this is the only memory store available. Paivio conceded that it is difficult to distinguish these two memory systems because we cannot estimate how much each contributes to memory.

Anderson and Bower (1974) insist that any imaginal memory theory is too "peripheral" in its conception of the memory trace. For them, "the principal representation in memory is neutral with respect to the question of modality . . . information is represented in abstracted, conceptual, propositional structures." (p. 453.) They argue that we store abstract interpretations of scenes rather than "raw, unanalyzed, textured details." This abstract character, they say, shows up in the schematic and sketchy character of memory images, focused only on salient features. They refer to Wiseman and Neisser (1971) who found that complex visual patterns are recognized only if a person sees something in the picture the first time, and recognizes it when he sees it again. Apparently, what is stored in memory depends on the interpretation of the scene by the perceiver. Anderson and Bower also argue that some conceptual distinctions, easily remembered, cannot be represented as images (e.g., "he forged a name to the check"; "only a few babies are unloved;" "the bell isn't there.") Hence they conclude that the "imagery effect" on the memory of verbal material is the result of a combination of factors, from special coding strategies to the encoding of propositions using spatial relationships. Anderson and Bower point out that instructions to make up sensible sentences including the noun-pair to be learned give as good retention as do imagery instructions. Some people, instructed to learn some pairs by imagery and other pairs by making up a sentence could remember the pairs equally well but could not remember which method they had used for a given pair.

The facts Anderson and Bower mention do not argue against the effective use of imagery. Images are not literal copies; they may be vague, sketchy, often inaccurate, but they do represent the important features of a scene as the person has perceived it. Images are not paintings. They are action sequences in which the words to be remembered provide actor and action. Whenever subjects were told to imagine the two nouns as two pictures on opposite walls, their retention was no better than when they learned noun-pairs without forming either images or sentences about them (Bower, 1970). Indeed, mnemonic systems recommend that the learner should incorporate the words he wants to remember in active, dramatic visual sequences. The fact that the subjects could not remember whether they had made up a sentence or formed an image for a given noun-pair speaks for the suggestion that these sentences were also accompanied by images, just as images relating the two nouns can be described in a sentence. The sentences Anderson and Bower quote ("he forged a name to the check") cannot be pictured in one image but can be imagined easily as a sequence of images.

Anderson and Bower's criticism misses the point. They assume that if imagery is effective, a still picture should suffice. Anything that cannot be so pictured, they say, owes its effect to the propositional structure of the relationship between the two members of the pair. The point is that all kinds of relationships between concrete objects can be far more easily imagined in a sequence of pictures than couched in a propositional statement. We imagine spontaneously, al-

most without knowing it, but have to make a special effort to form a propositional sentence.

The fact that we cannot attribute the exact proportion of memory to visual and
to verbal memory is no more threatening to scientific exploration than the fact
that we do not know what proportion of human personality is the result of genetic
endowment and what proportion comes from environmental interactions. We
take for granted that we have visual as well as verbal memory. We also have
auditory, olfactory, taste, and touch memories and recall them when needed.

Sensory memory is not "an internal photograph, videotape, or tape recording,
which we can activate and replay in remembering" as Anderson and Bower say.
We recall what has attracted our attention in the first place, what we consider
important for us. Often, a memory comes uncalled when we encounter a similar
situation. Our visual memory images may be sketchy, vague, evanescent, but
they do serve to recall the scene as we have encoded it. Visual or auditory recall
is not the replaying of a videotape or tape recording but a recalling of images,
visual and auditory, which we recognize as memories. Anderson and Bower ask:
"What is the homunculus that sits inside our head and 'reads' and interprets
these internal pictures?" (p. 454.) The answer is simple: We do not need a homunculus to see a scene, to hear a melody, either actually or in imagination;
neither do we need a homunculus to recall the scene or the melody. We use our
verbal, visual, auditory etc. memory to remember, just as we use our eyes and
ears to see and hear.

Anderson and Bower seem to prefer to reduce all memory to propositional
verbal memory because this is what they can encode in their computer program
(HAM). But there is no reason at all why a human being should remember in
exactly the same way a computer does. The computer cannot see and does not
have visual, auditory, etc. imagination or memory; but the human being can and
does. In the last analysis, it is a question of fact, not theory: Do human beings
have visual, auditory, olfactory, taste, and touch memory as well as verbal memory? I discuss evidence for the fact that they do in Part II, chapters 12 and 16.

SENSORY EQUIPMENT OF ANIMALS

For some years, it has been accepted without question that man is different from
animals only because he has a more complicated neural system. This is not the
place to argue the point. But at the risk of being thought anthropomorphic, I must
discuss the sensory equipment of animals and contrast it with that of human
beings.

All psychologists accept the fact that animals as well as human beings can
see, hear, taste, smell, and can feel heat or cold. They also can touch, and feel
when they are touched, and are aware of their own movements. They must have
an integrative sense, or they could not react to patterns and objects. Animals

learn, which means that they must be able to remember and imagine. In fact, such memory and imagination is modality-specific, as it is in man. In our own laboratory, we have tested rats on visual, auditory, tactual, taste, and olfactory discriminations; in all these experiments, the cues were carefully restricted to one modality at a time. All these discriminations could be selectively impaired by different brain lesions (see chapter 20) although the sensory capacity of the animals remained unimpaired.

Animals also must be able to make intuitive appraisals of things around them, and of their own actions, or they would not be motivated toward any goal, nor would they be able to better their performance. By the same token, they must have affective memory: without it, they could never go on repeating successful actions, nor could they keep away from things that have hurt them in the past. Animals are able to attend to certain things and leave others aside, which means that they can appraise something as "good to explore."

What they cannot do is to employ attention, memory, and imagination deliberately, as can human beings. Nor can they form concepts, that is, abstract the essential feature of a thing and see it as member of a class. They see this chair, jump up on it, adopt it as their own. They may jump on other chairs, thus react similarly to similar things; but they do it because of their affective memory, which leads them to expect the same effects from a similar situation. They do not make value judgments nor do they go beyond their personal experience. If they had conceptual knowledge, they would be able to understand, if not to speak, conceptual language.

Animals do not form concepts nor do they make hypotheses. Morgan's canon has been curiously reversed: Psychologists do not impute higher activities to animals when lower ones would suffice for a performance; rather, they seem to be saying that forming concepts and hypotheses cannot be high level activities because animals are capable of them. But animals' "concepts" are no more than images: When Köhler's ape managed to fit two bamboo sticks together and used them to rake in a banana, the sight of the extended stick was sufficient to recall earlier attempts to rake things in with a long stick, to imagine doing it, and do it successfully. The ape had no conception of the stick as a tool, or as a means to a goal. This is clearly shown by a report that apes can pile boxes one on top of the other and jump up to grab a banana hanging from the ceiling. They pile the boxes helter skelter and try to jump up on them so quickly that they may reach the banana before the boxes topple. If they had any concept of arranging the boxes in steps to achieve stability, they would pile up the boxes so that they would be stable and form steps. All they have is an image of something high and themselves atop—and an image is not a concept.

To sum up: I have tried to show that everything we experience is registered; and that this memory material is available for imagination as well as for recall. We cannot imagine something unless we know enough about it or unless we have experienced similar things before. In recall, a particular memory pattern is activated and recognized as familiar. In imagination, earlier memories are reorganized and recombined for a particular purpose. Hence imagination can complement memory. When recall is only partly successful, imagination closes the gap and fills out the picture.

Animals have a homologous sensory apparatus and can learn. Hence, they must have modality-specific and affective memory, they must be able to recall earlier experiences and find them familiar, and must be able to imagine what may happen and what to do. They cannot use their imagination deliberately, nor can they recall their experiences intentionally. Both imagination and recall remain spontaneous, set off by similar experiences, while the human being can set himself to recall and imagine at will.

7 Recognition

Once something has been preceived and registered, it will be recognized at the next encounter. This recognition is possible in every sensory modality: We recognize something seen, but also a melody, a perfume, a taste, the touch of velvet. This recognition is immediate, and brings with it a sense of familiarity.

In psychology, recognition is usually paired with recall, yet it seems to have a fundamentally different character. When we recall something we have seen, we form a visual *image* of it. When we recognize something, we experience a *sense of familiarity*. We do not always manage to recall the original experience, to recover the name of the person or of the scent we have recognized as familiar. In some cases, we may not even know what it is that has given rise to this feeling of familiarity. In such a case, we have a "déjà vu" experience. Since recognition is as direct as sense experience, it is difficult to define or describe it. All we can say is that the situation arouses a sense of familiarity that sometimes is combined with modality-specific recall, but sometimes stands alone.

THEORIES OF RECOGNITION

Most theories of recognition are based on the results of recognition experiments in which words or designs are shown to the subject and he is asked to say which of them have been shown before. Often, these theories apply to recognition experiments but not to the experience of recognition in daily life.

There are at least five different explanations of recognition (Crowder, 1976): the search, tagging, strength, context retrieval, and encoding specificity theories. The *search theory* goes back to William James (1890) who held the view that recognition is the last stage of recall: Recall is a search that ends when an item is recalled and recognized as a memory. This explanation has found many adherents.

As evidence for the search explanation of recognition, Sternberg (1966, 1967, 1975) published several experimental reports. He showed sets of scrambled digits (from 1 to 6) and two seconds afterwards asked whether a test digit had been included in the original ("positive") set. In half the trials the test digit shown on the screen had been included in the positive set, in the other half it had not. A new list of digits was shown as the positive set on each trial. Sternberg found that the longer the set, the longer the subjects' reaction time. Each additional item in the positive set increased the reaction time by the same amount (38 msec). The reaction time for items recognized and for items not recognized was the same. In this experiment, recognition was practically perfect. In another experiment, Sternberg used the same positive set for over hundred trials in succession rather than a different set for each trial. The rate of scanning was almost exactly the same. This scanning rate comes to about 26 digits per second, which clearly rules out subvocal speech as a means of recall; subvocal speech has a rate of roughly six digits per second. Sternberg obtained the same results when he used photographs of faces and nonsense forms.

On the basis of these experiments, Sternberg concluded that recognition requires a search through all the items shown and a comparison of every item with the test item. Obviously, this holds true only for the special case of recognition in a laboratory experiment in which the subject has to recognize an item included in a set shown before. In everyday life, we recognize things and people without any scanning or comparison. Only when we are uncertain do we try and visualize the face of the person we think we recognize, or compare the object we see here and now with our memory image of it. Even then we do not scan a number of faces or things.

Later investigators (Morin et al., 1967; Raeburn, 1974) found in similar experiments that recognition was faster when the test item was the last item in the positive set. In that case, reaction time dropped to 8 msec. Apparently, when the test item repeats the last item shown, the subject has the vivid image of this item still in mind and recognizes it immediately, without having to scan the other items.

Strength Theories. These theories are based on the notion that the memory traces of the most recent events are strong, while those of more remote experiences are weaker. Hence the memory network carries stronger and weaker traces. Repeated occurrences raise the strength loading. The subject recognizes an item according to the strength of a memory trace at a particular memory location. Hence the decision that an item is familiar is based on a threshold, set at a certain amount of strength (threshold theory). Above that threshold, items are recognized as familiar (Wickelgren & Norman, 1966; Bernbach, 1970). Other theorists hold that the subject must apply a decision criterion, a rule that above a certain strength he should recognize an item as familiar (Kintsch, 1970a,b; Murdoch, 1974).

The strength threshold seems to provide the trigger for recognition. When it is exceeded, the subject reports recognition. But how does he detect the threshold? The decision criterion is not a mechanism of recognition so much as a rule for reporting. When it is set at low strength, the subject will report many falsely "recognized" items; when it is set high, he will fail to report many correct instances. Here also, it is unclear how a person senses the various degrees of strength, either for setting a criterion or for acting on it.

Bernbach (1967) found that the subject either recognized an item or did not. When asked to give a confidence rating, he was either completely confident that he had recognized it or he had no confidence in his judgment. If there were intermediate strengths, as the theory assumes, the subjects were not able to distinguish between them. This seems to show that recognition is an all-or none process. We either find something familiar or unfamiliar. When we are in doubt, it seems to be almost certainly unfamiliar. This excludes any search and comparison process.

The *frequency theory* complements the strength theory. It maintains that the person judges the relative frequency of the stimulus presentation. Repeated presentations strengthen the trace so that it is more easily recognized. Underwood (1969) distinguishes background frequency and situational frequency. Frequently occurring events (digits, letters of the alphabet, words or word fragments) represent the background frequency. The task items in a memory experiment represent the situational frequency. During a study trial, the item to be remembered acquires additional frequency from seeing or hearing the item, pronouncing and rehearsing it (Ekstrand et al., 1966). On the test trial, the subject recognizes these items on the basis of the frequency difference established during study. Hence recognition should be poorest whenever the difference between the items to be memorized and distracting items is minimal. This has been found to be true in many studies. Noble (1953, 1954) found that judged familiarity is a function that shows negative acceleration, increasing with stimulus frequency. According to Underwood and Freund (1968), when the subject had to pronounce both words in a paired associate list (so that both acquired additional frequency), learning of the second member of each pair was inhibited; pronouncing these words without pronouncing the first member of each pair enhanced recognition. The studies of Gorman (1961) and Shepard (1967) support this explanation. They used high- and low-frequency words from the Thorndike and Lorge (1944) word count, and found that high-frequency words were less easily recognized than low-frequency words. The high-frequency words have a high background frequency, to which the situational frequency is added, making them relatively difficult to distinguish from other words with high background frequency. The low-frequency words, however, having a low background frequency, have a better chance of being distinguished on the basis of background plus situational frequency. There is a greater relative distance between a background frequency of 10 plus 2 situational frequency counts, and the 100,000 background frequency of high-frequency words, than between 100,000 plus 2 and 100,000 in the case of high-frequency words.

However, there are some findings that cannot be explained on the basis of a frequency difference. For instance, Strong (1913) and Bahrick and Bahrick (1964) have found that recognition is poor for abstract patterns, words, or digits that are difficult to distinguish from other test items. This is particularly true if the items to be recognized are shown during the test together with a large number of similar items (Davis et al., 1961; Postman, 1950; Peixotto, 1947). In the case of abstract patterns, the situational frequency was the same, whether these patterns were easy to distinguish or not. In the case of words or digits, the situational frequency was the same whether the test digit to be recognized was included in a large or a small array of similar items. Apparently, distinctiveness of the items is as important as their frequency. An item is distinctive when it can be easily distinguished from similar items. The more distinctive, the less likely that they will be confused when many test items are shown.

Tagging.   This explanation was proposed by Yntema and Trask (1963). They suggested that items seen on a list are given tags to mark the time of occurrence in a network of word memories. To discover whether a test word had been included in the list, the subject consults his word memories and finds that one of them has a tag: He recognizes the word immediately. This theory sounds intriguing because it can explain why nonlist words that are strongly asssociated with the tagged word are sometimes recognized erroneously; or how subjects can know that they saw the list recently. But the theory does not explain how the subject manages to attach tags to words in a list, or how he recognizes the tags. It really is a ''search theory'' with recognition displaced from words to tags.

Context Retrieval.   Hollingworth (1913) and more recently Tulving (1975) suggested that recognition happens when the familiar item recalls the context in which it had originally occurred. In recognition tests, the given item recalls the context; in recall tests, the context is given and the special items in it have to be recalled. In contrast to the strength and the tagging theories, which attribute recognition to a change in the memory trace, the context retrieval theory conceives recognition as the result of retrieving the background information in which the original item was embedded.

Anderson and Bower (1974), for instance, insist that the item must be associated with a memory of the relevant time and place when it first occurred. A word is recognized when the subject associates it with the memory of the most recent list, but also with a host of physical and psychological cues noticed at the time. The authors assume that recognition of a particular item or object always goes with a recall of the situation in which it occurred. Nothing is further from the truth. In everday life, we recognize a friend even if we cannot recall the time, place, or circumstances in which we have first seen him. The theory may barely hold for the recognition of a hammer or a lawnmower as ours. It could be argued that we recognize them because we remember the time they were slightly damaged. But it is more likely that we recognize the hammer because of a slight nick in the handle, although we don't know how it occurred. In the same way, we recognize a word included in a recent list not because of its position in the list or because of the way it is printed but because of its meaning. When the test item is presented, we recognize a word that may look different but means the same as the word seen before: not the associations connected with word or object at the time of first encounter determine recognition but the fact that we have seen it before. Associations with its context may help recognition but they don't account for it.

Encoding Specificity. According to this theory, the individualized perception of an object leads to later recognition, not the associations at the time of its first occurrence. Tulving and Thomson (1973) say: "Specific coding operations performed on what is perceived determine what is stored, and what is stored determines what retrieval cues are effective in providing access to what is stored." (p. 369.) The retrieval cue for recognition, according to this view, is the item (object) that brings with it the particular cognitive state experienced originally. For Tulving and Thomson, the item seen here and now does not necessarily remind us of the original item unless it carries the same meaning. In one example, they point out that the item LIGHT may have been perceived (encoded) originally as illumination; but at the time of recognition testing, the subject may think of LIGHT as the opposite of HEAVY. If so, he will not recognize the word. Acceptable as this theory is, it is not specific for recognition. As Crowder (1976) points out, it applies to all forms of remembering, recall as well as recognition.

THE PROBLEM OF RECOGNITION

None of these theories explains how it is that we *recognize* something, that we feel a sense of familiarity. We may search for an item, find a tag on some memories, and we may sense a certain strength of memory trace, but how do we decide that a certain item, a tag, or a certain trace strength means we have encountered this item before? And how do we recognize the context when it is recalled by the item? How do we recognize the cognitive state that is reinstated? Recognition requries a kind of insight that we have experienced something before. Without such an insight, the process of locating the item, sensing a strong trace, finding a tag, having the context or the cognitive state reinstated remains just that, it does not become recognition. What these theories are saying is that there are certain conditions under which recognition can occur—but it does not have to occur. Such failure of recognition despite repetition is illustrated by patients with traumatic amnesia.

One young man I talked to had fallen from his truck two years before and had suffered a severe concussion. Despite his long stay in the hospital, he did not recognize the doctors, patients, or nurses. Everything was strange to him and he was worried and puzzled. When he was reminded of things he had done or people he had talked to just a while before, he could not remember. Although the ward routine repeated day after day, he was continually surprised by it. Sheer repetition does not ensure recognition; and without recognition, there is no memory.

That sheer repetition does not necessarily trigger recognition has been shown experimentally. Tulving and Thomson (1973) and Watkins and Tulving (1975) have shown that subjects may fail to recognize words seen in a paired-associate list although they used these words in free associations. For instance, in the Tulving and Thomson experiment, subjects studied word pairs like CHAIR-GLUE. When they were later asked for free associations to the word *table,* they produced the word CHAIR 66% of the time, but they did not always recognize this word as having been on the original list. Only a little more than a third of the time did the students recognize the target words they had brought up in free association as belonging to the paired-associate list.

Recognition Versus Recall. Since recall must end in recognition to be experienced as a memory, it is not surprising that a great deal of research has been devoted to the question of whether the two factors can be reduced to one memory process or whether they represent two distinct types of memory. It would seem that this question could be settled if it could be proved that recall and recognition differ qualitatively from each other.

Recognition—Superior to Recall? Recognition is usually superior to recall (Luh, 1922; Postman & Rau, 1957). Subjectively speaking, recognition is not only faster than recall but requires no effort (see Kintsch, 1970a). When we recognize something in everyday life, the recognition is immediate and needs no search. Sometimes a person seems vaguely familiar; but such an undefined feeling of familiarity is not identical with recognition.

However, under certain circumstances recall seems to be at least as effective as recognition or even more so. For instance, Tulving (1968) asked students to learn 48 pairs of words by giving the response word when the cue word was offered. They learned this list in an average of 7.2 trials. All students could recite the responses perfectly after the first errorless recall; hence Tulving concluded that they achieved 100% correct recall. Next, they were tested for recognition of the response terms alone. Tulving used pairs like AIR-PORT, BACK-LOG, BASE-BALL, BIRTH-DAY. In the recognition test, he used 96 words, 48 of which were response terms (PORT, LOG, BALL, DAY), arranged alphabetically among words that also formed "idioms" with the stimulus words (PLANE, LESS, PLACE). The students were asked to say which words had been on the original list. They recognized 90% of the words but mistakenly identified 2%. Hence Tulving concluded that in this experiment recall was more effective than recognition.

The reason for the superiority of recall over recognition in this experiment is not far to seek. Words are not only remembered as letter combinations, they also have a meaning, and that meaning is incorporated in a visual image. An airport is quite a different place from a port; a backlog is very different from a log. A baseball is a special kind of ball, just as a birthday is a special kind of day. When the students saw the response words and visualized them, they did not find the visual images of port, log, ball, and day familiar; or at least, they had to make an effort to detach the meaning of the response terms in their original list from the meaning of the cue-response combination.

That recognition is more effective than recall under normal circumstances is shown by reports that many more items can be recognized than can be recalled. This is illustrated by three experiments reported by Shepard (1967). In one experiment, Shepard investigated the recognition of words, in another, of sentences, and in the third, the recognition of pictures. The words and sentences were printed on cards. The subject went through the whole deck at his own pace. The pictures were shown by a stripfilm projector that the subject advanced at his own pace. There were 540 words, 612 sentences, and 612 pictures. At the end of the inspection, the subject was shown cards with word or sentence pairs, or a stripfilm pair. One number of the pair was old, one new. The median percent correct was 90 for words, 88.2 for sentences, and 98.5 for pictures, which shows a rate of recognition after one presentation that cannot be matched by recall.

Word Frequency.   Shepard (1967) reported that recognition was better for low-frequency words than for high-frequency words, regardless of the frequency count of the distractor words. In contrast, recall is better for high-frequency words than for low-frequency words (Deese, 1961; Kinsbourne & George, 1974). The latter authors also found that recall was reduced if low-frequency words were shown beforehand so that their frequency was increased for the subject.

Intentional Versus Incidental Learning.   It has been shown repeatedly that subjects have better recall when they are warned that they would be tested for retention, as compared with an experimental set-up in which the subjects are led to believe that they will not have to pass such a test (Hyde & Jenkins, 1969; Eagle & Leiter, 1964). For instance, Eagle and Leiter tested three groups on a

36-word list. One group was told to learn and remember the words, another group was told to classify each word as a part of speech. The third group was told to classify the words but also to learn and remember them. The three groups were then tested, first for free recall, and then for recognition. The group that was asked to remember the words recalled an average of 15.2 words while the group that was asked only to classify them recalled only 11.4 words. But in the recognition test, the incidental learning group recognized 27 words, the intentional learning group only 23.7 words.

The reason for the reversal might be that the incidental learning group paid undivided attention to the words in the list as parts of speech. The intentional learning group was so intent on learning the words in sequence that the charcteristics of each word did not stand out. In general, it would seem that recognition is a more direct process, depending only on the perceptual image; while in recall the subject must translate the perceptual image into a motor response.

Retention Time.   Postman and Rau (1957) showed that recognition remains practically perfect while recall deteriorates with time. Their students learned twelve nonsense syllables to a criterion of one errorless repetition. An independent group learned twelve meaningful words to the same criterion. One group recalled their material after twenty minutes, another after one day, and still another after two days. Recognition was tested in different groups at the same intervals. At all intervals, recognition was practically perfect. Free recall was good after twenty minutes; after one day, it dropped considerably, and after two days, recall recovered somewhat for nonsense syllables but further declined for words. Two other measures of recall (relearning and anticipation) gave results similar to free recall (Adams, 1967, Fig. 9.2, p. 255).

Shepard (1967) also tested retention time. Subjects tested for recognition of pictures after two hours had 100% correct; in tests after three days, 93%, and in tests after seven days, 92% correct. Finally, subjects tested after 120 days recognized 57% of pictures.

TWO-PROCESS THEORIES

Since recognition and recall differ in important respects, it would seem reasonable enough to conclude that they are two different processes. But as long as memory theorists assume that recognition will occur automatically once the appropriate conditions are provided, and does not deserve a separate explanation they will find it difficult to concede any qualitative difference between recall and recognition. According to Kintsch (1970a), the two-process hypothesis has been neglected because of its introspective appeal, and introspection has been the *bête noir* of American psychology for a good many years.

Current Theories.   Recently, the possibility that recall and recognition are two processes has had renewed discussion. The learning theorist, Estes (1960), concedes its plausibility. He insists that the notion of one-trial learning must be tested separately for recognition and recall because findings on recall do not necessarily apply to recognition. Even theorists who deny a real difference between recognition and recall are forced to make a distinction. For instance, Mandler (1979) says that "the distinction between recall and recognition is a remnant of vague, common-language usage and it is difficult to find a useful and serviceable psychological distinction." (p. 306.) Yet he suggests that recognition is based on integrative factors, and recall on elaborative factors. Also, he admits that both processes are employed in recall and recognition tests. In the former, the subject searches his memory to retrieve the desired items and later checks them for familiarity; in the latter, the subject finds certain items familiar, but checks those he does not recognize by searching among recalled items. This distinction surely implies one process, recall, and another, recognition, defined as a sense of familiarity. Despite Mandler's protests, the "vague, common-language usage" seems to indicate a distinction he is forced to employ himself.

Still, for theorists favorably disposed toward the two-process theory, there is always the problem how to account for recognition. Adams (1967) is a good example of a theorist who supports this theory but has no explanation for recognition. He objects to the notion that the same memory trace should be the basis for both recall and recognition, which is implied in the strength (threshold) theory of recognition. His own explanation is that any sensory experience establishes a perceptual trace, which is reactivated by the original stimulus in the recognition test. Adams points out that this perceptual trace is identical with the sensory image (immediate memory). Adams distinguishes the "memory trace" laid down at the time of *response,* from the perceptual trace. It is this memory trace of the response that is activated in later recall. Put differently, he distinguishes between a sensory and motor trace. The former serves recognition, the latter, recall. In Adams' words, "there is enough preliminary empirical evidence to indicate the existence of two traces . . . a perceptual trace that grants the power of recognition and a memory trace that governs recall by being the associative agent that fires the response when its stimulus is presented" (p. 270).

According to Adams, the second presentation of a given stimulus directly activates the earlier perceptual trace and this produces recognition. But an activation of a perceptual trace can only be the re-experiencing of the original perceptual trace: I see a Koala bear for the first time and have an image of the bear that lasts for a short time. I see the bear a second time and the image is re-experienced—but how do I recognize it? Like most recognition theorists, Adams does not recognize the omission. If the sheer repetition of the image or perceptual trace "grants the power of recognition," how does it do that? Like other memory theorists, Adams evades the question.

It is difficult not to agree with Adams (1967) when he says:

> Recognition, frankly, does not seem to be getting anywhere conceptually . . . On the assumption that recall and recognition mirror the same memory state, investigators might hve thought that the measure of retention does not make much difference and, feeling a freedom of choice, tended strongly toward recall. This hypothesis (and that is all it is) may be true, and recognition and recall may indeed be sides of the same memory state. On the other hand, the hypothesis may be false. (p. 263.)

Unfortunately, his own solution leaves the nature of recognition still in limbo.

Alternative Two-Process Theory.   It seems to me that the differences between recognition and recall are so striking that they cannot belong to the same class of phenomena. However, considering the weight of opinion arrayed against this view, the only way to make a two-process theory acceptable is to specify recognition and recall in such a way that the qualitative difference between them is clearly apparent. This is not a difference between recognition and recall *tests;* as I have pointed out before, recall must always be complemented by recognition. By recall I mean the retrieval of information up to but not including the final recognition of the recalled items as memories. And by recognition, I mean the unwitting, unconscious, and entirely spontaneous judgment that "this is something encountered before." This appraisal completes recall, just as a good/bad appraisal completes and complements perception. We are not reflexively aware of the appraisal of something as a recurrence, we merely experience a sense of familiarity—just as we are not reflexively aware of an intuitive good/bad appraisal but merely like or dislike what we have so appraised.

In recognition experiments, this judgment is both unconscious, implicit, and conscious, explicit: The subject consciously judges whether his sense of familiarity is strong enough to decide that the item recognized was included in some earlier array. The stronger this sense of familiarity, the stronger will be the reported confidence in his judgment.

When we see something, we appraise it as good to know; hence we attend to it, spontaneously remember similar experiences (modality-specific memory) and their effect on us (affective memory). With that associative recall comes recognition—the intuitive appraisal that we have seen this before. We are not reflexively aware that this is a recurrence, we merely experience a sense of familiarity.

Since recognition is an appraisal of something perceived, it must be mediated by brain structures that receive afferents from sensory cortex. It would seem that the limbic cortex bordering on the various sensory and memory areas mediates this appraisal of recurrence just as it mediates the appraisal of something as good or bad.

Recognition is faster than recall because it is an intuitive judgment based on spontaneous modality specific and affective memory. It requires no effort because no search is necessary. As soon as we encounter this thing, it automatically arouses memories of similar experiences. When the object is difficult to distinguish from other things, or when the item to be recognized is difficult to perceive as a whole (for instance, an abstract design), this recognition may be uncertain. For difficult items, repeated presentation may be necessary for reliable recognition. This hypothesis does not require "tagging" of a memory trace. Indeed, the sense of familiarity is usually experienced without any reference to the time or date of an earlier occurrence. Something or somebody is recognized as familiar, even if we do not recall a specific earlier encounter.

This is illustrated dramatically by word recognition. We listen to a speech or read a book at a very fast rate. This feat implies that every sound or visual form is recognized immediately. If a word is interposed that we do not know, we immediately recognize it as unfamiliar. We do know that we have never seen or heard this word before, but we have no way of knowing when or how often we have encountered the many words we read that are familiar.

Norman (1969) demonstrates this immediate recognition in the following passage:

> If shown a new word—this chapter emphasizes the mantiness of memory—we know that the word is new . . . "mantiness" does not exist in your memory, hence your ability to discover this fact indicates that you did one of two things. Either you scanned the entire contents of memory and discovered the absence of "mantiness" or you examined that part of memory where the word "mantiness" would have been, had it been present, and discovered its absence. The first hypothesis can be rejected as implausible . . . The second alternative also seems implausible but at least conceivable. It means, however, that we are able to use either the sound or the sight of the word "mantiness" to get to the part of memory where it ought to be stored. (p. 162.)

As Norman says, the first alternative can be rejected out of hand, but the second alternative is implausible, also. We are not conscious of any search in recognizing "mantiness" as unfamiliar. Indeed, no search is needed. The word arouses a feeling of unfamiliarity based on the immediate intuitive judgment that it has never occurred before. And that judgment is based on the fact that the word has brought up no visual or affective memory when we saw it. In postulating such an unwitting, implicit appraisal (recognition) based on spontaneous, immediate, visual and affective memory, we are relieved of the necessity of using either of the two implausible alternatives.

Of course, recognition is based on the memory of earlier encounters with the things or people we recognize. When we see a friend, we recognize him because we spontaneously remember past encounters and the joy they brought. The appraisal that we have encountered this person before brings past affection into the present. Lack of recognition means that we have no memory of past meetings and experience no feelings of affection. Our friendship might as well never have been.

To sum up: Recognition is an intuitive, unwitting judgment that we have encountered this person or thing before. It is experienced as a sense of familiarity. The intuitive appraisal of recurrence, like the intuitive good/bad appraisal, is unconscious. Recognition is founded on the spontaneous recall of relevant experiences (modality-specific memory) and the revival of intuitive good/bad appraisals that went with these experiences (affective memory).

We can recognize actual sensory experiences, something seen, heard, touched, tasted, or smelled. But we can also recognize sensory images. We recall verbal, visual, and auditory images and appraise them as familiar. Such recognition verifies these images as memories, and helps to distinguish memory from imagination. The lack of confidence in what we remember usually indicates that memory has been contaminated by imagination; or better, that imagination has at least partially replaced memory.

8

Memory Models

Recently, theorists have attempted to follow the complete process of registration, retention, and recall, and to build memory models that trace the fate of sensory impressions right through registration, retention, and the eventual reponse. Such models correspond to the "flow-chart" of computer programming.

Model builders have various purposes. Some of them want to build a model that will handle particular learning or memory experiments mathematically. Others want to establish a flow chart that can be used for computer programming. Still others base their model on the decision process used in signal detection theory and clearly separate the process of extracting information from the decision and response based on that information.

CURRENT MEMORY MODELS

There are excellent surveys of recent memory models (Norman, 1970; Spence & Spence, 1967, 1968; Spence & Bower, 1970) that the interested reader should consult. In this chapter, I discuss three representative models to discover whether they adequately explain the psychological processes involved and whether they help us to identify the neural correlates of these processes. I have not included a computer model. However stimulating and helpful for computer programming, a memory model cannot be considered adequate unless it helps us to understand the actual memory processes as they occur in human beings. We neither perceive nor remember the way a computer does; and the human brain has no similarity with the electronic system of a computer.

Most theorists postulate a sensory information storage which derives from the presentation of the stimulus; from this sensory storage, the material is transferred to a different storage system, after encoding it into a new format—this is short-term storage. When the material is rehearsed frequently, or properly organized, or more attention is paid to it, the information is consolidated or transferred into a third memory system, long-term memory. Some theorists interpose an intermediate storage between short and long-term memory. All theorists agree that new material is quickly forgotten after presentation unless it is rehearsed; there is disagreement, however, as to what is the reason for the forgetting (decay, interference, or a combination), and the reason for long-term retention (transfer to long-term storage, slowing up of rate of decay, increase of trace strength). These disagreements we have discussed already. What is new in the memory models is the addition of a mechanism of retrieval which again is formulated appropriately to the different theories.

The Single Replica Model

Harley A. Bernbach (1970) suggests a single replica model. He postulates a single memory store, in contrast to most of the memory models that postulate several memory stores (STM, ITM, LTM). Bernbach's theory refers to post-perceptual memory; that is, he admits that "very-short-term" or immediate sensory memory exists as "part of the perceptual process," but his model starts with the memory processes that follow after such immediate memory is registered.

For Bernbach, the memory process has the following sequence (abbreviated):

1. On presentation of an item, a single replica is stored in memory.
2. Immediately on presentation, the item is rehearsed, producing a storage of additional replicas.
3. This rehearsal of the individual item is followed by general rehearsals of all the items previously presented that can be recalled. Each general rehearsal occasions the storage of one additional replica of each item rehearsed. All items not forgotten have an equal chance of being rehearsed.
4. On presentation of a new item, any or all of the previous items may lose exactly one replica.
5. When the subject is tested, he will recall every item of which at least one replica is still in storage. If every replica of this item is lost, he must guess.

Replicas may contain more than the minimal necessary information; indeed, they have to do so to explain incidental learning. But for purposes of the model, each item is considered to yield one unit replica. As a result of presentation and rehearsal, a stack of replicas is stored. The subject is aware only that he has a replica but not of how many replicas he has—similar to a push-down stack which presses down as another item is added so that its level does not depend on the number of items in a stack. Thus the rehearsal of an item is independent of the number of replicas; of course, an item that has no replicas cannot be rehearsed.

According to the analogy with a push-down stack, the probability of a correct response also is independent of the number of stored replicas. As long as there is at least one replica, there is certainty of recall ($p = 1.$). An item without any replicas in storage is forgotten. This follows from the assumption that each replica is a unit. It leads to problems because a subject often recalls the beginning letter of a word but is scored incorrect on the word itself.

Forgetting is less likely if there are many replicas in storage. However, the number of replicas affects only the likelihood of forgetting, not the likelihood of recall. When other material is stored in memory, there is storage interference and the loss of replicas. But an interfering event can at most cause the loss of one replica. Burnbach tested this model against experimental data and found that it can explain many results. It can explain the *recency* effect of memorizing, that is, the fact that subjects remember the last items better than the rest of a list they are memorizing. The last item in the list is recalled perfectly, then recall drops off for the earlier items, with a rise for the first items on the list. When graphed, the performance has an S shape (Fig. 8.1), the more pronounced the longer the list to be learned. That the last items are remembered better can be explained by Bernbach's assumption that replicas are stored with every rehearsal so that more than one replica is stored for every item in the list. Forgetting (loss of all replicas) cannot occur until there is at least the same number of new items as there are replicas in store. Thus the last few items in the list are saved from forgetting. The first few items are recalled best because of Bernbach's assumption that each rehearsal of a new item is followed by a general rehearsal of all former items. The first item is rehearsed most often and so builds up most resistance to forgetting. This resistance is partly cancelled out when the list becomes longer. Bernbach points out that this model eliminates the necessity for postulating long and short term memory stores.

Bernbach reports that mathematical predictions from his model can handle single item recall, memory for individual paired associates and continuous paired associate learning; his model can also handle repeated presentations in single item recall, and repeated presentations in paired associate learning. To explain a continuous memory task, Bernbach has to make a change in his assumptions. For such a task, Atkinson and Shiffrin (1968) used a set of four, six, or eight items, and created new items by using a different response paired with the cue stimulus. Once a subject had given the response, he was shown the same stimulus paired with a new response, which now had to be recalled. In this experiment, the performance curve was markedly different from the usual S curve (see Fig. 8.2). This time, the curve showed an abrupt loss after the first item, and then a rapid leveling off.

According to Bernbach, this experiment is not applicable to his model because it implies a memory *structure* while his model assumes the rehearsal of

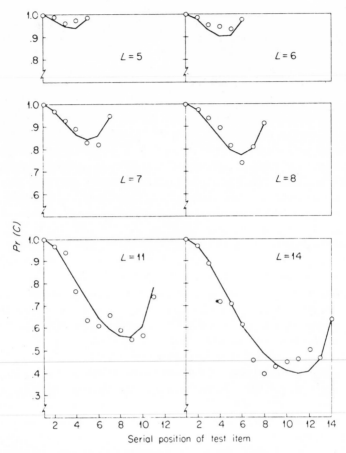

FIG. 8.1   Observed and theoretical probabilities of a correct response as a function of serial position for several values of list length, L (data from Phillips *et al.*, 1967). Note that serial position is counted from the end of the list, so that recall performance for the last item of each list is shown in position 1. From: D. A. Norman, 1970.

individual non-structured items. Since items that can be held in memory in a structured form are known to be easier to remember, he suggests that a change in his model, called the structured register model, will account for this difference. Bernbach assumes that the subject creates a memory structure containing the number of stimuli used in the list together wth their current responses. When he is shown the first new pair, he stores one replica in the register. Instead of rehearsing, however, the subject places the new response in the appropriate slot. The chances of accomplishing this depend on the size of the register. The item in the register is secure in the slot and cannot be lost as easily on presentation of a new stimulus item.

Critique.   It is obvious that this change in Bernbach's model is really more far-reaching than appears. The change in assumptions is far more than a simple model change. If the human being is able to use a structured register, or even better, if he can devise his own structures (and there is evidence that he can and does), it is more than doubtful that remembering is a simple accumlation of replicas, or forgetting a loss of replicas pushed out of storage by new experiences.

Even apart from a such a fundamental consideration, Bernbach's model cannot accommodate or explain the fact that a word in the middle of a long list is recalled almost perfectly if it is, for instance, printed in red, with every other word printed in black. In his model, every item has an equal chance of being rehearsed and so remembered. In human memory experiments, however, it is well known that attention can be directed toward some items, either involuntarily as in the example of the word printed in red, or voluntarily, by appropriate instructions. When a man is told to remember the word just before or just after a marker signal, he can do so. He can also be instructed to pay attention (and remember) the right or left member of a pair; and he can remember words by visualizing the objects to which they refer in a continuing scenario. This factor of selective attention is completely left out of Bernbach's model.

Finally, it is doubtful that a dynamic neural system could mediate such bits of information as proposed in this model. We know that there is continuity even with stimulus discontinuity. For instance, eye movements do not provide static

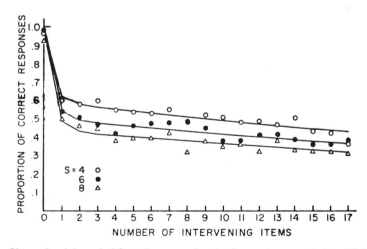

FIG. 8.2   Observed and theoretical forgetting curves for stimulus set sizes, s = 4, 6, and 8 (data from Atkinson *et al.*, 1967). From: H. A. Bernbach, 1970.

snapshots but a continuity of the scene at which we are looking. Turning around does not produce an impression of different scenes but a continuous field of which we see first one, then another aspect. A succession of replicas on the analogy of a push-down stack seems to provide the possibility of mathematical prediction in strictly limited situations but bears no resemblance to our known psychological activities.

Bernbach's model has all the advantages and disadvantages of oversimplification. It can do without a long-term storage system and the mechanisms of consolidation by relying on the sheer number of replicas in storage. But on the other hand, this mechanical piling up of a stack of replicas makes the theory as vulnerable as are all merely mechanical models. Little attention is paid to the retrieval process. Bernbach simply assumes that a response is somehow hooked up to each stack of replicas and will pop out when needed as long as there is at least one replica in store. But this is a model of an automat, not a man. Even in learning a list of paired associates, the human being searches for clues, often uses home-made mnemonic devices, or organizes the list in some way, as Reitman (1970) has observed. Retrieval is automatic only when the list is overlearned.

The Model of Norman and Rumelhart

These authors (1970) propose a far more sophisticated model, in which retrieval is as carefully discussed as storage. They assume that stimulus representations (images) are stored in a Sensory Information Store (SIS) but start to decay as soon as the stimulus has gone. Before the image has a chance to decay, "a pattern recognizer extracts information from the image . . . to construct the perceptual vector" (p. 30). The rate of extraction is determined by the clarity of the image and the amount of material stored. When more than one item is presented, attention is divided equally. In sequential presentation, the subject attends to an input proportionally to the clarity of the image.

Next, various features or attributes of the sensory material are extracted. Visual material is represented by a list of spatial properties, speech by a list of phonemes, ordered into perceptual vectors. The vectors are then named; in the naming process that identifies the material, a "dictionary" is used to match names to physical features. According to the authors, "this process continues either until the naming system manages to identify the signal unambiguously or until the image of the signal has disappeared from the sensory system" (1970, p. 23). The feature extraction mechanism slows up as more signals arrive. This mechanism is a parallel, not a serial process.

The naming system is modeled after Bower's (1967). This theorist assumes that the vector of features is now matched with all relevant dictionary items. When two names match equally well, naming depends on a conservative or liberal perceptual bias. Most subjects are conservative, refusing to name when the match is ambiguous. Others, when forced to respond, guess randomly among approximate matches. When the presentation time is increased, there is more time to build up vectors. The same thing happens when some items are eliminated, or the subject is led to expect fewer items. In the first case, the rate at which perceptual vectors are developed is increased; in the second, the number of features needed in the perceptual vectors is decreased (for instance, when English words are used, only an English dictionary is necessary).

The output of the naming system is an ordered list of attributes, formed into a memory vector, which contains name and context. In recall, the subject goes to the information about the context in which these attributes are stored. If the link between context and attribute is missing, the attribute is missing.

Recognition occurs by checking the attributes of the item with their stored representatives. We are given the attributes and try to recover the contextual information. We do not store or remember individual attributes, we operate only on their links and associations. Only if the attribute, or rather, a sufficient number of attributes, contains the context will the item be recognized.

In recall, we assume that we are given the contextual information and use it to recreate the individual attributes. For instance, the subject is given context A from which he can recover attributes a, c, d (Fig. 8.3). But these attributes must be used to complete the entire memory vector. This is done by entering the three retained attributes into a dictionary of possible responses. If they uniquely identify the item, the subject recalls it. If the identification is ambiguous, he either guesses or remains silent. The authors assume a content-addressable storage sys-

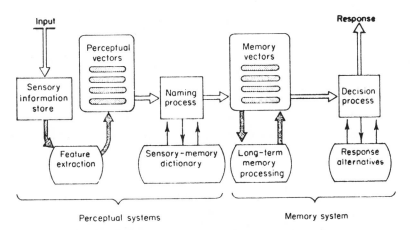

FIG. 8.3 Outline of the general system. Physical inputs are stored in their sensory form by the SIS while critical features are extracted from each item and placed in the appropriate perceptual vectors. The vectors of perceptual features are transformed into vectors of memory attributes by the naming system. The type of response is based on the question asked of the decision process, the set of possible response alternatives, and the attributes remaining in each memory vector, either temporarily (as STM attributes), or more permanently (as LTM attributes). From: Norman and Rumelhart, (1970).

tem: Given a list of attributes, we find them in storage without search. Similarly with contextual material: It is always available and always found.

Short-term memory is entered from the naming process as a vector of attributes. As more items enter, some are lost or degraded, and so cannot always be retrieved. The development of the long-term trace is quite similar to that of the perceptual vector. Long-term differs from short-term memory mainly in the permanence with which contextual information is attached to the attribute. Also, contextual information is more complete. When information is retrieved, Norman and Rumelhart consider only the number of attributes retained and make no distinction between short- and long-term storage. The likelihood that the attributes of an item will become stored permanently depends in part on the length of time the item has been in short-term memory.

Critique.   Norman and Rumelhart assume that recognition is simply a process of checking each item with its representative already in storage. But checking must end in a decision that this is something encountered before, or there will be no recognition. This must occur either at the feature extraction or at the perceptual vector stage, else naming will be impossible. Hence, even at the sensory and perceptual stage we have to draw on long-term memory. The same difficulty arises in the naming system. How do we recognize the appropriate name? The authors simply assume that the name given to the perceptual event depends on the match between it and a "relevant" dictionary item. What determines its relevance?

The notion of a "content-addressable dictionary" is ingenious but difficult to defend. The naming process would already have to know the content before looking up the name in the dictionary. Something red, round, bouncing, made of rubber—how would we look it up in a dictionary? Perhaps a computer is fast enough to search among all possible names for something red, next for something round, next for something bouncing, and finally for something having all these attributes and also made of rubber, and come up with an answer in the time it takes a person to give the response "ball." But a human being certainly could not do it. And even computers have thus far not been programmed to recognize and name objects.

How the naming process produces memory vectors is similarly difficult to understand. The authors seem to assume that the context of the situation within which the items occurs is laid down in these vectors, so that the name can later be recovered from these context replicas. But suppose the trigram RMZ occurs in list A and the subject is later shown this trigram together with several others. Or suppose the subject is asked to learn a series of paired associates (set A), then is shown another series (B) and afterwards is asked to recall the second member of the pair when the first member of Series A is shown. In his attempt at recall, he would have to locate the context to, say, "dog." Suppose the other member of the pair was "cat" in set A, and "house" in set B. The subject has as memory vectors contextual cues for set A and set B in which these pairs are embedded. But now where did the context come from? How did it get into the memory vectors? We have traced the items from SIS through perceptual vectors to the naming process; up to that stage, apparently there was no context, so how did it slip by? If it was there from the beginning, so that the subject remembered "dog-cat in Series A," "dog-house in Series B," what need is there for memory vectors?

To do the authors justice, what they intend to cover in memory vectors is the organization imposed upon the material by the subject, and not the organization arranged by the experimenter, although their example (p. 26) gives the latter. But supposing the subject organizes the material: Where is that organization provided for in the model? To say, as the authors do, that the organization comes from long-term memory gives us no hint how this particular organization is selected.

The authors realize these deficiencies and admit that because of them they are "forced to restrict the model to situations that use simple, homogeneous lists of stimulus items" (p. 62). To be sure, they mean that precise prediction is restricted to such application. But the point is that the model is rally too elaborate for such simple memory material, yet misses out in some very important aspects.

Norman and Rumelhart's model assumes that recall consists essentially of a search through a passive memory store but it is not quite clear who does the searching. There are various active systems (perceptual system, naming system, memory system, etc.); but it is really an anthropomorphic notion to suggest that the naming system uses a dictionary, or that the decision system decides between response alternatives. Of course, we really are speaking about anthropos, so that anthropomorphic notions seem in order. But it is the man himself who names an object and decides on the response, not systems either in his head or his mind.

THE PROBLEM OF THE AGENT

There are several ways to solve this problem of the agent in memory search and decision. One is to postulate an "executive routine" as Neisser (1967) does. He says:

> As recently as a generation ago, processes of control had to be thought of as *homunculi,* because man was the only known model of an executive agent. Today, the stored-program computer has provided us with an alternative possibility, in the form of the *executive routine* . . . Most computer programs consist of largely independent parts, or "subroutines." In complex sequential programs, the order in which the subroutines are applied will vary from one occasion to the next. In simple cases, a conditional decision can lead from one subroutine to the next appropriate one: "transfer control to register A if the computed number in register X is posi-

tive, but to register B if it is negative or zero.'' In other situations, however, the
choice between register A and register B may depend on a more complicated set of
conditions, which must be evaluated by a separate subroutine called ''the executive.'' Common practice is to make all subroutines end by transferring control to
the executive, which then decides what to do next in each case. (p. 295–6)

Neisser admits that existing computer models are not satisfactory from a psychological point of view because the executive routine must be established by the
programmer from the beginning. No computer can make major changes in its
executive routine. It is curious that Neisser, who insists that memory traces are
not ''activated'' but *used*, does not consider that other mechanisms also could be
used, and used not by a homunculus but by the human being who possesses
them.

Another way of dealing with the problem of the agent is to consider the individual himself as an active agent. This notion avoids the difficulty of having an
active system that does things only a human being can do: use a dictionary, decide on what is relevant, or name the perceptual object.

Atkinson and Shiffrin's Memory Model (1968).

These authors postulate an active system. They assume permanent, structural
features of the memory system but also active control processes directed by the
subject. When and how such control processes are used depends on the instruc-
tional set, the experimental task, and the past history of the subject.

Structural features include the sensory register and the short- and long-term
stores (Fig. 8.4). Incoming sensory impressions are registered in the sensory register. Unless transferred to the short-term store, the items in the sensory register
decay almost immediately (within less than a second in the case of visual images); other sensory systems also may have such images that quickly decay, but
there has not been sufficient research to decide that question.

Information from the sensory register is next encoded and stored in the short-
term store. A word seen may be encoded into an auditory-verbal-linguistic
(a-v-l) short-term store. Since the available research has been done mostly in this
area, the authors concentrate on it without denying that other storage systems
may exist. Perhaps we let Atkinson and Shiffrin speak for themselves:

In the case of the transfer from the visual image to the a-v-l short-term store, it
seems likely that a selective scan is made at the discretion of the subject. As each
element in the register is scanned, a matching program of some sort is carried out
against information in long-term store and the verbal ''name'' of the element is
recovered from long-term memory and fed into the short-term store . . . This communication between the sensory register and long-term store does not, however,
permit us to infer that information is transferred directly to long-term store from the
register. (p. 14)

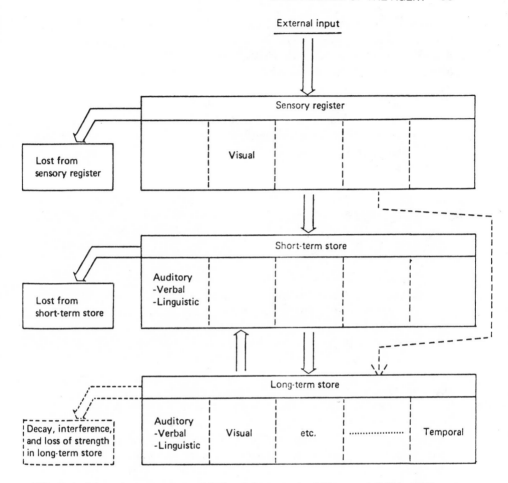

FIG. 8.4   Information-processing model of verbal memory by Atkinson and Shiffrin (1968).

In other words, a-v-l short-term store receives information directly from the long-term store and only indirectly from the sensory register. But a visual image might be entered into the short-term store directly without a verbal coding.

Unless rehearsal maintains the information in the short-term store, it decays and is lost within about 15–30 seconds. Since little information is available about decay rates in other than the auditory-verbal-linguistic modalities, the authors do not offer any values for them.

Finally, the long-term store is relatively permanent. While all information not further processed is eventually lost from both the sensory register and the short-term store, the information in the long-term store may be destroyed, replaced, modified, or no longer retrievable, but it does not decay. The authors assume that this store contains information not only in the a-v-l mode but also memories in other modalities. There may also be memories that do not belong to any modality; for example, temporal memory.

Atkinson and Shiffrin assume that the long-term store has many traces or copies of information which may be partial or complete. In scanning, only one or a small number of these copies may be found, none complete enough to produce correct recall. But when an associated item is offered and recognized, access is gained to other copies. This theory, the authors claim, explains the "tip of the tongue" phenomenon. When a person is asked to recall something, he often feels that the name is on the tip of his tongue. If he is then asked to predict whether he will be able to choose the correct answer from four alternatives, he is very often able to do so. Indeed, Brown and McNeill (1966) found that his subjects could often recall the first letter of the name they later recognized as one of four alternatives.

More recently, Shiffrin (1977) mentioned that the sensory register has been combined with the short-term store in their theory, so that it now has a single short-term store in addition to the long-term store. Apparently, evidence has accumulated that perceptual information is coded and recoded repeatedly and persists for varying periods of time.

The control processes are largely directed by the person. They control the information flow from one store to the other. Copies of the selected information flow from one store to the next, while the copied memories remain in their original store, eventually to decay and disappear. To initiate this flow, the subject scans the input from sensory modalities into the sensory register and, as a result, searches through the long-term store to find relevant information that is introduced into the short-term store. From this store, information is continually transferred to the long-term store in the form necessary for the purpose of the moment. Atkinson and Shiffrin suggest (but are not certain) that a direct transfer from the sensory store to long-term store may occur as well.

Information is transferred continually from long-term to short-term store in problem solving and thinking. Attention is one of the control processes that select particular parts of the sensory input for transfer to the short-term store. The subject must decide to which sensory register he should attend and what to scan within the memory system. He also must decide which strategy to use for matching items in the register against the long-term store to identify the input.

Another control process is retrieval. Recall has a search component that is absent in recognition. This search through the short-term store is less elaborate than through the long-term store because of the smaller capacity of the former. Since rehearsal capability is restricted, and traces in the short-term store decay quickly without rehearsal, scanning time is limited. If the trace in the short-term store is partially decayed, the subject may have to scan the long-term store as well, so as to match the partial information with complementary information in the long-term store. However, by rehearsing them, the subject can hold a small number of items in the short-term store immediately available.

Each rehearsal regenerates the short-term trace and delays decay. To extend the life of the items in the short-term store, the subject may replace one item at each rehearsal by a new item, so that a constant number will be rehearsed at least some of the time. Atkinson and Shiffrin call this a *rehearsal buffer* and suggest that it is attached to the short-term store. The maintenance and use of the buffer is entirely under the control of the subject. Items enter the buffer either from the sensory register or from the short-term store. When a new item enters the buffer, an old item is pushed out, either into the long-term store (if a trace has been built up during rehearsal), or it is lost through decay. Every item in the short-term store can be transferred to the long-term store, provided it is rehearsed or re-corded before it decays.

Any search through the long-term store must locate the desired memory trace and recover it as soon as it is found. If only a partial trace is recovered, the sub-ject must either guess at the missing part of the trace or search further to match the partial trace with other known information. Each search is ordered in some way, either by association or by some other strategy; it may be directed along a temporal dimension or use categories of thought helpful in the search.

In more recent work, Schneider and Shiffrin (1977) have distinguished controlled search, which is a serial comparison, from automatic detection, which automatically draws attention to a habitually perceived signal. Automatic proc-esses are either built in or acquired as habits and do not need attention. They operate in parallel with other control or automatic processes. Controlled proc-essing is initiated by the person, may be altered from time to time or from trial to trial, proceeds serially, and requires attention. Examples of automatic processing may be found in a variety of perceptual habits (e.g., reading), or skilled motor sequences (e.g., grammatical speech, dancing, swimming).

Critique.   The advantage of this model over most others lies in the addition of voluntary control processes operating on the structural memory system. As Atkinson and Shiffrin say," these control processes are such a pervasive and in-tegral component of human memory that a theory which hopes to achieve any degree of generality must take them into account" (p. 109). Such an assumption avoids the difficulty of postulating active processes (Norman and Rumelhart's executive routine) that can program themselves and switch their programming at will. As for Atkinson and Shiffrin's automatic control processes, there is no doubt that learned reactions can become automatic; but some control must be exercised by the person, even in the most automatic of response sequences, or dancers would cannon into others, skiers would come to grief, and speakers would free-associate instead of delivering a reasoned address. Even in built-in automatic activities, as for instance in walking, running, or instinctive consummatory responses, the person exercises a modicum of control. It would be preferable to postulate subject control in all control processes but stipulate that some response sequences may be carried out automatically.

In their sketch of the structural memory system, consisting of three (later two) different but communicating memory stores, the authors are not nearly as credible. Perhaps that is their own feeling as well, because Shiffrin (1977) remarks that it is not sensible to ask for proof that separate memory stores exist; rather, the theory should be evaluated "in light of its entire set of major assumptions and . . . judged in light of its ability to organize previous findings, to predict new results, and to give rise to new experiments" (p. 2). This cliché was originally meant to deny that a theory has to be true. To see it used as a way to evade proof or evidence is a new wrinkle.

While Atkinson and Shiffrin in their latest version have combined sensory register and short-term store, other theorists have combined short-term and long-term stores (Wickelgren, 1970; Murdock, 1974). This also seems to indicate that it is difficult to conceive of three separate stores, even for theorists who propose them. Despite Shiffrin, the notion of two or three memory stores should be open to verification. If they exist, their memory traces should be located somewhere in the brain. The sensory register would seem easy to identify. It should be identical with the association cortex to each primary sensory area. This would allow for modality-specific registration, as provided for in the sensory register. But where could we find the short- and long-term stores? If they include primarily the auditory-verbal-linguistic memories, Wernicke's area in the temporal lobe next to the auditory area, and Broca's area in the frontal lobe next to the face motor area would be prime candidates. That would mean that Wernicke's area would have to serve both as auditory register and auditory short-term store, but Atkinson and Shiffrin's later combination of sensory register and short-term store could accommodate that. It would also serve to extend this double storage by analogy to other sensory association areas. But when it comes to the long-term store, it is difficult to know where to look. Atkinson and Shiffrin seem to imply that the hippocampus stores long-term memories, although they admit that bilateral hippocampal lesions may merely block the retrieval of such memories.

Bilateral hippocampal lesions leave short-term memory intact but prevent new memories from being added to the long-term store. After such lesions, patients are able to rehearse new information for many minutes, but forget the material as soon as they are interrupted. Since their intelligence is unimpaired (Milner, 1968b), the long-term store must be intact, for they are able to draw on general information acquired long ago. Hence the hippocampus cannot contain a long-term memory store—and other locations in the brain are more than doubtful.

Atkinson and Shiffrin suggest that control processes directed by the individual transfer copies of selected information from sensory register and short-term store into the long-term store. If this transfer is by way of rehearsal, the trace in the long-term store will be weak and open to interference. The subject may also use various coding processes, altering or adding to the information in the short-term store, which will increase the strength of the memory trace in the long-term store. Such information can be reordered, coded and recoded, transferred and retransferred. In addition, control processes also conduct the search in retrieval, which includes both short- and long-term stores. This means a great deal of to-and-fro traffic between the two stores and makes us wonder how retrieval processes could be kept separate from transfer processes.

Finally, Atkinson and Shiffrin assume that the input into the sensory register and short-term store soon decays; but that memories once transferred to the long-term store no longer decay, although they may become altered or inaccessible. Why should we assume decay in the two earlier stores but not in the long-term store? There is no evidence either way. It may just be possible that none of the memory traces decay; perhaps they simply become inaccessible.

The authors seem to consider recall and recognition as control processes, similar but for the fact that recall includes both a search and a recognition component while recognition does not have a search component. Hence both recall and recognition would seem to be stages of one process. I have mentioned before that recognition must follow an insight that a particular item has been encountered before.

Of the theories discussed here and other theories published in recent years (Anderson & Bower, 1973; Baddeley, 1976; Murdock, 1974), Atkinson and Shiffrin's model stands out. Any criticism must take into account their own statement that they are offering a general framework but not a complete theory. As they continue to formulate precise models perhaps they will reconsider the problem of separate memory stores and will attempt to define recognition.

In the next chapter, I outline an alternative theory of memory and cognition which, I hope, can explain psychological findings and can, in turn, be verified by evidence from neurophysiological research.

9 A Psychological Theory of Cognition and Memory

Our discussion of memory theories and memory models has made it clear that an adequate theory of human memory requires a comprehensive theory of human psychological functioning. As several memory theorists have discovered (Neisser, 1967; Reitman, 1970), neither memory registration nor recall can be explained apart from other cognitive functions. Indeed, they cannot be explained apart from the whole complex of psychological functions, just as the neural substrate of memory cannot be sketched apart from the functioning of the brain in other psychological activities. The realization that memory must be seen in the context of other cognitive functions has led Neisser and Reitman to insist that remembering is a problem-solving activity, similar to all other instances of problem-solving.

AN INTEGRAL THEORY OF PSYCHOLOGICAL FUNCTIONS

Since memory cannot be explained isolated from all other functions, it is necessary to present a theory that embraces the whole of human psychological functioning. Once that is done, it will be possible to fit the various memory mechanisms into their appropriate place. This theory cannot be sketched in the form of a simple flow chart of what goes on in recall and recognition because many activities go on in parallel, and a flow chart implies a serial process. What can be done is to sketch the various psychological functions as we experience them and show that they can work in series or in parallel, or in series-parallel; next, how they are used by the human being. To round off the theory, I will try to indicate which functions are either not available to the animal or are not used in the same way as human beings use them.

Such a theory of human functioning has to start with a description of the activities involved in sensory experience and bridge the gap between experience and action. It has to account for the activities directed by the human being but also for quasi-automatic functioning. In the first few chapters, I have discussed the functions involved in various psychological activities. Now I want to sum up this discussion by sketching the sequence from perception to action, discussing the functions as they occur in the sequence.

From Perception to Action.   The accompanying chart (Fig. 9.1) describes the activities as they occur. They are sketched as following each other serially, in several rounds of appraisals. Actually, they may go on in parallel. As one aspect is appraised, triggering recall, imagination, and affective memory, another aspect begins to affect us, favorably or unfavorably, and initiates a similar sequence of rounds.

The *first appraisal* is of the object as "good to know," leading to *attention.* As we attend to it, we recall earlier experiences with similar things and relive their effect on us; we imagine what this thing may do to us. In the light of what we recall and imagine, we appraise it anew, which leads to an impulse to do something about it. This is the *second round.*

Now we recall what we did in similar situations in the past, relive the good or bad effect of such actions; imagine what we could do this time and appraise possible actions. This appraisal, like the first, is intuitive, unconscious, and results in an emotion: love, fear, anger, with an impulse to welcome, flee, fight, depending on our appraisal. This is the *third round.*

The urge to approach or flee is now appraised as well. We recall similar approaches or escapes and relive past consequences of our action. We imagine possible consequences this time, which leads to a new appraisal of the proposed approach or withdrawal. We also judge consciously and deliberately whether this action is suitable or desirable—unless the emotional impulse was so strong that it has led into action without further deliberation. If the *fourth round* appraisal of this particular action is favorable, we stop imagining further possibilities and decide to act. Since this is the only action impulse left, it automatically leads to action. If the appraisal in the last round is that the action is unsuitable, we can either imagine other possibilities and decide on one of them, or stop imagining and decide that no action is required.

These rounds may follow each other so fast that we are hardly aware of them; or they may go on for a long time without resulting in any decision. We may go on appraising different aspects of the situation and imagining different actions until we are lost in confusion.

I now turn to the various psychological functions that are engaged in these rounds of trying to come to a decision.

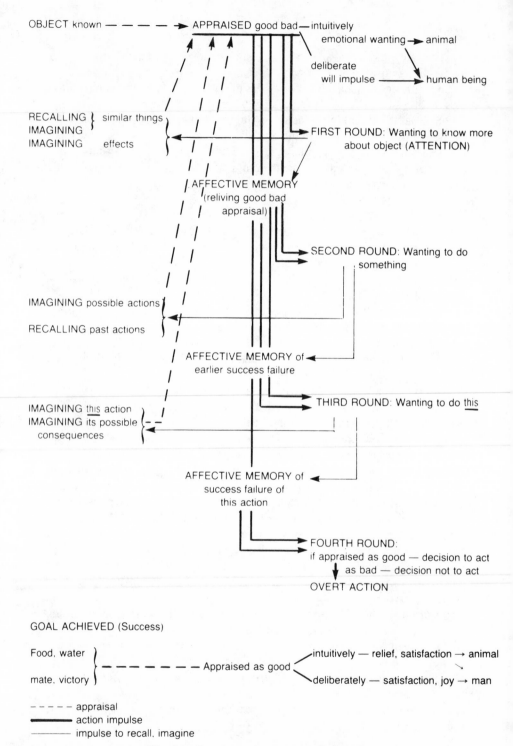

FIG. 9.1 From Perception to Decision and Action.

COGNITIVE FUNCTIONS

The broad distinction among cognitive functions is between sensory knowledge and intellectual or conceptual knowledge. Sensory functions are spontaneous, direct, and non-deliberate. We open our eyes and see, provided there is light enough; we stretch out our hand and can touch anything that is close enough. Sight, touch, hearing, taste, and smell are direct experiences that require no effort on our part. Conceptual knowledge is based on sensory experience but requires judgment and logical thought.

The Sensory System.

Each sensory system provides sensory experience in a particular modality. Seeing, hearing, tasting, touching, and smelling, are sensory reactions to stimuli acting on particular receptors. But over and above the specialized senses that provide experience in their own modality, there must be some integrative sensory function that makes it possible to see objects rather than patches of color, to realize that the sound we hear comes from the bell we see; that the fleeting touch impressions we sense on tracing an outline indicate a three-dimensional object. This integration must be a sense function because we experience patterns and objects as directly as we sense red and green. Such integration is inherent in the perceptual process. We may call it the integrative sense.

The Integrative Sense. This sense produces an awareness of its integrated product: of an object, a situation, a melody, or a visual pattern. It also mediates the implicit awareness of myself, the observer, seeing, hearing, or otherwise sensing it. The fact that I see *an object* is the result of this sensory integration in which the patches of color given by the visual sense are integrated into a whole; and the awareness that I *see* (and not hear), and that *I myself,* do the seeing, is implied in this integration.

The integrative sense is active not only in sensory experience but in movement. I know that I am *doing* something, and *what* I am doing; and I know that *I* am doing it. This is true for animals as well as for human beings. In both, this knowledge is implicit but direct, not in any way reflexive. The very fact that the dog hears a sound and immediately pricks up his ears to listen, that he turns towards it and looks in the direction of the sound, shows convincingly that he expects to see something that up to now he has only heard. Unless a dog is aware that he sees a hare (rather than touching it), he would not run after it. If he were not aware that he smells the hare (rather than seeing it) he would not keep his nose to the ground to follow the spoor. Such awareness is implicit in all sensory experience and all movement, and is as simple and direct as sensation and movement itself.

It is clear that the sense of sight or smell cannot give such awareness. The sense of sight can only produce visual sensations, the sense of smell, olfactory sensations. In the same way, the sensory experience of successive positions of limbs, or of muscle contractions, comes after each position is reached and cannot mediate the awareness that I intend to move, or that I am now moving. These are experiences that must be ascribed to the integrative sense.

Obviously, the integrative sense has no peripheral sensory receptors but uses the information provided by each of the external senses. Its neural substrate would have to be the cortical feltwork, at least in human beings and higher mammals. There is evidence that the various layers of the visual cortex mediate the perception of pattern and the direction of movement (Hubel & Wiesel, 1968; Dykes, 1978); this is also true of the somesthetic cortex (Dykes, 1978).

The integrative sense seems to articulate not only sensory experience and movements but also sensory and motor images. We can imagine ourselves moving, seeing, touching; we can visualize a tree, a landscape, or hear a melody in imagination. We can do so because such images are produced together with sensations and can be revived in recall and imagination. They also occur together with movements and can be used in planning skilled actions. They are identical with the "immediate memory" discussed in chapters 4 and 5.

Modality-Specific Memory. When we encounter a new situation, we use our senses but also memory and imagination to investigate it. We come to know it by recalling earlier experiences that are similar, we appraise its significance for us, and fit it into the context of related knowledge. Anything that proves to be uninteresting or unimportant we quickly drop and as quickly forget. Even among the things we do remember, we select relevant features and leave out those that are of no interest. Such selection is controlled by us, not by a sensory or memory system.

Memory is not a unitary function but is modality-specific. Memories are registered and preserved as neural dispositions to be reactivated in recall. On the basis of evidence I review in chapter 12, I am suggesting that sensory memories in the various modalities are registered in the association cortex close to the various primary sensory areas. Hence each memory modality is represented in one area, adjoining the same sensory modality.

Reactivation of memory traces requires access to these memory areas. If access is not established immediately after each sensory experience, it is lost and the memory can be retrieved later only by special techniques or under special circumstances. For instance, we may forget a dream completely, but something heard or seen during the day will recall it. In hypnosis, access to long-forgotten experiences can be established again because all other access lines are immobilized by the hypnotist's instructions; the long-disused access to the forgotten memory will now stand out and can be used to revive the memory.

Access is established either by rehearsal (e.g., in motor skills) or by drawing on the immediate memory for further encoding. When such memories are used to formulate sentences, judgments, or plans, they are registered also in motor (speech) memory areas and in auditory memory areas. If we use these memories a great deal in thinking and planning, they will be anchored firmly within a familiar context. By fitting new facts into larger and larger contexts and so connecting them, a system of related memories (Bartlett's "schemata") is formed that is continually changing, either extended as interests widen, or contracted as interests change.

What is never used is forgotten because access to it has not been maintained. Whether access is not maintained for lack of interest, out of fear (as in Freud's "repression"), or simply from preoccupation with other matters is immaterial. Neural pathways are either facilitated by use, or their learned patterning disintegrates. This explains why immediate memory quickly escapes our grasp but becomes more durable the more it is incorporated into other memory modalities, and the more these memories are used. There is no need to postulate several different memory stores with different decay times.

Recall.   Since maintaining access to memories is so important in my theory, recall is the key to permanent retention. Spontaneous recall together with immediate memory bridges the immediate past and the present. Spontaneous recall also occurs when we encounter something we want to identify. It revives relevant past experiences without any effort.

Deliberate recall is initiated and directed by the person and consists in focusing on the immediate area of interest until the relevant memories are revived. It is not a search or scan. A search implies looking through a large array of memories laid out for our perusal until we spot what we are looking for. But that is not the way memory works. When we try to recall a fact or a name, we try to recall peripheral facts and gradually move closer until the desired memory "pops up." The very fact that we often spend fruitless minutes trying to recall something, only to have it come unsought as soon as we relax our attention, shows that it is not in our power to force its appearance. The memory suddenly comes to mind, we do not discover or find it. A memory scan is based on the assumption that the memories are all there, ready for our inspection, so all we have to do is to run through them until we find the right one. But memories are never "there," they are *potential* dispositions to be actualized. There are traces in the brain, but they are not images that only need to be lit up to be recalled.

Imagination.   The sensory and motor images that remain after every perception and action provide the raw material for memory and imagination. As Bartlett (1932) has shown, memory and imagination go hand in hand. When memory fails, imagination rounds out the picture. Imagination also is a sensory function working spontaneously in producing images of possible events and action. Without imagination, man or animal would remain a slave of the past, able to repeat actions but not to adapt them to new circumstances. While recall attempts to revive past experiences in their exact temporal and spatial pattern, imagination enables us to use such memories in picturing other possible situations, and in planning action. In animals, imagination, like recall, is set in motion by an unconscious spontaneous appraisal. In human beings, it is initiated both by an intuitive (unconscious) and by a deliberate appraisal. When we want something, we spontaneously imagine possible ways of obtaining it. But we can also set ourselves to imagine just anything at all.

In dreams and hallucinations, imagination works autonomously, released from conscious control. But even during waking, when imagination is used in storytelling, it works autonomously, following the storyteller's habitual emotional attitudes. For that reason, it is possible to sample products of imagination to discover a person's emotional preoccupation (for instance, in the Thematic Apperception Test; see Arnold, 1962).

Like memory, imagination has no external receptors but uses the material provided by the senses. Like memory and the integrative sense, imagination could be called an internal sense.

Conceptual Memory. In the human being, all sensory functions are accompanied by intellectual functions that depend on sensory experience but are not bounded by it. The integrative sense allows us to experience a well-articulated field in various modalities; but we are also able to order objects into categories, form concepts that apply not only to concrete things but also to abstract matters, relations, and activities. Thus we develop a complicated linguistic system that allows us to analyze sounds and signs with extraordinary facility. We may see, hear, trace, or pronounce letters and words; but the meaning of words and sentences does not depend on their sound or visual appearance. Helen Keller could neither see nor hear, yet she was able to communicate as well as anyone who has both sight and hearing. Conceptual knowledge rests on sense knowledge and complements it, but goes far beyond it.

Conceptual knowledge allows an expansion of every sensory function. Memory, in particular, cannot be explained without conceptual knowledge. The fact that memories can be ordered into more and more inclusive schemata cannot be explained on the basis of rehearsal or even free access to modality-specific memories. Rehearsal maintains access; but in addition, we can devise rules according to which each item of knowledge is categorized and assigned to particular schemata that can be employed to retrieve every needed item.

Both memory and imagination can be used deliberately by human beings, though not by animals. Imagination can be used to picture abstract relationships as well as concrete objects. We can construct scientific systems as well as creating works of art. All these endeavors are inconceivable without conceptual memory. Sensory memory is supplemented by conceptual memory so that we can structure memories according to their meaning, systematize them and so expand our memory span. The elaborate mnemonic systems that have been devised from time immemorial bear witness to the expansion of memory possible in man.

Sensory Appraisal.   Everything we experience or do, we appraise as good or bad, pertinent or irrelevant. This appraisal complements sensory experience and relates it to us personally. Without an appraisal, we cannot act. As long as the world of things and people is merely there, apart from any connection with us, we cannot attend to it, think about it, or act upon it. Action requires a wanting or intention. And before we can want anything, we must have realized that it is "wantable." If there is something we do not want, we are either indifferent to it and leave it aside; or we find it undesirable, and want to avoid it or escape from it. In either case, we must have appraised it as good or bad, desirable or undesirable, before we can want to approach or avoid it. Indeed, we need a preliminary appraisal in encountering anything at all, before we want to attend to it. Without this appraisal, we would let things pass us by without a second thought.

These appraisals seem to be mediated by a special appraisal system. It has a cortical component, the limbic areas, which receive fibers from the periphery as well as the association cortex, and are connected via the hippocampus with the motor cortex (Arnold, 1960, vol.2). I discuss these "appraisal" areas and their connections in various chapters in the second part of this volume.

We do not experience spontaneous appraisals, that is, we are not reflectively aware that we are making a judgment of good or bad. This judgment is direct, intuitive, and entirely unconscious. We only experience the action impulse that springs from it: we feel attracted to something we have appraised as good, repelled from something appraised as bad. In addition to this spontaneous appraisal, we also judge anything we encounter consciously and deliberately, assessing its impact on us. We may find it valuable or without further interest. But every deliberate judgment has an undercurrent of like or dislike, stemming from the simultaneous spontaneous appraisal. These feelings may support our reasonable judgment or run counter to it. The more a boy is teased, the more he wants to fight, although he may realize that he has no chance against a bigger and stronger opponent.

There is another kind of unconscious judgment we seem to make without knowing it: When we *recognize* something as familiar, we are judging that this is something we have experienced before, rather than something we see for the first time. When we try to recall a word list or a poem, the intuitive judgment that we have seen, heard, or said these words or lines before is the necessary affirmation that we are *recalling* something, not just imagining it. Hence recall is always accompanied by recognition, but recognition does not presuppose deliberate recall. Recognition is experienced as a sense of familiarity, just as the appraisal of something as good to touch or good to look at is experienced as a feeling of pleasantness.

Affective Memory.   Any appraisal of good/bad is registered and retained, just like sensory experience; and like such experience, it can be reactivated as "affective memory.'' Since the original appraisal was intuitive and unconscious, its revival is also. Like the original appraisal, this reactivated appraisal produces an action impulse toward anything appraised as good, and away from anything appraised as bad. This emotional action tendency is *experienced here and now, it is not a revived memory.* Affective memory, evoking a here-and-now emotion, biases our deliberate judgment, results quite literally in prejudice, and can only be changed by a corrective experience.

In remembering something, modality-specific and affective memory normally work together. We recall a new acquaintance, an interesting discussion, or a concert, and also relive the feelings and emotions these experiences have afforded us. While modality-specific memory provides sensory images as a faint afterglow of the original experience, affective memory duplicates the original emotional tone. Affective memory cannot be deliberately initiated. It appears spontaneously when we encounter an object or a situation similar to the original one. But with affective memory added to the here-and-now appraisal, our emotional reaction may be out of proportion to the present occasion.

Value Judgments.   Not only do we intuitively estimate people and things as good, bad, or indifferent for us here and now, we also consciously and deliberately judge their effect on us. Hence sensory appraisal is complemented by conscious value judgments that are not restricted to what is ''good or bad for me'' but what is of value to others, be it individuals, nations, or humanity as a whole. This deliberate value judgment is an extension of the sensory appraisal, just as conceptual knowledge is an extension of sensory knowledge, and conceptual memory is an extension of sensory and motor memory. Affective memory, which creates and maintains positive and negative attitudes toward things, also allows us to form such attitudes to ideals, systems of belief, and social institutions.

In this brief outline of cognitive functions and the memory systems embedded in them, I have built upon foundations laid by the perennial philosophy. These foundations may be ancient but the superstructure can accommodate the findings of psychological experimentation, as well as facts gleaned from everyday experience, while many a theory cast in a more up-to-date framework cannot.

However, a cognitive framework is not enough to account for memory phenomena. To explore memory, the experimenter must depend on recall and recognition as reported by human beings, or on the performance of animals in various kinds of learning and retention tasks. For this reason, we have to explore the way in which perception leads not only to appraisal and recall but to overt action. While the cognitive part of this chapter summarizes the earlier chapters, the discussion of appetitive functions to follow anticipates conclusions based on evidence given in Part II. Where necessary, I refer to the chapters that deal with these matters in detail.

APPETITIVE FUNCTIONS: ACTION IMPULSES AND ACTIONS

Every appraisal, whether intuitive or deliberate, results in an impulse to action. The intuitive appraisal arouses a spontaneous impulse (a wanting), a deliberate appraisal arouses an intention (a will impulse).

Attention.   The first action impulse produced by appraisal is the desire to know something or know it better, which leads to closer investigation: This is attention. It is involuntary, based on an intuitive appraisal, when something breaks in on our train of thought: a loud sound, a garish color, a quick movement. Attention is voluntary, based on deliberate judgment, when we decide to focus on something to explore it. Attention is the prelude to knowledge but is itself not a cognitive function. It is, as it were, the first-fruit of sensory appraisal, based on the preliminary intuitive estimate of something as worth knowing, and leads to knowledge.

The next intuitive appraisal may arouse an impulse to recall similar things, or an impulse to imagine what will happen or how to cope with the situation. In short, each appraisal produces an impulse to action. This action may either be further exploration of the object or situation encountered, it may be the accomplished recall of a memory, or it may be the production of a fantasy image.

Once object or situation is identified and appraised as "good for me," there is an emotional wanting if the appraisal was intuitive, or an intention to approach if the appraisal was deliberate. Action impulses, emotional or intentional, are appraised in turn. We may want to do something, be ready for action, but a reflective evaluation of the proposed action may show it to be unsuitable, and we delay or put off action altogether. Habitual positive or negative attitudes toward things and people, stemming from earlier appraisals revived by affective memory, will influence deliberate decision. A student who throughout the year has preferred partying to studying will find it very difficult to stay home and study even when he knows examination time is near. An emotional impulse will become a motive if the action to which it urges is deliberately and reflectively evaluated as suitable and leads to overt action. We have many desires but not all of them become motives. A desire that is simply there but leads to no perceptible action may be a wish but can hardly be called a motive.

Appraisal and action impulse represent the transition from sensory experience to action. I hope to show in Part II that the brain structures I have suggested as mediating appraisal actually have direct connections from all sensory areas to subcortical pathways running to the cortical motor areas. Appraisal is still on the sensory side because it indicates the effect of things or people on us; but the action impulse is already the forerunner of action.

Action.   When an emotion or an intention has been evaluated and found appropriate here and now, there is only one course open: overt action. Now there is no longer any impulse to recall further aspects of the situation, or to imagine further possibilities of action. The individual turns away, as it were, from further thought and launches himself into action. If this is something he has often done before, motor memory takes over and he runs through a complex sequence of movements with no delay and hardly a thought. If all or part of the action is new, or has never been practiced in this precise pattern, he will plan his motions. This plan may either be conscious, explicit, worked out almost like a blueprint, or it may be simple motor imagination, as, for instance, imagining a new dance step before actually trying it. Motor imagination is sequential rather than spatial and consists in a preliminary innervation of the muscles used in a particular pattern. The tension in such muscles can be picked up by electrodes, as Jacobson (1934) has shown. It is in the oculomotor muscles when the individual visualizes something, in the arm muscles when he imagines lifting his arm, and in the speech muscles when he imagines saying something. Motor images can also be *recalled* in this way, when, for instance, we imagine demonstrating how to hold a golf club and swing it. But ordinarily, as soon as we form the intention to make a particular practiced movement, the disposition becomes actual, and motor memory is activated and leads into the desired sequence.

Executive Control.   What remains to be discussed is how all these sensory and motor activities mesh to make up daily living. Within limits, a man can decide whether and in what way he will use his sensory system. He can attend to one thing almost exclusively so that he neither hears nor sees anything else; or he can shut his eyes, plug up his ears, relax his muscles, and so fall asleep. Obviously, he cannot do so indefinitely because the boredom that comes from lack of interest and disuse of his sensory and motor equipment will soon force him into activity.

Gradually, in the course of infancy, the child develops his motor integration. He learns to adapt his reach, he learns to walk, he learns to use his hands for the most varied skills. In the beginning of such motor learning, whether it occurs in infancy, childhood, or during his adult life, he must focus on every movement, correct each mistake, until the integrated sequence is well established.

Attention, as a desire to know what is going on, is the *sine qua non* of executive control. It can be relaxed for a while in routine activities, but is never abolished completely. The difference between learning a skill and exercising it when it is well-learned lies in the direction of attention. During learning, attention is narrowly focused on the mechanics of movement, and the goal of action recedes, often to the point where such lack of attention detracts from the performance. Once a skill is acquired (e.g., tennis), the player's attention is kept on the goal, and the mechanics of movement are left to the learned integration of the motor system. That is possible because an inherent steering mechanism takes over: The sensory system keeps the player informed of the progress of the game; and by means of the appraisal system he can appraise the ball in flight, its course and the appropriate return much faster than he could by deliberate judgment. In this way, the tennis player can map out his strategy while almost automatically returning one ball after another.

The only danger is that the player may become emotionally involved. He may become discouraged by a few bad breaks so that he no longer appraises each ball from the point of view of his overall strategy but appraises it as it affects his chances of winning. This immediately influences his game; he "loses his cool," "goes on walkabout," and steadily worsens his chances. Becoming emotionally involved breaks up the learned integration that had made each stroke swift and sure. Now he focuses on the way his playing affects him instead of keeping his focus on the game. Before, he had appraised each stroke according to "what is good for my game," but now his appraisal becomes "what is good for me as a person." He is thinking about himself instead of planning the strategy of the game, and so interferes in what had been a smoothly-flowing motor integration.

Executive control does not mean a hierarchy of *systems*. It is always the person who sees, hears, and appraises the situation and his possibilities for action. He sets the goal, e.g., to play tennis, and then keeps his attention on the goal without interfering with the learned integration of sensory and motor activity. It is he who has learned such integration, and it is he who carries it out, albeit not by conscious deliberation but by an interplay of sensory, appraisal, and motor activity that no longer needs special attention.

Limited Autonomy of Functions.   Even when executive control is relaxed in the performance of well-practiced acts, they are under the control of a "set" or intention that permits autonomy as long as it serves the person's purpose. This is particularly true in speaking and writing, and in artistic expression. A man's intention sets his visual, auditory or speech imagination in action and leads to the well-practiced performance that gives expression to his intention. But it is the person who exerts the final control, who likes one formulation, one drawing or painting and lets it stand, or is dissatisfied with it and looks for a better way to give expression to what he wants to convey.

In routine matters, the intuitive appraisal may suffice. For instance, in colloquial speech, where it does not matter how something is expressed, executive control is exercised only when a strong cultural taboo is about to be violated. But in creative writing, such personal control is exercised frequently because the writer is concerned about the form in which his meaning is expressed.

The same situation obtains in recall. In spontaneous recall, where something seen or heard immediately recalls the image of an earlier situation, the experienced sense of familiarity suffices to give the conviction that this is something that has happened before. But when recall is uncertain and has to be implemented by imagination, there may be no decisive sense of familiarity; in such cases, the individual has to decide how sure he is of recognizing this particular item. The ratings of certainty in recognition experiments are such deliberate decisions.

It has become clear from our discussion that psychological functions mesh in a complicated way in the sequence from perception to action. Perception is completed by appraisal, which produces an action impulse and eventually action. But this progression is complicated by the fact that an object or situation is usually appraised from many points of view so that one appraisal is pyramided on another. At every round of appraisal, the situation is evaluated in the light of what is recalled of similar objects or situations, and what can be imagined as to their effects, and possible ways of coping with them.

Every possible action is appraised, sometimes so briefly that appraisal, rejection, and turning to another possibility, are not distinguished as separate. If a habitual course of action is available which in the past has been appraised as suitable both in intuitive and reflective appraisals, the appropriate action will follow almost without thought. Often, undesirable emotions and actions are perpetuated in this way. For somebody who is timid, for instance, every new situation will immediately call out the affective memory of earlier reluctant action or earlier defeat, and the present challenge will almost inevitably be biased in favor of withdrawal rather than advance.

Affective memory, the reliving of past appraisals, is always spontaneous, unwitting; but at the same time, we may also have formed a reflective attitude on the basis of past deliberate appraisals. That is shown best in areas where for one reason or another the deliberate judgment goes against the emotional attraction; as, for instance, in the case of the diabetic who wants to eat more, or more palatable foods than his diet allows. He feels the accustomed appetite; but, if he has habitually followed the doctor's prescription, he also experiences an immediate impulse to turn away from the temptation. Obviously, the intuitive and deliberate appraisals act in parallel, and so do the action impulses that spring from them.

It is clear, then, that not only appraisal but action impulses may be and are both spontaneous (unconscious) and deliberate (conscious) in the human being. For the animal, an emotional impulse can be countered only by another emotional impulse. But for man, an emotional impulse can be in conflict with a choice of action stemming from a deliberate judgment. The fact that appraisal and action impulse act in parallel adds poignancy to the conflict: We are aware that we both want and do not want to do something, and yet have to make a choice.

This difficulty can only be resolved by another round of appraisal which assesses the consequences of the contemplated action. We recall what the results of such action have been in the past; we imagine what they might be today; we feel again the shame or embarrassment we have felt in the past: and we appraise the proposed action anew. This appraisal, again, is both intuitive and deliberate. The intuitive appraisal produces either a renewed attraction to this course of action or a reluctance based on affective memories of the consequences. The deliberate appraisal now leads to a definite choice of action (the decision), or alternatively, to a choice of no action (see Fig. 9.1).

Even this description, though complicated, is only a first approximation of what actually happens. Instead of four rounds, there may be ten or twenty—and there are, when a man is indecisive. He cannot decide to act because he goes over all possible actions repeatedly, and repeatedly finds that a given action is desirable, but has undesirable aspects as well. A man is free because he has innumerable possibilities of action that he can imagine and appraise as suitable or unsuitable and can eventually choose. His past history may have biased his appraisal so that he thinks undesirable what another may think desirable. His past history has also influenced his inclination to look for more and more choices, or to make an appraisal of his choice and be satisfied with it. A man for whom every decision is a heavy burden has brought himself to this attitude over the years; whether he kept looking for more and more possibilities of action out of conscientiousness or out of a desire to have the choice made for him is beside the point. The fact is that the way he has acted till now has brought him to his present predicament.

All this complicated activity is always the activity of a person. The individual appraises, he attends to something, recalls what he needs to identify it, imagines what is going to happen and what he is going to do about it; he feels emotion and decides whether to give in to it or overcome it. The final decision for action is his, no matter what environmental, physiological, or psychological influences have played upon him. It is he who has executive control and it is he who can on occasion let go of it. And when he relinquishes control, he is still in command: What is happening is merely that intuitive appraisal and spontaneous impulses to action take over; but they have been shaped by his previous convictions and actions, so that he still acts as he is. *In vino veritas:* the drunk who becomes aggressive and ornery is acting out his own disposition. When sober, he may have his impulses under tight control, but he really believes that everybody is out to get him, although he may never admit it. If he really felt friendly toward people, he would have acted considerately and put himself out for them habitually, and his intuitive appraisal would be in accord. As it is, his friendliness is superficial, a counsel of expediency; his underlying aggressiveness is expressed in his intuitive appraisals and lies open for everyone to see when he relaxes his deliberate control.

The sequence from perception to action moves in many or few channels, in series and in parallel, doubles back on itself repeatedly before it ends in the final appraisal and decision for action. The flow chart is as simple or as complex as the situation and the person requires. But however complex, the basic ingredients have been spelled out. What remains now is to try and identify the structures and pathways in the brain that are activated when the psychological activities described in the flow chart go on.

II NEUROPHYSIOLOGICAL CORRELATES

10 Localization of Psychological Functions

I am less impressed with the analogies of various machines and neural activity such as are discussed in "cybernetics." There has been a curious parallel in the histories of neurological theories and of paranoid delusional systems. In Mesmer's day the paranoic was persecuted by malicious animal magnetism; his successors, by galvanic shocks, by the telegraph, by radio, by radar, keeping their delusional systems up-to-date with the latest fashions in physics. Descartes was impressed by the hydraulic figures in the royal gardens and developed a hydraulic theory of the action of the brain. We have since had telephone theories, electrical field theories, and now, theories based on the computing machines and automatic rudders. I suggest that we are more likely to find out how the brain works by studying the brain itself and the phenomena of behavior than by indulging in far-fetched physical analogies. The similarities in such comparisons are the product of an oversimplification of the problems of behavior.

K. S. Lashley
Discussion in AMA Archives of Neurology and Psychiatry, 1952,
67, p. 195

In a discussion of brain function, there are several questions that have to be raised: (1) What is really "localized" in the brain? (2) If there are areas in the brain that mediate memory registration, how are these memory areas reactivated? (3) How can psychological activities be localized in the brain? (See Luria, 1973).

Registration of Sensations and Movements.   As to the first question, we must distinguish between the localization of sense impressions or movements, and the localization of sensory and motor memories. There is no doubt that separate, highly specific areas in the cortex mediate visual, auditory, tactual, olfactory, and taste experience; and a motor area that, when stimulated, produces well-defined movements. The sensory receiving areas in the cortex are highly specialized and often have a point-by-point projection from the receptors. The motor cortex also is quite distinctive. Different areas within it produce movements of specific parts of the body. It is generally accepted that excitation modifies the sensory cells in some ways to produce sensory experience in a particular modality. Vision, hearing, touch, taste, and smell are "localized" in the cortex in the sense that these sensory areas are the endstations of their sensory systems. Although it is possible to experience light, sound, taste, or touch, even without the cortex if the sensory thalamic nuclei are intact, the cortex allows us to experience objects, visual and auditory patterns, and melodies. Movements are "localized" in the motor cortex in the sense that this area is necessary for finely structured movements (see Chapter 13).

Registration of Memories.   As to the second question: If memory areas exist, they must be connected with the sensory projection and must receive neural impulses for memory registration during sensory experience. What is preserved cannot be the original impression (that can only be experienced as sensation) but its analogue or image. Obviously, this image cannot be a picture, even for a visual memory; but it can be a disposition to relive the image of the original sense impression. This disposition can only be preserved as a modification of cortical cells similar but not identical to the changes occurring in the sensory areas. When reactivated this disposition allows us to experience the image of the original sensation.

The question of how memory is recalled has found little interest and fewer answers. Most of the research effort has been directed toward identifying the mechanism of memory registration. It seems to be assumed that once we know that mechanism, the question of recall will solve itself. But whatever the mechanism of registration, how could we recall (spontaneously or deliberately) exactly what we want to (despite occasional lapses), and how could we draw on our memory store in free imagination unless there were some circuit over which a given memory pattern could be reactivated? There are enough reports of retention deficits after lesions in different parts of the brain to allow us to trace such a circuit (see Chapters 11, 12, 13).

Localization of Mental Activity.   The third question, how mental activity can be localized in the brain, has been partially answered in an earlier publication (Arnold, 1960). I have tried to show that a careful analysis of the sequence from perception to action will provide hints as to the brain pathways and structures that mediate these psychological operations. I have spelled out the psychological functions involved in greater detail in the first part of this book and summarized them in Chapter 9. The brain structures and pathways activated during the sequence from perception to action will be discussed in this second part.

Our earlier discussion of memory theories and memory models has shown that a psychological theory of memory is impossible unless memory is seen as part of the total cognitive and appetitive human functions, and finds its place in the chain of activities from perception to action. To understand and identify the neural "substrate" of memory, it is similarly important to identify, as far as may be, the structures mediating sensory and motor functions before attempting to single out the particular structures mediating memory registration, recall, and recognition. In fact, we cannot be sure of having identified the substrate of memory until we have succeeded in showing how the various psychological functions are mediated by neural structures and pathways. This implies a theory of brain function that accounts not only for neural pathways serving memory but for all psychological functions. In an earlier publication (Arnold, 1960, vol. 2) I attempted to formulate such a theory on the basis of hundreds of published research reports. This theory is not intended to be a "model" of brain function but is a set of inferences based on actual research data.

Since any one psychological function can only be discussed as part of the interlocking network of human functions, and the underlying brain processes are similarly structured, I propose now to parallel the discussion of psychological functions in Chapter 9 with a review of what we know about the brain functions mediating such psychological activities. My emphasis is on research after 1958, although some earlier evidence must be mentioned. For much of the evidence before this cut-off point, my earlier volume provides the references.

It is necessary to sketch my theory of brain function in outline before giving a review of some of the more recent research. Lest this procedure seems too didactic, it is well to remember that the brain, that "great, ravelled know," is an extraordinarily complex organ. An inductive exposition, going from the data to their significance for brain function and finally presenting the complete theory, would be difficult to follow and would lack any persuasive power. Although the theory was developed inductively, on the basis of published research reports, clear exposition demands that the theory be stated first and then tested against the available data.

There are two main problems that have to be solved by a theory of brain function: one, what areas in the brain mediate the registration of sensory experience so that it can be recalled; and the other, how the sensory areas are connected with the motor cortex so that sensory experience produces a motor reaction. We know something about the cortical areas that mediate sensory experience and there are some suggestions as to the areas that register memory engrams; but there is hardly a suggestion, let alone agreement, on the question of what pathways connect sensory and motor cortex. We know that the long association fibers cannot constitute such a pathway because it was found that a cut around sensory cortical areas severing these fibers did not interfere with learning in animals. After such a cut isolating the visual, auditory, or tactual area, animals were still able to make a learned response to the correct visual, auditory, or tactual stimulus. But the animals were unable to learn or retain such a response when the relevant association area was undercut and so isolated from the subcortex; yet their sensory experience was not impaired, for they still reacted to food or pain. Hence there are areas in the brain that seem to mediate memory and learning via pathways through the subcortex to the motor cortex.

Views of the Localization of Psychological Functions.   In the course of neurological investigations of the cortex of the brain, expert opinion on the localization of sensory and motor functions has made several pendulum swings. From Gall's phrenology (1825), which had the whole cortex mapped out for various complex mental faculties (e.g., hope, justice, self-esteem, sociability, etc.), to Lashley's (1929) dictum of "mass action" and "equipotentiality of the brain," opinion has swayed back and forth. At first, localization was understood to mean centers producing or at least representing particular mental qualities or abilities.

Even at the time of Gall, there was opposition to such a view. Flourens (1842), for instance, had found that shortly after the destruction of circumscribed areas on the bird cortex, behavior becomes normal once more. Crossing the extensor and flexor nerves of a wing in a rooster, he found that the wing functioned normally after a short time. Hence, he insisted that the cerebral hemispheres are homogeneous masses rather than a combination of centers serving specialized functions. However, first Bouillaud (1825) and later Broca (1861) insisted on the basis of both anatomical and clinical evidence that there must be special areas in the brain that serve special functions. Broca showed that brains of patients with disturbance of articulation showed lesions in the posterior third of the inferior frontal convolution of the left hemisphere (Broca's speech center). He concluded that this area is a "storehouse of movement images of articulated speech." Some years later, Wernicke (1874) showed that a lesion of the posterior third of the superior temporal gyrus of the left (dominant) hemisphere resulted in loss of language comprehension. He concluded that the "sensory images of speech" are localized in this area (Wernicke's language comprehension center). These discoveries were followed by other investigations that resulted in a description of centers of visual memory (Bastian, 1869), a writing center (Exner, 1881), and centers of ideation (Broadbent, 1872, 1879). At about the same time, Fritsch and Hitzig (1870) discovered that electrical stimulation of certain areas in the cortex of a dog resulted in movements. Such "motor centers" were also found in other animals and in man. Betz (1870) observed giant pyramidal cells in the anterior central gyrus, from which area movements had been obtained by electrical stimulation, and concluded that these cells are responsible for movement.

During the years that followed, agreement was reached that sensory experience is mediated by various areas of the cortex. The receiving area for visual impressions is area 17 in the occipital lobe while area 42 in the temporal lobe mediates auditory experience, and the olfactory lobe seems to be the receiving station for olfactory impressions. The anterior part of the parietal lobe, areas 3, 1, 2, receive touch and other somesthetic impulses; and the most lateral region in this area, overlapping with the area mediating touch on tongue and palate, mediates taste experience. In modern times, this kind of localization of sensory experience as well as movement has never been seriously disputed. What has been questioned is the localization of "higher mental functions," including intellect, will, judgment, or learning.

The investigations of Vogt (1951) who showed that there are marked differences in the cell structure of various parts of the cortex tended to support the concept of localized sensory and motor areas. Unfortunately, the large number of cortical fields with different cell structure but without known sensory or motor function also encouraged speculation about their role in higher mental functions. While speculative excesses deserved criticism, the neurologists who opposed such speculation contributed nothing to a genuine knowledge of brain function and its correlation with psychological activities. Goltz, for instance, lesioned various cortical areas in animals in the years between 1876 and 1884 and found that the resulting behavioral disturbances disappeared after a short time. He concluded that brain lesions produced a general "lowering of intellect." He also found that the impairment was the more severe the more cortical tissue was destroyed and thought that this was sufficient evidence against cortical localization.

The notion was reemphasized by Lashley (1929) who investigated the performance of rats in running a maze after he had destroyed various areas of the brain. The impairment varied with the mass of brain destroyed; hence he postulated that the brain acts as a whole in learning and that the function of lost brain tissue can be taken over by other areas of the brain (mass action and equipotentiality of the brain[1]). Lashley's views have had considerable influence on the thinking of psychologists, for he was the first psychologist who not only was interested in brain function but also did a great deal of experimental work in this field. His conclusions gave rise to such ingrained doubts in the possibility of any kind of correspondence between brain function and psychological activities that for many years the brain was almost completely disregarded by psychologists.

The notion of a localization of functions received another setback from Hughlings Jackson's formulation of principles of neural functioning. In the

---

[1]*Equipotentiality*: There are alternative explanations for Lashley's findings. A rat running a maze can use visual, tactual, and movement cues. If the occipital area is removed, visual cues can no longer be used, which will impair but not prevent correct performance. If tactual cues also are excluded by removing the parietal cortex, the performance is impaired again, but as long as the movement pattern in running a maze can be learned and remembered, performance is still possible. While it is true that correct performance becomes more difficult as more brain tissue is removed, this can be the result of removing more and more areas needed to use various sensory cues.

Mass Action: While it is true that most of the brain is active in learning, this need not be mass action. It has been shown that the electrical potentials in the brain show a precise sequential patterning during learning, which indicates that learning occurs via definite pathways rather than activating the brain en masse.

1860's, Jackson studied motor and speech disturbances and found that local brain lesions never led to a complete loss of speech or movement (Jackson, 1884). Although the patient may be unable to make a movement or pronounce a word on command, he may be able to do so when the movement is embedded in a habitual action or when it is part of emotional expression.

Eventually, Hughlings Jackson proposed that psychological activity depends on a vertical type of organization in the nervous system. It is organized first on the lower level of spinal cord and brainstem, then at the middle level of cortical sensory and motor areas, and finally at the highest level, the frontal lobes. His work was not published in England until 1931 and his ideas took a long time to penetrate the professional world. What was immediately taken up were his strictures against cortical "centers" and his suggestion that psychological activities are highly complex, "symbolic" processes that cannot be localized in particular areas of the brain.

In psychology, this type of thinking was implicit in the theories of the Würzburg School and Gestalt psychology. Perhaps the most eminent representative of this point of view was Kurt Goldstein, (1949), who worked with the neurologist Ernst Gelb in the rehabilitation of brain-injured veterans of the first World War. He came to the conviction that brain injury interferes with a person's ability to organize the environment: It results in a loss of "categorical behavior." Frontal lobe injury, in particular, creates an inability to assume an "abstract attitude" (e.g., the patient can drink out of a glass, can comb his hair, but cannot pretend to do so).

As Luria (1966a) points out, both views, localization and antilocalization, led to (or perhaps resulted from?) important discoveries. On the one hand, protagonists of localization could point to the evidence for cortical sensory and motor areas, and the importance of Broca's and Wernicke's areas for speech and the understanding of language. On the other hand, investigators who insisted on the holistic functioning of the brain have shown that various psychological functions could be restored after cortical damage, and have insisted that the brain is far more plastic than could be expected if the cortex consisted of separate centers. But as Luria also says, both schools had a similar view of the connection between brain and mental processes, namely, that they can be "directly correlated with the brain structure without intermediate physiological[2] analysis." (p. 22). Both schools, those who accepted localization and those who did not, were quite willing to believe that not only sensation and movement but will, intellect, self-esteem, ego, id, and superego, are separate isolable phenomena. This indiscriminate attitude of belief or disbelief and the attendant unwillingness to analyze psychological functions has finally resulted in an abiding distrust in the possibil-

---

[2]Luria, Like all Marxist psychologists includes in this term both the physiological and psychological analysis of functions.

ity of localizing any complex mental activity. Today, only the localization of sensory and motor areas is generally accepted.

Russian neurologists, following Pavlov, have had a more flexible view of psychological functions and a correspondingly different approach to localization. For Luria, "individual areas of the cerebral cortex cannot be regarded as fixed centers but, rather . . . (as) 'staging posts' or 'junctions' in the dynamic systems of excitation in the brain and . . . these systems have an extremely complex and variable structure." (1966a, p. 29). Following Pavlov, the Russian school postulates cortical sensory and motor "analyzers"; that is, areas in which information from the peripheral receptors is analyzed and processed for further use. This is a far more fruitful notion than postulating cortical "centers" for various functions. For Luria, it is a simplified and obsolete notion "to assign a function to a particular area of the brain or to an isolated group of nerve cells." It should be replaced by Filimonov's "principle of graded localization of function" coupled with that of "functional pluripotentialism" of the brain. The first of these principles means that "functions are localized, not in fixed centers, but in dynamic systems whose elements maintain strict differentiation and play a highly specialized role in integrated activity." (Luria, 1966a, p. 28). The principle of functional pluripotentialism impies that "no formation of the central nervous system is responsible for only a single function. Under certain conditions, a given formation may be involved in other functional systems and may participate in the performance of other tasks." (Luria, 1966a, p. 27.)

Perhaps such pluripotentialism exists in brain formations like the visual cortex, which mediates not only the perception of colors but of outlines, patterns, and movements. But a single cell may have only one function. In the visual cortex, for instance, there are columns of cells that mediate the perception of outlines or direction but do not mediate the perception of color. Even brain structures may not necessarily have more than one function. Among the examples of pluripotentialism Luria mentions, two are rather doubtful: He claims that the "olfactory structures of the cerebral cortex" (i.e. hippocampus and hippocampal gyrus) must have another function as well because they are found also in anosmic animals like the dolphin. However, it has been found that the hippocampal system is a general correlation system connected with all sensory and motor systems; it is not an "olfactory structure" at all (Kaada, 1951). The other example is doubtful, also. Luria mentions Lashley's report that maze performance in rats was more impaired by lesions of the visual cortex than by blinding the animal; hence he concluded that the visual cortex also must have another function. But in all likelihood, such lesions destroyed not only the visual cortex but the underlying portion of the hippocampus which is important for learning (see chapter 20–21) and Arnold, 1960, vol. 2). Hence, in both cases, even a given brain structure may only have one function but be closely connected with another system having a different function. Incidentally, if the first principle mentioned by Luria is taken seriously, that "the elements of dynamic systems maintain strict differentiation and play a highly specialized role,'' it really is incompatible with the second principle of functional pluripotentialism.

Among psychologists interested in theory, it has become fashionable to construct speculative models of particular "complex functions" like memory or learning, patterned on information theory and computer models, rather than on the actual functioning of the brain. And experimental psychologists interested in brain function and learning who have contributed to the abundance of valuable neurophysiological research, have rarely gone beyond the structures or systems they have studied and so have failed to develop a theory of brain function.

My own theory of brain function has grown out of the effort to account for the arousal of emotion (Arnold, 1960, vol. 2). Not surprisingly, I discovered that it is impossible to trace the pathways that serve a given psychological function, without having some notion how this function can and does mesh with every other psychological function, and how their neural pathways connect.

Unless a theory of brain function takes into account the psychological reality of human experience and action, it is doomed from the beginning. Human experience never starts out of the blue, it is connected with everything that went before or it cannot be woven into purposeful action. We may arbitrarily isolate some unit in this continuous flow from perception to action, but we must realize that this is an arbitrary cut-out from an ongoing living process.

If we talk about cortical centers at all, we must realize that these are centers for the analysis and synthesis of sense impressions and for structuring movements. A sensory center does not manufacture sensations nor does the motor cortex act like a switch that is somehow operated by the "will." Via the sensory areas in the cortex, we sort out sensory impulses from the periphery and organize them into coherent experiences of the world around us and of our own body. The brain does not act of itself and by itself. It is always the person who acts; and whenever he or she acts, the brain functions in a particular way. The living brain is not like an intricate electrical system, it is an integral part of the living being. It is not the brain that produces sensations, images, memories, or thought, we do. We sense, we imagine, we recall something. *We* think, not our brain. It is not the motor cortex that produces a movement, *we* do. When we sense, imagine, think, or move, certain pathways are active and communicate activity to a widespread area. But our muscles are innervated because we intend to move, and they relax because we intend to rest. It is conceivable that at some future date we might be able to discover exactly how the brain functions when a person is experiencing a particular situation, but it will never be possible to predict from brain activity how a given person will react to this experience. There are so many possibilities of reaction, with emotion or without, with anger, fear, or curiosity, with a reasonable plan for action or impulsively; and the person's motives, convictions, as well as the particular circumstances and his past experience will influence his action.

My Theory of Brain Function.   Briefly, my theory starts from the fact that the sensory projection areas in the cortex as well as their neighboring association areas receive impulses from the various sensory organs (see Hubel & Wiesel, 1965, 1968); when these impulses reach the primary cortical projection area, we experience integrated objects and situations.

Part of the projection from sensory thalamic nuclei goes to the neighboring association cortex, which mediates the experience of sensory images. We usually speak only of visual images, but a sound just heard, an odor, or a touch just felt also remains as an auditory, olfactory, or touch image. A movement just made remains as a kinetic image, so that we can imagine making the same movement over again. These sensory and motor images are preserved as dispositions in the appropriate cortical association areas and can be recalled, either as memory or as fantasy images.

What is seen, heard, or otherwise experienced, is next appraised as "good or bad for me here and now" and this appraisal, I suggest, is mediated by the limbic cortex adjoining the appropriate sensory areas. We know that the initiation of integrated action depends on the motor cortex: and I am postulating that the appraisal of actions and action impulses depends on the neighboring limbic cortex. These appraisals of situations and actions are preserved as dispositions for recall in the same regions of limbic cortex.

To recall something in any modality, that is, to revive a memory disposition, impulses must travel from the appraisal (limbic) areas to the hippocampus, where they are transformed into an impulse to act. From the hippocampus, neural impulses travel to precommissural fornix and brainstem and return via thalamic sensory nuclei to the appropriate cortical association areas. This is the *memory circuit,* mediating modality-specific memory.

When we imagine something or plan action, impulses travel from the appraisal area to the amygdala where they are transformed into impulses to form appropriate images. From the amygdala, these impulses are relayed via thalamic association nuclei to the relevant cortical association areas. This is the *imagination circuit.*

In reviving earlier appraisals, impulses travel from the appraisal area via hippocampus, postcommissural fornix, and mamillary bodies to the midbrain and return via anterior thalamic nuclei to the cingulate gyrus and other cortical limbic areas. This is the *affective memory circuit.*

Every intention to remember, recall, imagine, or act necessarily starts from an appraisal that this is good to do. Accordingly, neural impulses traveling over modality-specific memory circuits, the imagination circuit and the affective memory circuit must be initiated by impulses from the limbic appraisal areas.

Finally, I am postulating that impulses to action, whether emotional or deliberate, are mediated by the action circuit, which also originates in an appraisal mediated by some region of the limbic cortex, and runs via hippocampus, midbrain, and cerebellum, returning via ventral thalamic nuclei to the prefrontal and frontal cortex. When these impulses arrive in the prefrontal cortex, they are registered as motor memory engrams; when they arrive in the premotor cortex, we experience an impulse to action, which may be an emotional impulse or an intention to act. This impulse leads to action when nerve impulses arrive in the motor cortex.

This is a brief outline of my theory of brain function, which is fleshed out in the succeeding chapters. On the basis of a great deal of research published in the last few decades I discuss the brain structures that form these circuits and the psychological experiences that follow when they are damaged or stimulated.

11 Cortical Areas Mediating Sense Experience: Sensory Areas and Appraisal Areas

The ultimate goal of studies of the neurobiology of memory is to understand how the nervous system processes, stores, and utilizes information. The problem is not one simply of determining the mechanism underlying the neural trace of an experience. We need to know how such traces are produced, where they occur and how they are used when required to control learned behavior . . . .The particular neuroanatomical and neurochemical systems activated by any new experience will depend upon the type of information (visual, auditory, etc.) to be stored . . . .Consequently, it does not seem likely that there are unique neuroanatomical systems or unique neurochemical systems that store many different types of memories. But, it may be that some brain systems are involved in certain processes which promote the storage of most if not all information. Thus, although it may not be possible to locate specific "engrams" it should be possible to locate the neural systems which are involved in the processing and storing of information and, eventually, to understand the anatomical interactions and neurochemical bases of such systems.

J. L. McGaugh and P. E. Gold, 1974, p. 189

We have considerable information about the various cortical areas that mediate sense experience. Our knowledge of the association areas is far less exact, and what is gleaned from experimental or clinical findings is not generally accepted.

THE PRIMARY SENSORY CORTEX

The cell structure of the primary sensory areas differs from that of the surrounding cortex. Layers II and IV (external and internal granular layers) of the six-layered cortex contain numerous small granular cells. The internal granular layer

117

IV forms the afferent plexus and receives relays from the subcortical relay stations of the afferent sensory pathways. Layers III and V, the internal and external pyramidal layers of the cortex, contain pyramidal cells that relay impulses to other layers. However, in the sensory cortex, layer III consists mainly of granular cells which occasionally spread even to layer V. Hence the sensory cortex is granular cortex.

The primary sensory cortex is needed for the experience of patterns and objects. Sensory thalamic nuclei are sufficient for appreciating the quality of a sensation (light and dark, sound, touch), but at least in higher mammals the primary sensory cortex is necessary to distinguish outlines, shapes, spatial and temporal patterns; and the primary motor cortex, to move purposefully. This would imply that the cortical feltwork of the primary sensory cortex is responsible for integrating sensations into objects, that it is the "organ" of the integrative sense. While the afferent plexus (layer IV) receives relays from sensory receptors, the remaining layers seem to provide for the integrative function of the cortex and for relays to other cortical and subcortical areas.

For a long time, most of our knowledge of brain function in man had been derived from accidental damage to parts of the brain, from brain tumors, cerebral accidents, gunshot wounds, and the like. But during the last few decades, stimulation of the exposed brain of conscious patients has added much to our knowledge. In addition, there has been a great deal of brain research on animals.

It used to be thought that the sensory cortex is exclusively a receiving area while the motor cortex has only efferent connections with the periphery. Today we know that the sensory cortex not only receives afferent fibers from the periphery but also sends out impulses to afferent relay stations and even to the receptor organs. And the motor cortex not only sends impulses to subcortex and muscles, it also receives impulses from these areas, so that movements can be continually monitored. This two-way connection of cortex and periphery should be kept in mind throughout our discussion although it may not be specifically mentioned. The sensory process is not a passive reception of afferent impulses but a reaction to stimulation, which is passed on throughout the nervous system.

Auditory Cortical Area.   The primary auditory area consists of the transverse gyri of Heschl (area 41 and part of area 42), each of which receive auditory fibers from both ears (Fig. 11.1). The sound frequency determines the part of the cochlear membrane that reacts to it, and also the area of cortex that is maximally activated. In mapping the boundaries of the primary auditory cortex, a regular increase in the frequency best recorded was found as the recording electrode moved from posterior to anterior areas. Two complete representations of the cochlea were found in the primary auditory cortex; the boundary of these fields were correlated with the boundaries of areas with different cell structure (Dykes,

FIG. 11.1   Cytoarchitectural maps of human cerebral cortex by Brodmann (1914). Above, convex surface of hemisphere; below, medial surface.

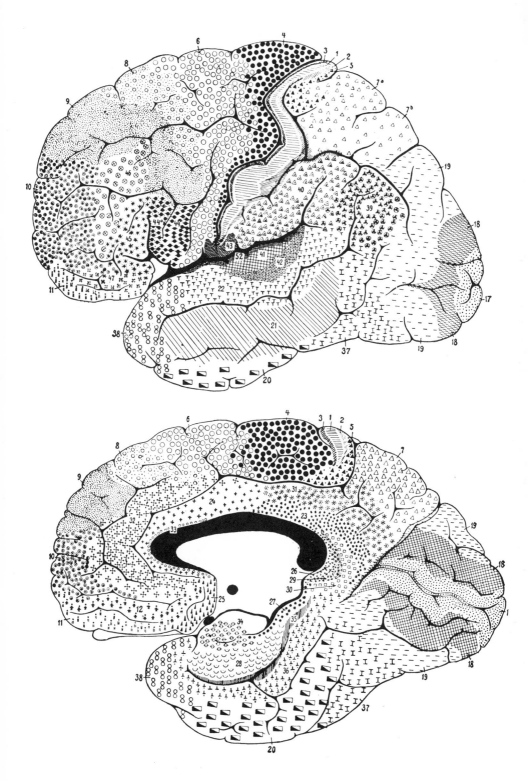

1978). The mediation of tonal frequency is but one dimension of the extent of the primary auditory cortex; the other dimension of auditory cortical maps is still undefined (Woolsey, 1961).

Unlike the visual cortex, which mediates spatial patterns, the auditory cortex mediates temporal patterns, such as speech or music. When this area is damaged, there is no permanent loss of hearing but the patient is no longer able to distinguish speech sounds, and may lose the ability to understand spoken language. Such a patient cannot distinguish rhythmic patterns and so cannot reproduce them, particularly if the pattern is more complicated. Writing also is affected because both the articulation and the writing of words become uncertain if the ear cannot distinguish between similar sounds. When the patient is asked to repeat letters like g and k, or b and p, he cannot do so correctly unless he can see the letters as well as hearing the sounds. Damage of the auditory area also produces a disintegration of auditory patterns. According to research reports, unilateral damage impairs auditory localization on the contralateral side.

Bocca et al. (1955), for instance, reported that it was difficult for a patient with a temporal lobe tumor to recognize speech made hard to distinguish by a low-pass filter, or to comprehend language when spoken very fast. The patient had these difficulties when listening with the ear opposite his temporal lobe tumor, whether the tumor was in the right or left hemisphere. This report has been confirmed for patients with atrophic lesions of the temporal lobe. No such impairment was found in a control group of patients with lesions in other parts of the brain. According to Luria (1966a), "a disturbance *in the analytic-synthetic activity of the auditory cortex* (in the form of a disturbance of the differential system of speech sounds), *may be regarded as the fundamental sympton of a lesion of the superior temporal region of the left hemisphere*" (p. 107, original emphases). Hence the primary auditory cortex seems to be responsible for the integration of sound patterns.

Visual Cortical Area 17.   Visual fibers from the retina run via the optic tract to the optic chiasm where the optic tracts cross over and go to the lateral geniculate nuclei in the thalamus and to the visual cortex. The optic tract from each eye contains fibers from both the left and the right visual field. But at the optic chiasm, only part of the fibers cross over, so that fibers from the left visual field of both eyes now go to the right hemisphere while fibers from both right visual fields go to the left hemisphere. Area 17 receives association fibers from the secondary visual areas (the neighboring association areas 18 and 19) and sends fibers to them. It also sends fibers to the lateral geniculate nucleus from where fibers go back to the retina.

The fibers of the retina project in an ordered arrangement to the lateral geniculate nucleus and the visual cortex, so that each area in the retina projects to a definite area in the lateral geniculate and the visual cortex. Talbot (1940, 1942) described projections from the retina to the primary visual area 17 and also to a smaller mirror image in area 18 for cat and monkey. Hubel and Wiesel (1965) reported evidence for a separate projection to areas 17, 18, and 19 in the cat. These projections are retinotopically organized and were mapped on the basis of short-latency electrical potentials.

Destruction of small parts of area 17 leads to a strictly localized degeneration in the lateral geniculate and the retina, causing a dark spot in the corresponding area of the visual field. Electrical stimulation of various points in area 17 produces visual experiences described as "colored light," "white light," "flame," "blue fog," and the like (Hoff & Pötzl, 1930; Penfield, 1954). Hubel and Wiesel (1962, 1963, 1968) have shown that there are columns of cells in the visual cortex that respond to vertical, horizontal, and oblique outlines, and to the direction of movement. This provides the mechanism for the perception of shapes and patterns, so that we see stationary or moving colored objects rather than a medley of colored patches. As Hubel and Wiesel put it: "the visual cortex appears to have a rich assortment of functions. It rearranges the input from the lateral geniculate body in a way that makes lines and contours the most important stimuli." (1963, p. 10).

When the primary visual area is severely damaged, the patient can still distinguish light from darkness, but he can no longer make out objects or patterns. When the occipital lesions are less extensive, the patients experience a disintegration of form (Faust, 1955; see discussion in chapter 1). They may see forms and patterns when they first look at them, but these patterns disintegrate after a short time.

Apparently, the cortical feltwork performs the integrative functions that allows us to see colored moving objects or complex patterns. The electrical stimulation of visual cortex is perceived as colored light rather than colored objects because the cortical cells so stimulated cannot draw on information provided by the underlying cell columns. Indeed, these flashes of light may come from the excitation of efferent fibers from visual cortex to the lateral geniculate nucleus.

Somesthetic Areas 3, 1, 2, in the Postcentral Gyrus. The postcentral gyrus receives afferents from touch, movement and other somesthetic receptors, which run in the posterior funiculi of the spinal cord, form relays in the nuclei of the dorsal column and the ventrobasal nuclei of the thalamus, and finally end in the postcentral gyrus. In this area, there is a well-defined projection of different bodily zones, corresponding to the motor projection of area 4 just in front of it (see Fig. 11.2).

The primary somatic area has been mapped by recording the cells that show short-latency electrical potentials when a part of the body is stimulated. The medial part of the somatic area receives afferents from the lower limbs; the more lateral cortical areas receive projections from sites higher up on the body, until the face is represented at the base of the lateral aspect of the postcentral gyrus. The cortical projection is most extensive for body parts that are used most exten-

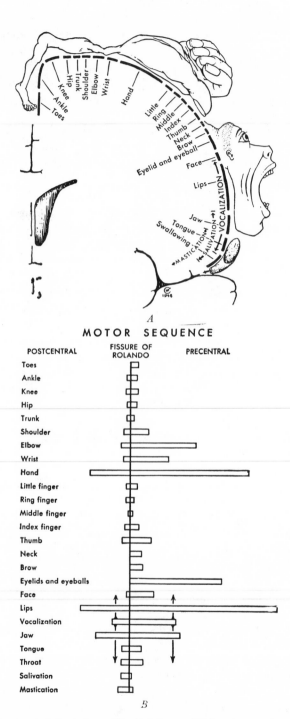

MOTOR SEQUENCE

FIG. 11.2 Motor representation in human Cerebral Cortex. (A)Motor homunculus; (B) Extension of the motor representation into the postcentral gyrus. Reprinted with permission of Macmillan Publishing Company from *The Cerebral Cortex of Man*, by Penfield & Rasmussen. Copyright 1950 by Macmillan Publishing Company, renewed 1978 by Theodore Rasmussen.

sively. In primates, and particularly in man, mouth, larynx, tongue, and pharynx project over a considerable area; so do hand and fingers. Body and limbs have a comparatively small projection. In primates, the area representing the head and face is so large that it disrupts the body sequence. The face area is separated from the area representing the back of the skull by the area serving the hand. Recently, several investigators have found that there are two complete body maps, one in are 3 and the anterior part of area 1, and the other in area 2 and the posterior part of area 1 (Dykes, 1978).

When the primary somatic sensory area is damaged, the patients show obvious disturbances of touch and muscle sensations. They do not feel the affected limbs, nor can they move them smoothly and easily. Since they do not sense the exact position of the affected limbs, they contract the muscles in a mass movement that rarely reaches its aim. In the most severe cases, according to Foerster (1936), the patient was altogether unable to move the affected limb. According to Luria (1966a), the electromyogram of the hand movements of such a patient showed gross differences in innervation when compared to that of an intact person. Luria concluded that "a lesion of this region leads to a disorganization of spatial integration . . . or to disturbance of those 'kinesthetic schemes' of movement upon which the construction of the motor act is based" (p. 180).

When the inferior part of the postcentral cortex of the left hemisphere is damaged, the patient has difficulty in using his speech organs. He cannot articulate sounds or words without concentrating on his articulation. Not feeling the pattern of lip and tongue positions, he has difficulty in moving them precisely as required. Sometimes, habitual expressions or short phrases may be pronounced rather easily, but the patient fails in repeating sounds or words that require precise articulation. However, retraining is possible because the motor area is unimpaired.

Taste Area.   Taste nerves from the tongue run in the seventh nerve trunk (via chorda tympani and lingula nerve) and also in the ninth and tenth nerve to the nucleus of the tractus solitarius. Comparatively recently, it has also been established that from there, taste fibers are relayed via the thalamic arcuate nucleus, which also receives touch fibers from the face (Patton et al., 1944), to the posterior operculum of the parietal lobe (Brodmann area 43). It coincides almost exactly with the touch area for the tongue. By itself, the sense of taste can only mediate the qualities of sweet, sour, bitter, or salty. We experience complex taste sensations when taste combines with smell. In manipulating something, the senses of touch and taste can give us the experience of an *object* (solid or liquid) that has a certain taste.

Olfactory Area.   The olfactory system is the only sensory system whose afferent nerves do not travel through the thalamus to the cortex. All other sensory systems have a peripheral receptor system which sends afferents through sensory thalamic nuclei to end up in sensory cortex. In an attempt to find a similarly lengthy afferent pathway, earlier anatomists have ascribed the experience of smell to a complex structure they called the rhinencephalon. However, Kaada (1951) has shown convincingly that the hippocampus, the main structure of the rhinencephalon, is not a higher center for smell but a correlation center for all sensory systems. Mammals without a sense of smell (seacows, whales) have a well developed hippocampus, although their olfactory lobes are practically non-existent.

Unfortunately, no consensus on the olfactory system has developed since Kaada's work. We know that olfactory nerves go from receptors in the upper part of the nasal cavity to the olfactory bulb, and in the olfactory tract to the anterior olfactory nucleus and the olfactory area (in man) or the olfactory tubercle (in macrosmatic mammals) and connects with the prepiriform and periamygdaloid cortex. According to Macleod (1971), the projection area of the lateral olfactory tract is the primary olfactory cortex, that is, the anterior external border of the olfactory tubercle, the prepiriform area and the periamygdaloid area. Yet he admits that this region appears "more like a relay than like a final integrative projection area" (p. 193). Indeed, the periamygdaloid cortex and the amygdala receive afferents from all sensory cortical areas (see Ch. 23). Like the hippocampus, the amygdaloid complex seems to be a correlation center for various sensory systems rather than part of the primary olfactory cortex.

Unlike other sensory systems, the olfactory system does not send relays via the thalamus to the cortical receiving area. But it is possible that the olfactory bulb serves a similar function as do the sensory thalamic relay nuclei. The olfactory bulb merges into the anterior olfactory nucleus. Once considered no more than a degenerated cortical border, its importance has not been recognized until comparatively recently. According to Lohman and Mentink (1969), the anterior olfactory nucleus extends from its anterior part in the olfactory bulb caudally toward the prepiriform cortex and receives extensive projections from the lateral olfactory tract. Its anterior part consists of clusters of large cells. Their axons run along the anterior limb of the anterior commissure and project to the contralateral anterior olfactory nucleus. Its lateral part extends toward the prepiriform cortex and blends with it. The medial part is continuous with the lateral part and reaches without interruption into the orbital cortex. It sends fibers to the contralateral bulb via the anterior limb of the anterior commissure. Scalia (1966) found another contingent of fine fibers, probably stemming from the bulb, crossing in the anterior commissure and distributing to the deep layers of the whole cortical projection area of the lateral olfactory tract.

Since the amygdaloid complex is connected with all sensory cortical areas, it cannot have a purely olfactory function. In chapter 23, I try to show that it may well serve the initiation of imagination and give rise to the imagination circuit. Hence the primary olfactory cortex will have to be located at a point well before the olfactory projection reaches the prepiriform area. The anterior olfactory nucleus seems to be a likely candidate for this role. It has a simple type of cortex, but this type seems adequate for a sensory system that mediates no more than a particular chemical attribute of the environment. Smell, like taste, cannot give us the experience of objects or patterns, or even the location of the odorous object. For such information, we must depend on vision, touch, and movement.

Many odors are pungent, and stimulate not only olfactory receptors but also receptors of the sensory branches of the trigeminal system, although in different degree. Tucker (1971) has shown that the threshold concentration for most odorous compounds is different for olfactory and trigeminal electrical responses. Trigeminal fibers from the nasal mucosa reach the olfactory tubercle and connect with the sensory trigeminal nucleus. It is possible that the tubercle represents the primary cortex for the trigeminal afferents from the nasal mucosa. The olfactory tubercle is well developed not only in macrosmatic animals but even in animals with poorly developed olfactory lobe. It is particularly prominent in animals with a well-developed snout and in the chameleon with its long flexible tongue (Clara, 1959). *Movement* can be perceived either by one sense alone (e.g. vision) or by several senses together, aided by exploratory body movements. For instance, the direction of a sound can be followed as it moves from right to left before looking for its source.

A moving object can be detected by its odor as it is carried by the wind. So the hunter tries to keep downwind to prevent the deer from detecting him. The direction of movement can be perceived by integrating experiences from several senses; all primary and secondary sensory areas are connected by short and long association fibers.

In summary, then, the primary sensory cortical areas seem to mediate the integrated experience of objects by sight and touch, the experience of sound patterns, of tastes and smells. While the afferent layer brings sensory impulses from the receptors, other layers in the sensory cortex serve the completion and integration of sensory experience. This is best demonstrated for the visual cortex but holds analogously for the auditory and somesthetic cortex. The taste cortex also is complex because its cells are interspersed in the touch area for the tongue and palate. The only exception is the olfactory cortex, which solely serves for the discrimination of odors and does not seem to have an integrative function. The more complex the sensory cortex, the more varied are the functions it mediates. It could be said with justice that the cortical feltwork mediates an integrative experience, that it is the organ of the integrative sense.

APPRAISAL

The sheer experience of things around us cannot lead to action unless they are appraised for their effect on us. I must relate what I experience to myself, I must want something or want to avoid it. There must be some motive for action. This has been readily admitted for voluntary action but not for spontaneous behavior, particularly when such behavior does not seem to be connected with instinct or drive. Indeed, it is difficult to argue that all behavior is motivated by instinct or drive; but there is every reason to say that all behavior has its roots in some kind of appraisal, intuitive or deliberate. Even so-called "expressive behavior," the infant's smile, its gurgling and cooing, is an expression of an emotional state; and such a state depends on the baby's intuitive appraisal of the situation and its own organic state. Mannerisms, like twiddling one's thumb or pulling one's hair, spring from the desire to do something, anything, in a situation where nothing constructive can be done—and this again depends on the intuitive estimate of the situation.

Without appraisal, we would not be conscious either of the world around us or of our own body. Merely seeing, hearing, touching, smelling, or tasting things would remain disconnected shreds of sensory experience devoid of any significance. Only when we assess something as it affects us, when we connect it with past experiences and decide whether this thing is good, bad, or indifferent, are we conscious of the environment and able to deal with it. We must know something in relation to ourselves and assess its significance before we can say we are aware of our environment; and we must appraise our bodily sensations as good, bad, or indifferent, and our action impulses and actions as suitable or unsuitable, before we can say that we are aware of ourselves.

Hence appraisal is essential to consciousness; and the cortical system that mediates appraisal is necessary for conscious experience and action. Clinical reports provide evidence that the cortical limbic system is necessary for awareness. Bailey (1965), for instance, mentioned the case of a woman patient who did not regain consciousness after a thyroid operation but lived for a year. According to Bailey, "she lay quietly with eyes open and eyeballs wandering aimlessly." At autopsy, the brain was found shriveled, the cortex yellow and shrunken, but the brainstem and thalamus were intact. There was patchy degeneration in the mesocortex of the anterior limbic region, in the posterior orbital region and the hippocampal gyrus. The hippocampus proper was intact.

The subcortical part of the appraisal system also must be intact for conscious functioning. The relation of this system with the cortical limbic system is discussed in chapter 18.

Appraisal is a psychological function of which we become aware when it is deliberate or prolonged (e.g., deciding whether we like a new model car), but of which we are unaware most of the time when it is spontaneous, intuitive, and followed by emotion (for instance, seeing a snake and getting scared). But we are aware of the action impulse that follows appraisal, whether that is an impulse to run away or attack, a simple liking or disliking, or even the impulse to recall something or investigate it. Liking and disliking, pleasure and pain, satisfaction and dissatisfaction can be experienced in connection with any sense experience and any movement or action. Even when the somesthetic cortex is destroyed, mammals react with pain to a sharp pinch, prick, or blow. Apparently, a rudimentary appraisal of sensory stimuli is mediated by subcortical relays to medial thalamic areas (see chapter 18).

The Neural Appraisal System

I have argued (1960, vol. 2, p. 34 ff.) that these appraisals are mediated by a special neural system that receives relays from sensory and motor systems. It includes the afferent connections from sensory receptors to brain stem reticular formation, intralaminar and midline thalamic nuclei, and the limbic cortex. I have proposed to call this system the *estimative system* or *appraisal system* because it mediates appraisals or estimates—just as the sensory system is so called because it mediates sensations. The appraisal system, then, functions on three levels; the peripheral-spinal, subcortical, and cortical level.

A rudimentary kind of appraisal is needed even for a reflex. When we step out of a dark house into bright sunlight, the pupil contracts, and the strength of contraction depends on the degree of contrast. When the contrast is very strong, light is felt as painful, implying a rudimentary appraisal. The connecting link of the reflex arc seems to represent such automatic appraisal and gives rise to the reflex contraction. As higher levels of the estimative system are involved, the connection between receptor and effector becomes more complex and the resulting action impulse is consciously experienced. On the thalamic level, for instance, man or animal can expereince pain, but without the somesthetic and adjoining limbic cortex exact localization is impossible.

If appraisal complements perception and forms the link to action, as I have argued, the cortical area mediating such appraisal should be closely connected with the areas serving sensory experience. In an earlier publication (Arnold, 1960, vol. 2, pp. 34 ff.) I suggested that the limbic system (excluding the hippocampus) might be the cortical region mediating appraisal. This system has changed little from mouse to man during evolutionary development (Fig. 11.3). The simple intuitive judgment that something is good or bad, desirable or undesirable, needs no evolutionary refinement. It is only the things that are so judged that become more complex as we move from animal to man, and eventually include abstract concepts as well as concrete situations. Hence the neocortex has expanded vastly from mouse to man while the limbic appraisal areas have remained comparatively unchanged. The structures included in the limbic appraisal area are the subcallosal cortex, the cingulate, retrosplenial, and hippocampal gyri, and the insula. Histologically, these structures consist of three-layered "transitional" cortex, forming a transition between the oldest type of cortex without any distinct layers and the neocortex with its six layers. Hence limbic cortex represents a more primitive type of cortex than sensory or motor neocortex. The superficial (supragranular) layer covers a well-developed receiving (granular) layer, separate from and superimposed on the third layer consisting of pyramidal cells. As the limbic cortex shades into neocortex, the

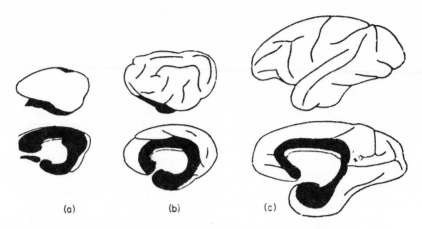

(a)   (b)   (c)

FIG. 11.3   Relative size of limbic lobe in rabbit, cat and monkey. The upper drawings show the lateral view, the lower drawings, the medial view (From P. D. MacLean, 1954a).

layers gradually become separated into regions of differently specialized cells until the six layers of typical neocortex can be distinguished.

Since appraisal is a process of evaluating sense impressions and memories from many sense modalities, and of estimating movements and movement impulses as appropriate or inappropriate, it is not surprising that the areas serving such appraisal should be connected with all sensory, motor and association areas. The granular cells in the limbic cortex receive relays from these areas while the pyramidal motor cells relay the impulses to action, produced by appraisal, to other structures.

Only in rare instances is one sensory modality sufficient for appraisal and action. A sharp blow is felt as painful; but to decide on appropriate action, we must be aware where it comes from, and what is the best way to deal with it. Usually, the information from several senses must be assessed before we can decide on action. Hence, we would expect the areas serving appraisal to be connected with one another and with sensory and motor areas. This is exactly what has been found, not only anatomically but by neuronography.

Connections of the Appraisal System.   The main pathway connecting limbic areas with each other and with neocortical regions is the cingulum. It consists of transverse as well as long and short longitudinal fibers. The transverse fibers connect the various parts of the cingulate gyrus throughout its length, from the rostrum of the corpus callosum to the splenium, with the hippocampus (Gastaut & Lammers, 1961). According to Glees et al. (1950), the transverse fibers connect the posterior orbital region (areas 11, 12) with the parolfactory region (area 25), the prefrontal cortex (areas 6, 8, 9, 10) with the anterior cingulate gyrus (areas 24, 33), and the parietal and occipital association areas (7, 18, 19) with the retrosplenial region (areas 26, 29, 30). These connections would enable the individual to appraise information from every modality: smells, via relays from posterior orbital cortex; movements and movement impulses, via relays from frontal and prefrontal cortex; somatic sensations can provide data via relays from parietal association areas; and things seen could be appraised over relays from occipital association areas. Finally, something heard can be appraised as soon as relays from the auditory association area reach the hippocampal gyrus. In the monkey, according to Adey and Meyer (1952), there are also fiber connections from the temporal pole (area 38) and the inferotemporal area (36, 20, 37), to the hippocampal gyrus; and the inferotemporal cortex is necessary for visual discrimination (Mishkin, 1966, 1972).

Pribram and MacLean (1953) have verified these connections by neuronography. They have found five different limbic regions in the monkey brain that have two-way connections with relevant sensory and motor areas (Fig. 11.4). The medial occipitotemporal region, for instance, connects the visual sensory and association areas with the limbic cortex of the posterior hippocampal gyrus. The medial parieto-occipital region connects the somatosensory primary and association cortex with the limbic cortex of the posterior cingulate and parasplenial gyri. The medial frontoparietal region embraces the superior frontal neocortex (motor and premotor region) and the limbic cortex of the anterior cingulate gyrus. The medial frontal region includes the ventromedial neocortex of the frontal lobe (including the olfactory areas) and the limbic cortex of the subcallosal and medial frontal orbital surface. And the medial frontotemporal region shows the connection between the neocortex of the frontal pole plus the ventromedial aspect of the anterior temporal pole with the limbic cortex of the limen insulae, prepiriform area, and anterior insula. Finally, there is a medial temporal region that represents a one-way connection from the superior and mid-

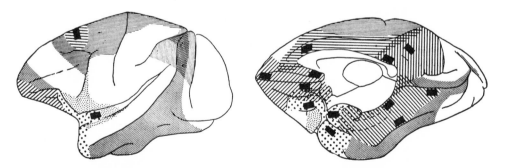

FIG. 11.4 Lateral and medial surface of a monkey brain, showing the distribution of limbic and extralimbic regions. Coarse stipple or striation indicates regions with two-way connections as mapped by physiological neuronography. Finer stipple or striation shows additional cortex activated in one direction from a point within the region. Black rectangles show sites of strychninization (From Pribram & MacLean. 1953). Stippling ∴: fronto-temporal; rostroventral striations \\\\: medial occipitotemporal; vertical striations ⅠⅠⅠ: medial parieto-occipital; horizontal striations ≡: medial frontoparietal; dorsorostral striations ////: medial frontal.

dle temporal gyrus (the area for hearing and equilibrium) and the posterior operculum (somatosensory face area including the taste region) to the limbic cortex of
the posterior insula.

These limbic appraisal areas seem to be identical with the "third sensory
areas" that have been reported within the last decades. Talbot (1940, 1942)
found a third visual area in the cat, and Tunturi (1945) reported a third auditory
area in the dog. Showers and Crosby (1958) stimulated various points along the
cingulate gyrus of the monkey, a third motor area. They found a pattern of movements characteristic of emotional expression; this pattern was repeated in reverse
order on stimulation of the posterior cingulate gyrus.

No localization was found in these third areas. Indeed, if these are appraisal
areas that initiate emotion and action, any intense sensory stimulation may produce the same appraisal ("bad for me here and now") and the same emotional
reaction. Since the posterior cingulate revealed a reverse pattern of movements
from that in the anterior cingulate, which resembles the reverse localization in
the somatosensory cortex, it seems that the posterior cingulate serves the appraisal of touch; and the anterior cingulate, the appraisal of movement. That
stimulation of the posterior cingulate produces a similar movement pattern in reverse as stimulation of the anterior cingulate is not suprising. Whether a monkey's foot or ear is pinched, the monkey will protest and pull back. Similarly, if
the monkey moves in a way that is painful, he will pull back whimpering.

On the basis of these and similar research findings, I have proposed (Arnold,
1960, vol. 2) that the anterior cingulate gyrus mediates the appraisal of movements and movement impulses and the posterior cingulate, the appraisal of touch
and other somesthetic experiences in legs and body. The subcallosal or
parolfactory area beneath the rostrum of the corpus callosum would serve the
appraisal of odors and the medial olfactory tubercle, the appraisal of pungent
odors, sensed via trigeminal afferents.

Anything seen seems to be appraised via retrosplenial and posterior
hippocampal gyrus, anything heard, via the anterior and middle hippocampal gyrus. The island of Reil, also part of the limbic system, borders on the face region
of motor and somesthetic cortex. Accordingly, the anterior insula should serve
the appraisal of head movements, facial expression and speech, while the posterior insula should mediate the appraisal of taste, also of touch or pressure applied
to face or head. Whether touch to hands and arms and movements of hands and
arms are appraised via insular cortex or cingulate gyrus is uncertain. Future research will have to decide.

A recent report by Turner et al. (1980) confirms the proposed connections
from sensory association areas to limbic cortex. They investigated the projections from sensory cortical areas to the amygdala and found them to come only
"from the modality-specific association areas one or more steps removed from
the primary sensory areas" (p. 515). They found the second somatosensory area
to project to the dorsal half of the posterior insula (the appraisal area for touch on

face or head in my theory); the taste area apparently projects to the neigboring dorsal part of the anterior insula, ventral to the taste area in the cortex. The visual association area projects to the claustrum. The visual, taste, and auditory projection then reaches the peri- and prorhinal areas, the anterior part of the hippocampal gyrus; branches also reach various amygdaloid nuclei. The hippocampal gyrus is a region of limbic cortex that receives afferents from all sensory areas (see chapter 20).

Turner et al. point out that only the olfactory system is an exception to the rule that the projection from sensory systems comes from secondary sensory areas. He, of course, considers the piriform cortex as the primary olfactory cortex. But if the primary cortex is the anterior olfactory nucleus, as I have suggested, there would be no exception to the rule. The periamygdaloid cortex in the piriform lobe is the olfactory *limbic* cortex, according to my theory.

Since we cannot experience intuitive appraisals consciously, it is difficult to demonstrate the neural substrate experimentally. The best we can expect is a demonstration of affective arousal or the action impulses that follow from it.

APPRAISAL AREAS

The Cingulate Gyrus. The effect of cingulate gyrus lesions was first reported by Ward (1948). Monkeys with such lesions acted impulsively without regard for their fellows. They took food wherever they found it, even out of the hand of another monkey. They sat wherever they wanted to, even on one of their fellows. They ceased to groom themselves and others and showed no affection toward their companions.

These lesions destroyed both the anterior and posterior cingulate gyrus. The anterior cingulate gyrus, according to my theory, mediates the appraisal of actions and action impulses. The effect of such lesions is discussed in chapter 14. The posterior cingulate gyrus, on the other hand, seems to mediate the appraisal of touch. Ward's monkeys no longer felt touch as pleasant, so that they no longer wanted to groom either themselves or their fellows. They showed no affection because touching or being touched was no longer attractive. Ward's monkeys had lost the pleasure of touch because the area needed for the appraisal of touch had been destroyed.

There is some direct evidence that the posterior cingulate gyrus mediates the appraisal and hence the pleasure of touch. MacLean (1954b, 1958) stimulated the posterior cingulate gyrus electrically and observed enhanced grooming, as well as pleasurable and sexual reactions. The pleasure of grooming and of sex is the result of the appraisal that such touch is "good" and results in an impulse to prolong that pleasure.

Other sensory appraisal areas are discussed in chapter 12, and the extensive reports on damage to the cingulate gyrus, in chapter 18.

12 Cortical Memory Registration: Sensory Memory and Affective Memory

Synaptic and growth changes . . . could well be the primary changes constituting the so-called engram or permanent memory trace. At the same time . . . the law of effect . . . says there must be something more than just the use of synapses; there must be, in addition, some kind of retroactive feedback for reinforcement of good effects versus bad effects . . . Responses that have a good effect tend to be retained, repeated, and remembered, while those that do not fit in are abandoned, lost, and forgotten.

R. W. Sperry, 1965, p. 146

It has long been assumed that the "association cortex," bordering on the primary motor and sensory cortex, has something to do with memory associations. The term "association centers" was first used by Flechsig (1876) to distinguish the primary sensory and motor areas from the wide expanse of cortex found to have neither sensory nor motor functions. These association areas increase in size from lower mammals to higher apes, and cover the greater part of the cortex in man. Although the primary sensory areas also are more extensive in man than in the ape, human association areas by far surpass in extent those in the higher apes, both relatively and absolutely. These areas, like the primary sensory areas, receive projection fibers from the sensory thalamic nuclei.

The association cortex develops later than do the primary cortical areas; myelinization takes several years to complete. Layer III, which contains association fibers, increases in width gradually, from birth to adulthood. In contrast to the primary sensory areas where cells are large, giving them a granular appearance, the cells in the association cortex are small with widely branching fibers.

The primary areas project mainly to the association cortex, so that electrical stimulation of the primary cortex produces potentials mainly in the neighboring secondary sensory areas. But the association cortex is connected with widely separated cortical fields.

The association areas have often been called "silent areas" because direct electrical stimulation does not produce reportable psychological experiences. This fact has given rise to the widely held notion that the human being uses only a small part of his brain capacity, despite the finding that stimulation of such areas can interfere with normal functioning, and that their damage or destruction results in serious impairment. When sensory receptors are stimulated electrically, short-latency potentials (registered through electrodes placed on the pial surface after skull and dura are opened) appear not only in the primary sensory cortex but also in neighboring association areas. By means of this evoked potential technique, such "secondary areas" are mapped in every sensory system.

More recently, the sensory areas have been further subdivided. In addition to the primary areas, at least three cortical projection areas have been mapped in the association cortex of the visual, auditory, and somatosensory system.

SENSORY MEMORY AREAS

At this time, it would be difficult to assign functions to each of these projection areas; but it is conceivable that at least the secondary areas may register the memory images that are produced together with primary sensations. These areas could be called sensory memory areas, to be reactivated during recall. Like the primary sensory area, these memory areas are modality-specific (Fig. 12.1).

The notion that the secondary sensory areas are memory areas is not new. In modern times, the well-known neurosurgeon J. M. Nielsen (1943, 1956) has held it and has reported many clinical cases with severe modality-specific memory loss after damage in various regions of the association cortex. His views have met considerable resistance from theorists who deny that any functions except sensory and motor functions can be represented in the brain. I propose to review recent experimental as well as clinical findings that suggest that memories are registered in various modality-specific areas of the association cortex.

Perhaps the fact that neither Nielsen nor other theorists have proposed a neural pathway to activate memories during recall accounts for some of the resistance to cortical memory areas. My theory does provide a recall circuit that branches off to various memory areas and reactivates the registered memory dispositions.

This theory is based on a great deal of experimental and clinical evidence. Too often, theories that go beyond the immediate facts are considered armchair speculation. Experimenters who are not theoretically sophisticated persist in confusing inductive reasoning with speculation. Reasoning starts from ascertained facts, tries to explain them, and tests the explanation by checking it with other facts. Speculation relies on hunches, disdains facts and builds models that have no counterpart in reality.

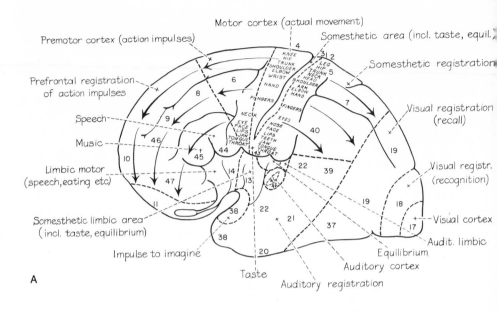

A

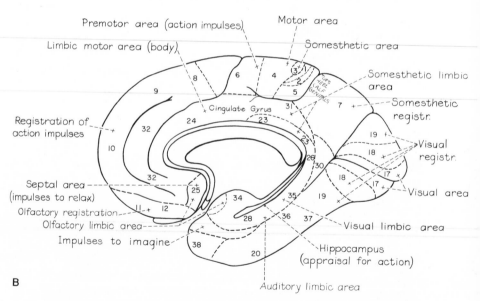

B

FIG. 12.1 (A) Lateral view of human brain with insula spread out, showing sensory, motor, association, and limbic areas, and the functions they mediate. (B) Medial view of human brain, showing sensory, motor, association, and limbic areas, and the functions they mediate. Arrows indicate that motor and somesthetic representation continues into the association area. Numbers indicate Brodmann cortical areas. Amy. - amygdala. (From M. B. Arnold, 1960)

Visual Memory Areas

The visual association areas 18 and 19 differ in their cell structure from the primary area 17. Their fourth (afferent) layer is much narrower while the second and third layers, which serve mainly associative functions, are much more extensive. In cats and monkeys, both striate and peristriate cortex (areas 17, 18, 19) receive visual fibers. In the cat, Hubel and Wiesel (1965) found three visual projection areas. Histological examination led them to conclude that these areas are practically identical with areas 17, 18, and 19. In a later report (1968), they mentioned that the divisions of the peristriate area into histologically defined regions was less sharp in the monkey. However, cells in all these areas responded to retinal stimulation. This confirms my suggestion that something seen (via area 17) is at the same time registered in the visual memory areas (18, 19).

Stimulation Effects.   More recently, the primary and secondary regions were found to include at least four different projections. In the visual area, three regions (areas 17, 18, 19) have retinotopically organized projections. Evoked potentials at the limbic border of the striate cortex define the fourth projection area (Seiden & Dykstra, 1977).

When electrically stimulated, the primary area induces potentials only in areas 18 and 19; but stimulation of these areas produces excitation not only in the same areas of the opposite hemisphere but also in the "frontal eyefield" (area 8), and several other cortical areas. Area 18 sends fibers to areas 17 and 19, and to all parts of area 20. Both areas 19 and 20 are connected with the primary auditory areas 41 and 42, and the associated areas 22 and 21. Area 19 projects to the superior colliculi, pons, and tegmentum (Clara, 1959).

Lesion Effects.   If areas 17, 18, and 19 are damaged unilaterally, one side of the visual field may be missing and eye movements do not seem to compensate for it. Since nothing is seen on one side, the eyes cannot be directed toward it. If both hemispheres are involved, but only areas 18 and 19 are damaged, the patient can see but does not recognize what he sees (visual agnosia). In severe cases, he cannot recognize even the simplest things. When the lesion is widespread, he may recognize simple objects but not complex ones. As Luria (1966a) says, such a patient focuses on a particular feature and then tries to infer what the whole thing could be. For instance, when he sees a picture of a pair of spectacles, he will say: "a circle, then another circle, and some sort of crossbar . . . it must be a bicycle?"

The same disintegration of the visual field is revealed when the patient tries to copy a drawing (Fig. 12.2). Apparently, he is unable to see the picture as an integrated whole and so is unable to draw it. If the cortical feltwork serves the integrative sense, as I have argued, the visual image as well as a visually perceived object will disintegrate if the cortex is severely damaged. In other cases,

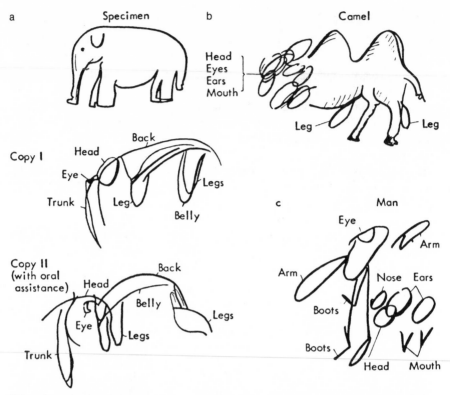

FIG. 12.2   Drawings by a patient with optic agnosia from a bilateral wound of the occipital region. (*a*) Copying a specimen. (*b*) Completing a drawing that had been started. (*c*) Drawing from spoken instructions. (From: *Higher Cortical Functions in Man* by A. R. Luria (1966a) translated by Basil Haigh. Copyright (1980) by Consultants Bureau Enterprises Inc. and Basic Books, Inc., Publishers. Reprinted by permission of the publisher.)

the patient can recognize things but can perceive only one of them at a time. Such patients cannot keep their eyes fixed at a point and cannot look from one object to another at will. Their gaze keeps wandering. Considering the close connection of the visual association area with the motor area, the visual eyefield, it is not surprising that they can no longer look where they want to look, that they lose the object they are looking at, and cannot see more than one object. The patient has difficulty reading. He may not be able to read whole words although he may recognize individual letters. He may confuse similar letters, or recognize them only when clearly printed, not when written or crossed out. Tracing the letters with his finger helps the patient to identify letters: the motor image, as traced out, makes up for the difficulty in recognizing the visual shape.

Combined Lesions.   The temporo-occipito-parietal regions (areas 39 and 37) are often considered to involve all three systems, the visual, auditory, and somatosensory systems, because area 39 is connected with the somatosensory association areas 7 and 40, and the visual association area 19; while area 37 is connected with area 39, the visual areas 18 and 19, and the auditory association areas 20 and 21. Damage of area 39 results in severe disturbances in spatial orientation. Since vision is the only sense that allows us to see a simultaneous side-by-side, vision really is at the base of all spatial orientation. Of course, vision is not the only sense that is used. Very soon after birth, the infant can follow a moving light with his eyes. Later, he begins to reach for something he wants. Even though he may not be able to estimate how far he has to reach, he does reach in the right direction. The child is also continually busy investigating first with his mouth and later with his hands so that he begins to know the shape, consistency, and volume of the things he sees. The visual side-by-side of things gradually becomes oriented in relation to this own body in such a way that eventually he is able to estimate vertical and horizontal relationships in space even when his own position is changed.

Of course, a lesion may not be confined to areas 39 and 37. It may affect also the more anterior and superior part of the cortex, in which case there will be difficulty in recognizing objects by touch alone (tactual agnosia); or it may also affect the more posterior portion, so that the symptom picture will include a defect in recognizing what he sees (visual agnosia). The central difficulty, however, with lesions of areas 39 and 37 is a pronounced impairment in orientation. A patient with such a lesion may lose his sense of direction—go right when he should go left—and is unable to copy geometrical figures or arrange blocks in patterns. The more complicated the spatial relationships, the greater the patient's difficulties. He cannot tell the time according to the position of the clock hands, read a map or point to various countries on the map; he cannot point to his fingers when he is asked to point to index, ring finger, or thumb because he confuses their position. When the damage is in the non-dominant hemisphere, the naming of countries on a map or the telling of time by the clock may be less disturbed because the speech area (44) in the dominant hemisphere is not involved (Luria, 1966a). When the lesion is confined to areas 39 and 37 in the right (non-dominant) hemisphere, the visual agnosia for spatial relationships may be confined to the left visual field.

The patient also has difficulty in visualizing spatial relationships when asked to do so. He is unable to understand a prose passage, whether long or short, if it contains spatial terms. For instance, the terms "above," "below," "right of," and "left of," convey nothing to him; he is unable to draw a triangle below a circle, or a triangle to the right of a cross (Luria, 1966a). He is also unable to make comparisons that require visual imagination, for instance, "Kate is paler than Sonia" or "Sonia is paler than Kate." He cannot distinguish the meaning of "taking to someone" from "taking from someone" or the difference between "father's brother" and "brother's father." Luria quotes one patient as saying: "Of course, I know what brother and father mean, but I cannot imagine what the two are together!" This nicely illustrates the patient's real difficulty: to understand the phrases, he would have to imagine his father, with the father's brother at his side; and to picture his brother beside their common father. True, we do not ordinarily use visual imagination to understand such constructions, but they are based on visual imagination. If the memory of such experiences of visual side-by-side is wiped out, the meaning of the language constructions is lost as well.

Animal Experiments.   In animals also, the visual association area (peristriate cortex) is necessary for visual memory. This has been established comparatively recently. Lashley (1942) had reported that the striate cortex, that is, the primary visual area, is sufficient for visual discrimination in rats. But in the last decade, it has been shown that the peristriate area is involved in learned visual discrimination. Fields (1969) inserted electrodes in peristriate as well as striate cortex and reported that information about the size of visual patterns is received in medial areas of the occipital cortex and that information about the shape of the pattern is received in more lateral areas. His data indicate a localization of these two functions within the striate and peristriate area. Hall and Diamond (1968) and Kaas et. al. (1970) found an area of posterior neocortex in the hedgehog brain that is active in pattern discrimination. Lesions of this area produced severe pattern discrimination deficits, although the striate cortex was essentially intact. This area receives impulses from the lateral thalamic nucleus and seems to be homologous to the peristriate area in the rat.

Research with cats and monkeys clearly shows that peristriate cortex is necessary for learning a visual discrimination. Meyer (1963) and Wetzel (1969) found that cats with large occipital lobe lesions, sparing part of the striate areas, showed deficits on pattern discrimination. Mishkin (1966, 1972) reported that lesions of peristriate cortex in the monkey resulted in pattern discrimination deficits, hence an impairment of visual memory.

The extent of the visual memory area has been determined also. Mishkin (1966) reported that impairment in visual pattern discrimination resulted from either peristriate or inferior temporal cortex lesions in monkeys. In this species, the visual association cortex extends to the inferior and middle temporal cortex in one direction, and into the parietal cortex in the other (Fig. 12.3). Hence the cortex necessary for visual discrimination includes not only areas 18 and 19, but also areas 37 and 39. In the human being, the temporo-occipito-parietal region (areas 39, 37) involves not only the visual but also the auditory and somesthetic system. It is possible that this holds good for the monkey also; but Mishkin did not investigate auditory and somatosensory discrimination at the same time.

Deficits in visual pattern discrimination after inferior temporal cortex lesions have been reported in monkeys (Spiegler & Mishkin, 1981), size discrimination deficits in several species of primates (Olson et al., 1967). Wegner (1968) reported that extensive lesions of areas 18, 19, and 21 in monkeys left simple pattern discrimination intact, but more complex tasks were impaired. Butter (1965, 1968), Butter and Doehrman (1968), and Butter and Gekoski (1961) found several types of visual discrimination deficits after inferior temporal cortex lesions in the monkey.

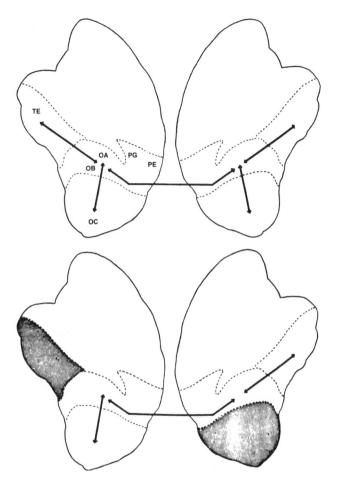

FIG. 12.3 Visual Association Cortex in Monkey. In the monkey, the striate area projects to the prestriate region and also to the gyri in the depth of the parieto-occipital junction, to the caudal bank of the upper half of the superior temporal sulcus, and to the banks of the caudal part of the intraparietal sulcus. This projection field of the striate cortex projects, in turn, to the visual area in the inferotemporal lobes (Mishkin, 1966). Letters refer to von Bonin and Bailey's (1947) cytoarchitectural areas.

Auditory Memory Area

The primary auditory area was mapped in the middle ectosylvan gyrus of the cat; and the secondary area, in reverse tonotopic order, immediately lateral to and below the first. The second auditory area was later found to have a dual representation. One part continued to be called auditory area II, the other was termed Ep (posterior ectosylvan area). Ep may have more than one representation. There is another short-latency auditory projection in an anterior region that overlaps the second somatosensory face area; it is now called auditory area III (Dykes, 1978).

Although the auditory projection is bilateral, the contralateral projection is dominant. When the temporal lobe association cortex is extensively damaged on one side, the patient finds it difficult to recognize sounds heard with the contralateral ear (Bocca et al., 1955). This means that auditory sensations must be registered on both sides (the patient can recognize sounds with both ears) but that the main area for registration is contralateral (he has difficulty doing so when he hears sounds with the ear contralateral to the lesion).

Stimulation Effects.   Direct electrical stimulation of the secondary auditory areas 22 and 21 produces potentials in Broca's area in the frontal lobe (area 44), and also in areas 46 and 10. These connections make auditory analysis and clear speech possible. To understand speech, we must be able to distinguish the varying sounds in the continuous speech melody, and know what the sounds mean. We need both sound and word memory. In learning a foreign language, it is very difficult at first to hear and understand connected speech because the sounds are not readily distinguishable into words, and the words we can distinguish, we have to translate. Reading a foreign language is simpler because we see the words, recognize them, and can take time to recall what they mean. In listening to a lecture, we have to guess at the words and guess at their meaning and never seem to catch up with the speaker. It takes considerable practice not only in hearing but in speaking a foreign language before auditory analysis becomes effortless.

This process is similar to the language learning of the child. According to Luria (1966a), during the first years the child listens by attempting to articulate the words as he hears them. Gradually, he is able to understand without such help; and by the time he enters school, he is able to understand most words without having to articulate. Wernicke's area in the left temporal lobe (in right-handed people) seems to register the sound images that make the recognition of speech possible. And the connection of the secondary auditory areas (21, 22) with Broca's area in the frontal lobe (area 44) seems to revive the motor images of speech articulation that help in such recognition.

Lesion Effects.   When a stroke or other injury damages the temporal lobe, this damage is not necessarily restricted either to the primary or the secondary auditory area; hence the resulting impairment may be the result of partial damage to both areas. This should be remembered when evaluating the impairment after such lesions. According to Luria (1966a), the ability to hear and reproduce rhythmic patterns of tapping is seriously disturbed in patients with lesions of the superior part of the left temporal lobe. They can reproduce such patterns only if the tapping is done so slowly that they can count out the taps. Although such patients have no difficulty in articulation when they merely have to imitate the position of someone else's mouth, or when they pronounce a word spontaneously, they find it hard to pronounce a word correctly when they have to repeat it after someone else. Either they pronounce the word incorrectly, or they replace it with another word having a similar sound or a similar meaning. Often such a patient is not able to find the words he needs. When he listens to someone talking, he may hear only a meaningless jumble of sounds (auditory aphasia), or, in milder cases, he may have only an approximate notion of their meaning. As a result, he may try to describe something rather than naming it. When he is shown grains of wheat, for example, he may say, "you know, flour is made of it." This disintegration of words and conceptual structure is revealed in milder cases only by special tests. For instance, when a patient is asked to point to his eyes, ears, and nose, in quick succession, he may understand the words but soon becomes confused when try-ing to obey the commands. If he is asked to repeat one or two words after a short pause, he cannot do so and again resorts to paraphrases.

All these difficulties seem to indicate an inability to organize sounds into pat-terns, as well as a loss of auditory memory images. The superior part of the tem-poral lobe includes the primary auditory areas 41, 42, and part of the secondary area 22. Damage to this region leads to impaired integration of sequential sounds (the function of the primary auditory cortex) and to a loss of memory images of such sequences (because of damage to the secondary area); and this, in turn, leads to difficulties in motor performance.

The middle part of the lateral surface of the temporal lobe (area 21 and 37) receives fibers from thalamic association nuclei and is connected with the visual association cortex, as well as with the limbic system, hippocampus, and amyg-daloid nuclei. After lesions of the middle segment of the temporal lobe there is no disturbance of auditory discrimination or synthesis (Luria, 1966a). The patients can repeat individual words or sounds without distortion. But as soon as they are told several words (even as few as three or four) they fail. Usually, they keep repeating one or two short words. The same thing happens when they are told several short phrases. In particular, they cannot retain the order of words or phrases, and cannot change the order if asked to do so. When such patients are told to name several objects, they may name one and then give the same name when pointing to the others, without noticing that it is incorrect. This implies a clear loss of auditory word engrams and an impairment in organizing those still available. When the patient is no longer able to organize his auditory memory images, he also loses the ability to associate them with visual memories or to recall the corresponding speech sounds. These findings suggest that the middle temporal association area serves the registration of sequences of sounds and their association with memory areas in other modalities.

Many investigators have found that the impairment after such lesions is not a general defect in intelligence or abstraction. Patients with auditory aphasia can grasp the meaning of abstract ideas, they can carry out various operations involving geometrical relations or numbers, make spatial analogies, as long as this can be done in writing, and they can read the instructions (Ombredane, 1951).

In recent years, detailed investigations have shown that lesions interfering with auditory memory do not necessarily interfere with visual memory. Two patients reported by Luria et al. (1967) were unable to repeat spoken words, letters, and simple sentences but had no difficulty when the same material was shown to them. In this case, auditory memory was impaired while visual memory was intact. Similarly, Warrington and Shallice (1972) reported a detailed investigation of a patient who could not repeat strings of one to four numbers, letters, or words; but his recall of the same material was much superior when it was presented visually. The opposite defect was reported by Kinsbourne and Warrington (1962): A patient with a lesion of the left anterior occipital lobe (verified at autopsy) could accurately report single visual stimuli such as digits and letters, but could not do so if two such stimuli were presented simultaneously. When the digits and letters were read to him, his difficulty disappeared. Apparently, his auditory memory was intact. Hence Warrington and Weiskrantz (1973) concluded that "there are strong reasons for postulating the existence of modality-specific short-term memory systems" (p. 391).

Animal Experiments.   There is evidence for auditory memory areas in animals as well. Stepien et al. (1960) reported that the auditory association cortex (the first and second temporal convolution in the monkey) is necessary for auditory discrimination. And Strominger et al. (1980) found that ablating the anterior part of the lateral surface of the superior temporal gyrus in monkeys produced severe deficits in successive auditory discrimination.

Somatosensory Memory Area.

The primary somatosensory projection from the medial lemniscus, spinothalamic, and trigeminothalamic tracts runs via the thalamus to the postcentral gyrus. The thalamic somatosensory relay nuclei are the ventroposterolateral and ventrobasal nuclei. Both these nuclei project to the primary and association areas. The small-celled part of the posterior group of thalamic nuclei apparently projects to somatosensory area 5a, which also reacts to moving touch stimuli, to the movement of several joints, to touch, and reacts differently to active than to passive movements. The posterior nuclear group projects to area 5 from its rostral part. The primary somatosensory area projects to the secondary area and to area 5; but the secondary area does not seem to project to area 5. The main projections from the somatosensory area go to motor and premotor cortex; there are no direct connections to the primary visual and auditory areas.

Stimulation Effects.   In the somatosensory cortex, the secondary area seems to be smaller than the primary area, and receives afferents from both ipsilateral and contralateral sites, although contralateral stimulation evokes responses almost twice as large as ipsilateral stimulation. Localization seems to be slightly less detailed, with more overlapping than in the primary somatosensory cortex, and a slightly slower latency of evoked potentials, although the differences are not absolute. Some experimenters have found that the primary area also receives bilateral afferents. The taste area receives bilateral afferents in both primary and secondary regions. Somatosensory area III has been identified recently as area 5, the region immediately behind areas 3, 1, and 2 (Dykes, 1978).

These somatosensory association areas connect with areas 37, 39, and 40, with the premotor, motor, and prefrontal areas 6, 4, 8, and 44, with each other, with the primary auditory and auditory association areas 42, 20, and 21, and with the visual association areas 18 and 19 (Peele, 1954).

Lesion Effects. Nielsen (1946) reported tactile agnosia in patients after lesions of the postcentral gyrus (areas 3, 1, 2, and 5), the inferior parietal lobule (area 7), or the supramarginal gyrus (areas 39, 40). The patient may be completely unaware of his own limbs on the side opposite the lesion and may not recognize them as his. He feels touch, pressure, or movement but neither recognizes them as his own nor recalls them. When the somatosensory association cortex remains intact, there is no such deficit. To be aware of one's own body implies continuous somatosensory recall. It means spontaneously remembering what the limbs feel like, and keeping in mind the changes in sensation produced by motion. When the areas serving the registration of somesthetic impressions are lost, such memories will disappear.

Bender (1952) reported that patients with lesions of the somatosensory association areas cannot distinguish two touches from one touch. They feel being touched but quickly forget it. They do not recognize a figure traced on their skin. Although somatosensory experience seems to be normal, the memory of such experiences cannot be preserved because the sensory image cannot be registered. The patients cannot recognize touch impressions because they cannot compare them with the memory images of earlier impressions.

Some reports indicate that somesthetic memory registration, like visual memory registration, occurs primarily in the right hemisphere in righthanded people. Corkin (1965) found that patients with right hemisphere lesions were significantly inferior to patients with left hemisphere lesions in learning a tactually guided maze. Similarly, De Renzi (1967) reported that patients with right posterior hemisphere lesions were impaired in a tactually presented spatial task (formboard). However, this problem of hemisphere function in memory registration is discussed in detail later (Ch. 19).

Animal Studies. There is considerable evidence from animal studies that somatosensory memory is impaired after lesions of the parietal association cortex. Bates and Ettlinger (1960) found that bilateral posterior parietal ablations in the monkey produced significant impairment in tactile shape discrimination; and

Ettlinger and Kalsbeck (1962) found that the impairment was restricted to the contralateral hand in unilateral ablations. According to these authors, "the nature of the disorder of tactile shape discrimination in animals having posterior parietal ablations remains obscure . . . . contralateral removals gave rise to significantly more impairment than ipsilateral removals but the greatest impairment resulted from bilateral (successive) removals" (p. 267).

According to Pribram and Barry (1956), parieto-occipital lesions in monkeys resulted in tactual and weight discrimination deficits, although the animals could relearn. But after the operation, new learning of a length discrimination was no longer possible.

Taste discrimination in monkeys was also impaired by parietal lesions. Since taste is represented in the face region of the somatosensory cortex, the parietal association area seems to serve the registration of taste memory as well.

Olfactory Memory Area

If the primary olfactory area is the anterior olfactory nucleus, and the primary olfacto-trigeminal area is the olfactory tubercle, as I have suggested (chapter 11), the olfactory memory area should be the cortical area closest to them; that is, the posterior orbital cortex.

This suggestion is supported by several findings. First of all, Pribram et al. (1950) reported that the olfactory tubercle is connected with the posterior orbital cortex and the medial subcallosal (septal) area. And Lohman and Mentink (1969) mentioned that the medial part of the anterior olfactory nucleus reaches without interruption into the orbital cortex. Even more recently, Takagi (1979) reported that electrical stimulation of the olfactory bulb has evoked electrical potentials in the lateral part of the posterior orbital cortex (Fig. 12.4). Since such stimulation also evoked potentials in the dorsomedial thalamic nucleus, magnocellular part, it would seem that the posterior orbital area to which this nucleus relays may be the olfactory memory cortex (Fig. 12.5). According to my theory, the dorsomedial thalamic nucleus is a relay station in the imagination circuit, mediating motor imagination via its small-celled part and olfactory imagination via its large-celled part. Olfactory imagination necessarily has to draw on registered olfactory memories in the posterior orbital cortex (see discussion in chapter 18).

Experimental Studies. Behavioral experiments seem to support the suggestion that the posterior orbital cortex is the olfactory memory cortex. Allen (1940) reported that dogs lost all olfactory discrimination after removal of the frontal lobes. They could still find meat by smell, showing that they could smell it and appraise it as good to eat. Bilateral removal of the temporal lobes with the hippocampus did not disturb olfactory discrimination, which means that the rhinencephalon (the supposed "smell-brain") is not necessary for olfactory discrimination, nor is the prepiriform and periamygdaloid cortex, considered to this day the primary olfactory cortex. And Caldwell (1958) found that psychiatric patients with prefrontal lobotomy (which cuts the connections from the posterior orbital cortex to the hippocampal rudiment, so interrupting the olfactory memory circuit) were unable to distinguish between common odors. They usually reported a different odor as a change in intensity. Control groups of psychiatric patients without lobotomy distinguished odors as easily as did healthy people.

Interestingly, R. Thompson (1980) recently reported that bilateral destruction of the occipito-temporal, parietal, lateral frontoparietal, dorsal frontoparietal, or cingulate areas did not impair the retention of an olfactory discrimination. The orbital cortex was almost the only cortical region left untouched. Despite this omission, Thompson concluded that "the neocortex is not the storehouse of all engrams." The reason for his neglect of the orbital cortex as the registration area for olfactory impressions is probably the conviction that the piriform area is the primary olfactory cortex.

Altogether, there seems to be enough evidence for the conclusion that the extensive areas of so-called association cortex adjoining the various sensory areas serve the registration of sensory memory. In recent years, secondary and even tertiary areas have been located in the association cortex. Whether these areas mediate different functions is uncertain. But at least the secondary areas seem to

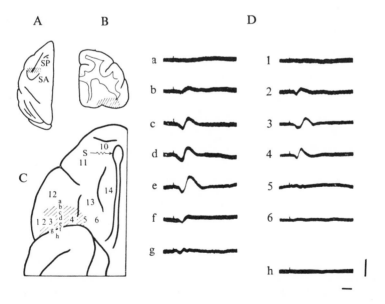

FIG. 12.4   Posterior orbital olfactory potentials. (A) Dorsal surface of monkey hemisphere; SA Sulcus arcuatus, SP Sulcus principalis. (B) Frontal section of monkey brain at site of electrode insertion (hatched area). (C) Diagram of orbitofrontal cortex; numbers from 10-14 indicate cortical areas, numbers from 1-6 and letters from a to h show recording sites. On stimulation of the olfactory bulb (OB), as indicated by an arrow and S, potentials were evoked in the hatched area from 2 to 4 and from b to g. (D) Records obtained at orbitofrontal sites shown in C. (From Tanabe et al., 1975)

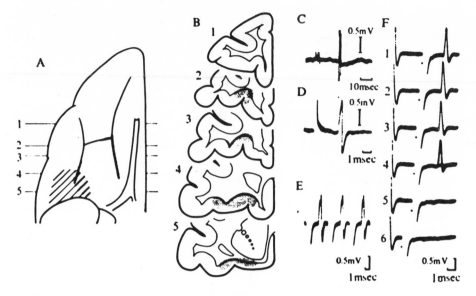

FIG. 12.5   Posterior orbital projection area. (A) Posterior orbital cortex of monkey. (B) Frontal sections of monkey frontal lobe. (C) Spike potentials following stimulation of olfactory bulb. (D) Spike potentials after above-threshold stimulation of central and posterior part of orbitofrontal cortex. (E) Potentials after repetitive stimulation of the same areas. (F) When stimulation was applied to these areas at various intervals after spontaneous spike potentials, the potentials collided when the interval was 3 msec or less (5 and 6). Stimulation of the dotted regions in A and B evoked a field and spike potential in the medial part of the dorsomedial thalamic nucleus. On stimulation of the olfactory bulb, potentials appeared in the hatched area of A. (From S. F. Takagi, 1979. Reprinted by permission from the Proceedings of the Japan Academy, vol. 54, Ser. B. 30–34, 1978.)

mediate the registration of memory images, dispositions to reexperience them, either in recall or in imagination. These memory areas are modality-specific. Several memory modalities seem to combine into a unitary memory picture, just as several sensory modalities combine into a unitary sensory experience. This integration of both sensory and memory functions can be ascribed to the working of the integrative sense embodied in the feltwork of the neocortex.

AFFECTIVE SENSORY MEMORY

We know that we can remember and recall sensory impressions. But we also seem to re-experience the corresponding feelings and emotions. These feelings as well as the original liking or dislike are generated by an appraisal. Appraisals are not experienced as such when they are spontaneous or intuitive, generating feelings and emotions. Our only experience is the feeling or emotion that follows the appraisal. When something we encounter here and now revives the appraisal, we again experience only the feeling, not the appraisal. This would suggest that the appraisal, registered as a disposition to be revived, needs no special memory area. It can be revived in the limbic area in which it was registered. Hence the sensory appraisal areas discussed in chapter 11 are also the areas that reactivate the appraisal registered there.

Every learning task demands not only modality-specific memory but an appraisal of the cue as good or bad, to be approached or avoided. Indeed, since all animals can learn, they as well as human beings must have a mechanism that allows *affective memory,* that is, the revival of earlier appraisals so that they can find food more successfully and escape a threat more quickly. Modality-specific memory almost certainly is a late arrival on the evolutionary scene because it depends on the neocortex. It has often been said that frogs see only small moving things. That is truly an anthropomorphic assumption: Because the experimenter only sees the frog's reactions to small moving things, he assumes that the frog sees only what he reacts to. The frog may well see everything there is to see around him, but he is interested only in what he can find to eat. He feeds by snapping at small moving things, and what does not move he leaves aside. What does not move is unfit to catch, as far as the frog is concerned, although he may see it well enough. Indeed, if the frog didn't see things that do not move, how ever would he find his way around? Like all reptiles and amphibians, the frog has a minuscule cortical area, and probably no sensory memory, so that he cannot recognize the resting fly as identical with the moving fly. He has to depend on his affective memory that small moving things are good to eat. In contrast, mammals and particularly human beings use modality-specific memory together with affective memory. They can remember what happened before and what they did in response, and imagine what to do here and now. Hence they can explore what to do about it and decide on what is best to do.

AFFECTIVE MEMORY AREAS

In the last chapter, I discussed some of the evidence for my suggestion that the cortical limbic areas are appraisal areas. Like modality-specific sensory experience, the experience of pleasure or pain, pleasantness or unpleasantness, is remembered also. Unlike sensory memory, affective memory is the reactivation of the original appraisal, generating an actual emotion. Hence the affective memory circuit starts from the appraisal area and returns to it; damage to the limbic appraisal areas impairs both appraisal and affective memory. In Chapter 11, I discussed some of the findings that demonstrate impairment of appraisal and the difficulties that flow from it. In the following I mention some research that clearly involves affective memory.

Retrosplenial and Hippocampal Gyrus.   The effect of damage to these limbic areas is difficult to estimate because lesions also damage afferents from other limbic areas. We do know that visual stimulation of waking monkeys has resulted in potentials from the posterior hippocampal gyrus, the parahippocampal portion of the lingual gyrus, and the retrosplenial gyrus, while auditory stimulation has produced potentials in the posterior insula. Gustatory stimulation has resulted in potentials from the insula in the neighborhood of the frontal operculum, the sensory area for taste (MacLean, 1975). Apparently these are limbic appraisal areas.

Posterior Orbital Cortex. It is well known that damage to this area has effects that differ from those of medial or dorsolateral frontal lesions (Pribram, 1973). According to Pribram, the orbital surface includes three different divisions: the medial, lateral, and posterior region. The latter is sandwiched between the orbital extensions of the medial and lateral frontal cortex. It receives projections from the magnocellular portion of the dorsomedial thalamic nucleus (in my theory, the projection of the imagination circuit to the medial orbital area), and is connected with the neighboring anterior insular, periamygdaloid and temporal polar cortex (all of them limbic areas).

The medial subcallosal area, adjoining the posterior orbital cortex, seems to be the limbic area for the appraisal of odors. Its connection with the anterior insula, motor appraisal area for head movements, makes it possible for the animal immediately to move its head in the direction of an odor and sniff. An odor may be felt as pleasant or unpleasant, whether it is pungent or not. As mentioned in chapter 11, olfactory sensations often have a trigeminal component. But when the trigeminal receptors are stimulated, the animal usually reacts more intensely, with changes in respiration and heart rate, and often with incipient movements even when anesthetized. For instance ammonia, a decidedly unpleasant odor, strongly stimulates the trigeminal system. When the trigeminal ganglia were blocked experimentally with xylocaine, the animals no longer showed the usual physiological responses. Their EEG showed the slow waves of sleep instead of the usual fast arousal reaction (Stone et al., 1966). I would suggest that pungent odors and odors significant for some instinctive activity may be appraised via the medial olfactory tubercle, the appraisal area for the olfactory trigeminal system. (For discussion of the afferents to these limbic areas, see Ch. 11.)

Some recent reports seem to support this suggestion. For instance, Powers et al. (1979) report that male hamsters were no longer attracted to female vaginal secretions placed on a wall after their olfactory receptors were blocked. But they were still attracted to such secretions rubbed on one of two anesthetized castrated hamsters. Apparently, the males could no longer appraise female secretions as pleasurable because of their lack of functioning receptors. But the sight of the hamsters recalled previous pleasurable experiences (visual limbic system intact). Coupled with the presence of the odor (appraised but not smelled), there was sufficient attraction. This interpretation is supported by a further finding. When Powers et al. blocked only the vomeronasal and not the olfactory receptors, the attraction of female vaginal secretions was significantly reduced only for males with a severe mating impairment. These animals had no affective memory of pleasure associated with female secretions. Without the connection of vomeronasal nerves with the hypothalamic sexual centers, the odor did not induce approach. Powers et al. also reported that combined olfactory and vomeronasal deafferentation in male hamsters eliminated copulation in all hamsters, but blocking of the olfactory system alone did not. Paradoxically, the odor remained attractive although the animals could not smell it.

The Island of Reil (Insula).   The *posterior* insula seems to be the appraisal area for touch on head and (perhaps) forelegs, and for taste. In our investigations at Loyola University in Chicago we found that both bilateral and unilateral posterior insula lesions produced a significant deficit in successive olfactory and visual discrimination. The successive olfactory discrimination required that the rat choose between lemon-flavored water and vanilla-flavored quinine-water, when shown one cup at a time. In the visual discrimination, the animal had to press a bar for water when the home lights were flashing. If it pressed the bar when the lights were steady, it was punished by a shock to the hind feet. The memory impairment can be explained on the basis of my theory: In the successive olfactory discrimination, the animals could not remember the bad taste of quinine, an impairment in taste memory, not olfactory memory. In the visual discrimination, they could not remember that the steady light was "bad" and brought on a shock.

The *anterior* insula, in my theory the appraisal area for head and perhaps foreleg movements, is discussed in Chapter 14.

Cingulate Gyrus.   The anterior cingulate is a motor appraisal area while the posterior cingulate is a somatosensory appraisal area for body and hindlegs. There is considerable research concentrating on this area. However, some lesions involve posterior and anterior cingulate so that it is difficult to distinguish between motor appraisal and sensory appraisal deficits. I discuss the experimental evidence in Chapter 18.

AFFECTIVE MEMORY IN SIMULTANEOUS AND SUCCESSIVE DISCRIMINATION

Normally, sensory and affective memory are used simultaneously in recall. But in some tasks, affective memory alone may be sufficient for learning a sensory discrimination. For instance, after large lesions of the visual association cortex, simultaneous discrimination of visual cues is unimpaired (Thompson, 1969; Thompson & Malin, 1961; Milliser, 1972) but successive discrimination of pattern and brightness reveals a severe deficit (Milliser, 1972).

Similarly, Pinto-Hamuy et al. (1957) reported that large neocortical ablations of the anterior temporal lobe impaired successive visual and olfactory discrimination. Their lesions involved the temporal pole and various parts of the anterior temporal lobe. They decided that the temporal pole, the only cortical area removed in all animals, must be the area mediating both visual and olfactory discrimination. However, many later reports confirmed that the area necessary for successive visual discrimination is the inferior temporal convexity and not the temporal pole (Brown et al., 1963; Mishkin, 1966, 1972). It is much more likely that the lesions damaged connections with hippocampus and amygdala. In a successive discrimination, the animal must be able to imagine the other cue and what to do about it.

Brown et al. (1963) reported a similar difference between a simultaneous and a successive olfactory discrimination. Monkeys with lesions of the temporal pole and the superior temporal sulcus, which also encroached on the anterior tip of the prepiriform cortex and the amygdaloid complex, performed normally on a simultaneous olfactory discrimination but were significantly impaired on a successive one. Here also, the lesion broke the connection between amygdala and olfactory memory area.

Van Hoesen et al. (1976) reported a sizable projection from the cortex of the inferior temporal area of the Rhesus monkey to the medial portion of the olfactory tubercle. Such a direct connection between the visual memory area and the olfactory/trigeminal appraisal area might make it possible for the animal to see something and know immediately whether it is food or mate by its remembered smell.

The difference in memory retrieval between a simultaneous and a successive discrimination perhaps requires additional explanation. When two cards are shown side by side, one signaling reward, the other punishment or no reward, the animal learns that the positive cue is "good," to be approached, the negative cue "bad," or at least indifferent, to be avoided. Affective visual memory is sufficient for this task. In contrast, successive discrimination requires that the animal recall the positive cue when the negative cue is present, and vice versa. As long as both cues can be inspected, the animal feels an attraction to one but not the other. But with only one cue, the impulse toward food is strong enough to mask the lack of attraction to the negative cue. Hence most errors in successive discriminations (the go/no go problem) are approach errors to the negative stimulus. To refrain from approaching the negative cue, the animal must imagine and recall the positive cue when the negative stimulus is shown, and, so to speak, convert the successive into a simultaneous discrimination. If that can be done, the attraction will be clearly confined to the positive cue which is not in sight, and the animal will not approach the negative cue. Once the task is overlearned, the negative cue will have developed enough negative value so that affective memory alone may suffice for the task. But for learning a successive discrimination, the visual memory area as well as the visual appraisal area must be intact and connected with memory, imagination, and action circuits.

The difference between easy and difficult visual discriminations is essentially the difference between simultaneous tasks that can be learned by affective memory alone, and those that require visual recall in addition. Such difficult tasks are, for instance, successive discrimination (which the animal must convert into a simultaneous one), discrimination reversal, or even an increasingly complex simultaneous discrimination where the two patterns are similar enough to confuse the animal. Mishkin and Hall (1955), for instance, reported that monkeys with inferotemporal lesions were consistently inferior to intact monkeys in learning a visual size and pattern discrimination when that task became gradually more difficult so that the two stimuli were more difficult to distinguish.

Strictly speaking, a simultaneous discrimination is restricted to visual stimuli. Sounds, tastes, touches, and smells, must be experienced one after the other. However, as long as the animal is permitted to smell, touch, or taste both objects shortly before making a response, the task remains within his attention span and no recall is necessary.

BIOCHEMICAL TRANSFER OF TRAINING

This type of research has occasioned a great deal of controversy and still lacks a believable explanation. The report that animals can learn by having an extract of ribonucleic acid (RNA) from trained donor animals injected parenterally into untrained animals who then learn faster than untrained animals without such injections, has been as often disproved as confirmed. Positive reports, I believe, can be explained on the basis of affective memory; negative reports are based on learning tasks the animal cannot remember on the basis of affective memory alone.

Babich et al. (1965) trained rats to approach the food cup on hearing a click produced by the experimenter operating the pellet dispenser. After training, the animals were killed and their brains (except for frontal areas and the areas caudal to the superior colliculus—1 g of tissue) treated so that the RNA was precipitated. This precipitate was then injected intraperitoneally into untrained rats. A control group was injected with RNA from untrained donors. All rats were then tested 4, 6, 8, 22, and 24 hours after injection. The experimental animals approached the food cup area significantly more often when hearing the click than did the controls.

In another experiment, Luttges et al. (1966) tried to replicate this result by training mice in a two-choice brightness discrimination in which the animals had to swim in a water Y-maze to the non-preferred darker alley. Another group was trained always to turn left regardless of the light's position. At the beginning of the trial, the platform was submerged so that the animals were forced to swim to one of the alleys. After training, the brains of the animals in each of the groups were homogenized and centrifuged; the nucleic acid was precipitated with ethanol. The two experimental groups of naive mice were then injected with the nucleic acid from the trained donor mice. Eighteen hours later, their spontaneous activity was tested. Two hours later, the experimental animals were given six trials in the water maze, as were a group of control animals. No differences were found between the three groups. In a second experiment, the authors trained rats on a light-dark discrimination in a shuttle box. In this experiment also, no differences were found between rats injected with nucleic acid from trained donors and those injected with nucleic acid from naive rats.

In a third experiment, Frank et al. (1970) used brain homogenate and liver homogenate from mice trained in a two-way shuttle box. One group of donors were shocked as soon as they entered the black compartment while another group were not shocked in this compartment. A third group was made up of "stressed" mice, animals that had been placed in a ventilated glass jar and rolled back and forth five times. Immediately after these procedures, the mice were killed, the brain and liver removed and separately homogenized with distilled water. Next, a single injection of either brain or liver homogenate was given to naive animals. Six hours after injection, all animals were tested in the same shuttle box. All animals that had received homogenates of either brain or liver from *shocked* animals hesitated longer before entering the black compartment than did mice that had injections from non-shocked donors. But mice that had received either brain or liver homogenates from stressed donors had the longest delays. The authors concluded that the homogenates from shocked or stressed animals contained a stress factor that accounts for the difference between experimental and control animals.

While a "stress factor" may explain Frank et al.'s results, it does not explain Babich et al.'s results because no stress was involved in their experiment. But an analysis of the psychological factors involved can explain the stress factor as well as the success of some experiments and the failure of others. The experiment of Babich et al. required a simple approach response to a click. The animals appraised the click as good, approached the food cup and were fed. Affective memory of the click as "good, to be approached" was all that was required to solve the task. Such simple liking of the click could well be transferred from one animal to the other if we assume that increased amounts of serotonin could be generated in response to the click and that this increase in the homogenate could sensitize the same cortical area in the recipient. Similarly, the electric shock and stress by tumbling could be transferred as a simple affective memory of "bad" things to happen, expressed in changes of noradrenaline concentration.[1] This might result in a disinclination to enter the black compartment, or, even more simply, in a fear of exploring. In both cases, we are dealing with very simple likes and dislikes, similar to hereditary preferences, which could conceivably be transmitted by RNA or DNA. The required action is simple approach or avoidance. In contrast, the experiment of Luttges et al. required a complicated response on the basis of a brightness discrimination. This cannot be solved on the basis of affective memory. The animal must distinguish light from dark and must organize and plan the response, which requires imagination. Finally, it must remember to avoid the dark box—which requires modality–specific memory. No simple biochemical substance could be expected to provide all this information. Hence we can conclude that "memory" can be transferred biochemically from one animal to another as long as the experimental response is a simple approach or avoidance, based on affective memory. But as soon as modality-specific recall is involved, such a transfer is impossible.

---

[1]For a discussion of serotonin and noradrenaline and their connection with good/bad appraisals, see chapters, 24–25.

13 Cortical Areas Mediating Movement: Motor Areas and the Initiation of Action

The motor system of the brain exists to translate thought, sensations and emotions into movement.

E. Henneman, 1974

MOTOR AREAS

The motor area of the cortex is perhaps the best-known part of the brain. Electrical stimulation of the motor cortex (area 4) has produced various movements, both in man and animal. From human stimulation experiments, investigators have constructed maps that show the particular areas of the motor cortex that mediate movement in head and body, limbs and joints (see Fig. 11.2). The conscious human being experiences a movement produced by electrical stimulation as something outside his control, a passive movement. Deliberate movement, on the other hand, is produced by a conscious intention to move: We intend to move, we do, and know that we move. It is important to emphasize this fact because scientists sometimes assume that we are only aware of what we experience through our senses. This assumption had led psychologists of an earlier day to talk about "feelings of innervation," so confusing the issue by their very terminology. We do not feel innervation, we consciously intend to move and we are aware of moving. This awareness of our intention is present before the intention is translated into movement, hence it cannot have anything to do with "feelings of innervation," because this term implies that we sense the innervation of motor nerves after the movement has begun.

When we form an intention to move, this intention must be translated into nerve impulses that will activate the required muscles in exactly the right sequence and pattern. We set the direction and the way in which we want to move, but the movement is carried out by a complex combination of individual muscles. In computer terminology, we could say that our intention provides the task but the actual programming of muscles has to be done by the brain. We are not aware of this programming of our muscles although we know that we are moving according to our intention and even that we are moving more quickly and easily after several repetitions. This programming of muscles requires an integrative process that transforms the intention into the pattern of nerve impulses that will move the muscles to accomplish our goal.

Stimulation of the motor cortex does not result in the contraction of particular muscles. It produces a final set position of limbs or body, no matter what their position at the time of stimulation (Ward, 1952). This is just what we would expect if the cortex carries out intentions. We intend a particular movement, not the contraction of a set of muscles—in fact, we would not know which muscles to contract to carry out our intention. Apparently, the motor cortex integrates the neural pattern required, no matter what the muscles that need to be contracted or what sequence of innervation is required. Hence the motor cortex, like the sensory cortex, has an integrative function. This integration is immediate and direct, as is sensory integration; neither motor nor sensory integration is in need of conscious guidance. In fact, if we attempt to contract muscles deliberately to perform a movement, the smoothness and swing of the movement will be disturbed. We are not aware of the way in which the motor system organizes movements just as we are not aware of the way in wich the visual or auditory system works to let us see or hear. We intend to move in a particular way and let brain and muscles do the rest. But we know that we move just as we know that we see.

Such an integrative functioning of the cortex can explain the structuring of our sense experience and movements as well as the results of electrical stimulation of the cortex. When sensory cortex is stimulated, what we experience is unlike any experience through ordinary sensory channels. Stimulation of the visual cortex does not result in seeing objects but in seeing flashes of light; stimulation of the somatosensory cortex produces an experience difficult to describe, something between burning and tingling. Such stimulation activates cells randomly, quite different from the patterned activity produced by sensory stimulation. Electrical stimulation of the motor cortex produces simple movements which may vary according to stimulus intensity from a flick of the finger to massive convulsive movements. Stimulation of the motor cortex will not lead to a complete action, for instance, taking an apple and eating it, because such stimulation activates points in the motor cortex but not the intention, which alone can give aim to a movement.

We could say quite generally that without integrative sensory functions that structure sense impressions and so allow us to know the world and our own body, and without integrative motor function that structures our movements according to our intentions and so allows us to move in the real world, we could neither know anything nor act upon this knowledge. That it is the cortex that mediates goal-directed movement is shown by the effects of decortication, which are more severe as we go from lower mammals to primates. The cat or dog deprived of his cortex can move but is not able to find his food or mate; the decorticated monkey or ape cannot even move and is doomed to death unless spoon-fed and maintained.

Motor Area 4.   The cell structure of Brodmann's area 4, the motor cortex, differs sharply from that of the sensory cortex. It measures about 5 mm in width, as against the barely 1-½ mm width of the visual cortex. This is accounted for by the increasing number and size of pyramid cells as we go from the surface to the depth of the cortex. Even layers II and IV, the external and internal granular layer, contain some pyramids; and layer V, broader than in other cortical areas, has pyramid cells of all sizes, including clusters of giant pyramids, the Betz cells. Because of this dearth of granular cells and dominance of pyramid cells, particularly in layer IV, the motor cortex is said to be agranular. The small and large pyramid cells relay motor impulses to subcortex and spinal cord. Area 4 lies mainly along the precentral gyrus, including its anterior and posterior banks. In front of it is area 4s, the "suppressor" strip, with large pyramids in layer IV. Electrical stimulation of area 4s produces suppression of movement or relaxation of muscles.

Stimulation experiments have established that area 4 is arranged in such a way that mouth and head movements are obtained on the lateral extent of the precentral area, at the foot of the central fissure. When the stimulating electrode is moved toward the top of the central gyrus, it produces movements of fingers, hands, arms, and trunk, in that order. The hips are represented at the upper lateral limit of the precentral gyrus, legs and feet on the medial side (see Fig. 11.2). In man, damage of the motor area results in paralysis of the affected limbs, but some movement returns after a short time. However, the movement of individual fingers and toes is usually lost permanently if the hand or foot area is damaged.

The main motor pathways from the motor cortex are the corticobulbar and the corticospinal tracts. The corticobulbar fibers run part of the way together with the corticospinal tract, and finally decussate near the cranial motor nucleus for which they are destined. But some of the fibers do not cross over so that most of the striate muscles of the head are activated from both sides of the motor cortex. The corticospinal fibers pass through the internal capsule together with the corticobulbar fibers and finally decussate in the medulla, where they form the medullary pyramids. Not all the fibers cross, so that there is always a slight innervation from the same side. But the main innervation comes from the opposite side of the motor cortex.

The pyramidal tract can be defined as consisting of the fibers that emerge from the pons to form the medullary pyramids. They include the corticobulbar and corticospinal tracts as well as some smaller bundles. Before reaching the medulla, pyramidal tract fibers distribute to the ventrolateral nucleus of the thalamus, the red nucleus, the pontine nuclei, and the medial and dorsolateral midbrain tegmentum. About half the pyramidal tract fibers disappear in the bulb (medulla); these are identified as the corticobulbar tract. In the spinal cord, the pyramidal fibers terminate primarily in the dorsal horn and intermediate zone; a few terminate in the ventral horn (Towe, 1973).

The cell bodies that give rise to the pyramidal tract are concentrated along the border between the frontal and parietal lobe. But they are also scattered sparsely through other cortical areas. In man, about 60% of the myelinated pyramid fibers come from area 4, 6, and possibly 8, and about 40% from areas 3, 1, and 2 (the somatosensory fields) and areas 5 and 7 (the somatosensory association areas) in the parietal lobe. Fibers from frontal cortex mainly innervate motor interneurons in the dorsal horn and intermediate zone. Fibers from parietal cortex mainly innervate sensory interneurons (Towe, 1973).

One third of all fibers in the medullary pyramids are unmyelinated. Their origin has not yet been traced. The pyramidal tract consists primarily of small fibers. About 90% of the pyramidal tract fibers are less than 3 micron in diameter, which means that their conduction time is relatively slow (Towe, 1973). Apparently, these small fibers mediate various physiological changes whereas the large fibers, coming from the Betz cells, initiate movement. Thus Wang and Lu (1930) have found that stimulation of the motor cortex produced not only movement but also a psychogalvanic response and a lowering of blood pressure. These responses were abolished by section of the cerebral peduncles (including the pyramidal fibers) but not by destruction of the hypothalamus. And Sachs and Brendler (1948) have found that stimulation of area 4 produced blood pressure and respiratory changes at lower threshold levels than was required for the production of movement.

The fact that fibers in the pyramidal tract originate in postcentral as well as in precentral areas is one reason why it has often been said that there is no clear distinction between the motor and sensory cortex. The other reason is the fact that stimulation of both precentral and postcentral cortex produces movement. However, there is a decided lengthening of reaction time as the stimulating electrode moves from frontal to parietal and occipital cortex—which might mean that stimulation of postcentral cortex produces movement by way of the motor cortex. Seeing a light flash or having a peculiar somesthetic sensation, as the result of occipital or parietal stimulation, would normally arouse an intention to look toward the flash or toward the point of somatic sensation, or to dislodge whatever seems to produce the disturbance. The movement that appears when parietal or occipital cortex is stimulated may thus be the motor reaction to sensory stimulation, even when the animal is lightly anesthetized. The recent report that fibers from parietal cortex mainly innervate sensory interneurons in the spinal cord confirms this suggestion.

There is considerable evidence for an afferent influence on the motor cortex. According to Luria (1966b), "the higher we climb up the evolutionary ladder, the smaller the relative volume of the Betz 'trigger' cells and the greater the relative volume of the controlling, afferent apparatus, regulating the activity of the Betz cells, and the greater the importance in the regulation of movement assumed by the complex afferent systems of the cortex'' (p. 135–6).

Recently, it has been found that the pyramidal cells in the motor cortex are arranged in columns perpendicular to the surface, with several hundred cells in each column. Several columns may be engaged in a given movement. When the motor cortex is stimulated via microelectrodes, for instance in the thumb area, so that the thumb moves, the cells producing this movement all lie in neighboring columns. If, next, the skin of the thumb is stimulated at the points represented by these motor areas, this stimulation affects pyramidal cells in exactly the area in the motor cortex that is activated when the thumb moves toward the point on the skin which was stimulated before. As Eccles (1977) says, this means that the thumb moves to explore the skin contact.

Area 6, Premotor Cortex.   German and Russian anatomists include in motor cortex or ''motor analyzer'' not only area 4, but areas 6, 8, and 44. English and American anatomists do not include area 6 in the motor cortex. They classify it with area 4 only because it also is agranular. On the surface of the medial hemisphere, this area lies in the anterior third of the paracentral lobule. On the lateral surface, it lies on the posterior part of the frontal gyri and the anterior part of the precentral gyri. Although it does not have giant Betz cells in layer V, it does have large pyramid cells in layers II to V. In area 6, there are more axo-dendritic connections than in area 4, hence the association layer III is broader and almost indistinguishable from layer IV.

In lower monkeys, area 6 is much smaller than area 4, but in man the relationship is reversed to that area 6 amounts to 80% of the combined motor and premotor region (Glezer, 1955). Electrical stimulation of area 4 spreads only to neighboring regions, that is, the somatosensory cortex, but stimulation of area 6 spreads to somatosensory areas 3, 1, and 5, to the motor cortex 4, and also to areas 8 and 39. According to Wyss and Obrador (1937), when area 4 is stimulated with shocks lasting 10–15 milliseconds, there is a contraction of individual muscles. But when this stimulus is applied to the premotor area, this movement spreads to more and more muscles after a latency of 10–15 seconds. Soon this movement is converted into a series of motor impulses forming an integrated motor act, a progressive and purposive movement, for instance, withdrawing the leg, turning the head, and the like. Hence, organized movement seems to be the result of activating area 6 and through it, area 4.

Lesions of area 6 produce a disintegration of complex motor acts (Sittig, 1931), also motor restlessness, impulsiveness, forced grasping, and a disturbance of inhibition in established actions (Bianchi, 1920, Fulton et al., 1948).

Since area 6 has become so decisively dominant in man, only findings from brain damage in human beings will bring us closer to an explanation of its functions. Of course, clinical reports, on which we have to depend, do not provide information as precise as that from lesion experiments in animals. Tumors or wounds are never strictly localized in one particular cortical area. Also, the reported functional impairment is only rarely based on systematic psychological investigation. Such testing has been done only in the last few decades, and even then has often been done with standard tests that do not necessarily reveal specific impairment.

As long ago as 1936 Foerster had reported that a lesion of the premotor area causes loss of precise sequential movements. Complex motions disintegrate because each element seems to require a special effort. And in the last thirty years, Russian investigators have made a concerted effort to demonstrate specific psychological deficits. They have shown that lesions of the premotor cortex produce symptoms that are essentially different from lesions of the primary motor cortex. While a lesion in area 4 interferes most of all with the ability to move fingers and toes voluntarily, lesions of area 6 do not disturb simple isolated movements, nor do they reduce the strength of these movements. According to Luria (1966a), the central symptom produced by premotor lesions is the "disintegration of the kinetic structure of motor acts" (p. 196), which agrees with Foerster's report. Typists lose their facility and begin to type with one finger, "moving the finger from one key to another by a conscious effort every time" (p. 196). With a lesion of the premotor area in the dominant hemisphere, it is the contralateral limb that is mainly affected, but the limb on the same side shows some impairment, too. These patients find it all but impossible to learn a sequence of complex motions. When a patient is asked, for instance, to make a fist with one hand and stretch out the other with palm up, he usually has to make one movement after the other. He cannot change from one rhythm of tapping to another, or from drawing circles to drawing squares, particularly if he has to draw circles and squares alternately. Instead, he keeps on drawing the same figure.

Luria also points out that spoken language is a highly complex system of kinetic structures; that is, it is a motor performance that also is affected by lesions of the premotor area. Patients with such lesions lose the fluency of speech because the articulation of each word requires a special effort. A lesion of the superior part of the premotor region may give rise only to slight interference with fluent speech, but a lesion of the inferior part of the premotor zone of the dominant hemisphere, closely associated with Broca's speech area (44), produces pronounced disturbances.

Luria (1966b) has reported his investigations of two patients with lesions in the parasagittal premotor area. He found that these patients used a separate impulse for each phase of one continuous act. Shortly after the operation, they were completely inert, could not raise the arm on command, but could brush away a fly from the forehead. They repeated simple movements because they did not seem to know how to go on with the next step. When instructed to tap with his fingers in the order 1st–2nd, 1st–5th, one patient could not keep up the sequence, even after practicing for two months after the operation. He complained: "The general instruction does not get through so that each finger has to carry out the instruction separately" (p. 230). The other patient complained: "I cannot think, my brain doesn't work." Although he was fully oriented and had no difficulty seeing or hearing, he could not write spontaneously or tell a coherent story. Luria concludes that there is a "disturbance of successive internal schemes by means of which highly automatized skilled movements or intellectual actions (mental arithmetic, storytelling) are performed" (p. 292).

In short, the patients seem to be unable to organize their intention into a sequence of movements, whether these are speech movements or movements of the hands or arms. In the first days after the operation, the impulse to move seems to be lacking altogether. The conclusion seems to be that the premotor area mediates the impulse to organized action. The highly developed association layer seems to make possible the organization of successive impulses to highly complex movement sequences.

In lesions of the premotor area we also have to consider that such a lesion breaks the continuity of impulses from prefrontal cortex to the motor area. The sequential structure of a learned movement, registered in the prefrontal cortex, can no longer be relayed to the premotor and motor cortex to influence the ongoing action. Hence complicated movements lose their dynamic structure and have to be broken up into several simple movements and started one by one, by a separate intention.

Another defect noted in patients with damage of the premotor area is the loss of expressive speech. They do not seem to be able to give the proper emphasis to the appropriate words in a sentence. Luria has reported that patients find it difficult to emphasize different words in a sentence so as to give it a slightly different meaning, or to express different emotional nuances. This also can be explained as loss of an action impulse, this time an emotional impulse. I have suggested that emotion is a felt impulse to action, experienced when subcortical impulses arrive in the premotor cortex. After a lesion in this area, such emotional impulses are no longer experienced—hence the curious "emotional flattening," which is part of the frontal syndrome. The patient can still appraise a situation as good or bad, but he can no longer experience the emotional impulse produced by this appraisal. This results in expressionless speech and also in the indifference that is a well-known symptom of frontal damage.

Experimental lesions of the premotor area in animals have not been extensively investigated from a psychological point of view, although there have been many reports of deficits after frontal lobe lesions. But these lesions have usually included both prefrontal and premotor areas or even the whole frontal lobe.

The Frontal Eyefield, Area 8.   Anatomists do not agree on the exact boundaries of this area. According to Foerster (1936), this region forms a 2–3 cm strip covering the medial and lateral extent of the superior frontal gyrus and narrows almost to a point as it extends to the operculum. The most numerous elements in this area are small pyramid cells. Stimulation in the region overlying the end of the middle frontal gyrus has produced eye movements.

The frontal eyefield receives afferents from area 18, the visual association cortex, and sends relays to this area. It also receives afferents from areas 41, 42, 22, and 37, the auditory and auditory-visual association cortex. While relays from these areas do not seem to initiate action[1] they may prime the eyefield neurons so that the impulse to look will more easily lead to action. When we see or hear something not immediately in front of us, we have the impulse to look for it and keep it in sight. When one eyefield is eliminated in the monkey, head and eyes begin to deviate toward the side of the lesion. The intact side of the brain, initiating the impulse to look, is no longer balanced by the other side, hence the monkey overreacts toward the damaged side.

Like areas 4 and 6, the frontal eyefield is agranular, hence a motor type cortex. It is approximately at the level of the eye representation in the motor cortex. It seems that the activation of this area mediates the impulse to look toward something, an impulse that is carried out as soon as relays from the eyefield arrive in the motor cortex.

MOTOR APPRAISAL AREAS

Each action impulse (emotional or deliberate) must be appraised for action, as suitable or unsuitable. This allows either delay of action or planning for action. Planning may be deliberate, carried on in words and concepts, as it usually is in older children and adults, or a spontaneous gauging of action possibilities, as it is in infants and animals. As the action continues, its success or failure must also be appraised before an individual can decide whether the goal is reached and action should be stopped.

Action impulses could be appraised via the limbic cortex nearest areas 6 and 8, the areas that serve the experiences of emotion and the intention for action. There is enough evidence to suggest that the anterior cingulate gyrus (areas 32, 24) is the appraisal area for movements of the whole body, and for action impulses involving the body; the anterior insula (area 14), for movements and movement impulses of head and mouth (including speech movements), and perhaps hand movements as well.

The connection of the premotor areas 6 and 8 with the limbic appraisal areas seem to be the so-called "suppressor strips" in the frontal lobe, areas 4s and 8s. In the anesthetized animal, electrical excitation of these strips produced suppression of activity. However, later experiments showed that stimulation of these areas in the waking animal does not produce a suppression of activity but can

---

[1]According to Kuypers and Haaxma (1975), cutting the occipito-frontal long association fibers prevented monkeys from grasping a pellet sunk in a well in the center of a disk by inserting finger and thumb into two white grooves. The monkey brought up his hand to the pellet but was unable to insert his fingers into the white grooves. Apparently, the occipito-frontal connections serve accurate visuo-motor manipulation, although they do not initiate reaching.

produce faciliation and activation as well as a reduction of activity. Sloan and Jasper (1950) have concluded that these responses are produced via subcortical pathways. They believe that the anterior limbic areas have a regulatory rather than a suppressor function. But to call it a regulatory function does not explain under what circumstances either a decrease or an increase of activity could occur. We can call an appraisal of action and action impulses a "regulatory" function; but an appraisal means a psychological activity that can explain increased or decreased activity: Activity is increased if the action is appraised as suitable, and is decreased or even suppressed if the action is found unsuitable.

Perhaps the unraveling of frontal lobe function has led to so many difficulties and even paradoxes because the frontal lobe mediates a number of functions: overt action, the intention to act, the appraisal of action and action impulses, and the registration of motor memory. Without an attempt to identify the regions that mediate these functions, additional research will only find additional problems. For instance, damage to the premotor area may mean that man or animal finds it difficult to initiate action; but it is also possible that the lesion has interrupted the fiber connections to the appraisal area in the anterior cingulate gyrus. If so, there will also be problems in evaluating action impulses and actions themselves. Luria's patient who could not alternate a tapping pattern may have suffered from an appraisal difficulty. To alternate the fingers in tapping, he must appraise his movements. When no longer appropriate, he must change or stop them. When such direct appraisal of movements or movement impulses is impossible, the patient may have to wait until he *sees* that his movements are incorrect (visual appraisal is unaffected) and only then will he be able to change them.

Since appraisal areas and affective memory areas are identical (see chapter 12), I first discuss affective motor memory and then give evidence for motor appraisal and affective motor memory areas in chapter 14.

THE INITIATION OF ACTION

Until comparatively recently, it was assumed that movements are initiated from the motor cortex via the pyramidal pathway and supported by impulses via the extrapyramidal pathway originating from the basal ganglia. While the pyramidal pathway was known to descend directly to the spinal cord, the extrapyramidal system was supposed to consist of several relays coming from the striatum and converging via red nucleus and reticular formation upon the motor cells of the spinal cord. Striopallidal, pallidorubral, pallidoreticular, rubrospinal, and reticulospinal relays were considered to be the principal links in this extrapyramidal system.

Within the last three decades, this view has suffered a radical change. In the first place, the connections of the basal ganglia have turned out to be much more complicated than had been believed before. And secondly, the basal ganglia and their connections do not constitute a separate system independent of the motor cortex and the pyramidal system (Fig. 13.1):

According to Nieuwenhuys (1977), the basal ganglia are relay stations in several circuits: The most important is a projection from all parts of the neocortex to the striatum (caudate and putamen), which sends fibers to the phylogenetically older globus pallidus. From there, fibers run through the fasciculus thalamicus to the anterior and lateral ventral thalamic nuclei; and the anterior ventral nuclei project to the frontal association cortex while the ventro-lateral thalamic nuclei connect with areas 4 and 6 of the motor cortex. Hence the major projection of the striatum goes to the motor cortex via the ventral thalamus; and the ventral thalamus receives direct relays from the cerebellum. The motor cortex not only initiates relays to the pyramidal tract but also sends out fiber systems that connect with the striatum and other "extrapyramidal" relay stations.

There are several reciprocal connections from striatum to other subcortical structures: from striatum via globus pallidus to centromedian thalamic nucleus and from intralaminar thalamic nuclei to the striatum; from striatum via globus pallidus to subthalamic nucleus and back to globus pallidus; from striatum via globus pallidus to substantia nigra pars reticulata, and from substantia nigra pars compacta back to the striatum. There is also a connection from the striatum via the substantia nigra to the ventral, lateral, and dorsomedial thalamic nuclei. Finally, the striatum is a relay station in the projection from brainstem reticular formation and midbrain tegmentum to the frontal cortex.

Contrary to earlier views, there is no direct projection from the globus pallidus to the red nucleus. Rather, the red nucleus receives a strong projection from the motor cortex, which together with the descending rubrospinal tract and the pyramidal tract, seems to mediate finely differentiated limb movements. Via the substantia nigra, the striatum projects to the reticular formation and the superior colliculus. Both these structures give rise to descending spinal systems. The reticular formation also receives a substantial projection from the motor cortex, so that once again, the system is under cortical control. Fig. 13.1 shows diagrammatically the older and newer view of the relationship between pyramidal and extrapyramidal systems (Nieuwenhuys, 1977, p. 14–15).

There has been considerable interest and a great deal of research on the connections between the various structures in communication with the motor system. Eccles (1977), for instance, discusses at length cerebello-cerebral interac-

FIG. 13.1   (*Opposite page.*) Two views of the extrapyramidal motor system. (A) embodying the classical concept of the pyramidal (PY.) and extrapyramidal (E.P.) Motor systems, and (B) our present-day knowledge of the fiber connections of the motor cortex and the striatum. Abbreviations: C., nucleus caudatus; F.R., formatio reticularis; G.P., globus pallidus; G.P.E., globus pallidus, pars externa; G.P.I., globus pallidus, pars interna; H.L., lateral habenular nucleus; I., intralaminar nuclei; M., motor neuron; P., putamen; R., nucleus ruber; S.N., substantia nigra; SUBTH., corpus subthalamicum; TECT., tectum mesencephali; THAL., thalamus; T.P.P., nucleus tegmenti pedunculopontinus, pars compacta; V.A., nucleus ventralis anterior; V.L., nucleus ventralis lateralis. From: R. Nieuwenhuys, 1977, p. 14.

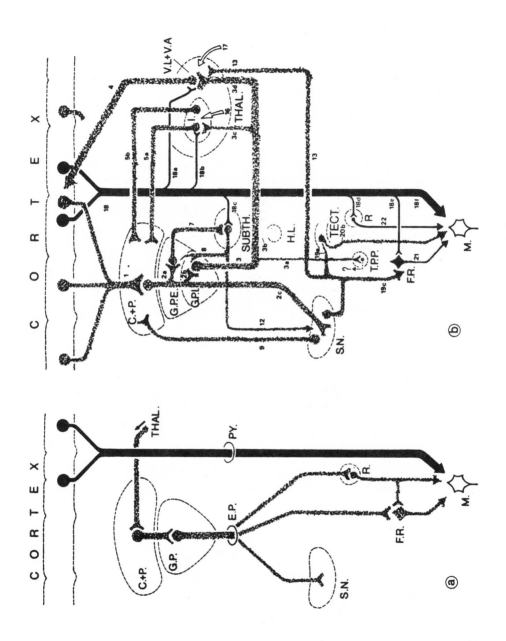

163

Circuits in Fig. 13.1

1. Projection from all parts of the neocortex to the caudate/putamen.
2a. Fibers from striatum to globus pallidus external segment
2b. Fibers from striatum to globus pallidus internal segment
2c. Fibers from globus pallidus via cerebral peduncle to substantia nigra pars reticulata (transmitter = GABA)
3a. From internal pallidal segment to mesencephalic tegmentum, terminating in nucleus tegmenti pedunculopontinus, pars compacta.
3b. From internal pallidal segment via stria medullaris to lateral habenula
3c. From globus pallidus to centrum medianum nucleus
3d. From internal pallidal segment via Forel's field H as fasciculus thalamicus to thalamus, to the nucleus ventralis anterior and lateralis; topically organized.
4. From nucleus ventralis lateralis to areas 4 and 6 of frontal cortex
5a. From centromedian thalamic nucleus via internal capsule to caudal part of putamen and in corpus of caudate nucleus
5b. From rostral intralaminar nuclei to rostral part of caudate nucleus and putamen
6. Collaterals (from 5b) to frontal cortex
7. From globus pallidus to corpus subthalamicus
8. From subthalamic nucleus to globus pallidus
9. From substantia nigra to striatum (dopaminergic, but not exclusively)
10. From substantia nigra to caudate/putamen
11. From globus pallidus external segment to substantia nigra pars compacta
12. From subthalamic nucleus to substantia nigra
13. From substantia nigra pars reticulata via field of Forel H to thalamic VL, VA and DM nuclei
14. From reticular formation at caudal mesencephalic and pontine levels, to striatum
15. From dorsal raphé nucleus to neostriatum (serotonergic)
16. From brain stem reticular formation to intralaminar thalamic nuclei, projecting point to point to caudate/putamen.
17. From dentate cerebellar nuclei via brachium conjunctivum to thalamic VA, VL nucleus. Projection overlaps terminals from striopallidum
18a. Projection from motor cortex to VL thalamic nuclei
18b. Projection from motor cortex to CM thalamic nuclei
18c. Projection from motor cortex to subthalamic nucleus
18d. Projection from motor cortex to red nucleus
18e. Projection from motor cortex to brain stem reticular formation
18f. Projection from motor cortex to pyramidal tract
19a. Nigrotectal fibers to deeper layers of superior colliculus
19b. Tectoreticular fibers to mesencephalic reticular formation to spinal cord
19c. Tectoreticular fibers to rhombencephalic reticular formation to spinal cord
20a. Tectoreticular fibers from tectum to reticular formation
20b. Tectospinal fibers from tectum to spinal cord

tions. He assumes an open loop circuit between the two structures ''so that there is an ongoing 'comment' from the cerebellum within ten to twenty milliseconds of every motor command'' (p. 133). He suggests that a second open loop runs from the association cortex to the basal ganglia, and from there via the ventral thalamic nuclei to the motor cortex. This system, he thinks, is in parallel with the open loop from the cortex to the cerebellar hemispheres, which project via dentate cerebellar nucleus and ventral thalamic nuclei to the motor cortex. Both systems are necessary for smooth movement: Degeneration of the basal ganglia results in Parkinsonism or Huntington's chorea, and cerebellar lesions produce ataxia and tremor.

In recent years, voices have been raised insisting that this is not the whole story. For instance, in a volume on *Efferent Organization and the Integration of Behavior,* Maser (1973) says:

> Although the traditional approach to the neurology of movement regards pyramidal and extrapyramidal organization as the most salient feature, the efferent response view stresses the role of limbic nuclei such as the septal region, cingulate gyrus, frontal granular cortex, hippocampus and hypothalamus. Furthermore, it is suggested that extrapyramidal structures not only influence the role of gamma motoneurons in regulating muscle tone, but also participate in fixed action patterns and interact with limbic response mechanisms (p. 10).

Unfortunately, none of the authors in this volume specify the interaction between motor and limbic systems. Granted that the motor cortex is interconnected with all the relay stations of the so-called extrapyramidal system, as well as with the limbic system, what is needed is some suggestion of the sequence in which these relays are engaged. There are open loop systems not only in the motor system but throughout the brain. Most structures are connected indirectly if not directly so that they receive relays from the structures to which they project. The problem is to identify the main relays from sensory areas to the motor system.

For such a task, two assumptions are necessary: First, we have to assume that a nervous impulse does not start out of the blue but is initiated either by a receptor organ or by a relay from another structure. Open as well as closed loop systems must provide an entrance from the sensory side and an exit toward the spinal motor pathway. Secondly, we assume that the sequence of relays from sensory areas to motor area must conform to the sequence of psychological activities from perception to action. There may be continuous loops, but they cannot be excited at random. Just as there is no gap between one psychological activity and the other, from perception to action, so there cannot be a gap between the neural relays that mediate them.

The Intention to Act

An impulse to goal-directed action has to be motivated; and the motive is involved in the appraisal of the immediate situation. We want something we have appraised as good. We want to escape from something we find dangerous. We recall an omission and want to repair it. We have an idea for a story and hurry to write it down. In all these examples, an appraisal is the necessary link between some experience and the ensuing intention and action. I have argued that the limbic cortex mediates appraisal—and this includes not only the appraisal of anything we see, hear or otherwise experience, but also the appraisal of things remembered, imagined, or thought about. To go from such an appraisal to action, we must want or intend something; such an intention is the first step to overt action. The appraisal is a cognitive act, but wanting or intending is a felt action impulse. Since every step in the chain of psychological activities must be mediated by neural relays, there should be a relay from the appraisal area (limbic cortex) to a structure that can convert the cognitive appraisal into an impulse to action. in my theory, this structure is the hippocampus.

According to my theory, limbic cortex serves as appraisal area for neighboring primary and association cortex. Indeed, all areas of limbic cortex are connected both with the striatum and with the hippocampus. According to Yakovlev & Locke, (1961), the efferent pathway from the cingulate gyrus contains three kinds of fibers: those stemming from cells in the anterior cingulate gyrus and running forward over the knee of the corpus callosum to end in the striatum (Fig. 13.2); those arising from cells in the posterior cingulate gyrus and running caudally toward the subiculum of the hippocampus; and finally, fibers that origi-

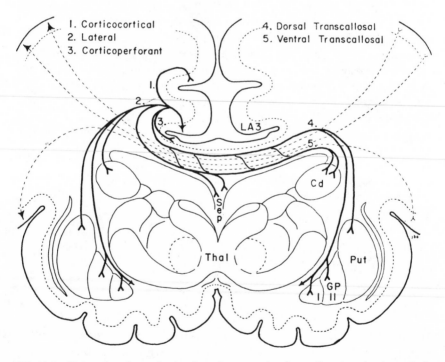

FIG. 13.2 *Major branches of cingulum in coronal plane. Superior* (corticocortical), *callosoperforant* (lateral, dorsal, and ventral transcallosal), and *corticoperforant* branches are shown. Contralateral projections to lenticular nucleus are only tentative. (From Yakovlev et al., 1966)

Cd - caudate nucleus	Put- putamen
GP - globus pallidus	Sep - septum
LA-layer	Thal- thalamus

nate from pyramid cells in all parts of the cingulate gyrus and bifurcate, one branch running forward toward the striatum and the other running backwards toward the fascia dentata of the hippocampus. The anterior cingulate gyrus receives afferents from the anterior motor and premotor cortex, and hence seems to be the appraisal area for action and action impulses. The posterior cingulate gyrus receives afferents from the parietal sensory and association cortex and seems to mediate the appraisal of touch and other somesthetic experiences. Efferents from limbic areas mediating the appraisal of sights, sounds, and smells, also connect both with the striatum and the hippocampus. These relays from limbic cortex to striatum seem to prime striatal cells for action while the relays from limbic cortex to hippocampus seem to initiate action directly via the cerebellum.

The Action Circuit

The intention to act may be an intention to make a particular movement, mediated by the action circuit. But this intention may also be a spontaneous or deliberate impulse to recall something or to reexperience an earlier appraisal. In my theory, the hippocampus is the central relay station for all these impulses, or rather, their origin. Here, the appraisal of experience is transformed into an impulse to action.

I propose to postpone the discussion of hippocampal structure and function until chapter 19. In the meantime, let us accept provisionally that the hippocampus is the origin of the action circuit, and follow the further course of this pathway. Corresponding to its diverse functions, the hippocampus has connection3 to various structures. Its main efferent pathway is the fornix, which connects the hippocampus with the septal area, the mamillary bodies, and finally the tegmentum. From there, relays run to the reticular formation, the inferior olivary nuclei, and the cerebellum. From the cerebellum, relays go both directly and also indirectly, via the hypothalamus, to the ventral thalamus and motor cortex.

The Cerebellum.   That the action circuit from hippocampus to motor cortex includes the cerebellum can be inferred from many reports. Green and Morin (1953), for instance, reported that stimulation of the fornix and the hippocampal commissure produced electrical potentials in the frontal, temporal, parietal, and occipital cortical areas, and also in the cerebellum. These potentials were quite similar to the electrical activity in these structures after visual stimulation or stimulation of sensory nerves. Similarly, Saint-Cyr and Woodward (1980) found that stimulation of the fornix produced excitation of the cerebellar cortex. And Lennox and Robinson (1951) found that electrical stimulation of various limbic regions induced an afterdischarge not only in these structures but also in hippocampus and cerebellum. Finally, Gastaut (1954) showed that sensory stimulation, reinforced by metrazol, produced electrical activity in the cerebellum and motor cortex. I discuss the structure of the cerebellum, its afferents and efferents, in connection with the action circuit, in chapter 26.

Many authors who concede that the cerebellum is involved in motor control assume that it is part of a loop from motor cortex to cerebellum and from cerebellar nuclei back to motor cortex. According to Eccles (1979), the plan of movement is formulated in the association cortex and then this plan is programmed via the basal ganglia and the lateral dentate nucleus in the cerebellum and projected to the ventral thalamus and motor cortex. Next, the motor cortex initiates the programmed movement and also sends a second loop via the intermediate cerebellar zone and interpositus nucleus back to the motor cortex. Eccles suggests that this relay from interpositus nucleus back to motor cortex provides a continuing "comment" on the evolving movement. Hence the pars intermedia within this executive loop "makes an important contribution by updating the movement that is based upon the sensory description of the limb position and velocity upon which the intended movement is to be superimposed. This closed-loop operation is a kind of short-range planning as opposed to the long-range planning of the association cortex and the cerebellar hemispheres" (p. 16).

Because Brooks (1978) questioned the proposed "long-range planning" of the cerebellar hemispheres, Eccles suggests that such long-range planning may be restricted to the association cortex, while the programming of the plan involves the basal ganglia and cerebellar hemispheres. According to Eccles, in very rapid movements like piano playing or typing, we must rely entirely on the programming by the basal ganglia and cerebellar hemispheres because "there is no time for on-target correction by the pars intermedia once a fast movement has begun" (p. 16). But surely, even a slow movement, once begun, is carried out without continuous correction. The notion that such correction is necessary has been derived from goal-seeking missiles which track the target as it moves. Human movement ordinarily does not track a target. It is aimed toward a stationary target, hence aimed in a given direction, never changing its aim. The only difference between slow and fast typing is that the muscles have become superbly organized during years of practice until the fingers have learned to move at speed. The same muscles engaged in the slow movement (and hence the same muscle pattern organized by the cerebellum) will be used in the fast movements, except for undue muscle tension, which gradually drops out with learning.

Eccles assumes that the nucleus interpositus in the cerebellum also influences the motor impulse through efferents to the spinal cord. But is is doubtful whether the connection from cerebellum to the spinal cord can materially influence a movement in progress. Mettler and Orioli (1957), for instance, have reported that ataxia cannot be produced in animals by sectioning the descending limb of the brachium conjunctivum and the rubrospinal tract, so interrupting the connection between cerebellum and spinal cord. Ataxia can be produced only when the ascending brachium conjunctivum is cut, so interruping the connection between cerebellum and motor cortex. Hence the influence of the cerebellum seems to be exerted upstream, on the motor cortex.

Not only does the coordination and timing of movements seem to depend on the relay from cerebellum to motor cortex, but so also does the strength of movement. Meyer-Lohman et al. (1975) found that cooling the cerebellar nuclei decreased the intensity of the intended component of the motor cortex discharge, while the pyramidal tract neurons showed no change.

The connection from motor cortex to cerebellum seems to report the movement in progress. As a result, the cerebellum can adapt the continuing action pattern in such a way that the following movement builds on the movement last made and reported.

In skilled movements like tennis, basketball, or baseball, where shoulder and arm muscles are used, the interposited as well as the dentate nuclei would have to be active in the programmed motor sequence. Strick (1979) recorded the electrical activity in these nuclei during the preparation for movement in monkeys. He trained the animals to pull a handle when a green light was shown and to push it when the light was red. The monkey had to wait until the handle he grasped moved automatically before starting to push or pull. Strick found that a reaction time interval of 70–100 msec intervened before the animal moved the handle. During this interval, the handle kept moving toward the animal automatically regardless of later push or pull. When potentials were recorded from interposited and dentate nuclei during this reaction time interval, Strick found that changes in electrical activity occurred in the interposited nuclei before changes in the dentate could be seen. Different motor sets (push or pull) did not affect the activity of interpositus neurons but profoundly influenced the response of dentate neurons. When the animal prepared to push, dentate neurons showed a short-latency increase in activity; when the animal prepared to pull, they showed a short-latency decrease.

Strick suggested that the short-latency changes in the interposited nuclei signaled the afferent input induced by the handle movement. However, he also mentioned that some ventrolateral thalamic neurons showed short-latency activity changes when the handle held by the animal was moved, and suggested that these changes relate more to the animal's corrective movements than to the afferent input. The same may apply to the activity changes in interposited nuclei. The short latency responses of dentate neurons, in contrast, depend on the animal's set or intention, and also on the direction of the intended movement. Such changes in electrical activity before movement, indicating an earlier "reflex" and later "intention" component, occur well after the corresponding changes in interposited and dentate cerebellar nuclei.

Hence it would seem that the cerebellum is part of a relay from association cortex to motor cortex, a link in what I have called the action circuit. Allen and Tsukahara (1974) seem to share the opinion that the cerebellum is a relay station in a circuit from association areas to the cerebral motor cortex. From the fact that the main afferents to the cerebellum come from the sensory cortical areas, they conclude that the cerebellum is involved in planning movements rather than executing them—which would imply a relay from the sensory cortical areas via the cerebellum to the motor cortex.

Cerebellar lesions and their effect on movement support the notion that the

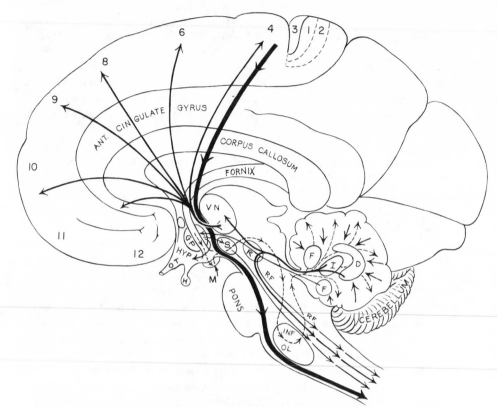

FIG. 13.3 The action circuit. When an appraisal produces an *intention to act,* relays run from limbic cortex to hippocampus. This generates an *impulse to act,* mediated by relays from hippocampus via fornix to mamillary body, reticular formation, inferior olive,and cerebellar cortex. Amplified and organized, motor relays go from there to (a) cerebellar dentate nucleus, ventrolateral and ventral anterior thalamic nucleus and frontal lobe; (b) interpositus nucleus, and either directly or via red nucleus to ventral thalamus and frontal lobe; (c) interpositus and fastigial nuclei to substantia nigra, striatum, ventral thalamus and frontal lobe. From the motor cortex, corticobulbar and corticospinal tracts run to medulla and spinal cord. _ _ _ _ Relay from hippocampus to cerebellum. ▬▬▬ Relay from cerebellum to frontal lobe. ▬▬▬ Relay from cerebellum to extrapyramidal and hypothalamic effectors. ▬▬ Corticospinal tract.

D dentate nucleus. F fastigial nucleus. GP globus pallidus. H hypophysis. HYP hypothalamus. I interposited nucleus. INF OL inferior olive. M mammillary body. OT optic tract. R red nucleus. RF brain stem reticular formation. S substantia nigra. VN ventral thalamic nuclei. (From M.B. Arnold, 1960)

170

cerebellum organizes limbs and muscles in spatial and temporal patterns of activation and relays the impulse to organized action to the motor cortex. After cerebellar lesions, movements become weak and ataxic, that is, abrupt, irregular, and clumsy. When such lesions are large, the patients cannot carry out smooth movements that involve several joints but have to make the movement joint by joint. One of Holmes' (1922) patients who had half his cerebellum shot away, described his impairment thus: "The movements of my left hand are done subconsciously, but I have to think out each movement of my right arm. I come to a dead stop in turning and have to think before I start again." Such a situation is intelligible if the cerebellum organizes body and limb movements and relays the organized pattern to the motor cortex. In addition, the feedback loop from the motor cortex back to the cerebellum would insure continuing coordination of intention with movement. But with one side of the cerebellum lost, the organization of the arm movement on the other side is disturbed, although the connection from association cortex via reticular formation to motor cortex could still supply the intention. With the overall organization of the movement pattern missing on one side, the patient has to initiate each link of a combined sequence separately.

From all these facts we can infer that a pathway from limbic cortex via hippocampus/fornix, cerebellum, and ventral thalamus to frontal cortex mediates the intention to act and relays an integrated action pattern to the motor cortex. The direction or goal of action seems to be provided by the motor cortex, which initiates action via the pyramidal and supporting pathways to the spinal cord (Fig. 13.3).

14 Motor Memory Registration

There are types of learning, especially in man, that appear to involve more than a simple linkage between sensory perception and motor performance. An important affective component has been added which appears to serve a function in the acquisition of the learned behavior, to be associated in its retrieval, and to guide its performance . . . [In] an interesting experiment . . . Ivanitskii . . . conditioned rabbit pups for the first five days of life to lift their heads in response to an odor presented during suckling. Then, after five days without this olfactory stimulus, during which the pups acquired their normal patterns of locomotion, the odor was again presented. Now, instead of merely lifting their heads, they ran toward it in a behavioral response that had never been coupled with the odor before. Obviously what had been learned was not a performance but an affective association (or, if you will, an appetitive drive).

S.S. Kety, 1976, p. 323

Although the functions of most cortical areas have been fairly well determined, the extensive prefrontal area anterior to the motor and premotor area (4 and 6) is still a minor mystery. Not only the old phrenologists but modern neuroanatomists (Kleist, 1934; Krieg, 1957) have suggested that this area serves "judgment and reasoning" or mediates "the elaboration of thought processes" despite the fact that prefrontal lobotomies and ablations undertaken to alleviate intractable pain have shown that patients with damaged frontal lobes are still able to think, reason, and judge (see Freeman & Watts, 1942). The notion that higher thought processes are "elaborated" in the brain seems to be based on the assumption that concepts, judgments, and thoughts, have to be produced by a particular part of the brain—and an area to which no other function can be assigned seemed to be the best candidate. This is on a par with the notion of earlier neurologists that the soul must have its seat in the brain; and because nobody has been able to discover it there with scalpel or electrode, it was finally decided that there cannot be a soul.

Surely, concepts are not tied to any particular sensory modality nor are they tied to particular words. They are abstracted from sensory experience and denoted by a particular speech, visual, or auditory pattern, a pattern that varies from language to language. Words expressing concepts are used in every human language and can be translated from one into the other. Since concepts are abstracted from experience, they depend on the normal functioning of the brain and cannot be tied to any one structure. The same is true for thinking or reasoning.

The experience of patients with damage in various brain areas confirms this point. If it is impossible for a patient with brain damage to *read* the word "chair," he may still be able to pronounce it and know what a chair is. As long as even one memory modality is intact, concepts can be used and understood because the relevant words can be spoken, heard, traced, or distinguished by touch (as the blind do in reading Braille).

More recently, it has been suggested that prefrontal damage results in a loss of the "abstract attitude" (Goldstein, 1949), so that the patient can no longer use concepts. However, it was found later that such patients can form and use concepts as easily as people with intact brain. What seems to have been impaired is motor imagination: The patient can no longer *pretend* to drink water or comb his hair, although he can carry out these actions when a comb or a glass of water is available. Pretending to do something requires a particular kind of imagination, not a general abstract attitude.

MOTOR MEMORY

Any purposeful movement implies a patterning of muscle action that depends on a knowledge of the object and the direction in which it can be reached. I must know that a ball can be caught with one or both hands; that in walking, movements in one direction will take me toward my goal, in another, away from it. Neurologists have talked about a "body schema" within which individual movements can be carried out. This means essentially that we can register movements and can preserve the disposition to repeat them when wanted or to draw on such memories in imagining various other movements. When a movement is registered, cortical cells have to be changed in such a way that a disposition to move in the same way is preserved. When this disposition is reactivated, it is strengthened and will eventually become a habit or skill.

Deficit after Prefrontal Damage.   There are many reports of prefrontal damage that imply a deficit in motor memory and imagination. Nielsen (1941), for
instance, mentions that frontal lesions have produced disorientation in space.
The patient can visualize directions and distances, yet cannot find his way. In
other words, he can neither remember nor imagine *what to do* to reach a particular place, no matter how well he has known his way in the past. That the prefrontal cortex is the motor association area seems also indicated by the fact that destruction of Broca's area (44) in the lateral part of the prefrontal cortex of the
dominant hemisphere produces an inability to speak, that is, a loss of speech
(motor) memories. This area lies at the level of the motor representation for
mouth and larynx. An area dorsal to Broca's area, at the level of the motor representation of hand and arm, is critical for writing. When it is damaged, the patient
is unable to write spontaneously, although he can copy what is put before him
(Nielsen, 1941, 1946; Luria, 1973a). Apparently, he can no longer draw on the
remembered movements that would form the appropriate letters. But when he
sees the letters, he can make the necessary movements.

At the time, these findings were generally discounted. But there are more recent reports, both from animal experiments and clinical findings, that allow the
same conclusion. For instance, Ghent, et al. (1962) reported that patients with
penetrating wounds of the frontal lobe were not impaired on spatial tasks (which
require visual memory) and digit span (which require auditory memory because
the patient has to listen to a series of digits); but patients with unilateral injury in
the left parieto-temporal region (visual and auditory memory area) showed a decided impairment. This report shows that patients with prefrontal injury do not
have a "short term memory deficit" as has sometimes been suggested; nor are
they impaired in visual or auditory memory.

That prefrontal damage produces a motor memory deficit can be inferred form
many reports of a delayed response deficit in animals. Wilson *et al.* (1963) investigated some suggestions as to the cause of this deficit. They showed that it cannot be explained on the assumption that the animal is "less able to overcome the
strongest response tendency," or as "intertrial interference," or an inability to
use position as a "bridging response." But such damage can be explained as a
deficit in motor memory. The animal has to remember *the intended movement*
toward the hidden food. When not distracted, the animal usually can retain the
response tendency and perform correctly if the delay is not too long. This means
that it can retain the motor image but cannot recall it. It is also possible that some
animals may recall where they *saw* the bait, which might account for the finding
that monkeys with prefrontal lesions often respond above chance on delayed response problems (Wilson, 1962).

There is a consistent and severe deficit in right/left alternation after bilateral
damage to the lateral frontal cortex (Mishkin & Pribram, 1955, and many others). This task depends on the animal remembering which way it had gone before
and imagining which way it has to go this time. Again, this deficit is a deficit in

motor memory: Alternation between two objects (e.g., cup/ash tray) is intact after prefrontal lesions because it depends on visual memory.

Kinetic versus Kinesthetic Memory.   There has been extraordinary resistance to the notion of motor memory, even in Russia, despite Pavlov's dictum that the frontal lobe represents the "motor analyzer." Of course, it is also possible that the English translator, aware of the ruling fashion, always translates "kinetic" as "kinesthetic."[1] Often, experimenters and theorists have said that animals with large lesions of the lateral frontal lobes do not seem to remember what happened before; but they always end up with complicated explanations that such memory is really kinesthetic memory. For instance, Pribram (1969) says: "When the frontal cortex of a monkey is damaged, the animal has difficulty performing tasks in which he has to remember what happened just a few seconds earlier" (p. 84). But he concludes that the mechanism organizing such memories is not located within the frontal association areas; these merely exercise control over the input via brainstem structures (Pribram, 1969, p. 86).

The reason for Pribram's failure to infer that the prefrontal cortex might be involved in registering motor engrams seems to be "an assumption that has never been satisfactorily answered, namely, that the performance of alternation tasks depends on some proprioceptive or kinesthetically maintained memory trace" (Pribram, 1961, p. 434). Since it is known that somatosensory discrimination demands an intact posterior association cortex, and that at least in primates "the posterior association areas are located among the various primary sensory areas and consist of subareas that are specific for each of the senses" (Pribram, 1969, p. 79), we would reasonably expect that proprioceptive and kinesthetic memories would be registered in the parietal association cortex. There is enough evidence to show that parietal lesions impair tactile as well as proprioceptive learning (e.g., weight discrimination). But parietal lesions have never produced impairment in right/left or up/down alternation. If alternation problems tap kinesthetic memory, as Pribram believes, that is passing strange. Prefrontal lesions, however, do produce impairment in right/left, up/down alternation— which should be reason enough to infer that this kind of performance depends not on kinesthetic but on kinetic (motor) memory, registered in the frontal association cortex.

One reason why the notion that motor learning depends on kinesthetic memory has become so entrenched is the conviction that movement is not possible

---

[1]For intance, Konorski (1973) says: "lesions sustained in the motor, or rather kinesthetic, centers also affects the instrumental CRs to various degrees. . . . The "movement center" in our model represents that area of the brain in which the kinesthetic pattern of the trained movement is being formed. In fact, we have good evidence to show that lesions in the premotor area have detrimental effects on the performance of manipulatory instrumental movements" (p. 179).

Here Konorski talks about the premotor area as a movement center, which surely means kinetic, not kinesthetic.

without afferent feedback. And this conviction was based on Sherrington's (1934) report that monkeys do not use a limb that has been deprived of sensory nerves, at least in their exploratory or goal-directed activity. If motor learning, as well as voluntary movement, depends on sensory feedback, the argument ran, motor learning must be kinesthetic learning.

In recent years, however, the notion that goal-directed movements require sensory feedback has been neatly demolished. Taub and Berman (1968) deafferented one arm in monkeys; and found, like Sherrington, that the monkeys did not use the deafferented limb. But when the intact arm was immobilized, they began to use the deafferented limb with no sign of impairment. In fact, when both arms or both legs were deprived of their sensory feedback, the monkeys began to use them normally after a short period of reluctance. Eventually, their movements were like those of intact animals, even when they were blindfolded. Taub and Berman speculate that the monkeys did not use the deafferented arm because the intact limb has an inhibiting effect on the damaged limb—analogous to the Schiff-Sherrington effect. Schiff and Sherrington found that decerebration produced plastic rigidity in all four limbs, which increased when the spinal cord was afterward sectioned at the midthoracic level. Hence, they claimed that "lower extremities ordinarily seem to have an inhibitory effect on forelimbs."

Release from Inhibition?   There was a time when a host of effects produced by brain lesions was thought to be the result of "release from inhibition." But today, even decerebrate rigidity is no longer thought to be a sign of release from inhibition but the result of the excitation of reticulospinal and vestibulospinal motor neurons (Ward, 1947). In Taub and Berman's monkeys, the motor system was intact, hence there was no reason for an inhibition of the deafferented limb by the intact limb. At any rate, the monkeys did use the arm deprived of sensory nerves after the other arm had been deafferented also—and this despite the supposed "inhibition" by the legs. It is far more reasonable to assume that an arm without its sensory nerves is not used because its position and movement can no longer be felt. As a result, the intact arm is used when arm movement is necessary. When the monkey has no intact arm to use (either because the intact arm is immobilized or because both arms have been deprived of their sensory nerves) his impulse to reach for something will finally lead to arm movement despite the lack of sensation. At any rate, the monkeys' movements eventually became normal: with both arms deafferented, they could learn and retain conditioned responses, could climb vertically and laterally with reasonable speed, could pick up raisins, could walk and run. Since then, it has been shown that motor tasks can be learned and retained without any visual or kinesthetic feedback (Linke, 1977).

Since motor learning is possible without kinesthetic feedback, it would have to depend on motor engrams, the residue of each movement, which are registered and later reactivated. It seems reasonable to suggest as I have done (Arnold,

1960), that the prefrontal association cortex is a motor memory area, that is, the area where motor memories are registered.

Registration of Movements and Movement Impulses.   Sensory memories are registered at arrival of the sensory projection in the cortical sensory association areas; but motor memories must necessarily be registered as soon as there is a movement or even an impulse to move. This means that movements are either registered on the way from motor cortex to periphery, which is extremely unlikely; or they have to be registered when the intention to move is experienced, that is, on arrival of impulses in the frontal lobe. When a movement is executed, relays in the action circuit reaching the prefrontal cortex would serve the registration of motor engrams. Next time a similar action is intended, relays can reactivate these engrams and relay them to the motor cortex.

When we are set to carry out a well-remembered action (playing tennis, typing, reciting a poem) this intention is carried out via the action circuit, which activates the motor engrams in the prefrontal lobe. According to Krieg (1954), the number of cortico-cortical association fibers conducting impulses increases progressively from the frontal pole to the motor cortex. Apparently, neural impulses are conducted from all prefrontal areas to the motor cortex—which would agree with the notion that the prefrontal areas register motor engrams that are later activated by relays over the action circuit and so influence the initiation of action via the motor cortex.

Every action is remembered, that is, registered and retained as a motor engram. This means that movements must be registered in sequence and retained in structure. Motor memory is registered in the course of motor action just as sense memory is registered in the course of sensory experience. Like sense memory, motor memory is registered not in the primary area (the motor cortex) but in the appropriate association cortex (prefrontal areas). In the course of a well-practiced action, for instance in playing golf or tennis, in swimming and skating, the action here and now is the end result of many previous movements that serve to make each movement fluid and certain.

Motor memories seem to be registered with every movement, but also with every intention to move, that is, whenever impulses arrive in the frontal cortex via the action circuit. Even when a movement is only imagined, it seems to be registered in the prefrontal area and to activate the premotor and motor cortex sufficiently to bring about action currents in the muscles. Jacobson (1932, 1934) has shown that such action currents can be recorded from the arm or leg muscles when a person imagines moving arm or leg, and from the eye muscles when he imagines looking at something. More than that, it is possible to learn a simple skill by imagining it in detail. Thus Beattie (1949) found that dart throwing could be learned just as effectively by imaginary practice as by real practice. This would indicate that imagined movements must be registered like actual movements. The intention to imagine movements, like the intention to move, initiates impulses via the action circuit which fans out over the frontal cortex and allows the registration of such imagined motions. When the actual movement is made (in testing dart throwing after imaginary practice), the action impulse activates the registered motor memories and effectively guides the movement.

Action does not only consist of overt movements. There is also an array of physiological changes that accompany these movements (Wang & Lu, 1930; Landau, 1953). Hence, when a movement is registered, the autonomic pattern that goes with it is registered as well. Such registration seems also to be mediated by various areas of the prefrontal cortex. This would explain, for instance, why prefrontal lobotomy produces an immediate relaxation of blood vessels. As soon as the fourth quadrant is cut, the patient's face loses its waxy pallor and becomes pink and healthy-looking (Freeman & Watts, 1942). Apparently, the autonomic memory pattern can no longer be activated and the chronic constriction of blood vessels resulting from anxiety is released.

In conclusion, I suggest that there is sufficient evidence to infer that the prefrontal association cortex mediates the registration of motor impulses (emotions, intentions) and actions. Just as the arrival of afferent impulses from sensory receptors in sensory cortical areas mediates the experience of objects, so the arrival of impulses in the premotor and motor areas indicates the intention to move. Such motor impulses are registered in the prefrontal cortex and preserved as dispositions to the same kind of movement. The corpus callosum and the various commissures serve the transfer of such motor memory engrams from one hemisphere to the other. The registration of motor impulses occurs during all motor activity, including motor learning and motor imagination.

AFFECTIVE MOTOR MEMORY

Affective motor memory, like affective sensory memory, is mediated by the limbic areas that serve the registration of appraisal, namely, the anterior cingulate gyrus and the anterior insula, and the medial orbital cortex.

A simple appraisal of something seen, heard, even imagined, is sufficient to arouse an action impulse: We like or dislike it, want to approach or withdraw. But to feel a definite emotion like fear or anger, love or hate, we must appraise not only the situation but also the required action. We may dislike something and turn away from it: We feel aversion. But if we feel that it is threatening serious harm, we are afraid and try to escape. If, on the other hand, we feel strong enough to overcome it, we are angry and attack. An emotion requires both an intuitive appraisal of the situation and an intuitive appraisal of possible action. I would paraphrase William James' dictum, "we run, therefore we are afraid" by saying, "we feel an urge to run—we are afraid." The beginning of fear comes with the appraisal of the situation as dangerous. Fear is full-blown following the intuitive (unconscious) appraisal that running is the thing to do.

Every appraisal of an action or action impulse is registered and will be reactivated when we appraise a similar action. Habitual actions feel "good, suitable" and are done without thinking. When the original impulse was to attack or flee, we are twice as ready to do so in a similar situation. The emotion we experience has added urgency because affective motor memory adds to its impulsion. Affective motor memory is a disposition to re-experience the appraisals of similar earlier actions and feel anew the emotions felt before. It accounts for the cumulative urge to run in fear, to attack in anger, to withdraw in despair. Every new appraisal of a situation as threatening induces an impulse to flee, which is strengthened by earlier fear impulses and in turn adds its weight to theirs.

Since fear is accompanied by various physiological changes, and the whole complex is touched off by the intuitive appraisal, every new fear, given in to, increases the urge to flee. If someone gives in to fear repeatedly and avoids confrontation, his fear will grow and spread. If narrowly focused, fear may become phobia. If directed toward new situations, it can become anxiety. Fear becomes "generalized" because it is preserved in affective memory as a revived appraisal of similar situations that leads to similar actions.

With every fear impulse, associated motor impulses induce the secretion of adrenaline from the adrenal medulla, raise blood pressure and heart rate, and produce muscular tremor (see Arnold, 1960, vol. 2). When fear becomes chronic anxiety, the continuing effect of these physiological changes leads to the typical fatigue, reduction of performance, and even exhaustion so prevalent in anxiety neurotics.

Prefrontal lobotomy prevents the activation of affective motor memories because the motor memory circuit is cut between thalamus and prefrontal cortex. Hence the immediate muscular relaxation as soon as the fourth brain quadrant is cut (see Freeman & Watts, 1942). Anxiety is also reduced, but usually the effect wears off after a while. Prefrontal lobotomy prevents only the reactivation of the affective motor memory pattern with its physiological symptoms. The disposition to appraise a situation as dangerous remains. Everything that used to arouse fear will still be appraised as dangerous and will arouse fear. The only gain is that the patient is no longer overwhelmed by the cumulative impulses to flee with their cumulative physiological changes. But without some help in appraising a situation more objectively, the patient will experience the same shrinking and be urged to the same actions.

Affective Memory of Success and Failure

The motor appraisal areas (anterior cingulate gyrus, anterior insula, medial orbital area) are important also for appraising the consequences of action. Children learn that they cannot say or do everything they want. In the course of growing up, the girl or boy learns what to do and what not to do to be popular. All of us have to learn to guard our tongue and to refrain from impulsive action. Such discipline requires the evaluation of our action impulses before they are ex-pressed in action. Though it may be learned slowly, such evaluation becomes automatic with time. It becomes an affective motor memory ready to be reactivated with the next action impulse. When such memory no longer directs the appraisal of action impulses because the circuit activating the frontal ap-praisal area is cut, as in prefrontal lobotomy, the patient does and says what his momentary impulse dictates. According to Yakovlev et al. (1950), the cingulate gyrus, the anterior and dorsomedial thalamic nuclei and the insula are all dam-aged in lobotomy; hence the patient's impulsiveness in speech and behavior, and his difficulty in planning action (see Freeman, 1951).

LIMBIC MOTOR MEMORY AREAS

The Anterior Cingulate Gyrus

Ward's (1948) experimental ablation of the cingulate gyrus in monkeys, dis-cussed in chapter 11, included both the anterior and posterior portion. The de-struction of the anterior cingulate gyrus seems to account for most of the behavior changes. As Ward said, the animals took food wherever they found it, even out of the hand of another monkey. They showed no concern for their fellows, would push them aside or even sit on them. According to my theory, the anterior cingu-late gyrus mediates the appraisal of action impulses and actions. No longer able to appraise their impulses, the monkeys acted impulsively, completely oblivious to the reactions of their fellows.

Affective Motor Memory Deficit after Lesions.   Stamm (1955) and Slotnick (1967) reported that cingulate lesions disrupted the maternal behavior of rats. The animals no longer built nests. They might begin to retrieve their young but soon dropped them again. Instinct apparently urged the rats to pick up their pups, but they could no longer appraise their actions, so they never finished what they had started. They had the urge to pick up strips of paper but soon dropped them again instead of using them to build a nest. According to Wilsoncroft (1963), anterior cingulate lesions disrupted maternal behavior far more than posterior cingulate lesions.

Undercutting of the cingulate gyrus has been used in psychosurgery. Obsessional and ritualistic behavior disappeared, but the patients became irrita-ble and impatient (Tow & Whitty, 1953). Without the intuitive appraisal of their action impulses, they gave free rein to their impatience no matter how petty the cause. They could do without their obsessional ritual because they could no longer appraise the possible consequences of omitting them, and suffered no longer from the fear the ritual was meant to prevent.

That the anterior cingulate gyrus is involved in the appraisal of success or failure has been shown by Niki (1979). He trained monkeys to depress a key for food, after depressing a "hold" lever which illuminated the key. If the monkey held the lever for at least two seconds, the illumination was turned off and a juice reward appeared. When the monkey had reached a criterion of 90% correct responses, recording electrodes were installed in various cortical areas. In the banks of the anterior cingulate sulcus, Niki found several units that increased firing when the monkey had made an error, but also when the juice did not appear after a correct response, or the juice was delayed. As soon as the juice was given, normal electrical activity returned to these anterior cingulate sulcus cells. This experiment illustrates nicely that the anterior cingulate gyrus mediates the appraisal of success or failure. It does not merely detect an error, as is usually assumed. The non-appearance or delay of a reward after a correct response is not an error.

Thompson and Langer (1963) reported that precallosal limbic cortex lesions produced a significant deficit in learning to reverse a position habit. Rats with lesions in the caudal part of the anterior cingulate gyrus had no deficit. In this task, the rat had to run to the safe compartment in one end of a T-maze by knocking down an unlocked card. When pushing against a locked card in reversal training, the rat was shocked through the feet. In this situation, the animal had to remember the turn that brought the shock, and on the next trial take the turn into the other arm of the T-maze. Learning the reversal required motor memory but also the affective motor memory that the turn is now "bad." Precallosal limbic cortex lesions eliminated affective motor memory. Rats with lesions in the caudal part of the anterior cingulate gyrus had no deficit because their affective motor memory was largely intact; and so was at least part of the posterior cingulate gyrus, which mediates the affective memory of shock.

Barker and Thomas (1965, 1966) found that animals with anterior cingulate lesions were greatly impaired in mastering a single runway problem in which they were rewarded only on alternate trials. The impairment was related to the amount of retrograde degeneration in the anterior thalamic nucleus (which is a relay station in the affective memory circuit). Barker (1967) also found a deficit in learning alternating bar presses for reward. And Pribram et al. (1962) reported that anterior cingulate lesions prevented the retention of delayed alternation. All these deficits stem from the animals' inability to appraise their actions and recall their success or failure. In a similar vein, Glass et al. (1969) suggested that the lesioned animals are unable to anticipate the emotional consequences of their behavior, whether reward or punishment. They consider the deficit a failure of anticipation, which is essentially a failure to imagine what is likely to happen. This could be part of the explanation because such lesions interrupt relays from amygdala to limbic cortex, including the anterior cingulate gyrus, so preventing relays from the imagination circuit to reactivate the affective memory of success or failure. But in Conneely's (1967) lesions, this connection was spared, yet the animals had a passive avoidance deficit. In the end, it is a question of internal consistency on which the value of any theory must be decided. Glass et al. only explain anterior cingulate lesions. My theory can explain these lesions together with lesions in other limbic structures on the basis of one well-integrated theory.

Anterior Insula

Lesions of this structure, whether bilateral or unilateral, impaired successive olfactory and successive visual discrimination in our experiments at Loyola University of Chicago (unpublished). According to my theory, the anterior insula
mediates the appraisal and affective memory of head and probably foreleg movements. After the lesion, the animals could no longer remember that dipping the
head to drink brought shock (deficient affective motor memory for head movements), hence the impairment in the successive olfactory task. And they could
not remember that pressing the bar for water was good during flashing light but
bad when the light was steady (deficient affective motor memory for paw movements); hence the impairment in a successive visual task. In contrast, rats with
anterior insula lesions were unimpaired in learning an active avoidance and a
single alternation task. These tasks depended on whole body movement, appraised via anterior cingulate, and this structure was intact.

Similar results were reported by Kaada et al. (1962) and Kveim et al. (1964).
They found that rats with anterior insula lesions kept on drinking from a dish
through which they had been shocked before, hence revealed a passive avoidance
deficit. Even when animals refrained from drinking, Kaada et al. reported, they
would "remain motionless for several seconds, leaning over the dish and then
suddenly withdrawing" (p. 662). This nicely illustrates the difficulty such animals have in remembering whether drinking had brought pain.

Damage to the frontal lobes has to be carefully assessed if the impairment of
the lesioned animals is to be correctly explained. The animal may not remember
what to do, or it may no longer be able to plan or appraise its movements, and so
respond to the negative as well as to the positive cue. Failure to distinguish between motor memory impairment and impairment of affective motor memory accounts for many contradictory findings. Some of these problems are discussed in
chapters 15 and 16.

15 Motor Memory Deficits After Frontal Lesions

Numerous observations have . . . . revealed the role of the frontal lobes in the execution of complex programs of activity . . . and the organization of strategy. Further, their role in . . . matching the effect or consequence of action to the initial intention . . . is the basis of the . . . modification of action . . . . (p.22)

The frontal lobes do not present a single and homogeneous system and the role played by their separate parts in the organization of behavior is not uniform. It is . . well known that the polar and medial (and perhaps also mediobasal) parts of the frontal lobes participate in the regulation of the state of activation . . . Furthermore, we know that the convexal parts of the frontal lobe (and especially the posterofrontal parts of the cortex) preserve an intimate connection with the cortical parts of the motor analyzer and that [a] lesion in this location as a rule, leads to . . . a derangement in the complex forms of organization of movements. (p. 23)

A. R. Luria, 1973b

Every learned performance includes a motor component in addition to the required sensory discrimination. If the frontal lobe serves movement, movement impulses, and motor memory, as I am suggesting, frontal lesions should result in a significant impairment of learned responses and also of any sensory discrimination that requires more than simple approach or avoidance. There is a vast literature reporting on the result of frontal damage, both in human beings and in animals. I can mention only a selected sample. Of course, the evidence must be interpreted with caution. In most lesions, whether produced by disease, accident, or surgery, more than one structure or functional unit is damaged. A lesion may disturb fibers of passage in addition to cortical cells. Anyone who tries to interpret the resulting deficit as the effect of a circumscribed lesion, without considering the neighboring areas or the fibers of passage that may have been affected, runs the risk of misinterpretation.

I believe that the effects of such lesions can only be explained on the basis of some scheme of overall brain function such as my theory has tried to provide. The circuits I have postulated (recall, affective memory, imagination, and action circuits) often run side by side for some distance and can be identified only if the results of a variety of lesions are compared. These circuits have been inferred from a wide array of research findings in the literature up to the late fifties (see Arnold, 1960, vol. 2). I propose to examine relevant research reports since that date to show that later findings provide additional support.

MEMORY IMPAIRMENT AFTER FRONTAL LESIONS

Clinical reports of deficits after various kinds of brain damage are often difficult to evaluate. During the patient's lifetime, it is not easy to find the exact site and extent of the lesions, and post-mortem reports are not always available. In addition, the reported memory impairment is not always based on a systematic and exhaustive psychological investigation, so that it is often difficult to assess the psychological deficit. For instance, most of the time, the personality change often found after frontal lobe damage is described in such general terms that it is difficult to know just what brain function could be impaired.

Luria's Results

The Russian school, following Pavlov, considers the prefrontal area the third area of the motor analyzer, serving the highest synthesis and the most delicate differentiation. Despite this theoretical stance, Russian psychologists, like their Western colleagues, have made no attempt to locate motor engrams in this area. They seem to accept the notion that motor learning is essentially kinesthetic[1] learning. At the same time, the painstaking and extensive work of Luria and his school has provided a wealth of material that supplies evidence for the motor and motor memory function of the frontal lobe. For instance, Luria (1966a) mentions that patients with frontal damage "proved almost untrainable (in the occupational therapy workshops) despite the absence of signs of pareses or apraxia" (p. 249). As an example, he mentions a patient who began to work in the carpenter shop of the hospital and "kept on planing a plank until he had planed it completely through and started to plane the bench. "These patients could understand

---

[1]According to English translations.

and repeat verbal instructions (for instance, to tap three times, or squeeze the doctor's hand three times), but they might tap or squeeze any number of times. Despite the patient's intact auditory memory (he could understand and repeat the instructions), he was unable to stop tapping or squeezing when the specified number had been reached. This indicates an inability to evaluate his performance and stop it at the right time because the connection with the anterior cingulate gyrus and the anterior insula, the motor appraisal areas, was broken by the frontal lesion.

Luria also mentions that patients with massive lesions of the frontal convexity have great difficulty in carrying out a complex motor program. Instead, they "perseverate," that is, they continue with the same action. For instance, a patient was asked to draw spectacles, and did so. Next, he was asked to draw a watch. Instead, he continued to draw spectacles despite his effort to follow instructions. Eventually, he added figures and watch hands to one spectacle lens. This illustrates the patient's inability to use motor imagination. In a massive lesion, not only the motor registration area but the imagination circuit is affected as it spreads out from the dorsomedial nucleus into the frontal lobe. To draw spectacles or a watch, the patient must visualize each of the two objects and then draw them. When drawing the eyeglasses, he lays down a motor engram which is reactivated as he attempts another drawing. Without motor imagination to plan and guide his movements, his drawing follows the facilitated path—and he draws another pair of spectacles. The same inability to imagine or plan what is to be done is implied by Luria's report that such a patient does not look around or look for the significant features of a picture even when instructed to do so.

Finally, Luria mentions the difficulty these patients experience in memorizing a series of words or numbers. A normal person pays particular attention to the words he has missed on the first presentation of the series and gradually increases the number of words learned. The patient with frontal damage learns three or four words and repeats these, however often the series is given, without any improvement. As Luria points out, such patients are unable to correct the mistakes they make and go on repeating them. It seems fairly obvious that these patients cannot evaluate their performance, nor can they make any corrections because they can no longer imagine what to do. This seems to point to damage of the imagination circuit and the connection with the motor appraisal area. Luria's interpretation implies these deficits but is couched in such general terms that it is impossible to form any opinion as to the structures involved. He says:

> Characteristically, the preliminary investigative stage required for a complex activity is omitted or becomes too unstable, the system of associations that should regulate the subsequent course of the mental process is not formed, and the patient's actions fall under the influence of inert afterimages of past experience or of extraneous stimuli and, consequently, irrelevant associations. In the absence of continuous comparison between the plan of action as prescribed by the instruction and the re-

sults actually obtained, the mistakes that arise are not rectified by the patient himself. (1966a, p. 292)

In other words, the patient cannot plan (imagine) the correct action, hence lets himself be guided by irrelevant motor memories and cannot correct his action.

Russian investigators also report that premotor lesions disturb the comprehension of complex sentences. For instance, the sentence: "To rule the country, the monarch relies on the aid of the governing classes, and is subservient to their will," poses a difficult problem for such patients. One patient said: "If I read it through once, I grasp only a few words and do not understand what it means . . . I have to read it many times, to pick out the ideas and put them together, and then I can understand it" (Luria, 1943). It was still more difficult, if not impossible, for him to comprehend the sentence if he was told that he must not read it aloud. Reading the sentence aloud brings in auditory memory in addition to visual memory, both of which are intact. Also, reading aloud focuses the patient's attention on what he is doing. Since easy distractibility is another symptom of frontal lobe damage, this focusing of attention is of considerable help. Such patients have the same difficulty in arithmetic problems. Here as in the comprehension of complicated sentences, the patient does not seem to know what to do—or better, how to make a plan and translate it into action. This indicates an inability to imagine what to do and also, to set his intention. The former is the result of the interrupted imagination circuit, the latter, of the premotor lesion itself. I have suggested that the premotor area initiates motor impulses, including attention (see Ch. 17, also Arnold, 1960).

Despite these reports of seriously disturbed functioning, the patients' tested intelligence seems to be unimpaired after prefrontal lobotomy or frontal lesions (Mettler, 1949; Hebb, 1950; LeBeau, 1954; Ghent et al., 1962). Hence, says Luria, "the frontal syndrome is characterized by an inherent contradiction—the potentially preserved 'formal intellect' and the profoundly disturbed intellectual activity" (1966a, p. 292).

Actually, these findings are not necessarily contradictory. In the first place, most of the reports of intact intelligence concern lobotomized or topectomized patients (Mettler, 1949, LeBeau, 1954), whose motor appraisal areas certainly were intact. Secondly, intelligence tests do not require motor imagination; the only test item that does is the "open field" test in the Binet scale. Other tests that require motor imagination are the Porteus Maze test, as well as the form board and the Kohs block test; and in all these tests, lobotomized patients and patients with frontal damage are deficient. Regular intelligence tests require intact visual and auditory memory rather than motor imagination.

Ghent's Results

Even when psychologists try to go beyond these tests of general intelligence and devise special procedures to test impairment after frontal damage, they do not test motor memory or motor imagination. For instance, Ghent et al. (1962) tried to devise tasks analogous to the delayed response tasks that have shown significant impairment in animals with frontal lesions. The six tasks selected were: line test, tactual point localization, visual point localization, digit span, form span, and body tilt. It may be instructive to discuss these six tests to discover the functions they require.

1. Line Test.   The patient had to judge the point at which the tilt of a fluorescent tube, turned by the experimenter, matched the original tilt. This task requires visual memory and appraisal (visual memory areas 18, 19, and the posterior hippocampal gyrus). There is no reason why prefrontal lobotomy should interfere with it.

2. Tactual Point Localization.   With eyes closed, the patient sat with palm upturned on his knee. The experimenter touched a point on his palm with a blunt stylus for two seconds. Either immediately afterwards, or after a delay of 15 seconds, he touched the palm again several times and the patient had to decide which touch matched the original one. This task requires touch memory and appraisal, mediated by the somesthetic memory area in the parietal lobe and the somesthetic appraisal area in the posterior cingulate gyrus and posterior insula.

3. Visual Point Localization.   The patient had to match the position of a target moving on the perimeter with the original positions. This task, like the line test, requires visual memory and appraisal areas.

4. Digit Span.   The digits were given orally. This means that auditory memory and appraisal were involved (via temporal association area and posterior insula). Again, there is no reason why frontal damage should produce impairment.

5. Form Span.   Ten forms from the Seguin-Goddard form board had to be memorized with eyes closed. Next, sample blocks were placed randomly and the patient was instructed (either immediately or after 15 seconds) to locate them and reconstruct them in the original order. This task also can be solved by using visual memory and appraisal.

6. Body Tilt.   The patient, blindfolded, sat in a chair which was tilted 20° for five seconds. He was told to remember the tilt. The chair was then returned to the upright position. Next, the chair was tilted slowly until the patient reported that it had reached the original tilt. This was described as a "spatial orientation task." Functionally, it required kinesthetic memory and appraisal. In all these tasks, the appraisal was always "this is familiar or unfamiliar."

The patients used in this study were male veterans with penetrating wounds of the frontal lobes. The controls were veterans with leg wounds and veterans with brain injury outside the frontal lobes. None of the tests showed any difference between the three groups. According to the authors, these tests were intended to sample short-term memory in various dimensions because delayed response impairment in animals has often been described as a defect in "short-term memory." Obviously, frontal lobe damage in these patients did not produce short-term memory impairment. The authors also mention another hypothesis, namely, that delayed response impairment is a "defect in recall mediated by kinesthetic-orientational cues." They mention the line test and the body tilt test as providing such cues. There was no impairment in either test.

As I have tried to show, memory is not a unitary function but is modality-specific; and there is no reason to expect a defect in visual, auditory, tactual, or kinesthetic memory after lesions of the frontal lobes. The delayed response impairment in animals with frontal damage is not a defect in a generalized "short-term memory" or in kinesthetic recall but the result of impaired motor memory. If there is a delay, the animal is unable to remember what it had intended to do. Without the delay, the intention is formed and carried out immediately via the action circuit and its connection with the premotor and motor area.

It is difficult to duplicate the task the animal is facing. The human being has means at his disposal that help him remember his intention: He can remember hearing the instructions, he can repeat them to himself (which will produce a motor speech memory), or he can visualize the task and so renew his intention. The animal who cannot understand instructions or repeat them is completely dependent on his memory of the intended move.

In this connection it is interesting that patients with prefrontal lesions could correctly assess whether lines shown to them were vertical or oblique as long as they themselves were in an upright position. But when they were tilted, they made gross errors (Teuber, 1959, 1964). To judge whether the lines were tilted when they themselves sat in a tilted chair, the patients would have to imagine themselves upright. Only motor imagination, based on motor memory, could have provided the basis for comparison. Apparently, their prefrontal lesion made it impossible for them to imagine themselves upright because it interfered with the motor recall and imagination circuits.

There is a considerable literature on the psychological impairment after frontal lesions. In particular, the works by Luria (1966a,b, 1973a,b) are recommended reading. The reported deficit, complicated though it seems, can be explained as a deficit in motor imagination (planning), motor memory and (in premotor lesions) the impulse to action. The memory deficits in split-brain patients have also contributed to our knowledge of frontal lobe function (see Chapter 19).

Animal Experiments

In animal experiments, it is possible to destroy a particular structure or area and compare the performance of the lesioned animals with the performance of intact animals. Pribram (1973) has pointed out that there are at least three subdivisions of the frontal lobe that represent functional units. If these differences in function are not recognized, there is bound to be confusion when the effects of frontal lesions are assessed. As he says, "differences in results obtained in various investigations might well be expected when different amounts of cortex from each of these categories have been included in the lesion" (1973, p. 294).

The first of these subdivisions is the lateral and polar extent of the frontal lobes. This area receives impulses from the major small-celled part of the dorsomedial thalamic nucleus. The second area, the medial frontal lobes, receive projections from the anterior and other limbic nuclei of the thalamus (see chapter 16, p. 213). And the third region, the posterior orbital cortex, receives impulses from the magnocellular portion of the dorsomedial nucleus and is connected with the neighboring anterior insular, temporal polar and periamygdaloid cortex.

According to my theory, the dorsolateral frontal cortex serves the registration of motor memories. Its connection with the parvocellular portion of the dorsomedial nucleus represents the thalamocortical part of the motor imagination circuit (see Fig. 16.4). It also receives the projection from the caudate and the ventral anterior thalamic nucleus, which is the cortical part of the action circuit. In my theory, the action circuit is associated with the motor memory circuit which serves the registration and recall of motor memories; the motor imagination circuit activates the same memory areas but allows us to rearrange and recombine motor memories.

The medial frontal lobe with the anterior cingulate gyrus serves the appraisal of body and limb movements and of movement impulses, and also the registration of such motor appraisals, that is, affective motor memory. The anterior insula mediates the appraisal of mouth, hand, and head movements, including speech movements in the human being. Many research findings support my theory of frontal lobe function.

Delayed Response.   Since Jacobsen (1935) first found delayed response deficits in animals with frontal lesions, this impairment has been reported regularly in such animals (Mishkin & Pribram, 1956a). In the simplest version of delayed response experiments, a peanut is placed under one of two cups in a monkey's view; then a screen is lowered. After a variable delay, the screen is lifted to let the monkey find the peanut under the cup. Jacobsen (1935, 1936) suggested that the monkey's inability to do so is the result of a "loss of recent memory," and this notion has lingered despite the fact that specific visual, auditory and tactual discriminations, which also are based on recent memory, are not impaired after frontal lesions (Ghent et al., 1962). Many other explanations have been proposed, but experimental tests have not supported them. Wilson (1962) and Wilson et al. (1963) reviewed some of these theories and found that the deficit cannot be explained as "lack of inhibition," nor an "inability to overcome the strongest response tendency." It is neither "intertrial interference," nor an "inability to use position as a 'bridging response'." All these possibilities have been ruled out by experiment. These authors also pointed out that animals with frontal lesions are no more active on incorrect than on correct choices, hence their well-known hyperactivity also does not explain the deficit. When such an animal is not distracted, it can learn to make the correct response; it has been shown that animals with frontal lesions are more distractible than intact animals. All these deficits stem from a loss of motor memory.

Alternation and Delayed Alternation.   The standard procedure for left/right alternation is to bait one of two covered cups so that each cup contains food on alternate trials. The monkey has to try one cup. If he finds a peanut there, the peanut will be in the other cup on the next trial (baited procedure). If he finds no peanut on the first trial, he must choose the other cup on the next trial to find the peanut (unbaited procedure). Both procedures use either left/right or up/down alternation.

In delayed alternation tasks, the monkey watches one of the cups being baited. Then a screen is lowered and, after a short delay, removed again so that the monkey can reach for his peanut. After each trial the screen is lowered. The peanut is always in the alternate cup and the monkey has to remember in which cup he found the peanut on the last trial.

THEORIES OF FRONTAL FUNCTION

As with the delayed response problem, so with alternation and delayed alternation: a great many different theories have been offered to explain the reason for the impairment in this task after frontal lesions (Wilson, 1962; Mishkin, 1964; Pribram, 1973; Grueninger & Grueninger, 1973), but none of them have accounted for all the results. I would like to discuss two of the more recent theories.

Pribram's Views.   Pribram (1973), for instance, feels

> reasonably sure that the dorsolateral frontal cortex, like the limbic formations of the forebrain (including the medial and orbital frontal cortex) are concerned in the inhibition of interference among brain events. With respect to lesions of the frontal cortex, this involvement becomes manifest on the input side as a difficulty in attention, a difficulty in registering novelty so that habituation, or assimilation, fails to take place. On the output side, the feedback to actions from their outcomes is impaired and reinforcers become relatively ineffective. The intact frontal brain tissue must help to accomplish registration and reinforcement. (p. 306)

Pribram suggests that the frontal cortex is needed to supply "executive programs when these are necessary to maintain brain organization in the face of insufficient redundancy in input processing and in the outcomes of behavior" (p. 312). This is the reason, he thinks, why monkeys are successful when they are given visual or auditory tasks that supply them with external cues. Only when such external organization is not available must the animal draw on his frontal cortex for an internal "executive program."

Pribram uses a computer analogy to describe psychological reality—which prevents him from identifying the psychological functions involved. On the input side, Pribram sees the impairment after frontal lesions as a difficulty in registering novelty so that habituation fails. But frontally lesioned animals learn a visual or auditory discrimination as quickly as do intact animals. Attention may be disturbed if the lesion encroaches upon the premotor cortex and interferes with the impulse to look and listen. On the output side, Pribram mentions that feedback from action outcomes is impaired so that reinforcement fails. This happens when the limbic cortex is involved. According to my theory, motivation fails if the animal can no longer appraise the outcome of its actions. There is no doubt that the frontal cortex is needed to supply an "executive program"—it registers motor engrams that must be recalled for effective action. An executive program means that the animal must plan for action; in other words, the animal needs motor imagination in addition to motor memory. Several subdivisions of the frontal lobes are involved in one or other of these functions: the anterior cingulate and subcallosal limbic cortex, in the appraisal of action impulses, actions, and their outcomes; the dorsolateral cortex, in imagining (planning) action and in drawing on past motor memories; and the premotor cortex, in the impulse to attention and action.

The Views of Grueninger and Grueninger (1973).   These authors speculate that

> "the frontal eugranular isocortex evolved as part of a biological interface that couples the flickering evanescence of the neocortical information processing systems to the plodding neural elements of the more primitive layers of the brain. The dorsolateral frontal cortex in particular has been portrayed as part of a buffer register which stabilizes allassostatic[2] readjustments until appropriate internal or external responses have been completed. If anything at all is stored within the substance of the frontal cortex, even temporarily, it is not the dying image of a spatial past, but a pattern of efferent activity that promotes the completion of any Plan being executed." (p. 288)

Shorn of the poetry, the authors are saying that the prefrontal cortex is intimately connected with the limbic system; the dorsolateral area is involved in planning, not memory. The "Plan" is the plan of action as outlined by Miller et al. (1960). Grueninger and Grueninger explain: "The biological buffer register functions to maintain the relative facilitation of the Plan being executed, thus suppressing irrelevant inputs as well as suppressing possible competing re-

---

[2]Allassostasis: a process whereby the basic homeostatic systems are influenced by external events (Grueninger & Grueninger, 1973, p. 271).

sponses or response tendencies . . . . By allowing relevant inputs to both set and reset the system, the mechanism . . . does parse the temporal flow (as Pribram & Tubbs, 1967, suggested), and, by maintaining stability until resetting occurs it makes it possible for the organism to compare the outcomes of its actions with its expectancy or intention'' (p. 287). Grueninger and Grueninger's insistence on plan and intention emphasizes motor imagination at the cost of motor memory. They do say, however, that the biological buffer registers functions (in my terms: every action is registered in the frontal lobe as a motor memory) which can be said to suppress competing response tendencies. Thus they imply something like motor registration but put the function of the frontal lobes into negative terms. Motor imagination and motor recall do provide an organized behavioral sequence and incidentally suppress irrelevant action tendencies. The setting and resetting of the system occurs because the intact animal can appraise its actions and the outcome and change its behavior as required.

My Theory.   Alternation and delayed response also can easily be explained on the basis of my theory. The dorsolateral frontal cortex, with premotor and motor cortex the projection area of the ventral thalamic nuclei, mediates the registration of motor memories whenever the action circuit is activated; and the projection from the small-celled part of the dorsomedial thalamic nucleus to dorsolateral frontal cortex serves motor imagination. In delayed response tasks, the animal with lesions in the dorsolateral frontal cortex no longer remembers his *impulse to move* toward the cup under which he saw the experimenter hide the peanut. The animal is "distractible." When the animal is not distracted, for instance when he sits in the dark during the delay, he can make the correct response. Apparently, he remembers *seeing* the experimenter hide the peanut because no other visual experiences interfere, and so can form the intention to move toward the correct cup as soon as the screen is lifted. Frontally lesioned animals can learn a delayed response when the delay is short and is lengthened gradually, and for the same reason. The shorter the delay, the easier it is to recall the visual image. Gradually, the animals learn to depend on their visual memory instead of their motor memory. In fact, some animals may use their visual memory on occasion even in tasks with a longer delay, which would account for the finding that monkeys with mid- or dorsolateral lesions often respond above chance on delayed response problems (Wilson, 1962).

Left/right, up/down alternation and delayed alternation are impaired because the monkey can no longer remember what he did in the last trial, whether he went to the right or left cup, the cup above or the one below. In the delayed response task, the frontally lesioned monkey forgets during the delay that he wanted to move to this or that cup; in the alternation task, he forgets during the intertrial interval what he did in the last trial. In both cases, there is an impairment in motor memory because the area that ordinarily registers these memories has been destroyed.

EXPERIMENTAL EXPLORATIONS

In an attempt to discover the factors that account for the impairment after frontal lesions, experimenters have explored many variations of these two types of problem. I now examine some of these variations.

Go/No Go Problems. Mishkin and Pribram (1956b) reported that monkeys with lateral frontal lesions who had failed to learn a classical delayed response task were successful when the problem was changed to a go/no go task. In this task, a peanut and an empty hand were shown alternatively above a single cup. The monkey found a peanut in the cup after a peanut had been shown over it, and no peanut if the empty hand had appeared. In this problem, the monkey had to remember the "good" peanut (affective visual memory) and go, or the "bad" empty hand and refrain from going. The difference between the delayed response task on which monkeys with frontal lesions are impaired and the go/no go task on which they are not lies in the fact that they have to use motor memory in the delayed response task (to remember to which cup they wanted to go) and can use visual affective memory in the go/no go task (i.e., they have to remember the "good" or "bad" object).

Similar results have been obtained with the so-called indirect method (Mishkin & Pribram, 1956b). A positive and a negative object were shown on top of two cups in the predelay period; after the delay, the monkey had to go to the cup on which he had seen the positive object to find the peanut. All animals with lateral frontal lesions were unable to learn this task but monkeys with inferotemporal lesions had no difficulty. Frontal lesions prevented the monkeys from remembering their intention to go left or right; inferotemporal lesions did not. But when Mishkin and Pribram used a single cup with either the positive or the negative object on top of it, monkeys with both types of lesion learned this go/no go task, although the monkeys with frontal lesions took slightly longer.

Rosvold et al. (1961) reported that chimpanzees, like monkeys, are impaired in delayed response tasks after lateral frontal lesions, but they can relearn a go/no go delayed response almost perfectly. Unlike monkeys, they are also able to improve their performance on delayed response with two cups to above 70% correct. The difference between monkeys and chimpanzees seems to lie in the greater flexibility of the chimpanzee who can employ affective visual memory (via posterior hippocampus) and affective motor memory (via anterior cingulate gyrus) when motor memory itself is no longer available (left cup and going left is "good," right cup and going right is "bad"). Visual and motor appraisal areas were intact.

Object Alternation. Pribram and Mishkin (1956) reported that monkeys with lateral frontal lesions are also severely impaired on object alternation. In this task, they have to choose the object (tobacco tin or ashtray) that had not been rewarded on the previous trial, regardless of its position (left or right). Inferotemporal lesions did not interfere with learning. Since the position of the object changes, the monkey must remember not only which object he had approached successfully, he must also plan to which cup he should go this time. He needs affective motor memory (anterior cingulate) which is intact, but also motor imagination (projection from dorsomedial thalamic nuclei to dorsolateral frontal cortex) which is obliterated after lateral frontal lesions. In contrast, monkeys with inferotemporal lesions, with both affective motor memory and motor imagination intact, learned without difficulty. The authors mentioned that one of the four monkeys with lateral frontal lesions learned normally. A later additional lesion of the inferotemporal cortex did not impair his performance. On the other hand, when the three monkeys with inferotemporal lesions, who had performed normally on this task, were given an additional lateral frontal lesion, their performance dropped and never reached criterion. Pribram and Mishkin pointed out that all these animals had been trained on many simultaneous and successive discrimination problems in which the same objects had been employed: one of these objects had always been rewarded, the other left always unrewarded. They suggested that these objects had acquired sufficient "distinctiveness" during these experiments, and that accounted for any above chance performance. Surely, "distinctiveness" means that the monkeys had learned that one object (ashtray or tobacco tin) was always good, to be approached, the other indifferent, not worth approaching. Hence the monkeys could use affective visual memory in addition to the required visual and motor memory, and motor imagination. It is quite likely that the one monkey with lateral frontal lesions who learned normally used affective visual memory, just like the chimpanzees with lateral frontal lesions who reached above chance (70%) correct performance. However, in delayed response and spatial alternation, motor memory seems to be necessary for criterion performance.

The Impulse to Move.   Some recent reports show even more clearly that the dorsolateral frontal cortex serves the registration of motor memories, and the premotor cortex, the formation of the intention to move. Stamm (1969) and Stamm and Rosen (1973) reported that electrical stimulation of the dorsolateral frontal cortex in monkeys disturbed a learned delayed response when stimulation was applied during the first few seconds of delay. When electrical stimulation was applied to the premotor area, the monkey did not respond until stimulation stopped. Apparently, the monkeys could not intend to move when the premotor area was stimulated (and so preempted); and they could not draw on their motor memories when the dorsolateral cortex was stimulated. Electrical stimulation of a structure prevents the normal use of that structure.

Affective Motor Memory Impairment After Frontal Limbic Lesions.   There are not nearly as many experiments exploring the behavioral deficits after medial frontal lesions. But there are enough to confirm that the deficit is different from that revealed after lateral frontal lesions.

Pribram et al. (1952) made ventromedial frontal lesions in the brains of baboons. These lesions included the medial aspect of the frontal pole and the medial orbital, anterior cingulate, and subcallosal gyri, the areas I have included in the appraisal areas for smell and also for body, leg, and perhaps arm movements. Two out of four of these animals showed impaired retention of a delayed response postoperatively, but they did relearn. Although they were impaired, they did better than animals with dorsolateral frontal lesions. In learning the delayed alternation task after surgery, they performed well above chance but did not reach criterion. However, one of the intact control animals did no better. It is clear that both these tasks require motor memory, but once learned, the memory of the "good" object and the "suitable" response (affective motor memory) may suffice. Apparently, affective motor memory helps learning more than retention. Perhaps it would be important to know how much subcallosal and precallosal damage had been inflicted, and whether the limbic projection had been damaged as well.

Pribram et al. (1962) used a delayed alternation problem and found that in postoperative retesting all monkeys with cingulate lesions (removal of pre-, sub-, and supracallosal cingulate cortex) retained the task perfectly. However, postoperative learning of this task was severely impaired. Apparently, the animal must be able to assess its action impulse and the success of its action to learn a motor task like delayed response or alternation. But once acquired, motor memory alone is sufficient for effective performance.

Barker and Thomas (1965, 1966) reported that rats with cingulate lesions were unable to learn or retain an alternation task in which the food box was alternately baited and unbaited. In this task, the animals had to run to the food box whether it was baited or not. The running speed (fast to baited box, slow to unbaited box), indicated learning. The lesions affected the anterior cingulate gyrus to a far greater extent than the posterior cingulate. Consequently, the greatest retrograde degeneration was found in the anteromedial thalamic nucleus, which projects to the anterior cingulate gyrus. Damage to the anterior cingulate prevents the appraisal of movement and movement impulses, and blocks affective motor memory. The animals with such lesions remembered approaching the food box, but could not remember whether their approach had been successful. Hence they did not know whether to expect food or not, and ran at the same speed each time.

The control group had lesions of similar size in the neocortex between the anterior pole and the splenium. Since these lesions did not damage the anterior cingulate gyrus, the rats remembered that the last approach had been successful and slowed down on the next approach because they expected it to be unsuccessful.

There is evidence that orbital frontal lesions impair the performance of animals in a go/no go task, not because they are unable to discriminate between negative and positive cues but because they do not withhold responses on negative trials (Brutkowski et al., 1963). And Butter et al. (1963) reported that monkeys with orbital lesions did not extinguish a bar pressing habit as quickly as did normal animals, and animals with lateral frontal lesions. These authors concluded that "orbital frontal animals appear to have abnormal difficulty in suppressing strong, habitual modes of response." In other words, they can no longer appraise the "impulse to move" as suitable or unsuitable—so they move, regardless of the consequences. Monkeys with lateral frontal lesions extinguished as quickly as intact animals, evidently because they could and did evaluate bar press without reward as inappropriate.

Butters and Rosvold (1968b) found in a follow-up experiment that monkeys with septal lesions were similarly impaired in extinguishing a conditioned bar press, and so were monkeys with lesions of the ventrolateral sector of the head of the caudate nucleus, which connects with the orbital cortex. They concluded that the ventrolateral part of the head of the caudate nucleus, the septal area, and the orbital cortex represent one functional unit regulating response tendencies. However, they did not find a deficit in delayed alternation in monkeys with septal lesions while monkeys with caudate lesions were significantly impaired. This would mean that the caudate nucleus together with the lateral frontal cortex forms a functional unit, as Divac et al. (1967) have suggested,[3] but that the septal area is not part of this system.

Another task on which animals with orbital lesions are impaired is object reversal learning (Mishkin, 1964). Divac et al. (1967) noticed the same impairment after lesions of the ventrolateral sector of the head of the caudate nucleus.

In my theory, the ventral thalamic nuclei, the caudate, and the lateral frontal cortex form the last link of the action circuit which registers motor memories and reactivates them. The subcallosal and anterior cingulate gyri are part of the affective motor memory circuit. The septal area, on the other hand, is a very complex structure, connected with the hippocampus/fornix system. I discuss the behavioral effects of septal lesions in chapter 22.

According to my theory, the posterior orbital cortex is the olfactory memory area, and the adjoining adolfactory area, ventral to the subcallosal gyrus, is the olfactory appraisal area. None of the experiments used olfactory discrimination. The anterior orbital surface, according to Pribram (1973), is the orbital extension of the dorsolateral and medial frontal cortex; in my theory, it would serve motor memory and motor appraisal. The impairment in go/no tasks and object reversal seems to have resulted from the animals' difficulty in appraising their impulse to action—an affective memory deficit. The impairment in reversing or extinguishing a discrimination habit seems to have had the same root.

It seems clear that animals use both motor and affective motor memory in learning a task that requires a complicated motor response. Under some circum-

---

[3]This connection is discussed in chapter 28.

stances and with some tasks, either motor memory alone or affective motor memory alone may suffice for learning or retention, although learning may be retarded. When motor memory is necessary, as in two-cup alternation (so-called "spatial" alternation), it may be possible for the animal instead to use other memory modalities if suitable helps are given. Let us now discuss some of these aids.

Delayed Right/Left Alternation: Aids to Learning.   Battig et al. (1960) found that monkeys with bilateral lesions of the dorsolateral surface of the frontal lobes had some impairment in delayed alternation but could relearn. However, animals that had learned the task preoperatively in the same apparatus could not learn delayed alternation in the Wisconsin General Testing Apparatus (WGTA) after surgery. In the original apparatus, no screen was interposed between the animal and the food container. After pressing one of two bars on the first trial, the monkey had to press the other bar on the second trial to obtain food. The food dish was illuminated when food was delivered from the feeder. After each bar press, the house light was turned off and came on again at the end of the delay. After an error, the house light was turned off. But when the light came on again for a new trial, the bar not pressed before was again correct. In this apparatus, there were several visual cues that defined the trials and emphasized the reward. The dark interval during the delay prevented distraction so that nothing else provided a contrary impulse to move.[4] Finally, the delay was increased gradually from one second to five seconds, in one-second steps.

In the WGTA, a screen was interposed and the animals were started postoperatively with a 5-second delay. In this situation, they failed to learn. When the opaque screen was eliminated and the delay was increased gradually, the monkeys were able to learn, though some impairment remained. Other workers have reported that gradual lengthening of the delay promotes relearning in animals with prefrontal lesions (Campbell & Harlow, 1945; Mishkin & Weiskrantz, 1958).

Similarly, Pribram and Tubbs (1967) were able to provide helps that enabled monkeys with large prefrontal lesions to learn a 5 second delay spatial alternation problem that they had failed before. These workers interposed a 15 second delay between every right/left alternation. If the monkey made an error, the 15 second delay was repeated, thus initiating another trial. Pribram and Tubbs suggested that normal frontal lobe function is "critically involved in the proper programming—the parsing of the stream of stimulation" (1967, p. 1766). Although this change in the task improved postoperative learning, it did not bring it to criterion performance.

---

[4]Malmo (1942) found that animals improved in delayed response tasks if the room was darkened during the delay to prevent distraction.

What seems to be happening when the delay is gradually increased from one second to five seconds is that the animals learn to recall the visual memory and form the intention to move anew, instead of trying to recall it. Similarly, when only one right/left alternation has to be remembered, as in Pribram and Tubbs' "parsing of the stream of stimulation," the animal can learn to use the intact visual memory of the cup found baited and the left bar pressed on the last trial, and to imagine the cup with bait and the right bar to be pressed in the next move, instead of having to recall its last move. Apparently, an animal who has lost his motor memory can learn to use additional sensory cues to supplement its performance, if it is allowed additional trials.

Sensory Discrimination after Frontal Lesions.   Originally, Jacobsen (1935) had reported that frontal lesions left visual and auditory discrimination untouched, a view that had been tacitly accepted until some recent studies forced a reassessment. While frontal damage does not produce a specific impairment, as for instance the impairment in visual discrimination after inferotemporal lesions, or the impairment of tactual discrimination after posterior parietal lesions (see chapter 12), the general learning deficit produced by frontal lesions is considerable. However, this deficit is found only under particular circumstances; or rather, it is revealed only if the problem cannot be solved by a simple response, so that the animal needs motor memory to perform correctly. For instance, animals with frontal lesions are impaired on some variations of sensory discrimination, such as the "learning set" and "oddity" problems.

Learning Set.   Brush et al. (1961) investigated the performance of monkeys with frontal lesions, monkeys with temporal lesions, and intact monkeys on a series of learning set problems. Each series consisted of 200 problems, and each problem employed a new pair of small objects. On half the problems, the first trial had both objects baited; the object chosen by the monkey was considered positive and its choice was rewarded on the ten following trials. On the other half of the problems, neither object was baited on the first trial, and the object chosen was considered negative. The baited-unbaited "preference" trials were given in a balanced sequence. Three problems had to be learned daily until 100 "baited" and 100 "unbaited" problems were completed. This experiment represents a simultaneous visual discrimination with twenty reversals between "baited" and "unbaited" problems. All groups made more errors on "unbaited" problems, but intact animals and monkeys with temporal lesions reduced their errors on "unbaited" problems almost to the number of errors on "baited" problems. Frontally lesioned monkeys showed little improvement.

Brush et al. suggested that the initial choices of all animals are often guided by object preferences or aversions, which explains the poorer showing on "unbaited" problems. Animals with frontal lesions, they think, have "greater difficulty in learning to suppress these normal tendencies" (p. 323). Next, they tried to induce preferences or aversions experimentally by using 40 pairs of objects and one member of each pair as the training stimulus for that problem. The well covered by the training object was baited on half the problems, unbaited on the other half. When it was unbaited, the monkey had to uncover it five times in a row without finding a peanut. After the five training trials, which established an "aversion" or a "preference," the training object together with the other member of the pair was used in ten simultaneous discrimination trials. On half the problems, the training stimulus was baited, on the other half, it was not baited.

The investigators found that the monkeys avoided a negative training object 95% of the time during the test trials, and chose the other object instead. The positive training object was chosen only 55% of the time, with the other (new) object chosen 45% of the time. This was true for all three groups. When the negative training object was unbaited in the test trials, all three groups performed equally well. When the positive training object was baited during the test trials, monkeys with frontal lesions did as well as monkeys with inferotemporal lesions, and almost as well as intact animals. However, when the positive training object was unbaited in the test trials, all groups made more errors; but the inferotemporal group made more errors than the intact group, and the frontally lesioned group almost doubled the errors of the inferotemporal group. When the negative training stimulus was baited during the test trials, all groups made more errors than under the other conditions, but again the frontally lesioned animals had the largest error score.

This second experiment clearly establishes that the impairment of frontally lesioned animals is not simply an inability to inhibit incorrect responses. The preferences and aversions established in this experiment resulted in just as much inhibition of unrewarded responses (e.g., negative training stimulus unbaited in training and test trials), but animals with frontal lesions did as well as the two control groups. Only when the positive training object was unrewarded in test trials, or the negative training object was rewarded in test trials, did the frontally lesioned animals show a deficit. The authors concluded that "an abnormal difficulty in suppressing either trained or spontaneous stimulus preferences or aversions would appear to be specific to frontal animals" (p. 325).

But the problem remains: What accounts for this inability to suppress preferences and to change the responses when experimental conditions change? The answer seems to be that large lesions of the dorsolateral frontal cortex, as these were (from the frontal pole to the arcuate sulcus, including its anterior bank, i.e., the entire dorsolateral convexity), prevent not only the registration of movement and movement impulses, but also their appraisal because there is no longer any connection between the area mediating impulses to action and the limbic motor areas. In addition, large lesions interfere with motor imagination so that the animals cannot plan alternative responses. Hence a change (reversal) of experimental conditions from positive to negative object and vice versa is difficult.

Oddity Problems.   The impairment of animals with frontal lesions in learning oddity problems can be explained in a similar way. In an oddity problem, three objects are shown on every trial; two of them are identical. The monkey has to choose the odd one to earn a reward. Harlow (1952) reported that monkeys with frontal lesions as well as monkeys with inferotemporal lesions showed significant deficits in performing this simultaneous visual discrimination.

In this problem, the monkey must compare the three objects; he must recognize two as similar (familiar), the third as unfamiliar (affective visual memory). On each trial, the monkey must remember that he has to make this comparison-appraisal (motor memory) and must plan to approach the object he will single out (motor imagination). Monkeys with frontal lesions are impaired because they do not remember what is to be done (comparison-appraisal) and cannot plan their approach. Monkeys with inferotemporal lesions are impaired because they do not remember what visual aspect they have to appraise (the odd object); since the inferotemporal cortex connects with the visual limbic cortex, the visual appraisal area is disconnected so that they cannot make the comparison and appraisal. Since both visual and motor memory and the corresponding affective memory are involved, monkeys with either type of lesions will be impaired but will be able to learn eventually on the basis of the remaining memory modalities.

Go/No Go Problems.   In successive sensory discrimination, only one card or object is shown in a given trial. The animal must approach the positive cue and refrain from approaching the negative cue. This is a "go/no go" problem (see p. 193). In this task, animals with prefrontal lesions show significant learning and retention deficits. (For visual discrimination: Brush et al., 1961; auditory: Weiskrantz & Mishkin, 1958; touch: Ettlinger & Wegener, 1958, and many others.)

All successive discriminations, like the complex simultaneous discriminations discussed earlier, depend on four types of memory: the sensory memory modality employed (e.g. visual, auditory, tactual recall); the affective sensory memory of the good or bad object; the motor memory of the go or no go response; and the affective motor memory of the response as suitable or unsuitable. They also require motor imagination, i.e., what to do this time. After large prefrontal lesions, when motor memory, affective motor memory, and motor imagination are no longer available, the animal has to depend on its sensory memories of the object seen, touched, and smelled, along with its affective memory of this object as good or bad. When an animal is hungry, the fact that it sees something that has been associated with food or may promise food, is enough to want and approach it. Since the animal can no longer remember that an approach to the negative object is useless (loss of affective motor memory), it will approach no matter what cue has been given. Hence animals with frontal lesions make more approach responses to negative cues than withholding responses to positive cues.

However, when an approach to the negative stimulus is punished (e.g., by electric shock), it will then be appraised as "bad, to be avoided" instead of being indifferent. Pain is now registered as affective somatosensory memory, which enables the animal to remember the object as "bad." According to Rosvold and Mishkin (1961), frontally lesioned animals learn such a problem as easily as do intact animals. When the punishing electric shock is omitted, these animals are again impaired. As soon as shock is restored, they once more perform like intact animals. Here, the affective somatosensory memory of the pain serves the animal as substitute for the lost affective motor memory.

Another experiment illustrates the value of additional sensory cues. In a successive tactual discrimination, reported by Rosvold and Mishkin (1961), monkeys had to displace a lid in the dark to find food. When moving the lid was effortless, monkeys with frontal lesions showed the usual impairment. But when both the negative and the positive lid were difficult to move, frontally lesioned monkeys learned the difference between the positive and negative lid as quickly as intact monkeys. Here, the difficulty of moving the lid gave the animal the opportunity of concentrating on the difference in touch; the touch memory and the affective memory of the "good" touch were now sufficient to make the correct choice.

Of course, Rosvold and Mishkin do not explain the impairment after frontal lesions as a defect in motor and affective motor memory. But they agree that the impairment is not sensory in nature and that it cannot be explained as inhibition of response, of drive, or of stimulus. In a later article, Mishkin (1964) suggested that frontally lesioned animals suffer from perseverative interference, that is, there is a "perseveration of central mediating process"—but as there may be many such mediating processes, he could not specify any particular process.

That not only sensory but motor memory is needed in a delayed visual discrimination is shown by an experiment reported by Cohen (1972). Monkeys were trained on a task in which a 3-second display of two identical patterns was followed by an 8-second delay, and then by the illumination of both windows with identical colors. Responses during the test trial were rewarded if made to the left window when one pair of patterns was displayed, and to the right window for another pattern pair. During the pattern display, the monkey had to recall which turn was indicated by these particular patterns, and form the intention of taking that turn. This required visual memory and an impulse to action. During the delay, the monkey had to remember the intention to turn in the indicated direction. Correct performance could be disrupted during the pattern display by 3-second stimulation of the inferotemporal cortex; or during the early part of the delay, by stimulation of the dorsolateral frontal cortex. Obviously, visual memory requires a functioning inferotemporal cortex, and motor memory, a functioning dorsolateral frontal cortex.

Stamm and Rosen (1973) investigated the electrical activity in the frontal cortex of monkeys during a delayed reponse task. They recorded surface negative steady electrical potential shifts (NPS) from the dorsolateral frontal cortex. These started at sight of the cue, reached maximum amplitude at the beginning of the delay, and returned to the base line before the delay was over. A second NPS started after the response and returned to base line during the intertrial interval. The first shift could be associated with the intention of approaching the cup. The second shift could be related to the evaluation of success: According to the authors, omitting the sugar pellet after a correct response markedly reduced this potential. Whatever the interpretation of these negative potential shifts, it is clear that the monkey was doing something while looking at the display—he was not simply holding back the response. And he was doing something after the response, something that apparently "reinforced" the response. After ablation of the frontal cortex, these negative potential shifts can no longer occur—but why should this loss of activity be called disinhibition, as the authors do? The electrical activity in the intact frontal cortex was not associated with inhibition.

My suggestion that the first NPS indicates an intention to move and the second, an appraisal of success, is in line with other evidence and is exactly what could have been predicted on the basis of my theory.

It would seem that the effect of frontal lesions has been so difficult to explain because most theorists have been looking for a single function mediated by the frontal lobe—or, if not a single function, at most one function each for the three subdivisions defined by Pribram (1973): the orbital, medial, and dorsolateral frontal regions. Also, insisting that motor learning must be based on kinesthetic rather than motor memory has left the frontal lobe without any recognizable basic function and has given rise to a host of theories suggesting esoteric higher functions.

Once we assign motor and affective motor memory, motor imagination and the appraisal of motor impulses to the dorsolateral and medial precentral frontal lobe, and olfactory memory and appraisal to the posterior orbital cortex, we resolve the apparent contradiction between lesion effects in animals and human beings. Many authors have tried to duplicate the impairment after frontal lesions in animals by devising tests they thought would show a similar impairment in patients with frontal lesions, and have failed. No wonder, since they assumed the deficit to be a loss of short term memory, and devised tests accordingly (see p. 186 ff.). Human beings as well as animals suffer a loss of motor and affective motor memory and an impairment of motor imagination after dorsolateral and medial frontal lesions. Luria's (1966a) reports leave no doubt about that. Russian psychologists should have no difficulty realizing that the frontal lobe serves such functions. Western psychologists and neurophysiologists will find it far more difficult to adjust their perspective.

16 Memory Retrieval

In the consolidation experiments . . . we followed what might be called a "frontal assault" on the problem of memory formation. Our experiments were predicated largely upon traditional behavioristic concepts of learning and memory and relied exclusively upon conventional neuropsychological research methods. We have gradually come to the view that our frontal assault failed to attain its intended objective because we knew neither how our treatments actually affect the nervous system nor what neural mechanisms are actually involved in memory trace initiation. Furthermore, we have learned enough about the problem to realize that all similar efforts, aimed at identifying specific morphological or functional changes in the mammalian brain in relation to "experience," are likewise bound to remain unsuccessful to the extent that they continue to be based solely upon the narrow conceptual foundations of operational neobehaviorism."

S. Chorover, 1976, p.570

Memory can be tested only by recall. We may report what we have experienced, recite a poem or play a game of tennis or chess. Whenever our performance falls short, we cannot assume that the memories we are trying to recall have not been registered. Usually, we judge that we have not attended to what we have seen or heard, or that we have not practiced what we have learned. It is well known that a person may recall what he has seen or heard word for word under hypnosis, although he is normally unable to recall more than a very few things. Hence all recall implies speech or motor memory and active attention. A learning or memory deficit may indicate a defect in motor memory or attention in addition to a

203

possible deficit in sensory or affective memory. There may even be a difficulty in anticipating cues and in planning appropriate action—that is, a defect in imagination.

A deficit in sensory or motor memory after a brain lesion does not necessarily mean that the lesion has damaged one or other memory area. It could also happen that the memory engrams are intact but cannot be reactivated. Hence the way in which engrams are activated in recall must be our next concern. In addition, we must explore how memory images are activated in imagination. We know that memory images can be restructured and recombined at will (in waking imagination) or unwittingly (in dreams).

MEMORY RETRIEVAL

The problem of memory retrieval has been all but forgotten by researchers and theorists. Their interest has been centered almost exclusively on the registration and storage of memories. Up to the most recent past, neither psychologists nor neurophysiologists seem to have realized the importance of a memory retrieval mechanism. A few years ago, Rosenzweig (1976) pointed out this omission in his summary of a conference on "Neural Mechanisms of Learning and Memory" held in 1974. He says:

> Certain widely shared assumptions may limit or restrict research at any given time . . . Let me try to indicate one . . . . I refer to the implicit assumption . . . that THE problem of the neural basis of learning and memory is how information can be stored in neural terms. In other words, what is the form of the engram? An equally important problem is how stored information can be retrieved, in terms of neural processes. This may well be a more difficult problem than that of storage, especially since few investigators have addressed the question or seem to have a handle on it (p. 597).

The problem of retrieval is difficult enough. But in addition, several retrieval systems seem to be involved in a given learning task. In particular, motor memory is involved in almost every case. Human learning often means memorizing series of digits, words, or nonsense syllables; this involves speech, which is a motor activity and requires motor memory. Animals cannot tell us what they remember, and we have to depend on their performance in learning tasks to gauge impairment after frontal lesions. Learning may be impaired not only in typical motor tasks but also in various sensory discriminations because these also require a motor response. In the last decades, thousands of experiments have been undertaken employing different learning tasks under widely differing conditions to investigate learning deficits after brain lesions in animals. Unfortunately, without some theory of brain function, much of this research has been a groping in the dark. The results have been ambiguous and often contradictory and have done little to advance our knowledge of brain function. That is not surprising because the various learning tasks involve many different memory systems—and hardly any fit into generally accepted categories.

Learning a given task requires the recall of the relevant modality–specific memories on the basis of sensory cues; an impulse toward the "good" and away from the "bad" cue (affective sensory memory); the recall of the appropriate action (motor memory) and its success or failure (affective motor memory). Also, the learner must expect (imagine) the cue and must plan (imagine) the action required here and now, which requires intact memory areas but also intact retrieval and imagination circuits.

The learner may fail to learn for a number of reasons. He may not be able to recall which is the positive or negative cue (impairment of sensory and affective sensory memory) after lesions of parietal, temporal, or occipital association cortex and the associated limbic cortex; he may not be able to recall the appropriate action (motor memory loss), or to evaluate his action impulse (defect in affective motor memory) after lesions of the prefrontal areas and frontal limbic cortex. Brain lesions may interfere with the imagination circuit so that the learner can no longer experience fear and is unable to avoid punishment; or he no longer expects the cue because he can no longer imagine it, and so pays no attention to it. On the other hand, if the learning task is so simple that it can be solved by affective memory alone, the animal may not seem impaired even if the necessary sensory memory areas are heavily damaged.

But the damage may not be in the areas that register memories, it may be in areas necessary for retrieval. My task in this chapter is to sketch the circuits which, I believe, must be intact for memory retrieval. However, before concentrating on a theory of memory retrieval via definite brain circuits, I would like to discuss the rival theory of memory storage and consolidation in the light of known brain function.

Memory Consolidation.   Given the single-minded concentration of both psychologists and neurologists on information storage in the brain, it is not surprising that all efforts have been bent on investigating the fate of memory traces. Müller and Pilzecker had suggested as early as 1900 that nervous activity accompanying perception goes on for some time and is responsible for the consolidation of the memory trace. Much work has been done since then, but the main features of the consolidation view have remained.

In a recent review, McGaugh and Gold (1976) discuss the modern view that the process of consolidation has two stages: The first a dynamic, labile memory trace, the after-effect of sensory experience, which is transitory and can be blocked or disrupted by various treatments like drugs or electroshock; the second stage consists of the establishment of a long-term, relatively permanent memory that can no longer be disturbed easily. There has been considerable discussion whether this view implies one or two storage areas. The consensus seems to be that the first phase implies a short-term storage (STM) from which those memories that survive are transferred into long-term memory (LTM). Just where in the brain the short term memory is stored, how it is transferred into long term storage, and where the storage could be has not been hinted at by consolidation theorists.

A great deal of work has been done on the consolidation phase of memory storage. McGaugh and Gold (1976) report that consolidation is influenced by a variety of treatments following learning: antibiotic drugs, convulsant drugs, cortical spreading depression, electrical cortical shock (ECS), and brain stimulation. The effect of such treatments varies. Under some conditions, ECS and convulsant drugs block retention only if administered within a few seconds or minutes after training. Under other conditions, treatment affects retention if given as long as two or three days after training. McGaugh and Gold point out that interference with memory by various treatments does not imply that the time during which such treatment blocks memory indicates the time required for memory consolidation.

McGaugh and Gold also mention an alternative interpretation of these treatment effects, namely, that the treatment interferes with retrieval processes rather than disrupting memory consolidation. The treatment may disrupt the retrieval of recently stored information without affecting earlier storage. There are research findings that would support such a hypothesis. For instance, rats that were given a post-trial treatment that interfered with learned performance can later perform correctly if given some cues or "reminders" to assist retrieval. McGaugh and Gold comment, however, that "the reminder effect can be readily explained (on the basis of consolidation theory) as resulting from the combination, through generalization, of the punishing effect of the reminder stimulus with a weak memory of the original inhibitory avoidance training" (1976, p. 551).

Actually, the reminder works even if it does not punish. Moreover, McGaugh and Gold do not make clear how generalization manages to combine the present "punishing effect" with the original memory. Neither consolidation nor retrieval theorists have thus far explained the temporary loss of retention as the result of treatment. The consolidation theorists do not specify what kind of process results in consolidation and how posttrial treatment can interfere with it. They seem to assume that consolidation simply "stamps in" the original trace. How it is reactivated is anyone's guess. And consolidation or retrieval theorists do not explain where memory is stored nor do they offer any hint how stored memories are retrieved.

A simpler alternative is to assume that repetition (whether in memory, imagination, or reality) improves learning by synaptic facilitation of retrieval over neural memory circuits. Our guide to the search for the pathways of memory registration and retrieval must be the psychological sequence from perception to action.

Chorover (1976) has remarked that experiments based on behavioristic concepts will remain unsuccessful in their search for neural correlates of behavior. Behaviorism, the theory of the empty organism, has no tools for dealing with either experience or brain function. Clearly, the individual perceives experimental conditions, assesses them and responds according to this appraisal. If we are willing to follow this sequence, we may find a similar sequence of neural relays from sensory to motor cortex.

Memory: Unitary or Multiple? Another common assumption is the view that there is only one mechanism of memory storage. As Gazzaniga (1976) says, memory theorists seem to assume that there is one mechanism for the storage of information, a mechanism that is used in all storage processes. If such a mechanism implies a single storage site in the brain for memory storage, this assumption should have been quietly discarded as soon as the first reports of split-brain patients were published. Such a patient, when asked, can retrieve something he saw in his left visual field (registered in the right hemisphere) with his left but not with his right hand (which is controlled by the left hemisphere). Since each hemisphere functions independently after transection of the corpus callosum, the split-brain patient can only draw on memories stored on the same side. Memories registered in the right hemisphere are available for retrieval with his left hand. But the left hemisphere, controlling the right hand, has no visual engrams of the object. Such a patient cannot report what he saw in his left visual field; apparently, speech memories are registered in the left hemisphere. The patient's right hemisphere visual engrams now have no connection with his left hemisphere speech engrams.

Alas, the information-processing computer model is too persuasive. The computer stores information in one way and in one place—so the brain should do the same. However, on the basis of his research with split-brain patients, Gazzaniga has concluded that "we may be faced with the fact that memory storage, encoding and decoding is a multifaceted process carried out in different ways in different areas in the brain" (1976, p. 65). In chapters 12 and 14, I have shown that there is good reason to believe that sensory and motor memory images are registered in different areas of the brain. These engrams surely have to be reactivated by different relays.

Immediate Memory. Most theorists agree that there is a short-term memory (immediate memory) at least for vision and hearing. According to Simon (1976),

there is another sensory memory whose existence is quite firmly established: the "echo box" or echoic memory, which permits us to retain, for a second or two, an incoming sound stream to which we have not been attending, and to bring it into STM (short-term memory) if our attention is called to it before it disappears. The echoic memory may be thought of as the aural analogue to the visual iconic memory, although information survives substantially longer in the former than in the latter—several seconds as against a few hundred milliseconds (p. 90).

The difference in time may have its root in the difference between the visual image of objects existing side-by-side and a temporal sequence (the auditory or echoic memory). Sounds linger, and the last sound heard often explains the sequence heard before; while in visual perception, many things are seen at the same time, as a total configuration, and thus obliterated by new impressions more easily.

Spontaneous Rehearsal.   In immediate memory, each image is held in mind until it merges into the next one. If we look out the window, we see a stationary background and against it a procession of people, dogs, cars, trucks. We know that they are coming from somewhere and going somewhere because we recall the scene as it looked a moment, a minute, an hour ago. Perception is completed by appraisal which provides the meaning; and this requires continuous recall, so providing the continuity and unity of mental life (see chapter 1). Such spontaneous recall includes not only sensory and motor memory but affective memory. If we see a dog killed by a speeding car, we are upset not only at the moment it happens, but for quite a while afterwards. It is this spontaneous memory rehearsal that seems to account in part for the "consolidation" of memories.

Since this spontaneous rehearsal does activate the registered engrams, this activation has some similarity with the "reverberating circuits" of the consolidation theorist. However, spontaneous rehearsal is not automatic but is directed by attention (see chapter 2). This means that rehearsal is selective, so that we remember (rehearse) what is important to us and disregard (forget) what is irrelevant. This view of spontaneous rehearsal has the advantage that we do not have to postulate a special mechanism of "consolidation." Every rehearsal, whether spontaneous or deliberate, facilitates the neural pattern reactivating the memory, and so increases the chances of later recall. Once something is experienced, the disposition to recall it is established, ready to be activated. If the memory is not recalled (spontaneously or deliberately) within a short time, access to it will be lost.

This would account, for instance, for cases of traumatic memory loss, usually after a longer or shorter period of unconsciousness. During this period, the immediate spontaneous rehearsal is not possible. At the moment of trauma there were memories that had not been rehearsed, or not rehearsed sufficiently, hence access to them is lost. Because it rests on a bone shelf, the hippocampus, which seems to be the switching station for memory recall, is peculiarly sensitive to concussion or near-concussion. Memory loss happens not only after concussion but also after metrazol or electroshock, which activates all circuits in the brain; we can assume that such strong excitation overrides synaptic connections in the memory circuit that are still fragile and so disturbs the recently established memory activation patterns. In concussion, we can assume that these fragile synaptic connections have been disarranged by the trauma. Some time after trauma or shock, the patient usually recovers some of the memories registered before. But in severe cases, a core of memory loss remains, covering a period beginning some time before the trauma and ending some time after recovery from unconsciousness.

Spontaneous recall, directed by imagination, goes on during sleep. At irregular periods, the slow wave pattern of sleep is interrupted by a series of faster waves, the so-called K-complex. This variation in EEG pattern has been called "paradoxical sleep" because it shows EEG activation as during waking, yet the individual is asleep. It has been found that such paradoxical sleep is necessary for memory retention. When it is prevented by waking the subject every time a K-complex begins, the performance of a learned task deteriorates. Since such activation of the EEG pattern occurs both in man and in animals and is connected with dreaming in human beings, we can assume that animals, like human beings, dream about the events of the past day and, in dreaming, rehearse the learned task.

Spontaneous rehearsal ordinarily is complemented by deliberate rehearsal in learning, or by a set repetition of performance. It is through this rehearsal that access to our memories is maintained. Spontaneous rehearsal keeps the gate open, as it were, but we must walk through the gate if we are to remember our way.

THE MECHANISM OF MEMORY RECALL

Psychologists and neurophysiologists have paid scant attention to the mechanism of memory recall. Except for my own, there are no theories to account for it. Indeed, if memory is conceived as a unitary function, with its engrams widely—and perhaps randomly—scattered over the cortex, it is difficult to conceive how we could recall particular events. How could we choose among all our memories from childhood to the present day? How is it possible to remember a trip we took years ago, a play we saw, or a conversation we had with a friend? There may be memory lapses, but by and large we do manage to recall what we want to recall, despite the failure of memory theorists to explain it. But when we realize that there are memory modalities just as there are sensory modalities, and that memory images are registered in the association cortex close to sensory and motor cortex, we can look for the circuits that could activate engrams in different modalities and so perhaps find an explanation.

Memory and Imagination Circuits.   A pattern of sensory images registered as dispositions to be activated at some later date can be recalled in its original form, order, and sequence: We *recall a memory.* Or sensory images may be restructured, combined at will with images registered at different times: We use them in *imagination*. Both recall and imagination depend on memory images, registered in various association areas. Because recall means reviving memory images in the original order and sequence, the circuit that reactivates them must repeat the pattern and sequence in which they were laid down. This cannot be the same circuit as that mediating imagination because imagination ranges over the whole memory field and is not bound by the time or order in which memory images have been registered. Hence the imagination circuit must be different from the memory circuit. Whether the reactivation of memory images occurs in recall or in imagination, it implies that a particular engram pattern must be selected and activated. Such activation can only be initiated and guided by an intention to recall or imagine a particular scene, phrase, melody. This intention is an action impulse produced by an appraisal (via limbic cortex) that this is good to do.

To recall a particular memory, the registered memory pattern must be activated in its proper form, order and sequence. This means that at least over part of its course, the circuit must follow the pattern and sequence of the original impulses. In addition, there has to be a selector station that can channel the impulses to the appropriate memory areas and into the appropriate pattern. This selector station seems to be the hippocampus. Bilateral hippocampal lesions, whether made by the surgeon's knife, or resulting from disease or trauma, are responsible for true amnesia (Milner, 1966, 1968a).

The Sensory Memory Circuit.   The impulse to recall something may be spontaneous, as in seeing someone and immediately recalling his name and the fact that he is a friend. Both man and animal immediately "associate" something seen with the context in which it was experienced before. But the human being may also deliberately intend to recall something because he has judged that this is something he wants to do. He may intend to visualize a scene, to hear a melody in imagination, or to recall a name. Deliberate recall is practically limited to the visual and auditory modality, or to motor memory (e.g., when performing a dance, playing a well-learned duet on the piano, or reciting a poem). Recall in any memory modality, whether spontaneous or deliberate, would have to be relayed over neural pathways in substantially the same temporal and spatial sequence as the original experience or movement pattern, so as to reactivate the intended engram pattern in the association cortex.

Recall or the intention to recall does not appear suddenly, out of the blue. When spontaneous, it is brought about by something we see, hear, smell, taste, or feel; or it may be brought back with some movement or word of ours. When deliberate, recall is based on the judgment that there is something we need to remember here and now. Spontaneous or deliberate, recall always has its roots in an appraisal, intuitive or deliberate, that this is good to do. This appraisal produces an action impulse, the intention to recall something. I am suggesting that this action impulse is relayed from limbic cortex serving appraisal (subcallosal and orbital area, cingulate, retrosplenial, hippocampal gyri, and insula) to the precommissural fornix and septal area, hypothalamus and midbrain, and returns via thalamic sensory nuclei to the various cortical association areas. This is the proposed sensory memory circuit (Fig. 16.1).

Motor Memory Retrieval. Motor memory is different from every other modality-specific memory. When we try to remember dancing or skating or moving a pencil in a blind maze, we find ourselves imagining these actions or even visualizing them instead of remembering. Yet we know that we can dance or skate, and when we actually start dancing or skating, the movements are easy and familiar.

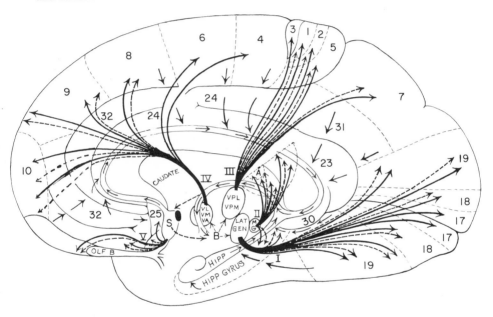

FIG. 16.1   The memory circuit—reception and registration, recall. Sensory impulses travel via thalamic sensory nuclei to cortical sensory and association areas, mediating sensory experience. Associated impulses are relayed to limbic areas, mediating appraisal. This appraisal of sense experience initiates spontaneous recall of similar things and situations, mediated via hippocampus, thalamic sensory nuclei, and the various association and limbic areas. Motor impulses travel via ventral thalamic nuclei to frontal areas.
_____ Reception and registration. _ _ _ _ _ _ Recall. Arrows indicate the direction of conduction. Short arrows indicate the connections for appraisal and recall.
I visual system. II auditory system. III somesthetic system (including taste). IV motor system. V olfactory system. Arabic numerals represent Brodmann areas. A cortical auditory area. B brain stem. HIPP hippocampus. LAT GEN lateral geniculate nucleus. MG medial geniculate nucleus. OLF B olfactory bulb. S septal area. VA anterior ventral nucleus. VM ventromedial nucleus. VL ventrolateral nucleus. VPL ventroposterolateral nucleus. VPM ventroposteromedial nucleus. (From M. B. Arnold, 1960)

The process of recalling something seen or heard is quite different. In recalling a landscape or a song, we form a visual or auditory image and recognize it as familiar. But in visual and auditory recall, the image is formed automatically, as soon as we form the intention. Only when memory fails, as in old age or when trying to remember something seen fleetingly or heard only once, do we have recourse to putting the memory together piecemeal. But in every case, our recall includes a feeling of familiarity that springs from the appraisal that we have seen or heard this before.

In contrast, an effort to recall a movement always turns into an effort to imagine how to do it. The only way to recall a movement directly is to make the movement and in making it recognize it as something we have done before. We hear the band, we start dancing, and feet and body do their familiar best. The intention to dance or skate, to catch the ball and run with it, seems to activate the relevant motor memories as the action progresses. Every time we repeat a movement, we lay down additional motor memories so that next time we can move more smoothly, more quickly.

Corresponding to the experiential difference between motor and sensory recall, the motor memory circuit is different from the sensory memory circuit. In the first place, the only way in which registered motor engrams could be revived to influence action is via some circuit coursing through cells in the motor memory areas and connecting with the motor cortex. Unlike visual, auditory, or other sensory memory, the remembered movements immediately modify the execution of the planned action.

Moreover, there is a difference in the muscular pattern depending on the action that is planned, for instance, dancing versus playing tennis. In both cases, this pattern is initiated almost as soon as the intention is formed. In playing tennis, relays from the visual appraisal area on seeing the ball will touch off the intention to hit it via the hippocampus; this impulse is patterned for body and arm movements via the cerebellum, which relays this pattern not only to the ventral thalamus but also to the tegmental reticular formation, red nucleus, central gray, parafascicular and centromedian thalamic nucleus, the posterolateral and reticular nuclei, field H_1 of Forel, and the dorsolateral hypothalamus (Cohen et al. 1958). These areas connect with the striatum and the frontal lobe. When we recall a movement so as to correct it, for instance in target shooting, relays from the motor appraisal area go to the hippocampal rudiment from where fibers turn ventrally toward the precommissural fornix, which connects via midbrain reticular formation with the cerebellum and frontal lobe, forming part of the action circuit. It seems likely that the route via the ventral thalamic nuclei, as well as the route via the red nucleus, substantia nigra, and striatum, is involved in the muscular pattern of movement and the aim of movement, while other relays are involved in the pleasure/pain aspect of moving (see chapters 26, 27, & 28).

The Affective Memory Circuit.   Not only do we re-experience a previously registered memory image, we also relive our earlier appraisals; or, to be precise, we experience the action impulse, often emotional, that springs from it. Obviously, the original appraisal was not experienced as an image. In fact, it was not *experienced* at all; there was only the experience of the action impulse initiated by the appraisal. When this appraisal is revived, we again do not experience the appraisal, we only experience the feeling, the emotional action impulse, that is generated by it. Thus affective memory is different from every other type of memory because it is the revival of an earlier appraisal that generates a new feeling or emotion. (See chapters 7 and 9.)

There is no doubt that such affective memory exists. When I read in the paper about a reception honoring a celebrity, a reception which I attended, I spontaneously recall not only the guest of honor and the acquaintances I saw, but also the impression I gained. I experience the liking or dislike, the respect or admiration he or she inspired in me—an experience as spontaneous as the visual image of seeing the guest of honor in the reception line.

Since both the visual recall and the emotional attitude are based on appraisal, both the sensory memory circuit and the affective memory circuit would have to start from the limbic cortex; and both would have to run through the hippocampus, the memory switching station. But from here, the affective memory circuit seems to run via fornix to the mamillary bodies and to return via the mamillothalamic tract and the anterior thalamic nucleus to the cingulate gyrus and other limbic areas. Such a circuit actually exists. The cingulum, running from the cingulate and retrosplenial gyrus to the hippocampus, the postcommissural fornix going from the hippocampus to the mamillary bodies, and the mamillothalamic tract are among the best-marked pathways in the brain. It is also known that each area of the limbic cortex receives projections from the anterior thalamic nuclei, the end stations of the mamillo-thalamic tracts.

According to Yakovlev et al. (1960), these thalamic nuclei project to all areas of the limbic cortex. They form a crescent on the mediodorsal border of the thalamus, beginning with the anterior medial nucleus (AM) in the most anterior position, which projects to the septal area. The anterior ventral (AV), anterior dorsal (AD), and lateral dorsal (LD) nuclei overlap and follow each other. Their cortical projections also overlap, although the AM, AV and AD project mainly to the anterior cingulate gyrus, and the lateral dorsal nucleus projects mainly to the posterior cingulate gyrus. Of the smaller nuclei of the medial thalamus, the parataenial nucleus projects to the subcallosal allocortex, the anterior paraventricular nucleus to the indusium griseum, and the superior central nucleus to the taenia tecta. Finally, Yakovlev et al. suggest that the ventral anterior nucleus and the magnocellular part of the dorsomedial nucleus should also be considered thalamic limbic nuclei because they project to cortical limbic areas: the former, to the anterior insula, and the latter, to the orbital surface of the frontal lobe (Figs. 16.2, 16.3).

The Hippocampus. In my theory, the hippocampus is the central relay station for both memory circuits as well as for the action circuit. I discuss the struc-

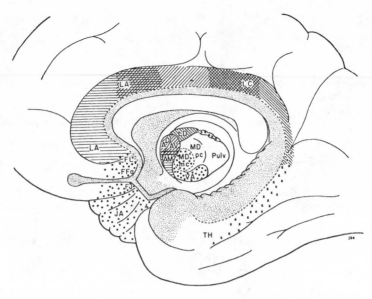

FIG. 16.2 Projections of the limbic nuclei of the thalamus in sagittal plane. Note extensive overlap of projections to cingulate gyrus. (Cortical areas after Economo and Koskinas, 1925.)

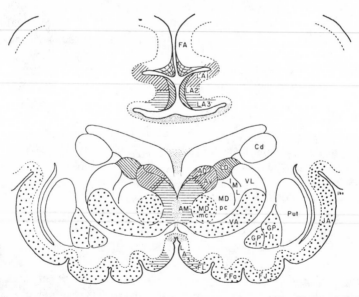

FIG. 16.3 Projections of the limbic nuclei of the thalamus in coronal plane. Note laminated arrangement of projections to cingulate gyrus, athalamic zone at the limbic lip (part of LA3 bordering the allocortex), and nonlimbic character of medial part of AM nucleus (appears to project to septum). (Cortical areas after Economo and Koskinas, 1925.) (Figs. 16.2 and 16.3 From Yakovlev et al., 1966)

ture and function of the hippocampus in detail in Chapter 20. Here I merely want to point out that the hippocampus does receive relays from all sensory and motor areas. Sensory stimulation produces electrical potentials in limbic regions that send relays to the hippocampus. According to MacLean (1975), the connections from sensory areas to limbic cortex are strictly modality-specific, with no intermingling that would suggest integration. His view seems to be that the hippocampus does not integrate incoming information but might be, in computer terms, a "coordinator of requests for various services" (p. 197). I am suggesting that the appraisal of events and actions mediated by limbic cortex is relayed to the hippocampus and there gives rise to various action impulses. The information (appraisal of situations and actions) reaching the hippocampus from limbic cortex is converted in the hippocampus to motor impulses and relayed either in the memory circuits for recall, or in the action circuit for overt action.

From the hippocampus, impulses are relayed via the postcommissural fornix to the mamillary bodies, the anterior thalamic nuclei, and the cingulate gyrus as well as other cortical limbic regions. This is the *affective memory circuit* (Fig. 16.4).

Other relays go from the hippocampus via the precommissural fornix to the mamillary bodies, and return via midbrain to sensory thalamic nuclei and sensory memory areas in the *sensory recall circuit* (see Fig. 16.1). Finally, there are relays from the hippocampus via the postcommissural fornix and mamillo-tegmental tract to the midbrain reticular formation and cerebellum, returning either directly or via the midbrain reticular formation to ventral thalamic nuclei and frontal lobe, in the *action circuit*. The latter is active also in the registration and revival of motor memories (see Fig. 13.3).

The Imagination Circuit. That recall and imagination always go together has been shown by Bartlett (1932) many years ago. In our attempt to recall a scene, a conversation, a happy encounter, we always supplement our memory by imagination. Deliberate recall, unless carefully trained, is accurate for features that have impressed us, but the unimportant details have to be supplied by imagination. Eidetic imagery is probably the only example of deliberate recall bringing back the original image in all its detail.

Imagination creates dreams and fantasies, but also functions in planning for action. In imagining something, we use the same memory material we use in recall, but we disregard its sequence, reorder and restructure it. To achieve this play of imagination, we have to retrieve memory images over a circuit that allows their selection at will. This circuit should include a relay station that can be activated by perception and appraisal but also by physiological appetites like hunger, thirst, and sexual tension. We all know the wealth of images that come unbidden as soon as we are under such physiological tensions.

Such a relay station would have to receive afferents from sensory and limbic areas as well as from the hypothalamic regions active in hunger, thirst, or sexual

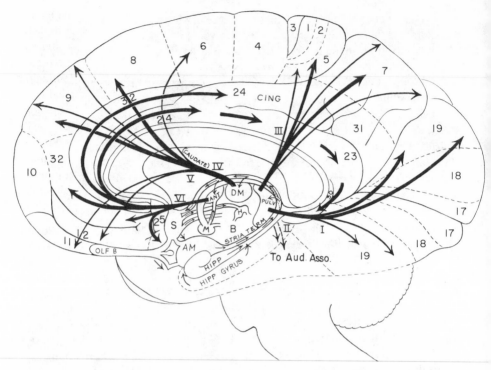

FIG. 16.4 Circuits mediating imagination and affective memory. We identify things by recalling similar objects (relays from association cortex to limbic areas, and from there via hippocampus-fornix circuit to the brain stem and back to thalamic sensory nuclei and sensory association cortex) and remember their effect on us (affective memory circuit from association cortex to limbic areas, and from there via hippocampus and postcommissural fornix to anterior thalamic nuclei and cortical limbic areas). This results in imagining possible effects of this thing on us and possible ways of coping with it (imagination circuit from cortical limbic areas via amygdala to thalamic association nuclei and cortical association areas).

I–IV imagination circuits: I visual, II auditory, III somesthetic, IV motor, V olfactory imagination. VI affective memory circuit.

AM amygdala, AT anterior thalamic nucleus, B brain stem, CING cingulate gyrus, DM dorsomedial thalamic nucleus, H habenula, HIPP hippocampus, M mamillary body, OLF olfactory bulb, PULV pulvinar, S septal area, STRIA TERM stria terminalis. (From M. B. ARNOLD, 1960)

desire. It would have to project to cortical association areas to activate the engrams used in imagination, but in such a way that memory images could be reactivated in any temporal or spatial order. Moreover, since we can imagine movements and plan action, and such imagined movements actually innervate the needed muscles (see Jacobson, 1932), this relay station would have to connect with the frontal lobe as well.

The Amygdaloid Nuclear Complex.   This nuclear complex lies in the anterior temporal lobe and has the required connections. To judge from the voluminous research studies, the amygdala could serve as the relay station in the imagination circuit. For instance, Lesse et al. (1955) found distinct changes in the electrical activity of the amygdala and rostral hippocampus every time a patient with implanted electrodes vividly imagined or thought about something. Visual, auditory, and olfactory images all produced such an increase in electrical activity.

The amygdaloid complex includes several subcortical nuclei. It is present in vertebrates from fishes to mammals and reaches its greatest complexity in human beings (Humphrey, 1972). Its connections are widespread, ranging from hypothalamus to cortex. In the last decades, a great deal of work has been done elucidating these connections and correlating amygdaloid stimulation with behavior. I describe and review these findings in a later chapter (chapter 23). At this point, I would like merely to mention a few reports which make it likely that the amygdala is indeed the central relay station in the imagination circuit.

Sensory stimulation in all modalities and electrical stimulation of many brain areas evoke potentials in the amygdala or influence the activity of individual cells in it. These responses from the amygadala have a long latency and sometimes continue after the stimulation has ended. Often, stimulation of widely divergent cortical areas triggers potentials in the same amygdaloid cell, but many cells do not respond to any of the stimuli provided (Goddard, 1972). Some cells respond to complex rather than simple stimuli: in a cat, meows rather than clicks, mice rather than flashes of light. These findings are exactly what we would expect in a relay station of the imagination circuit. Meows and mice mean something to a cat, flashes of light do not. Whether the cat sees or smells or hears a mouse, it imagines investigating or catching it. Even after the mouse is gone, the cat may go on preparing for action.

The amygdala seems to mediate motor imagination via its projection to the dorsomedial thalamic nuclei and the frontal lobe. These nuclei also project to the pulvinar and the lateral and posterior thalamic nuclei, which connect with occipital, parietal, and temporal association areas (Fox, 1949). The amygdala is directly connected with olfactory association areas. Because of these connections, the amygdala can mediate imagination in all modalities. In addition, it can be excited from various hypothalamic nuclei. Endocrine secretion and the accompanying hypothalamic excitation can activate the amygdala to initiate images of mate, food, or water, and plan appropriate action. Conversely, particularly in human beings, sexual images can arouse sexual desire, images of food or drink can arouse the desire to eat or drink. Imagination easily leads to action.

When we see something, for instance, but cannot interpret it immediately, we imagine what it could be and imagine possible ways of coping with it. A pleasant odor can induce the image of food and a pleasurable anticipation of its taste ("it makes the mouth water"). To do that, the imagination circuit relays impulses from olfactory areas and the limbic subcallosal area to the amygdala, and from there via thalamic association nuclei to visual and taste association cortex. Since the amygdaloid complex connects with the hypothalamus and the pituitary gland, it can induce endocrine and gastric secretions. It is well known that the expectation of a particular kind of food (meat, lemon), produces the kind of gastric secretion necessary for digesting it.

The imagination circuit projects to the same cortical association areas as does the recall circuit, but reaches them via a different route (see Figs. 16.1 and 16.4). Thus the same memory engrams are used in imagination as are used in recall. But they are reactivated over a different circuit and so can be reshuffled, recombined and reorganized as needed. My hypothesis of the amygdala as a central switching station in the imagination circuit can explain how imagined situations (for instance, in sexual fantasies) can lead to autonomic and hormonal changes, and how imagined movements can produce motor innervation. Whether something is actually experienced or imagined, it is appraised for action and produces action impulses that lead to the innervation of muscles and glands, even if we choose to withhold overt action.

It is clear that the impulse to recall anything at all is an impulse to do something, to focus on a particular context and recover the needed memory. Similarly, the impulse to imagine something implies an intention to see or hear or do in imagination what we have appraised as good to do. The fact that we look toward the thing we imagine, we listen for the melody we hear in imagination, we innervate the appropriate muscles when we imagine lifting arm or leg, as Jacobson (1932) has shown, surely proves that the impulse to imagine is part of a motor pattern. When we imagine doing something, we activate relays from amygdala to the dorsomedial nucleus which projects to the dorsolateral part of the frontal lobe. Hence motor imagination activates the frontal lobe as does the intention to act. Indeed, the amygdala also sends relays to the striatum and the ventral thalamic nuclei and so connects with the action circuit.

If the amygdala is active in planning action, as I am suggesting, such motor imagination should be mediated by impulses from the amygdala to the dorsomedial thalamic nucleus, septal area, and frontal lobe. Indeed, Brazier (1972) reports that theta waves of waking human patients recorded in the amygdala consistently lead those recorded from the dorsomedial thalamic nuclei (by 7 milliseconds), and those recorded from the septum (by 15 milliseconds). Brazier recorded these time relationships during normally occurring electrical activity via implanted electrodes and did not rely on electrical stimulation, which produces "an abnormally concentrated barrage of impulses at the next synapses" (Brazier, 1972).

In summary, I am suggesting that *sensory memory* is activated by a memory circuit that starts from limbic appraisal areas, runs via hippocampus and precommissural fornix to hypothalamus and midbrain, and returns via thalamic sensory ("extrinsic") nuclei to the sensory association areas which have registered the original impressions. When these memories are reactivated, we experience memory images, not the original sensations. *Motor memory* is both registered and reactivated by the action circuit. Motor engrams are registered in the prefrontal cortex during movement and reactivated when the movement is repeated. The action circuit runs from limbic areas via the hippocampus and postcommissural fornix to the midbrain reticular formation and cerebellum and projects via cerebellar nuclei, reticular formation and ventral thalamus to prefrontal, premotor, and motor cortex. Hence, motor memory is automatically activated with every relevant action and guides its further progress.

Finally, the reactivation of *affective memory,* also initiated from the limbic appraisal areas, is achieved via the affective memory circuit running to hippocampus, postcommissural fornix and mamillary bodies, and returning via mamillo-thalamic tract and anterior thalamic nuclei to the various limbic areas. Affective memory is a reactivated unconscious appraisal that generates the same action impulse as did the original appraisal. As a result, we experience a new emotional impulse, not the memory of an appraisal.

Imagination uses the same sensory memories as does recall, but activites them via different relays. The central switching station of the imagination circuit is the amygdaloid complex, which receives relays from limbic areas and sends impulses via the thalamic association (intrinsic) nuclei to the various sensory memory areas. Motor imagination is activated via amygdala and dorsomedial thalamic nuclei connecting with the frontal lobe. Since the dorsomedial thalamic nuclei are connected with the anterior part of the ventral thalamic nuclei and these receive relays from the cerebellum, the motor imagination circuit seems to feed into the last link of the action circuit. This would explain why imagining a movement innervates the same muscles as the actual movement. The imagination circuit has access to all engrams in a given memory area. Hence, imagination is not constrained by the original spatial or temporal memory pattern and can recombine and reorganize memory images as the immediate situation requires.

ELECTROPHYSIOLOGICAL EVIDENCE

Recent neurophysiological research has brought confirmation that learning includes the activation of several subcortical structures that influence behavior. John (1966) found that spontaneous activity in various brain areas has no intertrial rhythm when a cat begins to learn to jump a hurdle to avoid an electric shock at a cue of a 10 per second flickering light. After training for ten days, a rhythm of half the frequency of the conditioning stimulus appeared during the intertrial intervals. This rhythm occurred in the visual cortex and also in the superior colliculus, fornix, septum, reticular formation, and amygdala, and was apparently simultaneous in all regions. As soon as the cat was returned to its living quarters, these rhythms disappeared. When the cat was fully trained, the rhythms were less apparent.

These changes during learning have been confirmed in other experiments. The intertrial rhythms became even more obvious when a waiting period of one second was interspersed between cue and response. In this experiment, the rhythms were at about the flicker frequency. It would seem that in the waiting period or between trials, the animal rehearses the flicker (via fornix, septum, reticular formation, and visual cortex) and imagines the required responses (via amygdala and septum). When an animal is trained to respond to a 10 cycles per second (cps) flicker, and is then shown a 6 cps flicker it will often respond with a wave form conforming to the 10 cps flicker rather than the actually seen 6 cps flicker. In differential conditioning, with a 10 cps flicker as the positive and a 6 cps flicker as the negative stimulus, the waveform before responding is that characteristic for the positive stimulus, even when the 6 cps flicker was shown. In other words, the negative 6 cps flicker actually seen was interpreted (recalled, imagined) by the cat as the positive 10 cps flicker (John, 1966). Still another experiment showed that during an incorrect response, that is, a response to the negative stimulus, the wave form of the positive flicker was observed in the motor cortex. Apparently, it was this (positive) wave configuration that resulted in the erroneus response (Stern et al., 1960).

According to John (1966), the evoked potential after a light flash has two components in trained cats, one early and one late. The early component represents the primary response arriving over the classical visual projection pathways in the visual cortex. The later, much slower deflection is greatly reduced by nembutal, hence seems to arrive over multisynaptic pathways. As John says: "During generalization (from positive to negative stimulus) there appear, not in the geniculate but in the reticular formation and the visual cortex, waveforms which seem to include a component based upon prior experience as well as a component derived from the present event" (p. 179). I would add that the late component seems to be the impulse mediating memory recall via the visual memory circuit.

John's next experiment was devised to show which of these components are crucial in further processing. After training cats to respond to a 4 cps flicker by jumping a hurdle, he stimulated the visual cortex in such a way that each 4 cps central stimulation was either simultaneous with the early component of the evoked potentials, or arrived together with the late component. The electrical stimulation that coincided with the early component caused little or no interference with the conditioned response. But when such stimulation coincided with the late component, the conditioned response was severely disrupted. As John says, "there is something crucial to the processing of information . . . by the visual system which takes place at the time of the arrival at visual cortex of the late influences of the nonspecific system" (1966, p. 181).

There is a similar sequence of early and late components in evoked potentials from the cortex when a human subject hears and repeats nonsense syllables (Morrell, 1961). The early negative potential (sometimes with preceding early positive deflection) reaches a maximum around 90 msec after the word is given, and the later positive potential peaks around 160 msec. The largest deflection is recorded from the left parietotemporal area (which includes Wernicke's auditory memory area). The recording over the Rolandic area was taken from the region that includes the representation of muscles of vocalization; these potentials were equal on the right and left side. Finally, the potentials recorded from the frontal leads were from a region that includes Broca's speech (motor) area. These potentials were larger in the left hemisphere.

Potentials can also be recorded just before the subject repeats the syllable. They seem to indicate the intention to speak. These potentials have the same form over the frontal and the rolandic leads, indicating that the muscles of vocalization are activated in the pattern of the motor speech memory. The late deflection in the potentials recorded after the subject heard the word indicate that in man also, imagination and recall accompany perception.

The process of learning is further illustrated by studies of electrical potentials recorded from visual cortex, ventral anterior thalamic nucleus, mesencephalic reticular formation, and hippocampus of the cat (Morrell, 1960, 1961). When a tone is sounded and followed by 10 cps light flashes, the visual cortex shows potentials from the onset of the light flashes. The ventral anterior thalamic nucleus continues firing spontaneously; the hippocampus reacts only to light flashes, but the reticular formation reacts to both stimuli. As training continues, the hippocampus begins to react to the tone as well as to the light, potentials in the anterior thalamic nucleus are suppressed, as are those in the reticular formation. Finally, in the last period, when the tone has been conditioned to the light, the visual cortex reacts to the tone as well as to the light, and so does the ventral anterior nucleus of the thalamus, while the reticular formation and the hippocampus are no longer reacting. This seems to mean that during learning, the tone brings about recall of the flash (via hippocampus). As soon as training is complete, the tone is recognized (via direct connection from auditory limbic cortex to ventral anterior thalamic nucleus) and the light expected (amygdala to visual cortex) so that there is no longer any necessity to recall the light flash (reticular formation and hippocampus silent). This would explain why the hippocampus is necessary for new learning but not for a well-practiced performance.

17

The Neural Substrate of Attention and the Medial Appraisal System

The technical barriers that have for so long separated the brain/ mind question from the rest of the neurosciences are now being overcome . . . . It requires little prophetic insight to predict that when the breakthrough occurs the limbic system will provide bridges that link brain, mind and behaviour in a functional continuum.

Acceptance of the limbic system concept, when it comes, will be revolutionary—a quantum leap in enlightenment that will change the profile of the basic and clinical neurosciences, and have major impact on medical education and on the social sciences as well. We can conclude today that a good deal is known about some of the individual components of the limbic system, that a moderate amount is known about some of its first order interactions, but that rather little is known about its global performance over extended periods of time. It is this latter area that remains the great engima—how do the pieces fit together to create a performing whole?

K. E. Livingston, 1976

Often, we cannot recall what we have encountered because our attention was elsewhere. Although such experiences may be brought back by special methods, for instance hypnosis, they are unavailable for deliberate recall. Attention seems to be the precondition for normal recall.

In Chapter 2, I have shown that attention is an active process. The human being or animal turns toward something, looks and listens, and concentrates on it. It follows that the neural mechanism mediating this activity cannot be a passive filter automatically varying the sensory process. Indeed, it has been found that the spontaneous or deliberate focusing on a particular experience intensifies the cortical potentials evoked by the sensory excitation and reduces the potentials in other areas of the cortex. For a brief but adequate review of the work in this area, see Hernández-Peón (1966).

Attention seems to be a response to the unasked questions: "What is it?" "How will it affect me?" and "What do I do about it?" I have suggested that attention is aroused by the appraisal that "this is good to know, good to explore," resulting in the impulse to look and listen and to disregard everything else for the time being. Hence every sensory avenue over which the object of attention can be experienced is engaged while the sensory pathways not in use may be inhibited. The impulse to look and listen is an action impulse, mediated by relays from limbic cortex via hippocampus to the frontal lobe.

NEURAL MEDIATION OF ATTENTION

In animals, attention can be studied by observing the "orienting reflex." It consists of a pricking up of ears, turning toward a novel stimulus and eventually exploring it. The synchronized electrical activity recorded by the EEG during rest is replaced by low-amplitude fast desynchronized activity over most of the cortex (arousal or activation of the EEG).

Perhaps the most extensive studies in this field have been done by Sokolov (1959). He described the first reaction to a novel stimulus as a general desynchronization of the EEG, which is gradually replaced by a localized reduction in EEG amplitude. For instance, the first reaction to a light touch was a change of this kind. After 25 repetitions, the EEG pattern only showed a slight diminution of amplitude over the motor cortex. This does not mean a reduction in sensitivity: The animal can become completely habituated to an intense stimulus, yet show a strong orienting response after a new low-intensity stimulus. According to Sokolov, the animal develops a "neuronal model" of its reaction to the stimulus. When it encounters a new stimulus that does not conform to this model, it shows an orienting reaction and EEG arousal.

Attention and the Amygdala. There is recent evidence that the amygdaloid complex is involved in attention. Animals show attention not only by turning toward a new stimulus, pricking up their ears, looking and listening but also by a change in heart rate and respiration, a galvanic skin reflex (GSR) and EEG arousal. Electrical stimulation of the amygdala produces a similar set of changes, indistinguishable from the orienting reaction induced by stimulation of the brainstem reticular system, except that it habituates more rapidly. EEG activation is produced by stimulating the anterior amygdaloid area, the lateral and magnocelluar part of the basolateral nucleus, and an area along the ventral amygdalofugal path, the zona incerta and the subthalamic nucleus to the mid-brain (Hassler, 1956). Using combined stimulation and ablation techniques, Ursin and Kaada (1960) have shown that this arousal response is mediated by the stria terminalis, the projection from amygdala to cortex.

When the amygdaloid complex is removed bilaterally, the animals continue to prick up their ears and show EEG activation; but GSR, heart and respiratory rate no longer change (Bagshaw & Benzies, 1968).

According to Pribram (1967), intact monkeys flick their ears when confronted with a novel stimulus, but this flick disappears as soon as they have learned the task. After amygdalectomy, monkeys show these ear flicks for a much longer time, particularly in tasks in which they are deficient. Hence Pribram suggested that the orienting response has two components, "one an alerting reaction indicated by the ear flick, the other a focusing function which allowed registration of the event which produced the alerting. It is this second stage which involves the amygdala and is signalled by the appearance of a GSR" (p. 327).

True, this dissociation of behavioral alerting and physiological changes indicates clearly that two functions are involved: one an overt action (ear flick, looking) accompanied by EEG activation, which does not require the amygdala; the other a set of physiological changes which do. Pribram links these changes with memory registration because the amygdalectomized monkey is slow to habituate—which might indicate a memory deficit. But such monkeys do learn, albeit slowly, and learning presupposes memory registration and recall. They fail to habituate as quickly as intact monkeys not because they cannot remember but because they cannot imagine how the cue might affect them. Ablation has eliminated imagination so that only recall is left.

The functions involved in the total process of attention are: Appraisal, recall, imagination, and action. The monkey encounters something new, appraises it as unfamiliar (via limbic cortex) and wants to know more about it. This desire to know leads not only to looking and listening but to imagination and recall, both of which produce EEG activation. Imagining what may happen alerts the animal to possible danger, which brings about a GSR, changes in heart rate and respiration. Without amygdala, Pribram's monkeys could still appraise something new as unfamiliar (via affective memory), want to know more about it, and recall similar situations. This is indicated by the ear flick, looking, listening, and EEG activation. Since they could no longer imagine anything, good or bad, they were not alerted, showed no change in heart rate or respiration, and no GSR. Without imagination, they could still learn the discrimination task, now exclusively on the basis of visual and motor memory. They were slow to habituate because the situation remained "new" until the task was practically learned. Without imagination, only successful responses can make the stimulus familiar.

This interpretation is supported by Bagshaw and Coppock's (1968) report that amygdalectomized monkeys showed normal GSR to skin stimulation but failed to develop either anticipatory or conditioned GSR to a light that signaled a mild electric shock. Without amygdalae, the monkeys could not anticipate the shock, felt no fear, and thus showed no anticipatory or conditioned GSR. In contrast, skin stimulation produces a GSR directly, as a reaction to the appraisal of the stimulus as pleasant or unpleasant.

Attention and the Prefrontal Cortex. According to Grueninger and Grueninger (1973), monkeys with lesions of the dorsolateral frontal cortex that also included the orbital cortex showed EEG desynchronization and orienting after a light flash or a tone, but the GSR was no longer present. The dorsolateral and orbital frontal cortex is the projection area of the amygdaloid complex; without these areas, the animals can no longer imagine what to do. The dorsolateral premoter area (area 6) is necessary for the initiation of the GSR (Schwartz, 1937), hence the authors' lesions would effectively prevent it. Like animals with amygdala lesions, these animals were extremely distractible; they were no longer able to organize their actions, hence reacted to any chance stimulus. The authors mentioned that an electric shock to the wrist did produce a GSR. Such a shock can be immediately appraised as painful, hence the GSR, which represents an impulse to escape from it. In this situation, imagination is not needed.

According to my theory, the amygdaloid complex is involved in attention because it is the main relay station in the imagination circuit. Since appraisal and recall are part of the total process of attention, as I have mentioned, the appraisal system and recall circuit should be involved as well. A pin prick, a flash of light or a loud sound is appraised on the spinal and brainstem level as well as on the cortical level. Indeed, stimulation of the brainstem reticular system in waking animals produces the orienting reflex.

Attention and the Brainstem Reticular System. To put this system into perspective, I now sketch briefly its topography.

The brainstem includes the medulla, pons, midbrain, thalamus, and basal ganglia (caudate, putamen, globus pallidus, and amygdala). The brainstem is continuous with the spinal cord. Like the spinal cord, ontogenetically it is derived from the dorsal (sensory) plate of the original neural tube and the ventral (motor) plate. The dorsal part, derived from the alar plate, includes the colliculi and dorsal tegmentum in the midbrain and the thalamus and epithalamus (habenula and nuclei of the caudal commissure) in the diencephalon. The ventral part, derived from the basal plate, includes the ventral tegmentum together with other ventral structures in the midbrain, the hypothalamus with its motor and secretary nuclei, and the subthalamus (globus pallidus, subthalamic nucleus, ansa lenticularis nucleus, zona incerta, and nucleus of the field of Forel) in the diencephalon. The subthalamus is thought to be part of the extrapyramidal motor system.

The midbrain or mesencephalon includes the anterior and posterior colliculi dorsally, and reaches from the mamillary bodies to the pons ventrally. Its most dorsal region contains the colliculi, which are covered by the tectum. The next ventral layer is the tegmentum, which contains the aqueduct and surrounding central gray, the reticular nuclei, red nuclei, interpeduncular nucleus, and substantia nigra. In the ventral part of the midbrain course many fibers of passage, some within the cerebral peduncles, some dorsal to them. Near the midline in the tegmentum are the oculomotor and trochlear nuclei.

The brainstem reticular formation continues the gray substance of the spinal cord and gradually concentrates around the aqueduct. It stretches from the caudal part of the medulla through the brainstem until it terminates in the reticular nuclei of the thalamus. The small, poorly myelinated fibers of the dorsal longitudinal fasciculus of Schütz run throughout the central gray just ventral of the aqueduct and fourth ventricle, and connect with the midbrain tegmentum and the medial thalamus. The central gray also has connections to cortical limbic and motor areas, to the amygdala, the thalamic limbic nuclei, and to the secretory and motor nuclei of the hypothalamus. Because of these widespread connections, Clara (1959) calls the diencephalic central gray the functional center of the organism, the bridge between mental and physical processes.

The Ascending Reticular Activating System.   In 1949, Moruzzi and Magoun reported that EEG arousal can be produced by repetitive high-frequency stimulation of the reticular core of the brainstem, as well as by sensory stimulation. Magoun (1952) called this projection the "ascending reticular activating system." Much later, Steriade et al. (1980) attempted to verify this notion that this reticular system activates the whole cortex. They identified neurons in the brainstem reticular formation of intact cats and stimulated them via implanted electrodes. From sites in various thalamic nuclei and also from the zona incerta and the preoptic region of the hypothalamus, they recorded the evoked potentials. They found that all these sites receive relays from the dorsal aspect of the midbrain reticular formation, the nucleus cuneiformis. Steriade et al. also stimulated the animals through electrodes inserted into the bulbar and pontine reticular formation and the superior raphé. They reported that most of the direct ascending relays to the forebrain arise in the midbrain rather than the pontine or bulbar reticular fields. This agrees with Moruzzi and Magoun's findings that the ascending reticular system reaches from the upper pons to the cortex. In addition, Steriade et al. found that those neurons that receive multiple afferents from thalamic levels and the spinal cord are not the neurons that project to thalamus and cortex. Hence there are receiving and projecting neurons. This might mean that the system can be activated from the forebrain as well as from the spinal cord.

According to Scheibel (1980), most reticular core neurons in the midbrain tegmentum, particularly in the cuneiform nucleus, are multimodal, that is, they respond to visual, somatic, and auditory stimuli. Combinations of the last two are most numerous. These neurons respond to stimuli coming from approximately the same direction. For instance, a unit responding to a tap on the hind limb will also respond to a sound coming from the rear. Such a somatic-auditory map is coextensive with the visuotopic map in the overlying colliculus. Scheibel suggests that a deep tectal-tegmental motor map is in apparent accord with this three-dimensional map.

THE MEDIAL APPRAISAL SYSTEM

My suggestion would be that these units in the reticular core are part of the appraisal system closely connected with the affective memory circuit. The animal must appraise the stimulus before it can want to turn and see what is going on. Next, it will find the situation good or bad (via affective memory) and will imagine what might happen and what to do about it. Hence the midbrain appraisal system is activated whatever the stimulus modality. If the situation is recognized as "bad" the animal will want to escape. Hence electrical stimulation of such neurons may also produce movement. That may account for the fact that the same neurons that respond to visual, auditory, or somatic stimuli may also produce movement when stimulated electrically.

According to Rocha (1980), when a novel stimulus is repeated, the orienting reaction subsides and the electrical potentials recorded from brainstem reticular neurons decrease. Such "attenuating" neurons have been found in spinoreticular afferent areas, in the reticular formation at bulbar and pontine levels, and in the midbrain. When the novel stimulus is either incorporated in a learning task or has no harmful consequences, the animal's emotional state subsides. With it, the excitation in the affective memory circuit subsides to normal levels.

Attention and the Medial Appraisal System.   Although the total process of attention embraces appraisal, action impulse, recall, and imagination, the most important factor is probably the appraisal, which touches off the urge to know what it is all about. When we see something but cannot appraise it, we do not really experience it. During anesthesia, when the medial appraisal system is suppressed, we do not experience anything, we do not remember, and we do not use our imagination voluntarily. In contrast, when we encounter something we appraise as exceedingly pleasant or unpleasant in the waking state, our awareness is heightened and our imagination stimulated.

Since the medial appraisal system is so important for attention, I discuss the connection between the somesthetic pathways and the relevant appraisal path here. While impressions in all modalities are appraised as good or bad, pleasant or unpleasant, the appraisal of somesthetic sensations carries with it the most intense pain and pleasure. Compared to physical pain and pleasure, visual, auditory, olfactory, and taste sensations are rarely more than mildly pleasant or unpleasant. A flash of light, the smell of burning, or a loud sound may quickly draw attention, but only if danger threatens is it actively avoided. It is the threat of possible danger that arouses imagination and produces EEG activation.

I have suggested (Arnold, 1960, vol. 2) that the small fibers of this system have their origin in the various sensory receptors and feed into the medial appraisal system.

Peripheral Afferents in the Appraisal System

All sensory systems seem to have fine afferents that travel with the modality-specific fibers and connect with limbic thalamic nuclei and cortical appraisal areas. I discuss three systems for which there is sufficient evidence for these connections: the visual, somatosensory, and olfactory system.

The Visual Appraisal System.   The fine fibers in the medial part of the optic tract that run to the magnocellular ventral part of the lateral geniculate body seem to belong to this system. They also connect with the tectum and midbrain reticular formation (Clara, 1959). And Marg (1973) reported a fiber tract with receptors in the retina that travels together with other fibers in the optic tract and chiasm, to end in the transpeduncular tract in the midbrain. This tract is connected with the basal nucleus of the optic tract and with the ventrolateral reticular area in the midbrain, the interpedunuclar nucleus, and the substantia nigra. Other fibers in this tract run to the ventral nucleus of the lateral geniculate body, which is connected with the visual cortex. MacLean (1975) found a projection from the ventral part of the lateral geniculate body to the posterior hippocampal gyrus, and also a projection from the inferior pulvinar to that gyrus. On visual stimulation, only the direct pathway from the ventral lateral geniculate nucleus to the posterior hippocampal gyrus responded with electrical potentials. This seems to be the postulated afferent projection of visual appraisal fibers to the visual limbic cortex.

The Somatosensory Appraisal System.   This system also has fine afferents that seem to belong to the medial appraisal system. Bishop (1959) found, for instance, that five pathways from somesthetic receptors run in the spinal cord to the brain. Three of them go directly or indirectly (via brainstem reticular formation) to the medial thalamic nuclei (intralaminar nuclei) and connect with the cingulate gyrus, prepiriform cortex, insula, and claustrum. This is the spinoreticular thalamic system. The fibers in these pathways are small in diameter and conduct very slowly. One of these pathways is the so-called pain and temperature tract, which mediates diffuse pain. This spinoreticular-thalamic system projects bilaterally and is found only in mammals.

Two of the five somesthetic pathways, phylogenetically much younger, go to the sensory thalamic nuclei (ventroposterolateral and ventroposteromedial nuclei) and the somesthetic parietal cortex. This projection is mainly contralateral. One of these tracts is the medial lemniscus, which mediates touch and other somatic sensations. The other, the neospinal tract, forms the spinothalamocortical pain system and mediates sharp, well localized pain. The neospinal tract (ascending in the cord as the lateral spinothalamic tract) connects with the more diffuse spinoreticular-thalamic system on the spinal, bulbar, and thalamic levels. Many fibers of this tract end in the centrum medianum nucleus in the thalamus. The fibers in the neospinal tract are small when compared with the fibers in the medial lemniscus but larger than the fibers in the spinoreticular-thalamic system (Bishop, 1959). Since nerve conduction is slower the smaller the fiber, the nervous impulses initiated by touch, pinch, or electrical stimulation of the sciatic nerve arrive much later in the brainstem reticular formation than at the same level in the medial lemniscus or the neospinal tract. Hence the long delay of evoked potentials in the tegmentum, as reported by Starzl et al. (1951a,b).

I am suggesting that these small fibers in the spinoreticular-thalamic system and the slightly larger fibers of the spinothalamocortical system mediate not only the pain from pressure, prick, or cut, but also the pleasantness of touch or tickle, warmth and coolness, and the pain or unpleasantness of cold and heat (Fig. 17.1). In addition, they mediate sexual pleasure as well as the malaise of various internal sensations. It is well known, for instance, that sectioning the lateral spinothalamic tract at a high thoracic or medullary level (tractotomy) relieves intractable pain—but it also abolishes sexual pleasure (Clara, 1959). After tractotomy, diffuse pain may remain. It is abolished when the centrum medianum nucleus is coagulated. When that is done, even without tractotomy, both sharp and diffuse pain disappear.

Like the ventral magnocellular part of the lateral geniculate body, the large-celled part of the ventroposterolateral thalamic nucleus seems to belong to the appraisal system. According to Yakovlev et al. (1966), this region, together with the laterodorsal thalamic nucleus, projects to the supracallosal and retrosplenial limbic cortex. It is quite possible that the magnocellular parts of other sensory thalamic nuclei project to limbic cortex while the small-celled parts project to the modality-specific sensory cortex.

The Olfactory Appraisal System.   The afferents ending in the appraisal areas in the medial part of the posterior orbital cortex seem to come from special receptors in the nasal mucosa. One type of receptor is connected with the terminal nerve, the other with the vomeronasal organ in the accessory olfactory bulb.

The terminal nerve occurs in all mammals, including the human being. In animals, it is closely associated with the vomeronasal organ, which is present in the human embryo but has atrophied in the adult. The terminal nerve seems to run to the subcallosal limbic area and the septal nuclei (Tucker, 1971). Riss et al. (1969) have reviewed the olfactory connections in a number of vertebrates and suggested that the terminal nerve, which projects directly to limbic structures, is proof that the olfactory lobe belongs to the limbic as much as to the olfactory system. Indeed, they suggested that olfactory structures may have evolved from limbic structures. For instance, amphioxus possesses no olfactory nerve but does

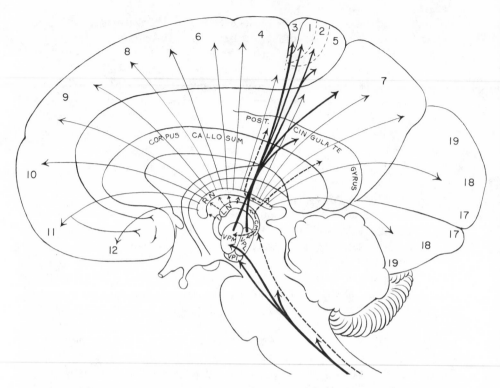

FIG. 17.1.   The APPRAISAL system. Peripheral fibers project in spinothalamic and spinoreticular tracts to posterior cingulate gyrus. The associated somesthetic projection is also shown. (Appraisal fibers from other sensory systems are not sketched.) The diffuse projection from the intralaminar thalamic nuclei reaches every area of the cortex via the thalamic reticular nuclei. ——— Sensory projection. - - - - - Projection of appraisal system. ——— Diffuse projection. Arabic numerals refer to Brodmann areas. CM centrum medianum. ILN intralaminar nucleus. RN reticular nucleus. VPI ventropostero-inferior nucleus. VPL Ventroposterolateral nucleus. VPM ventroposteromedial nucleus. (From M. B. Arnold, 1960)

have a terminal nerve; the later evolving lamprey has both a terminal and an olfactory nerve. Human beings, who have lost the accessory olfactory bulb, still possess a terminal nerve. As part of the limbic system, the terminal nerve may mediate the appraisal of odors and, like the fine afferents in the somatosensory system, belong to the medial appraisal system.

Bennett (1968) reported that unilateral removal of the olfactory bulb does not impair retention of an olfactory discrimination. Only when more than 50% of both anterior limbs of the anterior commissure were transected was retention impaired. After complete transection of the anterior commissure on both sides, the learned performance was completely lost but could be relearned. Apparently, the intact terminal nerve made it possible for the animal to retain the olfctory discrimination. After ablation of the bulb, the animal was still able to appraise the positive odor as good and approach it. But after transection of the anterior commissure on both sides, the major part of the nerve distribution was lost, and retention was lost with it. However, the unilateral connection of the terminal nerve would make it possible for the animal to relearn.

Pribram (1973) mentioned that the part of the posterior orbital area that adjoins the medial orbital cortex is closely connected with the neighboring insula— which is not surprising because animals sniff to detect an odor. Sniffing is a motor reaction; and the appraisal of snout movements is mediated by the anterior insula, according to my theory. Appraising the smell as "good to know," the animal attends to it and sniffs. Any olfactory experience, registered in the posterior orbital cortex and appraised via its medial region, is accompanied by electrical activity in the anterior insula.

The Vomeronasal Organ.   In addition to the main olfactory bulb, most animals also have an accessory olfactory bulb with a vomeronasal organ. This organ receives bundles of fibers that are intimately associated with myelinated, presumably trigeminal, fibers from receptors in the nasal nucosa. Like the main olfactory bulb, the accessory olfactory bulb is connected with the anterior olfactory nucleus, the olfactory tubercle and the amygdala. It is also connected with the hypothalamus and midbrain. I would suggest that the vomeronasal system may mediate the appraisal of odors that stimulate the trigeminal system; or, perhaps, of odors significant for instinctive activities (food, mate, young). Its cortical limbic area seems to be the medial olfactory tubercle.

Wold and Brodal (1974) stimulated the posterior orbital cortex and found electrical potentials in the nucleus interpolaris of the sensory trigeminal nuclear complex. They suggested that relays from this nucleus go to the cerebellum— which connects with the ventrolateral thalamic nuclei and the motor cortex. Hence something smelled and appraised as harmful or pleasurable would result in approach or withdrawal.

An odor may be felt as pleasant or unpleasant even if it does not appreciably affect the trigeminal system. But when this system is stimulated, the animal usually reacts to the odor with changes in respiration and heart rate, and often with incipient movements, even when it is anesthetized. For instance, ammonia, a decidedly unpleasant odor, strongly stimulates the trigeminal system. When the trigeminal ganglia were blocked with xylocaine, the animals no longer showed the usual physiological responses. Their heart rate and respiration remained unchanged. In fact, the EEG showed the slow waves of sleep instead of the usual arousal reaction in response to an odor (Stone et al., 1966). It would seem that the EEG changes and autonomic reactions are triggered by trigeminal stimulation rather than by purely olfactory sensations.

Halpern and Frumin (1979) found the same connection between the vomeronasal system and active approach in garter snakes. After vomeronasal nerve lesions, the snakes would no longer attack and eat pieces of earthworm. But when the snakes were given many sensory cues while learning to attack earthworm bits, they retained such prey attack even after their vomeronasal system was disrupted. Sensory cues recall the affective memory of earlier experiences with earthworms, hence prey attack remains intact for such snakes.

My suggestion that the appraisal of pure odors is mediated by the terminal nerve and posterior orbital limbic cortex, and the appraisal of pungent odors by the vomeronasal system, seems to be contradicted by the fact that human adults no longer have a vomeronasal organ and birds have neither a vomeronasal organ nor a terminal nerve. Yet human beings are repelled by ammonia; and birds, although not endangered by smells as much as are land animals, must be able to avoid a forest fire before they see it. But it is surely possible that there are nerve fibers that have the same function and even the same location without being numerous enough to be combined into a conspicious vomeronasal organ.

Thalamic and Midbrain Levels of the Appraisal System

These sensory appraisal fibers are connected not only with limbic cortex but also, and more directly, with the medial appraisal system at the thalamic and midbrain levels. Even after decortication, an animal is able to react to pain, an odor, or a flash of light. And attention is attracted to something painful or threatening long before man or animal can correctly perceive it.

If the activity of this medial appraisal system is suppressed, for instance during anesthesia, man or animal becomes unconscious. French et al. (1953) reported that barbiturates or ether first depressed the evoked potentials in the brainstem reticular formation (elicited by sciatic nerve stimulation), and after a short time abolished them. The evoked potentials in the sensory pathway, the medial lemniscus, were not affected. As soon as the potentials in the reticular formation were reduced, the EEG waves slowed. When these potentials dropped out altogether, the EEG showed the slow waves of deep sleep. The authors pointed out that sensory impulses run via both the medial nonspecific and the lateral sensory system to the cortex. Evoked potentials from sciatic stimulation were found not only in the brainstem reticular formation but also in the somatosensory cortex, the centrum medianum in the thalamus, and the frontal lobe.

According to Steriade et al. (1980), "projections through lateral thalamic nuclei and the specific thalamo-cortical pathways coexist with those through the medial thalamus" (p. 139). These pathways seem to serve different functions: The route from receptors to sensory thalamic nuclei and cortex seems to carry the appraisal fibers of the modality-specific sensory system, while the route from collaterals to the brainstem reticular system via medial thalamus to medical cortex seems to be a link in the afferent pathways of the appraisal system from midbrain reticular system (connected with the sensory system) to various regions of the limbic cortex. That the medial thalamus projects to limbic cortex was confirmed by Robertson and Kaitz (1981), who reported that the thalamic midline and intralaminar nuclei project to all limbic cortical areas.

Finally, Rocha (1980) reported that the brainstem reticular system receives crossed afferents from specific sensory systems but also from spino-reticular sources, and sends relays to sensory thalamic nuclei, hypothalamus, and cortex, but also to the spinal cord. Rocha believes that this system is involved in attention, via relays to the thalamic reticular system. He found no somatotopic relation of points in the brainstem reticular formation with points on the body surface when he stimulated cats by taps. Potentials in the reticular formation ranged over a wide area, although the face region registered more rostrally than the body region. On electrical stimulation of the brainstem reticular formation, the potentials in the thalamic somatosensory area were more restricted but also showed no somatotopic relationship. This is in line with the lack of any somatotopic relationship of recorded potentials in the posterior cingulate gyrus with points of the body stimulated. Obviously, the affective reaction to such stimulation is not restricted to the point of contact.

The thalamic level of the medial appraisal system seems to be identical with the "unspecific system" of Lorente de Nó, so called because it seemed to use unspecific pathways of unknown origin, unlike the sensory system that runs from receptors via specific thalamic nuclei to specific cortical sensory areas. Other investigators called it the "diffuse" thalamic system; but Skinner and Lindsley (1973) preferred the term "non-specific system" because "the electrocortical responses are neither unspecific in their projection nor diffuse in their distribution."

Facilitation and Inhibition of Sensory Experience.

The medial appraisal system in the brain stem also seems to be responsible for the facilitation and inhibition of sensory experience. This occurs during attention and particularly during the concentrated attention found in hypnosis. Hernández–Peón (1961) has reviewed the experimental evidence showing that the midbrain reticular formation can both facilitate and inhibit sensory relays at all levels of the sensory pathway. In one study, the experimenter recorded the potentials evoked by touching the face of a cat that carried implanted electrodes. When the mesencephalic reticular formation was stimulated for three seconds, the cat became alert and the potentials evoked by touch and recorded from cortex and trigeminal nucleus were significantly reduced. The greater the alertness produced by stimulating the reticular formation, the smaller were the evoked tactile potentials. Apparently, repetitive stimulation of the activating system inhibits the conduction of sensory impulses.

Stimulation of the reticular formation not only reduces sensory potentials, it also inhibits conduction in non-specific pathways. Normally, repetitive electrical stimulation of the amygdala (basolateral region) produces electrical afterdischarges. When the reticular formation was stimulated, the animal became alert and attentive and the same repetitive stimulation of the amygdala now produced no afterdischarge. The amygdala, I have postulated, is active in attention and imagination. When attention is produced by stimulating the reticular formation, the animal focuses on its surroundings; this activates the amygdala and the additional electrical stimulation has no further effect.

Sensory inhibition is possible as long as the brainstem reticular formation is intact. Hernández–Peón and Brust-Carmona (1961) experimented with cats whose brainstem was completely transected at the rostral midbrain level. They recorded evoked tactile potentials from the lateral spinothalamic tract. Next, they transected the spinal cord just below the medulla and found that these tactile potentials were now greatly enhanced. This means that there must have been an inhibitory influence originating in the midbrain, not the cortex.

Attention can bring about facilitation as well as inhibition. Hernández–Peón (1961) recorded simultaneously the evoked potentials in the olfactory bulb, the spinal trigeminal sensory nucleus, and the cochlear nucleus, in waking cats. When they brought a mouse into the cat's cage, the olfactory bulb showed bursts of increased rhythmic potentials, so-called "arousal discharges," and the tactile potentials in the trigeminal sensory nycleus were enhanced; however, the auditory potentials were reduced. In a few seconds, when the cat focused its attention on the mouse, the olfactory potentials were further increased, but both the tactile and auditory potentials were reduced. As soon as the mouse was taken away, the electrical activity in the olfactory bulb and the evoked responses to clicks and tactile stimuli returned to their earlier size.

This is an excellent illustration of the way attention facilitates some sensory systems and inhibits others. When the cat concentrates on the olfactory experience and disregards other sensory stimuli, potentials are facilitated in the olfactory bulb but inhibited in auditory and tactile pathways. Facilitation and inhibition are consequences of appraisal. What is appraised as good to know (to see, to sniff, etc.) will result in facilitation of the sensory pathway used, and in inhibition of all other sensory pathways. Since both facilitation and inhibition are the result of appraisal and attention, they must normally be cortically induced.

Motor facilitation and inhibition can also be produced via the medial appraisal system. Potentials in the brainstem reticular formation can be evoked by electrical stimulation of various cortical areas: the frontal eye field, the cingulate gyrus, the orbital surface of the frontal lobe, the sensorimotor cortex, and the superior temporal gyrus (French et al., 1955). According to these authors, the cortical regions that evoke potentials in the reticular system show a striking resemblance to the so-called "suppressor strips" in the cortex. Since the conduction of neural impulses resulting from such cortical stimulation is from cortex to brainstem, this was said to be a "descending" reticular system. According to Hernández–Peón (1966), this descending systems seems to reach only to the rostral border of the pons.

I have suggested before (Arnold, 1960/II) that the suppressor strips in the cortex represent the areas in the cortex that connect with the neighboring limbic areas which serve the *appraisal* of movement and movement impulses, and also of sensory experience. Depending on a given appraisal, movement may be initiated, facilitated, or inhibited. The appraisal system can prime or inhibit the action circuit. The "ascending activating system" seems to represent the brainstem levels of the appraisal system projecting to the frontal lobe; the "descending activating system" seems to represent the connection of sensory and motor cortical areas with limbic appraisal areas, and the connection of the appraisal areas with the action circuit.

The appraisal of something as "good to smell" seems to result in the inhibition of various motor reflexes that are not appropriate at the time. For instance, Sauerland and Clemente (1973) reported that on stimulating the orbital gyrus (the memory area for smell that connects with the adolfactory appraisal area), the soleus (calf muscle), and the masseter (jaw muscle) reflex were inhibited simultaneously. The same inhibition was produced when the ventromedial reticular formation was stimulated. This is Magoun and Rhines' (1946) "inhibitory" region. In my theory, it is the brainstem level of the appraisal system. When Sauerland and Clemente stimulated the orbital gyrus with a single pulse, they could record evoked short-latency potentials from precisely those points in the medullary inhibitory area which, when stimulated, had induced reflex inhibition. But on stimulating the orbital gyrus, they could also record evoked potentials from the reticular area of the pons known to produce reflex facilitation. They concluded that neurons in the orbital cortex send axons directly to the facilitatory and inhibitory areas in the brainstem. No synaptic relays seem to be involved. Apparently, the appraisal of something as "good to smell" facilitates some movements and inhibits others. The facilitated movements (masseter reflex in chewing) are connected with the action to which the appraisal may lead.

APPRAISAL AND ACTION

The appraisal system functions not only in gauging the environment and attending to it, but in appraising something for action. The action circuit functions as soon as an individual decides on attention and action. From the evidence we can conclude that stimulation of the brainstem reticular formation excites the action circuit as well as the appraisal system. It is not surprising that more than one function is represented in the "ascending and descending reticular system." It is a highly organized system and is understood to comprise heterogeneous nuclear structures. For instance, Sprague and Chambers (1953) have shown that the stimulation of waking animals via electrodes implanted in the bulbar reticular formation does not produce simple inhibition or facilitation but coordinated posturing.

From the spinal reflex to voluntary action we see the relation between appraisal, attention, and action. In the scratch reflex, the receptor link mediates the sensation of touch or tickle, the connector (medial) link the estimate of "unpleasantness," which activates the effector link and leads to attention and scratching. On the thalamic level, we experience the quality of sensation but also its affective complement: Sudden bright light draws our attention but is felt as unpleasant, hence the pupil contracts and we close our eyes. On the cortical level, finally, we appraise things in the light of experience, attend to them, and plan our action according to conditions as we see them.

The Descending Reticular System. This system seems to be a link in the action circuit, or at least, connected with it. According to my theory, the action circuit runs from limbic cortex via hippocampus to brainstem and cerebellum, to return via thalamic ventral nuclei to the motor cortex. While consummatory action (e.g. chewing) may be directly inhibited or facilitated by the limbic cortex of the orbital surface, as Sauerland and Clemente suggest, actions that are not instinctive require intuitive or deliberate appraisal via the cortex of the limbic system, and inhibition or facilitation via the action circuit. Hence, sciatic stimulation is appraised as painful via the thalamus, and the posterior cingulate gyrus or posterior insula, and leads to action via hippocampus, midbrain, cerebellum, and frontal lobe in the action circuit. Indeed, Moruzzi (1954) has shown that cerebellar polarization results in facilitation of reticular neurons and EEG arousal when 1.5 mA current is used, but inhibition of reticular neurons at lower current intensity (0.5 mA). The medial anterior lobe of the cerebellum is responsible for this effect. Moreover, von Baumgarten et al. (1954) have shown that the same bulbo-reticular units may be influenced by relays from sensory, cerebellar, and motor cortex. This means that the action circuit can be excited from sensory and motor cortex but also from the cerebellum, which is exactly what we would expect if normal excitation is the result of an appraisal of sensory experience and of action, and if the action circuit runs via the cerebellum.

Cerveau Isolé and Encéphale Isolé. That the motor memory and imagination circuits are involved in activating the EEG is also shown by the fact that the cerveau isolé, an animal whose brainstem is cut between the superior and inferior colliculi, or just below the inferior colliculi, a cut which interrupts the memory circuit, is asleep and paralyzed. Its EEG shows the slow waves of deep sleep. Only olfactory stimulation can produce EEG arousal for a short time. The appraisal of olfactory impressions via the adolfactory area can activate the amygdala and the frontal lobe via the dorsomedial thalamic nucleus and so produce EEG arousal. Optic stimulation has no effect on the EEG, despite the fact that the optic as well as the oculomotor nerve are included in the cerveau isolé. Since the action and memory circuits from hippocampus to midbrain are interrupted in this preparation, optic stimulation cannot result in moving the eyes or activating recall, and so cannot bring about EEG arousal.

In contrast, an animal with its brain stem cut behind the pons (encéphale isolé) has a normal sleeping and waking rhythm. Visual, olfactory, and trigeminal stimulation wake it and produce EEG arousal. So does electrical stimulation of the cortex (Bradley & Elkes, 1957). In fact, even when the brainstem is cut just rostral to the trigeminal roots, so that all tactual sensations are excluded, the cat could follow a moving object with its eyes and react with pupillary dilation to the sight of a mouse (Batini et al., 1958). Encéphale isolé animals have a normal sleeping and waking rhythm, hence a normal EEG, because the memory and imagination circuits are included in this preparation. According to my theory, only when the animal is able to remember similar experiences and so can identify and appraise them, when it can plan action and appraise its possibilities of success or failure, will it be able to sustain wakefulness for any length of time and so show a normal EEG.

Directed Attention.   In human beings, attention can be directed at will, either to something present or absent, even something remembered or imagined. In experimental situations, the subject can be asked to pay attention to a particular stimulus that will be shown to him. Grey Walter (1973) has reported that such expectation of a signal produces distinctive slow waves (expectancy waves) first in the frontal cortex, later in other cortical areas. When the instruction is revoked and the subject no longer expects a signal, these waves disappear. The expectancy wave occurs among the desynchronized waves of the normal EEG.

Ordinarily, attention to a novel stimulus lapses quickly but is revived if the stimulus changes. But when the subject is instructed to watch for changes in the stimulus, or to count the number of stimuli, or to press a key in response to each signal, his attention is riveted on the stimulus; and the GSR, EEG arousal, and other physiological changes may persist for a long time. This is true also for patients with postcentral, temporal, or parieto-occipital lesions despite their kinesthetic, visual, or auditory defects. However, after lesions of the polar, medial, and mediobasal frontal lobes, verbal instructions did not lead to cortical arousal, or such arousal lasted only for a short time (Luria, 1973b). This means that the limbic motor appraisal areas are necessary for voluntary attention, which supports my suggestion that attention is a desire to know, an impulse to turn, look, and listen. This action impulse must be appraised as suitable, via medial and mediobasal frontal limbic cortex, before the individual will attend to the situation and concentrate on it.

Inattention.   Normally, inattention may be the result of drowsiness, daydreaming, distractibility, or deliberate "turning off." In every case, the person is inattentive because he is focused on something more engrossing than the situation to which he is supposed to pay attention.

When inattention is the result of a brain lesion, the lesion has made it impossible to show the usual signs of attention: in animals, pricking up of ears or ear flick, turning eyes or head toward the object, GSR, and changes in heart rate and respiration. Such inattention is often called "sensory neglect," because the animal does not react to a sensory stimulus. But the term is a misnomer. The animal does not neglect the stimulus; rather, it cannot react to it. Since this lack of reaction is the result of a lesion, the lesion seems to have interrupted the action circuit somewhere between sensory areas and motor area.

Iwai et al. (1979) have reported that a narrow band of the inferior parietal cortex, when ablated, results in behavioral blindness in the monkey. After bilateral lesions, the monkey completely disregards anything in the environment. Unilateral lesions produced "a visual neglect of objects in the contralateral visual field." Apparently, the lesion has disturbed relays from the occipital association cortex to the visual limbic cortex (Fig. 17.2). Brodal (1978a,b) has shown that most fibers projecting from the occipital area to the pontine nuclei and cerebellum originate in the medial (limbic) cortex of area 19, overlapping fibers from the parietal association cortex. Hence it is a reasonable conclusion that the lesion has interrupted these projections. Since the behavioral blindness only lasted a short period, additional connections from the visual area to the retrosplenial limbic area and hippocampus must have been sufficient for the animal to react after the initial disorganization.

According to Wiesendanger et al. (1979), unilateral lesions of the brachium pontis, which damage the cortical projection to the cerebellum, also result in inattention, this time at the side of the lesion. Stimulation of cerebral sensory areas evokes responses in the opposite cerebellar hemisphere because these fibers cross

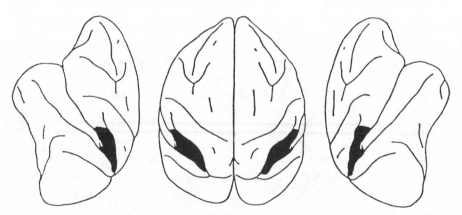

FIG.   17.2.   Inferior parietal lesion causing behavioral blindness. Representative reconstruction of inferior parietal lesion, based on stained cross sections. Lesioned areas are shown in black. This monkey, 78-J-57, received the smallest lesion within the IP-group monkeys, but showed clear behavioral blindness. The lesion included the ventral bank of the intraparietal sulcus and the dorsal banks of the superior temporal sulcus and lateral fissure. (From E. Iwai et al., 1979)

in the pons before reaching the cerebellum. Since the lesion has interrupted the relays from the pons to the cerebellum, the cerebellum cannot send a "motor command" (see chapter 26) via the ventral thalamic nuclei to the motor cortex, hence the animal is unable to react to anything seen in the visual field at the side of the lesion.

Lesions of the action circuit between cerebellum and frontal lobe also produce inattention to objects seen, but on the side opposite to the lesion. Ungerstedt et

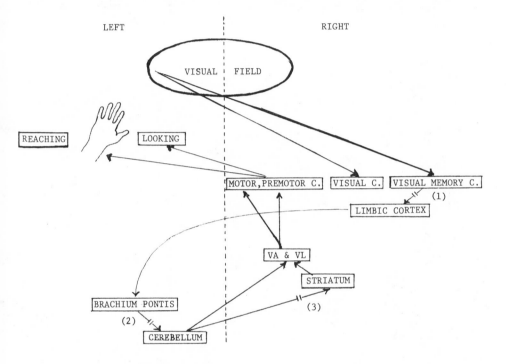

FIG. 17.3. Unilateral lesions within action circuit. (1) Lesion in right inferior temporal area; interrupts relays from visual association cortex to adjoining limbic cortex. Prevents appraisal of object seen in left visual field, hence no impulse to turn toward it: *inattention contralateral to lesion*. (Iwai et al., 1979) (2) Lesion in left brachium pontis interrupts the projection from right visual association area to left cerebellum. Object in left visual field is seen and appraised, but the impulse to turn and look cannot be experienced because cerebellum cannot relay impulse to ventral thalamic muclei and right premotor and motor cortex. Hence *inattention ipsilateral to lesion*. (Wiesendanger et al., 1979.) (3) Unilateral lesion to one of : lateral hypothalamus, striato-nigral or nigrostriatal pathway, striatum. Object in left visual field is appraised, impulse to turn and look is conducted via brachium pontis to cerebellum; but the ascending limb of the action circuit is interrupted so that the motor impulse cannot be experienced and carried out (via ventral thalamic nuclei to premotor and motor cortex.) This results is *inattention contralateral to the lesion*. (Ungerstedt et al., 1977.)

VA - ventral anterior ⎫
VL - ventrolateral   ⎬ thalamic nucleus
C. - cortex   ⎭

al. (1977) reported a profound contralateral sensory neglect after unilateral destruction of the nigro-striatal dopamine path or the lateral hypothalamus which contains this pathway. This also happens after lesions of the striatum or the striato-nigral pathway. Figure 17.3 illustrates the pathways interrupted after various lesions and the side (ipsilateral or contralateral to the lesion) which is "neglected" by the animal.

These results illustrate my point that attention requires an appraisal of the object and an impulse to turn toward it, look at it, and perhaps approach it; that is, an overt action, no matter how abbreviated.

18 Damage to the Appraisal System and the Affective Memory Circuit

> By a curiosity of evolution, every human skull harbors a prehis-
> toric vestige: a reptilian brain. This atavism, like a hand grenade
> cushioned in the more civilized surrounding cortex, is the dark
> hive where many of mankind's primitive impulses originate.
>
> Lance Morrow, in Time, April 13, 1981

> (Man) has inherited the structure and organization of three basic
> cerebral types. . . : reptilian, old mammalian, and new
> mammalian. . . . Despite great differences in structure and chem-
> istry, all three brains must intermesh and function
> together. . . . Man's brain of oldest heritage is basically reptil-
> ian. It forms the matrix of the upper brainstem and comprises
> much of the reticular system, midbrain, and basal
> ganglia. . . there are indications that the reptilian brain "pro-
> grams" stereotyped behaviors according to instructions based on
> ancestral learning and ancestral memories. . . it seems to play a
> role in. . . instinctually determined functions.
>
> P.D. MacLean, 1970

MacLean's flight of poetic fancy has been taken seriously by many a layman who supposes with a delicious shudder that he still has a piece of the old reptile in him (Fig. 18.1). Sober consideration of the evidence (see Chapter 17) indicates, on the contrary, that the "reptilian" medial system is an indispensible part of the nervous system of all vertebrates. It serves reflex appraisals on the spinal level, and the appraisal of sensory qualities on the thalamic level. On the cortical level, the limbic cortex mediates the appraisal of people, things, and situations. With- out this appraisal system, neither man nor animal would ever be able to react to

241

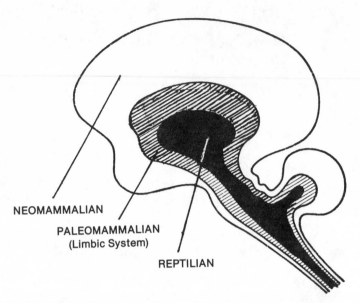

NEOMAMMALIAN

PALEOMAMMALIAN
(Limbic System)

REPTILIAN

FIG. 18.1.   Three basic brain types. Scheme of hierarchic organization of the three basic brain types which, in the evolution of the mammalian brain, become part of man's inheritance. They are referred to here as the reptilian, paleomammalian, and neomammalian brains. (From P. D. MacLean, 1967).

the environment. The appraisal system is the link between the afferent sensory system and the efferent motor system. I venture to say that even invertebrates, down to unicellular animals, must have some way of appraising what they encounter, to react appropriately.

In the mammal, the appraisal areas in the limbic cortex orginate the affective memory circuit that loops via hippocampus, postcommissural fornix, and anterior thalamic nuclei back to various limbic areas. Today's appraisals are always influenced by past appraisals and attitudes. For that reason, I have delayed the discussion of memory impairment after limbic cortex lesions until this chapter so as to treat the affective memory circuit together with the appraisal and affective memory areas. I have discussed the midbrain and thalamic levels of the medial appraisal system in chapter 17, and the cortical appraisal area in chapters 11, 12, 13, 14.

AFFECTIVE MEMORY AND TWO-STAGE BRAIN LESIONS

Often, bilateral brain lesions that fall within the memory circuits obliterate memory when made in one stage. But if the same lesion is made first on one side, and after some recovery time on the other, the animal is usually able to relearn the task with further training. Apparently, in the interval after the first lesion the animal learns to use affective memory, which is intact on both sides, in preference to sensory memory, which is impaired on one side. For instance, successive discrimination normally requires modality-specific memory as well as affective memory because the animal must recall the absent cue to make sure that the cue actually present is negative or positive. But with overtraining, the "good" cue may become so firmly fixed in affective memory that modality-specific recall is no longer needed. When complex, the required response needs organizing and planning, and that is often beyond the lesioned animal's capacity. But a simple response like bar pressing for food or water may become so automatic that the positive cue immediately elicits the response. The cingulate gyrus is linked not only with the hippocampus but also with the caudate. Very likely, such connections also obtain in other limbic cortical areas. Hence the positive cue, as soon as evaluated as good to approach, could immediately lead to the response.

Hippocampal Lesions. This double connection of the limbic areas may account for the oft-reported finding that one-stage ablation of both hippocampi results in severe impairment while a two-stage ablation does not. In the one-stage operation, the animal is deprived of modality-specific recall and is also unable to initiate the usual motor response via the hippocampus. Although the affective memory circuit may be intact because of the direct connections from limbic cortex to anterior thalamic nuclei, the animal cannot use this memory without the damaged modality-specific memory circuit. But in a two-stage ablation, the animal can use the intact modality-specific memory circuit of one side as a guide while becoming proficient in using the affective memory circuit alone. It may come to prefer using the undamaged affective memory circuit because the modality-specific memory circuit functions only on one side. After the second lesion, the animal continues using affective memory, which now is the only memory available.

Stein et al.'s (1969) report bears out this interpretation. These authors used a successive and a simultaneous light/dark discimination (Y-maze) and a reversal of these tasks. As passive avoidance task, they used a straight alley with a water spout at the end. The group with one-stage hippocampal lesions performed poorly on all three problems, which is the usual finding. The group with two-stage surgery (30 days between lesions) was not significantly different from sham-operated controls. Although simultaneous discrimination can be learned by affective memory alone, the choice of either arm of the Y-maze required motor memory which is normally initiated by the hippocampus. In two-stage ablations, the 30 days before the second lesion allowed the animals to become accustomed to using the affective memory of the "good" arm and of turning into it (via caudate).

Amygdala Lesions. These authors also tested retention after one- and two-stage amygdala lesions. The group with one-stage lesions were significantly impaired in the two visual discriminations, but even the animals with two-stage lesions showed a deficit. Amygdala lesions mean interruption of the imagination circuit that is normally used in learning. After the one-stage bilateral lesions, the animals could form neither the image of food and water, nor of their plan of action. Amygdala lesions do not prevent learning, they merely retard it because the animals have to depend exclusively on memory. Learning with imagination intact and then repeating the task without it would produce a significant impairment. This is true even for two-stage lesions because there is no substitute for the missing imagination. While affective memory can be used under some conditions without the help of modality-specific memory, neither affective memory nor modality-specific memory can substitute for imagination. What does happen when these circuits are intact but the imagination circuit is damaged is that the animal has to learn to depend on memory alone, without knowing what to expect or what it can do. With a simple task this is possible; but when an animal has to perform a complex task yet cannot imagine what comes next, the impairment is noticeable. The passive avoidance task did not show impairment after amygdala lesions, either in the one- or the two-stage method. But in this task, amygdalectomized animals have an advantage because this lesion retards their response (see chapter 23).

Stein et al. concluded that the intact performance of the animals with two-stage lesions suggests that there are no areas in the brain that are absolutely necessary for complex behavior (presumably excepting sensory and motor areas) and that the remaining tissue must have taken over the function of the ablated tissues. I have tried to show that a quite different inference can be drawn from Stein et al.'s results: Brain-damaged animals learn to do without certain psychological activities that are normally used in learning. In the interval between the two stages of surgery, they achieve sufficient practice in using the remaining affective memory circuits alone instead of in tandem with modality-specific memory circuits. When the two memory circuits are intact but the imagination circuit is interrupted (after amygdala lesions), the delay caused by the animal's inability to imagine what is to be done is sufficient to mimic the delay in approaching the water, as seen in intact animals.

DAMAGE TO THE APPRAISAL AND AFFECTIVE
MEMORY AREAS

I have discussed the effect of lesions of the sensory appraisal areas in chapters 11 and 12, and of the affective motor memory areas in chapters 14 and 15. However, I have not discussed the effect of combined lesions of affective motor memory and affective sensory memory areas, as, for instance, in ablations of the cingulate gyrus.

The Cingulate Gyrus.   The most widely investigated effects of cingulate lesions have been their influence on active and passive avoidance. McCleary

(1961) was the first to report that cats were unable to learn a two-way active avoidance task after bilateral lesions of the anterior and middle cingulate gyrus, but performed normally in passive avoidance. Peretz (1960), Moore (1964), Lubar (1964), Thomas and Slotnick (1963), and others confirmed these findings.

McCleary (1961) also reported that bilateral septal lesions in cats produced a deficit in passive avoidance but did not interfere with two-way active avoidance. Taking his cue from Kaada's (1951) report that stimulation of the subcallosal gyrus produced inhibition of cortically induced movement, and stimulation of the anterior cingulate gyrus produced facilitation, McCleary suggested that the subcallosal area represents a motor inhibitory region, and the anterior cingulate gyrus, a motor facilitatory region.

But there is reasonable doubt that a lesion of the anterior cingulate gyrus eliminates a facilitatory motor system. Such lesions inhibit active avoidance but do not eliminate escape from shock—yet both actions require the same motor system. Moreover, Thomas and Slotnick (1962) found that cutting the projection fibers from the anterior thalamic nuclei to the cingulate cortex impairs active avoidance but leaves maze learning intact (in rats). In a later experiment (1963), these authors found that rats with cingulate lesions acquire active avoidance as easily as do intact rats when they are hungry, but show a deficit when they are sated.

These findings cannot be explained as the result of damage to a facilitatory system; but they can be explained on the basis of my theory. A large lesion of the cingulate gyrus destroys both the appraisal area for movement and action, and that for touch. Maze learning is not impaired after cingulate lesions because hunger or thirst is the impulse that induces running the maze, not the fear of shock. Since these animals can no longer remember the painful shock, they do not avoid it—so showing an active avoidance deficit. They can escape from shock because the pain, felt via the medial thalamus, arouses an impulse to flee. They cannot run to the safe compartment on cue because they cannot appraise buzzer or light as "bad, to be avoided," since they do not remember that they experienced pain.

When the fibers from anterior thalamic nuclei to cingulate are cut, the animals can no longer remember either the painful shock or its successful avoidance, hence they have no impulse to run. Since their modality-specific memory cirucit is intact, they still remember their response to the conditioned stimulus, but they have no motive for repeating it. When hungry, they are impelled to find food, and repeat the former response—to find food, not to flee from danger (active avoidance response). When sated, they have no such impulse; since fear is eliminated, they stay in the home compartment (active avoidance deficit).

When the lesion includes both anterior and posterior cingulate gyrus, there is a double impairment because the animals cannot remember either the shock or its successful avoidance. In all these experiments, foot shock was used (Peretz, 1960; Thomas & Slotnick, 1963; Lubar & Perachio, 1965; Trafton et al., 1969). In McCleary's passive avoidance experiments, in contrast, the animals were shocked through the mouth (see discussion below).

Active Avoidance. There are some conflicting reports on active avoidance. Lubar et al. (1966) found that shallow lesions of the cingulate gyri that did not encroach on the underlying white fibers did not prevent cats from learning active avoidance in a two-way shuttle box when massed trials were used. Massed trials enable the animals to profit from immediate memory. Since the cingulum was intact, the affective memory circuit for harmful touch was active. Even with the cingulate gyrus damaged, pain can be experienced and remembered via thalamic nuclei, at least during the animals' attention span in massed trials.

However, Lubar et al. found a significant active avoidance impairment in his cats after lesions of the medial aspect of the midlateral gyrus and the medial aspect of the posterolateral gyrus (homologues of the visual sensory and association cortex in man). Since lesions of the lateral gyrus in the cat have resulted in an impairment of visual discrimination (Fischman & Meikle, 1965), Lubar and his coworkers suggested that the reported impairment in active avoidance after cingulate lesions must be the result of incidental damage to the underlying white fibers running in the projection from the lateral geniculate nucleus to the visual cortex. This cannot be the correct explanation. In rats, ablation of the homologue of the cingulate gyrus (area 29b) does not impinge on visual fibers. Thus Kimble and Gostnell (1968) found that cortical control lesions which were more likely to interrupt the visual system than cingulate lesions did not affect active avoidance in rats. And Trafton et al. (1969) reported that lesions of different regions of the anterior cingulate gyrus, far removed from the visual system, did impair active avoidance.

The results of Lubar et al. can be explained differently. Inevitably, the animals have to appraise the barrier they see as "good to jump." The buzzer they hear, announcing the shock, does not direct the response. Cats with lesions of the posterolateral gyrus cannot jump into the safe compartment because the lesion has made it impossible for them to remember what they see, and appraise it as safe. Lubar et al. reported that the cats seemed to show no visual impairment; visual placing also was intact. This would indicate that the lesions destroyed visual association cortex rather than primary visual cortex. Without visual association cortex, the animals cannot appraise visual impressions because the connection with the visual limbic area is broken. Lubar et al. reported that the cats became quite emotional, yet did not jump. The animals apparently expected the shock because the posterior cingulate gyrus homologue was intact and they could remember that buzzer meant shock. The lesioned cats eventually did learn, but it took many days before they made the first avoidance response; once they did, they learned quickly. In making the jump, the cats had to disregard their neutral visual perception and jump blindly, as it were, as soon as the buzzer sounded.

Passive Avoidance.   In passive avoidance, the animal must remember that it has been shocked in its approach to food and water and must appraise an impulse to approach the food cup again as "bad" because it remembers the pain and expects another shock. This affective memory of pain induces it to refrain from approaching. This is no "go/no go" problem but an approach/withdrawal paradigm in which approach is replaced by withdrawal when the situation changes from expected reward to expected punishment. For instance, Ursin et al. (1969) arranged an apparatus with the start box in the middle and runways at opposite ends. When the runway to the baited end was electrified, intact rats did not merely stop to approach the goal box but ran into the opposite alley.

Everything else being equal, animals with large cingulate lesions show a deficit in passive as well as active avoidance because they should be unable to remember the pain suffered on being shocked through the electrified grid. Indeed, a significant passive avoidance deficit was found after cingulate lesions when grid shock to the feet was used (Blanchard & Fial, 1968; Thompson & Langer, 1963; Thomas & Slotnick, 1962, 1963). However, in many experiments testing passive avoidance, mouth shock was used. So McCleary (1961) reported that rats with cingulate lesions performed normally in passive avoidance (mouth shock) but showed a severe deficit in active avoidance (foot shock). Such lack of any deficit in passive avoidance after cingulate lesions when mouth shock was used was confirmed by Kaada et al. (1962), Lubar (1964) and Cornwell (1966). All these investigators used the McCleary apparatus in which the animal was shocked in the mouth as it started to eat or drink. According to my theory, the limbic cortex mediating appraisal of painful touch to the mouth is the posterior insula; the limbic area serving appraisal of head and mouth movements and perhaps paw movements, the anterior insula. Cingulate lesions leave the appraisal areas for painful shock to the mouth, and for head movements, intact—hence the animals remembered the shock and appraised dipping the head to drink as "bad." They refrained from drinking and showed no passive avoidance deficit.

In our own laboratory at Loyola University of Chicago, Conneely (1967) found retention deficits in rats with cingulate lesions in several tasks where errors were punished by foot shock. This is a type of passive avoidance of cues that are followed by shock. The deficit in successive visual, auditory, and tactual discrimination and in T-maze single alternation was an impairment of affective somatosensory memory, not of modality-specific memory. In successive olfactory discrimination, errors resulted in tasting quinine water. In this task, the animals were not impaired because the appraisal of taste, according to my theory, is mediated by the intact posterior insula. Conneely's lesions were rather large, more than 4 mm^3, and reached caudally into areas 29b and 29c. Apparently, the lesions destroyed enough posterior cingulate cortex and cingulum to obliterate the affective memory for painful foot shock. Without it, the animals were unable to appraise the approach to the cup as bad.

NEURAL CONNECTIONS IN THE APPRAISAL
SYSTEM

The Cingulum.   The cingulum is the most important pathway from limbic cortex to hippocampus (see chapter 20). It connects all medial cortical areas with the hippocampus. Hence cingulate gyrus lesions may not necessarily have the same effects as lesions of the cingulum.

Fedio and Ommaya (1970) have reported that electrical stimulation of the left (but not the right) cingulum in human beings produced a deficit in verbal memory; but bilateral lesions of the cingulum did not. They suggested that the memory defect produced by left cingulum stimulation might be the result of activation of relays to other structures, particularly the hippocampus. According to my theory, excitation of the left hippocampus would disturb recall via left speech memory area. Transection of the cingulum would have no effect on recall because such a lesion would affect only the affective memory of body (not speech) movements.

Schneider et al. (1963) have reported that cancer patients gain relief from pain and anxiety when the cingulum is sectioned about 1 cm caudal of the genu of the corpus callosum. No personality changes like those occurring after lobotomy have been observed. Such a cut would prevent any appraisal of the impulse to flee, hence the patients would not be frustrated by the impossibility to run away from pain. The patient feels pain, and even the impulse to flee from it, but as something devoid of affect. I venture to suggest that this transection would not benefit patients with pain in face or head (e.g. tic douloureux) because the insula, the appraisal area for the head, is still intact.

In experiments in our laboratory at Loyola University of Chicago, we tried to confine electrolytic lesions to the cingulum with as little damage as possible to the cingulate cortex. Mead (1969) trained rats in four tasks: successive olfactory discrimination (quinine water as punishment for errors), successive visual discrimination (foot shock), active avoidance in the two-way shuttle box, and passive avoidance with either foot or mouth shock. After a preoperative retention test in all five tasks, the animals were given small bilateral midcingulum lesions. Incidental damage to cingulate cortex, dorsal hippocampus and fornix was slight. This lesion did not impair retention of any of these tests. Thompson and Langer (1963) also found no passive avoidance deficit after midcingulum lesions. Apparently, sufficient fibers from the anterior cingulate gyrus perforate the corpus callosum and reach the anterior thalamic nuclei to make it possible for the animals to appraise the approach to the negative cue as bad (affective motor memory); the posterior cingulate gyrus and cingulum were intact, hence the animals remembered the pain of shock and tried to avoid it.

However, when Mead made a second bilateral cingulum lesion at the genu of the corpus callosum, the combined lesions produced a deficit in retaining the passive avoidance task with foot shock as punishment. All other tasks were unimpaired, as was passive avoidance with mouth shock. After foot shock, intact rats avoid the water dish. But damage to the cingulum at the genu of the corpus callosum prevents the appraisal of body movements so that cingulotomized rats no longer experienced any reluctance to move toward the dish: They showed a deficit in passive avoidance. Even when the rats refrained from drinking, they often ran to the cup, placed their forepaws on the insulated platform surrounding it and held their head over the water. Since their appraisal of head movements was unimpaired (intact anterior insula), they were able to refrain from dipping their head to drink. Only the animals who ran to the cup and immediately drank showed impairment in passive avoidance. When mouth shock was used, the animals' performance was normal, despite many "almost-errors." These rats were not reluctant to approach the cup, but held off. Remembering the mouth shock, they were apparently able to appraise drinking as "bad" and refrained from doing it.

The Insula.   Mead's experiment is a good example how a seemingly slight change in procedure (mouth shock *versus* foot shock) can give entirely different results because different neural pathways are engaged.

In another experiment, we placed lesions in the anterior insula of rats (five with bilateral, seven with unilateral lesions) and then trained the animals in a successive olfactory and a successive visual discrimination, and also in single alternation. The lesioned animals learned the visual discrimination and the single alternation task normally, but they were severely impaired in learning the olfactory discrimination. This problem is very easy for intact animals: They run to the end of a narrow box and sniff at each successive cup as it passes in front of a cutout in the anterior wall. But the lesioned animals had great difficulty; even shaping them took a long time. They did not seem to know what to do and often ran back and forth instead of running to the front and waiting for the cup. Since this lesion prevents the appraisal of head movements, the animals apparently found it difficult to put their nose close to the cup, or decide whether to drink (Arnold, 1970).

In a companion experiment, we placed lesions in the posterior insula of 12 rats (3 with bilateral, nine with unilateral lesions). These animals had a highly significant learning deficit in successive olfactory discrimination, but performed normally on successive visual discrimination, single alternation and active avoidance (foot shock). The learning deficit on the olfactory task seems to stem from their inability to remember the unpleasant taste of quinine water, an appraisal mediated by the posterior insula, according to my theory. This interpretation is supported by Bagshaw and Pribram's (1953) report that monkeys refuse quinine as long as the posterior insula is intact.

All cortical limbic areas send relays to the hippocampus via entorhinal cortex, subiculum, and parasubiculum (Turner et al., 1980). According to Berger et al. (1980), the primary role of the hippocampus during learning is to "amplify a specific activity pattern projected to it by the entorhinal cortex." In terms of my theory, the limbic appraisal areas send an action impulse to the hippocampus. And the hippocampus seems to organize the necessary impulses to recall and react, and relay the pattern to midbrain and cerebellum. According to my theory, the modality-specific memory circuit runs from hippocampus via precommisural fornix to the septal area and connects via medial forebrain bundle with the midbrain, while the affective memory circuit runs via postcommissural fornix to the mamillary bodies, which send relays to the anterior thalamic nuclei and back to various limbic cortical areas. The precommissural fornix spreads from the septal area into the anterior commissure; hence both septal lesions and damage to the anterior commissure should produce memory impairment. Cutting the anterior commissure does indeed produce a severe deficit in visual and auditory discriminations (usually the only modalities tested), according to Doty and Overman (1977), and Overman and Doty (1979). Septal lesions result in a passive avoidance deficit but facilitate active avoidance (McCleary, 1961). I discuss the effect of such lesions in chapter 22.

The Postcommissural Fornix.   This tract is not the only connection between the hippocampus and the anterior thalamic nuclei. Direct fibers from cingulate gyrus and hippocampus to the anterior thalamic nuclei have been found in most animals, so that the affective memory circuit is rarely completely interrupted by postcommissural fornix or mamillary lesions. Moreover, it is difficult to interrupt the postcommissural fornix without damaging fibers of the precommissural fornix. Considering these facts, it is not surprising that lesion results are ambiguous.

For instance, Migler (1961) found that rhesus monkeys with fornix lesions performed like intact animals on a DRL task. Hostetter and Thomas (1967) reported that fornix lesions did not prevent rats from learning a four-unit maze, but Thomas (1971) found a retention and relearning deficit after pre- and postcommissural fornix lesions. Fischman and McCleary (1966) reported that fornix lesions did not affect food-reinforced passive avoidance but interfered with learning a position reversal. Van Hoesen et al. (1969) found that such lesions produced no or only a slight deficit in passive avoidance, while active avoidance was actually enhanced. The lesions were placed in the horizontal fornix, hence damaged both pre- and postcommissural fibers.

In human beings, Dott (1938) and Garcia Bengochea et al. (1954) have cut the descending (postcommissural) fornix columns on both sides and found no untoward effects, neither memory loss nor any clinical impairment. This can probably be accounted for by the fact that the direct fibers from hippocampus to anterior thalamic nuclei were untouched; hence affective memory was intact.

Mamillary Bodies and Mamillothalamic Tract.   These are the next links in the affective memory circuit from hippocampus/fornix to the anterior thalamic nuclei and limbic cortex. Lesions of these structures have sometimes produced a learning or retention deficit and at other times have not done so. The outcome seems to depend on the locus and size of the lesions, that is, whether it blocked access to the anterior thalamic nuclei.

For instance, Thompson and Massopust (1960) reported an active avoidance deficit in rats after lesions of both mamillary nuclei. And Thomas et al. (1963), as well as Krieckhaus (1964), found that interruption of the mamillothalamic tract resulted in poor retention of active avoidance in a two-way shuttlebox in cats. In contrast, Thompson and Hawkins (1961) found that bilateral lesions of the mamillary bodies did not impair active avoidance in rats; and Dahl et al. (1962) reported that complete bilateral lesions of either the mamillary bodies or the mamillothalamic tract did not produce an active avoidance deficit in cats. According to Ploog and MacLean (1963), coagulation of the mamillary bodies did not result in an active avoidance deficit in squirrel monkeys.

Krieckhaus (1964) repeated the experiment of Thomas et al. (1963), hoping to clarify these contradictions. He changed the procedure so that the cats with lesions of the mamillothalamic tract had to avoid electric shock signaled by a buzzer and a light by jumping into the "safe" compartment. After learning this active avoidance, they had to learn a reversal. Now they were shocked as they alighted, so that the cue of buzzer and light now indicated shock in the formerly safe compartment. As his learning criterion, Krieckhaus set 19 out of 20 responses correct for three consecutive days of distributed trials. After training, he made small lesions by focused ultrasonic sound, lesions practically confined to the mamillothalamic tract. The lesioned animals had a significant active avoidance deficit, related to the extent of the lesion. Even unilateral lesions of the tract impaired the retention of active avoidance. Krieckhaus pointed out that each mamillary nucleus projects to both anterior thalamic nuclei, hence a unilateral mamillothalamic tract lesion actually means partial bilateral damage.

Krieckhaus discussed the possibility that the lesions might have produced accelerated extinction of fear, but decided against it because the impaired animals showed the usual autonomic signs of fear while cats that had learned to avoid shock were "nonchalant and relaxed." Also, cats retrained in the one-way task after mamillothalamic tract lesions learned the avoidance response but took more trials to extinguish, which would mean that they were more afraid of shock than intact animals. I would say that the lesion interrupted the affective memory circuit so that the animals were unable to remember the pain or to recall it when they heard the buzzer and saw the light. These cues still activated modality-specific memory of buzzer and light, and of jumping into the other compartment. But without affective memory of the pain of shock, they might at first jump automatically, but would soon stop. This is exactly what Krieckhaus reports.

Moreover, the animal with such a lesion is able to appraise the situation. The pain experienced in past trials has induced an action impulse (fear) with its autonomic accompaniment, relayed in the action circuit via hypothalamus to the frontal lobe and registered as motor memory (see chapters 14, and 15). After lesions of the mamillothalamic tract, the animal sees the light, hears the buzzer, and recalls the motor response accompanied by the associated physiological disturbance, the accompaniment of fear. Without affective memory, the recalled motor response soon drops out because it is no longer relevant; but the associated autonomic changes still occur and are reinforced with every experience of pain following upon the cue signals.

If the signal announcing shock is made aversive in itself (as in Dahl et al.'s, 1962, experiment in which a loud buzzer is sounded at the back of the compartment from which the animal is to escape), or if the safe place is made attractive (a lighted pedestal to which the monkey has to jump, as in Ploog and MacLean's, 1963, experiment), the deficit after mamillothalamic tract lesions may not be noticeable. There are some experimental procedures that facilitate learning and some that reveal a deficit. On the basis of my theory, it is possible to show why a particular procedure does what it does. Unfortunately, without an adequate theory, experimenters may unwittingly change the procedure to one that yields contradictory results.

Whenever affective memory is necessary to motivate a task, the animals will be impaired by mamillothalamic tract lesions that obliterate all relays to the anterior thalamic nuclei. But when a task is motivated by a physiological drive, such lesions will not substantially interfere. For instance, Krieckhaus and Lorenz (1968) found that cats were impaired by mamillothalamic tract lesions when learning to press a lever to avoid shock, but were unimpaired when learning to press a lever for milk. Krieckhaus and Randall (1968) reported that such animals were not impaired in learning a right/left discrimination for water in a T-maze, but were slower than normal animals in leaving the start box.

Thompson and Langer (1963) found that rats with lesions of the mamillary bodies, the mamillothalamic tract, or the anterior thalamic nuclei were impaired in learning to reverse a position habit in which errors were punished by foot shock. In this experiment, the animals had to remember the arm of the T-maze in which they had been shocked. In the next trial, they had to choose the other arm. Any one of these lesions disturbed affective touch (pain) and affective motor memory. Since the two arms were identical, the animals' intact modality-specific memory was little help. They were reluctant to move from the start box because they could not appraise the action they were about to take as "good" or "bad." This impaired affective motor memory also accounts for the reluctance of Krieckhaus and Randall's animals to leave the start box.

Animals with such lesions can learn and retain a discrimination for a reward but are deficient in learning and retaining a task in which errors are punished or which is motivated by pain. When a physiological drive supplies the motive, they seem unimpaired because modality-specific memory alone is sufficient to guide their action: The animal sees the positive cue, imagines the food or water to follow, appraises it as good and runs toward it. When pain is the motive, a lesion that interrupts the affective memory of pain is bound to disturb learning.

The animal sees the light or hears the buzzer and recalls that it ran or jumped into the other compartment, but there is nothing in that compartment that can be appraised as good to approach. And without affective memory of pain, the animal can sense nothing in the home compartment from which to run. Pain can be recalled via modality-specific memory only as neutral touch; only affective memory could bring back the pain connected with this touch.

Affective memory enables us to relive pleasure as well as pain. What is sometimes called "psychic" sexual stimulation (looking at pornographic pictures or reading salacious material) seems to depend on such affective memory of formerly experienced sexual pleasure. Apparently, sexual pleasure can be revived via the affective memory circuit. Ploog and MacLean (1963) have reported that electrical stimulation of the mamillary bodies resulted in penile erection in squirrel monkeys.

The Anterior Thalamic Nuclei.   According to Gerbrandt (1965), lesions of the anteromedial thalamic nuclei retarded learning of a passive avoidance task. Passive like active avoidance requires intact affective memory of pain. The lesion interrupted the affective memory circuit, hence impaired learning.

Fear and anger depend on affective memory. Unless we remember that something has harmed us, we will not be afraid of it or try to attack it on sight. This connection between affective memory and emotion can be inferred from Schreiner et al.'s (1952) report that destruction of the anterior thalamic nuclei made it more difficult to arouse anger and fear in cats. Baird et al. (1952) and Crosby et al. (1962) reported the same change in human beings.

In our laboratory, we trained rats in single alternation and in successive olfactory, tactual, auditory, and visual discrimination. Errors were punished by footshock, except for olfactory discrimination where errors resulted in the animal's drinking quinine-water. After bilateral lesions of the anterior thalamic nuclei, the animals were significantly impaired in all tasks, except for intact olfactory discrimination (Arnold, 1969, 1970). Histological reports showed that the lesions obliterated the anterior thalamic nuclei, but also damaged the stria medullaris and habenulae.

The lesioned animals could smell and appraise the odor. They could also recall the positive or negative odor (via piriform cortex and posterior orbital area) and could remember the bad taste of quinine (via posterior insula). Turner et al. (1980) reported that the posterior insula, the limbic area for taste, is directly connected with the anterior insula, the appraisal area for head movements. The rats smelled the "good" odor, realized the water was good to drink, dipped their head and drank. Hence no deficit in olfactory discrimination.

Electric stimulation of the anterior thalamus in waking patients has resulted in smiling and laughing (Hassler, 1961). Apparently, such stimulation activates the affective memory circuit. Hassler also reported that bilateral stereotactic coagulation of the anterior thalamic nuclei resulted in the disappearance of tactile and auditory hallucinations in a schizophrenic patient. At the same time, he became completely disoriented in space and time and could not even recognize his own family. Recognition, as I have discussed in chapter 7, requires an appraisal that "this has occurred before," based on the revival of earlier affective memories. The patient could no longer recognize anything he saw, so he became disoriented in space; he could no longer appraise what occurred before or after something else, hence he was disoriented in time. The bilateral lesions seem to have abolished his hallucinations because they no longer carried any meaning for the patient. Without affective memory, he would neither recognize them nor be disturbed by them.

Patients suffering from Korsakoff psychosis usually have considerable damage to the anterior thalamic nuclei, the mamillary bodies, and the dorsomedial thalamic nuclei. They do not recognize anything because their affective memory circuit is interrupted. With damage of the dorsomedial thalamic nuclei, they also would have difficulty in planning action. Weiskrantz and Warrington (1975) showed incomplete pictures or words to such patients. When a patient failed to recognize them, he was shown a more complete form until he identified it correctly. When the same forms and words were shown afterwards, the patient needed less information to identify this material, that is, he was able to learn. Since his modality-specific memory circuit was intact, it is not surprising that the patient eventually was able to recall the words or names of the things he had been shown. But with the affective memory circuit damaged, he would not be able to recognize what he recalled, and without such recognition he could never be sure of his memories.

Butters and Cermak (1975) found that Korsakoff patients were almost normal in immediate recall of a list of eight words read to them. They were, however, significantly impaired when they were asked to recall words from different categories contained in the list (animals, professions, vegetables, names). They were also impaired on free recall. Immediate free recall was considerably better than recall according to categories. In contrast, alcoholic patients with memory defects improved when asked to recall according to categories. Hence Butters and Cermak concluded that Korsakoff patients are deficient in semantic encoding. Such encoding implies the recognition that a category embraces different things; and such recognition requires intact affective memory. It is easier for Korsakoff patients to recall words according to acoustic or associative linkages because such recall requires only modality-specific memory, not recognition.

Even more instructive is the result of the "false recognition" test employed by Butters and Cermak (1975). In this test, the patient was shown a 60-word list at the rate of one word every two seconds, and was asked to indicate which words were repeats. The list contained some repetitions but also words that sounded alike (homonyms such as bear and bare), associated words (table and chair), or words that have the same meaning (synonyms like robber and thief). Whenever the patient reported that a homonym, associate, or synonym was a repeat, it was scored as "false recognition." The Korsakoff patients recognized as many genuine repeats as did the alcoholic controls, but they also falsely recognized many homonyms and associates, and almost no synonyms or neutral words. Apparently, they indicated as repeats words that had a similar sound or shape, or had common associations, but not on the basis of their meaning (semantic encoding), which requires affective memory.

DAMAGE TO BOTH MEMORY CIRCUITS

Ordinarily, human beings as well as animals use both modality-specific and affective memory. However, in simultaneous discrimination, as I have suggested before, they can use affective memory alone, particularly when they have been overtrained. When simultaneous discrimination is used to motivate the animals with foot shock, brain lesions placed within both memory circuits impair retention. But without a theory of brain function it is extremely difficult to isolate the connections.

This is illustrated by the extensive research of Thompson (1969) and his group, who tried to identify the visual memory system. They systematically placed lesions at various brain sites and retested rats on three simultaneous visual discrimination problems overlearned before surgery. The rats had to push the positive unlocked card aside to enter the safe goal box. If they approached the negative, locked card, they were punished by a mild shock to the feet. Of the three discriminations, the first was white vs. gray card, the second, horizontal vs. vertical black-white stripes, and the third, a white cross vs. a white disk on black ground. The animals learned these tasks in sequence. The third problem proved to be the most difficult. Only animals with bilateral lesions in the occipital cortex, destroying areas 17, 18, and 18a of Krieg (1946), or the ventral posterior thalamus, or the red nucleus were severely impaired in all three discriminations. Animals with bilateral lesions of one of the following structures were significantly impaired on one or two problems: anterior-medial thalamus, posterior-subcollicular thalamus, interpeduncular nucleus, and substantia nigra.

Thompson mentions that ablation of the ventral nucleus of the lateral geniculate body abolished a brightness discrimination, and that this nucleus sends fibers to the posterior thalamic nucleus (Horel, 1968a, b), which might account for the pathway from the visual cortex to the posterior thalamus. Thompson also found that bilateral cuts through the brainstem at the junction between diencephalon and midbrain, as well as ablation of the posterior thalamus, abolished a brightness discrimination. Rats with such lesions were inferior to controls after overtraining, showed less disturbance after foot shock, and had difficulty in correcting errors after punishment. On the basis of his effective lesions (Fig. 18.2), Thompson assumes that the visual memory pathway runs from occipital cortex via posterior thalamus to the ventral midbrain in a diagonal orientation, parallel to the habenulo-peduncular tract. The only descending tract in this area is the thalamo-mesencephalic tract, which ends in the red nucleus.

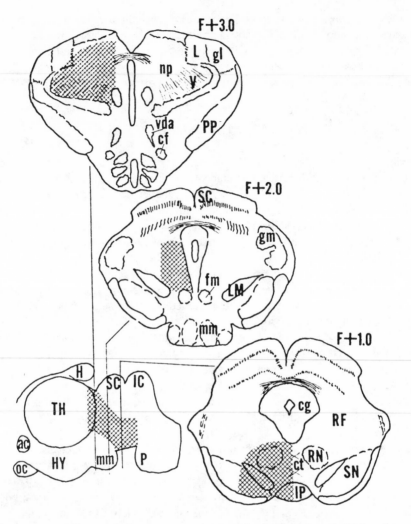

FIG. 18.2. Critical subcortical visual areas. Schematic drawing of parasagittal section of brainstem (lower left) and three frontal sections derived from the Massopust (1961) atlas showing critical subcortical areas (cross hatched) for normal performance of visual discrimination habits. (ac = anterior commissure; cf = column of fornix; cg = central gray; ct = central tegmentum; fm = habenulo-peduncular tract; gl = lateral geniculate nucleus; gm = medial geniculate nucleus; H = habenula; HY = hypothalamus; IC = inferior colliculus; IP = interpeduncular nucleus; L = lateral posterior thalamic nucleus; LM = medial lemniscus; mm = mammillary bodies; np = nucleus posterior; oc = optic chiasma; P = pons; PP = cerebral peduncle; RF = reticular formation; RN = red nucleus; SC = superior colliculus; SN = substantia nigra; TH = thalamus; V = ventral thalamic nucleus; vda = mamillo-thalamic tract.) (From R. Thompson, 1969. Copyright 1969 by the American Psychological Association. Reprinted by permission of the author.)

Considering all his experiments, Thompson suggests that visual discrimination tasks may involve two memory systems, one for visual discrimination and a second "which is specifically concerned with the suppression of some 'error-producing' tendencies" (1969, p. 26). I am suggesting that it is the affective memory system that makes it possible to remember the punishment for errors, and so suppress them. In Thompson's experiments, damage to the occipital cortex impairs the visual memory system while damage to the ventral nucleus of the lateral geniculate and its connections damages the affective memory circuit and produces impairment in simultaneous pattern and brightness discrimination.

As I have shown in chapter 12, simultaneous discriminations are possible as long as the affective memory circuit is intact and the animal can distinguish between the two cues. When the occipital cortex is ablated, the animals have lost their visual memory cortex, hence can no longer distinguish one visual pattern from another. When the visual memory cortex is intact, simultaneous discriminations could be abolished only if the affective visual or affective somatosensory memory circuit is interrupted so that the animals could not remember the "good" card or the "bad" foot shock. Simultaneous discrimination would also fail if the motor memory circuit was interrupted; Thompson used a rather complicated procedure (the rat had to push the positive card aside to enter the goal box) which requires motor memory.

In Thompson's experiments, bilateral destruction of the posterior thalamus seems to have prevented the animal from remembering the response (via connection of posterior thalamus to red nucleus) or from carrying it out. The lesions that impaired learning of two simultaneous discriminations either interfered with affective visual memory (anterior-medial thalamic lesion), or interfered with conduction in the motor memory circuit (relays from posterior thalamus to red nucleus), or, finally, interfered with other connections to the motor memory circuit (interpeduncular nucleus and substantia nigra—see chapter 28).

According to Thompson, lesions of the amygdala or dorsomedial thalamic nucleus did not affect retention. No doubt the imagination circuit was not needed because the rats were overtrained, hence the sight of the cue, appraised as good, immediately initiated the motor pattern. Animals with ablation of up to 18% of prefrontal cortex often had to be forced to run (by applying foot shock) and had difficulty in pushing aside the cue card. Such lesions would damage motor memory and perhaps premotor areas. Rats with lesions of the corpus striatum, thalamus, subthalamus, posterolateral hypothalamus and substantia nigra had similar difficulties. These lesions damaged the motor memory and action circuits, so that the animals were reluctant to move. I would think that bilateral anterior cingulate lesions would also have impaired the animals' performance, but there is no record of such lesions in Thompson et al.'s report. I discuss the effects of damage to the action circuit in chapters 26–28.

Stimulation and Lesions of the Medial Thalamus. In chapter 17 I have shown that the medial thalamus is connected both with the cortical appraisal system and with the sensory and motor cortex. Lesions and stimulation of this area are bound to have profound effects.

Grossman et al. (1965) placed minute amounts of carbachol (a cholinergic drug) into the thalamic midline nuclei of rats five minutes before each training session in a two-way shuttle box. This cholinergic stimulation significantly impaired active avoidance learning. The rate of improvement as well as the performance level suffered. However, once learned, the performance of the experimental group did not differ from that of the control group.

When carbachol was placed in the reticular thalamic nuclei, most animals failed to respond during the first 60–90 trials and the performance of the whole group never exceeded 22% avoidance throughout 150 trials. The rate of acquisition as well as the final performance of this group was significantly poorer than that of the midline group or that of sham-stimulated controls. When the experimenters discontinued stimulation after 150 trials, the animals' avoidance responses gradually increased during the next 165 trials; at the end, performance was indistinguishable from that of the other two groups.

Cholinergic stimulation of both midline and reticular thalamic nuclei significantly reduced locomotion, but it became normal again after 48 hours. Application of crystalline methylatropine (a cholinergic blocker) to midline nuclei increased locomotor activity significantly, with return to normal after 24 hours. Similar applications to reticular nuclei also increased locomotion ten minutes afterwards, but produced a more marked increase after 24 hours; after 48 hours, the animals moved at a normal rate.

Cholinergic stimulation of the midline nuclei reduced bar pressing for food. The animals sat quietly in front of the food cup and pressed the bar only occasionally. Cholinergic stimulation of the reticular nuclei reduced bar pressing even more. Both groups also reduced bar pressing after the application of methylatropine, the cholinergic blocker. The animals were hyperactive and kept exploring the familiar apparatus.

The midline nuclei lack direct cortical projection but are connected with the reticular thalamic nuclei which project diffusely to the cortex. The midline nuclei seem to be involved in learning rather than in retention, while cholinergic stimulation of the reticular nuclei seems to impair retention as much as learning. The midline nuclei are connected with the medial appraisal system of the brainstem; the reticular nuclei are assumed to be the last relay in the diffuse (nonspecific) projection system; but they are connected with the dorsomedial nucleus and may project to the cortex via this structure. Hence the appraisal of the light cue as dangerous (via visual limbic and medial thalamic structures) would facilitate active avoidance, while the appraisal of the bar as good to press would facilitate bar pressing. The fact that carbachol and acetylcholine reduced bar pressing, active avoidance, and locomotion seems to suggest that such stimulation engages cholinergic inhibitory fibers. This interpretation seems to be supported by the increased locomotion after methylatropine. With the inhibition lifted, the animals began running about, exploring the apparatus. Since this drug not only cancelled the inhibitory effect of cholinergic stimulation, but also neutralized the conduction over the memory circuit, it reduced bar presses even more than did cholinergic stimulation. The reticular thalamic nuclei are connected with the dorsomedial nucleus (according to my theory, a relay station in the motor imagination circuit) and also with sensory memory areas. With memory and imagination circuits depressed, the animals became hyperactive, exploring the apparatus instead of pressing the bar because they could not remember or imagine what was to happen or what they were to do.

High frequency stimulation of the midbrain reticular formation or the medial thalamus alerts animals or arouses them from sleep, and produces EEG activation (Moruzzi & Magoun, 1949; Monnier et al., 1960). Such stimulation also excites the dorsomedial thalamic nuclei projecting to the prefrontal cortex, which means activation of the imagination circuit, hence EEG arousal.[1] High-frequency stimulation of the midbrain reticular system has the same effect through its connection with the medial thalamus.

In contrast, low-frequency stimulation of medial thalamic nuclei produces inattention, drowsiness, and eventually sleep. The EEG waves become synchronized, show spindle bursts and slow waves (Tissot & Monnier, 1959; Monnier et al., 1960). Such spindles and slow waves also appear in the cortex when barbiturates or ether are given. As the anesthetic takes effect, the evoked potentials in the brainstem reticular system, produced by sciatic nerve stimulation, are first reduced and finally eliminated, as the EEG waves in the cortex are slowing and show spindle bursts. Such a slowing of EEG frequencies always indicates a slowing of brain function, experienced as drowsiness and a difficulty in attending to a situation, appraising it, and reacting to it.

The same effects are produced by a lesion in the midbrain reticular formation. After such a lesion, the animal can no longer appraise incoming impressions nor can it recall or imagine anything because the afferent appraisal system has been damaged. A larger lesion renders the animal unconscious so that even painful stimuli do not produce activation (Hernández-Peón, 1966). Low-frequency stimulation of the medial thalamus does not have such a severe effect because it merely slows conduction but does not interrupt it.

Lesions in the medial thalamus also produce inattention; but with it, EEG activation rather than spindle bursts. After such lesions, the animal still sees, hears, and smells, but is unable to imagine what to do because the connection with the motor imagination circuit (via dorsomedial thalamic nucleus) is broken. It will be inattentive because it literally does not know what to do. At the same time, the modality-specific memory circuit is intact and enables the animal to remember past situations—which induces EEG arousal.

---

[1] While it is true that electrical stimulation of the medial thalamus will supersede normal functioning, hence will not result in actual planning of action, it does activate the pathways involved in motor imagination.

19 Hemisphere Functions and Memory Impairment

It has been known for a considerable time that the two sides of the brain do not serve exactly identical functions. The majority of human beings prefer using the right hand for skilled movements. Hence the left motor area in the frontal lobe, which activates the right hand, is more active and probably more highly differentiated. This superiority of one hemisphere over the other is called cerebral dominance. The left motor area is dominant in righthanders, the right motor area in lefthanders.

LEFT HEMISPHERE FUNCTIONS

In 1861, Broca reported that the left frontal lobe seems to be dominant for speech as well. Unilateral lesions in what later was called Broca's area, in the left frontal operculum (area 44), produced aphasia, an inability to speak. Still later, Wernicke (1874) demonstrated that lesions of the left association cortex close to the auditory area (posterior part of the left superior temporal gyrus) impaired the comprehension of speech. In 1891, Déjérine reported that lesions of the left angular gyrus impair reading and writing. And in the following year, Déjérine reported a case with pure alexia as the result of left occipital damage. In 1881, Exner proposed a "writing center" in the left prefrontal cortex (inferior part of areas 9 and 8). Since impaired writing (agraphia) had been reported after lesions of the angular gyrus, Exner's suggestion was not taken very seriously.

While the location of speech-related areas, and particularly their extent, has been disputed by later investigators, their location in the left hemisphere for righthanders has been rather generally accepted. Several authors have reported that Broca's area can be excised to remove a tumor without permanent speech defect (for instance, Zangwill, 1975). However, Rasmussen (1975) has pointed out that slowly growing tumors often displace the frontal operculum. When the tumor is removed, the displaced tissue may move back and soon again mediate speech. Also, stimulation of Broca's area but also of the area just in front of it (areas 45, 47) have produced speech arrest. And Yakovlev (1975) has pointed out that extensive studies on the structural variability of the frontal cortex (Kononova, 1935) have found that areas 45 and 47 showed a much greater surface area and much greater structural differentiation in the left than the right hemisphere. Hence it seems that Broca's area should be extended rostrally (Figs. 19.1 and 19.2A).

In the Midsixties, Geschwind (1965) suggested that the speech reception center (Wernicke's) in the left temporal lobe and the expressive center (Broca's) in the frontal lobe, connected by the arcuate fasciculus, form a system that allows the imitation of speech sounds. However, Rasmussen and Milner (1975) reported that the integrity of the cortex around and between these two centers was not essential for intact speech. They suggested that the integration and coordination between these centers would have to be carried out by subcortical pathways. See Fig. 19.2B.

Hécaen (1979) pointed out that damage of the temporal lobe extending from Wernicke's area toward the angular gyrus increases the severity of reading and writing disorders. This seems to confirm Déjérine's suggestion that alexia and agraphia follow damage of the left occipital lobe and angular gyrus.

There is a vast literature on aphasia and related disorders. Unfortunately, differences in terminology used by various writers make it difficult to define the various disorders. For instance, the inability to comprehend speech has been called "asymbolia" by Meynert (1868), "imperception" by Hughlings Jackson (1884), and "sensory aphasia" by more recent writers (Hécaen, 1979). Sensory aphasia could include auditory aphasia as well as an inability to read. In contrast, motor aphasia could be called any difficulty in speech or writing. This would distinguish sensory aphasia from agnosia, which is the inability to recognize things by sight, hearing, touch, or smell; and motor aphasia from apraxia, which is the inability to perform skilled movements.

Perhaps the greatest obstacle to an understanding of the effects of lesions in the "language" areas has been the assumption that these lesions have damaged a language *function*. If language were a function, similar to sensory and motor functions, stimulation of these areas should produce speech, just as stimulation of sensory areas produces sensory experiences and stimulation of motor areas produces movements. Instead, stimulation of the Broca, Wernicke, and Déjérine areas produces aphasic arrest (see Fig. 19.2A). In contrast, electrical stimulation of the face area in the precentral and postcentral gyrus of patients has produced vocalization or, more frequently, speech arrest (Rasmussen & Milner, 1975). Such stimulation may also produce movements of face or head because the muscles involved, like the speech muscles, are excited from the motor cortex via the pyramidal tract. Postcentral stimulation produces the same movements

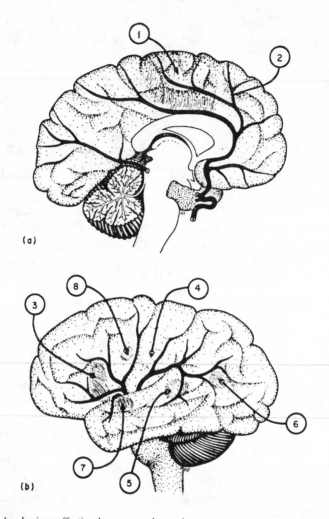

FIG. 19.1. Lesions affecting language and speech.

(1) Area supplied by the anterior cerebral artery—involves fronto-parietal region and the corpus callosum with only transient loss of speech as a result of inclusion of the supplementary motor area.

(2) Supplementary motor area of either hemisphere—stimulation of which produces arrest of ongoing speech and initiation of repetitive, nonvoluntary vocalizations (similar to epileptogenic lesions in the left hemisphere of that area). Lesions result in abnormalities in initiation, continuation, and inhibition of speech.

(3) Broca's area—lower part of the pre-motor zone—typically produces agrammatism, poor articulation, and abnormal writing of events required both for pronunication of words and fluent speech.

(4) Retrocentral area—lesions result in apraxia of the lips and tongue, leads to disintegration of speech as a whole.

(5) Temporal region—lesions affect the ability to generalize and differentiate phonetic sounds, cause disintegration of phonetic hearing. It always produces abnormal speech production and poor reading and writing.

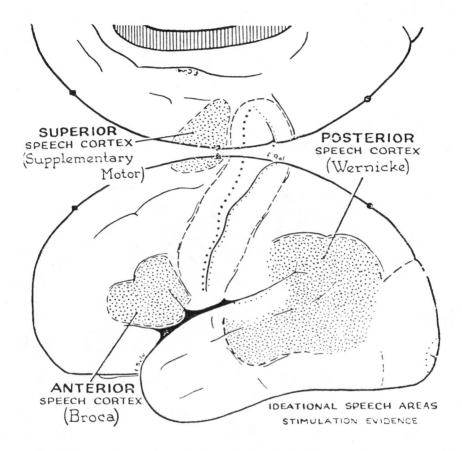

FIG. 19.2A. Cortical speech areas. In the dominant hemisphere, stimulation of these areas may interfere with speech or induce vocalization. (From Penfield & Roberts, 1959.)

(6) Temporo-parieto-occipital region—lesions do not change the external articulated speech, but prevent mental integration of separate elements (disturb simultaneous synthesis). Leads to disintegration of rational speech and to disturbance of the understanding of logical, grammatical constructions (semantic aphasia).

(7) Bilateral lesion of the temporal lobe, posterior 2/5 of the first and second temporal convolutions, plus posterior half of the Isle of Reil, extending to the inferior parietal lobe—shows word deafness, severe motor aphasia, more muteness than paraphasia.

(8) Near Broca's in the motor area of the lateral side of the left hemisphere—electrical stimulation results in perseveration of speech. (From M. S. Gazzaniga, 1975).

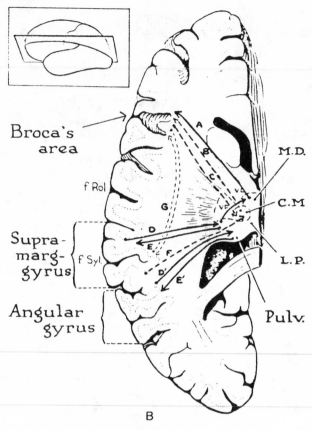

Broca's area

f Rol

Supra-
marg-
gyrus

f Syl.

Angular
gyrus

M.D.

C.M

L.P.

Pulv.

B

FIG. 19.2B.   Cortical language areas: Their connections with thalamic nuclei. (From Penfield & Roberts, 1959.)

because sensations experienced on face or head usually arouse the impulse to move the head, or facial muscles, and to contract the voice musculature so as to dislodge whatever has caused the sensations. In monkeys, stimulation of the motor cortex has not produced vocalization, but stimulation of various limbic and connected subcortical regions has done so (Ploog, 1981). This may not be a direct stimulation of motor pathways but the stimulation of a system of emotional expression that originates in limbic and brainstem areas (see Fig. 19.3). In human beings, stimulation of the face motor area produces speech arrest when the patient is speaking because the speech musculature he uses is now preempted by the electrical current applied to it. In contrast, stimulation of the language areas preempts the pathways used when the patient tries to recall the form of words and letters in reading, the pattern of sounds in listening, and when he produces sounds in speaking and words or letters in writing.

The ability to speak and understand language depends on the skilled production of sounds that can be recognized as referring to certain things, activities, or

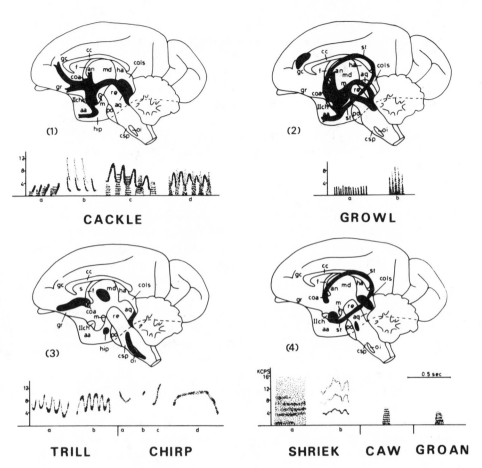

FIG. 19.3.   Vocalization elicited by electrical stimulation of the squirrel monkey's brain. General view of the cerebral system (in black) yielding cackling calls (1), growling calls (2), chirping calls (3), and shrieking calls (4). The calls are represented as frequency–time diagrams. Abbreviations: aa, area anterior amygdalae; an, nucleus anterior; aq, substantia grisea centralis; cc, corpus callosum; coa, commissura anterior; cols, colliculus superior ; csp, tractus corticospinalis; f, fornix; gc, gyrus cinguli; gr, gyrus rectus; ha, nucleus habenularis; hip, hippocampus; m, corpus mammillare; md, nucleus medialis dorsalis thalami; oi, nucleus olivaris inferior; po, griseum pontis; re, formatio reticularis tegmenti; st, stria terminalis; IIch, chiasma nervorum opticorum. (From D. Ploog, 1981).

concepts. It demands motor memory for articulation and writing, auditory memory for the comprehension of speech sounds, and visual memory for reading and also for writing. Apparently, area 44 and perhaps also the inferior part of areas 45 and 47 serve the registration of speech motor patterns, Wernicke's area the registration of speech sounds heard, and the lateral occipital area, the registration of visual images of figures, letters, and words. A lesion can disturb the comprehension of language in a given modality: comprehension of written or printed words, of words and sentences heard or traced. To understand a word, we must be able to associate it with the object or activity to which it refers by means of visual, touch, olfactory, or auditory memory. If a patient can read the word "apple" but does not know what it means, we may assume that he can recognize the word (via visual limbic cortex) but cannot imagine an apple or recall that this is what the word means. He cannot recall either the appearance of the apple when he sees the word, nor the feel of the apple or its fragrance. This would indicate damage to the fiber connections from visual limbic area to hippocampus and amygdala, that is, to the recall and imagination circuits.

Both alexia and agraphia can follow deep lesions in the neighborhood of the angular gyrus because the visual speech memory area is now disconnected from Exner's writing memory area in the left prefrontal cortex. I have suggested that the hippocampus serves as relay station for recall; and the angular gyrus region overlies the retrosplenial and posterior hippocampal gyri, which are the appraisal areas for things seen, and have relays to the hippocampus.

Damage to connections via the hippocampus would also explain the cases in which damage to the splenium of the corpus callosum has produced alexia and, in some patients, an inability to recognize letters in the left visual field by tracing their contours with the left hand (Hécaen, 1979). In these cases, the hippocampal commissure underneath the splenium of the corpus callosum was probably damaged as well, so that the words seen in the left visual field (via the right occipital area) could not be reported via the left motor area.

It seems reasonable to conclude that all forms of aphasia and agnosia are the result either of damage to verbal and nonverbal memory areas, or damage to the connections of these areas with the recall and imagination circuits. After deep lesions, there may be damage to both. Aphasia is not an impairment of an obscure "language function" but an inability to use visual, auditory, or motor verbal memory for the comprehension and production of speech.

RIGHT HEMISPHERE FUNCTIONS

In the last few decades, there have been many reports that the right hemisphere is important for other than language functions. For instance, right hemisphere lesions have resulted in difficulty in recognizing faces, an absence of proper form in drawing or writing, difficulty in dressing and other habitual tasks, impairment on the Kohs block and trailmaking test, and in map drawing (Levy, 1974). Similarly, Corkin (1965) reported that patients with right hemisphere lesions were inferior to patients with left hemisphere lesions in a tactually guided maze. And De Renzi (1967) found that patients with right posterior lesions were deficient in a tactual formboard task.

Hécaen and Marcie (1974) reported disorders of writing after lesions in the right hemisphere; but they insisted that such impairment is very different from the agraphia found after left hemisphere lesions. In left hemisphere lesions, the patient is unable to write. In right hemisphere lesions, he seems unable to arrange his writing on the page. Such patients leave extremely large left margins, they slant their writing toward the upper right corner, and often duplicate strokes and letters. Apparently, the right occipital lobe registers the memory of proper spatial ordering; and the right parietal lobe, memories of touch. Hécaen and Marcie mentioned that patients with such writing disturbances had lesions in the posterior part of the right hemisphere. Apparently, the same disturbances of spatial ordering can be traced in disturbances of reading and arithmetic after lesions of the right posterior hemisphere. Hence Hécaen and Marcie call these disorders spatial dyslexia, spatial discalculia, and spatial disgraphia.

In recent years, it has been reported that left hemisphere lesions produce difficulty in reading, writing, or speaking for both right- and lefthanders. Indeed, it has been suggested that lefthanders draw on both hemispheres for their linguistic skills. Hence in lefthanders, the right hemisphere is not totally devoted to visuomotor skills, which accounts for their significantly inferior performance in these skills (Levy, 1974). According to Gloning et al. (1969), lefthanders become aphasic, at least for a short time, after lesions of either hemisphere, while righthanders almost never become aphasic after right hemisphere lesions. And Luria (1970) reported that permanent aphasia in lefthanders is more likely to result from left rather than right hemisphere lesions.

THE SPLIT-BRAIN PATIENT

Considerable light has been thrown on hemisphere function by a technique that originally had the purpose of confining an epileptic focus to one side of the brain. Surgeons split the corpus callosum down the middle, disconnecting the hemispheres and probably also dividing the hippocampal commissure. Hence impulses from the limbic appraisal area on one side can now reach only the hippocampus of that side, which confines the action impulse to that side. This technique and the experiments undertaken with split-brain patients have done much to increase our knowledge of hemisphere function in language comprehension and speech production. Gazzaniga (1970) has published a survey of this work, covering both human beings and animals. Before we discuss some of his examples, let us remember that the sensory projections to the cortex cross over to the other side well below the level of the corpus callosum; and that the motor pathway from the cortical motor areas to the spinal cord crosses over in the medulla at the level of the pyramids. Hence the sensory projection to both hemispheres and the motor pathway from cortex to spinal cord remain intact and cross over even in the split-brain patient.

Effects of Disconnecting the Hemispheres

In such patients, each side of the brain works on its own. This can be demonstrated by various tests. If, for instance, one of ten objects is placed in a patient's hand while he is blindfolded, and then dropped into a grab bag, he can pick that object out with the same but not with the other hand. What has happened is that the patient has recognized the object by touch via the somesthetic memory area on the opposite side, which is connected with the motor area of that side. Since the motor pathway crosses over in the pyramids, he is able to find the object with the same hand he used in recognizing it. When he tries to find it with the other hand, he cannot recognize it because that hand has no connection with the tactual memory area which had registered the impression.

Such a patient can put together simple 2–piece cutouts with either hand, but cannot do so with both hands, holding one piece in each hand. He can imagine how the picture should look by drawing on the visual memories of the left hemisphere, which is connected with the left motor memory area and the left motor region innervating the right hand. Thus he succeeds easily with the right hand. He also succeeds with the left hand because he can visualize the picture via the right visual memory area and carry out the task via the right motor area. But if he tries to complete the picture holding one piece in each hand, he cannot do so because he cannot imagine both hands moving together, only each hand moving by itself. However, he is able to use both hands in tasks well-practiced before the operation, for instance, in dressing himself, tying his shoelaces, and the like.

When either side of his face, neck, the top or back of his head are touched and his eyes are closed, the patient can locate the touch with either hand. This is possible because the touch receptors in the head and neck project to both sides of the brain so that the motor region of both hemispheres can innervate the hands. But when he is touched anywhere below the neck, he can locate the point touched only with the ipsilateral hand. For instance, when the fingers and the palm of one hand are touched, the thumb of that hand can point to the stimulation point but the other hand or thumb cannot. The division of the hemispheres prevents the other hand from finding the touch point because that hand is not connected with the somesthetic memory area that registered the touch. Below the head and neck, somesthetic impulses are relayed only to the opposite side of the brain. Normally, sensory impressions would be relayed also to the hemisphere on the side that is being touched, and motor impulses initiated on that side would also be relayed to the opposite side, so that both hemispheres would have access to the somesthetic memory. But with the brain split through the middle, this is no longer possible.

The coordination between hearing and moving either one or both hands is good, so long as the instructions are within the attention span of the split-brain patient. According to Gazzaniga, when the patient was told through an earphone in his left ear to take a particular object, he could do so, either with the left or the right hand. He could also move the right and left hand as instructed. Writing to dictation could be done without difficulty when patients were using their right (dominant) hand. Two out of three patients could also do simple writing to dictation with their left hand. This was possible because sounds heard in either ear project to the auditory areas in both the right and the left hemisphere, and so are connected with the motor areas on both sides of the brain.

This is true also for vision. The left visual field of both eyes projects to the right occipital lobe, and the right visual field of both eyes projects to the left occipital lobe. To exclude one hemisphere, the patient must fixate a central point while objects or pictures are shown either in the left or the right visual field. Since it is not possible to keep such central fixation for any length of time, Gazzaniga flashed his pictures for 1/10 to 1/100 of a second on a tachistoscope either into the left or the right visual field. The split-brain patients showed considerable impairment, particularly when they had to report what they had seen, either verbally or in writing.

An experiment demonstrates the difference between fixating a central point and focusing on the object. In "condition A" Gazzaniga asked the patient to look at the illuminated button in his left visual field and then touch it with his right hand. In this condition, the patient accurately located the button. In "condition B" Gazzaniga asked the patient not to look at the button but, keeping his fixation on the midpoint of the visual field, to touch the button with his right hand. In this condition, the patient did not succeed in touching the button. Normal people respond easily and accurately in both conditions. When the patient looked directly at the button, he saw it with both eyes and so could respond with either hand because the visual memory was accessible to both hemispheres.

Verbal Report of Split-Brain Patients.   The most profound impairment was shown when the patient was asked to say what he had seen or touched. For instance, when a split-brain patient was asked to say on which point on his left side he was being touched when his eyes were closed, he could not do so, although he was able to point to it with his left hand. When he was given a pencil in his left hand and asked what it was, he said it was a can opener or a cigaret lighter, or something similar. According to Gazzaniga, "such guesses came presumably from the dominant left hemisphere and were based on whatever indirect cues happened to be available to that hemisphere" (p. 117). Visual stimuli to the left visual field also could not be reported correctly (Fig. 19.4) As Gazzaniga says:

> When visual stimuli such as triangles, ovals, squares, or pictures of objects such as pencils, spoons, apples, oranges, and so forth, were presented exclusively to the right hemisphere, the subjects would claim they saw nothing (i.e., the left hemisphere was talking, as it were) but then, with the left hand, they would retrieve the match from a series of objects. After each correct response, the subject was asked what had been retrieved. All replied they didn't know. Here again, it was the left hemisphere "talking," and it did not "know." It neither "saw" the visual stimulus nor had direct access to the tactual information. But because the right hemisphere performs consistently and well on such tests over a long period of time, it is assumed that it "knows" and is "aware" of the test stimulus: it isn't able to "talk" about it. (p. 27)

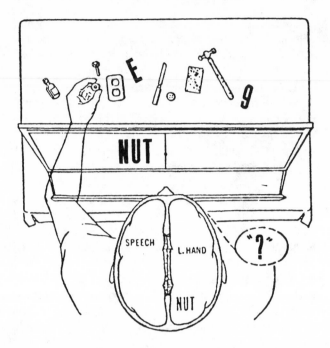

FIG. 19.4. Visual stimulation and verbal report. Names of objects flashed to left half-field can be read and understood but not spoken. Subject can retrieve the named object by touch with the left hand, but cannot afterwards name the item or retrieve it with the right hand. (From Sperry, 1970.)

Surely to speak of a hemisphere "talking" or "knowing" is sheer anthropomorphism. It is the patient who cannot say anything about the objects seen in his left visual field ("presented to the right hemisphere" as Gazzaniga puts it) but who can retrieve them with his left hand. Since his hemispheres are disconnected, stimulation on the left side, projected to the right visual cortex, cannot connect with the speech memory area which is confined to the left frontal lobe (Broca's area 44). This area is needed if the patient is to report on the objects shown.

It cannot be "the left hemisphere talking" as Gazzaniga has it, because the motor areas in both hemispheres innervate the speech muscles. But in the split-brain patient, only the right hemisphere contains the visual memory engrams and these had no connection with the speech memory engrams in the left hemisphere. The patient could talk about anything, he could respond to the experimenter's question as to what he saw on his left side, but the left speech memory area had received no input from the right visual memory area, so there was nothing the patient could say about the things he saw. The patient could use his left hand to select the picture or object he had seen in his left visual field or had felt in his left hand because the visual and tactual memory engrams registered in the right hemisphere had an intact connection with the right motor cortex which guided his left hand. He could not make the choice with his right hand because the visual and tactual memory engrams registered in the right hemisphere did not provide any input to the left motor cortex which governs movements with the right hand. Fig. 19.5 is a simplified diagram of the circuits used in these tasks. (Compare with Fig. 19.6, stimulus shown in right visual field.)

In the auditory sphere, the situation was quite similar. When the patient was told three digits through his left earphone, and three others through his right earphone, he could report the digits heard with the right ear but not those heard with the left ear. Apparently, auditory impulses project to auditory cortex in both hemispheres (the patient could carry out commands spoken into one ear with either hand) but the projection to the auditory memory area goes exclusively to the opposite side (the patient could not report digits heard with the left ear). The auditory image projected from the left ear to the right auditory memory area has no connection with the left auditory speech memory area (Wernicke's area) and the left motor speech memory area. The former is necessary for understanding spoken language and the latter is required for reporting what was heard. The split-brain patient could neither understand nor report the digits heard through his left earphone.

There is increasing evidence that the left (dominant) hemisphere is specialized for language functions while the right hemisphere mediates nonverbal memory functions (Reitan, 1966; Levy, 1974). In fact, it has been shown that the left temporal plane, which contains Wernicke's area, is considerably more extensive than the right temporal plane (Geschwind, 1974). Geschwind has also pointed out that this asymmetry in the temporal lobe, as indicated by the angle of the Sylvian fissure, was present in Neanderthal man but is either much reduced or absent in subhuman primates.

Immediate Memory vs. Recall.   Another test demonstrates the difference between so-called "immediate memory," which is really the image that accompanies the sense experience (see chapter 5), and a memory that must be recalled, which represents the reactivated sensory image. When a normal person hears two sounds, one through the left earphone, the other through the right earphone, and is asked to write down whether he heard the sound first in the left or the right ear, he is more accurate when there is more time between the two sounds. Split-brain patients do worse as the time lag between the two sounds increases. The explanation is simple. As long as the two sounds are close together, they are within the immediate "echoic" memory (see chapter 4). When the sound is heard through the left ear and the report can be given immediately, there is no need to recall either sound. The patient merely concentrates on the sound heard through the right ear which is projected to the left auditory cortex and so has connections with his speech and writing memory area in the left frontal cortex. He can report, either in speech or writing, whether he heard this sound before or after the other sound which he hears but cannot report. When there is some time between the two sounds, he must recall the sounds in both ears. Since

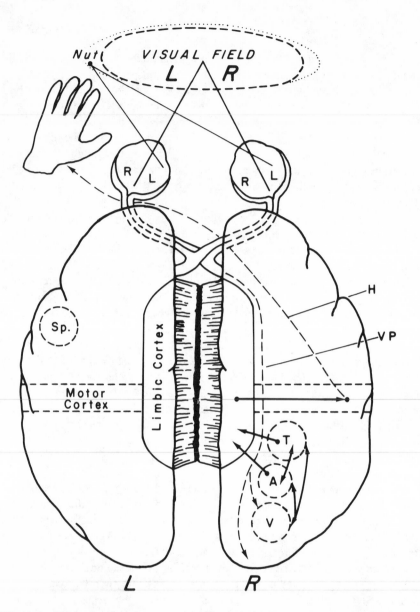

FIG. 19.5.   Effect of corpus callosum section: Stimulus shown in left visual field. Visual impression is projected to right cortical visual area and right visual memory area; the visual image is connected with the tactual memory image of object (nut). Impulse from visual and tactual memory areas to adjoining limbic cortex. Appraisal: "good to pick up." This produces a motor impulse from right limbic area to right cortical motor area. Subcortical crossover of motor impulse to left hand enables patient to pick up nut with that hand. The word (NUT) cannot be reported because right motor memory area has no connection with speech motor area in left hemisphere. Patient cannot pick up the nut with his right hand because the right limbic area, mediating appraisal "good to pick up" has no connection with left motor area which controls movement of right hand. (A) auditory memory area, (Sp) speech memory area, (T) tactual memory area, (V) visual memory areas, (VP) visual projection to cortical sensory area and visual memory areas, (H) subcortical crossover to hand.

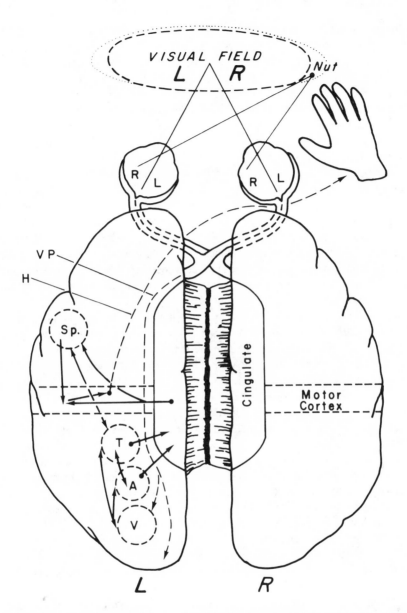

FIG. 19.6. Effect of corpus callosum section: Stimulus shown in right visual field. Visual impression is projected to left visual cortical area and left visual memory area; visual image is connected with left auditory memory and left tactual memory areas. Hence patient knows what the word sounds like and what the object feels like. Both memory areas connect with limbic cortex, hence patient can appraise object as good to remember, good to report, good to pick up. Impulse from limbic cortex to left speech memory area and left motor area for hand. Subcortical crossover to speech muscles and right hand enables patient to report the name of the object and reach for it with his right hand.

the auditory memory area in the right hemisphere has no connection with the left motor speech and motor writing area, he cannot report either the sound or its timing.

Similarly, the split-brain patient cannot compare visual stimuli, one shown in the left visual field, the other in the right one. When such a patient was asked to move his head from side to side to indicate that the two lights (one green, one red) were different, he was unable to do so. If both lights were green or both red, no patient was able to nod his head to tell that they were alike. This task requires that the patient compare the lights and judge whether they are the same or different. But a comparison is possible only when both lights can be remembered and reported. With these patients, one half of the brain had registered the red light, the other half, the green light. Since the judgment similar/different is a verbal judgment, it requires the left hemisphere, and that is connected only with the right visual memory area. But the right visual memory area has registered only one color—hence any comparison is impossible. The patient sees two colors, but can talk about only one.

Split-brain patients could write to dictation without difficulty when they were using their dominant right hand. Two out of three patients could also do simple writing to dictation using their left hand. All were able to write with their right hand what they saw in their right visual field or felt with their right hand. But when the same objects were shown in the left visual field (with eyes focused on the midline) they could not report them in writing with either hand. Obviously, writing from dictation and reporting in writing are rather different performances. In writing from dictation, the patient sees with both eyes and hears with both ears. He understands and remembers what he hears via the left auditory word memory area, and he sees what he has written and recognizes it via visual word memory and visual limbic areas. Since the left auditory memory area (Wernicke's auditory speech area, 22) is connected with the left speech memory (Broca's) area 44 and the left writing memory (Exner's) area as well as with the left motor area, which governs the right hand, he has no difficulty at all in writing to dictation with the right hand.

Knowledge vs. Report.   The situation is vastly different if the patient is asked to write down the names of objects seen in the left visual field or felt with the left hand. The visual and tactual memory engrams in the right hemisphere have no connection with the motor speech memory and writing memory area in the left frontal lobe. Hence the patient cannot recall and write the name of the object or identify it in writing. He should be able to draw the object with his left hand, but Gazzaniga apparently did not ask him to do so. Gazzaniga did report that the patient was unable to write down the name of the object seen or felt on his left side, either with his right or his left hand, although he was able to write a few words with the left hand. The patient was unable to write down the name of the object with the left hand for the same reason he could not write it with the right hand: the tactual and visual memory area in the right hemisphere was no longer connected with the speech and writing memory areas in the left frontal lobe. On feeling or seeing the object on his left side, the patient could not recall its name (i.e., appropriate speech movements) via the left speech memory area, nor could he write it down because he could not recall the appropriate writing movements via the left writing memory area.

When a light was flashed to different quadrants of the visual field shortly after the operation, the patients could describe and report only the flashes in the right visual field. But as testing and recovery progressed, the patients became able to describe the flashes in the left visual field. Gazzaniga asks: "Was this because the right hemisphere could now 'talk'? Was this becasue a subcallosal neural network became active in the interhemispheric transfer of visual information?" (1970, p. 92). He suggests that neither of these explanations are correct; "rather, it appears to be . . . the right hemisphere cuing in the left hemisphere that a light had come on by effecting a momentary shift of gaze from the midline to the illuminated point in the visual field." He seems to mean that the stimulus in the left visual field, projecting to the right hemisphere, initiated the shift of gaze to the left, so that both hemispheres now had access to the visual experience and the patient was able to report it. Apparently, immediately after the operation, the patient did not shift his gaze.

Explanations.   It is important to realize that the patient knew that a light had flashed in the visual field, although he was unable to talk about it. It is the patient who knows, not his right or left hemisphere. But it depends on the connection of the hemisphere that is activated by the stimulus whether he will be able to draw on his speech and writing memories and so be able to report what he has experienced.

When flashes of light were directed simultaneously into both visual fields, the patient reported only the light falling into the right visual field. But if he could push a button with the right hand and another with the left hand to indicate a flashing light, both hands responded correctly and *with equal speed*. This is the best proof that the split-brain patient can see the light in both fields and can report both if he is allowed to do so non-verbally. When a verbal or written report is demanded, he can do so only if his perceptual experience and sensory memory is mediated by the left hemisphere because only that hemisphere is connected with the verbal motor memory area in the left frontal lobe.

When the word "pencil" is flashed in the left visual field, and the patient is asked to select the corresponding object from several things on the table with his left hand, the patient can do so. But when the commands "laugh," "smile," "tap," "hit," are flashed in the left visual field, there is no response; when these commands are flashed to the right visual field, the patient obeys them. Gazzaniga concludes that the right hemisphere does not understand verbs, only a few simple nouns. He says: "The overall language capacity of the right hemisphere is limited, and of a particular kind." (1970, p. 130.) But there is another explanation.

When the word "pencil" is flashed in his left visual field, the patient sees it (via right hemisphere) but cannot understand or report it because he has no access to his visual and motor speech memory in the left hemisphere. But when he sees the pencil on the table, he sees it *with both eyes,* that is, both sides of his brain are now active. The sight of the pencil recalls the word "pencil" and its visual image. This visual image of the word, recalled and understood via the left hemisphere, recalled in its shape by the right hemisphere, now feels familiar (affective memory) and he recognizes it as having seen it a moment ago (via right hemisphere). This feeling of recognition, mediated by the limbic area of the right hemisphere (retrosplenial and posterior hippocampal gyrus) can now initiate the impulse to pick up the pencil with his left hand. It is not the right hemisphere that understands a few simple nouns but the patient who recognizes the shape of the word he saw before, as soon as his word memory is accessible to him. He cannot smile or tap on command when the command is flashed in his left visual field because he cannot understand the word via the right hemisphere, and there is nothing that will later bring it to mind.

Another proof that the patient really knows what he sees but cannot report it when it is flashed in his left visual field is Gazzaniga's statement that a split-brain patient can press a button to indicate which of a series of five nouns, flashed one after another in the left visual field, matches a word heard previously. When the patient first hears the word, the sound pattern is registered bilaterally in the auditory memory areas in both temporal lobes. He understands it via his left auditory verbal memory area (Wernicke's area). Hearing the word and understanding it, the patient will automatically recall its visual image via the visual memory areas in both hemispheres. When the five words are flashed to his left visual field, their visual pattern is registered in the right visual memory area. The shape of the word recalled a moment ago will seem familiar (via right limbic cortex), and he can now press the button with his left hand to indicate that he has recognized the word. Similarly, one split-brain patient, a carpenter, saw the word NUT in his left visual field and was then asked to retrieve the object to which the name refers from an array of various objects spread out on a table but hidden from his view. He could do so with his left hand although he was unable to say what he had seen or retrieved. As a carpenter, the patient would have associated the word NUT, the object it names and the feel of it during many years of working with nuts and bolts. When he touched the nut, the touch recalled the image of the object as well as the image of its name. He had an immediate feeling of familiarity, of having experienced this before (the word NUT flashed in his left visual field). As I have mentioned before, every sense experience immediately recalls the memory images associated with it. Recognizing something by touch because it feels familiar and recognizing the image of its name merely requires the limbic tactual and limbic visual memory cortex of the right hemisphere; it does not require verbal memory. If the picture of the nut instead of the word were flashed in the left visual field, it would have the same effect: The patient could retrieve the nut itself with his left hand because visual shape and tactual feel have become firmly associated (Fig. 19.5).

Gazzaniga interprets these results as meaning that language functions are represented to some extent in the right hemisphere. As Moscovitch (1973) points out, this interpretation contradicts the findings from lesion studies. Patients with left hemisphere lesions have a profound defect in language comprehension despite the fact that the right hemisphere is functioning normally. Even small lesions in the left hemisphere may leave the patient word-blind or word-deaf so that he is unable to identify simple words like "nose" or "eye" (Geschwind, 1965, 1970; Luria, 1970; Gazzaniga, 1972). Moscovitch tries to solve the problem by suggesting that "verbal functions, though represented in both hemispheres, are functionally localized in the dominant side," and that "removing the dominant hemisphere's influence releases the minor hemisphere's verbal behavior." (1973, p. 117.) He considers this suggestion confirmed by the fact that some patients are able to speak, though poorly, immediately on regaining consciousness after a left hemispherectomy.

But it is at least as likely that such speech memories were laid down in the right hemisphere before the operation, during the time—sometimes protracted—when the left hemisphere had been nonfunctional. At any rate, gradual relearning after left hemispherectomy is well documented and seems to be achieved through speech engrams registered in the remaining hemisphere. In cases where a stroke damages the right speech area after such relearning, the patient remains mute for the rest of his life. The hypothesis that motor speech engrams are registered on the right side when the left hemisphere is nonfunctional is a simpler explanation of the facts and needs no ad hoc hypothesis of "suppression" by the dominant hemisphere.

Such notions of suppression and release from inhibition have been a favorite expedient when no better explanation was available. I have mentioned (chapter 14, p. 176) that "suppression and surgical release" was the first hypothesis to explain the finding that monkeys do not use a deafferented arm as long as the other arm is intact, but use both arms when the intact arm is deafferented as well. Another popular hypothesis to explain a behavioral defect (e.g. in go/no-go problems) is to postulate a "lack of inhibition." Both explanations are ad hoc hypotheses that explain nothing.

Word recognition has usually been equated with comprehension; that comprehension is not necessarily involved has been shown by Glass et al. (1973). Global aphasic patients with left hemisphere lesions were able to distinguish words from non-words printed on cards, by sorting the cards into two piles. They were able to identify only 50% of the words, however. These patients also were able to form words out of three letters when the letters would give a word only in one order. But when the whole alphabet was available, they were unable to form words. Gazzaniga (1970) suggested that the patients manipulated the three letters randomly until a word was produced that "corresponded to an internal gnostic or visuo-verbal unit." In other words, they eventually hit upon a word they recognized as familiar—which is exactly my explanation. Apparently, the right hemisphere is better at recognizing the shape of a word than the left hemisphere. When normals saw a study word with both eyes, and then had to judge whether another word, flashed either in the right or left half of their visual field, was the same or different, they made fewer errors when the test word was flashed in their left visual field (projected to their right hemisphere), according to Gibson et al. (1972).

Finally, the notion that the right (non-dominant) hemisphere registers nonverbal memories seems to be confirmed by Gazzaniga's report that split-brain patients can copy geometric figures or reconstruct patterns in a block design better with the left than the dominant right hand. Apparently, the visual and motor structure of these figures is registered in the association cortex of the non-dominant right hemisphere. Bogen and Gazzaniga (1965) found that right-handed patients with right hemisphere lesions do worse on "spatial" tests such as drawing a Necker cube, than do right-handed patients with left hemisphere lesions. In two of their three patients with right-sided lesions, these drawings improved quickly after the first few months, which seems to show that engrams can be laid down in the intact hemisphere after the other hemisphere has become nonfunctional. Another patient did not improve and showed the same impairment when retested eight years after surgery; but this patient had additonal brain lesions.

According to Bogen and Gazzaniga, the two patients improved because there is some ipsilateral as well as contralateral motor innervation, and the right hemisphere eventually assumed good control over the right hand. But it would seem that ipsilateral control of movement is not sufficient for accurate drawing. Even excellent contralateral control does not enable a righthander to write fluently or draw competently with the left hand. It needs considerable practice to establish a dynamic motor structure that is gradually refined and preserved, and can be revived when needed. There is no reason why such motor memories of drawing could not be registered in the dominant (left) frontal lobe when the earlier motor memories are no longer available on the damaged right side.

Gazzaniga's own conviction is that most patients improve because they employ gradually more and more sophisticated methods of cross-cuing. But this notion only poses another problem: How does one hemisphere cue the other? Once the two hemispheres are disconnected, there is no way of relaying information from one to the other. Giving a cue implies that the giver must know that a cue is needed, he must recall the cue and pass it on. If only the right hemisphere "knows" the left signal, it would have to know also that the left hemisphere needs a cue and then would have to devise an action that supplies it (for instance, looking to the left side, pointing with the left hand). Surely such an assumption is unrealistic because it ascribes much too high a degree of sophistication to a hemisphere. According to Gazzaniga, the patient did occasionally look at the picture directly and so saw it via both hemispheres, increasingly so as testing went on. This may not indicate that the right hemisphere has cued the left one, as Gazzaniga seems to think, but merely that the patient knows that there is something to see on his left side and so is looking to make sure.

The problem is complicated only because Gazzaniga assumes that it is the hemisphere that does or does not know, not the patient. But if we assume that the patient does know what is happening, even if he cannot report it, the problem becomes much simpler. There is no question of two minds, one in each hemisphere, as is sometimes suggested. Normally, the split-brain patient experiences any stimulation over both the right and the left hemisphere. This is certainly true of seeing and hearing, also of smelling and tasting. But even touching something with his left hand, the patient experiences the touch, sees the object he touches via both hemispheres, and so can talk about it and reach for it with his right hand. Only when he is prevented from looking at it does he have difficulty talking about it or retrieving it with the right hand. He is aware of the left touch without knowing that it is the right hemisphere that mediates it; all he knows is that he can talk about it when he sees the object and cannot when he is blindfolded.

This impairment is quite different from the deficit that follows a lesion in Broca's area. A patient with a lesion in the left frontal lobe in area 44 can report that he saw something in his left visual field, even if he cannot say what it is. His right visual memory area is connected with the left visual memory area for words so that he can read and understand a word flashed in his left visual field, and can usually communicate his knowledge by circumlocutions. He knows that he cannot speak as he wants to; but the split-brain patient is unable to say anything at all about this particular experience, although he is able to talk about anything else. The split-brain patient is aware of such visual experiences in his left visual field but he cannot talk about them, either to himself or to others; that is, he cannot reflect on his experience. Hence he says he saw nothing in his left visual field and then is surprised when he sees himself picking up the orange that was shown in that field.

If a right-handed person were deprived of his left (dominant) hemisphere, he would still be aware of his environment and could react to it by moving his left arm and leg. But he could no longer use words to reflect on it, think about it or communicate his experience in any way. He might be able to relearn to speak but he would have to go about it as a child does. Neither a teacher nor his previous experience would be of much help because he could not understand instructions or remember earlier knowledge. In contrast, a patient with damage to the motor speech memory area can follow instructions and make use of his previous knowledge. One such patient was able to relearn to speak as well as before his cerebral accident, within a year's span (Lewis, 1946).

Gazzaniga actually raises the question ''what the predominant function is of one entire half of the human cerebrum. The meager list of its assets unearthed to date hardly appears adequate to explain its role in light of the amount of neural tissue involved'' (1972, p. 142). Here Gazzaniga refers to the association cortex of the non-dominant hemisphere. Surely the answer is clear: Modality-specific memory engrams for all sensory experiences are registered in the opposite hemisphere and used for appropriate action. Apparently, auditory, visual, and motor memory engrams for speech are registered in the dominant hemisphere, while those for nonverbal sensory experience are registered in the non-dominant hemisphere. Since we need sense organs on both sides of the body, we also need the memory of the experiences they provide. And we need motor memory engrams for fluent speech, manual skills, and other skilled movements (for instance, dancing or playing a musical instrument) just as we need the patterned innervation of motor nerves for movement of all our limbs. It is possible to live with one side paralyzed, or with only one hemisphere, but it certainly is a severely restricted life. For normal living, there are no unused or superfluous areas in the brain.

THE SPLIT-BRAIN ANIMAL

The split-brain procedure was used in animals to study the functions of each hemisphere in greater detail. Research workers not only separated the two hemispheres by cutting the corpus callosum and the hippocampal commissure; they also divided the optic chiasm, and the anterior, habenular, and posterior commissures (Fig. 19.7). An animal with such complete transection shows little obvious disturbances of behavior. The deficit becomes apparent only when it has to perform various tasks.

When the sensory inflow is experimentally confined to one hemisphere, the memory patterns can no longer guide performance controlled by the other hemisphere. For instance, a cat with both the corpus callosum and the optic chiasm sectioned can no longer perform a visual task learned with one eye when that eye is blindfolded and only the other eye is available. The same cat can learn a negative response to a stimulus when trained with one eye open, and a positive response to that stimulus when trained with that eye blindfolded and the other eye open. When only the optic chiasm is cut but the corpus callosum is intact, cats can make a visual discrimination, learned with one eye, either with the "trained" or the "untrained" eye. If the corpus callosum is transected after this problem has been learned, the cat can still perform correctly, using the "untrained" eye (Myers, 1955, 1956; Myers & Sperry, 1958). Indeed, the cortex on the trained side can be ablated after learning with intact corpus callosum, and the discrimination can be performed with the "untrained" eye (Myers & Sperry, 1958). According to Sperry, the corpus callosum relays a mirror-image of the engram on the trained side to the untrained side.

When the cat had to distinguish touch and pressure on the surface of the forepaw, the same independence of the two hemispheres was found in callosumsectioned animals. Indeed, not only sensory discrimination but the motor pattern

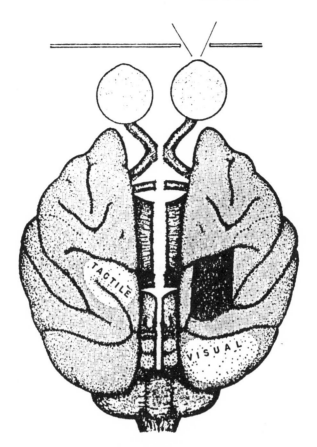

FIG. 19.7. Split-brain of monkey. *Stylized representation of monkey-brain hemispheres and underlying midline structures, split through the quadrigeminal plate to the level of the trochlear nerve (11), as prepared for a study of visuotactile integration.* (From R. W. Sperry. Copyright 1961 by the American Association for the Advancement of Science)

required to operate a pedal was restricted to the trained side in callosum-sectioned cats (Stamm & Sperry, 1957). The same situation was found in the monkey (Downer, 1958, 1959; Sperry, 1961).

Results obtained with the split-brain technique show that memory engrams are normally located on both sides of the brain (at least in animals); this is true also for simple motor memory which is registered in the frontal lobes. For instance, it has been found that the impairment in delayed response tasks after bilateral removal of the frontal lobes, or even after large bilateral prefrontal lesions, can also be produced by unilateral prefrontal lesions in split-brain monkeys (Sperry, 1965; Glickstein et al., 1960, 1963). These lesions destroyed the side of the prefrontal lobe that contained the memory of *going to the well* to find the hidden food. The other, intact side did not register this motor memory because the corpus callosum was sectioned.

Visuo-motor coordination can be studied particularly well in a monkey who has the left occipital cortex and the right frontal cortex ablated and the left optic tract cut behind the chiasm (Fig. 19.8). In such an animal, the right occipital cortex receives visual impulses from the right visual field of both eyes and registers these visual memories. The right occipital lobe, normally connected via the action circuit with both frontal lobes, now connects only with the left motor area. Since the pyramidal pathways cross over, the intact left motor area governs movements with the right arm. The animal is able to use vision to aim at both stationary and moving objects (Myers, 1955). But any complicated movements guided by vision are so disrupted that they require prolonged retraining. Such movements depend on motor memory and motor imagination. The monkeys' motor habits had been formed on the basis of visual input from both the right and left visual field. With only the right visual field available to guide movements the established habits no longer function and have to be reestablished on the basis of the visual input from the right visual field alone.

However, simple movements apparently can be retained after extensive ablations and sectioning of commissures. Sperry (1965), for instance, reported that a

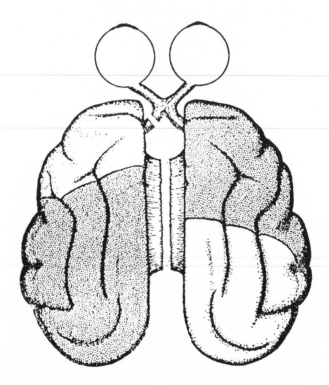

FIG. 19.8   Split-brain and complementary lesions. *Basic complementary lesion pattern used with variations for analyzing conditioned response learning and visuomotor coordination.* (From R. W. Sperry. Copyright 1961 by the American Association for the Advancement of Science)

split-brain monkey with right frontal cortex ablated and left optic tract cut behind the chiasm, who was trained to flex the right arm on seeing a flashing light, retained this reponse after near-total removal of right hemisphere neocortex, and section of anterior, posterior, hippocampal, and habenular commissures, as well as midline section of the massa intermedia and the quadrigeminal plate. This was possible because the monkey still had affective memory (light flash—good for bending arm), mediated by the right limbic cortex which relays impulses to hippocampus and fornix; relays from there return via the supramamillary decussation and both mamillary bodies to the limbic cortex of both hemispheres. Relays to both hippocampi can then engage the action circuit to the intact left motor cortex which allows the monkey to bend the right arm. It might not be possible to train an animal who has its brain lesioned in this way; but once trained, affective memory is apparently sufficient for a simple movement.

Spreading Depression.   To study hemisphere function, it is also possible to eliminate one hemisphere by the technique of "spreading depression," a topical application of KCl to one hemisphere. Bureš (1959) has shown that spreading depression represents a functional ablation. The hemisphere so treated is inactivated for several hours. In a study by Russell and Ochs (1965), a group of rats were trained to press a bar in a conditioning chamber. When the bar was pressed, a light flashed, the apparatus rumbled and a pellet was discharged into the food pan. Before training, spontaneous bar presses averaged 8 per hour. When an animal was trained, these responses increased to an average of 171 per hour. The rats were trained with one hemisphere depressed. Twice during training, and at the end of training, the "trained" instead of the "untrained" hemisphere was inactivated by spreading depression. As a result, the rats pressed the bar about eight times per hour, as before training. Apparently, the memory engrams were registered exclusively on the "trained" side, the same side as the functioning motor cortex. Whenever this side was inactivated by spreading depression, the animal had no memory of the training. This did not depend on handedness or motor preferences. The animals learned as easily whether the left or the right hemisphere was depressed.

Although only one hemisphere was "trained" in these animals, and only this hemisphere could have contained the required memory traces, transfer to the other hemisphere was instant as soon as the animals were allowed to press the bar while both hemispheres were functional. When they were removed from the apparatus immediately after such a single response and tested an hour later with the "trained" hemisphere depressed, their response rates equalled those obtained when the "trained" hemisphere was functional.

These experiments allow the conclusion that sensory and motor memory is normally registered bilaterally (at least in animals) but that the engrams of one side suffice when the other hemisphere is excluded. Moreover, bilateral registration of motor engrams occurs with every response; and these engrams are located in the frontal lobe.

20

The Hippocampus: Relay Station of Memory and Action Circuits

There is an intuitively obvious truth relevant to the general question of the function of the septo-hippocampal system . . . namely that this system almost certainly does not have one single function. It is patently absurd to take any large component of the brain and to try to attribute to it a single function, spatial mapping, some sort of retrieval function, behavioral inhibition, affect, or whatever . . . . The behavioral effects of hippocampal lesions are as diverse as those observed after destruction of any other major component of the brain, if not more so. The worst we could do is to argue whether it has one function or another. What we should do instead is to try to reach agreement on the nature of the multiple functions the septo-hippocampal system appears to have, and to discuss whether they might be related in some sensible way; in order to discover whether there is some reason why those functions are located together in this part of the brain (p. 417)

S. P. Grossman 1978b

In my theory, the hippocampus is the central relay station for the modality-specific and affective memory circuits, as well as for the action circuit. It forms the bridge between sensory experience and action. The structure and connections of the hippocampal formation are such that it could serve these functions.

STRUCTURE OF THE HIPPOCAMPAL FORMATION

The hippocampal formation includes the hippocampal gyrus and the hippocampus proper (Ammon's horn) with the dentate gyrus. This structural complex has developed from the hippocampal primordium found in primitive vertebrates. In

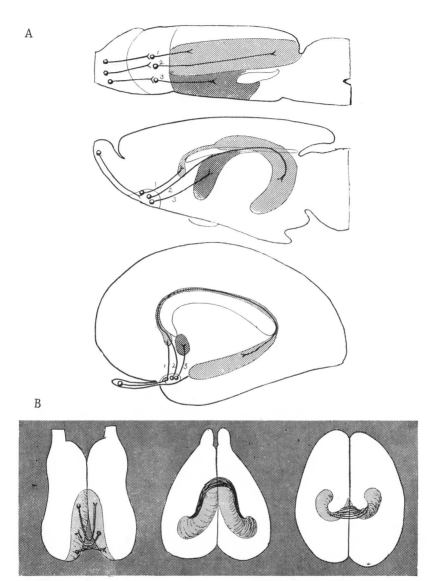

FIG. 20.1. Evolution of hippocampal formation: newt, rat and man. A—medial view. Medial olfactory striae: 1, to anterior end of hippocampus; 2, to hippocampus proper; 3, to septal nuclei. Light hatching, hippocampus; dark hatching, septal nuclei. B—Dorsal view. Hippocampus in light cross hatching; hippocampal commisure in black. (From W. S. J. Krieg, 1942.)

marsupials, who lack the corpus callosum, the hippocampus arches from the septum dorsally and laterally into the temporal lobes (Fig. 20.1). With the development of the corpus callosum in placental mammals, the hippocampus was forced to stretch out lengthwise to accommodate the numerous callosal fibers connecting the two hemispheres. These fibers have grown right through the anterior part of the hippocampal complex (septum, fornix, indusium griseum, and the hippocampal commissure) so that hippocampal neurones can be found above, below, and within the corpus callosum. Above the corpus callosum, the hippocampus has been reduced to a few fiber bands, the medial and lateral longitudinal striae, the indusium griseum, and the fasciola cinerea. According to Angevine (1975), these correspond to the fimbria-fornix system, the hippocampus and the dentate gyrus. (The fasciola cinerea is continuous with the dentate gyrus.)

In mammals, the hippocampus arches around the thalamus. The part above the thalamus is often called the dorsal hippocampus, and the part reaching into the horn of the lateral ventricles, the ventral hippocampus. In the rat, the dorsal hippocampus is prominent, the ventral portion insignificant. The cat and dog have nearly equal dorsal and ventral parts. In the course of evolutionary history, the hippocampus gradually came to lie entirely in the temporal lobe, as it does in primates, particularly the human being. Hence the terms "dorsal" and "ventral" hippocampus are inappropriate for primates. It is more accurate to distinguish between anterior and posterior hippocampus, according to its location in the temporal lobe.

The medial part of the hippocampal formation is the hippocampus proper, capped by the dentate gyrus. The hippocampus proper consists of agranular cortex which has the same cell structure as the motor cortex; the dentate gyrus is a strip of granular cortex that has a similar cell structure as the primary sensory cortex (von Economo & Koskinas, 1925). Both the hippocampus and the dentate fascia are allocortex, a primitive three-layered type found in all vertebrates. In primates, the lateral part of the hippocampal formation is periallocortex, sixlayered, and forms the hippocampal gyrus, part of the limbic appraisal system. The hippocampal allocortex is surrounded by a ring of limbic cortex (callosal, precallosal, cingulate, retrosplenial, and hippocampal gyrus and the insula; (Fig. 20.2). These limbic cortical regions form the transition to the highly specialized neocortex.

The dentate gyrus caps the rolled-up hippocampus in such a way that the surface layer of the dentate is continuous with the surface layer of the hippocampus. (Fig. 20.3) The dentate fascia contains the superficial molecular layer, a granular layer, and a layer of polymorph cells. The afferent granular cells of the dentate fascia are in intimate contact with the large efferent pyramidal cells of the hippocampus. The axons of the dentate granule cells reach through the molecular layer toward the dendrites of the hippocampal pyramid cells. The polymorph layer contains basket cells which reach numerous granular cells (Chronister & White, 1975).

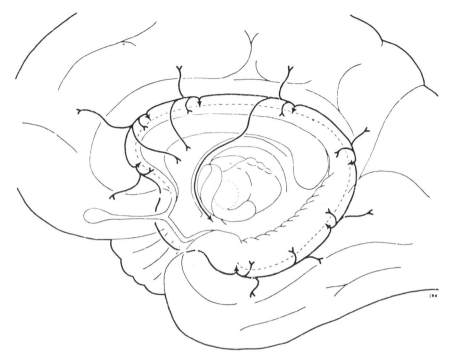

FIG. 20.2.   *The cingulum*. Major branches of cingulum in sagittal plane and disposition of cingulum and uncinate fasciculus within parahippocampal and orbitoinsular sectors of limbic cortex; respectively. Three major groups of branches are depicted: *superior* branches, to paralimbic cortex; *callosoperforant* branches, here shown entering septum and fornix; and *corticoperforant* branches penetrating the indusium griseum in the region of the sulcus of corpus callosum. Uncinate fasciculus interdigitates with cingulum at both anterior and posterior ends of orbitoinsular limbic sector. (From Yakovlev et al., 1966)

Basically, the hippocampus has three cell layers: the external plexiform layer (so called because dendrites and other fibers form a dense plexus), the pyramidal layer, and the polymorph cell layer. These layers have been subdivided again, but for our purposes this subdivision is not relevant. The polymorph layer contains basket cells (probably inhibitory) that synapse with numerous pyramidal cells and several other cell types. The pyramidal layer has a type of cell found nowhere else in the nervous system, the double pyramids—so called because their tufted dendrite trees reach in opposite directions, toward the surface and toward the alveus. The alveus lies beneath the lining of the lateral ventricle and covers the hippocampus in a net of myelinated fibers. It becomes continuous with the fimbria beneath the medial border of the hippocampus. The fimbria eventually joins the fornix.

The hippocampal formation is usually divided into four adjacent cortical fields, according to their connections: the most lateral field is the entorhinal area,

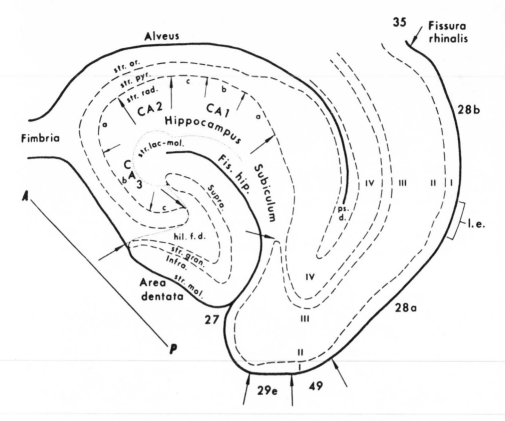

FIG. 20.3. *Diagram of hippocampus.* Nomenclature, areal and sector boundaries (long arrows), and subsector boundaries (short arrows). I.e., Transition zone between subareas 28b and 28a; ps.d., psalterium dorsale. (From Angevine, 1965)

next to it is the subicular complex, next the Ammonshorn or hippocampus proper, and finally the dentate fascia. The entorhinal area and the dentate fascia send relays only to other areas within the hippocampal formation. But the subiculum complex and the hippocampus proper project to the septum and mamillary body via the pre- and postcommissural fornix (Swanson, 1978).

Hippocampal Afferents.   Considering the position of the hippocampal formation within and around the lateral ventricles, afferents must follow one of three routes: one from the septum through the fornix/fimbria system, another over a supracallosal route via cingulum and longitudinal striae, and the third from the lateral border of the hippocampal gyrus, entering the entorhinal region (area 28) either superficially or in the angular bundle (Fig. 20.4). Afferents from the medial septal nuclei and the nuclei of the diagonal band run in the dorsal fornix and alveus to terminate in the hilus of the dentate fascia and fields CA2 and CA3 of

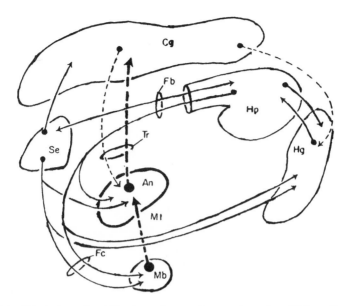

FIG. 20.4.   Principal septal and hippocampal connections are shown by solid lines. Broken lines represent some main secondary connections. An, Anterior nuclei (n); Cg, cingulate gyrus; Fb, fornix body; Fc, fornix column; Hg, hippocampal gyrus; Hp, hippocampus; Mb, mammillary body; Mt, mammillothalamic tract; Se, septum; Tr, thalamic radiations. (From E. W. Powell & G. Hines, 1975)

the hippocampus, with some fibers running to field CA1. These fibers continue beyond CA1 to subiculum, presubiculum, parasubiculum, to the area 28/35 border. Axons from the medial septal area enter the dorsal hippocampus and end there, while axons from the lateral septal area reach the ventral hippocampus (Siegel & Tassoni, 1971b; Chronister & White Jr. 1975). Lewis and Shute (1967) found that the fibers of this septo-hippocampal path use acetylcholine as the neurotransmitter.

The second pathway to the hippocampal formation is the supracallosal path, including the supracallosal striae and the cingulum bundle. The fibers of the cingulum enter the presubiculum, parasubiculum, retrosplenial, and entorhinal area and synapse with perforant fibers entering the entorhinal area. The cingulum fibers connect the frontal and parietal lobes as well as the anterior thalamic nuclei with the hippocampal formation. The anteromedial part of the frontal lobe seems to project only to the parasubiculum, a structure that has developed comparatively recently in evolutionary prehistory, parallel with the frontal lobe (White, 1959).

The third afferent fiber path enters the hippocampal formation from the entorhinal region. Since the entorhinal cortex is separated from the hippocampus by the subiculum and parasubiculum, all fibers entering the entorhinal area must perforate these structures to reach their destination. The lateral perforant path runs through the subiculum to end in the superficial molecular layer of the dentate gyrus and the deep regions of area CA3. The perirhinal area 35 receives afferents from the amygdala and sends relays to the dentate fascia, while the medial perforant path runs to the middle of the molecular layer of the dentate gyrus and the deep aspects of area CA3. According to Andersen (1975), entorhinal afferents enter a four-member neuronal loop consisting of the perforant path, mossy fibers, fimbrial axons, and Schaffer collaterals, and CA1 axons in the alveus (Fig. 20.5); schematically, the hippocampus consists of such loops. According to Lømo (1971), stimulation of perforant path fibers excited the dentate granule cells along narrow strips arranged at right angles to the hippocampal axis.

From the granule cells of the dentate gyrus, fibers project to areas CA4 and CA3, the hippocampal regions closest to the dentate gyrus. Axon collaterals from these areas, known as Schaffer collaterals, project to areas CA2 and CA1, the areas next in line; and axon collaterals from these two fields project primarily to the subiculum, the area next to CA1. At increasing stimulus rates, the synaptic effect increases so that more members of the neuronal loop discharge. At a low rate of perforant path stimulation (up to 5 per second), only the dentate granule cells discharge. With a slightly higher rate, both granule cells and CA3 neurons will fire, but CA1 cells are still quiescent. But when the stimulation rate is in-

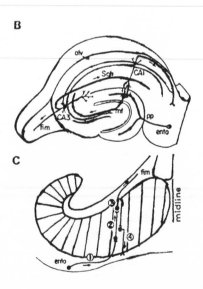

FIG. 20.5. Hippocampal formation from above. The transverse thin lines indicate the orientation of the various lamellae. The encircled numbers give the members of the neuronal loop as they would appear from above. (From P. Andersen, 1975)

creased to about 10–12 per second, neuronal impulses are driven all around the loop (Andersen, 1975)[1]

Sensory Origin of Hippocampal Afferents.   It has been known for a long time that some of the fibers entering the entorhinal region originate in the cingulum, and others in the olfactory system; but the origin of most of the other afferents to the entorhinal area has been in doubt until recently. In 1975, however, MacLean reported microelectrode and anatomical studies that showed clearly that these fibers have a sensory origin. Visual stimulation in waking monkeys resulted consistently in potentials from the posterior hippocampal gyrus (area 36), the parahippocampal portion of the lingual gyrus (area 26), and the retrosplenial gyrus (area 29). The lateral geniculate body and the lateral tegmental process of the pons also gave consistent responses. The shortest responses from the hippocampal gyrus showed more than twice the delay obtained from responses in the striate cortex (41 ms versus 20 ms). In lesion studies, MacLean found that fine fibers from the lateral geniculate body run to the hippocampal gyrus and neighboring areas in the lingual gyrus and fusiform cortex. He could not trace them to the entorhinal cortex. Lesions of the pulvinar produced degeneration of coarser fibers going to the same limbic and prelimbic areas. Hence MacLean suggested that the hippocampal potentials recorded after visual stimulation are produced over a pathway to the lateral geniculate and hippocampal gyrus.

According to MacLean, auditory stimulation (clicks and pure tones) produced potentials in cells of the posterior insula. The insular cortex overlying the claustrum receives projections from the medial geniculate nucleus. Apparently, this is a direct projection because some units responded after latencies as short as 7 msec. Somatic stimulation produced potentials only in the claustrocortex just anterior to the auditory zone. The stimuli employed were light touch, blunt and sharp pressure. Some units responded only to painful stimulation. Gustatory stimuli also produced potentials in the rostral insula in the neighborhood of the frontal operculum, the sensory area for taste. Electrical stimulation of the olfactory bulb produced potentials in entorhinal cells and, 2–2.5 msec later, in the hippocampus; and vagal stimulation was followed by potentials in the cingulate gyrus, half of them excitatory, half inhibitory.

MacLean's findings support my suggestion that sensory experience is evaluated via modality-specific limbic cortex, which results in an action impulse relayed to the hippocampus. MacLean emphasizes that the responding cells are modality-specific, which agrees with my suggestion that the limbic cortex receives sensory impulses from different cortical areas.

---

[1]The fact that excitation cascades from dentate fascia to CA 3, CA 1, subiculum and presubiculum, so that a number of cells in each field are excited by each dentate cell may explain the report that a lesion in the entorhinal area produces more extensive degeneration in the hippocampus than in the dentate gyrus (Rose et al., 1976).

Similar findings are reported by Turner et al. (1980). They examined all sensory cortical systems for efferents to amygdala and neighboring anterior hippocampal formation, and found that both structures receive afferents from the second and third sensory areas. Somatic area II projects to the dorsal half of the posterior insula; the association area for taste, to the dorsal half of the posterior part of the anterior insula; the olfactory projection goes to the entorhinal cortex; and all other projections from secondary sensory areas, to the perirhinal and prorhinal cortex. Turner et al. mention that they could find no direct relays in the somatosensory projection from the posterior insula either to the amygdala or the hippocampal formation. However, it is known that the insula is connected via the cingulum with the entorhinal cortex (Yakovlev & Locke, 1961, see Fig. 20.2); and the main limbic area for body and hindlegs seems to be the posterior cingulate, so that the cingulum seems to be the somatosensory projection to the entorhinal cortex. The posterior insula, according to my theory, is the limbic area for the appraisal of somatosensory impressions from head and paws.

The Dentate Receptive Area.   That the granule cells of the dentate fascia play a decisive role in hippocampal activation is shown by recent findings. According to Altman and Bayer (1975), the repeated irradiation of the hippocampus in infancy, which results in the death of large numbers of granule cell precursors, prevents the formation of all postnatally acquired dentate granule cells. The irradiated animals show all the symptoms of a surgical removal of the whole hippocampus, despite the fact that irradiation did not produce any reduction of hippocampal pyramids. The fact that a large proportion of dentate granule cells (5 out of 6) are formed after birth (Altman & Bayer, 1975) also supports the suggestion that these cells receive sensory-limbic input. Before birth, sensory stimulation is limited. As Douglas (1975) says, "the dentate gyrus can be considered to be a receiving or 'sensory' portion of the hippocampus . . . which probably processes information . . . from widespread cortical regions" (p. 336).

In a reversal situation, when the positive cue becomes negative, the dentate granule cells give responses different from those recorded from the hippocampal CA1 cells (Segal & Olds, 1972; Livesey, 1975). During learning, individual cells in both regions responded with increased firing rates to a tone announcing food. But when the tone suddenly signaled an electric shock, the CA1 cells continued their increased firing but the dentate cells stopped firing. If the tone was linked first with electric shock, the dentate cells suppressed firing but the CA1 cells showed little change. Apparently, the negative appraisal of the cue announcing shock (mediated by auditory limbic cortex) resulted in an inhibitory relay to the dentate gyrus, so that its cells stopped firing. But the previous response pattern, initiated by hippocampal pyramids, required some time to adjust.

Livesey (1975) found that continuous electrical stimulation over implanted electrodes in field CA1 interfered with learning and retaining a brightness discrimination. This happened even when this region was stimulated only between cue and response. In contrast, when CA1 cells were stimulated 5–10 seconds after each response, learning was delayed but retention was unaffected. But when the dentate gyrus cells were stimulated, the animal showed no significant learning deficit but a dramatic impairment when the cues were reversed. None of the animals so stimulated reached criterion, and most performed at a chance level. These findings can be explained easily enough on my theory. Stimulation of the dentate cells would not produce an impairment in learning because these cells signal only good/bad appraisals, and so long as any positive signal arrives, the hippocampal cells will follow suit. Since the CA3, CA2, and CA1 cells form the approach pattern after positive appraisals, stimulation of the CA1 region before the response disturbs learning. Stimulating them after the response, however, has no effect on the response, except that each response has to be initiated anew—hence a delay in learning, but no retention deficit. The motor pattern registered in the prefrontal cortex is activated during the response and is responsible for retention. In contrast, when the positive appraisal turns to a negative appraisal during reversal, and the dentate cells are stimulated electrically, the inhibitory signal cannot reach the CA1 cells and they cannot inhibit the established action pattern.

Zornetzer et al. (1977) found that mice with bilateral lesions in the dentate fascia were significantly impaired in passive avoidance in a step-through task, both after 15 minutes and after 24 hours. The group with lesions elsewhere in the hippocampus (mostly in field CA1), or with dentate damage on one side and extradentate on the other, were somewhat impaired in the 15–minute test, but unimpaired in the 24–hour test. Because Zornetzer et al. noticed that the CA1 region was always damaged to some extent after dentate fascia lesions, they suggested that CA1 and other hippocampal regions are involved in short term memory while the dentate fascia is necessary for long term memory. They seem to have assumed that the dentate gyrus and the hippocampus are functioning separately, so that only dentate damage is responsible for long term memory deficit, and only the hippocampus for the short term deficit. Actually, as I have mentioned before, the dentate cells activate the hippocampal pyramids; both are members of the 4–member loop from entorhinal cortex to alveus (see p. 290). Hence any damage to the dentate fascia leads to degeneration in the CA1 field. The difference between such degeneration and direct damage to CA1 would seem to be that the latter only impairs some of the connections from the dentate fascia. While hippocampal damage may impair memory 15 minutes after learning, the intact dentate fascia can still excite undamaged hippocampal cells, perhaps in the other hemisphere, so that performance is unimpaired as soon as such reorganization is complete, that is, after 24 hours. Both the dentate fascia and the hippocampus are involved in long term memory, but unilateral damage to the dentate fascia, or damage to the hippocampal pyramids can be compensated while bilateral damage to the dentate fascia cannot.

Zornetzer et al. also found a learning deficit after dentate stimulation, but Livesey (1975, see above) did not. However, Livesey used a brightness discrimination, in which learning consists in repeating the learned approach, while Zornetzer et al. employed a step-through passive avoidance task. This task depends on the appraisal that the movement, suitable before, is now unsuitable and must be suppressed. The appraisal is similar to that in a reversal problem, and Livesey found performance in a reversal problem impaired after stimulation of the dentate gyrus.

Finally, Zornetzer et al. (1977) found that memory was impaired when he stimulated the dorsal dentate region less than 15 seconds after learning; but stimulation of the dentate gyrus in the ventral hippocampus had no effect. The dorsal hippocampus receives relays from the cingulate gyrus, mediating the appraisal of movement—and the passive avoidance task employed by the authors depended on the appraisal that this movement is now unsuitable. In contrast, the ventral hippocampus has connections to the visual and auditory limbic areas but not to the cingulate motor appraisal area (MacLean, 1975). Hence damage of the ventral hippocampus, or its electrical stimulation, does not interfere with reversal learning or passive avoidance, but might interfere with visual or auditory discrimination.

The Hippocampal Rudiment.   If the hippocampus is a relay station in the modality-specific and affective memory circuits, as I have suggested, it would be important to know the effects of interrupting these circuits at various points. Part of this circuit, the indusium griseum with the medial and lateral longitudinal striae has had less attention than any other part of the hippocampal system. Yet Hines (1922) and Yakovlev et al. (1960) have pointed out that the indusium griseum in the embryo has the same structure as the hippocampus and is similarly connected with the fornix. For this reason, it is often called the hippocampal rudiment.[2] To my knowledge, there are no published research reports on the effects of damage to the hippocampal rudiment.

Experiments at Loyola University Behavior Laboratory.   Most of the learning tasks employed in hippocampal research have used visual and auditory cues. If memory is modality-specific, as I think, this concentration on visual and auditory memory has meant a neglect of other memory modalities. For this reason, we have attempted a series of experiments using all memory modalities, one at a time. We made small lesions, large enough to interrupt the modality-specific or affective memory circuit at a given point, but too small to destroy a significant portion of hippocampal or limbic cortex. In our first experiments, we trained rats

---

[2] Angevine (1975) mentions that in the supracallosal structures connecting the septum with the hippocampus, the fasciola cinerea corresponds to the dentate gyrus, the indusium griseum to the hippocampus, and the medial and lateral longitudinal striae, to the fimbria/fornix system.

in one discrimination and compared the results of postoperate learning and retention with the performance of an intact and a sham-operated group. Later, we realized that the concept of specific memory modalities could be tested only if we trained the animals in several tasks, each using a different cue modality, tested them for retention and, after surgery, compared their postoperative with their preoperative retention scores. If we could show that a retention deficit in one modality does not necessarily imply a deficit in another modality, we could determine the course of the modality-specific circuit. I discuss our experiments on modality-specific memory here; those on affective memory have been covered in Chapter 18.

Fagot (1962) found that rats with small lesions (about 1 mm in diameter) that destroyed the indusium griseum at the genu of the corpus callosum bilaterally were significantly impaired in learning and retaining a successive olfactory discrimination. Extract of pine or extract of hyacinth was introduced into an airstream. The animal had to press the bar in a Skinner box for water when the positive odor was introduced; a bar press in the presence of the negative odor resulted in foot shock.

Gavin (1963) reported that rats with a complete bilateral transection of the hippocampal rudiment at the point where motor and somatosensory cortex meet (Krieg coordinates 55.5) were unable to learn a single alternation T-maze after surgery, and unable to retain or relearn this habit when learned before surgery. Rats with unilateral lesions had no postoperative learning deficit, but a significant deficit in relearning the alternation they had learned before surgery.

Planek (1965) used a simultaneous tactual task (a Y-shaped elevated runway with one arm covered with smooth rubber, the other, with corrugated rubber). The animals were first trained in this task and next in a successive visual discrimination with a single bar and a small light. When the light flashed, a bar press triggered the appearance of a dipper with water. When the light was steady, a bar press triggered shock through the floor. After a bilateral electrolytic lesion of the hippocampal rudiment at the splenium of the corpus callosum, both learning and retention of the simultaneous tactual and the successive visual discrimination were unimpaired. A simultaneous discrimination, as I have mentioned before (see p. 150) only requires affective memory, hence a lesion of the hippocampal rudiment should not affect it. And a successive visual discrimination depends on the modality-specific memory circuit from visual limbic cortex (retrosplenial gyrus to hippocampus, and from there via fornix and midbrain to thalamic association nuclei and visual memory areas). A lesion of the hippocampal rudiment at the splenium of the corpus callosum would not interrupt this circuit.

Driessen (1965) used the same successive visual, simultaneous tactual discrimination task and the single alternation T-maze as Planek. In addition, he trained the rats in a successive auditory task in a box with a single bar. The animal could get water if it pressed the bar during clicks from a speaker suspended from the ceiling of the experimental room. (Driessen found that learning was greatly facilitated when the speaker was fastened to the rear wall of the box because the animal could feel the vibration; hence he excluded this additional cue.) When the rat pressed the bar during a silent interval it received foot shock. For the olfactory discrimination, Driessen used a small rectangular box with a glass wall in front. A tray with ten small cups was moved manually along a groove inside the glass. In random alternation, each cup contained either clear water, or quinine dissolved in alcohol. After a retention test (and necessary relearning) three weeks after training, Driessen transected both hippocampi by a 6 mm long knife cut starting at Krieg coordinates R 80, L 86, 3 mm from the midline, fronto-caudally. The cut was 5.5 mm deep, sufficient to transect hippocampus and fimbria. Unfortunately, mortality was high, so that only four animals with complete bilateral transection survived. They had a significant postoperative deficit in the auditory and visual tasks, but their performance in simultaneous tactual discrimination, successive olfactory discrimination and single alternation was unimpaired. This is what we would expect if olfactory and motor memory circuits join the hippocampal rudiment but not the hippocampus proper; and if relays from visual and auditory limbic areas reach the hippocampus via the retrosplenial and hippocampal gyrus, as my theory specifies.

Dufour (1967) trained rats on the same five discriminations but used a quinine-water solution with either lemon or vanilla odor as cues in the olfactory discrimination. For the tactual discrimination, he substituted a successive for a simultaneous task. The rat had to press the bar in the animal box to get water; but at irregular intervals, the animal received a foot shock instead of water. Intact animals quickly learned to stop pressing the bar after the shock and to start pressing again after a while until water appeared. At that time, they pressed the bar rapidly until they received another shock and no water. After learning and retention tests, Dufour placed electrolytic lesions to interrupt the hippocampal rudiment either at the genu of the corpus callosum (4 mm anterior to the bregma, 0.5 mm laterally, 6 mm deep), or at the splenium (3.5 mm behind the bregma, 3.2 mm deep, 0.5 mm laterally). Out of 12 animals, only 8 had a complete bilateral transection of the hippocampal rudiment. When the animals were tested in all five discriminations after surgery and had relearned them to criterion, those without deficit were given a second lesion at the previously not lesioned anterior or posterior location. Of the eight animals with bilateral transection,[3] two had an olfactory deficit and three had an alternation deficit. Of three animals with precallosal lesions, two refused to run in the olfactory apparatus (3 days' refusal); and of six animals with posterior lesions, three refused to run in the alternation task (1–5 days' refusal). None of the animals refused to work in the three bar press tasks (visual, auditory, tactual). Dufour explained these refusals on an individual basis: trauma in the ether chamber, incidental startle, head too

---

[3]One with bilateral transection of precallosal hippocampus and dorsal anterior olfactory nucleus; one with bilateral transection of supracallosal hippocampus at the splenium.

sore to push through the swinging door in the alternation task, etc. But it is difficult to explain the difference in the number of refusals between intact and lesioned animals. In this series, 6% of intact animals occasionally refused to run. But in Dufour's experiment, 50–60% of lesioned animals refused; but they only refused in the single alternation and the olfactory task. That an interposed swinging door did interfere with the performance of septally lesioned animals in an active avoidance task was mentioned by DeRyck et al. (1976). Both in Dufour's and DeRyck et al.'s experiments, motor memory was apparently impaired by the lesion so that it could no longer influence the animals' performance. In addition, they could no longer appraise their movements effectively because the lesion also interfered with relays from prefrontal area to the anterior cingulate gyrus. Hence the animals had to start running solely on the basis of their affective visual memory that the arm of the T-maze or the front of the olfactory apparatus was "good to approach." Without motor memory or motor appraisal, this was a feeble spur, hence the frequent refusals. Bar press tasks, as in Dufour's visual, auditory, and tactual discriminations, were not affected because the intact anterior insula (according to my theory the appraisal area for foreleg movements) had an intact inflow from the lateral prefrontal area so that the animals could properly appraise their remembered action. Finally, all of Dufour's animals were overtrained because they were given retention/relearning trials after the first lesion and again after the second lesion, in addition to the preoperative learning/retention trials. Dufour even added make-up trials for the animals that had refused to run. I have mentioned before that an animal with impaired modality-specific memory can learn a successive discrimination on the basis of affective memory alone provided that it has a great deal of additional training, which Dufour's animals certainly had.

We can conclude from this series of experiments in our laboratory that hippocampal rudiment lesions at the genu of the corpus callosum result in olfactory deficit and often refusals to run (Fagot, Dufour), while mid-rudiment lesions result in a severe alternation deficit (Gavin). Even lesions in the posterior hippocampal rudiment may result in olfactory memory deficits and a refusal to run the alternation task (Dufour). A transection of the hippocampus lateral to the hippocampal commissure results in auditory and visual memory deficits.

In all the experiments in this series, we only considered animals in which the rudiment lesions were well placed. Very few cases had slight unilateral damage to the cingulate gyrus. Hence the deficits must be ascribed to rudiment damage, or at least to damage of fibers connecting the indusium griseum with the anterior cingulate gyrus. In another experiment, Conneely (1967) attempted to make a complete transection of the cingulum at the junction of the motor and somatosensory cortex (empirically determined as lying 2 mm behind the bregma). However, in the process, Conneely also transected the hippocampal rudiment bilaterally in all but two animals. He trained the rats on the same five discriminations with the same apparatus as Dufour. After surgery, the animals were significantly impaired in all discriminations except the olfactory task, in which they improved.

Transection of the cingulum at the caudal end of the motor cortex should intensify any motor impairment produced by hippocampal rudiment transection because affective memory as well as motor memory would be impaired. However, the lesion also transected the cingulate cortex and the corpus callosum. Some lesions even encroached slightly on the hippocampus of one side. Hence it seems likely that afferent fibers from the anterior thalamus were damaged in transit to the posterior cingulate gyrus. As a result, the animals would not remember the shock to their feet and so be impaired in retaining and relearning all discriminations punished by foot shock. They improved in the olfactory task because the punishment for an error was an unpleasant taste—and the appraisal of taste, according to my theory, is mediated by the posterior insula, which was intact. In this experiment, the only deficit that can be ascribed to the transection of the hippocampal rudiment is the impairment in single alternation. The other deficits seem to be the effect of interrupting the affective memory circuit.

The above experiments are summarized in Fig. 20.6 which shows the sites in the rat brain where electrodes or knife were inserted. Another experiment, also shown, is described in chapter 22 (Synder, 1965).

ELECTROPHYSIOLOGICAL EVIDENCE

In the last twenty years, many experimenters have attempted to relate the electrical activity in the hippocampus to behavior. In more recent studies, chronically implanted electrodes in freely moving animals were used with rats, rabbits,

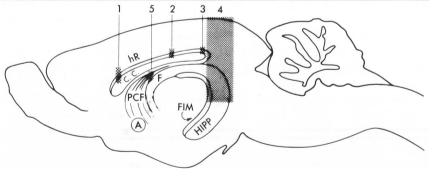

FIG. 20.6.   Schematic diagram of rat brain showing lesion sites. (1) Hippocampal rudiment at genu of corpus callosum (Fagot, 1962; Dufour, 1967) (2) Hippocampal rudiment caudal to motor area (Gavin, 1963) (3) Hippocampal rudiment at splenium of corpus callosum (Planek, 1965; Dufour, 1967) (4) Transection of hippocampus (Driessen, 1965) (5) Transection of precommissural fornix (Snyder, 1965). All lesions bilateral. hR hippocampal rudiment, cc corpus callosum, PCF precommissural fornix, F postcommissural fornix, HIPP hippocampus, FIM fimbria of hippocampus, A anterior commissure. From M. B. Arnold, 1967. In Appley & Trumbull (Eds.), Psychological stress. Reprinted with permission from Appley & Trummbull, the copyright holders.

guinea pigs, dogs, cats, and monkeys. Vanderwolf et al. (1975) reported that the rat hippocampus has an electrical frequency below 15 cycles per second (cps) at all times. But when the recording electrodes are moved to the dentate gyrus, the pattern consists almost exclusively of 15–50 cps waves. However, Winson (1975) has found that the dentate gyrus shows a slow wave pattern closely coupled with that of the overlying CA1 hippocampal field except that the phase is reversed.

Hippocampal Theta Waves

The amplitude of these spontaneous waves seems to be between 0.5 and 1.0 millivolt on the average, but may be up to 3 millivolt in some sites. The slow wave pattern is of three main types: first, rhythmic slow activity (RSA or theta waves), which usually has a frequency between 6–12 cps. A second type is large amplitude irregular activity (LIA), which has frequencies as low as 2 cps and does not show rhythmic wave trains. The third type is small amplitude irregular activity (SIA), which appears suddenly and rarely lasts longer than one or two seconds, in contrast to the other two types, each of which may last for many minutes. Vanderwolf et al. (1975) found that the fast activity recorded from the dentate gyrus or subiculum could not be further analyzed. These regions show large amplitude slow waves during sleep and irregular fast activity during waking much like the neocortex.

The RSA or theta pattern is the type of electrical activity in the hippocampus that was most frequently correlated with particular kinds of behavior. However, this is true for lower mammals rather than primates. In rats and rabbits, any voluntary (as distinct from instinctive) movement is accompanied by large amplitude theta waves. Novel sensory stimuli or electrical stimulation of the medial septal area, dorsal fornix, medial forebrain bundle and midbrain reticular formation produces hippocampal theta (Green & Arduini, 1954; Petsche et al., 1965). Usually, this is accompanied by EEG arousal, i.e., neocortical desynchronization. Green (1960) reported that monkeys show hippocampal theta only when they are extremely emotional.

Possible Functions of Theta. Theorists have tried to link RSA with a variety of psychological functions. Green and Arduini (1954) suggested that it is an arousal response to stimulation. Others thought that it is an attention or orienting response (Grastyán et al., 1959; Bennett, 1969, 1975), that it indicates information processing and memory consolidation (Adey et al., 1960a,b; Adey, 1966), or voluntary movement (Dalton & Black, 1968; Vanderwolf et al., 1975).

Grastyán found that hippocampal theta was invariably associated with orienting or attention. He recorded hippocampal activity during hypothalamic electrical stimulation, applied by the experimenter, which could be stopped by the animal stepping on a large pedal. Weak hypothalamic stimulation induced orienting or approach; strong stimulation at the same site, flight or withdrawal. When the animal stopped weak stimulation by stepping on the pedal, it avoided the pedal afterwards. When it stopped strong stimulation, it later approached the pedal. Grastyán called these "rebound" phenomena. Approach after weak hypothalamic stimulation, or as a rebound after strong stimulation, was characterized by slow 3–5 cps theta waves in the hippocampus. Avoidance was accompanied by hippocampal desynchronization. Hence Grastyán suggested that theta is associated with orienting followed by approach. In his view, the hippocampus directs information from outside toward approach or avoidance. Destruction of the hippocampus yields predominantly approach.

Adey et al. (1961) followed the change in hippocampal electrical activity in cats when they were learning a T-maze in which a visual cue indicated food reward. The resting hippocampal record showed various frequencies, but also a dominant 3–4 cps wave. Just before the reward signal appeared, rhythmic 4–7 cps waves were recorded in hippocampus and entorhinal cortex. The spectrum then shifted to a burst of 5–6 cps waves on each approach. After 10–20 trials, the rhythmic slow activity dropped out in the ventral hippocampus but remained in the dorsal hippocampus and entorhinal cortex. This slow rhythmic activity remained until the task had been learned (80–90% correct), then became less obvious. The slow wave theta disappeared during extinction and reappeared during retraining. Between trials, the record returned to the 3–4 cps rhythm. The same wave pattern was found when the animal learned a delayed response. When food was placed under one of two cans in sight of the cat, there was a delay period of 5–10 seconds in which the electrical activity showed a wide spectrum of 3–6 cps, but when the animal was permitted to approach, the same 5–6 cps waves appeared as were recorded during approach to food in the maze. During approach, bursts at these frequencies registered simultaneously in the reticular formation of the rostral midbrain, the subthalamus, the primary visual cortex, and the somatic cortex. During correct approach responses, the entorhinal cortex leads the dorsal hippocampus, but during incorrect responses the dorsal hippocampus leads (Adey et al., 1961). Apparently, when the cat decides on approach based on what it did before (motor and affective motor memory), the response is incorrect (dorsal hippocampus leading, afferents from cingulate cortex). But when it approaches on the basis of the visual memory of food hidden under the cup in *this* trial (afferents from visual memory cortex via limbic cortex to entorhinal region), the response is correct.

From his results, Adey (1966) concluded that hippocampal theta mediates not only attention to the environment but also some memory function. He says: "the deposition of a memory trace in extrahippocampal systems may depend on such wavetrains (theta) and subsequent recall in the stochastic reestablishment of similar wave patterns" (p. 25).

Bennett (1975), who had set out to reconcile the views of Grastyán and Adey, found in the course of his experiments that RSA (theta) accompanies the learning and performance of cats in any task that requires attention to environmental cues, for instance, successive or simultaneous brightness discrimination, auditory discrimination, and the like. In contrast, learning and performance of tasks that do not require environmental cues (CRF or DRL schedule in an operant chamber) are accompanied by hippocampal desynchronization. Bennett also showed that a task with 20 seconds delay between successive bar presses for a milk reward (DRL 20) was accompanied by hippocampal desynchronization. But when a light cue was added to signal the end of the delay, the bar press was again accompanied by RSA. This change from desynchronization to theta was only seen in cats. Rats showed hippocampal theta under both conditions. Hence Bennett suggested that hippocampal theta may be correlated with attention to environmental stimuli, but that the association of movement and hippocampal theta may hold only for rodents, not for cats. According to Bennett, scopolamine abolishes hippocampal theta but does not affect attention, learning, or performance.

Vanderwolf et al. (1975), proponents of the view that hippocampal theta is correlated with voluntary movement, reported that two hippocampal systems seem to be involved in the production of slow waves. One generates rhythmic slow activity with a frequency range usually between 5 and 7 cps, the other produces 7–12 cps activity, both in rabbits and rats. The slower frequency as well as irregular waves occur during immobility, licking or face washing, and automatic activities that are instinctive. It may also occur when an animal is preparing to move or when it hesitates to move. The faster activity always accompanies voluntary (appetitive) behavior. The slower 5–7 cps waves are depressed by atropine but resistant to ether. Since atropine counteracts acetylcholine, we might infer that this slower system is cholinergic. According to Vanderwolf et al., the faster type of theta (7–12 cps) correlated with voluntary motor activity and is in phase with neocortical motor discharges. It is resistant to atropine but is depressed by ether. Since ether depresses the medial reticular system, we might infer that this type of theta indicates an appraisal for action.

Animals can be conditioned to produce faster or slower frequency theta. Black (1975) conditioned dogs and cats to produce fast RSA, (normally accompanied by movement) while they remained immobile, washing their face or licking. Rats could not be conditioned to produce high frequency RSA while immobile but could be conditioned to produce low frequency RSA. This type of activity also occurs during so-called paradoxical sleep (see chapter 26).

Crowne and Radcliffe (1975) found that there is one situation in which RSA reliably appears in the monkey hippocampus, and that is the experimental extinction of a learned response. The first few nonrewarded trials produce slow wave trains, usually in all hippocampal leads, but most frequently in midhippocampus. These anticipate the animal's response. There are also short RSA trains between responses that usually occur only in one lead. These authors conclude that there is no serious break between mammals and primates. But they insist that RSA cannot represent merely the initiation of movement but must indicate a "highly abstract'' level of internal activity. They suggest that ''the functions of the hippocampus involve a process of anticipatory modulation or control of intended responses . . . . A very general way of stating the hypothesis is that changes in the valence of stimuli (from positive to negative, from reinforced to nonreinforced, from arousing to repetitive . . .) activate the intention system.'' (1975, p. 200, 201)

Crowne and Radcliffe acknowledge that the hypothesis says nothing about the process by which hippocampal efferents are coded, the nature of hippocampal afferents, the way in which inputs are collated, or the differences in hippocampal anatomy that could account for the species differences in electrical activity as related to behavior. Crowne and Radcliffe's notion that RSA indicates the formation of an intention is similar to my suggestion that this waveform represents an action impulse. But in my theory, this action impulse can be an intention to recall something as well as an intention to move in a particular way. The finding of Vanderwolf et al. that RSA includes two waveforms, one slower, generated by a cholinergic system, the other generated by a system not antagonized by atropine, lends credence to my suggestion that hippocampal theta may indicate either an intention to recall something or an intention to move. Since the relays from septum to hippocampus seem to be cholinergic, it is possible that this cholinergic slow-wave system represents the recall system. The other, faster, system generating RSA may mediate the intention to act.

Single-Cell Recording

Ranck's Results.   The electrical pattern recorded from the hippocampus represents a great number of cells firing together. According to Ranck (1975), recording from single cells would be more likely to yield behavioral correlates. He implanted microelectrodes at extracellular sites in the hippocampus and related regions of freely moving rats and observed the potentials recorded from each neuron while the animal was waking or sleeping, eating or drinking, while it was pressing a bar for food or water, or avoiding an electrified water spout. Eventually, he was able to classify these neurons into several groups, according to the behavior observed during their firing.

About 6% of the total cells increased their firing only if a regular theta rhythm could be seen in the hippocampus, whether during waking or during paradoxical sleep (see chapter 26). These cells he called *theta cells*. They fired fastest during voluntary behavior, and more slowly during well-learned activities, during bar pressing, eating, drinking, or grooming. These cells occurred in all areas of the hippocampal formation and also in the medial septal nucleus. They were nonspecific, that is, they fired during every type of behavior. They slowed during irregular slow wave activity in the hippocampus, when the rat was wakened from sleep, or immediately after an external stimulus while the rat was motionless.

The *complex spike cells* were different from the theta cells in that at one time or another they fired a complex spike, that is, a group of potentials, occurring within 1.5–6 msec of each other, and usually decreasing in amplitude. Complex spikes were never recorded from theta cells. Ranck could distinguish several types of complex spike cells, according to the behavior during which they fired. Most cells in presubiculum, parasubiculum, and medial entorhinal cortex were *specific orient cells*. They fired for about 2 seconds when the rat turned toward food, water, or other objects. In the dorsal fascia dentata, *appetitive cells* were the most common, but they could also be found in hippocampal fields CA1, CA2, and CA3. These cells fired during orienting or approach. Some of them were specific for objects or places (e.g., going toward food, the water bottle, etc.), some were firing during any kind of approach. In contrast, *approach-consummate cells* fired only during approach followed by consummatory action (e.g., approaching water and drinking). They were most commonly found in CA3, but also in anterior CA1 and dorsal CA2, CA3. In hippocampal fields CA1 and CA2, the cells most commonly identified were *the approach-consummate-mismatch cells*. They fired during the same type of behavior as did the approach-consummate cells, but they also fired when approach was unsuccessful, for instance, when the rat explored the water hole after the bottle had been removed. A few *motion-punctuate cells* were identified in dentate gyrus and hippocampal fields. These cells fired one to five action potentials at the end of some orienting movements or at some change of direction.

In the lateral septal nucleus, *approach-orient cells* and motion-punctuate cells were the major types of neurons. Their rate of firing did not change much, but they were identified because now and then their firing was synchronized with movement potentials. Approach-orient cells fired during orienting or approach, and motion-punctuate cells, at the end of such movements. Ranck did not observe any specificity in these cells.

In the medial septal nucleus, Ranck could identify four types of theta cells. Three of them were snychronized with hippocampal theta; the fourth, *approach-orient theta cells,* had components of both approach-orient cells and theta cells. Still another type, *tight group cells,* fired during specific consummatory behavior. In discussing the significance of his findings, Ranck suggested that ''specific orient cells excite appetitive cells, that appetitive cells converge with tight group cells of the same specificity to excite approach-consummate cells, that approach-consummate cells and appetitive cells excite approach-consummate-mismatch cells'' (1975, p. 243).

Ranck is saying that impulses from entorhinal cortex and the medial septal nuclei (and indeed, indirectly from all sensory and motor areas) are relayed to the dentate gyrus and the hippocampus; in this way, specific appetitive behavior, approach and consummate behavior, as well as the estimate of success or failure are mediated by the hippocampal formation. Allowing for the difference in terminology, this is at least partly the position I am advocating, namely, that the hippocampus organizes the intention to act in a particular way, when activated by a specific appraisal. But I have also tried to show that the hippocampus is, in addition, involved in the impulse to remember (modality-specific and affective memory), and can initiate imagination via amygdala.

Hippocampal Place Units.   Another function of hippocampal excitation has been described by O'Keefe and Black (1978). These authors found that some cells in the hippocampus of freely moving rats fire when the animal occupies a given place in his environment. Eliminating information from different sensory modalities (turning off the room lights or changing intra-maze cues) did not disrupt the firing of these cells. Only change of place did.

To discover whether these cells were receiving information over different sensory modalities or perhaps from the geomagnetic field, the authors employed a T-maze located within an enclosure. Outside the maze but within this enclosure were four cues (white card, dim light, buzzer, fan) placed so that each side of the enclosure had one cue. From trial to trial, the maze was randomly rotated within the enclosure so that the entrance was always between two different cues. On one half of the trials, the food was in the left arm of the maze; on the rest of the trials, in the right arm (Fig. 20.7).

The potentials recorded from several units in the rats' hippocampus were obtained from places in the maze that were related to the cues. On probe trials, some of the cues were removed. As long as two cues remained, the firing of

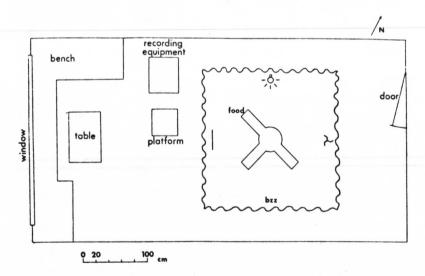

FIG. 20.7.   Layout of the experimental room in the single cell experiment. The cue-controlled enclosure is the curtained-off area just to the right of centre. -̗Ọ̖-, low wattage light; ⋋ , fan; I, card; bzz. buzzer. (From O'Keefe & Conway 1978.)

hippocampal cells remained undisturbed. When more cues were removed, particularly the light, the cells no longer fired when the animal was in the goal box but rather increased firing wherever the animal was in the maze. The authors concluded that the rats had formed a spatial map on the basis of the cues outside the maze that enabled them to find the food no matter what its location in the maze or the location of the maze in the enclosure. They think that the increased firing when too many cues were removed acts as a misplace signal and triggers exploration.

There is no reason why an animal should not have a "map" of various places in its environment. Both man and animal experience objects *in* an environment rather than *separated from* the environment. The same integrative sense that allows us to experience objects rather than a bundle of sensations also allows us to experience their relations in space.

Hippocampal Activity During Learning.   The hippocampus is engaged whenever the animal learns something: to press the bar for food, to avoid shock, or to learn to orient itself in O'Keefe and Black's apparatus. That the hippocampus actually paces the progress of learning has been shown recently by R. F. Thompson (1980) and associates, who used an airpuff to condition eyeblink in rabbits to a tone. He recorded unit spike discharges of neurons in multiple unit clusters in the hippocampus and also in the motoneurons of the final common pathway for nictitating membrane responses, the sixth cranial nerve nucleus. Thompson found, first of all, that the eyeblink responses and the potentials of the sixth nerve nucleus are very closely coupled. Whatever the neurons do, the nictitating membrane does also. Moreover, unit activity in the granule cell layer of the dentate gyrus and in the pyramidal cell layer of hippocampal fields CA1–2 and CA3–4 increased during learning and did not increase in control animals, which were given the airpuff without the tone. These animals blinked with the onset of the airpuff; the conditioned experimental animals blinked with the onset of the tone. In these animals, the hippocampal activity began to increase with the second trial of training. As Thompson says, it may well be the earliest sign of learning in the brain. The degree to which learning will occur can be predicted from the increase in the hippocampal potentials. Recordings from the lateral septal nuclei showed the same increase after an initial delay. Activity in the medial septal nucleus was evoked by onset of the tone but habituated with learning instead of increasing. Recordings from the mamillary nucleus resembled the response from the medial septum. Thompson mentioned that Swanson and Cowan (1975, 1977) had reported that the hippocampus in fact does not project to the mamillary bodies, the projection originates in the subiculum.

In addition to recording from a cluster of cells, Thompson and his coworkers also took recordings from single pyramid cells in CA fields of the hippocampus. They identified these cells by antidromic stimulation of the fornix, which ensured that the cells from which the potentials were recorded were actually projecting from the hippocampus via the fornix. Berger and Thompson (1978a) found that these cells paced behavioral learning, increasing their activity as soon as the animal began to learn. R. F. Thompson (1980) concludes that the hippocampus forms a temporal model of behavioral learning. He says:

> the growth of the hippocampal unit response is completely predictive of subsequent behavioral learning. If the hippocampal response does not develop, the animal will not learn. If it develops rapidly, the animal will learn rapidly . . . . Further, the temporal form of the response predicts the temporal form of the behavioral response. The only thing more that could be asked of any brain system in relation to learning would be to find the engram there. (p. 212)

The engram is not there to be found. It is registered in the sensory and motor association cortex. But Thompson's findings completely support my theory, according to which the hippocampus organizes the impulse to recall what happened after the tone, and what the animal did about it. This impulse was relayed via fornix (a) to septal area and tegmentum, returning via medial geniculate to the auditory association area, and (b) to anterior thalamic nucleus and auditory limbic area in the posterior insula, and (c) via the action circuit to the motor nucleus of the 6th nerve. We can conclude with Thompson that the hippocampus initiates the impulse to learn, and paces learning; however, the animal may be able to repeat a well-learned performance without hippocampal participation.

Berger et al. (1980) found that the increased hippocampal activity during learning is initiated by relays from entorhinal cortex. They suggest that the primary role of the hippocampus is to potentiate or amplify a specific activity pattern. This confirms my suggestion that the limbic appraisal areas, mediating an appraisal for action, send relays to the hippocampus; this structure then organizes the goal and direction of the required activity. The pattern of body and limb movements would next be organized via the cerebellum.

Berger and Thompson (1978b) found similar increased electrical potentials in the lateral septum and the mamillary bodies, which supports my suggestion that the hippocampus mediates memory recall via hippocampus, fornix, and midbrain. Berger and Thompson (1978a) suggest that the rapid growth of hippocampal activity during the initial stage of learning is parallel to the long-term potentiation of electrical activity found in the hippocampus by many investigators. A single train of 10–15 pulses per second, applied for several seconds, potentiates the cell population for an hour and longer. Such potentiation was found not only in the dentate fascia but also in the mossy fiber field CA 3 and the Schaffer collateral CA 1 field synapses. This potentiation was limited to the synapses stimulated and was not an increase in general excitability. Berger and Thompson suggest that this potentiation, which is thought by many investigators to be the neural substrate for learning and memory, is the same mechanism that accounts for the rapid increase of hippocampal activity during the first stage of learning. The authors point out that the increase of hippocampal activity during this stage depends on presenting the conditioned stimulus before the unconditioned stimulus; and in the potentiation procedure, the increased activity depends on grouping the stimulus train into 10–15 pulses per second, applied for 15 seconds. The suggestion may well be valid, but unless the increased activity in the hippocampus during learning can be shown to depend on the same frequency stimulation as long-term potentiation, it is at most an interesting parallel.

21
Hippocampal Damage and Memory

During the past three decades of intensive research, many investigators have proposed their favorite version of hippocampal function. Indeed, so many theories have been propounded that it would be too lengthy and too tedious to list them all. Except for my own, no theory has proposed more than one function for the hippocampus. But as research reports have accumulated, new explanations of hippocampal function had to be found to accommodate the increasingly disparate results. Of necessity, these explanations became more and more general. The hippocampus was seen as generator of internal inhibition (Douglas, 1967, 1975), or as a mechanism for the suppression of interference from earlier memories (Isaacson, 1974; Weiskrantz & Warrington, 1975). Such a theory is so general that it explains everything and nothing. It explains everything—because every response could be explained by internal inhibition, which excludes all other responses. And every incorrect response could be explained as interference by earlier memories because learning depends on memory. Such a theory explains nothing—it does not explain the positive response choice that dictates the inhibition of other responses. It does not explain either positive or negative interference from earlier memories because it does not supply the trigger that suppresses undue or unwelcome interference.

One problem for theorists has been the fact that hippocampal damage seems to have very different consequences for human beings as compared to animals. In human patients, the most striking result of bilateral hippocampal damage is a profound and enduring memory defect (Scoville & Milner, 1957; Penfield & Milner, 1958; Milner, 1964). In contrast, animals with such damage seem to learn some tasks more quickly than intact animals, and perform normally in others. They do show considerable impairment in a number of tasks, and vary from normal animals in many ways.

HIPPOCAMPAL DAMAGE IN HUMAN BEINGS

I propose to review first the effects of hippocampal damage in human beings and then the results of such damage in animals. A comparison of the two should make it possible to isolate the common features if they exist.

Memory disturbances that involve the hippocampus and related areas have been reported for many years. For instance, memory disturbances have occurred in patients with temporal lobe tumors (Simma, 1955), third ventricle tumors (Williams & Pennybacker, 1954), lesions of the midbrain reticular formation (Hernández-Peón et al., 1956), and damage to the hippocampus and the mamillary bodies (Grünthal, 1947; Ule, 1951). But the most conclusive evidence for the connection between hippocampal damage and memory disturbances has been obtained from studies of patients with bilateral or unilateral ablation of the hippocampus or the temporal lobes. Terzian and Dalle Ore (1955) reported severe memory loss in a patient after a two-stage temporal lobectomy, undertaken to control persistent and severe psychomotor epilepsy. After removal of one temporal lobe, no memory defects were noticed. But after ablation of the second lobe, the patient no longer was able to carry on a conversation, and could say only a few words, like "give me a cigarette." He remembered little of his childhood and nothing about recent events or actions. He did not recognize old friends, was unable to learn anything, and seemed to be motivated exclusively by physiological appetites. The authors concluded that this patient was the human analogue of the monkeys with Klüver-Bucy syndrome as a result of bilateral temporal lobectomy (Klüver & Bucy, 1939).

Less extreme but still serious memory defects followed a series of medial temporal ablations which included the uncus, amygdala, and anterior hippocampus. In several reports, Milner (1958, 1959, 1968a, 1970), has described the effect of these surgical ablations. Since these patients were studied exhaustively, we can learn a great deal from the kind of memory defects reported. Such patients can repeat up to nine digits and carry out mental arithmetic. But they cannot recall the test material after five minutes if they have done something else in the interval. They cannot recall words, sentences, stories, drawings, or objects. A patient may remember his old address but not the new one to which his family moved after his operation. He cannot recognize friends by sight, reads the same magazines over and over, and cannot find his way home. One of the patients Milner studied could not learn a visual maze with buzzers indicating errors, but learned mirror drawing easily. Motor skills, like cutting gloves or preparing blueprints, were preserved in all patients (Milner, 1965). Whether a patient later recognized what he had made seemed to depend on the extent of the hippocampal ablation.

One young man, H. M., with extensive medial temporal ablations, was studied for many years. During this time, he had normal immediate recall, normal digit span forward and backward, and a slightly higher I.Q. than he had before surgery (WAIS 118 versus 104). He was able to recall verbal and nonverbal visual and auditory material for a few seconds provided he was allowed to rehearse silently (Prisko, 1963; Sidman et al., 1968). He remained unable to recall daily events or to learn either verbal or nonverbal material. He could not learn a stylus maze with 28 choice points, but after 155 trials and 256 errors he was eventually able to do a stylus maze with seven choice points (Milner et al., 1968). However, he learned a mirror drawing design and a pursuit rotor task in a few days, despite his insistence every day that he had never seen the pursuit rotor before (Milner, 1968b; Corkin, 1968).

Undoubtedly, this memory loss is the result of hippocampal ablation. According to Milner (1959), the bilateral removal of uncus and amygdala did not affect memory if the hippocampus was spared. Indeed, she found a rough correlation between the extent of hippocampal removal and the severity of the memory loss. This loss, according to Milner (1965), is an "impairment of recent memory."

However, it cannot be an impairment of all recent memory because motor learning is preserved. Learning mirror drawing requires recent memory as much as does a visual maze. Rather, the defect seems to be a loss of visual and auditory memory. The immediate visual and auditory image is preserved (the visual and auditory association cortex is intact) but access to these engrams seems to be lost. What the patient hears and sees is registered, the visual and auditory image is formed and retained, and can even be reported as long as the patient is concentrating on it. Once his attention wanders, he can no longer gain access to it. I would hazard the guess that olfactory, taste, and touch memory are defective also, but these modalities are not usually tested.

Not only hippocampal damage but damage of related structures has produced severe memory losses. The Korsakoff syndrome, an effect of chronic alcoholism, brings with it degeneration of the mamillary bodies (which receive fibers from the hippocampal formation and send fibers to the anterior thalamic nuclei (see chapter 18, p. 250f.), the fornix, and often the hippocampus and dorsomedial thalamic nuclei. Victor et al. (1971) reported that the locus coeruleus shows cell loss and depigmentation in over two thirds of Korsakoff patients; indeed, such damage seems to be more frequent than hippocampal damage. This nucleus seems to be the origin of the noradrenergic system that connects with the hippocampus. I discuss its significance in chapter 24.

Like the patient with hippocampal ablation, the Korsakoff patient has both anterograde and retrograde amnesia. He remembers little if anything for a period of weeks, months, or years before the present, and he does not remember anything happening now. He is usually able to recall childhood memories and adolescent experiences, but may not be able to remember where he has lived or worked for the past few years. He does not remember current events, for instance, who is the president of the United States, nor can he remember the name of his physician or the hospital in which he is staying. When asked to recall something, he confabulates. Once started on a task, he finds it extremely difficult to shift to another. Such patients seem apathetic, lacking all motivation (Talland, 1965).

One difference between Korsakoff patients and patients after surgical removal of both hippocampi is the fact that the former confabulate, the latter do not. In Korsakoff patients, the damage is usually restricted to the mamillary bodies, and the anterior and medial thalamic nuclei. Since the hippocampus is largely intact, the impulse to remember can be relayed via precommissural fornix to the hypothalamus but is prevented from reaching the midbrain, sensory relay nuclei, and sensory association cortex (sensory recall); and also, from reaching limbic cortex via anterior thalamic nuclei (affective recall). But the patient can form the intention to remember (via hippocampus) and with it, the impulse to imagine the situation (connection from anterior hippocampus to amygdala). As we know, normal recall activates imagination as well as memory. The Korsakoff patient intends to remember but can only activate the imagination (not the memory) circuit. He thinks he is recounting a memory because that was his intention, but he has only activated the imagination circuit and so he confabulates instead. In contrast, the patient who has had a bilateral hippocampal ablation does not even know how to go about remembering: The intention to remember, I am suggesting, is formed in the hippocampus. As a result, he can activate neither imagination nor memory circuits and simply reports that he does not remember.

After unilateral hippocampal ablation, the memory loss is specific for left and right, quite similar to the memory defect after unilateral lesions of the visual or auditory association cortex (see chapter 12). Patients with right temporal lobectomies were impaired on Kimura' recurring nonsense figures (Kimura, 1963), in learning visual and tactile mazes (Milner, 1965; Corkin, 1965), in recalling tonal patterns (Milner, 1967), and in the recognition of faces after a short delay (Milner, 1968a). In contrast, patients with left temporal lobectomies had difficulty learning and recalling words, whether the words were spoken or displayed visually (Milner, 1967). According to Serafetinides et al. (1975), such patients could not remember messages, either oral or written, forgot appointments and dates, things of interest seen and heard on TV, radio, or read in newspapers. Most of them showed no dysfunction of the intact temporal lobe. In a later study, Cherlow and Serafetinides (1976) found that all right anterior temporal lobectomy patients were superior to all left anterior lobectomy patients both in short and long term memory. Intracarotid administration of sodium amytal into the dominant (left) hemisphere resulted in transient impairment in recalling learned verbal and numerical material. No such impairment followed injection into the nondominant hemisphere.

Electrical stimulation of the hippocampus in the left (dominant) hemisphere produced more interference with recall than stimulation on the nondominant side. Many patients showed severe confusion in approaching their task; this also was found more frequently during stimulation of the dominant side. Stimulation of the nondominant side led not to confusion but to altered sensory experience. The patients reported "feeling the room closing in," "feeling as if floating in outer space," or as "having an eerie experience." Serafetinides found a loss of consciousness in 13 out of 15 patients who were gradually injected with sodium amytal into the dominant hemisphere. Apparently, both memory and consciousness are closely connected with normal functioning of the left (dominant) hemisphere. Serafetinides suggests that the dominant hemisphere for speech is also dominant in alertness and memory, via the hippocampus of the dominant side.

There is no report of olfactory or taste memory deficits after hippocampal ablation—but these modalities have not been investigated in such patients. The finding that motor skills are unimpaired while visual, auditory, and tactual memory are impaired requires discussion. The patient's vocabulary, his facility with numbers, and early memory also seem to be unimpaired, except for the radical bilateral temporal lobectomy described by Terzian and Dalle Ore (1955). All these memories are motor memories, as I have argued earlier (chapter 14). Childhood memories are intact because they have been transformed into speech (motor) memories by frequently recalling and recounting them. Motor memories, according to my theory, are registered and recalled over the action circuit (see chapter 16). While the action circuit receives relays from the hippocampus, it can also be engaged by an appraisal for action directly via limbic cortex, medial thalamus, and reticular formation. Once an action pattern is initiated, the action draws on the motor engrams registered in the frontal lobe. Terzian and Dalle Ore's patient could no longer converse because the auditory memory and limbic area in the left temporal lobe seems to have suffered too much damage.

Patients with bilateral ablation of most of the hippocampi as well as Korsakoff patients seen to have as much difficulty in *recognizing* what they have seen or heard as they have in *recalling* it. This accounts for the fact that they may make a glove or a blueprint, but once finished, they do not recognize it as their own handiwork. When they are given cues during retention tests, their level of recall improves. Weiskrantz and Warrington (1975) have suggested that they make errors in recall because earlier memories intrude. When this intrusion is reduced by giving a cue, their recall improves. For instance, when the patients have to recall the word "table" in response to "chair" in a paired associate test, they can do it if given a letter or two (ta——). Such learning with cued retention is retained for months. As Weiskrantz and Warrington point out, the patients must have learned something, or they could not recall it even with the cue. Hence the memory deficit cannot be a loss of memory consolidation but must be an impairment in retrieval.

We can certainly agree that hippocampal damage impairs retrieval, that is, it prevents access to existing memories. If the hippocampus is the main switching station in the recall circuit, as I am suggesting, the loss or damage of this structure would prevent access to the memory engrams in the association cortex. The notion that hippocampal damage impairs retrieval because intrusions can no longer be prevented, only adds an unverifiable hypothesis. It implies that the intact hippocampus acts as guardian against unwanted intrusions. Obviously, it cannot prevent all intrusions because in everyday life we depend on continuous recall (memory intrusions) to deal with our present circumstances. In contrast, my own hypothesis merely states that the hippocampus normally provides access to the recall circuit, and spells out the various links in this circuit.

According to my theory, patients with bilateral temporal lobectomies that include the hippocampus cannot recall word associates because auditory and visual limbic cortex is either missing or has no access to the hippocampal remnant. With both amygdalae also missing, patients cannot use their imagination to hunt for the word to be recalled. But when the first two letters of the word are given and they pronounce them, they activate their speech memory via the action circuit and so can complete the word.

Such word memory functions best when there are no or few other words that fit the cue. Indeed, Weiskrantz and Warrington found that the patients' recall was best when a unique cue was given, that is, when the first three letters defined only one word (cue: oni; word: onion). As a matter of fact, under these circumstances, their recall was somewhat better than that of matched intact controls. In cases where the cue can be matched by only two words (moa: moat and moan), the patients' recall was essentially normal. In learning a reversal, however, where the formerly incorrect words were now correct, the patients were grossly impaired.

Weiskrantz and Warrington used to insist that the interference hypothesis can explain every type of memory impairment. However, they found more recently that false positives do not intrude excessively at first, but only emerge gradually in later repetitions. Also, when the patient does not have to distinguish successive lists of paired associates, interference effects do not appear to the same extent. Hence Weiskrantz (1978) concluded that cues do not work by constraining inappropriate responses—which disapproves at least one form of the interference hypothesis. Now Weiskrantz is suggesting that the hippocampus serves to sort out different alternative memories. If such sorting is not required, man or animal can dispense with the hippocampus.

But Gaffan (1978) denies that the difficulty lies in such a sorting process. He finds that amnesic patients cannot remember which of two pictures of faces they have seen before, even if they only have to point to it. Fornix-lesioned monkeys have the same difficulty of recognition, yet such monkeys can remember which of two objects has been rewarded. Gaffan comments that "equally complex control processes are surely required in the two kinds of tasks" (p. 403). Hence he suggests that it is recognition that is defective after hippocampal lesions. Amnesic patients cannot reliably assess whether an item is familiar, although they may still be able to form and store associations (Weiskrantz & Warrington, 1975).

Gaffan's hypothesis is close to my suggestion that recognition depends on the appraisal that "I have seen this before." Such recognition seems to be mediated by the appraisal system. We appraise something as familiar if we have encountered it before, just as we appraise something as good if we have found it satisfying in the past. As soon as I see a friend in the distance and appraise this sight as "good to know better," both modality-specific and affective memory are reactivated. Recalling his appearance, and our past affectionate association, I recognize him, that is, I appraise the person I see as having seen him often and loved him well. When brain damage in the Korsakoff patient involves the hippocampal formation or the affective memory circuit (mamillary bodies, dorsomedial and anterior thalamic nuclei), he may recall earlier impressions in cued recall but fails to recognize them as memories.

Such dissociation of recall and recognition has recently been investigated in various tasks. For instance, Weiskrantz and coworkers (Weiskrantz, 1978) conditioned the blink reflex to an airpuff in a postencephalitic amnesic patient and a Korsakoff patient. Both patients retained the conditioned reflex over the 10–minute rest pauses and an interval of 24 hours. But they could not recall the conditioning procedure, even when they were asked while still sitting in front of the apparatus. Similarly, amnesic patients can learn and retain motor skills, visual discriminations, anomalous pictures in the McGill Anomalies test, and various other tasks. But they never recall that they have learned the task or even that they have seen it before. Hence Weiskrantz suggests that their impairment results from a dissociation between levels of processing rather than a failure on any particular level. However, neither of these two explanations seems adequate. Rather, the sight of the tasks they have learned does not initiate affective recall so that the patients have no basis for the appraisal that they have seen or done this before. Their deficits as reported represent a failure of visual or motor affective memory. No doubt, olfactory and auditory recognition is similarly defective. So Caldwell (1958) has found that lobotomized patients are unable to recognize odors, while psychiatric patients equated for length of illness but without lobotomy, had no difficulty in doing so. In lobotomized patients, both olfactory and olfactory affective memory circuits are interrupted.

HIPPOCAMPAL LESIONS AND ANIMAL BEHAVIOR

After trying to investigate the results of hippocampal damage in animals and comparing them with clinical reports, most experimenters found no similarity between deficits in human beings and animals. Of course, "memory deficits" were translated as "learning deficits," to avoid "mentalistic" terminology; and learning, like memory, was assumed to be a unitary function. From their investigations we have learned that animals with large bilateral hippocampal lesions are impaired in some types of learning, but not in others.

Such animals are impaired in *successive* visual and auditory discrimination (Kimble, 1963; Arnold, 1967), in delayed response and delayed reinforcement, in reversal learning and experimental extinction. They perseverate in their responses and do not habituate in new situations. They are deficient in spontaneous and learned single alternation. Such animals are not distracted as easily as intact animals when engaged in a task. They repeatedly turn into the same blind alley, increasing their errors (see the excellent reviews by Douglas, 1967, 1975). They are deficient in passive avoidance, but active avoidance is intact (Isaacson & Wickelgren, 1962; Kimble, 1963; Teitelbaum & Milner, 1963; Kimble et al., 1966). Snyder and Isaacson (1965) reported that the larger the hippocampal lesions, the larger the deficit.

Animals with large hippocampal lesions show normal learning and retention in *simultaneous* black-white discrimination (Kimble, 1963), tactile discrimination (Teitelbaum, 1964; Webster & Voneida, 1964), size and brightness discrimination (Douglas & Pribram, 1966), and the discrimination of numerals (Kimble & Pribram, 1963). They show no impairment in learning a straight runway task (Wickelgren & Isaacson, 1963, and others), and are perhaps quicker than intact animals in learning to press a lever for reward (Clark & Isaacson, 1965; Schmaltz & Isaacson, 1966). Hippocampectomized animals are not impaired in acquiring an active avoidance response in the one-way shuttle box (Niki, 1962), and are better than intact animals in the two-way shuttle box (Isaacson et al., 1961, and others). They are also unimpaired in successive olfactory discrimination (Allen, 1940, 1941).

At first glance, such a medley of experimental results, including deficient, normal, and even improved learning, seems puzzling. But I hope that a systematic discussion of these findings will show the way to a consistent explanation.

Simultaneous Versus Successive Discrimination.   In chapter 12, I tried to show that there is a significant difference in these two procedures. In simultaneous discrimination, only affective memory is necessary. Such a discrimination can be learned so long as the sensory limbic cortex and its connection with the affective memory circuit are intact. In contrast, successive discrimination requires both sensory and affective memory. The discrimination can be learned only when both memory areas and their respective memory circuits are intact. I have suggested on the basis of published evidence that the limbic area for body touch is the posterior cingulate gyrus, and for mouth touch, the posterior insula; the limbic area for sight, the retrosplenial and posterior hippocampal gyrus. Since the affective memory circuit has direct connections from limbic areas to the anterior thalamic nucleus which sends relays back to limbic cortex, hippocampal lesions are not likely to disturb affective memory; and affective memory is sufficient for learning a simultaneous visual or tactile discrimination.

According to my theory, olfactory memory is registered in the orbital cortex; and the olfactory recall circuit travels via the medial olfactory striae to the hippocampal rudiment, and from there via the precommissural fornix to the midbrain, returning via the habenula to the orbital cortex. Accordingly, hippocampal damage does not disturb either simultaneous or successive olfactory discrimination.

When a simultaneous discrimination is no longer strictly simultaneous, the hippocampectomized animal is at a disadvantage. For instance, Niki (1962) used a Y-maze in which the rat had to choose between the arm with the lit bulb and the arm with the unlit bulb. The light bulbs were in front of the goal box, at the end of each arm of the maze. The animal had to look first toward one goal box, then turn and look toward the other, before deciding which goal box to approach. Such a set-up is closer to a successive than a simultaneous discrimination, and Niki predictably reported a learning deficit in his hippocampectomized animals.

Animals from rats to monkeys, and human beings as well, are impaired in successive discrimination after hippocampal ablation. So Stepien et al. (1960) found that monkeys with lesions including much of the hippocampus were unable to learn a task in which they had to respond when two visual or auditory stimuli, shown or sounded one after the other, were the same, and not to respond when they were different. The animals' failures were almost without exception the result of responding when no response was called for. This could indicate, as the authors suggest, that the hippocampus is involved in response inhibition. But these findings would also support my contention that this task requires visual and auditory memory (the animals had to remember the first stimulus when they saw or heard the second). This task resembles a successive discrimination and cannot be solved on the basis of affective memory alone. In another study, Stepien and Sierpinski (1960) used epileptic patients for a similar task. The authors assumed that hippocampal function was defective in these patients because hippocampal electrical activity was abnormal. Indeed, the epileptic patients were impaired in these tasks but they performed normally as soon as the interval between the two stimuli was shortened to less than a minute. Their performance was seriously impaired at longer time intervals, and even at short intervals when they were distracted. Apparently, the patients could use the perceptual image or trace, available in immediate memory, for correct performance. But if the delay lasted beyond their attention span, they could not recall the first stimulus.

It is instructive to see what happens with an apparently minor change in procedure. Correll and Scoville (1965) showed a single color to a monkey with hippocampal ablations, and rewarded the animal for touching it. After a short time, they showed two colors and rewarded the monkey for touching the color identical to that shown before. The color of the positive stimulus was varied from one trial to the next. The monkey performed normally and showed no sign of impairment. This procedure is quite different from that used by Stepien et al. It changes the task from one requiring both visual and affective memory to one requiring only affective memory. If, for instance, the monkey saw the color red first and was rewarded for touching it, red became the "good" color. When he next saw blue and red together, he could easily select the good (familiar) color.

The former successive discrimination had become a simultaneous discrimination, and could be learned easily.

Another variation is the delayed matching-from-sample technique (Drachman & Ommaya, 1964). Monkeys with combined lesions of hippocampus and amygdala were shown a sample stimulus. After an interval, the monkey had to match one of several stimuli present with the sample seen before. The authors found a significant learning deficit that increased as the time interval increased. But additional training enabled the animal to solve the problem, after up to 12 seconds delay. This problem can be solved in two ways; one with the help of visual memory, recalling the sample and on this basis choosing the familiar object as match. Animals deprived of their hippocampus cannot use visual recall, hence their failure. But the problem can also be solved by choosing the familiar object among the others as match, thus depending entirely on recognition and affective memory. This method is difficult if there are many objects to choose from, some of them familiar; and it becomes more difficult the longer the time interval before choosing the match. But extended training could bring success.

Douglas (1967, 1975), who interprets the impairment after hippocampal damage as a defect in internal inhibition, has great difficulty in explaining the deficit in successive discrimination. He seems to assume that the main difficulty is the complexity of the task, but this assumption is contradicted by Niki's (1962) simple light/dark discrimination, which also revealed a deficit. Douglas tentatively suggests that the experimental animals, unlike the intact controls, perseverate—that is, they develop position habits they cannot overcome. And perseveration, in turn, comes from lack of internal inhibition.

But to correct an error, more than inhibition is needed. The animal must make the correct response instead of the incorrect one. If only internal inhibition were involved, the correct response would be to stop responding. Yet this is appropriate only in passive avoidance.

Douglas has even more difficulty with Drachman and Ommaya's delayed matching-from-sample task. In this problem, the monkey does withhold his response until he matches the sample, hence loss of internal inhibition cannot explain the deficit. As an alternative, Douglas proposed the notion of a "working memory" that is lost after hippocampectomy. He defines it as a hypothetical function that integrates earlier memories with present stimuli. Without such a memory, says Douglas, the animals are unable to recategorize new stimuli. And human beings suffer a memory loss for lack of a mechanism that can order and organize stimuli for storage, so that they are unable to exclude irrelevant cues (Douglas, 1967, p. 434).

This notion has some similarity with Weiskrantz and Warrington's (1975) interference hypothesis. But the sheer inability to integrate new perceptions with stored memories and to exclude the irrelevant cannot explain the observed deficit. Patients with hippocampal damage are not confused, their memories are not just disorganized—they simply cannot be recalled. For instance, Drachman and Arbit (1966) found that their patients with hippocampal damage performed normally when the items to be remembered fell within their attention span, but were greatly impaired when they had to remember more items than their attention span permitted. Surely we must infer that these patients have normal immediate memory and that they can even store their memories; but they have no later access to them.

Delayed Response and Delayed Learned Alternation.   The hippocampectomized animal is impaired in these tasks, similar to the animal with frontal lesions. The latter lacks the area in which the motor impulse is registered while the former lacks the hippocampal areas that initiate the impulse to recall. To be able to delay the response, the animal must recall the intention to move in a particular direction. In delayed alternation, the animal must recall the impulse to move in a direction different from that in the earlier trial. Such recall is based on seeing the food cup under which the food was hidden, or seeing the 2–arm maze or two levers between which the animal is to alternate. This requires the limbic hippocampal gyrus (limbic visual area), which has been ablated.

Spontaneous and Learned Alternation.   The loss of spontaneous alternation in hippocampectomized animals has been explained by Douglas and others as perseveration, and that, as loss of internal inhibition. However, Winocur and Mills (1969b) have shown that hippocampectomized animals do not perseverate in an experiment that offers them the choice of four different runways instead of the customary two. If, as I maintain, these animals do not remember the direction in which they had turned the last time, every runway is equally new to them, so that they have three chances in four of not repeating their last choice. They "perseverate" in a two-runway task because each trial gives them a fifty/fifty chance of choosing the same runway. This results in a 50–53% alternation rate, as compared with the 85% rate for intact animals (Douglas, 1975). Not only bilateral hippocampectomy, but also total fornix transection, massive septal lesions, and bilateral subicular-entorhinal lesions reduce the alternation rate to chance.

Douglas (1966) has shown that animals with large hippocampal lesions cannot use spatial cues. And what are spatial cues but the side-by-side of things as the animal *sees* them? When these animals see the two runways, they cannot remember which of them they had entered before. Interestingly, Douglas (1975) reported that fear prevents spontaneous alternation in intact animals. Ungentled rats had an alternation rate of 50–65%, practically the same rate as hippocampectomized animals. These animals did remember their last turn and had found it harmless. Being fearful, they preferred to return to the harmless run instead of exploring the unknown one.

According to Douglas (1975), the beginning of left/right alternations is connected with the maturation of dentate fascia cells, which occurs at the same time. And I have suggested that these cells receive afferents from limbic cortex and send relays to hippocampal pyramid cells which initiate recall and response. Apparently, spontaneous alternation is a cholinergic phenomenon, enhanced by cholinergic physostigmine and abolished by anticholinergic scopolamine, supporting my suggestion that recall is mediated by cholinergic fibers.

Habituation. The lack of habituation noted in animals after hippocampal damage can also be explained as a loss of modality-specific memory. These animals keep on exploring rather than stopping after a while, as intact animals do. Pavlov considers this a particularly pure example of internal inhibition but Douglas (1975) pointed out that several interfering factors have to be ruled out. When they are, as in the study of Douglas and Pribram (1969), hippocampectomized animals are shown to lack habituation completely. But inhibition, like excitation, is produced by the organism, not the stimulus. In Kimble's (1975) objective language, the stimulus variety serves as reward when the animal explores the environment—which is not too far from saying that the animal likes to see something new. The animal stops exploring when there is nothing new to see. Without any visual memory, the animal does not remember what it has seen, and so continues exploring and does not become habituated.

Distraction. Animals with bilateral hippocampal damage are less easily distracted when they perform a learned task. Intact monkeys were startled by an incidental buzzer and stopped for a while before going on with their task. Hippocampectomized monkeys also were startled but continued with their task, often at an increased rate (Douglas, 1975). Intact animals hear the buzzer, appraise it in the light of earlier experience and watch for further developments. If there are none, they continue their task. Without hippocampi, the monkeys cannot recall similar sounds, nor can they imagine possible consequences. Hence they appraise the buzzer as harmless and go on with the task.

Reversal and Extinction. In reversal, a response formerly punished is now rewarded, and vice versa; in extinction, a response formerly rewarded is rewarded no longer. When a response that was formerly rewarded is now punished, the animal must recall what happened after the last (punished) response and must disregard the many similar responses that were rewarded in the past. This requires selective recall but also a new response. True, the animal inhibits a response, but this inhibition is no mechanical process. Rather, the animal refuses to repeat a response that is now inappropriate, and plans (imagines) an appropriate one. Without hippocampi, the animal cannot recall what happened; without the relay from hippocampus to amygdala, it cannot plan an appropriate response.

Thus the animal must depend on a slow build-up of his affective memory, which eventually turns the impulse toward the now negative cue to an impulse toward the now positive cue. This slow build-up of affective memory accounts for the fact that continued training enables the hippocampectomized animal to learn.

Active Avoidance. The first investigators regularly found facilitation in animals with hippocampal lesions. But McNew and Thompson (1966) suggested that the procedures used (two-way shuttle box, buzzer as shock signal, and massed practice) were responsible for it. They did not explain the reason but they did show that lesioned animals were significantly impaired in a one-way apparatus in which the door to the safe compartment was raised as the signal of shock to come; they learned in 5 trials a day for 11 days (distributed practice), a poor performance.

McNew and Thompson were right in imputing the apparent facilitation to the procedures used. As Olton (1973) pointed out, intact animals may associate both compartments in a two-way shuttle box with painful shock and so hesitate to approach either compartment when they hear the buzzer. In other words, the intact animals are "impaired" because they are afraid of shock whether they stay or run. The lesioned animals remember the shock when they hear the buzzer (the posterior insula, the limbic auditory area, is intact) but they cannot recall the compartment in which they suffered shock (without hippocampus, they have no modality-specific recall). Hence they are afraid only of the shock they expect in their compartment, and run to escape it. In contrast, in the one-way box, the compartment to which the animals run is always safe, hence the intact animals are not afraid of it and learn quickly. In comparison, the lesioned animals seem impaired.

Finally, Liss (1968) showed that animals with hippocampus or fornix lesions have no avoidance deficit on massed trials, but a severe deficit on distributed trials. In those experiments that reported either facilitation or no difference in the active avoidance task for lesioned animals as compared to intact animals, the trials followed one upon the other with intertrial intervals of a few seconds, so that criterion performance could usually be reached in one session. With such a procedure, the repetition occurs within the attention span of the animals, that is, within immediate memory, and no recall is necessary. As a result, the animals learn but do not retain the active avoidance task and have to be retrained (Niki, 1962; Moore, 1964; Andy et al., 1967).

There are other studies reporting impairment of active avoidance after hippocampal lesions despite massed trials. But these experiments, without exception, used a complicated active avoidance response. For instance, Musty (1966) used a Sidman (1966) avoidance apparatus in which the rat could delay shock by pressing a bar. He found a learning deficit after hippocampal lesions when white noise signaled the shock; and an even larger deficit when shocks were given every three seconds (without any cue), unless the bar was pressed before then. Similar learning deficits have been found after septal lesions (which damaged the fornix fibers coming from the hippocampus) when a complex motor response was required. In Hamilton's (1969) study, cats had to jump to a retractable shelf to avoid grid shock. In an experiment by Vanderwolf (1964), rats were placed in a shuttle box, face to the wall, and had to turn around to make the avoidance response. In all these cases, the animals were impaired in active avoidance, despite massed trials.

The reason is not far to seek. With a simple motor response, the affective memory of the shock (via limbic cortex and affective memory circuit) was sufficient to initiate the impulse to run (via direct fibers from limbic cortex to midbrain, engaging the action circuit). But the animal could not remember a complicated motor response because the motor memory circuit had no information from the hippocampus. Whether the motor memory circuit is interrupted by a hippocampal lesion or by damage to fornix or septal area is immaterial, what matters is the extent of the damage. If the interruption of the circuit is complete, the animal is unable to remember what to do.

Related areas are also involved in the active avoidance deficit. According to McNew and Thompson (1966), not only hippocampal lesions but lesions in the septal area, medial forebrain bundle, medial hypothalamus, amygdala, medial thalamus, and ventral mesencephalon produced a similar deficit. I have suggested that the amygdala is the relay station in the imagination circuit—and imagination is required in planning a complex response. All the other areas are links in the proposed modality-specific motor memory circuit.

In contrast, hippocampal stimulation seems to facilitate active avoidance learning. Erickson and Patel (1969) trained rats to press a bar during a 5-second buzz that signaled a foot shock. Ten seconds after each bar press, the rats received 3 seconds of brain stimulation in the dorsal hippocampus. High-intensity brain stimulation had no effect, but low-intensity (30 microamp) stimulation allowed the animals to reach criterion in less than half the time. An injection of atropine before the session prevented this effect. When the rats obtained brain stimulation over electrodes implanted in frontal cortex instead of dorsal hippocampus, learning was not affected. This report seems to indicate that the memory circuit, beginning from the hippocampus, uses acetylcholine as transmitter.

Passive Avoidance.   Most experimenters found that hippocampal lesions produced a severe passive avoidance deficit (Isaacson & Wickelgren, 1962; Kimble, 1963; McNew & Thompson, 1966). Usually, the animal is shocked by contact with the food or water in the cup. The deficit is usually measured in seconds of latency before the animal will approach the cup after the shock. In this situation, the animal must remember that the cup it sees at the end of the runway or in the goal box is harmful, and must refrain from eating and drinking. Without the hippocampus, the animal is unable to remember the shock on seeing the cup because the limbic visual area is either damaged or has no connection with the limbic regions mediating the experience of pain. Van Hoesen et al. (1972) reported that damage to the entorhinal area produces a severe passive avoidance deficit—which is exactly what we would expect if passive avoidance depends on appraising the food cup seen as bad (via visual limbic area to entorhinal cortex and hippocampus). According to these authors, fimbria/fornix damage did not produce such a deficit. Since the hippocampus sends relays directly as well as via fornix and mamillary bodies to the anterior thalamic nuclei, the affective memory circuit remains intact.

Shock through the mouth can be remembered, according to my theory, via the posterior insula, the limbic area for tactile impression (and pain) from mouth and paws. Indeed, Kaada et al. (1962) reported that rats with insula lesions, as well as animals with anterior or midline thalamic lesions, had a severe passive avoidance deficit. All these lesions have damaged structures within the affective memory circuit. In contrast, Kaada et al. found no passive avoidance impairment after hippocampus or fornix lesions, when mouth shock was used. Kveim et al. (1964) also reported that animals with hippocampal lesions showed no passive avoidance deficit when mouth shock was used while animals with bilateral lesions in the insula and septal area did. It would seem that passive avoidance after mouth shock is disturbed when the posterior insula (limbic area for touch to mouth) or its connections with the ventral hippocampus are damaged. After foot shock, passive avoidance seems to be impaired when the posterior cingulate gyrus or other limbic areas serving the appraisal of touch to hindlegs and body are damaged. Thus Kimble's (1963) control group of rats, which had the cortex, including the insula, removed by suction, had a passive avoidance deficit after mouth shock. And Snyder and Isaacson (1965) have found that cortical control lesions which damaged the insula produced a deficit in passive avoidance after mouth shock but no deficit after shocks to the feet through an electric grid. Large hippocampal lesions, which also included cortical lesions with insula damage, resulted in a significant deficit in both situations. Finally, animals with small hippocampal lesions that included small cortical lesions but left most of the insula intact showed a slight passive avoidance deficit with mouth shock but a pronounced deficit after foot shock. It would seem that effective passive avoidance learning requires an intact insula when mouth shock is used but an intact posterior cingulate gyrus and entorhinal areas when foot shock is used.

22 The Hippocampal Projection

There are many more fibers in the hippocampal fields and the subicular complex than there are fibers in the main efferent fornix/fimbria system. Apparently, relays from several neurons in the hippocampal fields connect with each neuron in the subicular complex. According to Swanson (1978), only 20% or less of the pyramidal cells send relays outside the hippocampal formation. All parts of the hippocampal formation except the dentate fascia and the entorhinal cortex project to various structures outside the hippocampal formation. As mentioned in chapter 20, the entorhinal region and the dentate fascia seem to be receiving areas for sensory-limbic afferents. They send relays to various hippocampal areas, and the pyramids in these areas then initiate an impulse to action—whether that is movement, recall, or imagination.

THE FORNIX SYSTEM

Chronister et al. (1976) have pointed out that the fornix system can be separated into discrete components starting from the hippocampus. Fibers from the presubiculum and parasubiculum course through the subiculum and can be followed through the alveus to the anterior thalamic nuclei. Other fibers from the dorsal subiculum run through the alveus and postcommissural fornix to the mamillary complex. The ventral part of the subiculum projects via the medial cortico-hypothalamic tract which arches behind the anterior commissure and dips toward the periventricular region, and via the anterior hypothalamus to the zone around the ventromedial hypothalamic nucleus. In addition, the ventral part of the subiculum and parts of CA 1 project via the precommissural fornix to the lateral septal nucleus, nucleus accumbens and nucleus of the diagonal band. Chronister et al. suggest that this distribution implies a functional difference between pre- and postcommissural fornix projections. Fields CA 3, CA 1, and the subiculum project via the fimbria to the lateral septal nucleus, the septofimbrial, posterior septal, and bed nucleus of the stria terminalis. The fimbria (i.e., fringe) is a bundle of fibers that follows the ventrolateral border of the hippocampus for some time before joining the precommissural fornix. The lateral septal nucleus connects with the medial septal nucleus.

The different origin of the two divisions of the fornix seems to support my suggestion that the postcommissural fibers connecting with the anterior thalamic nuclei and the mamillary bodies belong to the affective memory circuit while the precommissural fibers are part of the modality-specific memory circuit.

There is also a projection from the subiculum and field CA 1 to the perirhinal area, which is connected with the amygdala (Swanson & Cowan, 1975; Swanson, 1978). Hence any attempt to recall something also initiates imagination. Another projection runs from the entorhinal cortex via the precommissural fornix and joins the stria medullaris thalami, to be relayed to the habenula, and from there to the interpeduncular nucleus and the tegmentum (Chronister & White, 1975). Postcommissural fornix fibers also have access to the tegmentum via the mamillo-tegmental tract. The stria medullaris projection may serve to connect olfactory recall with the recall circuits for other sensory modalities; and the return projection from habenula to orbital cortex may serve the connection between the recall circuits for touch, hearing, vision, with the olfactory memory area.

The two main efferent pathways from the hippocampus, the pre- and postcommissural fornix, connect with the midbrain, but relays from there return to the thalamus and cortex. According to my theory, the modality-specific memory circuit runs via the precommissural fornix to the septum, connecting via mamillary bodies and mamillotegmental tract with the midbrain reticular formation. From there, relays run via thalamic sensory nuclei to the sensory cortical memory areas. The affective memory circuit runs either directly or via postcommissural fornix to the anterior thalamic nuclei, and connects with all limbic cortical regions. Hence, as Powell and Hines (1975) say, the major projections of the hippocampal formation are not aimed downstream, as is traditionally supposed, but rather toward thalamus and cortex (Figs. 22.1 and 22.2).

In contrast, the action circuit runs from the postcommissural fornix via the mamillo-tegmental tract and tegmentum to the inferior olivary complex and the cerebellum, according to my theory. Saint-Cyr and Woodward (1980) stimulated the postcommissural fornix and reported that such stimulation produced short-latency excitation of cerebellar Purkinje cells via both mossy and climbing fibers. The cerebellar receiving cells are in the anterior lobe of the cerebellum, overlapping with potentials from stimulation of snout and forelimbs. This means that there is indeed a connection from postcomissural fornix to cerebellum,

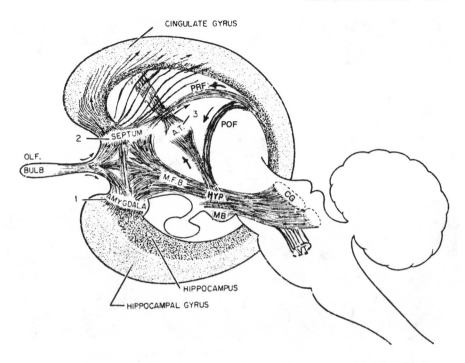

FIG. 22.1 Diagram of ascending connections within limbic system. Modified from MacLean, 1970. AT, anterior thalamic nucleus, CG central gray, MB mamillary body, MFB medial forebrain bundle, PRF precommissural fornix, POF postcommissural fornix, VT ventral tegmental area.

which seems to mediate the motor reaction to touch on snout and forelegs, hence a link in the action circuit.

According to my theory, the action circuit initiates action but also registers motor engrams. The associated motor memory circuit then reactivates motor memories, including the physiological accompaniment of action, on its course from cerebellum to ventral thalamic nuclei and frontal lobe. The various limbic regions relay not only to the hippocampus, but also directly to the midbrain reticular formation, so that they have direct access to the action circuit as well as to the two memory circuits. It follows that action can be initiated and repeated even without the hippocampus, although the hippocampus seems to be needed for any change in performance.

It is well known that there are connections between afferent and efferent pathways at every level of the neuraxis. At the spinal level, the reflex arc has a connecting link between sensory and motor fibers. I have tried to show that this link is part of the appraisal system (see chapter 17). At the midbrain and thalamic level, the connection is provided by collaterals to the medial appraisal system; and on the cortical level, by memory, imagination, and action circuits that have their relay stations in the midbrain.

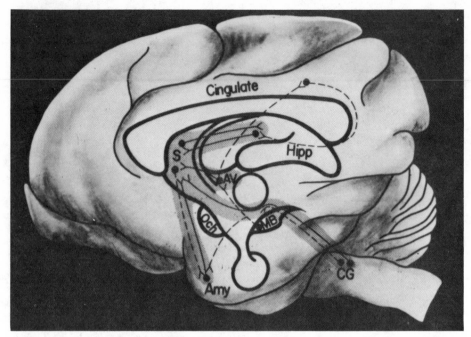

FIG. 22.2   Connections between limbic system and midbrain. Lateral view of rat's brain, showing the ascending system in the limbic area, receiving the reciprocating neural interconnection from the midbrain limbic area, the anterior amygdala, the hippocampus. AMY—amygdala, AV—anterior ventral thalamic nucleus, CG—central gray, MB—mamiliary body, OCH—optic chiasma, S—septal area: From N. Hagino and S. Yamaoka, 1976.

When these circuits are interrupted by a transection of the brain just below the inferior colliculi (in the *cerveau isolé),* the animal is not only paralyzed but asleep, as shown by the typical sleeping slow wave EEG. Olfactory stimuli can arouse it for a short time, but it quickly falls asleep again. In contrast, when the brain of an animal is isolated from the spinal cord by a cut behind the pons, producing an *encéphale isolé,* the animal sleeps and wakes normally, follows a moving object with its eyes, and expresses emotion despite being completely paralyzed. In such an animal, the memory and action circuits are intact. As in the normal animal, electrical stimulation of some brain areas produces EEG arousal, so does injection of adrenaline or amphetamine. In the cerveau isolé, EEG arousal does not occur, either after brain stimulation or injection of adrenaline. Amphetamine produces EEG arousal only if the mamillary bodies are included (Bradley & Elkes, 1957).

The Precommissural Fornix

Efferents from the hippocampus are organized strictly topographically. The perforant pathway from the entorhinal cortex excites the dentate granule cell dendrites of a segment perpendicular to the axis of the dentate gyrus. The mossy fibers of the granule cells connect with the dendrites of field CA 4 and CA 3 pyramidal cells in the same lamella. And the axons of the pyramidal cells enter the fimbria in the same topographical order so that progressively more temporal (ventral) neurons project through more lateral parts of the fimbria. This order is preserved in the septum, where fibers from rostral parts of CA 3, CA 1, and subiculum end dorsally in the lateral septal nucleus, and fibers from the temporal (ventral) pole project to the ventral part of the lateral septal nucleus, the posterior nuclei, and also to the bed nucleus of the stria terminalis (Edinger & Siegel, 1976; Swanson, 1978). This organization is invariant in vertebrates. In primates, the anterior hippocampus is a homologue of the ventral hippocampus of lower mammals while the primate posterior hippocampus is homologous to the dorsal hippocampus.

The efferent fibers from the hippocampus excite the septal receiving cells; but simultaneously, other parts of the septum are inhibited. Hence Edinger and Siegel (1976) believe that the septum "acts as a filtering mechanism to permit transmission of information only from that portion of the hippocampus whose pyramidal neurons are most active" (p. 248, 249).

These findings fit in well with the postulated modality-specific memory circuit via the fornix. Memory has to be specific—and this specificity can only be achieved if a focal excitation is accompanied by simultaneous inhibition of irrelevant information. And the fact that the topographical projection from hippocampus to septum is ordered according to dorsal/ventral hippocampal regions might mean that the modality–specific memory areas relay fibers to the hippocampus according to the order in which they are arranged around the hippocampal rudiment and the hippocampus. Hence the olfactory, body-motor, body-somesthetic memory areas project via the supracallosal pathways to the hippocampal rudiment and the dorsal hippocampus in that order, while the visual, auditory, head-motor, and head-somesthetic regions project to the ventral hippocampal region. Since the projection from hippocampus to septal area is ordered in the same way, ordered recall to different memory areas becomes possible. Of course, there is no evidence as yet that the connecting link from septal area via midbrain to the thalamic sensory nuclei is similarly ordered, although it could be inferred from the fact that these thalamic nuclei project to different cortical association areas.

Using autoradiographic methods, Swanson and Cowan (1976) found that the medial septal and diagonal band nuclei project through the fimbria and dorsal fornix to the hilar regions of the dentate gyrus, to fields CA 2, CA 3, and CA 4 of the hippocampus, to the subiculum and parasubiculum, and the entorhinal cortex. Fibers from the ventrolateral tip of the diagonal band nucleus course anterodorsally over the genu of the corpus callosum to terminate in the anterior limbic cortex. Some fibers, perhaps from cells close to the diagonal band nuclei, course even farther caudally to the splenium of the corpus callosum and the dorsal part of the subiculum. The medial septal and diagonal band nuclei send relays to the medial mamillary nuclei via the medial preoptic and lateral hypothalamic area.

According to Chronister et al. (1976), as well as Swanson and Cowan (1976), most afferents from the hippocampus seem to end in the lateral septal nuclei, particularly in the medial zone adjoining the medial septal nuclei. But they send a substantial number of fibers to the medial septal nuclei. These nuclei also receive afferents from the medial forebrain bundle, the piriform cortex, olfactory tubercle, and amygdala. Voneida and Royce (1974) have described a projection from the gyrus proreus in the cat (homologue of the prefrontal cortex) coursing caudally over the corpus callosum and around the splenium into the dorsal fornix to end in the lateral septal area. This may be part of the motor and olfactory recall circuit damaged by pregenual lesions (Fagot, 1962).

There have been few studies that have attempted to explore the effect of precommissural fornix lesions. In the first place, it is difficult to destroy the precommissural fornix without damaging the postcommissural fornix or the septal area. Moreover, the conspicuous deficits after septal lesions have centered the attention of researchers on this area; only incidentally have the effects of fornix lesions alone been explored as well.

In our laboratory at Loyola University of Chicago we attempted such lesions. Snyder (1965) trained twenty rats on successive olfactory, auditory, and visual discriminations, on a single alternation T-maze, and a simultaneous tactual discrimination (Y-maze with smooth floor in one arm, rough floor in the other). After a preoperative retention test for all five tasks, he lesioned the animals' precommissural fornix bilaterally. Some animals had additional damage to the postcommissural fornix, some to the hippocampal rudiment. Bilateral precommissural fornix lesions prevented the relearning of the auditory discrimination, whether there were additional lesions or not. It also impaired relearning of the olfactory and visual discrimination, and the alternation problem. Simultaneous tactual discrimination was unaffected by the lesions.

Although the animals could not relearn the auditory discrimination when the speaker was suspended above the chamber, they were able to do so when a small speaker was fastened to the rear wall. Apparently, the rats could sense the vibration as well as hearing the sound. Similarly, when quinine dissolved in ethyl alcohol was the negative cue, the animals had no olfactory discrimination deficit, apparently because the pungent smell affected the trigeminal nerve. When the negative odor was rosemary and the punishment an empty cup, the animals found the discrimination extremely difficult. The additional somesthetic cue in both tasks seems to have made it easy for the animals to use affective memory instead of modality-specific auditory or olfactory memory to relearn the two discriminations. Since the hippocampal formation sends direct relays to the anterior thalamic nuclei in addition to relays via postcommissural fornix to mamillary body and anterior thalamic nuclei, affective memory was functioning despite incidental postcommissural fornix lesions.

In recent years, severe visual and auditory memory deficits have been found after lesions or stimulation of the anterior commissure which carries precommissural fornix fibers (Doty & Overman, 1977; Overman & Doty, 1979). Overman and Doty applied 2–4 seconds' tetanizing electrical stimulation to the anterior commissure of macaques during a delayed match-to-sample task. Stimulation was applied either during the time the sample was shown or during the delay just before matching. The effect was slight with 2–second stimulation, but severe when stimulation was continued for four seconds. Unilateral tetanizing stimulation in the hippocampal area produced after-discharges but impairment of visual memory only at some sites. Stimulation in the anterior commissure did not induce after-discharges. Stimulation in the basal ganglia showed a nonsignificant deficit, while stimulation of other control sites had no effect. Interference with memory lasted for some time after the stimulation of the hippocampus had stopped, corresponding to the duration of the after-discharges. After stimulation of the anterior commissure had stopped, the monkeys immediately responded correctly. The authors concluded that the effect of anterior commissure stimulation was an impairment of visual memory, not a perceptual deficit; and that the basal ganglia are not involved in memory. In terms of my theory, tetanizing stimulation of the anterior commissure would prevent the monkey from recalling which match was correct. The slight deficit after basal ganglia stimulation would suggest that the monkey had difficulty recalling what to *do* (see chapter 28). Finally, the deficit after hippocampal stimulation results from the animal's inability to organize the desired action or to recall the appropriate match, depending on the site of stimulation.

The Septal Area

This area is not only a relay station for pathways to and from the hippocampus; it connects with many subcortical and cortical regions. Afferents from lateral preoptic and lateral hypothalamic areas project to medial septal and diagonal band nuclei. The ventromedial hypothalamic nucleus projects to the bed nucleus of the stria terminalis. This nucleus also receives afferents from both amygdala and hippocampus and projects to every nucleus in the hypothalamus. Hence imagination can influence various physiological appetites via the hypothalamus and is in turn affected by them. Via fimbria and precommissural fornix, afferents from the hippocampus reach the lateral septal nuclei. These connect with the medial septum and the nucleus of the diagonal band, and send relays to the lateral hypothalamus and mamillary bodies. Afferents from the hippocampus also reach the posterior septal nuclei which send relays to the habenular and interpenduncular nuclei (Swanson, 1978).

Considerable evidence has accumulated that noradrenaline and serotonin fibers travel via the medial forebrain bundle to the septum; and from there, via fornix and fimbria to the hippocampus and via amygdala to entorhinal area and subiculum. Both noradrenergic and serotonergic fibers are found in the hippocampus and the amygdala. Dopaminergic relays come from the region of the ventral tegmental area and run via amygdala to the lateral septal nucleus. Dopaminergic projections from the septum go to the cingulate gyrus and frontal cortex, but also via entorhinal area and subiculum toward the hippocampus. There is no evidence for dopamine fibers in the hippocampus.

But the most important pathway from medial septum via fornix and fimbria to the hippocampus is the cholinergic pathway. When it is cut, more than 90% of acetylcholine (ACh) disappears from the hippocampus (Storm-Mathisen, 1978).[1] This cholinergic pathway seems to be responsible for theta waves in the hippocampus. According to Vanderwolf et al. (1978), there are two theta systems ascending to septum and hippocampus from the brainstem: One runs via diagonal band and medial septal nucleus and contains cholinergic synapses; it is blocked by atropine and stimulated by cholinergic drugs. This system produces slow waves (4–7 Hz) in the hippocampus. Apparently, this system is part of the recall circuit, probably running from the olfactory and motor limbic cortex to the hippocampus, and from hippocampus via lateral hypothalamus to the septal area and prefrontal cortex. The other brainstem system produces theta only during movement and is not cholinergic. I discuss this system in the chapters on the action circuit (see chapters 26–28).

Lesions of the septal area produce an array of very different symptoms—which is not surprising considering the manifold connections of this region. The "septal syndrome" has been summarized by Grossman (1978a) but perhaps his categories could be further simplified. Septal lesions produce

1. Faster two-way shuttle box active avoidance learning.
2. Slower learning in other active avoidance tasks.
3. Impairment in successive discriminations (go/no go problems).
4. Passive avoidance deficit; decreased reaction to unavoidable shock; less food fighting; more shock-induced fighting; hyperreactivity.
5. Increased but inappropriate responding; hence impairment in extinction and reversal of learning tasks; increased exploration.
6. Decreased activity in activity wheel, tilt box, home cages.
7. Increased water intake, and intake of palatable solutions; sharp initial weight loss, later normal or increased intake of palatable food.

Grossman attempted an "experimental dissection" of the septal syndrome by transecting the main afferent pathways one after another. The first symptom, faster two-way shuttle box learning, and symptom 2, impairment in other active avoidance tasks, could only be reproduced by bilateral precommissural fornix

---

[1] Acetylcholine and other neurotransmitters and their function are discussed in chapters 24 and 25; and the route of their fiber systems through the hypothalamus, in chapter 27.

transections. Such lesions also impaired performance of other active avoidance and successive discrimination tasks. A systemic injection of atropine duplicated these effects in intact animals, but intraseptal injection of this drug did not. Grossman concluded that septal lesions or fornix lesions had interrupted a cholinergic pathway that does not have a synapse in the septum.

In terms of my theory, these lesions interrupted the modality-specific cholinergic memory circuit. Since the postcommissural fornix is intact, the animals still remember that the cue is "bad," to be avoided (in active avoidance) or "good," to be approached and manipulated (increased responding). But they no longer remember the place where they had been shocked or the change in the cue that demands a changed response (in extinction, reversal), or demands a period without response (DRL tasks).

Symptom 1. Facilitation in the two-way shuttle box after septal lesions has been confirmed for a number of animals by a number of authors (for rats, by Kenyon & Krieckhaus, 1965; Green & Schwartzbaum, 1968; Garber & Simmons, 1968; Green et al., 1967; Deagle & Lubar, 1971; for guinea pigs, by Lown et al., 1969; for mice, by Carlson, 1970; and for squirrel monkeys, by Buddington et al., 1967). In this task, it is the normal animal that is impaired and the lesioned animal that is unimpaired. The performance of lesioned animals is always judged against the performance of intact animals, and these are impaired because they hesitate to run to a compartment in which they have been shocked. In contrast, animals with septal lesions that include the fornix remember the painful shock (affective memory circuit is intact), but they do not remember that the compartment to which they are about to run is the place where they were shocked (modality-specific memory circuit is interrupted). Making the two compartments more distinctive in color, size, shape, helps the intact animals distinguish the safe from the dangerous compartment, hence they improve. But it does not affect septally lesioned animals because their modality-specific memory is impaired. Hence these animals show most "facilitation" as compared to intact animals when the two compartments are alike.

That animals with septal lesions are superior to intact animals only because they cannot remember the compartment in which they were shocked, that is, because they are suffering from a modality-specific memory loss, is shown by reports of impaired *retention* in the two-way active avoidance task despite facilitated learning (Moore, 1964; McNew & Thompson, 1966). Electrical stimulation of the basal septal area (which prevents normal functioning of this region) has also resulted in impaired retention of active avoidance (Lissak & Endröczi, 1967).

Active avoidance facilitation has also been reported in operant avoidance tasks, using both signaled and unsignaled foot shock (Duncan & Duncan, 1971; Morgan & Mitchell, 1969; Sodetz, 1970). The same active avoidance facilitation has been produced by hippocampal lesions (see chapter 21) and for the same reason: the interruption of the modality-specific memory circuit. In such operant avoidance conditioning, the animals no longer remember under what circumstances the shock occurs, hence they keep responding without hesitation.

Symptom 2.   The same animals are *impaired* in active avoidance in the one-way shuttle box (Hamilton, 1969; Kenyon & Krieckhaus, 1965) because they no longer have an advantage over intact animals. They are also impaired in a number of active avoidance tasks when a special action is required to avoid the shock. For instance, Hamilton (1969) had cats jump to a retractable shelf to avoid foot shock. In Vanderwolf's experiment (1964), the rats had to turn around before moving away from the grid through which they had been shocked. Dalby (1970) used a high hurdle the animals had to jump. In all these experiments, the animals had to remember a special action on the basis of a visual or auditory cue. Without motor memory and motor imagination, this was all but impossible. In the cases where lesioned animals learned more quickly than intact animals, they were simply running away to the only exit available. Thus DeRyck et al. (1976) found that rats with septal lesions learned faster in the two-way shuttle only when there was no obstacle in the way. When they found a door between the two compartments, their performance dropped to the level of intact animals. Lesioned animals were unable to plan or remember their action, even one as simple as pushing against a door to open it.

Symptom 3, Impairment in Successive Discrimination.   Cats and rats with septal lesions have severe deficits in successive discrimination (go/no go) tasks (Snyder, 1965; Zucker, 1965; Schwartzbaum et al., 1964); according to Grossman (1978a), because they respond on "no go" trials as well. That is true, but they do that because their modality-specific memory is impaired, and affective memory requires many more trials if the "bad" cue is to be recognized when appearing alone. What the animals remember is that the cue signalling food is "good to approach" hence they approach even on "no go" trials.

Harvey et al. (1965) found that extensive septal lesions, including pre- and postcommissural fornix, interfered with learning or relearning successive auditory and visual discrimination. The animals bar-pressed for water even after the negative cue, despite the shock. But the sham-operated controls did the same if they were extremely thirsty. The lesioned animals, deprived of modality-specific memory, continued bar-pressing because they could not distinguish between the positive and negative cue; the sham-operated controls did because their thirst urged them to do so despite the shock.

Animals with septal lesions learn and retain simultaneous visual, tactual, and kinesthetic discriminations as well as intact animals, but have great difficulty when the cues are reversed (Zucker & McCleary, 1964; Gittelson & Donovick, 1968). Affective memory is sufficient for learning when both cues are available; but reversing the cues means that their only means of discrimination has failed.

Without modality-specific memory, it takes a long time before the new positive and negative cues can become firmly established.

Symptom 4, Passive Avoidance. Animals with septal lesions are severely impaired in passive avoidance (McCleary, 1961; Kaada et al., 1962; Lubar, 1964). Grossman (1978a) and his coworkers tried to duplicate this deficit by selective lesions in various septal afferent and efferent pathways. Only when they cut the connections between amygdala and septum were they successful. Lesions of the hippocampus, entorhinal, and periamygdaloid areas produce the same deficit. Hence Grossman suggested that the pathway from hippocampus via amygdala to septal area may be responsible for the deficit in passive avoidance. Injection of atropine into the septum of intact rats produced the same deficit in "response to punishment" as he called it. Grossman concluded that the pathway involved is cholinergic, synapsing in the septal area. I would suggest that passive avoidance requires that the animal remember the shock and imagine the effect of the punished action. Since the imagination circuit was interrupted by cutting the afferents from amygdala to septum, the animals no longer expected a shock, hence did not stop responding. While I have postulated that the imagination circuit is dopaminergic, its fibers seem to be cholinoceptive.

Lesions of the amygdalo-septal connection also decreased the animals' aggression in feeding, and reduced food-connected fighting. This is a well-known result of some amygdala lesions (see chapter 23). Such lesions also resulted in hyperreactivity. Septal hyperreactivity and food-connected fighting is seen after bilateral lesions of the ventromedial hypothalamic nuclei. Hence it is likely that a pathway from the ventromedial hypothalamus to the amygdala is involved as well.

Clody and Carlton (1969) have found that lesions restricted to the medial septal nucleus do not produce an increase in rage or excitability. Since the amygdala projects not only to the medial septal nucleus but also to the ventral lateral septum (Swanson & Cowan, 1976), the connection with the amygdala is still preserved, hence excitability would not occur after this lesion. Such excitability occurs after amygdala lesions because the animal no longer is able to imagine what might happen when it encounters anything.

Hyperreactivity. After larger septal lesions, rats develop exaggerated reactions to harmless stimuli. This is often called septal hyperreactivity. According to Olton and Gage (1976), the animals show either aggression, attacking a glove or stick when it approaches them, or they back away from these objects. When the glove or stick is then moved toward them, they either back into a corner or leap to the top of the cage. As hyperreactivity gradually decreases, attack or flight occur only when the stick actually touches the animal.

Septal lesions damage the precommissural fornix, hence interrupt the modality-specific memory circuit, according to my theory. Larger lesions also interrupt the connection from posterior medial orbital area (olfactory limbic cortex) to the hippocampal rudiment and via fornix fibers back to septal area and posterior orbital cortex (olfactory memory area), so that the animal can no longer recognize anything by smell. Finally, septal lesions interrupt the projection from orbital area to the habenula, so preventing the recall of visual, auditory, and tactual memories on the basis of smell. Now the animal no longer recognizes anything by sight, hearing, touch, or smell, but can still imagine what might happen (intact connection from piriform cortex via amygdala and thalamic association areas to visual, auditory etc. memory areas (Fox, 1949), and can imagine what to do (via intact connection of amygdala to dorsomedial thalamic nuclei and prefrontal cortex). Not recognizing anything, hence expecting the worst, the animal is afraid or angry and shows "septal hyperreactivity."

Olton and Gage (1976) reported that the hyperreactivity following septal lesions could be prevented by earlier bilateral transection of either the pre- or postcommissural fornix, or by earlier bilateral lesions of the anterior hippocampus. Similar lesions of the posterior hippocampus did not protect animals from septal hyperreactivity. After the earlier lesions, the animals had sixteen days to recover before being given the septal lesions. Olton and Gage concluded that septal hyperreactivity requires an intact circuit from septum via precommissural fornix to anterior hippocampus, or from anterior hippocampus via postcommissural fornix to the hypothalamus. They did not venture any suggestion how these circuits mediate hyperreactivity.

On the basis of my theory it would seem that the bilateral transection of the *precommissural fornix* prevented the animals from remembering anything they saw, heard, touched, or tasted because the modality-specific memory circuit was interrupted. Since their affective memory circuit was intact, the animals were able to appraise what they saw, heard, or touched. They could recognize things by smell and verify what they saw and heard as good or bad by its good/bad smell (from visual and auditory limbic cortex via hippocampus to anterior thalamic nuclei and returning to subcallosal cortex (olfactory limbic area). The second (septal) lesion interrupted the connection between the olfactory limbic cortex and the hippocampal rudiment, thus impairing their olfactory memory (hippocampal rudiment via precommissural fornix to stria medullaris, habenula, and midbrain, returning via habenula to posterior orbital cortex, (the olfactory memory area); the lesion also impaired their olfactory affective memory (from olfactory limbic area via hippocampal rudiment and postcommissural fornix to anterior thalamic nuclei, returning to olfactory limbic cortex). The animals could no longer recall other modality-specific memories on the basis of smell (connection via stria medullaris and habenula to midbrain, returning via thalamic sensory nuclei to various sensory memory areas). In the interim between the first and second lesions, the animals had reacted to anything they saw or heard on the basis of their affective memory aided by olfactory memory, and had not been harmed. Now their olfactory and olfactory affective memory was lost but they could still appraise what they saw and heard—hence no fear, no hyperreactivity.

Lesions of the *postcommissural fornix* (if large enough) would practically eliminate the affective memory of touch, vision, hearing, taste, and even smell. But the animals could still recall earlier experiences via modality-specific memory and could recognize what they encountered. They might be apathetic but would not be afraid, hence no septal hyperreactivity. After the second (septal) lesion, many precommissural fornix fibers would be lost, so that their modality-specific memory would suffer. In addition, olfactory and olfactory affective memory would be eliminated as well. They would no longer recognize much, but they would not be afraid because they could not appraise anything as dangerous, either. Without fear, and without the possibility to appraise things for action, they would not be inclined to much activity.

Septal lesions are so devastating because they eliminate in one sweep all modality-specific memory together with olfactory affective memory. Not being able to recognize anything by smell, their most important sense, the animals find everything unfamiliar and appraise it as dangerous, hence react violently to every stimulus. They need time before they learn to depend on their affective memory of visual and auditory impressions and to react appropriately.

The *anterior* hippocampal lesions destroyed most of the anterodorsal hippocampus, hence eliminated its connection with the precommissural fornix. Although the animals had lost most of their modality–specific memory, they could still remember smells and imagine their effects; thus they remained calm. By the time they suffered the second (septal) lesion, they had learned to cope with things around them and continued to do so, even without the help of motor memory based on smell. They did not overreact.

Lesions of the *posterior hippocampal-entorhinal cortex* would not protect animals from the hyperreactivity produced by second (septal) lesions. After the first bilateral lesion, the animals would no longer recognize what they saw and heard, but would recognize things by smell. After the septal lesion they could no longer do that, were unable to appraise the environment according to past experience, hence were afraid of everything and overreacted.

Olton and Gage suggested that the decreased level of brain noradrenaline after septal lesions is responsible for septal excitability. They injected septally lesioned animals with L-Dopa and found that this injection rapidly and permanently abolished such overreaction. Since L-Dopa is the precursor of dopamine which then is converted to noradrenaline, this injection should raise the noradrenaline concentration in the brain. However, Hyppä et al. (1973) found that an injection of L-Dopa increased the dopamine content of striatum and hypothalamus threefold but did not affect the noradrenaline or serotonin content. This would mean that the injection of L-Dopa increases the activity of dopaminergic but not of adrenergic fibers; hence it cannot abolish hyperreactivity by virtue of its conversion to noradrenaline. But it would improve (dopaminergic) imagination.

In fact, Reis (1974) found that anger and aggressive attacks are accompanied by an increased turnover of noradrenaline in the brain. This produces a fall in the noradrenaline level because the emotional excitement uses more noradrenaline than can be replaced by neuronal synthesis. Reis points out that this NA depletion in the brain is always found in enraged animals. Apparently, it is the emotional excitement, the hyperirritability, that lowers brain noradrenaline; the lowered NA level does not *produce* this excitability.

It follows that L-Dopa must abolish excitability in septally lesioned animals because it enhances dopaminergic conduction. It is well known that denervation produces increased sensitivity to the transmitter used by the denervated fibers. Injected L-Dopa, converted to dopamine, could increase conduction via dopaminergic receptors in the imagination circuit and also in the intact motor circuit (see chapter 27). Hence the animals could more easily imagine what would happen when they saw, heard, or touched something, which to some extent compensated for the loss of olfactory and motor imagination as a result of the septal lesions. Their confusion would quickly disappear and with it, their hyperexcitability. Grossman's report that septal hyperexcitability could be reproduced by cutting the connection between amygdala and septum, thus interrupting the imagination circuit, would seem to confirm my suggestion.

Another reason for septal hyperirritability may be the fact that sex hormones can no longer affect the amygdala and imagination circuit, so that the animal can no longer form an image of mate and mating. After septal lesions, the animal also can no longer imagine what to do about the impulse he feels, hence sexual tension results in general irritability. Phillips and Lieblich (1972) report that the hyperexcitability after septal lesions can be prevented by castrating the rats before their thirtieth day of life. This would confirm my suggestion that circulating sex hormones result in hyperreactivity if the animals are unable to imagine and plan appropriate action.

Shock-induced Fighting.   This follows not only septal lesions but lesions of the ventromedial hypothalamic nucleus, a structure connected with the amygdala; its excitation mediates relaxation. Septal lesions deplete serotonin; and serotonergic pathways seem to induce ease and relaxation. According to Grant et al. (1973), the serotonin level after septal lesions drops sharply after some delay. On the sixth day after surgery, it reaches its lowest level. At that point, rats often kill mice even if they have never done so before.

Gradually, septal irritablility disappears, but an overreaction to foot shock remains (Lints & Harvey, 1969), as does an overreaction to flashes of light (Green & Schwartzbaum, 1968). Since the animals can no longer gauge their action nor anticipate possible consequences, they keep overreacting to sudden or intense stimuli.

Despite their irritability and increased aggressiveness toward harmless objects, animals with septal lesions try to escape an impending fight with other animals, even when they had fought successfully before surgery. When they had to fight, they were always defeated by intact animals. This was true both for mice and hamsters (Slotnick & McMullen, 1972; Sodetz & Bunnell, 1970). This change in behavior also seems to stem from the animals' inability to plan action. Haphazard fighting is not likely to achieve victory.

Schwartzbaum and Gay (1966) reported that bilateral lesions of the amygdala abolished the hyperirritability of septally lesioned animals and prevented the "freezing" of such animals in the open field. According to my theory, ablation of the amygdala would abolish visual, auditory, and tactual imagination in addition to the deficit in motor and olfactory imagination and memory brought about by septal lesions. Before amygdalectomy, the animals could imagine what might happen when they saw, heard, or touched anything, despite the fact that the septal lesions had deprived them of olfactory and motor imagination. They were inclined to "freeze" in the open field because they could no longer plan action. After the additional amygdala lesions, septal excitability and freezing disappeared because the animals could no longer imagine that anything they saw, heard, or touched might be dangerous. Instead, they became very active in the open field; they could no longer make sense out of the things they encountered, hence their continued attempt to investigate them. While septal lesions had blocked sensory memory and olfactory as well as motor imagination, the additional amygdala lesions blocked all other types of imagination so that the animals had no way of gauging the effect of anything they encountered.

Symptom 5. Increased Inappropriate Responding. Several investigators found that lesioned animals were impaired on DRL operant schedules when they had to wait several seconds between responses (Burkett & Bunnell, 1966; Ellen et al., 1964; MacDougall et al., 1969). Apparently, the animals could not gauge the time required between responses. Their response rates were higher than normal while correct responses declined. For instance, Kelsey and Grossman (1971) used a shuttle box in which the animals had to shuttle between two compartments and press alternate levers in each, thirty seconds after a reinforcement. Animals with septal lesions kept rushing into the opposite compartment to press the lever before the time was up, hence did not score as many rewards as intact animals.

Higher response rates by septally lesioned animals on fixed interval and fixed ratio schedules were found by Ellen and Powell (1962), Lorens and Kondo (1969), and Schwartzbaum and Gay (1966). This was especially striking when the animals were hungry (Johnson & Thatcher, 1972; Harvey & Hunt, 1965). The higher the drive, the more does the animals' behavior show their memory impairment. This is not a simple lack of response inhibition but an inability to remember what is the appropriate response. In addition, septal lesions interrupt the imagination circuit so that the animals cannot plan their action.

Animals with septal lesions are severely impaired in reversal learning and extinction. Without memory of the change in cue from positive to negative, they respond to the formerly positive cue until affective memory of shock is built up sufficiently to produce the correct response. For this reason also, they are slower than intact animals to extinguish responses, both in appetitive tasks (Donovick, 1968; Butters & Rosvold, 1968a; Schwartzbaum et al., 1964) and in two-way active avoidance (La Vacque, 1966). But they can extinguish an escape response from foot shock as quickly as intact animals (Brown & Remley, 1971) because memory is not necessary in this situation: They feel the pain and run. Lesioned animals do not respond regardless of the situation: Fallon and Donovick (1970) found that hungry rats, trained to press a lever for food, extinguished quickly when they were no longer hungry but thirsty. Hence such continued responding could not be called "disinhibition."

Thompson and Langer (1963) employed a T-maze to train rats in a repeated position reversal. The animals had to run to the end of one arm and knock down a card to obtain food. On the next run, the rat was shocked at that end and had to run to the other arm. Each trial consisted of an "information" run and a test run. Bilateral lesions of the medial septum produced a significant deficit, and so did bilateral lesions of the precallosal limbic cortex, hippocampus, precommissural fornix, and medial forebrain bundle. The authors remarked that "the reversal deficit reflects a genuine disruption of the . . . memory process—the lesioned subjects simply could not remember the side from which they received a shock 30 seconds previously" (p. 995). Each of these lesions interrupted the modality-specific memory circuit. In contrast, bilateral lesions of dorsolateral frontal cortex, supracallosal limbic areas, postcommissural fornix, medial, lateral, ventral or posterior thalamic nuclei, the habenular complex, lateral subthalamus, and amygdala did not produce a signficant deficit. These areas are outside the modality-specific memory circuit. The task required visual and motor memory and the affective memory of pain to the feet. Direct fibers from hippocampus to anterior thalamic nuclei were probably sufficient for this affective memory of pain.

Symptom 6.   *The decreased activity* of septally lesioned animals in activity wheel or home cage can also be explained as an impairment of motor imagination. If the animal cannot imagine what to do to compensate for the swinging wheel, or what to do in response to various objects in the home cage, it will move randomly, purposelessly, and soon stop.

Symptom 7.   *The hyperdipsia and hyperphagia* after initial weight loss, as well as the increased reaction to the taste of food was reproduced by Grossman (1978a) by a transection of the ventral afferents that connect the septum with the hypothalamus. The increased intake of palatable food seems to be another result of the lack of any satisfaction that comes from repletion; the same phenomenon is seen after ventromedial hypothalamic nucleus lesions (see chapter 27). Without the sense of relaxation and ease that comes from repletion (mediated by ventromedial hypothalamic nuclei), the animals have to depend on the taste of food for any satisfaction they obtain from feeding—hence their finicky eating habits.

STRIA MEDULLARIS AND HABENULA

Grossman (1978a) and his coworkers found a possible active avoidance deficit in the one-way task after lesions of the stria medullaris. And Van Hoesen et al. (1969) reported that animals with lesions damaging 80% of either the stria medullaris or the habenulae or both were almost as much impaired in passive avoidance as animals with septal lesions. Grossman did not find such a deficit after stria medullaris lesions and suggested that Van Hoesen et al.'s lesions must have damaged the projection to the interpedunuclar nucleus, which has caused such a deficit (Wilson et al., 1972). However, this suggestion is difficult to credit in the face of Van Hoesen et al.'s explicit description of their lesions. Since the passive avoidance apparatus used by Van Hoesen et al. consisted of a box with a food cup through which the animals received an electric shock, it may well be that the odor of the food was an important cue. From being "good to eat" it becomes "bad, announcing shock" as soon as the animal is shocked on touching the food. After bilateral damage of stria medullaris or septal area, this change in appraisal apparently is no longer possible.

The olfactory tubercle and olfactory limbic cortex are connected via hippocampal rudiment and dorsal fornix to the lateral septum and septofimbrial nucleus and project via the stria medullaris to the habenula, midbrain reticular formation, and interpenduncular nucleus. These pathways also carry relays back to the septal area (Raisman, 1966). Since the midbrain reticular formation is also connected with visual and somesthetic memory circuits, it is possible for man or animal to recall on smelling something what the odorous thing looks and sounds like and whether it is dangerous. Conversely, if we see or hear something, we can recall its odor. When either the septal area or the stria medullaris and habenula are damaged, the odor of the food the animal smells no longer connects with the memory of the shock. The animal no longer remembers on smelling the food that eating was followed by pain. He approaches and so demonstrates a deficit in passive avoidance.

The habenular nuclei are much better developed in macrosmatic animals than in primates. According to Clara (1959), the habenular apparatus is perhaps the only nuclear system that has been preserved unchanged in its connections throughout evolutionary history. In human beings, the habenular complex is small compared with the large habenula of fish or mouse. This reduction is not surprising, seeing how unimportant smell has become in primates.

23

The Amygdala: Relay Station in the Imagination Circuit

Although we are used to think of the amygdaloid body primarily as a modulator of hypothalamic activities, it is becoming increasingly more obvious that the functions of the amygdaloid body are considerably more complicated and diversified . . . . Sensory information is being channeled through a series of transcortical pathways, which finally reach the amygdaloid body, where the information somehow will have to match or interact with input reaching the amygdala from the hypothalamus and other subcortical areas known to be of importance for autonomic and motivational mechanisms. Exactly how and where this matching takes place is not known.

L. Heimer, 1981, p. 7

The amygdala is an almond-shaped complex of several nuclei in the anterior part of the temporal lobe in primate brains. A great deal of research during the last two or three decades has located many afferent and efferent connections. The overlying periamygdaloid area in the cortex of the piriform lobe sends many fibers to the amygdala, connecting mainly with the basal and lateral nuclei. In primates, the uncus is the homologue of the piriform lobe in lower mammals (Lammers, 1972). Apparently, the entire piriform cortex (excluding only the entorhinal cortex) sends fibers to the amygdala.

The amygdaloid complex is more prominent in primates than in other mammals. This increase in size may be connected with the far greater imaginal range of primates. Because of their greater range of movements, particularly the range of speech movements in human beings, they can form motor images in a variety unequalled by the motor imagination of lower mammals.

CONNECTIONS OF THE AMYGDALA

Both afferent and efferent fibers course in the two great pathways connecting the amygdala with other parts of the brain: The stria terminalis and the ventral amygdalofugal path.

The stria terminalis together with its bed nucleus forms a complex system of short and long axons that connects the amygdala with the septal area and olfactory bulb rostrally, and with the hypothalamus caudally. The three components of the stria terminalis all run to the bed nucleus of the stria and then divide. The dorsal component, coming from the cortical and a small band of medial amygdaloid nuclei, distributes to the nucleus accumbens, the medial olfactory tubercle, pregenual area 25, the anterior olfactory nucleus and the accessory olfactory bulb; caudally to the medial preoptic area, radiating through the hypothalamus and ending in the cell-poor capsule around the ventromedial nuclei. Some fibers continue to the premamillary nuclei. The ventral division stems from the lateral, basolateral, rostral cortical and medial nuclei, and projects through the preoptic-hypothalamic junction to the basal tuberal region, ending in the ventromedial hypothalamic nucleus and the premamillary nuclei. The commissural division, together with fibers from the dorsal component, connects the amygdala and its rostral projections with the opposite side (De Olmos, 1972; Fig. 23.1).

The ventral amygdalofugal system starts from the periamygdaloid cortex and the basolateral amygdaloid nuclei and connects rostrally with the prepiriform areas 51a and b, and caudally with the ventrolateral part of the entorhinal area 28. Other fibers reach the claustrum, the insula, the olfactory tubercle, and the medial prefrontal areas 25 and 32, as well as the anterior olfactory nucleus. Some fibers cross the anterior commissure to the posterior limb, distribute to the ventral part of the caudate-putamen and end in the anterior part of the lateral amygdaloid nucleus and the interstitial nucleus of the posterior limb of the anterior commissure. Another group of fibers, probably coming from the central nucleus and the rostral part of the medial amygdaloid nucleus, run in the medial forebrain bundle and distribute diffusely through the dorsal part of the lateral preoptic area and throughout the hypothalamus. A thick-fibered component runs in the medial forebrain bundle to the lateral hypothalamus, the nuclei gemini, the dorsomedial and ventromedial thalamic nuclei, and the lateral habenula (De Olmos, 1972; Krettek & Price, 1977).

Afferents from Cortical Areas. The amygdaloid complex receives afferents from all regions of the neocortex. There is evidence that sensory association and

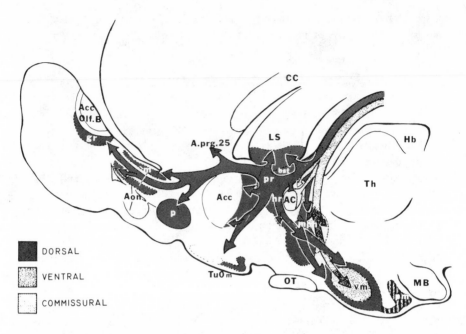

FIG. 23.1   Diagram of three stria terminalis components. AC—anterior commissure, Acc.—
nucleus accumbens septi, Acc.Olf.B.—accessory olfactory bulb, Aon—anterior olfactory nucleus,
aom—anterior olfactory nucleus, medial part, A.prg.25—pregenual cortical area 25, bst—bed nucleus of the stria terminalis, CC—corpus callosum, gr.—internal granular layer of accessory olfactory bulb, Hb—habenula, hr—hypothalamic radiation of supracommissural division of the dorsal
strial component, LS—lateral septal nucleus, m—medial part of anterior olfactory nucleus, MB—
mamillary body, mph—medial preoptic-hypothalamic junction area, OT—optic tract, p—posterior
part of anterior olfactory nucleus, pm—premamillary area, pr—parolfactory radiation of
supracommissural division of dorsal strial component, Th—thalamus, TuOm—medial olfactory tubercle, vm—ventromedial hypothalamic nucleus. From J. S. De Olmos, 1972.

limbic areas project both to amygdala and piriform cortex. Fibers from these
areas pass via the posterior limb of the anterior commissure to the piriform cortex
and the lateral amygdaloid nucleus (Van Alphen, 1969).

Mishkin (1979), Turner et al. (1980), and Turner (1981) reported that sensory
systems project to amygdala and hippocampal gyrus via limbic cortex, which
receives afferents from secondary sensory areas. Each sensory system projects in
separate relays that end in different parts of the amygdala. Turner (1981) concluded that each sensory system influences a restricted area of the amygdala by
means of modality–specific relays. He also pointed out that the monkey brain has
more relays between cortex and amygdala than the rat brain; and suggested that
this reflects either the greater cortical development of primates or their greater
functional specialization.

Turner et al. (1980) mentioned that the olfactory system is the only sensory
system that sends relays from the primary area (piriform cortex) to the amygdala.

To my mind, that is another reason why the piriform area is unlikely to be the primary olfactory area. In chapter 11, I have suggested that the anterior olfactory nucleus and the olfactory tubercle are the primary olfactory areas; and their medial part, the olfactory limbic area which projects to the piriform cortex, and the amygdala. Hence the olfactory system, like every other sensory system, sends relays from limbic cortex to the amygdala. Thus Koikegami (1963) reported a projection from the orbito-sylvian area in the cat (homologue of the orbito-insular area) to the lateral amygdala region; and Winans and Scalia (1970) found that fibers from the main olfactory bulb reach the nucleus of the lateral olfactory tract and the anterolateral part of the cortical nucleus of the amygdala; fibers from the accessory bulb, the posteromedial part of this nucleus (Fig. 23.2). According to Lammers (1972), the olfactory projection reaches the cortical and medial amygdaloid nuclei. Lohman and Russchen (1981) add that the subcallosal limbic area and the anterior olfactory nucleus project also to the medial central nucleus.

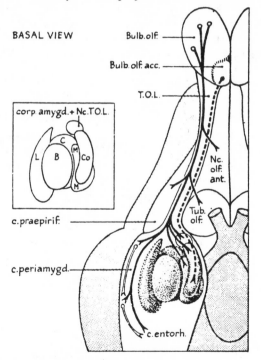

FIG. 23.2   Secondary olfactory projection. Black lines indicate the projection of the main olfactory bulb. White lines indicate the projection from the periamygdaloid cortex to the entorhinal cortex. The projection of the accessory olfactory bulb is indicated by the stippled line. B—basal amygdaloid nucleus, Bulb.Olf.—olfactory bulb, Bulb.olf.acc.—accessory olfactory bulb, Co—cortical amygdaloid nuclei, c.entorh.—entorhinal cortex, c.periamygd.—periamygdaloid cortex, c.praepirif.—prepiriform cortex, L—lateral amygdaloid nucleus, M—medial amygdaloid nucleus, Nc.olf. ant.—anterior olfactory nucleus, Nc.T.O.L.—nucleus of the lateral olfactory tract, T.O.L.—lateral olfactory tract, Tub.olf.—olfactory tubercle. From H. J. Lammers, 1972.

These connections from cortical sensory systems make it possible to imagine what might happen and what to do about it, as soon as man or animal sees or hears something, appraises it as "good to know," and attends to it. A projection to the amygdala from frontal (motor) limbic cortex can initiate imagination on appraising one's movements or action impulses. The amygdala is connected with the hippocampal formation, which can initiate imagination as soon as something is remembered, and initiate recall as soon as imagination is active.

Subcortical Afferents. The amygdala receives projections not only from cortical areas but from the thalamus, hypothalamus, and lower brainstem. Ottersen (1981) mentions a projection from medial thalamic nuclei to the amygdala, though Mehler et al. (1981) deny it. But there is general agreement that the paraventricular, interanteromedial, and peripeduncular thalamic nuclei in rat, cat, and monkey project to the amygdaloid complex (Mehler et al., 1981). The amygdala is also connected with the ventral globus pallidus (Ottersen, 1981).

The hypothalamus sends many relays to the amygdala. The medial preoptic area projects to the medial nucleus; the lateral and dorsal hypothalamic areas, to the central nucleus, while the ventromedial hypothalamus projects to both the central and medial nuclei, and sends some fibers to the basolateral nucleus. The lower brainstem projects mainly to the central amygdaloid nucleus (Ottersen, 1981). It is unlikely that the projections from hypothalamus and lower brainstem are activated directly by afferents from sensory receptors. Rather, they seem relay stations in the memory and action circuits. The relays to the amygdala would make it possible to activate motor images so that the animal can plan for action (see chapters 26–28).

In addition, impulses from the hypothalamus provide information as to the state of the body (cold or warm, hungry or sated, active or at rest), which trigger relays from the amygdala to various limbic and association areas, initiating images of food or water, warm or cold places, and images of what to do to find what is needed. The "drives" that are supposed to motivate cannot push man or animal blindly toward satisfaction. We must have some goal that draws us. Miller et al. (1960) call the impulse toward the goal a "plan" which, in the case of an animal, really is the image of an appropriate action. To form images is within the capacity of animals because imagination is a sensory capacity and does not imply conceptual thought.

Convergence of Afferents. While there are modality-specific projections from sensory systems to the amygdala, Van Hoesen (1981) and Lohman and Russchen (1981) also report a convergence of cortical projections in the central and lateral amygdaloid nuclei. And Kaada (1972) mentions that relays from several sensory modalities may converge on the same cell in the amygdala. This would suggest that experiences in any sensory modality may lead us to imagine very similar responses. It is the same with animals. Whether a deer sees, hears, or smells something strange, it will imagine the approach of an enemy and flee.

Relays from Amygdala to Limbic Cortex. Stimulation of the amygdala seems first to excite limbic cortical areas and later various areas in the association cortex. In human beings, such stimulation evokes complex formed hallucinations, as in a dream, or vague scenes like intruding fantasy images. Sometimes it produces simple visual or touch sensations, sometimes sensations of smell or taste, or sensations of nausea. According to Halgren (1981), most of these sensations are true hallucinations: amygdala stimulation that produces strong nausea usually does not affect gastric mobility. Amygdala stimulation can evoke fear or anxiety, and occasionally anger or pleasure. These emotions are usually accompanied by appropriate autonomic changes. Such stimulation sometimes arouses feelings of familiarity (déjà vu) and perceptual distortions as, for instance, feelings of depersonalization. According to Halgren, when after-discharges follow amygdala stimulation, they spread initially to the hippocampus and parahippocampal gyrus of the same side, in which case few of these phenomena occur. When such discharges spread to the limbic cortex of the same side, as well as to dorsomedial, center median thalamic nuclei and the pulvinar, emotional and hallucinatory phenomena are more likely. After-discharges seldom spread to neocortex, although neocortical areas may show fast waves in the EEG.

Gloor et al. (1981) reported that stimulation of amygdala, hippocampus, or parahippocampal gyrus in patients with temporal lobe epilepsy evoked such experiences in the majority of cases. These phenomena were not experienced by patients with epilepsy stemming from a brain site outside the amygdala. Like Halgren, these authors found that emotions (particularly fear) were experienced more frequently than hallucinations; and that amygdala stimulation yielded far more experiences of all kinds than either hippocampal or hippocampal gyrus stimulation. Neocortical stimulation did not evoke these phenomena unless the electrode was implanted close to the amygdala or anterior hippocampus. But Halgren, unlike Gloor et al., reported that stimulation of the amygdala produced the same type of experiences in nonepileptic patients.

Relays to Sensory Memory Areas. A given situation, appraised as good or bad, beneficial or threatening, seems to initiate imagination via relays from amygdala to limbic cortex which mediates affective memory and, in turn, activates relevant fantasy images via relays to sensory memory cortex. Dreaming or waking, imagination is guided by affective memory. If something has hurt us in the past, we expect (imagine) that it will hurt us again. Nightmare dreams are built around fears we have never managed to overcome.

The amygdala is connected with limbic cortex both directly and via the anterior thalamic nuclei. It is connected with sensory neocortex both via limbic cortex and via thalamic association nuclei, particularly the pulvinar. Lesions of the posterior thalamic nucleus, homologue of the pulvinar, impair learning visual and kinesthetic discriminations (Thompson et al., 1967); visual pattern discrimination is more affected than brightness discrimination. This holds also for bilateral occipital cortex ablations (Horel et al., 1966) and is consistent with the notion that the posterior thalamus is a relay station in the sensory imagination circuit. Rats with posterior thalamic damage were so reluctant to run in the test that they required frequent foot shocks to force a choice between the arms of the T-maze. They were disoriented in the apparatus and found it difficult to correct their response (Thompson et al., 1967). Without sensory imagination, the animals would not know what to expect in the experimental situation. They would not want to move because they could not imagine what to expect in either arm of the maze.

While visual pattern discrimination is impaired after posterior thalamus lesions, it is still possible; according to Thompson et al., because the occipito-geniculo-thalamic pathway to the brainstem was not severed completely. It is more likely that the animals could still learn, though slowly, because the visual and motor memory circuits were intact.

Olfactory imagination seems to be mediated via the projection from the magnocellular part of the dorsomedial thalamic nucleus to the posterior orbital area. As in other sensory systems, the relay from amygdala to olfactory memory areas seems to activate first affective olfactory memory (via subcallosal limbic area) and next the posterior orbital cortex. Both these areas are connected with the dorsomedial thalamic nucleus. Takagi (1979) has found that electrical stimulation of the olfactory bulb results in orthodromic activation of cells in the magnocellular part of the dorsomedial thalamic nucleus, and so does stimulation of the posterior orbital area.

Relays to Motor Memory Areas.   Not only do we imagine various situations, we also imagine ourselves acting in them. Such motor imagination seems to be mediated by the projection from the amygdala via dorsomedial thalamic nuclei to the frontal limbic and prefrontal motor cortex. Habitual affective motor memories of flight or attack (via frontal limbic cortex) will guide the appropriate motor images; these, in turn, intensify the emotion. According to De Olmos (1972), the amygdala projects via the stria terminalis to area 32 and 25 of the frontal limbic cortex; and via the dorsomedial nucleus, to the frontal association area.

Since the dorsomedial thalamic nucleus is connected with the ventrolateral thalamic nuclei and the frontal cortex, action images can influence behavior. McNew and Thompson (1966) reported that bilateral dorsomedial thalamic lesions produced a severe active avoidance deficit in rats. The animals were so reluctant to jump to the safe compartment that they often had to be shocked several times before they would move. These animals were no longer able to imagine what to do, hence their reluctance to move. Such delay in responding is typical for amygdalectomized animals (Isaacson, 1974). According to Kemble and Beckman (1970), such animals stop responding when they have to choose between alternatives or (in reversal problems) find no reward after the usual response. They extinguish quickly, but are slower than intact animals in learning the new problem after the reversal. These animals cannot imagine what to do and so are reluctant to do anything at all. When they finally move, they move at random, literally by "trial and error," which accounts for their slow learning.

In patients, surgical lesions of both dorsomedial thalamic nuclei resulted in a disturbance of memory and orientation (Spiegel et al., 1950). Without motor imagination, it would be very difficult for these patients to find their way. Medial thalamic lesions have similar results, either because they encroach upon the dorsomedial nuclei or because they interfere with the thalamic appraisal area connected with these nuclei.

Prefrontal lobotomy results in complete degeneration of the dorsomedial thalamic nuclei and partial degeneration of the anterior and ventral nuclei (Meyer & Beck, 1954). It produces a loss of alertness, general slowing and inertia. The speed of decision is strikingly impaired (Kalinowsky & Hoch, 1952; Landis & Clausen, 1955). The patients often sit without moving, not doing anything. Their spontaneity and general interest is much decreased. Their behavior indicates not only a loss of motor imagination (dorsomedial thalamic nucleus degeneration) but also a dearth of impulses to action because the degeneration of ventrolateral and ventro-anterior thalamic nuclei has blocked conduction to premotor cortex.

Imagination does influence action. In learning a skill, imaginary practice is as effective as actual practice (Beattie, 1949; Arnold, 1946). And Jacobson has shown that imagining a movement produces action currents in the muscles used for that movement.

Following my theory, the psychological and neurophysiological sequence would be something like this:

I see a big animal in the woods (via sensory projection to visual cortex)

appraise it as "good to know" (attention, via visual limbic cortex)

recall similar animals (via modality-specific memory circuit to sensory memory areas)

recognize it as a bear (appraise it as familiar, via limbic cortex)

appraise it as bad (dangerous) (via limbic cortex)

imagine what might happen (from limbic cortex to periamygdaloid cortex and amygdala; via anterior thalamic nuclei to limbic cortex (affective memory), and via thalamic association nuclei to sensory memory cortex—imagination circuit)

and what I might do about it (motor imagination circuit; via dorsomedial thalamic nucleus to motor memory area in prefrontal cortex)

I *feel fear* (limbic cortex to hippocampus, and via action circuit to midbrain and cerebellum, returning via thalamus to prefrontal and premotor cortex) *plan (imagine) how to escape* (from limbic cortex to amygdala, and via dorsomedial thalamic nucleus to frontal lobe—motor imagination circuit)

appraise an escape route as suitable (via anterior cingulate gyrus)

and run (to hippocampus and via midbrain, cerebellum, ventral thalmic nuclei to frontal lobe and motor cortex—action circuit.

As I have mentioned before, these circuits are activated in series as well as in parallel. Appraising the situation as dangerous, feeling fear, imagining what to do—all these activities go on practially simultaneously. Since one branch of the action circuit runs through the hypothalamus, according to my theory, it activates the nuclei initiating endocrine secretions and induces sympathetic symptoms during fear. These areas have already been primed by direct impulses from the amygdala during imagination. Connections from amygdala to limbic cortex activate affective and motor memory, so that action is influenced both by earlier motor memories and the motor imagination that sketches a plan for action.

Amygdala Ablation.   Many earlier studies have reported that bilateral ablation of the amygdala leads to increased aggression (Bard & Rioch, 1937; Bard & Mountcastle, 1947; Green et al., 1957). These results have been difficult to reproduce and difficult to explain. It is possible that a discharging focus had development at the rim of the lesions, because Green et al. mentioned that the cats that become more aggressive after surgery had epileptic seizures.

Most later studies found that total bilateral amygdalectomy results in tameness, with no evidence of rage or fear (Gastaut, 1952; Goddard, 1964a; Kling, 1966; and many others). Kling (1972) summarized the changes in the behavior of such animals: reduction of belligerence and fear; "oral" behavior, that is, a tendency to investigate everything by mouth and eat completely inedible things; increased and inappropriate sexual behavior. Kling added that such animals are severely impaired in social situations. Monkey mothers behave, says Kling, "as though the infant . . . [were] a strange object to be mouthed, bitten, and tossed around as though it were a rubber ball" (p. 512). These animals withdrew from their cage mates, became isolated, were attacked by intact cage mates, and soon died. The "oral" and odd sexual behavior was apparent only when several amygdalectomized monkeys were in one cage, probably because intact animals would not let them approach but attacked them. In a natural setting, such animals withdrew from the group and eventually disappeared.

All these behavior changes can be explained, quite literally, as a lack of imagination. The animals cannot anticipate the reactions of their cage mates and do not know what to do with the things they encounter. Sexual tension, mediated by hypothalamic areas, can no longer initiate images of mate or mating. They approach other animals indiscriminately, as soon as they feel a sexual impulse.

Without imagination, such animals are helpless when left to their own devices in a natural setting because they can neither anticipate danger nor the consequences of their own actions.

Small Amygdala Lesions.   More recently, experiments have investigated the effect of small lesions in amygdaloid zones that have induced attack or escape when stimulated. For instance, Fonberg (1965) reported that lesions restricted to the medial part of the amygdala increased tameness in dogs. In contrast, small lesions in the dorsomedial part, damaging the neighboring basolateral nuclei or the efferent path from this division, increased aggression. According to Fonberg (1965, 1981), the lesion must have damaged an inhibitory basolateral system and so released aggression.

True, as Kaada (1972) says, that is the obvious explanation. But we cannot simply postulate an inhibitory (or excitatory) system and let it go at that. There must be some psychological experience that produces inhibition and lifts it at the right time. When medial amygdala lesions reduce aggression in animals, these animals may no longer be able to imagine a situation that would call for attack. Conversely, a lesion in the dorsomedial amygdala, encroaching on the basolateral nuclei and their efferents, may have damaged parts of the amygdala that normally initiate images of affectionate contact, exploration, etc. Hence any situation will excite aggressive images more frequently than before.

PATTERNS OF EMOTIONAL EXCITATION

Many reports tend to show that there are different pathways leading from the amygdaloid nuclei to the limbic cortex, evoking different kinds of behavior (Van Hoesen, 1981). Some of these pathways have been mapped although exact details are still lacking. These relays seem to excite different kinds of emotion leading to different types of imagery.

Attention.   The orienting response in animals is most frequently evoked by stimulating the dorsal part of the anterior amygdaloid area, as well as the lateral and magnocellular part of the basolateral nuclei, and an area reaching medially through the central nucleus and the internal capsule toward the ansa lenticularis and the entopeduncular nucleus in the subthalamus (Kaada, 1972). Often, stimulation first evokes attention, which with continued stimulation eventually becomes rage. About half the orienting responses were accompanied by sniffing; but sniffing also occurred without orienting. The electrodes that produced sniffing were in the anterior and dorsal part of the lateral nucleus, the magnocellular part of the basal nucleus, and in the tract of the ventral amygdalofugal fibers running through the central amygdaloid nucleus (Kaada, 1972).

Sleep.   In contrast, stimulation of deeper fibers in the periamygdaloid and prepiriform cortex, the olfactory tubercle, and ventral amygdaloid areas resulted in slow waves in the EEG and sleep (Kaada, 1972; Kreindler & Steriade, 1964). Sleep also follows local application of acetylcholine to these structures (Hernández-Peón et al., 1967). Relaxation and sleep result, I believe, from the suppression of imagination and recall, producing EEG synchronization via cholinergic inhibitory fibers.

Rage, Attack.   Stimulation of a caudal and medial zone in the region of the central nucleus and the neighboring dorsal part of the lateral and basal nucleus results in a display of rage. The cat growls, hisses, flattens its ears, and crouches with dilated pupils and bristling hair (Kaada, 1972). Such a zone also seems to exist in the brain of primates (Ursin, 1971). According to Zbrozyna (1972), the area producing rage when stimulated includes part of the anterior amygdala, the basal nucleus (mainly its magnocellular part), and the central nucleus. Electrical stimulation along the stria terminalis produces the same effect, but lesions of the stria do not abolish the rage resulting from stimulation of the amygdala. Hence Zbrozyna concludes that rage is mediated via the ventral amygalofugal pathway. When that is destroyed in its entirety, stimulation of the amygdala no longer evokes rage. However, Hunsperger and Bucher (1967) could find no evidence that this connection is responsible for the display of rage. And Grossman (1972a) reported that a knife cut completely transecting this pathway does not prevent aggression in rats. Apparently, rage and attack are not produced by a direct relay from amygdala to the lateral hypothalamus.

It is well known that rage can also be produced by stimulation of the lateral hypothalamus. But when that is done, the animal is enraged immediately, and calms down as soon as stimulation stops. In contrast, when the amygdala is stimulated, the animal gradually increases its aggressive stance, and gradually relaxes when stimulation stops. If rage were the result of excitation via the ventral amygdalofugal pathway to the hypothalamus, stimulation of either area should have the same effect.

It seems more reasonable to assume that rage is produced by amygdala stimulation via relays to the cortical limbic system, engaging affective memory. These areas then initiate rage and attack over the action circuit connected with the hypothalamic "rage" zone. It would require some time before amygdaloid stimulation could excite the limbic areas sufficiently to activate the hypothalamic "rage" zone. Conversely, when amygdaloid stimulation stops, neurons in the action circuit may still be excited so that rage ceases gradually.

Local injection of acetylcholine in the prepiriform and piriform cortex and in the magnocellular part of the basal nuclei also produced rage (Hernández-Peón, et al., 1967). This was confirmed by Igic et al. (1970) who reported that local application of amitone (a cholinesterase inhibitor) in the basolateral amygdala produced increased aggression in rats, and in some cases mouse killing. This increased aggression was suppressed by atropine, the cholinergic antagonist. Apparently, aggression is mediated by cholinergic pathways.

Mouse-killing.   Rage can also be produced by ablation of the olfactory bulb. In 30% of non-killer rats, such ablation resulted in mouse-killing, provided the rats had been isolated for some time after surgery. Mouse-killing also occurred after extensive lesions of the prepiriform cortex (Vergnes & Karli, 1965). After ablation of the olfactory bulb or section of the pathways connecting it with the amygdala and hippocampus, the rat is unable to appraise other animals on the basis of smell and now treats a mouse simply as a moving thing. The more familiar a rat is with mice, the less likely that it will become a mouse-killer (Karli et al., 1972), which speaks for this explanation. Apparently, the central nucleus is crucial for mouse-killing. Complete bilateral ablation permanently abolishes mouse-killing, provided the lesions encroach upon the medial amygdaloid nuclei (Karli et al., 1972).

Suppression of attack, whether in mouse-killer rats or in cats stimulated in the hypothalamic "attack" center, was consistently achieved by stimulating the lateral part of the basal nucleus and the anterior and medial part of the lateral nucleus (Kaada, 1972). Excitation of these areas apparently evoked emotions and images incomptabile with rage.

Fear and Flight.   Fear and flight have been induced by stimulating a zone parallel to the "attack" zone, from the rostral part of the lateral nucleus and the preamygdaloid area through the region of the central nucleus into the ventral part of the internal capsule (Kaada, 1972). This is true for the monkey as well as the rat. Stimulation of this region in the human being has often resulted in feelings of fear (Gloor, 1972). Stimulation of the basolateral area via implanted electrodes inhibited fear and flight in animals, whether fear was evoked by electric shock or by stimulation of the hypothalamic fear zone. During such stimulation, the animals would run and play. This suppression of fear was not the effect of distraction; distracting stimuli, such as a loud sound, did not inhibit fear (Fonberg & Delgado, 1961; Egger & Flynn, 1963). These findings support my suggestion that imagination initiates and perpetuates fear. When an area outside the "fear" zone, but still within the amygdala, is excited, other images and emotions replace fear images.

INSTINCTIVE ACTIVITIES

Instinctive activities also are initiated by imagination, aroused by physiological changes (via hypothalamus), and guided by appetite or desire.

Feeding.   Most studies agree that the cortical and medial nuclei facilitate feeding, as does the adjoining parvocellular basal nucleus and the overlying periamygdaloid cortex (Lewinska, 1967; Kaada, 1972). Chronic stimulation of these areas resulted in increased feeding, particularly when the animals liked the food offered. If the amygdala were a "feeding center," such preferences would make little sense. But if the amygdala mediates imagination, as I maintain, the images of preferred food would be evoked most easily.

Lewinska (1967) found that cats increased their food intake after lesions of the posterior basolateral amygdaloid area. They became more aggressive after lesions of both magno- and parvocellular basal nuclei. In contrast, animals with lesions of the cortico-medial ara developed aphagia and became very quiet after surgery. Apparently, when lesions of the basolateral area make it impossible to imagine activities other than attack or eating, the attack and food imagery increases and leads to action. Conversely, when food imagery is impossible because the corticomedial nuclei are damaged so that odors can no longer excite the imagination, other images substitute and the animals lose interest in food.

Microinjection of adrenergic drugs, with the tip of the cannula in the cortical nucleus, has increased feeding but reduced drinking (Grossman, 1964a). While the lateral hypothalamus was similarly responsive to adrenergic and cholinergic stimulation, the effects were quite different. Hypothalamic stimulation leads even sated animals to eat and drink; but amygdaloid stimulation does so only when the animals are hungry or thirsty. Clearly, sated animals have no impulse to imagine food or drink, hence do not approach it. But hungry and thirsty animals imagine food and water, and therefore seek them. Hypothalamic stimulation engages the action circuit directly, hence the animals take food or drink whether they need it or not.

Sexual Activities. Electrical stimulation of the stria terminalis, the corticomedial, and possibly the parvocellular basal nuclei induces ovulation, milk secretion, uterine movements, and penile erection (Kaada, 1972). Stimulation of the amygdala has induced ovulation in rats after spontaneous ovulation was blocked by drugs or constant light. Ovulation was prevented by lesions of the stria terminalis but not of the ventral amygdalofugal pathway (Velasco & Taleisnik, 1969). Apparently, the animal must imagine mating (via stria terminalis connection to frontal cortex) before ovulation can occur. When spontaneous ovulation is blocked by nembutal, it can be induced by copulation. But a lesion at the anterior border of the preoptic area blocks such copulation-induced ovulation (Kalra & Sawyer, 1970). This lesion apparently blocks relays from amygdala to hypothalamus, activated during imagination; while lesions of the stria terminalis block relays to the dorsomedial thalamic nucleus and the cortical limbic area, so abolishing images of mate and mating.

These reports of stimulation and lesion experiments allow the conclusion that the amygdaloid complex contains nuclei and pathways that mediate special kinds of emotion and images—of attack, danger, food, drink, mate, and mating. Very likely, these pathways use different kinds of neurotransmitters (see chapter 24).

Electrical stimulation of the periamygdaloid cortex also produces rage and fear (Fonberg, 1968; Ursin, 1971), but no special zones have been reported. That might mean that the periamygdaloid cortex (and perhaps the whole piriform cortex) can excite special amygdaloid nuclei, depending on the type of situation the animal has encountered.

Lesion Effects in Patients. In recent years, surgeons have attempted to correct dangerous aggressiveness by making small lesions in the amygdala. Narabayashi (1972) reported on small bilateral lesions he made in the central and basal parts of the anterior amygdala. Since none of his patients have come to autopsy, the location of these lesions is only approximate. Only one patient showed "orality," hypersexuality, excitement, and polyphagia. This lasted for two months and then gradually subsided. About two thirds of his patients were children under thirteen years of age. Before surgery, they were hyperactive, violent and destructive, beating people and throwing or damaging things. The EEG of all patients admitted to surgery showed spiking in the amygdaloid area. After surgery, half the patients were dramatically improved, the other half showed moderate or slight improvement. The children became quiet and docile, were no longer destructive and had a much better concentration span. Many patients no longer had epileptic seizures or had them much less frequently. Electrical seizure activity in the EEG also was markedly reduced.

In these cases, as in the case of comparable amygdala lesions in animals, it would seem that aggressive motor images could no longer be formed, hence did not lead to aggressive action. The remaining relays from periamygdaloid cortex and amygdala to limbic and neocortical areas were sufficient to initiate other images more relevant to their tasks, hence their improved concentration.

LEARNING DEFICITS

Lesion Effects. Amygdala lesions have some effects similar to those of hippocampal lesions, and some that are entirely different. Lesions of both structures impair learning, although the animals are impaired for different reasons: animals with hippocampal lesions, because they cannot remember the other cue in successive discrimination, or cannot remember what they are to do; animals with amygdala lesions, because they cannot imagine what to expect and cannot organize their action.

One exception is maze learning. While hippocampectomized animals are severely impaired, animals with amygdala lesions are not (Goddard, 1964b). In a maze, the animal has to remember which turn had been "good" before. Seeing the entrance, the animal has to reactivate motor and affective motor memory— which is impossible for animals with hippocampal lesions. But the amygdalectomized animal, on seeing the path, remembers the "good" turn and takes it.

There are many other tasks in which hippocampal and amygdala lesions have different effects. For instance, animals with hippocampal lesions keep on exploring long after intact animals have stopped; animals with amygdala lesions stop exploring long before intact animals do (Schwartzbaum, 1964). Without hippocampus, the animals cannot remember what they have seen before, so they go on exploring. Without amygdala, they remember but cannot imagine what they could possibly find. They do not expect to find anything, so they stop looking.

Animals with amygdaloid lesions do not easily form a conditioned emotional reaction (CER; Isaacson, 1974; Goddard, 1964b). In contrast, hippocampal lesions do not affect such reactions (Nadel, 1968). When a tone is sounded that previously announced foot shock, intact animals press a bar for food more slowly while hearing the tone, and so do animals with hippocampal lesions. But amygdalectomized animals disregard the tone and press the bar at the same rate as before, because they cannot imagine how the tone could affect them; they do not fear the shock, hence do not hesitate pressing the bar. Hippocampectomized animals hear the tone, are afraid of the shock and press more slowly, like intact animals.

A number of authors report an active avoidance deficit in the two-way shuttle box in amygdalectomized animals (Brady et al., 1954; Kling et al., 1960; Horvath, 1963; and others), in contrast to the "facilitation" reported in hippocampectomized animals. King (1958) found that animals with amygdala lesions hesitated before running into the safe compartment; and Kling et al. (1960) reported that they required more trials than intact animals before they began making the first response. Once begun, they seemed to learn as quickly as intact animals. Isaacson (1974) made the same observation after stria terminalis lesions in rats. Intact animals also hesitate in the two-way shuttle box because they remember that they had been shocked in the "safe" compartment in earlier trials. But animals with amygdala lesions, who also remember the shock, cannot imagine what to do or why they should run on cue. Hence they delay much longer than intact animals—they show an active avoidance deficit. Once they make a successful response, they remember it and learn normally.

Grossman (1972c) investigated the active avoidance impairment after small lesions that selectively destroyed the cortical, central, or basolateral amygdaloid nuclei in rats. In another experiment, he destroyed the piriform cortex without damaging the amygdala. In the standard shuttle box, the rats had to go through a small door and jump into the other compartment. Grossman found that rats with these small lesions learned faster than intact controls. But animals with piriform cortex ablation showed a significant deficit. Grossman suggested that these lesions may have disinhibited active avoidance; and that the usually seen inhibition after ablation of the amygdaloid complex must be the result of the incidental destruction of the piriform cortex, which normally activates the amygdala.

But from the many reports on amygdala lesions and stimulation discussed above, it seems much more likely that there are several relays from piriform cortex via amygdala to limbic cortex and neocortex, each mediating different emotional imagery. One or the other of these relays could be blocked by a small lesion. For instance, damage of the basolateral nuclei seems to block images of what to do and what may be the outcome of a given action. Since the response is simple and the animal does not expect an ill outcome, it responds on cue. A small lesion of the cortical nuclei would block olfactory imagery, no doubt a potent factor in recognizing the compartment in which the rat had been shocked; again, the animal would not be reluctant to respond. A small lesion of the central nuclei (apparently in the fear zone) would reduce fear imagery to the point where the animals could respond immediately, not expecting to be shocked in the safe compartment. Actually, this group showed the greatest facilitation. In contrast, total ablation of the amygdala or destruction of the piriform cortex would prevent the animals from imagining either what could happen or what they could do about it, hence their reluctance to move.

According to Horvath (1963), animals with amygdaloid lesions are unimpaired in the one-way shuttle box. But McNew and Thompson (1966) and Robinson (1963) did find a significant deficit. The difference seems to lie in the kind of avoidance response demanded. If it is a simple run from one compartment to the other, lesioned animals have no difficulty; but if a complicated response is demanded, they fail. In McNew and Thompson's apparatus, the rat had to run through two open doors, cross a middle compartment, and jump three inches to the elevated end compartment. In Robinson's experiment, the rat had to touch a wheel in the white home compartment before running to the safe black compartment. Without amygdala, hence without imagination, the animals cannot organize such complicated actions, and show an active avoidance deficit.

Passive Avoidance.   Unlike hippocampal lesions, amygdala lesions in cats and rats do not impair passive avoidance (Horvath, 1963; McNew & Thompson, 1966). Since the affective memory circuit is intact, amygdalectomized animals remember the shock on seeing the food cup and refrain from responding. Of course, the animals' difficulty in starting to respond worked in their favor in passive avoidance.

In contrast to other investigators, Pellegrino (1968) found a significant passive avoidance deficit in rats after lesions of the basolateral amygdaloid region. Cortico-medial lesions had only a slight unfavorable effect. The deficit was not the result of increased thirst or increased activity. But I think it can be attributed to the experimental procedure. Pellegrino used a round metal chamber with water spout recessed in a 2–inch square opening just large enough for the rat to poke its head through. As soon as it did so, the circuit was closed and the rat received an electric shock. This is very different from the usual passive avoidance task in which the rat can see the cup, and remember that approaching it meant a shock. In this situation, the rat could not see the cup but had to remember that its own movement had brought on shock. But after such lesions the animal was unable to imagine (expect) that putting its head through the opening would be painful, because motor imagination was impossible. Since the corticomedial nuclei were intact, the rat could smell the water and expect it; hence it approached the cup and was duly punished. In contrast, damage to the corticomedial area abolished olfactory images of water; with the basolateral area intact, the animal could imagine the consequences of its action and expect the shock. It is surprising that these animals had even a slight passive avoidance deficit—unless more than the cortical nuclei was destroyed.

Bar Press and Reversals.   Pellegrino also found that rats with lesions of the basolateral nuclei were impaired in a bar pressing task in which they had to refrain from bar pressing for at least twenty seconds to receive a food pellet. The animals with corticomedial lesions were not significantly different from controls, but the rats with basolateral lesions showed a significant deficit. These animals were also impaired in learning to press the left and right bar alternately for a food pellet, while animals with corticomedial lesions were unimpaired. When a light above the bar indicated which bar to press, or the houselight indicated when to press the bar, all lesioned animals performed normally. When the cue was reversed, so that the light being turned off signaled the time for a bar press, all animals learned the reversal normally. With the visual cue, animals with basolateral lesions were able to imagine that food would follow, and pressed the bar accordingly. But they were unable to imagine what to do to obtain food if no visual cue was provided. Apparently, the basolateral nuclei initiate motor imagination.

Eleftheriou et al. (1972) found impaired learning of successive reversals in the deermouse after lesions of the cortical or basolateral nuclei but not after lesions of the medial group. That may mean that the lesion of the cortical amygdaloid nuclei has made it impossible for the animal to initiate imagery on the basis of olfactory impressions, which would severely reduce motivation. Lesions of the basolateral nuclei seems to have blocked motor images so that the animal could not imagine what to do.

Stimulation Effects.   Goddard (1964b) stimulated the amygdala of rats via implanted electrodes unilaterally, at very low intensities, every second day, during each test trial or in the five-minute period immediately following the trial. He found impairment in passive avoidance and a two-way active avoidance task, but normal performance in the one-way task. But McIntyre (1970) found that the learning deficit occurs only when posttrial stimulation produces seizure activity in the EEG. Goddard (1972) confirmed these findings and added that repeated low intensity amygdala stimulation always seems to result in "kindling," that is, in after-discharges that become bilateral after unilateral stimulation, spread to hippocampus and other limbic regions, and eventually result in convulsions. Such repeated stimulation has long-lasting adverse effects. It gradually lowers the convulsion threshold and eventually results in rage and violent attack at the same intensity which at first had merely produced sniffing or facial twitching. Massed trial stimulation, however, seems to result in adaptation to the stimulation and does not result in convulsions.

However, interference with learning may occur after amygdala stimulation even without kindling. Bresnahan and Routtenberg (1972) reported that stimulation of the medial amygdaloid nucleus during acquisition of a step-down passive avoidance task impaired next day's performance. Stimulation of other amygdala regions had no effect. From their electrographic record it seems clear that no after-discharges were involved. Since the medial nucleus lies within the "fear" zone, the animals seem to have been unable to anticipate harm, hence their passive avoidance deficit. Whether this zone is stimulated or ablated, it is not available for the animal's own use.

Apparently, appetitive learning, as distinct from passive avoidance learning, is not disrupted by amygdala stimulation. Kesner (1977) reported that rats learned normally to press a bar for sugar water despite stimulation of the amygdala after each trial. But when the animals had to refrain from pressing the bar because every bar press was punished by foot shock, they were unable to learn this passive avoidance problem when their amygdala was stimulated after every trial. They continued pressing the lever at the same rate as before when tested 64 seconds after the shock, and 24 hours afterwards. Intact appetitive learning after amygdala stimulation seems to be the result of a functioning recall circuit. The animal remembers that bar pressing brought sugar water, and presses again. When the bar press brings pain, the animal remembers the shock on seeing the bar, but cannot imagine what to do to avoid it. Stimulation of the amygdala makes it impossible to imagine anything. If Goddard is right, kindling had already occurred, so that the animal could not use imagination when it needed it.

Kesner (1977) also tested the effect of injecting cholinomimetic substances and cholinergic blockers into the amygdala. While rats were licking sugar water, they were given an electric foot shock. Immediately after the shock, or at various delay periods, carbachol or physostigmine (cholinomimetics) were injected into both amygdalae via implanted cannules. Animals injected immediately did not stop licking, that is, they had a passive avoidance deficit. Injections of the same drugs into the ventricles, or delayed injection (twelve hours after the trial) into the amygdala, had no effect. In contrast, when the animals were injected with atropine sulfate (a cholinergic blocker) immediately after the footshock, they stopped licking longer than the controls, that is, passive avoidance improved.

Electrical stimulation seems to disturb imagination so that the animals cannot imagine what to do to avoid the shock. And cholinergic drugs seem to produce rage when injected into the amygdala (Grossman, 1972b); this also would prevent the animals from using their imagination.

Routtenberg and his coworkers stimulated the medial nucleus of rats in a step-down situation. They stimulated this nucleus at the beginning of each trial, as soon as the animal was placed on the perch. Stimulation stopped when the rat stepped down on to the electrified platform. The stimulated animals learned to remain on the perch as quickly as did the control group—hence they showed no deficit in passive avoidance. However, when the animals were stimulated before the first trial next day, they immediately stepped down and received a shock (Bresnahan & Routtenberg, 1972). In a follow-up study, Gold et al. (1977) found that stimulation of points within the lateral amygdala disrupts retention. In their experiment, the animals were stimulated after each trial. Routtenberg and Kim (1978) suggest that the stimulation is "causing a jamming or disruption of the pattern of electrophysiological activity that would occur in this region during learning" (p. 308). That is certainly true, but I would add that the psychological activity blocked by electrical stimulation is not "learning" but imagination, which is needed to anticipate the shock. Stimulation during a trial does not disturb performance because in massed practice the affective memory of shock combined with the inability to imagine what to do is sufficient to hold back. But next day, stimulation before the first trial prevents the animal from anticipating shock, hence the retention deficit. In Gold et al.'s experiment, stimulation of the amygdala after a trial makes it impossible for the animal to anticipate the shock in the next trial, hence the deficit. In both experiments, the deficit is not caused by memory loss but by an interference with imagination.

24

Neurotransmitters in the Brain

*One of the neurochemical embarrassments of the brain is that it
has too many transmitters, or too many potential transmitters,
including those both for inhibitory and stimulatory functions. . . . This whole complex system makes one think that trying
to attribute any large, complex phenomenon to one transmitter,
under any conditions, is probably a futile venture.*

A. Yuwiler, 1978

At first glance, it might seem unlikely that a structure like the hippocampus
should serve as relay station for so many different psychological activities, as
postulated by my theory: sensory recall, the revival of appraisal (affective memory), the initiation of directed action and the physiological changes that go with
it, and finally, the revival of motor memory. It might seem just as unlikely that
another structure, the amygdala, should mediate different emotional and instinctive actions like anger and attack, fear and flight, eating and drinking. Yet we
know from studies reviewed in the last few chapters that this is what has been
found.

Perhaps these structures can mediate so many and such different activities because they serve as relay stations for several neural systems, each of which has a
different function. In recent years it has become possible to distinguish between
different neural systems according to the substances that serve as transmitters in
each of them. In addition to acetylcholine, which has been known as a transmitter in peripheral nerves for quite some time, many additional neurotransmitters
have been identified in the brain. The neurons synthesize transmitter substances
from a precursor through a series of enzyme reactions, store them in vesicles of

359

presynaptic nerve endings and release them into the synaptic cleft on arrival of a neural impulse. The released transmitter molecules bridge the fluid-filled gap between the presynaptic axon terminal and the cell membrane of the postsynaptic receiving neurons and are taken up by protein molecules precisely tailored to their configuration.

In the case of an excitatory neuron, the transmitter, combining with the receptor in the postsynaptic neuron, depolarizes the neuron, producing an excitatory postsynaptic potential (EPSP). If this potential reaches the firing threshold for that cell, it triggers a propagated potential that may result in conduction to the adjoining neuron, a muscle contraction, or a release of glandular secretion. When presynaptic excitation stops, release of the transmitter ceases. Since the transmitter still in the synaptic cleft is eliminated by enzymatic breakdown, reuptake, or diffusion, the postsynaptic neuron is repolarized. When an inhibitory neuron is excited, it liberates the inhibitory transmitter, which is received by specific postsynaptic receptors. The inhibitory transmitter now hyperpolarizes the postsynaptic membrane (inhibitory postsynaptic potential, IPSP), thus increasing the threshold for depolarization of the neuron and so preventing its conduction. When the presynaptic inhibitory neuron is repolarized, the inhibitory transmitter is no longer released, while the transmitter remaining in the synaptic cleft is eliminated. Hence the postsynaptic neuron returns to its normal state of polarization (Tapia, 1974).

Many receptors have a binding site for the transmitter molecule and, in addition, a pore that is selectively permeable to certain ions. When the transmitter is bound to the receptor, the pore is opened and ions inside and outside the cell membrane flow through according to their concentration gradients, either exciting or inhibiting the neuron's firing. Whether the transmitter generates an excitatory or inhibitory potential depends on the specific ions and the direction of their movement. For instance, acetylcholine (ACh) excites the muscle at the nerve-muscle synapse because it induces positively charged sodium ions to flow into the cell and depolarize the negative resting voltage. Thus ACh mediates transmission between a nerve and a muscle cell by a simple flow of sodium ions across the synapse. But in the brain, most cholinergic transmission seems to be mediated by a "second messenger" molecule, cyclic guanosine monophosphate (GMP).

Other transmitters, for instance the monoamines noradrenaline, dopamine, and serotonin, have a similar mode of action. In these systems, the receptor protein is coupled in the target cell membrane to the enzyme adenylate cyclase, which converts the adenosine triphosphate in the cell into cyclic adenosine monophosphate (AMP). When the enzyme adenylate cyclase is activated by the transmitter, it generates thousands of molecules of AMP so that the weak signal provided by the transmitter is amplified several thousandfold before it is passed on as a nerve impulse. This second messenger system works relatively slowly, compared to the rapidly acting receptors that mediate synaptic transmission by diffusion through a pore. Many transmitters act on two or more types of receptors. Dopamine seems to bind to two different types of receptor—D 1, which employs second messenger cyclic AMP, and D 2, which does not.

Once the nerve impulse has been transmitted across the synapse, the second messenger AMP or GMP is inactivated by an enzyme. The first messenger transmitters are taken up again into the presynaptic terminals. Some of the excess transmitter is inactivated by monoamine oxidase (MAO) for the biogenic amines, by acetylcholinesterase (AChE) for acetylcholine; the rest is converted to metabolites.

Many psychoactive drugs seem to act by either enhancing or decreasing the release of one or several transmitters from the axon terminals. Others block either the postsynaptic receptors or the reuptake into the presynaptic terminals. Still other drugs block the synthesis of the transmitter substance. For instance, tyrosine hydroxylase, the enzyme converting the precursor to dopa, can be inhibited by an antagonist, so that neither dopamine nor noradrenaline can be produced (see Fig. 24.1). Or the last step from dopamine to noradrenaline can be blocked, so that dopamine but not noradrenaline is available for transmission. I refer to some of these drugs later in the chapter.

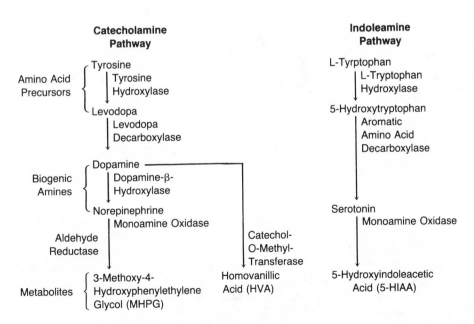

FIG. 24.1.   Catecholamine and indoleamine metabolic pathways.

Many neurotransmitters have been identified in the brain. Some brain neurons use acetylcholine, others use catecholamines (noradrenaline, dopamine) or indoleamines (serotonin) as transmitters. Conduction over still other synapses may require amino acids such a gamma-aminobutyric acid (GABA), glycine, glutamic acid, and others (De Robertis, 1972). More recently, it has been found that certain peptides (e.g., substance P and enkephalin) and even hormones (vasopressin, ACTH) can mediate nervous conduction. But these substances have a different mode of action.

Neurotransmitters alter membrane conductance by engaging specialized receptors at the synapse, thus changing the excitability of a single excitable element for a brief period of time, from milliseconds to seconds. In contrast, peptides directly alter the conductance of a membrane that is already activated by a transmitter. In other words, these substances modulate the action of the transmitter; hence they are called *neuromodulators*. Many drugs act as neuromodulators because they affect the postsynaptic membranes of neurons in the central nervous system, so altering either the receptor affinity for the neurotransmitter or the conductance activated by the transmitters.

Still another type of transmitter has been observed in axons that are not in synaptic contact with the neurons they influence. These are called *neurohormonal* transmitters. They induce long-lasting changes in the activity of various distant target cells. Their excitation may lead to autonomic, endocrine or motor activity. For instance, in mammals the central administration of angiotensin results in raised blood pressure, release of antidiuretic hormone and water intake (Barker & Smith, 1979). According to Chan-Palay (1977), both naradrenaline and serotonin fibers in the cerebellum have a synaptic and nonsynaptic mode of transmission; that is, they have both neurotransmitter and neurohumoral functions.

The techniques for studying these transmitters have only been worked out in the last two decades. The transmitter is collected at the presynaptic nerve endings—which is difficult because any excess not used by the receptors is immediately removed by a degrading enzyme or is taken up again by the presynaptic terminals. To collect samples of transmitter substances requires blocking of the removal mechanism by drugs; and these usually affect more than one transmitter. Even if the relevant transmitter can be preserved, its collection is possible only from surface structures in the living animal. Another difficulty is created by the "blood-brain barrier" which isolates the brain from the general circulation. Only those drugs can cross this barrier whose molecules are either very small or readily soluble in the fatty membranes of the glial cells. Hence only a few drugs can be given intravenously. Most of them must be injected into the ventricles or applied to particular brain sites by iontophoresis. However, the injected transmitter may diffuse to many cells or may affect more than one transmitter system.

Much information has been obtained by the study of brain slices that are stained selectively for neurons using a particular transmitter. One promising technique is to convert the transmitter into a fluorescent derivative that will glow under ultraviolet radiation. A second approach is to inject radioactively labeled molecules of a given transmitter into the brain and wait until they are taken up by the neurons using that transmitter. After the animal is killed, brain slices are placed on radiosensitive film so that these neurons can be identified.

These techniques have revealed that the transmitters are not distributed diffusely throughout the brain but are localized in discrete cells and pathways. Various transmitter systems have been identified. For our purposes, the most important transmitters in the brain are acetylcholine (ACh), dopamine (DA), noradrenaline (NA), serotonin (5-HT), and GABA.

ACETYLCHOLINE (ACh).

This substance has been known as a transmitter in peripheral nerves for a long time, but its role in the brain has only been explored comparatively recently. To identify ACh in the brain, brain slices must be stained for acetylcholinesterase (AChE), the enzyme that removes excess ACh from the synaptic cleft (Fig. 24.2). Since acetylcholinesterase is found not only in cell bodies but also in axons and dendrites, this technique does not indicate the direction of neural conduction. However, Shute and Lewis (1967) found that AChE accumulates on the cell body side of a cut axon and disappears at the side cut off from the cell body, so that the direction of conduction can be inferred. Combining lesions with staining of brain slices for AChE, these authors found cholinergic pathways, and published a comprehensive map of such pathways in the rat brain.

Cholinergic neurons contain AChE in the cell body and on the axonal membrane along its length, while cholinoceptic neurons (i.e., neurons that can receive cholinergic excitation but themselves use other transmitters) contain AChE on the membranes of dendritic spines but not along the axon. There are two main cholinergic pathways. The dorsal tegmental path originates mainly in the cuneiform nucleus on the dorsolateral part of the midbrain reticular formation and runs toward the tectum, pretectal area, the geniculate bodies, the thalamus, and septum.[1] The ventral tegmental pathway starts from the substantia nigra and the ventral tegmental area of the midbrain and runs toward the basal forebrain areas. From there, AChE containing neurons project to the cerebral cortex and the olfactory bulb. Of the cholinergic neurons in this pathway, the midbrain reticular

---

[1] After lesions of the medial septum or the septo-hippocampal pathway, less than 20% of AChE remains in the hippocampus. AChE piles up on the septal side of the lesion indicating that cholinergic conduction from septum to hippocampus has been interrupted (Storm-Mathisen, 1978).

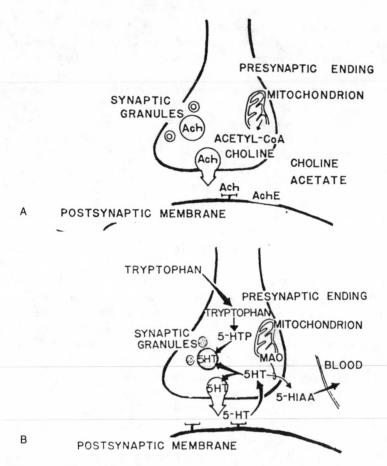

FIG. 24.2.   Models of cholinergic and serotonergic synapses. A: Model of a cholinergic synapse. B: Model of a serotonin (5-HT) synapse. ACh: Acetylcholine; AChE: acetylcholinesterase; 5-HIAA: hydroxyindoleacetic acid; 5-HT: 5-hydroxytryptamine; 5-HTP: 5-hydroxytryptophan; MAO: monoamine oxidase. From *Psychopharmacology: A Biochemical and Behavioral Approach* by L. S. Seiden and L. A. Dykstra. Copyright © 1977 by Van Nostrand Reinhold Company. Reprinted by permission of the publisher.

formation and a portion of the pallidum form part of the extrapyramidal system; in my terms, they form part of the action circuit (Fig. 24.3 A,B).

In mapping AChE-containing pathways arising from these structures, Shute and Lewis (1975) found that the striatum and the subthalamic nucleus are in the main cholinoceptive, with a small population of intrinsic cholinergic neurons. The red nucleus seems to be a cholinoceptive but non-cholinergic body. The limbic system and the cerebellum seem to be influenced by cholinergic excitation. These authors point out that the cholinergic system of the brain appears to be more extensive than the monoaminergic systems. Indeed, the presence of cells containing AChE in all sites occupied by monoaminergic neurons indicates that the monoaminergic systems are likely to be cholinoceptive.

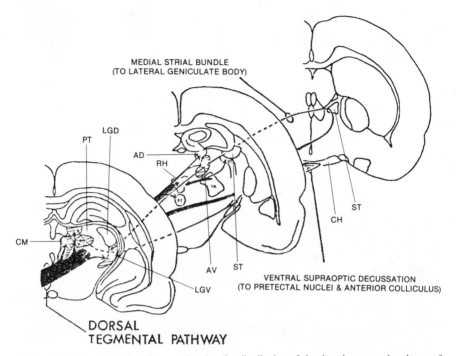

MEDIAL STRIAL BUNDLE
(TO LATERAL GENICULATE BODY)

LGD
PT
AD
RH

CM

AV   ST
LGV

ST
CH

VENTRAL SUPRAOPTIC DECUSSATION
(TO PRETECTAL NUCLEI & ANTERIOR COLLICULUS)

DORSAL
TEGMENTAL PATHWAY

FIG. 24.3 A.—Expanded diagram showing the distribution of the dorsal tegmental pathway of cholinesterase-containing fibres to the thalamus and metathalamus, with extensions entering the stria terminalis (medial strial bundle) and the ventral supraoptic decussation. Natural spacing of transverse sections increased five times. Areas of dense neuropil hatched. Abbreviations: AD, antero-dorsal thalamic nucleus; AV, antero-ventral thalamic nucleus; CH, optic chiasma; CM, centromedian (parafascicular) nucleus; LGD, dorsal nucleus of lateral geniculate body; LGV, ventral nucleus of lateral geniculate body; PT, pretectal nuclei; RE, nucleus reuniens; RH, rhomboid nucleus; RT, reticular thalamic nucleus; ST, stria terminalis; T, optic tract; VA, ventral thalamic nucleus, pars anterior. FIG 24.3 A, B, from Shute & Lewis, 1967, in *Brain* 90, 497–520. Reprinted by permission of Oxford University Press.

According to Iversen and Iversen (1975a), the dorsal system innervates the thalamus and corresponds to the thalamic reticular activating system while the ventral system projects to the cortex, striatum, and hypothalamus and also sends relays to the hippocampus via the septum. Both project back to the tegmentum. In terms of my theory, the ventral tegmental path would be a link in the motor memory circuit, projecting via hypothalamus to striatum and frontal cortex. The dorsal tegmental path seems to be active in modality-specific memory recall via sensory thalamic nuclei. The circuit from septal area to the hippocampus seems to mediate sensory recall as soon as man or animal smell something (connection from olfactory sensory and limbic areas) or imagine something (connection from piriform area and amygdala). Finally, the septo-hippocampal path mediates recall when the animal is hungry, thirsty, too warm, or too cold (connection from hypothalamic detector cells). This path also connects with the habenulo-interpeduncular tract (Fig. 24.4).

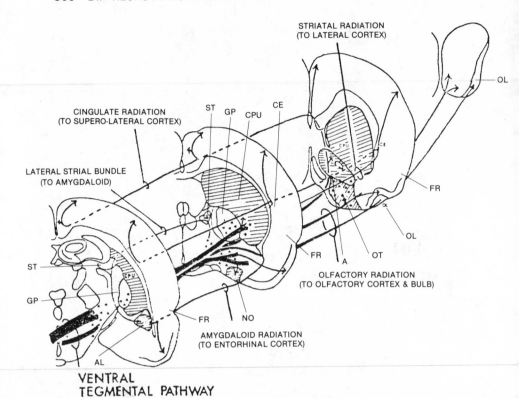

STRIATAL RADIATION
(TO LATERAL CORTEX)

CINGULATE RADIATION
(TO SUPERO-LATERAL CORTEX)

LATERAL STRIAL BUNDLE
(TO AMYGDALOID)

ST GP CPU CE

OL

FR

ST

GP

FR   A   OT

OL

OLFACTORY RADIATION
(TO OLFACTORY CORTEX & BULB)

FR   NO

AMYGDALOID RADIATION
(TO ENTORHINAL CORTEX)

AL

VENTRAL
TEGMENTAL PATHWAY

FIG. 24.3 B.—Expanded diagram, comparable to fig. A, showing the course of the ventral tegmental pathway of AChE-containing fibres through the subthalamus, lateral hypothalamus, lateral
preoptic area and olfactory tubercle, with an extension via the stria terminalis (lateral strial bundle) to
the amygdala, and radiations to neocortex, olfactory cortex and olfactory bulb. Areas of dense
neuropil hatched, location of AChE-containing cells indicated by asterisks. Abbreviations: A, nucleus accumbens; AL, lateral amygdaloid nucleus, CE, external capsule; CPU, caudate-putamen;
FR, rhinal fissure; GP, globus pallidus; NO, nucleus of lateral olfactory tract; OL, lateral olfactory
tract; OT, olfactory tubercle; ST, stria terminalis. FIG 24.3 A, B, from Shute & Lewis, 1967, in
Brain 90, 497–520. Reprinted by permission of Oxford University Press.

That AChE-containing fibers in the amygdala do affect the hippocampus has
been shown by Grossman (1972b). He injected minute quantities of ACh into the
basolateral nucleus of cats and found that these animals became highly aggressive and had repeated seizures with EEG spikes in amygdala, hypothalamus, and
hippocampus as well as in the motor cortex. After injection of carbachol (a
cholinergic drug that is not destroyed as rapidly as ACh) into the amygdala of
rats, these animals became similarly vicious and were unable or unwilling to
avoid painful stimulation (active avoidance deficit). Butcher (l978) and Mabry
and Campbell (1978) suggested on the basis of their investigations that ACh may
act as modulator on other transmitter systems. In any case, seizure activity in the

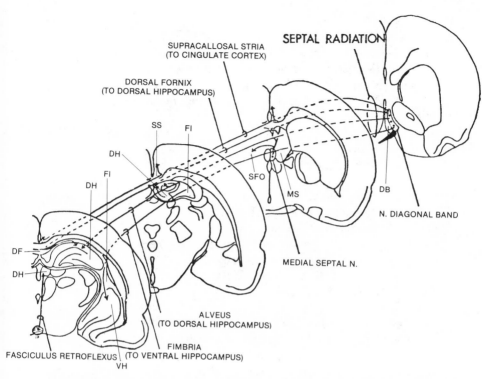

FIG. 24.4. Expanded diagram (natural spacing of transverse sections increased five times) showing the septal radiation of cholinergic fibres arising from the medial septal nucleus (MS) and the
nucleus of the diagonal band (DB), and supplying the subfornical organ (SFO), cingulate cortex via
the supracallosal stria (SS), dorsal hippocampus (DH) via the dorsal fornix (DF) and alveus (AL),
and ventral hippocampus (VH) via the fimbria (FI). The fasciculus retroflexus, with cholinesterase-
containing fibres running from the habenular nuclei (H) to the interpeduncular nucleus (IP), is also
included. From Lewis and Shute, 1967 in *Brain*, 90, 521–540. Reprinted by permission of Oxford
University Press.

amygdala would make it impossible for the animals to use their imagination to
plan action to avoid the shock—hence the avoidance deficit. Scopolamine, the
anticholinergic drug, counteracted the cholinergic excitation of the amygdala and
so restored active avoidance.

I would suggest that cholinergic excitation of noradrenergic neurons in the
amygdala produces anger and attack, while noradrenergic activity alone produces fear—hence improves active avoidance. Fear and anger are based on the
appraisal of something as bad, to be escaped (fear) or to be attacked (anger).
There must be a way for the nervous system to mediate these different emotions
and action patterns. Cholinergic stimulation of noradrenergic dendrites *versus*
noradrenergic stimulation of such fibers might provide the necessary distinction.

Actually, there is evidence that mouse-killing attacks in the rat are mediated
over cholinergic pathways. Bandler (1971) found that cholinergic stimulation in

the amygdala, lateral hypothalamus, and midbrain tegmentum induced such attacks; they could be aborted by blocking such excitation with atropine.

Acetylcholine has two types of action: fast action, called "nicotinic" because nicotine has the same effect; and slow "muscarinic" action, mimicked by muscarine, but also by pilocarpine. The fast nicotinic action is opposed by curare and similar drugs. Muscarinic action is antagonized by atropine and scopolamine. Physostigmine prevents the inactivation of ACh by AChE, hence facilitates its accumulation in the brain. This effect is antagonized by atropine. Acetylcholinesterase, which removes ACh from the synapse, can also be used to antagonize ACh action. Studies using ACh antagonists show that the ACh receptors in the hippocampus are mainly but not exclusively muscarinic. This would support my suggestion that the muscarinic action of ACh serves memory recall, while the nicotinic action serves the initiation of movements.

If the hippocampus is the switching station in the recall circuit, as I am suggesting, ACh should be the transmitter in hippocampal afferents. Indeed, a system of ACh-using fibers extends from the medial septal nucleus via the fimbria into the hippocampus and is connected with the limbic cortex (Kuhar, 1975; Siegel & Tassoni, 1971a,b; Lewis & Shute, 1967). Following lesions in the fimbria or medial septal nucleus, AChE, the enzyme that destroys ACh, and cholinacetylase, an enzyme that acetylizes choline to ACh, thus replenishing it, were abruptly reduced in the hippocampus. Apparently, most of the cholinergic components found in the hippocampus result from excitation via the medial septal nucleus. Indeed, stimulation of the surface of the septum caused a two-and-a-half fold release of ACh from the hippocampus. Stimulation of the caudate nucleus did not produce an increase (Smith, 1972; 1974). The neurons excited by ACh are found in the dentate fascia and the pyramids of the hippocampal cortex. The distribution of these cells differed significantly from that of cells sensitive to glutamate (Stefanis, 1964; Herz & Nacimiento, 1965; Straughan, 1975). The highest AChE activity was found in the layer that contains the basal dendrites of the hippocampal pyramids, in the supragranular zone and the hilus of the dentate fascia, hence in the region of cholinergic afferents (Kuhar, 1975).

The excitatory cholinergic septo-hippocampal pathway seems to terminate on muscarinic receptors: Atropine and other antimuscarinic substances antagonize responses to iontophoretically applied ACh and also antagonize hippocampal theta at 4–7 Hz. But according to Segal (1978), the hippocampus also contains nicotinic receptor sites. Indeed, they are more numerous there than anywhere else in the brain except in the hypothalamus. Microiontophoretic injection of ACh excites bursts of potentials in what presumably are pyramid cells and these bursts are reversed by atropine. But there are cells in the hippocampus that do not emit such bursts and do not respond to ACh. Iontophoretic application of nicotine reduces the spontaneous firing of these cells but does not affect the activity of burst cells. This action of nicotine can be reversed by nicotine antagonists (d-tubocurarine, gallamine). An intraventricular injection of carbachol or nicotine produces theta rhythms in waking rats. D-tubocurarine reduces theta produced by septal stimulation and spontaneous activity, except for the theta rhythm associated with movements. Apparently, pyramidal neurons have excitatory muscarinic receptors; and other cells, presumably interneurons, have inhibitory nicotinic receptors.

Vanderwolf et al. (1978) mentioned that there are two ascending brainstem systems that excite hippocampal theta. One runs via the diagonal band and the medial septal nuclei, and may contain cholinergic synapses because it is blocked by atropine and stimulated by eserine. This system produces slow theta (4–7 Hz) and can be recorded when the rat is immobile. The other system produces higher frequency theta (7–12 Hz) and is only active during walking or other goal-directed movements. This wave pattern is not affected by atropine but can be blocked by ether or urethane, just like actual movement. Morphine, on the other hand, abolishes this pattern without producing general anesthesia, although it does produce catalepsy. Atropine-sensitive theta still occurs during morphine catalepsy but can be abolished by atropine. Apparently, fast theta that appears during walking, running, or climbing, is mediated by the action circuit, while the slower rhythm, seen during immobility, seems to be mediated by the recall circuit.

According to Vanderwolf et al., two types of rhythm, similarly correlated with behavior, can also be observed in the neocortex. Electrical stimulation of the reticular formation produces low voltage fast activity (EEG arousal) in the neocortex, instead of the theta rhythm found in the hippocampus. After atropine, this fast activity is displaced by large amplitude slow waves that can be observed during immobility or stereotyped behavior. As soon as the animal starts walking or climbing, low voltage fast activity reappears. This atropine-resistant fast activity can also be produced by electrical stimulation of the hypothalamus or the brainstem reticular formation. It is abolished by ether or urethane. The atropine-sensitive fast activity seems to be cholinergic, paralleling the atropine-sensitive theta rhythm in the hippocampus. In terms of my theory, it seems to represent the cholinergic recall circuit. According to Vanderwolf et al., dopaminergic blocking drugs blocked atropine-sensitive fast activity in the neocortex, and atropine-sensitive theta in the hippocampus, but did not block movement-correlated atropine-resistant rhythms. This seems to imply that the atropine-sensitive fast activity can also be produced by the dopaminergic imagination circuit.

According to Fuster (1973), EEG arousal together with increased thalamic firing (particularly in the dorsomedial thalamic nucleus) occurs when a monkey sees a piece of fruit in a delayed response experiment, while he is attentive but immobile. Often, such thalamic activation continues during the delay. Distracting stimuli during the delay reduce thalamic activation and result in errors. Sudden noises or flashes of light evoked startle but no thalamic activation. Apparently, the monkey imagined reaching for the bait and recalled where it was hidden. Such imagination and recall would produce both EEG arousal and thalamic firing. Stamm (1969) reported that electrical excitation of the prefrontal cortex while the cue was shown markedly interfered with the delayed response—which is what we would expect, seeing that the prefrontal cortex is the projection area of the dorsomedial thalamic nucleus. All these reports support my suggestion that EEG arousal indicates activation of the recall and imagination circuits rather than of the action circuit.

Srebro et al. (1975) have found AChE-containing fibers projecting from the hippocampus via supra- and subcallosal fibers. They found heavy concentrations of AChE in the rostral part of the medial septal nucleus, the nucleus of the diagonal band and the dorsal septum, caudal part; also in the fimbrial fibers to the septo-fimbrial nucleus. These findings confirm that acetylcholine may be used as transmitter in the hippocampal projection to the septum as well as in the septal projection to the hippocampus. From the septum, the recall circuit seems to run to the midbrain tegmentum and, on its return loop via the sensory thalamic nuclei, to the sensory association cortex.

There is evidence that acetylcholine is the transmitter in this link of the modality-specific recall circuit also. For instance, Spehlmann (1971) has reported that ACh facilitates the excitatory response of visual cortex neurons to stimulation of the reticular formation, while atropine blocks it. And Phillis (1974) found cholinergic afferents in most regions of the neocortex. Excitation of cortical cholinergic neurons by somatic sensory, visual, and auditory stimulation, and by stimulation of the brainstem reticular formation, is slow in onset and lasts for some time. It is muscarinic because atropine abolishes it. Phyllis concluded that the afferent stimulation exciting the cortical cells must come from association fibers and non-specific thalamic afferents because the afferent sensory fibers are not cholinergic. Indeed, Mitchell and his coworkers (Collier & Mitchell, 1966, 1967; Hemsworth & Mitchell, 1969) have shown that a group of cholinergic thalamo-cortical and genicolocortical fibers is associated with the slow augmenting response. I am suggesting that these fibers belong to the recall circuit from limbic cortex via hippocampus to brainstem reticular formation, returning via sensory thalamic nuclei to association cortex.

Acetylcholine and Memory Research. That ACh is involved in memory has been shown in various research reports. It has been found, for instance, that anticholinergic drugs produce impairment of passive avoidance and spontaneous alternation, also defects in habituation and successive discrimination, effects similar to those of hippocampal lesions (Straughan, 1975; Douglas, 1975; see also chapter 21). In contrast, small doses of physostigmine (which facilitates cholinergic transmission) significantly increased spontaneous alternation in intact mice and in rats subjected to unilateral hippocampal ablation in infancy. However, physostigmine did not improve the alternation rate of rats with massive bilateral hippocampal lesions (Douglas, 1975), which indicates that memory recall via cholinergic fibers is mediated by the hippocampus.

That recall is mediated via cholinergic fibers has also been shown by Banks and Russell (1967). They used oral intubation of an anticholinesterase[2] (systox) to reduce the AChE level in the brain. Several groups of rats whose AChE level was chronically reduced to between 59% and 29% of normal were trained in serial problem solving in a closed field with squares painted on the floor. At 59% of the normal AChE level in the brain, the animals were unimpaired. Below that level, the lower the AChE concentration, the higher the error score.

Anticholinergic drugs abolished successive discrimination in a go/no go task (Russell, 1969). And Warburton (1972) showed that this deficit is caused by "sensory inattention" rather than by a loss in response control. Sensory inattention means that the animals paid no attention to the cue, hence failed the task. And they could not pay attention to the cue because they did not remember that the cue was the signal for action—again, a memory deficit.

Ilyutchenok et al. (1973) confirmed that cholinergic pathways are involved in memory. Working with dogs, the authors established a conditioned fear response: The animals were trained to step down from a platform and go toward the left cup when they heard a buzzer, and to the right cup when they saw a light. As soon as the dogs had learned the task, they were given a shock when they touched the cup. After one or two shocks, the dogs refused to approach the cup for several weeks. Next, the dogs were given 1 mg/kg benactizine (an anticholinergic drug) four times a day for three days. Fourteen days after this treatment, the dogs approached the cup again. Several weeks after their return to the food cup, the animals were given a weak shock when eating from a cup that had never been used for shock before. After this reminder, the passive avoidance response was reestablished. But with a higher dose of benactizine, the passive avoidance response was permanently lost and could not be restored by a reminder shock. The authors pointed out that the drug had not affected memory registration or consolidation but must have affected memory retrieval: Since the memory was restored by a reminder shock after a small dose, memory registration and consolidation must have been intact.

Finally, Deutsch (1972) and his colleagues showed that cholinergic synapses are involved in learning and that their effective conduction varies with time. They trained animals to avoid shock by running to the lighted arm of a Y-maze. After injection of anticholinesterases (physostigmine or d-isopropyl fluorophosphate—DFP) into rat hippocampal areas, the animals' performance varied with the time between learning and injection. Performance was *impaired* by injections given 30 minutes or 3–14 days after training. It was unaffected at 24 and 48 hours, and *improved* by injections after 28 days. The anticholinergic drug scopolamine had similar effects. Deutsch and coworkers concluded that the

---

[2]Anticholinesterase antagonizes AChE, hence prevents excess ACh at the synapse from being hydrolyzed so that the conductance of the neuron can be restored.

postsynaptic nerve endings in the cholinergic pathway become more sensitive shortly after initial learning and then their sensitivity gradually decreases. This point of view is interesting because it depends on the assumption of continual changes in synaptic sensitivity that can only apply to a recall circuit, not to registration or consolidation. It would apply nicely to the recall circuits I have postulated.

In human beings also, cholinergic pathways are involved in memory recall. Drachman (1977) reported that scopolamine strikingly impaired recall of a serial order of digits and the free recall of words. While verbal I.Q. was unaffected, the performance I.Q. was significantly lowered after scopolamine. Physostigmine by itself had no significant effect; but given after scopolamine, it produced a significant memory improvement and rising performance I.Q. Drachman also found that the performance of young people under scopolamine shows a similar profile as the performance of normal aged subjects. For instance, scopolamine produced a marked impairment of dichotic listening in young adults. In this experiment, the subjects heard a different series of nonsense syllables through each ear and tried to reproduce both series on an automated response panel. According to Drachman, this performance involved the auditory sensory and association cortex bilaterally; dividing the corpus callosum markedly impaired performance. When these young adults were compared with normal 65–85 year olds, the deficits in performance were strikingly similar. In both groups, normal hearing was unimpaired.

These reports make it seem likely that cholinergic pathways are used in recall, at least in the recall of modality-specific memory.

GABA, GLUTAMATE, ASPARTATE, AND GLYCINE

The most widely distributed inhibitory transmitter in the brain is gamma-aminobutyric acid (GABA). Almost a third of the synapses in the brain use GABA as a transmitter. Alone among transmitters, GABA is not usually found outside brain and spinal cord (Andersen, 1975; Iversen, 1979). GABA inhibits both spontaneous and induced hippocampal electrical activity at the soma of the cell. The enzyme that produces GABA from glutamic acid has its highest concentration at the soma where the inhibition occurs. Apparently, GABA can also produce excitatory effects but these occur at the dendrites (Storm-Mathisen, 1978). GABA is synthesized by the terminals of short axons, including cells in the hippocampal formation, and of long axon neurons in the cerebral and cerebellar cortex, the Golgi and Purkinje cells in the cerebellum, the granule cells in the olfactory bulb, and interneurons in the ventrobasal thalamus, the lateral geniculate nucleus, and the caudo-nigral and caudo-pallidal pathways.

Glutamate and aspartate are powerful excitants in the hippocampus and cerebral and cerebellar cortical regions. They act as transmitters in neurons that connect with perforant path and angular bundle terminals, hippocampal granule cells and pyramidal cell axons. Entorhinal terminals seem to release glutamate while pyramidal cell axons seem to release aspartate and possibly glutamate. Glutamate and aspartate are also transmitters in fibers projecting from the hippocampus to the septum and mamillary body.

Since these transmitters are used by interneurons within various structures, they have no independent psychological function. Interneurons simply function as relays between afferent and efferent fibers.

Glycine is an inhibitory transmitter in the brainstem and spinal cord. Glycine inhibits neurons in the cuneate nuclei, brainstem motor nuclei, Deiter's nucleus, reticular formation, red nucleus, substantia nigra, various thalamic nuclei, and in the cerebral cortex. Low concentrations of strychnine block this inhibition and produce convulsions.

MONOAMINE TRANSMITTERS

Comparatively recently, three monoamine transmitter systems have been identified in the brain by means of a fluorescent stain that revealed these fine fibers for the first time (Falck, 1962). Two of these transmitters, noradrenaline (NA) or norepinephrine (NE),[3] and serotonin (5-HT), are found in nerves that relay to the hippocampus. The third, dopamine (DA), does not act as transmitter in hippocampal afferents. These monoamine systems have their cells of origin in caudal parts of the brain but broadcast their axons to the forebrain. The transmitter substances are apparently synthesized in the cell bodies and transported slowly, a few millimeters per day, to nerve terminals by an axonal flow (Meek & Neff, 1972). All three transmitter systems send relays via the medial forebrain bundle to the limbic system and neocortex (Fuxe, 1965). After lesions of the medial forebrain bundle, there is a greater decline of these transmitters in the forebrain than after lesions of the cell bodies. Also, the fibers in the medial forebrain bundle do not directly terminate in all the areas found depleted after lesions in this bundle. Hence Heller (1972) has suggested that the polysynaptic fibers of the medial forebrain bundle can synthesize at least some neurotransmitters in the brain, the more so as it is known that excitation of this pathway increases noradrenaline and serotonin content. Heller's reasoning may hold also for relays in other parts of the brain.

---

[3]As between the terms "nor-adrenaline" and "nor-epinephrine" I have used the former because it indicates even to readers not acquainted with the literature that it is related to the adrenal gland and adrenergic conduction. I am aware that American workers in recent years have preferred the term nor-epinephrine, but apart from convention, there is no good reason to prefer the Greek form to the better known Latin form.

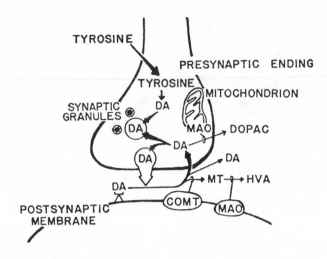

FIG.   24.5 Schematic model of a central dopaminergic neuron. Abbreviations—DOPAC: 3,4-dihydroxyphenylacetic acid; DA: dopamine; MT: methoxytyramine; HVA: homovanillic acid; COMT: catechol-O-methyltransferase; MAO: monoamine oxidase. Note that some of the monoamine oxidase is located on the postsynaptic membrane.

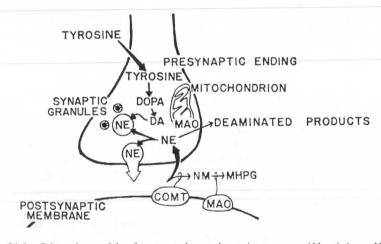

FIG.   24.6. Schematic model of a central noradrenergic neuron. Abbreviations—NM: normetanephrine; MHPG: 3-methoxy-4-hydroxyphenylglycol (note that this product is formed by the action of MAO on normetanephrine). In the peripheral nervous system, this reaction forms vanillyl-mandelic acid but in the central nervous system the acid is further released to the glycol, MHPG. COMT: catechol-O-methyltransferase;   MAO: monoamine   oxidase;   DOPA: 3,4-dihydroxyphenylalanine; DA: dopamine; NE: norepinephrine. FIGs. 24.5 and 24.6 from *Psychopharmacology: A Biochemical and Behavioral Approach* by L. S. Seiden and L. A. Dykstra. Copyright © 1977 by Van Nostrand Reinhold Company. Reprinted by permission of the publisher.

The two catecholamines, dopamine and noradrenaline, have a common precursor, tyrosine. Tyrosine is hydroxylated to L-dopa, and that, to dopamine (Fig. 24.5). Dopamine-beta-hydroxylase converts dopamine to noradrenaline (Fig. 24.6). Serotonin, an indole amine, is a close relative of the catecholamines. Its precursor is tryptophan, an essential amino acid, which is carried by the blood from the gut to serotonergic neurons. There, tryptophan is hydroxylated to 5–hydroxytryptophan (5–HTP), which requires a decarboxylase for the second step from 5–HTP to 5–hydroxytryptamine (5–HT), also called serotonin.

The Main Dopamine System[4]

This system has its cell bodies in the ventral tegmental region (A 8, A 10) and in the substantia nigra (A 9). One branch, the nigrostriatal system, runs forward close to the medial forebrain bundle. Some fibers go to the amygdala, but most of them enter the internal capsule and reach the caudate-putamen. The ventral dopaminergic bundle travels from the ventral tegmentum in the medial forebrain bundle. One branch runs along the ventral amygdalofugal path to the amygdala and piriform cortex; the second runs in the diagonal band to the lateral septum and frontal cortex. A third component goes to the anterior olfactory tubercle and a large branch enters the septo-hippocampal tract to the lateral septum, anterior limbic and frontal cortex (see Fig. 24.7, Iversen, 1979; Hamilton, 1976; Ungerstedt, 1971a). According to Lindvåll et al. (1977), the projection of the dopaminergic neurons in the ventral mesencephalic tegmentum closely coincides with the cortical projection of the dorsomedial thalamic nucleus. Dopamine fibers do not enter the hippocampus (Stenevi et al., 1977).

I would like to suggest that dopamine is the neurotransmitter in the imagination circuit. The amygdala, according to my theory the relay station in this circuit, is connected with the hypothalamus but also the striatum (caudate and putamen), the dorsomedial thalamic nucleus and the frontal cortex. The images themselves seem to be formed via the ventral dopamine system while their appraisal seems to be mediated by the serotonin and noradrenaline systems, which also distribute to the amygdala. The imagination circuit, like the sensory system, is apparently accompanied by fibers of the appraisal system. What we imagine, we immediately appraise as good or bad, and like or dislike it.

Blocking the ascending dopamine pathway in rats has resulted in a depression of motor activity and a severe impairment in learning an underwater swim maze

---

[4]Beside this dopamine system, which sends its axons to striatum, amygdala, septum, and frontal cortex, there is another dopamine system that is confined to the hypothalamus. Its cell bodies have been found within the arcuate nucleus and the ventral periventricular hypothalamic areas but also along the entire periventricular system of the hypothalamus and the preoptic area, some also in the zona incerta. These neurons send their axons to the medial eminence and the pituitary gland, and preoptic nuclei. This system seems to be involved in the regulation of the release of various hormones (Fuxe et al., 1978).

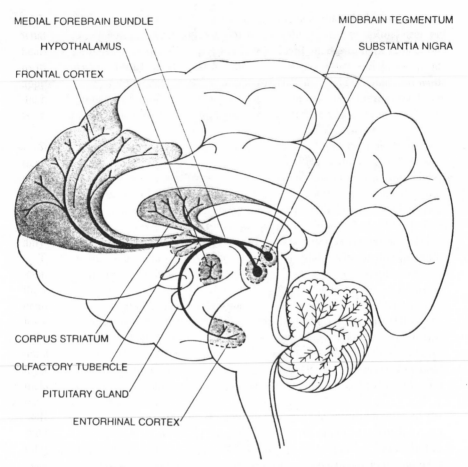

MEDIAL FOREBRAIN BUNDLE

HYPOTHALAMUS

FRONTAL CORTEX

MIDBRAIN TEGMENTUM

SUBSTANTIA NIGRA

CORPUS STRIATUM

OLFACTORY TUBERCLE

PITUITARY GLAND

ENTORHINAL CORTEX

FIG. 24.7. DOPAMINE PATHWAYS in the human brain are shown schematically. The neurons that contain dopamine have their cell bodies clustered in two small regions of the midbrain: the substantia nigra and the tegmentum. These neurons send out widely branching fibers that terminate in the corpus striatum, which regulates motor activity, and in the limbic forebrain, which is involved in emotion. A small set of dopamine neurons in the hypothalamus also regulates secretion of hormones from pituitary. Dopamine has been associated with two brain disorders: a deficiency of the transmitter in the corpus striatum causes the rigidity and tremor of Parkinson's disease, and an excess of dopamine in limbic forebrain may be involved in schizophrenia. From: Iversen, L. L. 1979.

(Ranje & Ungerstedt, 1976). Such an impairment could be expected if the animals are unable to imagine what to do.

Noradrenaline and Serotonin Systems

The noradrenaline terminals in cortex and hippocampus stem from cell bodies in the pons and medulla: cell groups A 1, A 2, A 3, A 4, A 5, A 6, and A 7. According to Olson and Fuxe (1972), the dorsal part of A 6 is the *locus coeruleus,* which sends axons to the thalamus, hippocampus, and cortex. The ventral part of A 6 together with A 7 form the *subcoeruleus* and send a rather thick bundle along the third ventricle to the hypothalamus and preoptic area. Another branch goes to the spinal cord to end in the lateral column. Cell bodies A 1, A 2, and A 5 send axons to the basal and lateral hypothalamus, preoptic area, amygdala, and stria terminalis. Before separating to reach their destination, these fibers merge in the medial forebrain bundle.

The serotonin-producing cell bodies in the raphé nuclei (cell groups B 5 to B 9) extend from the nucleus raphé pallidus in the caudal medulla to the dorsal raphé and centralis superior nucleus in the caudal midbrain. Some serotonin cell groups can be found more laterally in the nucleus paragigantocellularis and in the ventral part of the area postrema. Many fibers travel in the medial forebrain bundle. The terminals of serotonin axons innervate the basal ganglia, the midbrain reticular formation, the hypothalamus and preoptic area, the striatum, thalamus, amygdala, septum, hippocampus, and cortex. The suprachiasmatic nucleus and the ventral lateral geniculate nucleus contain particularly numerous serotonin terminals. The raphé cell bodies also send fibers to the spinal cord and the cerebellum (Dahlström & Fuxe, 1964).

The innervation of the septum seems to come from collaterals of axons that reach the hippocampus. In the septum, serotonin and NA fibers have a distinct but overlapping distribution (see Fig. 24.8). Serotonin and NA neurons distrib-

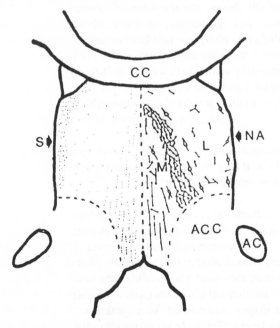

FIG. 24.8.   Diagram of the norephinephrine (NA) and serotonin (S) afferents to the medial and lateral septal nuclei in the rat. The open ovals with extended lines on the norephinephrine side are intended to represent the distribution of the densely innervated cells. From Moore, 1975.

ute to the same areas of the hippocampal formation. They end in a restricted region of the hilar zone of the dentate fascia, just beneath the granular layer, and on the apical dendrites of pyramidal cells in the hippocampus proper. Serotonergic neurons seem to be inhibitory, NA neurons excitatory. It would seem that these neurons serve the appraisal of action impulses initiated by the hippocampus; the serotonin system seems to mediate positive appraisals, the NA system, negative appraisals. When the appraisal is positive, no action is needed and conduction is inhibited. These two neuron systems also supply the anterior thalamic nuclei and their projections to all parts of the limbic cortex, which makes it possible to revive positive and negative appraisals via the affective memory circuit. Evidence for these suggestions is abundant.

The Noradrenaline System.   This system seems to be active during all kinds of stress and the aggression that often follows it. Repeated electrical foot shocks increase NA turnover in the brain and spinal cord (Thierry et al., 1968); electroconvulsive treatment (ECT) increases forebrain NA turnover; overcrowded conditions and forced activity deplete the NA level (Iversen & Iversen, 1975b). According to Ekkers (1975), aggressive men excrete significantly more methyl-NA than men who are inclined to blame themselves; the latter have higher methyl-adrenaline levels than aggressive men. Thus noradrenaline is connected with anger, adrenaline with fear (Arnold, 1960).

Improved performance on the continuous avoidance task with constant infusion of very low concentrations of noradrenaline was noted by Segal and Mandell (1970). Increased efficiency of noradrenergic nerves mediating the appraisal of threatened pain as bad would account for this finding. In contrast, higher concentrations (which block conduction) resulted in sedation.

It has been known for some years that reserpine abolishes the active avoidance of electric shock and disturbs the learned performance of various tasks for a food or water reward. Reserpine depletes noradrenaline in the nerve terminals, but depletes also dopamine and serotonin. However, alpha-methyltyrosine, which depletes only noradrenaline and dopamine, has the same effect, an effect that can be prevented or reversed by treatment with L-Dopa, the precursor of both dopamine and noradrenaline (Andén, et al., 1969). To discover whether dopamine or noradrenaline is more important for avoidance learning, they used the newer drug FLA–63 (see Table 24.1) to inhibit the synthesis of NA from DA. When the conversion of DA to NA was prevented by inhibiting dopamine-beta-hydroxylase, the injection of L-dopa did not completely restore active avoidance. This seems to show that noradrenaline is more important than dopamine for active avoidance learning. Fuxe and Hanson (1967) reached the same conclusion in a histochemical study. They treated rats with alpha-methyltyrosine to prevent the synthesis of both dopamine and adrenaline, then tested them for four hours on the active avoidance task. When the animals were killed and their brains treated with fluorescent stain, these authors found that the noradrenaline terminals were more

TABLE 24.1

Some commonly Used Drugs and Their Actions on Transmitter Systems

Type of action	Transmitter system			
	Noradrenaline	Dopamine	5-Hydroxytryptamine	acetylcholine
Receptor stimulant (+)[a]	Isoprenaline Clonidine	Apomorphine ET 495[c]	Tryptamine	Oxotremorine Arecoline Carbachol
Receptor antagonist (−)[b]	Propranolol	Chlorpromazine	Lysergic acid-diethylamide	Scopolamine
	Chlorpromazine Phenoxybenzamine	Pimozide Clozapine Haloperidol	Methysergide	Atropine Benztropine
Inhibitor of uptake (+)	Cocaine Amitriptyline Desipramine	Cocaine Amphetamine	Chlorimipramine	—
Inhibitor of metabolic breakdown (+)	MAO inhibitors: pheniprazine, iproniazid, pargyline, tranylcypromine, phenelzine		Imipramine	Di-isopropylfluoro-phosphate (DFP) Physostigmine
Inhibitors of biosynthesis (−)	α-Methyl-p-tyrosine Disulphiram, FLA-63[d]	α-Methyl-p-tyrosine	p-Chlorophenylalanine	Hemicholinium
Displacing agent (+)	d-Amphetamine	d-Amphetamine 1-Amphetamine	—	—
Precursor (+)	L-DOPA	L-DOPA	L-5- Hydroxytryptophan	—
False transmitter (±)	α-Methyl-m-tyrosine α-Methyl DOPA, Metaraminol			
Depleting agent (−)	reserpine, tetrabenazine, and related substances			

[a](+) = stimulates or enhances actions of transmitter.
[b](−) = antagonizes or decreases actions of transmitter.
[c]ET 495 = 1-3,4-methylenedioxybenzyl-4(2-pyrimidye) piperazine.
[d]FLA 63 = bis (4 Methyl-1-homopiperazinyl thiocarbonyl) disulphide.
From Iversen and Iversen, 1975b.

severely depleted than the dopamine terminals. Hence it must have been the depletion of noradrenaline that brought about the active avoidance deficit; the animals could no longer appraise the shock cue as "bad." Actually, learning to avoid the shock requires not only an appraisal of the shock as bad but also a plan to avoid the expected shock (via dopaminergic imagination circuit).

Sessions et al. (1976) reported that a lesion of the locus coeruleus (whose cell bodies produce noradrenaline), reduced cortical noradrenaline but did not impair one-way active avoidance, passive shock avoidance, acquisition or extinction of a conditioned taste aversion, or acquisition of bar pressing for food reward. As mentioned before, the locus coeruleus is only one of the regions that contain NA-producing cells. Its axons reach into the thalamus, hippocampus, and cortex. While the lesion may have interfered with negative appraisals of things and actions, either present or recalled over the memory circuit, the lesioned animals could still expect harm and plan action, and could still appraise such action as good or suitable. Hence they could learn and retain what they learned, as reported by Sessions et al. The lesion did impair running in an L-runway for food reward, but this may have resulted from the reduced psychomotor activity reported in animals with lowered NA level (see Wålinder et al., 1976).

In recent years, alpha and beta adrenergic receptors have been discovered in the brain as well as in the peripheral sympathetic nervous system. Adrenaline and noradrenaline stimulate both alpha and beta receptors, but in different proportions. Beta stimulation produces a rise in blood pressure and an increase in heart rate that can be abolished by pretreatment with a beta receptor blocker. Intraventricular injection of a beta blocker produces prolonged low heart rate and low blood pressure. Beta blockers reduce anxiety, and improve spontaneous activity in submissive monkeys and shy children (Koella, 1977). Hence beta receptor stimulation seems to account for the excitatory effects of noradrenergic activity.

The Serotonin System.   (Fig. 24.9) has not been investigated as thoroughly as the noradrenaline system until comparatively recently. A symposium volume (Haber et al., 1981) gives an overview of research studies during the last fifteen years. Jacobs et al. (1974, 1977) reported that the median and dorsal nuclei of the raphé not only have different projections but different functions. The dorsal raphé projects to amygdala and striatum; the median raphé, to the lateral geniculate nucleus (ventral part), and to the hippocampus (see Fig. 24.10). Bilateral lesions of the median raphé in rats produced a long-lasting, up to fourfold increase in locomotor activity as well as the almost total depletion of serotonin in the hippocampus. Despite this increased activity, rats with such lesions were no more aggressive after repeated electrical foot shocks than they had been before. In contrast, lesions of the dorsal raphé produced a short depression of activity, followed by a gradual return to normal levels. The hippocampal serotonin level

5-HT pathways

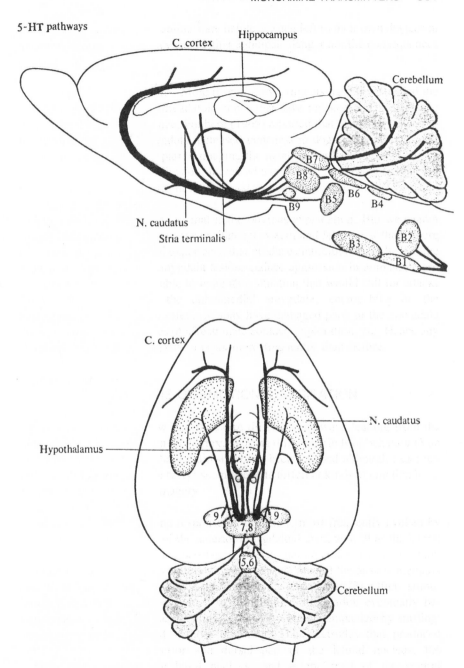

FIG. 24.9.   5-Hydroxytryptamine pathways shown in horizontal and sagittal projection. From Fuxe and Jonsson (1974).

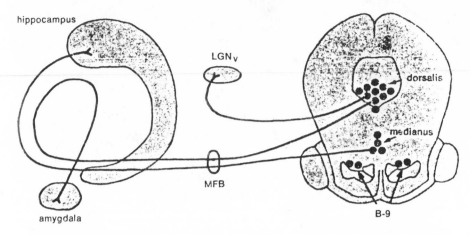

FIG. 24.10.   Projection of serotonin neurons. The axons of serotonin-containing neurons often project over great distances. Clusters of cell bodies *(dots)* of serotonin-containing neurons, both the dorsal and median raphe nuclei as well as the group of cells labeled B-9, are shown in cross section through the midbrain of the rat. Axons from these cell bodies ascend into the forebrain to make contact with structures such as the lateral geniculate nucleus (LGŇ, a portion of the visual system) and the hippocampus and amygdala (portions of the limbic system). The medial forebrain bundle (MFB) is one of the major pathways connecting the midbrain raphe neurons with their forebrain target cells. From B. L. Jacobs and M. E. Trulson, 1979.

was not affected significantly. However, these animals showed 83% more aggression after electrical foot shocks than before.

Karli et al. (1972) reported that the depletion of brain serotonin increased the aggression of rats and cats against other species, which is in accord with the findings of Jacobs et al. (1977). And Geyer (1978) confirmed the conclusions of Jacobs et al. that the larger dorsal and the smaller median raphé have not only different projections but different functions. He found that lesions of the median raphé increased startle and hyperactivity, reduced single alternation and antagonized morphine analgesia in rats. Injections of serotonin into the ventricles of rats decreased startle. The deficit in spontaneous alternation, reported by Geyer as a result of median raphé lesions, is also found after hippocampal lesions. Here, it seems to indicate the animals' difficulty in recalling whether the previous turn had proved successful.

According to my theory, lesions of the median raphé, which block serotonergic conduction to the hippocampus, would interfere with positive appraisals of remembered things and actions. The animals could no longer appraise anything they remembered as good, hence expected harm at every turn. Being apprehensive, they would tend to explore for possible danger — hence their increased activity. The situation is quite different after lesions of the dorsal raphé, which block serotonergic conduction to the amygdala and striatum. The activity level was depressed for a short time because the animals could no longer imagine possible actions.

But their memories of things and actions retained their habitual value, and the animals soon returned to their accustomed level of activity. They became increasingly aggressive after electrical foot shocks because they could no longer imagine anything pleasant happening to them; they expected the worst and attacked first.

Poschel and Ninteman (1971) pointed out that not the absolute level of a transmitter but the ratio of serotonin to other transmitters determines the response. When serotonergic activity dropped out after raphé lesions, activity in other neuron systems was found to increase. The same is true when the activity of raphé cells is inhibited by systemic injection of drugs like LSD or DMT (N,N-dimethyltryptamine), or by applying them directly to raphé cells by microiontophoresis. Serotonin also, so applied, inhibits the electrical activity of raphé cells. When neural activity drops out, whether through lesions or drug application, the postsynaptic neurons increase their activity because the presynaptic raphé cells normally inhibit their postsynaptic targets (Jacobs et al., 1977). That would imply that the axons of raphé cells can inhibit neurons using other transmitters, that is, neurons in the ACh, NA, and DA systems.

As Jacobs and Trulson (1979) have pointed out, we do not know the structures that project to the raphé. We do know that the dorsal raphé cells emit slow rhythmic electric discharges that hardly change during waking or slow wave sleep but cease almost completely during REM sleep (McGinty et al., 1973). But median and magnus raphé nuclei have more rapid discharges and reach their highest rate in REM sleep, their slowest rate in slow-wave sleep (Sheu et al., 1974). This striking rhythm can still be observed after complete transection of the brain rostral to the dorsal raphé nucleus and actually shows some increase in rate. Perhaps the slightly slower rate in intact animals is caused by the activity of forebrain structures; electrical stimulation of such structures has always produced inhibitory effects on raphé cells. This rhythmic discharge can still be seen in vitro, in 400 micron thick slabs of tissue containing the dorsal nucleus. This would suggest that this rhythm is a physiological discharge inherent in raphé cells (Jacobs et al., 1977).

Essman (1973) reported that electroshock given within 10 seconds of learning raised the serotonin content of hippocampus and cortex and interfered with a learned passive avoidance task. Intrahippocampal injection of serotonin, given within ten seconds of learning, also prevented recall and raised the serotonin content of the cortex. Interference with retention occurred to some extent even when the injection of serotonin was delayed for three minutes after training. Essman further found that these increases of cortical serotonin after hippocampal serotonin injection as well as after electroshock inhibit protein synthesis in cortex and limbic system. He suggested that this inhibition may cause the memory impairment.

As I have mentioned before, the underlying "memory substrate," which may well depend on protein synthesis, is not my concern in this work. What is relevant to this discussion is the fact that an increase in cerebral serotonin content, whether produced by electroshock or intrahippocampal injection, impairs passive avoidance. According to my theory, such an increase would bias appraisal so that the animal would make more positive than negative appraisals. This would reduce fear and malaise. Such animals would have little apprehension entering the chamber in which they had received a footshock shortly before. According to Essman, they entered the chamber within twenty seconds, while normal controls did not enter until 120 seconds had passed.

Not only fear but pain is counteracted by serotonin. Yunger and Harvey (1973) found that lesions of the medial forebrain bundle, which resulted in a reduction of serotonin in the forebrain, significantly increased reactions to pain. Treatment of the animals with the precursor of serotonin (DL–5–hydroxytryptophan) restored normal reactivity to pain. In general, it could be said that the effect of serotonergic excitation is relaxation and ease, in contrast to noradrenaline, which seems to be the transmitter in pathways that excite fear and aggression, and dopamine, which is connected with imagination and consequent activity.

HORMONES AND TRANSMITTERS

According to Telegdy and Kovács (1979), anterior and posterior pituitary hormones affect learning via aminergic mechanisms. Vasopressin facilitates passive avoidance by facilitating dopamine metabolism in the septum and striatum, while oxytocin facilitates extinction of active avoidance by decreasing noradrenaline and dopamine turnover in the striatum. Adrenocorticotrophic hormone (ACTH) improves passive avoidance and delays the extinction of active avoidance via an increased dopamine level in the striatum and midbrain. The local injection of dopamine receptor blockers into the substantia nigra prevents these behavioral effects. Small doses of corticosterone or raphé stimulation improve passive avoidance, while large doses or serotonin receptor blocking impair it. Hence vasopressin and ACTH apparently facilitate memory via the dopamine system, and small doses of corticosterone facilitate it over the serotonin system.

According to Hagino and Yamaoka (1976), estrogen or corticosterone activate both cholinergic and cholinoceptive noncholinergic neurons. Hence these hormones can affect both amygdala and hippocampus and so influence both imagination and memory. Since these hormones affect memory not directly but via the ACh and monoamine systems, we need have no further concern with hormone effects on memory as long as we can specify the effects of these transmitter systems on memory.

25 Neurotransmitters, the Reward System and Psychiatric Illness

The co-existence of so many transmitters of varying effectiveness and variable mechanisms demands that some theoretical assessment be attempted . . . . Clearly, nature could have devised a sophisticated and sensitive nervous system without this chemical redundancy . . . However, it is equally clear that this was not the way in which presently available nervous systems evolved. This fact, therefore, implies that some additional purposes must be served by the non-redundant properties of each transmitter substance . . .

It seems likely that when additional experimental results are available, it may be more appropriate to categorize the various chemical modes of transmitter actions along cytological or functional lines (e.g., special environmental or affective state monitoring circuits).

F. E. Bloom, 1974

THE NEUROPEPTIDES

The most recently discovered chemical messenger substances are molecules consisting of chains of amino acids: the neuropeptides.

The Enkephalins and Endorphins. These are neuropeptides, substances in the brain that seem to act like morphine and bind to sites at neuron receptor membranes. These opiate receptors were found by radioactive labeling of opiate compounds. The two enkephalins, methionine-enkephalin and leucine-enkephalin, are most heavily concentrated in the globus pallidus, which is five times richer in enkephalin than the next richest areas (central gray, nucleus accumbens, medial hypothalamus, and amygdala). They are found in lower concentrations in the brainstem, thalamus, septal area, other hypothalamic regions, and the hippocampus. They also occur in the spinal cord. (Kobayashi et al., 1977). They have been synthesized and are widely used in brain research. Both the enkephalins and the endorphins (which also act like morphine but are less effective than the enkephalins) are blocked by naloxone, a drug that blocks the binding of morphine to opiate receptors.

According to Belluzzi and Stein (1977), rats learned to press a bar that delivered one microliter of methionine-enkephalin or leucine-enkephalin into the brain ventricles. The rate of pressing was significantly higher for the enkephalins and for morphine than for Ringer's solution. Indeed, Ringer's solution soon stopped further bar pressing while the animals continued to press the bar for the enkephalins until they received up to ten milligram in 66 hours—a fluid intake into the ventricles that may have produced discomfort. Belluzzi and Stein pointed out that high concentrations of enkephalin have been found in brain sites that yield high rates of barpressing for electrical stimulation (e.g., pontine central gray, substantia nigra zona compacta, bed nucleus of the stria terminalis, and nucleus accumbens). Hence self-stimulation of these regions seems to depend at least partially on the release of enkephalin and the activation of opiate receptors. In a later test of this hypothesis, Belluzzi and Stein administered naloxone subcutaneously at weekly intervals immediately before testing the rats for self-stimulation, with the electrode in the central gray. They found dose-related decreases in the rate of barpressing in practically every case. Obviously, when the pleasurable effects of barpressing are reduced, self-stimulation is no longer desirable.

These authors also found a dose-related decrease of barpressing after different doses of diethyldithiocarbamate, which inhibits the synthesis of noradrenaline. When noradrenaline transmission is blocked, the animals feel no malaise, hence no desire to press the bar for surcease. The authors concluded that there are two different reward functions: "one corresponds to a state of incentive, and is the process by which behavior in pursuit of a goal is motivated and steered; this 'drive-inducing' reward function may be mediated by catecholamines. The second corresponds to a state of satisfaction or well being, and . . . (follows) the attainment (and consumption) of the goal; this 'drive-reducing' reward function may be mediated by an opiate peptide such as leucine-enkephalin" (1977, p. 558).

Belluzzi and Stein's suggestion is in line with my hypothesis that noradrenaline is the transmitter for negative appraisals that induce an impulse to action. Hunger or thirst is unpleasant and must be remedied. Anything annoying or threatening is "bad" and must be overcome or avoided. Malaise, however produced, can be overcome by activating relays in the serotonin system. This seems to be the true reward system, producing pleasure or satisfaction and reducing drive. Since activation of the serotonin system has morphine-like effects that can be counteracted by naloxone, and the enkephalins and endorphins have a similar action, it is possible that these peptides (in particular leucine-enkephalin) act as additional transmitters or neuromodulators affecting serotonergic nerves. The fact that fibers of the serotonin system are located in the same areas in which enkephalins and endorphins have been found, supports this suggestion.

Substance P. This substance is opposite in action to the enkephalins and endorphins. It is one of the neuropeptides, consisting of a chain of eleven amino acids, and is found in the brain but also in peripheral sensory nerves. Some of the sensory neurons, whose cell bodies lie in sensory ganglia along the spinal cord, contain substance P and release it at synapses with spinal cord neurons. Substance P is believed to be a transmitter from peripheral pain fibers to the central nervous system (Iversen, 1979).

According to Magnusson et al. (1976), synthetic substance P stimulates the formation of dopamine in the brain, but does not affect serotonin formation. When monoamine synthesis was blocked by a MAO inhibitor, synthetic substance P significantly accelerated the disappearance of dopamine, noradrenaline, and serotonin. Stimulation of dopamine formation by substance P would mean that the pain produced by substance P stimulates imagination, and that, in turn would increase fear. Enkephalin is found in small neurons in the same part of the spinal cord as substance P. It is known that enkephalin and opiate drugs can suppress the release of substance P from sensory fibers. Similar blocking of substance P by enkephalin may occur in the brain (Iversen, 1979).

According to Emson et al. (1977), substance P neurons in the medial habenula project to the ipsilateral ventral tegmental area, corresponding to the organization of dopamine dendrites. In the substantia nigra, the substance P projection also parallels the distribution of dopamine dendrites. Cholinergic neurons in the lateral habenula send efferents via the fasciculus retroflexus to the interpeduncular nucleus. Although medial and lateral habenulae are connected by substance P and cholinergic fibers, these fibers do not originate from the same neurons.

Hence it would seem that substance P influences the action of dopamine neurons and enkephalin influences the action of serotonergic neurons. Both noradrenergic and serotonergic fibers accompany the action circuit and the dopamine projection to the frontal lobe and are found in the spinal cord. I would suggest that noradrenergic and serotonergic pathways are part of the appraisal system and mediate the experience of pleasure and pain connected with sensory experience, with imagination and action.

PEA. Sabelli and his coworkers (1974) proposed that over and above the various transmitters in the brain, there are also many endogenous substances that modulate synaptic transmission. As one example, they mention 2–phenylethylamine (PEA), an endogenous amine found in the brain that, like amphetamine, produces wakefulness, alertness, EEG activation, and excitement. They point out that PEA is formed mainly by the decarboxylation of L-phenylalanine, hence its synthesis depends on the plasma levels of this substance, just as the rate of serotonin and noradrenaline synthesis seems to depend on the plasma levels of their amino acid precursors. PEA readily crosses the blood-brain barrier, so that PEA-sensitive neurons may be affected not only by brain PEA but also by PEA carried by the blood. PEA is found throughout the brain, including cortex and cerebellum. Sabelli et al. found that PEA affects the catecholamine system, sometimes increasing its effects but often counteracting them. For instance, exploratory activity in mice is decreased by noradrenaline and dopamine, but increased by PEA. According to Sabelli et al., PEA acts not only at synapses but also at non-synaptic sites. PEA levels in the brain are increased by antidepressants like pargyline and imipramine, and reduced by drugs that induce depression. On the basis of their investigations, these authors concluded that such antidepressants enhance the central effects of serotonin and PEA and block the action of acetylcholine and histamine. Since lowered PEA excretion is found in endogenous but not in reactive depression, they suggested that such a decrease is the primary cause of depressive illness.

In Parkinsonism, PEA excretion is also lowered. Normally, the striatum has a high concentration of PEA. Like amphetamine, PEA potentiates the stimulant effect of DOPA and can induce chorea-like movements in animals. These facts would suggest that PEA modulates the dopamine system. In terms of my theory, PEA would facilitate imagination. Together with serotonin, it would favor an optimistic frame of mind.

From this much abbreviated review we can conclude that the effect of brain transmitter systems on psychological activity can be explained on the basis of my theory. Relaxation, well-being, pleasure, and positive emotions seem to be mediated via the serotonin system, modulated by the enkephalins and endorphins; and pain, malaise, and negative emotions appear to be mediated by the noradrenaline system, modulated by substance P. Both systems seem to be part of the appraisal system, one mediating positive, the other negative appraisals. The dopamine system, modulated by substance PEA, seems to be part of the imagination circuit. Finally, cholinergic fibers with muscarinic slow action seem to mediate modality-specific recall; others, with nicotinic action, seem to be part of the action circuit.

Serotonergic and noradrenergic fibers are widely dispersed in the brain. They accompany sensory fibers via thalamic nuclei (sensory relay nuclei) to sensory cortical areas, and accompany dopaminergic fibers from the amygdala via the dorsomedial thalamic nucleus to the prefrontal cortex (Bloom, 1978). They are found in the reticular formation, olivary complex, cerebellum, and spinal cord, and project via ventral thalamic nuclei to premotor and motor cortex. Since both systems are part of the appraisal system, they are connected with the limbic appraisal areas. Hence they can provide the positive or negative feeling tone that accompanies all our experiences, all our actions.

The story of neurotransmitters is by no means complete. Many more have been identified and more are sure to be discovered. I have mentioned only those that have been investigated most thoroughly. While I am well aware that this area is still in flux and any suggestions must be tentative, I do believe that my interpretation of transmitter functions supports and is supported by the research findings discussed in earlier chapters.

NEUROTRANSMITTERS AND THE REWARD SYSTEM

In 1954, Olds and Milner reported that rats avidly press a bar for brain stimulation. They may do so continuously, hour after hour, until exhaustion sets in, if the stimulating electrodes are placed in particularly rewarding sites. During the years since that first report, many researchers have explored this phenomenon (Olds, 1956, 1960; Ray et al., 1968; Valenstein & Beer, 1964, and many others). They found that animals preferred brain stimulation at certain sites to food, provided stimulation was available continuously (Falk, 1961; Spies, 1965). Both rats and monkeys pressed a treadle for brain stimulation rather than another for food, actually starving themselves. Only one other reward has produced continuous responding for a long time—a mixture of saccharine and diluted sucrose (Valenstein et al., 1967). Like brain stimulation, this mixture does not produce repletion. Brain stimulation at other sites proved to be neutral or even aversive.

Reward sites in the brain include the hypothalamus, particularly the medial forebrain bundle, the amygdala, the entorhinal, retrosplenial, and cingulate cortex, the septal area, the caudate, thalamic reticular system and central gray, and the olfactory bulb (Gallistel, 1973), but also the medial frontal cortex, the pons, and medulla. All these areas are part of the medial appraisal system or connected with it (see chapter 17). Reward sites have been found in the rat but also in other animals and in the human being. Usually, the medial forebrain bundle has been the most rewarding site (Fig. 25.1, 25.2, 25.3).

In human beings, electrical stimulation of points in the ventromedial frontal lobe, hypothalamus, parts of the parietal and temporal lobe, and the upper midbrain produced ease and relaxation, smiling, and expressions of pleasure. Stimulation via electrodes in the septal areas produced sexual arousal, probably because the electrodes activated serotonin fibers from the anterior hypothalamus. Rewarding brain stimulation in the septal area has often suppressed pain for two to three days (German & Bowden, 1974).

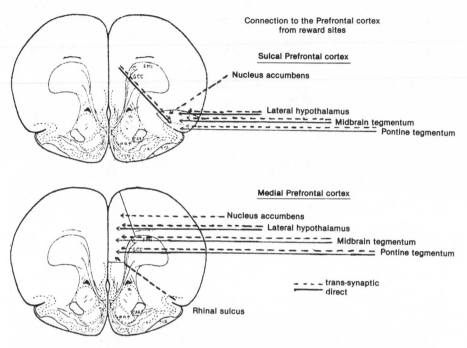

FIG. 25.1   Connections to the prefrontal cortex from reward sites in the rat. Recordings from single units in the prefrontal cortex showed that they were directly (solid line) or trans-synaptically (dashed line) activated from the different reward sites. The approximate extents of the medial and sulcal prefrontal cortices are indicated. Reprinted with permission from E. T. Rolls, *The Brain and Reward*. Copyright 1975, Pergamon Press, Ltd.

From human reports it is clear that electrical stimulation of some brain sites is pleasant and of others unpleasant. There is no reason to deny that animals have a similar experience. The sites reported coincide with the cortical, thalamic, and midbrain level of the appraisal system. The amygdala and its outflow, and the connections of the limbic system are a logical addition.

According to Olds (1977), brain stimulation can mediate drive (e.g., the animal approaches food and drink), reward (the animal keeps on pressing the bar), and aversion (the animal stops pressing the bar, or presses a bar that stops stimulation). Most stimulation sites produce mixed effects, but in far lateral and far medial areas of the hypothalamus, reward predominates. In areas in between, aversive and drive effects are about as frequent as reward (Olds, 1977).

If the electrode is in a drive center, the animal avidly approaches the drive object (food, water, mate) during stimulation, but as soon as the current is turned off, the animal stops. If the stimulating electrode is implanted in a reward center, the animal eagerly presses the bar. Indeed, rats cross an electrified grill and accept five times the shock level that would stop hungry animals from crossing to food—just to get to the bar to press for stimulation in a reward center in the lat-

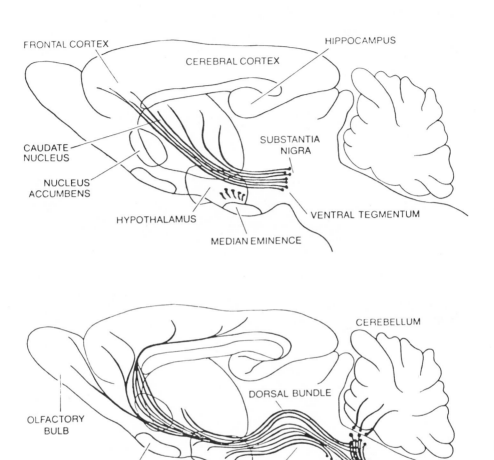

FIG. 25.2 NEUROTRANSMITTER PATHWAYS implicated in the reward system of the rat brain were mapped by fluorescence microscopy. The nerve cells that secrete dopamine (*top*) have their cell bodies concentrated in the substantia nigra and the ventral tegmentum of the midbrain; their axons project primarily to the caudate nucleus, the frontal cortex and the entorhinal cortex. The nerve cells that secrete norepinephrine (*bottom*) have their cell bodies localized primarily in the locus coeruleus of the brain stem; they project to the cerebellum, the cerebral cortex and the hypothalamus. Both the norepinephrine and the dopamine systems overlap much of the area that gives rise to self-stimulation behavior in rats. The dopamine fibers are found only in areas that mediate brain reward, whereas the norepinephrine fibers extend into other regions. This and other evidence points to a more critical role for dopamine in brain reward. From: A. Routtenberg, 1978.

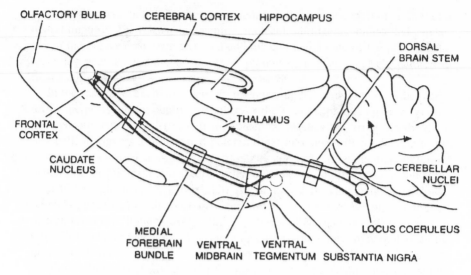

FIG. 25.3   PATHWAYS OF REWARD in the rat brain are outlined schematically in this longitudinal section. The pathways extend in both directions from nerve-cell bodies in the hindbrain, the midbrain and the frontal cortex, passing through the medial forebrain bundle in the hypothalamus. The circles indicate the locations of the cell bodies; the rectangles indicate regions where reliable self-stimulation behavior has been obtained in studies with the Skinner-box apparatus. From A. Routtenberg, 1978.

eral hypothalamus. With weaker stimulating current and the electrode implanted at different sites, animals could easily be stopped by a weak foot shock.

The effects of such self-stimulation do not last. The animal seems to forget over night, and may have to be "primed" by one or more stimulus trains the next day before it will press the bar for more stimulation. According to Gallistel (1969), reward stimulation is not necessarily the same as priming stimulation. He applied a stimulus train in the start box for priming, which induced the rat to run in the connecting alley to the goal box to press the pedal for brain stimulation over a different electrode. He achieved the best effects in animals with two implanted electrodes if he primed over one electrode and stimulated the other.

There is not much doubt that brain stimulation at reward sites is pleasurable, or that it is mediated by a specific "reward" system. The question widely disputed by investigators is the type of transmitter involved in this system. Many authors have insisted that the system that produces "reward behavior" is also the system that mediates reward (Olds, 1977; Stein, 1968; Stein & Wise, 1971; Routtenberg, 1978). Reward behavior, that is, bar pressing for brain stimulation, is facilitated by amphetamine and noradrenaline, whether injected systemically or into the brain ventricles. Intraventricular injection of 6–hydroxydopamine (6–OHD), which depletes brain catecholamines (but depletes NA more than it does DA, according to Uretsky & Iversen, 1969), reduces bar pressing for brain stimulation. Chronic injections of 6–OHD destroy noradrenaline terminals and block lever pressing for brain stimulation. Serotonin and serotonergic drugs also block such reward behavior. Hence Wise and Stein (1973) suggest that noradrenaline is the transmitter in the reward system while serotonin is the transmitter in a system mediating aversive effects.

But there is no reason why the system that induces reward behavior should also be the system mediating the reward. The intraventricular injection of noradrenaline is not itself rewarding, nor is the resulting activation of the noradrenaline system. If it were, the animal would have no need to press the bar for brain stimulation after the injection. The activation of the noradrenaline system produces malaise, which provides the impetus for bar pressing. Only when the animal has pressed the bar does it receive the reward in the form of brain stimulation. Hence the system that will induce bar pressing for brain stimulation must be a system that will arouse the animal and induce a state of malaise to motivate the animal to counteract it; and the system that mediates pleasure (reward) must be a system that can mitigate the malaise. Since the noradrenaline system increases reward behavior, it must be the serotonin system that provides relief and induces pleasure. Indeed, Poschel and Ninteman (1971) found that para-chloro-amphetamine, which releases serotonin from neural stores, suppressed self-stimulation shortly after administration. This effect was blocked by pretreatment with para-chlorophenylalanine, which blocks serotonin synthesis. These authors concluded that their results are incompatible with the adrenergic theory of reward, which ignores serotonin. I might add that the release of serotonin blocks bar pressing for brain stimulation because the animal has already received the reward via the drug-induced release of serotonin. In contrast, when serotonin synthesis is blocked, the animal experiences a malaise that induces bar pressing for the relief obtained by brain stimulation.

Stein et al. (1977) assume that the noradrenergic system is a reward system because injections of noradrenaline increase bar pressing for brain stimulation. From a variety of research reports they conclude that all three ascending noradrenaline paths (dorsal, ventral, and periventricular) are included in this reward system. They infer that serotonin mediates punishment and serotonin antagonists decrease the effect of punishment because such drugs induce animals to press a bar for sweet milk even when bar pressing is punished. In these experiments, hungry rats learned to press the bar for milk, obtained at infrequent intervals. During the punishment period, signaled by a tone, every bar press was rewarded—but also punished by a brief electrical foot shock. After several weeks of training, normal rats tended to stop responding as soon as they heard the tone. So did animals given chlorpromazine, amphetamine, or the specific noradrenaline blockers phentolamine and propranolol. But the benzodiazepines and other serotonin antagonists significantly increased punished responding because, as Stein et al. say, these drugs "reduce the effect of punishment."

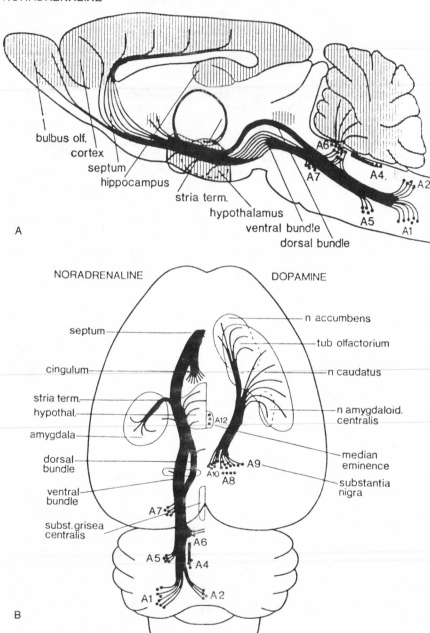

FIG. 25.4 Noradrenaline and dopamine systems in the rat (A) A lateral diagram of the rat's brain showing the major ascending norepinephrine system. (B) A dorsal view of the rat's brain showing the norepinephrine system (on the left-hand side) and the dopamine system (on the right-hand side). (From Ungerstedt, ©1971a.)

394

These facts can be interpreted differently. It is known that noradrenaline increases feeding. Noradrenaline antagonists should reduce the urge to feed, hence reduce punished responding. The benzodiazepines and other serotonin antagonists, according to my theory, block the pleasure of satiation, and so would increase the desire for food. With an increased urge to eat, the animal is willing to suffer the pain of shock to obtain milk, just as a female braves shock to cross to her young.

The excitation of "drive centers" in the hypothalamus seems to induce hunger, thirst, or sexual tension. With the drive object easily available, the animal can satisfy these impulses. Gallistel (1973) has argued that brain reward stimulation must provide a drive in addition to the reward, to induce the animal to continue bar pressing. He found that brain stimulation excites two kinds of neurons: one type with a refractory period around one millisecond, which seems responsible for the drive effect, and another with a refractory period of 0.5 to 0.6 milliseconds, which seems to mediate the reward effect. Psychologically speaking, the reward (felt pleasure) is derived from the appraisal that the experience mediated via the electrical current is good to have; and the drive, from the appraisal that bar pressing for more of the same is good to do. That the pleasure itself and the desire for it are mediated by different neurons and different neuron systems is exactly what I am suggesting.

As Olds (1977) points out, far lateral and far medial hypothalamic sites are predominantly reward sites. Both contain serotonergic fibers (Fig. 24.8, 24.9, 25.4). The area between lateral and medial sites, which may have reward, drive, or aversive effects, contain noradrenergic, serotonergic, and cholinergic fibers. Noradrenergic fibers seem to mediate a feeling of malaise, an aversive effect; cholinergic fibers may produce a drive state. Hence aversive and drive effects predominated, according to Olds, when the stimulating electrodes were in this area.

In the far lateral hypothalamic area, electrical stimulation is again mostly rewarding (Fig. 25.5). Ventrally, this area contains serotonin fibers; dorsally, dopamine fibers leading to the amygdala and striatum. Lesions in the lateral hypothalamus and the substantia nigra (the origin of the bundle of dopamine fibers) resulted in a loss of bar pressing for brain stimulation.

According to Routtenberg and Santos-Anderson (1977), bilateral lesions of the locus coeruleus, which contains the cell bodies of the noradrenaline axons, did not reduce bar pressing for brain stimulation when the electrode was in the brachium conjunctivum, although these lesions reduced the noradrenaline content in the cerebral cortex by 85%. Such lesions did, however, reduce bar pressing when the electrodes were in the medial forebrain bundle (Fig. 25.6). Lesions in the medial forebrain bundle revealed fiber degeneration running caudally through the stimulation site in the brachium conjunctivum. Degenerating axons were also found running rostrally through the medial forebrain bundle to the frontal cortex. Electrode sites in the ventromedial frontal cortex provided re-

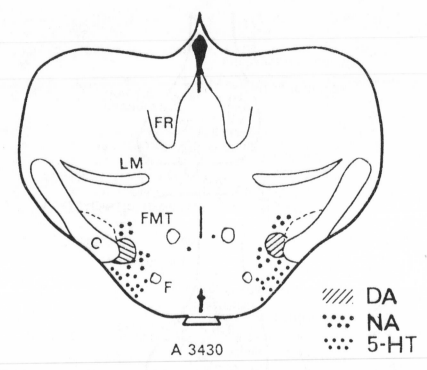

FIG. 25.5   Schematic illustration of the ascending monomine bundles in the lateral hypothalamic area. The 5-HT fibers are found mainly in the ventrolateral part and the NE (NA) fibers in the dorsolateral part of the lateral hypothalamic area. Some NE fibers to the cortex cerebri are found dorsal of the DA bundles to the telencephalon. From Fuxe & Jonsson, 1974.

warding stimulation while sites in the dorsomedial and lateromedial frontal cortex did not. Other data suggested that the pathway involved extends between frontal cortex and midbrain. Another site that produced reward was at the lateral edge of the frontal cortex, just above the rhinal sulcus (similar to the insula in primates). This pathway also projects caudally through the medial forebrain bundle to the brainstem.

However, Routtenberg and Santos-Anderson mentioned that the frontal cortex does not seem necessary for rewarding brain stimulation. Radical frontal ablation or complete decortication did not block the rewarding effect of posterior hypothalamic stimulation: decorticated animals learned to lift their head when rewarded with such brain stimulation. Hence the authors concluded that the medial thalamus as well as the frontal cortex can mediate the rewarding effect of brain stimulation and that the pathway involved seems to include both descending and ascending fibers.

To identify the fiber tracts involved, let us sketch the sequence of activities involved in bar pressing for brain stimulation. The "priming" stimulus reminds

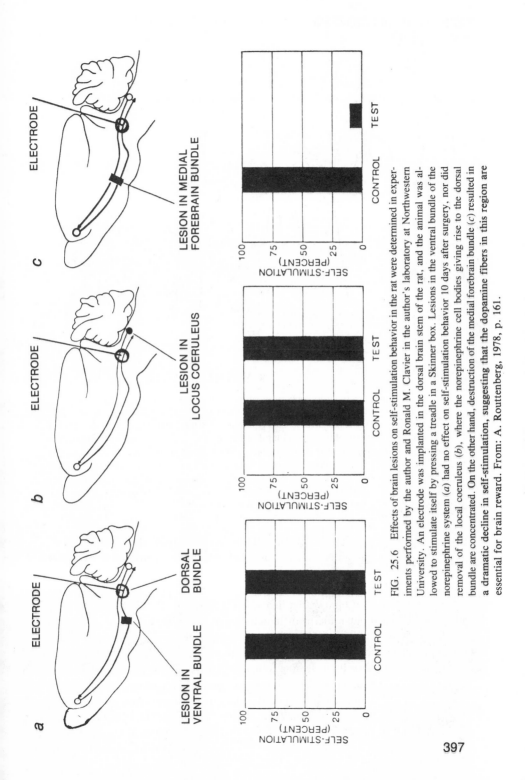

FIG. 25.6   Effects of brain lesions on self-stimulation behavior in the rat were determined in experiments performed by the author and Ronald M. Clavier in the author's laboratory at Northwestern University. An electrode was implanted in the dorsal brain stem of the rat, and the animal was allowed to stimulate itself by pressing a treadle in a Skinner box. Lesions in the ventral bundle of the norepinephrine system (*a*) had no effect on self-stimulation behavior 10 days after surgery, nor did removal of the local coeruleus (*b*), where the norepinephrine cell bodies giving rise to the dorsal bundle are concentrated. On the other hand, destruction of the medial forebrain bundle (*c*) resulted in a dramatic decline in self-stimulation, suggesting that the dopamine fibers in this region are essential for brain reward. From: A. Routtenberg, 1978, p. 161.

the animal of the pleasure obtained by bar pressing and arouses the impulse to press it (from anterior limbic cortex via hippocampus/fornix to midbrain, returning via cerebellum, thalamus and hypothalamus to the cortex (see chapters 26–28). Noradrenaline and dopamine fibers in the medial forebrain bundle relay excitation to the posterior orbital area, which urges action via the motor cortex. When the bar is pressed, the electrode site is excited and relays excitation to the posterior orbital and insular cortex via serotonin fibers, mediating a positive appraisal, felt as pleasure. There are also direct connections from posterior orbital and insular cortex via midbrain and cerebellum to motor cortex that can be activated even without the detour via hippocampus during strictly instinctive actions. Serotonergic fibers accompany the brachium conjunctivum to the ventral anterior nuclei, connecting with septal area and medial orbital cortex as well as the insula. As I have mentioned before, every pathway, sensory or motor, whether engaged in sensation, recall, imagination or intention to action, seems to be accompanied by both noradrenaline and serotonin fibers, so that sensory impressions, memory, and fantasy images as well as motor images and planned action may be appraised as pleasant or unpleasant, and may arouse positive or negative feelings.

Brain stimulation can produce pleasure even after cortical ablation because the appraisal system mediates a simple qualitative appraisal even on the thalamic level (see chapter 17). Just like the experience of diffuse unlocalized pain (thalamic pain), pleasure also can be mediated on the thalamic level via medial thalamic nuclei.

Routtenberg (1978) found that the dopaminergic pathway participates in the reward system. He found that electrical stimulation of the medial forebrain bundle, substantia nigra, or medial frontal cortex (all of them reward sites) when applied during learning of a simple task, impaired the animal's performance 24 hours later. Stimulation of the locus coeruleus, the origin of adrenergic neurons, had no effect. The dopamine system has its cell bodies in the ventral tegmentum near the substantia nigra and projects to striatum, amygdala, and via the amygdala to the septal area and the medial frontal cortex. The medial forebrain bundle connects the nonadrenaline and serotonin pathways with the amygdala and the striatum. When these areas are stimulated during learning, the dopaminergic imagination circuit is preempted by the stimulating current. Hence the animal cannot imagine what to do and has to depend entirely on motor memory. Since the task is simple, it can be learned in this way. But when set to repeat its performance at next day's test trial, the animal now imagines what to do instead of letting motor memory guide it. This is an instance of "state-dependent" learning. The animal had learned with the imagination circuit excluded and could not perform next day when it had full use of it. Its untrained imagination interfered with intact motor memory.

Dopaminergic fibers seem to mediate images of food, water, mate, and the action to be taken. They mediate a "drive effect," the impulse to approach what is appraised as good. But a drive effect should also be produced by stimulating the action circuit. Indeed, activating the nicotinic ACh receptors enhances bar pressing for brain stimulation and so does nicotine (German & Bowden, 1974). According to my theory, this amounts to stimulating the action circuit. However, according to these authors, nicotine does not facilitate bar pressing if the catecholamine stores are depleted by pretreatment with reserpine. In other words, action may be facilitated by nicotine; but only when animals need comfort or relaxation do they press the bar for brain stimulation.

According to Ito (1972), lateral hypothalamic cells are suppressed rather than excited by brain reward stimulation. In contrast, these neurons were active during morphine withdrawal and were suppressed when morphine was given to addicted animals (Kerr et al., 1974). During withdrawal, man or animal is distressed and wants relief—hence we would expect that both noradrenaline and dopamine fibers would be activated. If these fibers are suppressed during rewarding brain stimulation, they cannot be the fibers mediating pleasure. Olds (1977) found noradrenaline and dopamine neurons active in hungry animals— again, during a state of distress. They became even more active when the cue signal appeared and action was imminent. During eating, all electrical potentials in these neurons were suppressed.

Routtenberg (1978) and his coworkers found that drugs that raise the level of dopamine and noradrenaline in the brain (e.g., amphetamine) facilitate bar pressing for brain stimulation: Drugs that lower these levels (e.g., chlorpromazine) reduce such bar pressing. They also found that the dorsal (but not the ventral) noradrenaline bundle is associated with self-stimulation. However, the almost total destruction of the locus coeruleus, the site of noradrenaline-producing cell bodies, did not affect the rate of self-stimulation. But a lesion of the medial forebrain bundle which contains fibers of the dopamine, noradrenaline and serotonin systems, resulted in a dramatic decline (Fig. 25.6). That may mean, as Routtenberg says, that the noradrenaline system is associated with self-stimulation but not necessary for it. It may also mean that a lesion of the locus coeruleus does not stop all noradrenergic transmission; or even, that the lesion has interrupted conduction from the forebrain to the brainstem.

Since a lesion of the ventral tegmentum and the substantia nigra (which contains dopamine neurons) blocks self-stimulation, Routtenberg suggests that it is the dopamine, not the adrenaline system that is necessary for self-stimulation. He points to the fact that dopamine fibers are concentrated in the medial and sulcal frontal cortex, precisely the areas that produce reward on stimulation. Moreover, when haloperidol, which selectively blocks dopamine transmission, is injected into the caudate, self-stimulation stops.

Routtenberg, like many others, does not distinguish between the system that mediates "reward behavior," inducing the animal to press the bar for brain stimulation, and the system that mediates reward. Activation of the dopamine system may lead to increased imagination of what to do to obtain reward (pleasure).

Blocking dopamine transmission means that imagination is blocked so that the animal can no longer plan what to do. Noradrenergic pathways are associated with reward behavior because their activation results in malaise and an urge to find relief. Dopamine pathways are associated with reward behavior because their activation leads the animal to imagine what is required to relieve its malaise and what could be done about it. But the brain stimulation experienced when the animal presses the bar seems to mediate pleasure via the serotonin system.

Altogether, these findings allow the inference that serotonin is the transmitter in a system that mediates positive appraisals experienced as liking or pleasure, while the noradrenergic neural system mediates negative appraisals, experienced as malaise, fear or anger, depending on the appraisal of the situation. The report of Gromova et al. (1976), that conditioning under emotionally negative states depends primarily on the activation of the noradrenergic system while conditioning under emotionally positive states is tied to the activation of the serotonergic system, is completely in accord with this suggestion.

NEUROTRANSMITTERS AND PSYCHIATRIC ILLNESS

If serotonin and noradrenaline are transmitters in the appraisal system, and dopamine is the transmitter in the imagination circuit, as I have suggested, some psychiatric disorders could be explained as malfunctions in these systems. For instance, schizophrenic patients show paranoid suspiciousnes, have hallucinations and delusions. In schizophrenia, the patient seems to have involuntary visual and particularly auditory fantasy images (e.g., voices telling him what to do, or talking about him), so that he has the feeling that it is somebody else talking. As a result, the patient appraises such hallucinations as real. Paranoid suspiciousness seems to be based on biased appraisals: The appraisal system seems to be slanted toward negative appraisals, so that everything threatens harm—which arouses fear or anger. In delusions, the appraisal system itself seems to be disordered, so that the patient may find that rags are robes fit for a king, or believe himself to be Napoleon or Jesus Christ. In delusions and paranoia, the disordered appraisal is accompanied by an imaginative reconstruction of reality, a secondary attempt to explain the disordered appraisal. In hallucinations, the primary malfunction may be in the dopaminergic imagination circuit, although the limbic appraisal system may also show disordered function. In paranoia, the noradrenaline system should be overactive, according to my theory, while the serotonin turnover should be deficient. In patients with well-formed delusional systems, I would suspect that various limbic regions might be affected. However, the imagination circuit should be overactive, both in paranoia and in delusions.

In recent years, many investigators have delved into the connection between neurotransmitters and psychiatric disease. Many reports seem to support my suggestions.

Biogenic Amines and Schizophrenia. Iversen (1979) found an abnormally high concentration of dopamine and dopamine receptors in the brains of deceased schizophrenics, particularly in the limbic system. Chlorpromazine and haloperidol, drugs used in the treatment of schizophrenia, bind tightly to dopamine receptors in the brain and so prevent the natural transmitter, dopamine, from activating these receptors, so reducing imagination. Iversen suggests that in this disease the dopamine terminals may produce an excess of dopamine, or alternatively, that the dopamine receptors respond excessively. The high concentration of dopamine and dopamine receptors in the limbic system suggests either increased dopamine turnover and thus overactive imagination, which would fit most kinds of schizophrenia; or an excess of dopamine that would decrease conduction in the imagination circuit, explaining the blandness of hebephrenic schizophrenia.

According to Birkmayer et al. (1977), dopamine psychosis (i.e., the psychosis sometimes produced by long-time dopamine therapy for Parkinsonism) is characterized by an increase in the dopamine and noradrenaline level found in the gyrus cinguli, while an increased serotonin level is confined to raphé and substantia nigra. According to my theory, a raised level of dopamine and noradrenaline in the anterior cingulate gyrus would mean that imagined actions are increasingly appraised as unsuitable or unpleasant; thus planned movements would be slow and awkward. An excess of dopamine and noradrenaline would mean that planned movement could no longer be appraised; this might lead to the involuntary bizarre and repetitive movements of the catatonic. Abnormal functioning of the posterior cingulate would mean that somatic sensations would not be appraised as familiar but as strange and unpleasant—hence various somatic delusions. Should other limbic cortical regions be similarly affected, this might account for schizophrenic delusions in other modalities; for instance, friends not recognized, or various things experienced as strange. An increased serotonin level confined to the serotonin-producing cell bodies in the raphé would mean that serotonin is not transported along serotonergic nerves; such a condition would reduce positive appraisals, thus accounting for paranoid suspiciousness, the general malaise and unhappiness so striking in psychotic patients.

Stein and Wise (1971) and Wise and Stein (1973) reported that dopamine-beta-hydroxylase (DBH), the enzyme responsible for the final step in converting dopamine to noradrenaline, was significantly reduced in the brains of deceased schizophrenics as compared to normal brains. This reduction was somewhat more pronounced in hippocampus and diencephalon. They suggested that an aberrant psychotogenic metabolite, 6–hydroxydopamine, is formed from dopamine in schizophrenia and depletes brain catecholamines—noradrenaline more so than dopamine. This, they think, explains the antipsychotic action of chlorpromazine, which blocks the access of 6–hydroxydopamine to noradrenergic receptors.

These authors assume that the noradrenergic system is a reward system because noradrenaline increases brain self-stimulation in rats. They suggest that the lack of reward experienced by schizophrenics accounts for their lack of goal directed behavior. Earlier in this chapter I have shown that reward behavior (which is mediated by noradrenergic pathways) leads to rewarding brain stimulation; but the neurons providing reward do not belong to the noradrenergic system. The observed reduction of DBH in the brains of deceased schizophrenics may well indicate that noradrenergic terminals have stopped functioning. But the reduction of these terminals would account for the bland affect of the schizophrenic rather than for his lack of rewarding experiences.

The therapeutic effect of psychoactive drugs like chlorpromazine in the treatment of schizophrenia speaks for an overactivity of the catecholamine system in schizophrenia. Neuroleptics like chlorpromazine reduce the transmission in catecholamine systems, either by inhibiting the uptake of the transmitter by postsynaptic receptors, or by reducing the amount of transmitter available (see Table 24.1). All neuroleptics reduce transmission in dopaminergic and noradrenergic neurons, but to a different extent and over different mechanisms. They reduce agitation, anxiety, and disordered perception and judgment. They do not seem to affect serotonin transmission (van Praag, 1977).

Chlorpromazine and haloperidol, both receptor inhibitors, reduce dopamine and noradrenaline transmission but produce a compensatory increase in turnover, which subsides after three weeks. According to van Praag (1977), this may explain the fact that medication is not effective immediately but takes a few weeks, occurring at a time when the synthesis of catecholamines is normal but the postsynaptic receptors are blocked. The reduction of catecholamine transmission is significantly correlated with the reduction of delusions, hallucinations, and anxiety, the typical psychotic syndrome.

Patients with a comparatively low level of dopamine turnover before medication often developed Parkinson-like symptoms. Hence it has been suggested that Parkinsonism is connected with a low level of dopamine turnover, schizophrenia with a high level. Since chlorpromazine and similar neuroleptics reduce not only dopamine but also noradrenaline transmission, I would suggest that neuroleptics counteract not only the intensity of imaginative activity but also the bias toward inappropriate and negative appraisals of such images. However, the methods used in assessing dopamine transmission reflect mainly dopamine turnover in the nigrostriatal dopamine system. Van Praag suggests and my theory certainly implies that the dopamine transmission in the limbic system is of far greater importance for psychotic symptoms. Birkmayer et al. (1977) have made a beginning in determining an elevated dopamine level in the cingulate gyrus; but the dopamine level in the sensory limbic area, so far unreported, might be decisive for hallucinations and delusions.

On the basis of neurological and EEG examinations of schizophrenic patients, Stevens (1977) suggested impaired functioning in the mesencephalic nuclei in the ventral tegmental area. Application of microamounts of bicuculline, a GABA blocking agent, to these cells in freely moving cats resulted in an extraordinary state of intense arousal, with staring, fear, withdrawal, waxy flexibility, searching, and sniffing, accompanied by EEG spikes limited to the terminals of the dopamine projection from ventral tegmental nuclei to the amygdala and the nucleus accumbens, the same regions from which spiking has been reported in schizophrenics. Following such application of bicuculline, Stevens noticed the activation of tyrosine hydroxylase in the ipsilateral nucleus accumbens, a sign of dopamine synthesis.

When bicuculline was applied to the substantia nigra, spiking occurred in the caudate nucleus, together with ipsilateral circling, self-biting and grooming. In both areas, the reduction of GABA apparently released dopaminergic relays. If GABA is reduced in the ventral tegmental area of schizophrenics, Stevens suggests that this reduction might also account for the disinhibition of raphé cells, resulting in the high serotonin level found in Parkinson patients who died during L-dopa psychosis (Birkmayer, et al., 1977).

According to Kety and his coworkers (Pollin et al., 1961), tryptophan (forerunner of serotonin) combined with the MAO inhibitor iproniazid produced increased psychotic behavior in schizophrenics, which represents either a "biochemically induced acute flare-up of a schizophrenic process . . . or a toxic delirium superimposed upon chronic schizophrenia." Himwich and Narasimhachari (1974) repeated Kety's study but used L-cysteine as the amino acid and tranylcypromine as the MAO inhibitor. They found three psychotogenic compounds in the urine of schizophrenics and none in that of normals: N,N-dimethyltryptamine (DMT), bufotenin, and 5–methoxy-N,N-dimethyltryptamine (5MeODMT). This treatment increased the psychotic symptoms in schizophrenics but did not affect the behavior of normals. Himwich and Narasimhachari pointed out that an enzyme converting tryptophan into DMT and serotonin into bufotenin has been found in the brains of human beings as well as of several animal species. They implied that such conversion occurs in schizophrenics and is stopped by psychoactive drugs, like chlorpromazine or haloperidol. Simply discontinuing these drugs used in the treatment of schizophrenics also produced an aggravation of symptoms and the appearance of bufotenin and DMT in the urine. These reports make it likely that the conversion of tryptophan and serotonin into psychotogenic substances, together with the increased activity of noradrenergic and dopaminergic pathways could account for schizophrenic symptoms.

Biogenic Amines and Depression. Since the mid-sixties, an extensive literature has grown up discussing the possible role of biogenic amines in depressive illness (Bunney & Gulley, 1978). Reserpine, often used to combat hypertension, precipitated depression in 13–15% of patients; hence many investigators connected the resulting depletion of biogenic amines (dopamine, noradrenaline, serotonin) in the brain with the appearance of depression. American investigators usually ascribed depression to a deficiency of catecholamines, while European authors were more inclined to trace depression to a serotonin deficiency. The catecholamine hypothesis of depression assumed that unipolar depression results from a decrease in brain catecholamines while mania, the opposite of "bipolar" depression, results from an increase in these amines. The indoleamine hypothesis assumes that depression is caused by a decrease in brain indoleamines (mainly serotonin). More recently, Prange (1973) with his coworkers (Prange et al., 1974) have developed the "biogenic amine permissive hypothesis," according to which, depression occurs when a deficiency of brain serotonin becomes paired with a decrease of brain catecholamines; while mania is the result of indoleamine deficiency coupled with an increase in brain catecholamines (see Table 25.1). Gradually, the notion of a serotonin rather than a catecholamine deficiency in depression seems to be gaining ground (Akiskal & McKinney, 1975; Andén et al., 1971; Lapin & Oxenkrug, 1969) because an increasing number of research findings have shown that serotonin depletion in the brain is associated with depression (Shopsin et al., 1974, 1975; Wålinder, 1976; Wålinder et al., 1976). For instance, the antidepressant action of MAO inhibitors, which prevent the presynaptic reuptake of biogenic amines, is enhanced by tryptophan and 5–HTP, the precursors of serotonin, but not by L-Dopa, the precusor of dopamine and noradrenaline. Also, there seems to be a correlation of the antidepressant effect of niamid, a MAO inhibitor, with the degree of brain serotonin increase. The administration of tryptophan, the serotonin precursor, together with a MAO inhibitor, results in an elevation of mood rather than a change in motor activity, but it has resulted in substantial improvement even in severe depression (Lapin & Oxenkrug, 1969). On the other hand, L-Dopa results in increased motor activity

TABLE 25.1.
Biogenic Amine Hypotheses of Depressive Illness Comparison

Hypothesis	Predisposition	Melancholia	Mania
Catecholamine	(Unspecified)	Decrease in catecholamines	Increase in catecholamines
Indoleamine	(Unspecified)	Decrease in indoleamines	(Unspecified)
Biogenic amine permissive hypothesis	Indoleaminergic deficiency; normal level of catecholamines	Indoleaminergic deficiency; decrease in catecholamines	Indoleaminergic deficiency; increase in catecholamines

From Akiskal and McKinney, 1975.

without lifting the depression. It is useful in so-called retarded depression, in patients whose activity level is severely reduced. (Akiskal & McKinney, 1975). Levo-dopa treatment, useful in Parkinsonism, may result in depression, hypomania, and delirium. The treatment of agitated depression with L-dopa may cause a switch to hypomania without any lifting of the depression (Akiskal & McKinney, 1975). The noradrenaline level also seems to be involved in the motor activity that goes with agitated depression.

Birkmayer et al. (1977) found a significant decrease in the serotonin content of the amygdala, raphé, and substantia nigra in the brains of depressed patients. The dopamine level in the caudate nucleus of depressed patients was lower than that of normal controls. Serotonin deficiency seems to account for the depression of mood; the low dopamine level in the caudate and probably the amygdala, for the low level of motor imagination. According to Birkmayer et al., the low dopamine level in the caudate may account for the loss of drive and initiative— which is consistent with my suggestion: without motor imagination, no initiative or drive.

It seems, then, that a decrease of activity in the serotonin system may produce depression; and a simultaneous decrease in dopaminergic activity, retarded depression. Since serotonin-using fibers must be excited before serotonin can be released from the presynaptic vesicles, increased activity in the serotonin system means increased positive appraisals, according to my theory. When appraisals become increasingly negative after a loss of love or possessions, noradrenergic excitation dominates and results in grief and depression. Imagination is reduced or at best restricted to painful brooding. The difference between such a reactive depression and an endogenous depression lies in the temporal sequence of psychological and neurophysiological activity. In reactive depression, concentrating on painful images in disappointment or grief leads to dominant NA and DA excitation. In endogenous depression, the changes in transmitter turnover would cause rather than follow the increasingly pessimistic appraisals. In agitated depression, there seems to be increased dopaminergic as well as noradrenergic activation, resulting in negatively toned images that produce the agitated restlessness peculiar to this illness.

Serotonin and LSD.   Lysergic acid diethylamide (LSD), like serotonin itself, depresses raphé activity, which counteracts the inhibition normally exercised by raphé axons on other neurons. Other hallucinogens producing a similar effect (DMT, psilocin)—also depress raphé activity. In fact, drugs that decrease brain serotonin levels potentiate the effect of LSD; and drugs that increase brain serotonin levels reduce it.

Jacobs and his coworkers (1976) found that LSD activated the dopamine system while psilocin and similar indole nucleus drugs did not. When patients who were having "bad trips" after LSD were given dopamine receptor blockers (e.g. chlorpromazine) they reported reduced intensity but continued presence of hallucinations. Apparently, the reduction of raphé axon activity after LSD, which lifts the inhibition on dopamine neurons is sufficient to maintain fantasy images and thus hallucinations.

Serotonin and Morphine.   Apparently, the serotonin system mediates the effect of morphine and other opium derivatives (Somjen, 1978). Electrical stimulation of the periaqueductal gray and the midbrain raphé suppresses pain. This effect is reversed by naloxone, a morphine antagonist. It is well known that morphine not only abolishes pain but also produces a kind of elation, a "high." This is exactly what we would expect if the serotonin system mediated positive appraisals, experienced as pleasure or liking. After painful stimulation, intravenous morphine depresses the firing of the fine C and A-delta "pain" fibers of the spinal cord (Le Bars et al., 1978). It does not affect responses to light touch or stroking and may even enhance them (Belcher & Ryall, 1978). Since naloxone, the morphine antagonist, does not reverse the depressed firing of pain fibers, Le Bars et al. infer a direct action of morphine on these fibers. However, the serotonin system is also involved in the depression of pain fibers. Microinjections of serotonin depress the spinothalamic neurons that respond to various intensities of touch, from stroking to pinching (Jordan et al., 1978). Moreover, when the spinal level of serotonin is lowered while the brainstem level is maintained, morphine analgesia is reduced. Apparently, the brainstem raphé nuclei inhibit the spinothalamic "pain" neurons. Indeed, electrical stimulation of these nuclei produces analgesia; their ablation prevents the analgesia produced by morphine (Wolstencroft et al., 1978). When Haigler (1978) recorded potentials in the brainstem raphé via implanted electrodes, he found that painful stimuli inhibit most brainstem raphé cells, leave less than a third unaffected, and excite less than a third. Contrary to expectation, the iontophoretic application of serotonin to these nuclei did not excite these cells but inhibited some and left others unaffected. Intravenous or locally applied serotonin inhibited all cells in the midbrain raphé. Electrical stimulation of the dorsal and median raphé, the two midbrain raphé nuclei, excites the brainstem raphé, and so does stimulation of the periaqueductal gray. The analgesia produced by such stimulation probably acts via the brainstem raphé nuclei, which send serotoninergic relays to the spinal cord.

It seems likely that the circuit affected by morphine has an afferent as well as an efferent link. The afferent link seems to be part of the medial appraisal system, which consists of fine afferent fibers (see chapter 17). Morphine depresses the pain fibers directly but seems to excite fibers that mediate a positive appraisal of touch or stroking. This afferent appraisal system seems to make contact with the midbrain raphé, the medial thalamus, limbic cortex, and hippocampus. Thus Hill and Pepper (1978) found that morphine reduced the increased firing of neurons in the medial thalamus after painful stimuli. The morphine antagonist naloxone prevented this effect. And Siggins and coworkers (1978) reported that morphine excites the hippocampal pyramid cells, an effect that is antagonized by naloxone. This connection of the raphé complex with the limbic system and hippocampus seems to mediate the positive appraisal of the bodily state after morphine, inducing a feeling of well-being, ease, and relaxation. Via the hippocampus, fornix and midbrain, fibers of the action circuit seem to connect with the periaqueductal gray, the midbrain, and brainstem raphé, and the spinal cord. Vinogradova (1975) actually reported that electrical stimulation of the hippocampus (field CA 3) produced short latency (15–25 msec) spike potentials in the raphé, with longer latencies (30–40 msec) in the midbrain reticular formation. Since microinjections of serotonin in the midbrain raphé inhibit all cells and microinjections in the brainstem raphé inhibit most of them, it is quite likely that the fibers of the action circuit connecting with the raphé do not use serotonin as transmitter, but acetylcholine.

26

The Action Circuit: Ascending and Descending Links; Activation-Depression

THE ACTION CIRCUIT: DESCENDING LINK

In my theory, I am assuming that every goal-directed action is initiated by an appraisal of the situation. This appraisal is mediated by various cortical limbic regions which send relays simultaneously to the striatum and substantia nigra to prime the action circuit, and to the hippocampus to initiate the intention for action. This intention is an action impulse initiated by the hippocampus and patterned at various stages of the action circuit to terminate in the frontal lobe. The descending link of the action circuit includes the postcommissural fornix, the mamillary bodies and the mamillo-tegmental tract to the midbrain tegmentum (See Fig. 13.3).

The Midbrain or Mesencephalon

This structure includes the anterior and posterior colliculi dorsally, and reaches from the mamillary bodies to the pons ventrally. Its most dorsal region contains the colliculi and is covered by the tectum. The next ventral layer is the tegmentum, which contains the cerebral aqueduct and surrounding central gray, the reticular nuclei, the red nucleus, interpeduncular nucleus, and substantia nigra. In the most ventral part of the midbrain course many fibers of passage, some within the cerebral peduncles, some dorsal to them. Near the midline in the tegmentum are the oculomotor and trochlear nuclei.

The central gray is continuous with the central nucleus of the inferior colliculus. Rostrally, it continues into the diencephalic central gray and caudally, into the pontine periventricular gray. The small, poorly myelinated fibers of the dorsal longitudinal fasciculus of Schütz run throughout the central gray just ventral to the aqueduct and fourth ventricle and connect with the midbrain tectum and the thalamus. The central gray also has connections to cortical limbic and motor areas, to the thalamic limbic nuclei, and to the hypothalamic nuclei. Because of these widespread connections, Clara (1959) calls the central gray "the functional center of the organism and the bridge between mental and physical processes." In my theory, the central gray is the brainstem level of the appraisal system, connected both with the spinal and cortical levels. For this reason, lesions of the central gray and the regions in immediate contact have a profound effect on behavior.

The reticular nuclei in the midbrain are part of the reticular formation, which stretches from the lateral medulla oblongata through the tegmentum of pons and midbrain into the thalamic reticular nucleus. The midbrain reticular nuclei seem to have developed partly from the alar and partly from the basal plate, hence seem to have partly sensory and partly motor functions. I would suggest that the dorsal reticular nuclei are relay stations of the modality-specific memory circuit projecting to the sensory thalamic nuclei and cortical memory areas. The nuclei derived from the basal plate are relay stations from postcommissural appraisal fibers to the action circuit. Hence lesions in the tectum and dorsal reticular formation have different behavioral effects from those of the ventral tegmentum. Indeed, Schiff (1964) reported that lesions of the ventral tegmentum depressed and in some cases prevented the bar pressing of rats for septal stimulation. Lesions in the dorsal tegmentum had no such effect.

From Midbrain to Cerebellum.   Since the limbic cortex is connected with the striatum as well as with the hippocampus, a well-practiced task may be executed via the shortcut from limbic cortex to striatum and cerebellum. However, during learning a complicated task and during reversal, the long way via hippocampus/fornix to tegmentum, reticular formation, olivary complex, and cerebellum is probably mandatory. I would conjecture that the intention to act is mediated via the action circuit, which includes both noradrenergic and serotonergic fibers. These fibers seem to be present in the relays from midbrain to olivary complex and cerebellum (Chan-Palay, 1977). The action impulse itself may be cholinergic in nature, although there is no evidence to confirm it. However, the action impulse may be felt as good or bad, suitable or unsuitable, and the fibers responsible for that appraisal seem to be serotonin- and noradrenaline-using fibers.

The Cerebellum

Relays from the primary and association cortex run to pontine nuclei; and from there, mossy fibers project via the brachium pontis to the cerebellar cortex. The cerebellum consists of the anterior lobe, separated by the primary fissure from the posterior lobe, and the flocculonodular lobe. The flocculonodular lobe is called the archicerebellum, the oldest part in evolutionary history, and is mainly concerned with the maintenance of equilibrium.

The anterior division of the posterior lobe with the cerebellar hemispheres (neocerebellum) appeared late in evolutionary history and became greatly enlarged in primates, corresponding to the enlargement of the frontal lobes. The cerebellum has a completely homogeneous structure. It consists of numerous leaves of cortex folded like the leaves of a book, with the white association fibers on the inside. All incoming impulses arrive either via climbing fibers that twist around large Purkinje cell dendrites, or via mossy fibers that branch extensively and synapse on small granule cells. Their axons pass upwards to the molecular layer and bifurcate to form the parallel fibers which synapse with Purkinje cells, basket and stellate cells. Mossy fibers are widely dispersed and produce both excitation and inhibition. Climbing fibers are monosynaptic and are solely excitatory. Purkinje cells send their axons to cerebellar nuclei, except for Purkinje cells from the flocculo-nodular lobe, which send axons also to the vestibular nuclei directly.

Afferents.   The flocculondular lobe receives only vestibulocerebellar fibers; spinocerebellar fibers go to the anterior lobe and the posterior division of the posterior lobe. All parts of the cerebellum except for the flocculonodular lobe receive fibers from the primary and association cerebral cortex. When cerebral sensory areas are stimulated, long-latency potentials are evoked from the cerebellum, similar to the potentials observed on sensory stimulation (Henneman et al., 1952). On mapping the cerebellar areas that respond to stimulation of the somatosensory cortex, a double "tactile" projection was found, one on the dorsal medial cerebellar cortex and the other on the ventral surface of each hemisphere. Visual and auditory stimulation, or electrical stimulation of visual and auditory cortical areas, produced potentials in the cerebellar face region. It was at first thought that the cerebellum, like the cerebral cortex, has sensory (particularly somatic) areas (see Fig. 26.1).

However, cerebellar lesions have never produced sensory but only motor deficits. Hence it is now beginning to be generally accepted that this structure is involved in motor control (see Massion & Sasaki, 1979). Indeed, when any of the supposedly sensory areas in the cerebellum was electrically stimulated, short-latency potentials appeared in the motor cortex together with appropriate limb or trunk movements (Henneman et al., 1952; Hampson et al., 1946, 1952).

According to Wiesendanger et al. (1979), all cortical areas project to the ipsilateral pontine nuclei, but the densest projection is from the sensorimotor area. However, Brodal (1978a, b) reports heavy projections from visual and auditory association areas rather than from primary areas, although he also found considerable projections from primary sensorimotor areas and somatosensory as-

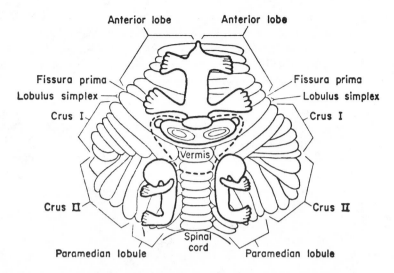

FIG. 26.1   CEREBELLAR REPRESENTATION OF THE BODY. When various body surfaces are touched, potentials appear in the dorsal cerebellar cortex and also in both paramedian lobules. Auditory and visual area overlaps the face region.
—Tactile projection. ---Visual and auditory projection. From R. S. Snider. 1950. Diagram specially redrawn from Monthly Research Report, Aug. 1950, Office of Naval Research, Washington, D.C.

sociation areas. The superior and inferior colliculi project to the same pontine areas as does the relay from visual and auditory cortex.

Wiesendanger et al. (1979) reported that the majority of pontine neurons are activated from two or more cortical sites. Apparently, there is no point-to-point projection from cerebral cortex to pons. Moreover, retrograde labeling techniques have shown that a given cerebellar site is connected with multiple pontine sites. These authors point out that considerable processing must go on before the cortical projection reaches the cerebellum.

This processing, I believe, is done in the hippocampus. I have argued (Arnold, 1960) that sensory impulses from cortical areas are converted into motor impulses in the hippocampus and relayed to the cerebellum and frontal cortex. Of course, there are shortcuts from limbic system to cerebellum that make movement possible in animals even after destruction of the hippocampus. The cerebellum organizes and amplifies the pattern of limbs and muscles required for a given action and relays this organized pattern to the motor cortex for the initiation of movements via pyramidal tract and coordinated corticobulbar and corticospinal fibers. While the cerebellum organizes limb and muscle movements into a consistent pattern, the motor cortex seems to determine the direction of movements toward the intended goal.

There are two other projections from association cortex: via lateral reticular nucleus of the medulla to the cerebellar interpositus nucleus and the cerebellar cortex; and from association cortex via inferior olive to the dentate nucleus and the cerebellar cortex. The pontine nuclei and the lateral reticular nucleus send mossy fibers to the cerebellum; climbing fibers come from the inferior olivary complex (Eccles, 1979). All these projections go to the neocerebellum, that is, to the middle lobe and the cerebellar hemispheres.

Saint-Cyr and Woodward (1980) have found that stimulation of the postcommissural fornix activates both mossy and climbing fibers. Apparently, more than one projection from cortical areas reaches the cerebellum via the hippocampus. Indeed, it is possible that all cerebellar afferents from the neocortex relay in various regions of the limbic cortex and project via hippocampus to the cerebellum (see Fig. 26.2).

The relay over limbic cortex and hippocampus is necessary because an experience must be appraised for action before the appropriate limbs and muscles can be organized toward the desired movement. Efferents from sensory cortex can only provide sensory information. There must be a way to use this information to initiate action. According to my theory, man and animal appraise what they experience and what they do (via limbic cortex) and decide on appropriate action as relays from limbic cortex arrive in the hippocampus. Thus the hippocampus receives motor and sensory appraisal impulses and sends action impulses to midbrain and cerebellum.

The cerebellum also receives direct relays from sensory afferents. From the vestibulary nerve and nuclei, vestibulo-cerebellar fibers reach the old cerebellum, that is, the homolateral flocculus, nodulus, uvula, and lingula, which in turn project to the fastigial cerebellar nucleus. Ventral and dorsal spinocerebellar fibers project mainly to the anterior lobe although some fibers end in the middle and posterior lobe. The vestibular projection reports the body's position in space; the spinocerebellar fibers provide somatosensory information. The human being needs sensory information via the cortex as well. We cannot maintain equilibrium unless we have some sensory cues. In fog and cloud, pilots must depend on instruments to maintain level flight. Similarly, information from somatosensory afferents to the cerebellum must be supplemented by relays from neocortex for effective action.

While the hippocampus seems to initiate the intention to move in a particular way for a particular purpose, the inferior olivary complex and cerebellum seem to organize the necessary pattern of limb and body movements (Fig. 26.3). The incoming impulses seem to bring information as to what action is required, what is the position of the goal, and what is the position of body and limbs.

Efferents.   The pattern for body and trunk movements is relayed by the Purkinje cells of the cerebellar cortex to the intracerebellar nuclei. In monkeys, according to Sasaki (1979), the neocerebellum projects via dentate nucleus and

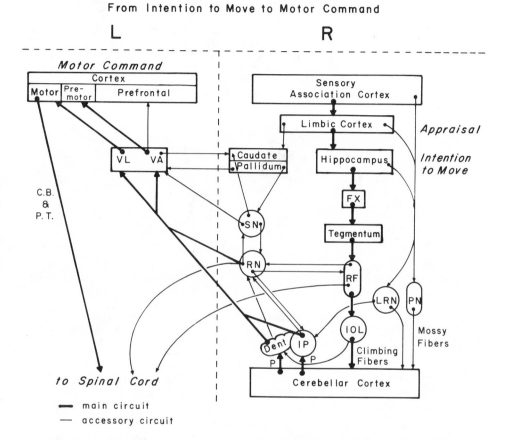

FIG. 26.2   From intention to move to motor command; Suggested relays from sensory to motor cortex.

Main circuit: Sensory experience is appraised via limbic cortex. Relays to hippocampus; as intention to move to fornix (Fx), tegmentum, reticular formation, inferior olivary nucleus and (via climbing fibers) to cerebellar cortex.

After amplification and organization, relay (via Purkinje fibers) to (a) dentate nucleus, ventrolateral and ventral anterior thalamic nuclei and frontal lobe; (b) interpositus nucleus, red nucleus, substantia nigra, caudate, pallidum, ventrolateral, and ventral anterior thalamic nuclei, to frontal lobe. From there, corticobulbar (C.B.) and corticospinal (C.S.) tracts to medulla and via pyramidal tract (P.T.) to spinal cord. Accessory connections: From association cortex and limbic cortex to lateral reticular nucleus, pontine nuclei, and (via mossy fibers) to cerebellar hemisphere.

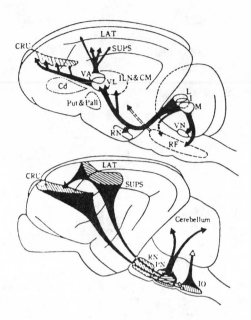

FIG. 26.3   Schematic illustration of the cerebello-cerebral (upper diagram) and cerebro-cerebellar (lower diagram) projections in cats. See text. CRU: cruciate sulcus. Lat: lateral sulcus. SUPS: suprasylvian sulcus. VA: anterior ventral thalamic nuclei. VL: lateral ventral thalamic nucleus. ILN & CM: intralaminar and centrum medianum thalamic nuclei. Cd: caudate nucleus. Put & Pall: putamen and pallidum. M, I, L: medial, interpositus and lateral cerebellar nucleus. RN: red nucleus. VN: vestibular nuclei. RF: brain stem reticular formation. PN: pontine nuclei. IO: inferior olive. From K. Sasaki, 1979.

ventral thalamus to the forelimb areas in the motor cortex; the intermediate part of the cerebellum, via the interpositus nucleus to the trunk areas, and the medial part of the cerebellum projects via the fastigial nucleus mainly to the medial part of the motor cortex, the hindlimb area. However, these projections overlap considerably. The relays may be dispersed in the ventral thalamic nuclei, but congregate again in the motor cortex, so that a given site in the cerebellar cortex produces potentials in a correlated area of the motor cortex.

The cerebellar projection to the frontal cortex is involved not only in deliberate movements but in emotion and integrated instinctive action patterns. For instance, Sprague and Chambers (1955) found that destruction of the dentate nucleus markedly reduced the responses to pain in trunk and limbs of the same side, and destruction of the auditory region on both sides of the cerebellum greatly reduces startle. These authors also mentioned that earlier investigators had reported increased sensitivity to touch, pain, auditory, and visual stimuli when the cerebellum was stimulated. The animals would howl, cry, snarl, back away, try to escape, cringe, or wildly lick and bite their own body. Actually, the animals were not necessarily more sensitive to stimulation; they merely reacted more strongly.

Lisander and Martner (1976) reported that stimulation of the rostral pole of the fastigial nucleus in unanesthetized cats produced licking and chewing, predatory attack, and other integrated behavior patterns. After decerebration, these cats no longer showed such behavior on cerebellar stimulation. However, when the cats were decerebrated at the intercollicular level and kept for 7–30 days, fastigial stimulation induced emotional responses such as crying, clawing, ruffling of fur, running movements, and sometimes licking and chewing. Apparently, stimulation of the fastigial nuclei in waking cats activated autonomic changes seen in emotion. After intercollicular transection, which excluded the cortex, stimulation no longer produced the complete action pattern but merely disconnected parts.

The cerebellum initiates action via relays to the motor cortex. When an animal moves, the cerebellar dentate nucleus fires just ahead of the neurons in the motor cortex that initiate the appropriate action. On the basis of her own experiments and the reports of previous work, Chan-Palay (1977) suggests that the cerebellum provides "a means for specification (of movements) in direction, space and time" (p. 44). The cerebellum also seems to amplify motor impulses. In primates, damage to the cerebellum does not interfere with the goal of action but destroys coordination and results in loss of muscle tone and general weakness.

Motor adaptation seems to require intact inferior olivary nuclei and an intact cerebellum. The oculo-vestibular reflex has been studied extensively in this connection. Normally, the eyes turn right when the head is turned left by the experimenter. Test subjects were fitted with reversing prisms so that objects seemed to move to the left when the head was turned to the right. The vestibulo-ocular reflex of turning the eyes to the left when the head is turned to the right exaggerated the effect of the prism. But in a few days, the subjects adapted to the prism so that now the eyes turned in the same direction as the head. Monkeys, rabbits, and cats have shown a similar adaptation. Destruction of the cerebellar flocculus abolished adaptation in these animals. Chan-Palay (1977) has shown that the cerebellar dentate nuclei also participate in this adaptation; and Ito and Miyashita (1975) found that destruction of various parts of the inferior olivary nuclei abolished or impaired vestibulo-ocular movements. Hence Chan-Palay suggested that the cerebellum is involved "in the regulation of motor output in response to volition and sensory stimuli" (p. 476).

It is sometimes said that the cerebellum is not necessary for retaining a learned task. According to Thompson (1969), bilateral cerebellar ablation did not impair the retention of simultaneous visual discriminations despite the animals' locomotor ataxia. However, this is true only for tasks in which motor activity is secondary to sensory discrimination. Thompson's animals had to choose one of two visual cues and approach it. It is quite different when the animal has to learn or retain a complicated motor task, as for instance in compensating for a unilateral lesion of the labyrinth. After such a lesion, the animal can no longer maintain a normal posture. Its body rolls toward the side of the lesion and turns in tight circles. The head is tilted, with the eye on the lesioned side looking down, that on the intact side looking up. Gradually, the animal begins to stand close to the ground but still turns in place. Head and eye position are straightened first, next the eyes begin to track. Eventually, the animal walks in widening circles, until in one or two days it walks and moves its eyes normally. As Llinas et al. (1975) point out, this is a model of motor learning and depends on an intact olivo-cerebellar system. If the inferior olive is lesioned or its connection with the cerebellum is interrupted, vestibular compensation does not occur. If the lesion is made after vestibular compensation is established, it breaks down again. There is little doubt that this compensation is genuine motor learning which requires a connection from cortex via hippocampus to inferior olive and cerebellum. The animal must sense its motor difficulty and try to correct it.

The inferior olivary complex and the cerebellum are supplied with serotonergic and noradrenergic fibers from raphé nuclei and locus coeruleus in the midbrain. There are return projections from the inferior olivary nuclei and cereballum to raphé and locus coeruleus, but this projection does not use monoamines as transmitters (Chan-Palay, 1977). These monoaminergic systems would make it possible to appraise the motor patterns integrated via olive and cerebellum as good (suitable) or bad (unsuitable) so that the movement would be felt as easy and pleasant or effortful and unpleasant.

THE ASCENDING LINK OF THE ACTION CIRCUIT

Several routes from cerebellum to frontal cortex are included in this link. According to Cohen et al. (1958), the brachium conjunctivum, the main projection from the cerebellum, decussates in a broad sheet from the border of the pons to the superior colliculus. Some of its fibers go to the red nucleus, but almost half of them run beyond it, either to the field of Forel and the dorsolateral hypothalamus, which connects with the basal ganglia via the medial forebrain bundle, or directly to the ventrolateral and ventral anterior thalamic nuclei and the frontal lobe. In man, some fibers go to the ventral intermedian nucleus with relays to frontal cortex (Jasper & Bertrand, 1966). Some fibers run to the dorsomedial thalamic nucleus (Chan-Palay, 1977), which connects with prefrontal and insular cortex (Papez, 1956), and some to centrum medianum and midline thalamic nuclei, which project to the anterior cingulate gyrus and diffusely to the whole cortex (Angaut, 1979).

The Midbrain Reticular Formation

Like the spinal cord, the brainstem (i.e., the part of the brain remaining after removal of cerebral cortex and cerebellum) is derived from the dorsal alar plate and the ventral basal plate. The former has sensory, the latter, motor functions. The brainstem consists of the medulla with pons, the midbrain, thalamus and basal ganglia. The alar plate includes the colliculi and dorsal tegmentum in the midbrain, and the massa intermedia and several small nuclear masses in the thalamus. The basal plate includes the ventral tegmentum together with other ventral structures in the midbrain, the hypothalamus in the ventral part of the diencephalon, and the basal ganglia in the telencephalon. While the dorsal tegmental nucleus is part of the alar plate, the ventral tegmentum is formed from the basal plate, hence has motor functions (Clara, 1959). According to my theory, it is a relay station in the ascending link of the action circuit and the associated motor memory circuit.

The medial two thirds of the reticular formation are considered an effector area. It sends mainly uncrossed relays to the intralaminar and reticular thalamic nuclei and also to spinal levels. These thalamic nuclei distribute fibers to the whole cortex (Carpenter, 1976). The ventral tegmental area also distributes widely to the whole cortex (Markowitch & Irle, 1981).

Stimulation of the midbrain reticular formation facilitates motor activity. Mild electrical stimulation, or stimulation by excitatory drugs like strychnine, picrotoxin, or amphetamine, when injected during the first few minutes after learning, improves learning and retention (Bloch et al., 1977; McGaugh & Herz, 1972). Stimulation seems to improve conduction not only in the action circuit but also in the motor memory circuit. However, when the midbrain reticular formation in rats is stimulated during the delay in a discrete trial delayed alternation task, retention is disrupted no matter whether the stimulation is applied early or late during the delay. Bierley and Kesner (1980) suggest that such stimulation directly interfered with the memory trace. I would suggest that it disrupted the conduction of impulses in the motor memory circuit so that the animals no longer remembered which bar they had intended to press.

The Red Nucleus.   This large nucleus in the midbrain reticular formation is part of the projection from cerebellum to ventral thalamic nuclei. It is a round, yellowish-red nuclear mass in the basal motor part of the reticular tegmentum. Its afferents come from the reticular formation at the level of the superior colliculus, from Deiter's nucleus, and the globus pallidus. The small-celled neorubrum also receives afferents from the cortex (Larsen & Yumiya, 1980). The neorubrum is larger in man than in any other species. Fibers from several modalities, sensory and motor, converge on it. These seem to come both from cortex and from afferent pathways (see Fig. 26.3). Irvine (1980) has reported short-latency potentials in the red nucleus after auditory stimulation, which seems to imply relatively direct brainstem connections, but also long-latency potentials, which seem to indicate cortical projections. The small neorubral cells send fibers to the striatum and ventrolateral thalamic nuclei and also to the inferior olive and the cerebellum. The large-celled paleorubrum is the origin of the rubrospinal tract, and sends relays to the midbrain tectum. The spinal connections have lost most of their significance in the human being while the projection to the ventrolateral thalamus has achieved increasing importance.

My suggestion that the projection from cerebellum to ventral thalamus, either direct or via the red nucleus, mediates the impulse to action seems confirmed by a report that the readiness potential, which occurs just before a movement, was absent in patients with degeneration of the dentate cerebellar nucleus and the superior cerebellar peduncle. It was severely depressed in patients with unilateral vascular midbrain lesions involving the red nucleus or dentatothalamic pathway, and also in Parkinson patients who were given a unilateral surgical lesion in the ventral intermediate thalamic nucleus (Shibasaki et al., 1978). The readiness potential seems to signal the intention to move, an impulse to action that is apparently blocked by a lesion between cerebellum and ventral thalamus. This may account for the difficulty these patients have in initiating action.

Damage to the Ventral Midbrain.   When both circuits are damaged, for instance, by bilateral lesions of the red nucleus, rats are significantly impaired in brightness and pattern discrimination (Thompson et al., 1967). These lesions also impaired the retention of a kinesthetic discrimination (T-maze with one arm tilting upwards, the other downwards). McNew (1968) confirmed that bilateral lesions of the red nucleus interfered with the retention of a size discrimination in which errors were punished by shock. Form discrimination was unimpaired. The red nucleus, one of the structures often called "polysensory" because fibers from several modalities converge upon it, is rather a motor relay station mediating the reaction to sensory experience.

In rats, damage to the ventral midbrain and central gray produced a severe deficit in active avoidance to visual and auditory signals (Thompson et al., 1964), in kinesthetic discriminations (Thompson et al., 1967), and successive reversals of a position habit (Thompson & Langer, 1963), when errors were punished by foot shock. According to Thompson (1969), lesions of the central tegmentum between the central gray dorsally, and the interpeduncular nucleus or the mamillary bodies ventrally, produced significant deficits in visual discrimination, whether the interpeduncular nucleus was included in the lesion or not. These lesions seem to have damaged the connection of the sensory system with the motor memory circuit so that the animals no longer remembered the motor pattern appropriate to the cues.

Ventral and deep ventral tegmental lesions resulted in increased saccharin preference thresholds, but dorsal lesions did not. Also, the quinine aversion threshold was considerably increased in ventrally lesioned rats; and finally, the animals consumed less water than did normal animals. Rats with ventral lesions were relatively inactive when undisturbed, compared to animals with dorsal lesions and controls. But when they were handled, they became vicious (Schiff, 1967). These animals seem to have had lesions in the action circuit, hence their inactivity. Ventral tegmental lesions would have damaged the dopaminergic imagination circuit, so that the animals reacted violently to handling; the lesions would also have damaged the noradrenergic and serotonergic pathways, so that the animals needed a more saturated quinine solution to appraise it as bad and avoid it, and a more saturated saccharin solution to find it good and prefer it.

Kesner et al. (1967) reported that small two-stage lesions in the medial and dorsal part of the midbrain reticular formation, which partly transected the midbrain, produced aphagia and adipsia for a few days. Afterwards, the animals were hyperactive, groomed excessively, and took some time to wake when stimulated. Apparently, this lesion produced edema that impaired function in the lateral as well as ventromedial hypothalamic pathways originating in the midbrain reticular formation. As soon as the edema subsided, only the damage to inhibitory fibers leading to the ventromedial hypothalamic nucleus remained. The animals were hyperactive because they could not relax; they groomed excessively because this was one source of pleasure that was not disturbed.

Small implant-produced lesions in the midbrain reticular formation facilitated appetitive learning (black/white discrimination in T-maze, bar pressing for food) while cholinergic stimulation, applied to the same sites, had the opposite effect. Also, it almost eliminated exploratory behavior. Atropine, a cholinergic blocking agent, also reduced bar pressing. These lesions seem to have damaged inhibitory fibers in the action circuit, hence the animals ran faster in the T-maze to obtain food, and improved their performance on the VR–5 schedule bar pressing task. The application of carbachol to the same sites impaired running, almost abolished exploratory behavior, and depressed bar pressing because it improved cholinergic conduction in the same inhibitory pathway. Atropine, on the other hand, depressed bar pressing because it impaired the motor memory circuit, which also has relays in the midbrain reticular formation. Grossman and Grossman (1966) pointed out that lesions in the same brainstem region in an earlier experiment had inhibited performance in escape-avoidance situations, while cholinergic stimulation had aided it. However, the action circuit contains both inhibitory and facilitatory fibers in neighboring sites in the midbrain. Only when it reaches the hypothalamus do they diverge; the facilitatory fibers toward the lateral hypothalamus, the inhibitory fibers toward the ventromedial hypothalamic nucleus. It is possible that Grossman and Grossman's earlier experimental lesions damaged the facilitatory fibers, hence the impairment in active avoidance. The cholinergic stimulation at the same sites then improved cholinergic conduction and produced facilitation of active avoidance.

The direct route to the ventral thalamus and perhaps the route via the red nucleus seem to mediate the action impulse that determines the strength of movement, its spatial and temporal organization. The indirect route via the hypothalamus, which in addition receives relays from the brainstem reticular formation, seems to mediate the movement patterns acquired through learning, as well as instinctive action patterns.

ACTIVATION OF THE ACTION CIRCUIT

If action is mediated over the action circuit, as I am suggesting, conduction over this circuit could be either enhanced or depressed. Enhanced conduction can be equated with increased activity, particularly locomotion; decreased conduction, with diminished activity, leading to relaxation and finally sleep.

The action circuit and associated motor memory circuit are of all suggested circuits the most difficult to trace. Not only do they include a loop from mibrain over the inferior olive and cerebellum, but one branch of both circuits traverses the hypothalamus before reaching the ventral thalamic "motor" nuclei and the frontal lobe. In the hypothalamus, these fibers are compressed into a narrow funnel, which makes investigation difficult. Much has been done in the last two decades, but more remains to be done. My theory is no more than a skeleton that needs to be fleshed out by future research. A thorough computer analysis of the structures and pathways suggested here should add materially to our knowledge.

One way to explore increased and decreased conduction over the action circuit is to manipulate the transmitters involved in motor function. This has been done to a considerable extent.

Transmitter Systems Involved in Hyperactivity

The Dopamine System.   Excitation of this system seems to increase activity, including locomotion. Amphetamine releases catecholamines from vesicle stores, hence facilitates activity via dopaminergic pathways.

Amphetamine-induced locomotor activity in the rat was not reduced by a microinjection of 6–OHDA into the dorsal and ventral noradrenaline bundle. Extensive (85–95%) depletion of noradrenaline in the hypothalamus, cerebral cortex, and hippocampus after such lesions did not affect either spontaneous or amphetamine-induced activity. Hence the noradrenaline system is not responsible for amphetamine-induced locomotor activity.

According to Pijnenburg et al. (1975), such activity could be inhibited by injection of haloperidol into the nucleus accumbens septi of the rat, but not by such injection into the caudate nucleus. It would seem that locomotor activity is induced via the mesolimbic dopamine system (Roberts et al., 1975). A 92% depletion of neostriatal dopamine after 6–OHDA injection into the substantia nigra severely reduced such activity but did not abolish it. But a microinjection into the nigrostriatal dopamine bundle completely prevented or abolished it (Roberts et al., 1975). According to Iversen (1977), the ventral mesolimbic dopamine system is not strictly separated from the fibers of the nigrostriatal system. An injection of 6–OHDA into the substantia nigra or the nigrostriatal tract might diffuse into the fibers of the ventral system. Apparently, the intranigral injection of Roberts et al. damaged but did not destroy the mesolimbic pathway, hence locomotor activity was reduced but not abolished. The injection into the nigrostriatal path, however, seems to have destroyed the mesolimbic as well as the nigrostriatal dopamine system, hence abolished locomotor activity induced by amphetamine.

Since the mesolimbic system is connected with the amygdala (hence the imagination circuit), it is entirely possible that the activation of imagination secondarily produces the increased running about. In animals, images are the precursor of action: food, mate, and enemies, are all potent goals, which might explain the incessant scurrying about.

In contrast to the mesolimbic dopamine system, the nigrostriatal pathway seems to mediate the impulse to goal-directed action. Complete bilateral lesions anywhere along the nigrostriatal dopamine pathway produce akinetic, cataleptic, and rigid animals which refuse to eat or drink and do not respond to stimulation. Overactivity of this pathway, on the other hand, as produced by amphetamine, induces stereotyped behavior in animals (licking, biting, gnawing, bizarre immobile postures). Such stereotypy is different in each species and even in each individual, but recurs after every similar application of amphetamine. It can be blocked by neuroleptics except for thioridazine and clozapine, which have no motor effects; it can also be blocked by 6–OHDA injection into the caudate nucleus, but not by injection into the nucleus accumbens septi. Hence such stereotyped behavior seems to result from the destruction of the nigrostriatal dopamine system (Iversen, 1977).

When haloperidol is applied systemically, it reduces dopamine activity in the striatum, as do most other neuroleptic drugs. This reduction cancels the inhibitory effect of dopamine on the cholinergic interneurons in the striatum so that they become overactive. Such overactivity seems to contribute to the muscular rigidity in Parkinsonism. Anticholinergic drugs decrease cholinergic activity, hence their usefulness in this disease. In contrast, dopamine transmission seems to be increased in schizophrenics, particularly in the mesolimbic system (Stevens, 1977). After prolonged treatment with neuroleptic drugs, schizophrenics often show choreic symptoms, apparently a result of the reduction of dopamine transmission in the striatum produced by these drugs.

The Serotonin System.   Median raphé lesions also produce hyperactivity (in rats) while lesions of the dorsal raphé do not (Jacobs et al., 1975). These authors also produced hyperactivity by the administration of p-chlorophenylalanine (PCPA), which blocks serotonin synthesis. Segal (1975) reported that 92% of hippocampal pyramid cells tapped by monitoring electrodes were inhibited by serotonin; and half these cell were inhibited by stimulating the dorsal or median raphé. When the rats were pretreated with PCPA, such stimulation did not inhibit hippocampal cells. Apparently, serotonergic excitation produces relaxation via the hippocampus and action circuit. When such relaxation is prevented by PCPA, the animals become hyperactive.

This serotonin-induced inhibition of activity may be mediated by inhibitory fibers in the action circuit from ventral tegmentum via ventromedial hypothalamus to the frontal cortex. GABA-using cells in the ventral tegmental area, perhaps connected with this inhibitory pathway, seem to depress activity in the mesolimbic dopamine system. For instance, Stevens (1977) applied small amounts of the GABA blocker bicuculline to cells of the ventral tegmental area in freely moving cats. This produced intense arousal, staring, fear, withdrawal, waxy flexibility, posturing, searching, sniffing, and hiding. EEG spikes occurred only in the nucleus accumbens which receives the dopamine projection from the ventral tegmental area. Such spikes have also been recorded in the nucleus accumbens of schizophrenic patients. Repeated brief electric shocks ("kindling"), applied to the ventral tegmental area induced similar behavior accompanied by ipsilateral EEG spikes in the nucleus accumbens in three of six cats. Since an activation of tyrosine hydroxylase followed the microinjection of bicuculline in the ipsilateral nucleus accumbens but not in the caudate, Stevens concluded that excitation of the mesolimbic pathway from the ventral tegmental area to the nucleus accumbens results in increased dopamine turnover. Stevens pointed out that schizophrenics also show evidence of mesolimbic dysfunction.

From all these experimental reports we can conclude that hyperactivity has many causes. It may be the result of apprehension (via NA system) and of increased imagination (via mesolimbic system) so that the animal runs about and explores. It may be the result of increased motor facilitation (via nigrostriatal dopamine system), which induces animals to repeat endlessly what they are doing (stereotypy); finally, it may come from an inability to rest and relax, brought about by a deficiency of serotonin.

DEPRESSION OF THE ACTION CIRCUIT

Sleep, Relaxation.

Activity is depressed during sleep and relaxation. During sleep, motor activity is suppressed (except for some involuntary movements) and EEG waves are slowing down. In deep sleep, the EEG shows large slow waves. This slow wave sleep (SWS) is interrupted from time to time by so-called rapid-eye-movement (REM) sleep, also called desynchronized (D) sleep, because it is associated with rapid eye movements and a fast desynchronized EEG. Human experiments have shown that such D sleep is associated with dreams. Since animals can remember and imagine, there is no reason to deny them dreams.

Sleep can be induced by mild repetitive stimulation of peripheral nerves, by low-frequency and low-intensity stimulation of the caudal and rostral brainstem, the midline and lateral thalamus, and the basal forebrain (including hypothalamus, the posterior orbital and parolfactory cortex). Higher frequency and intensity may produce arousal (Hess, 1943; Sterman, 1974).

Low frequency stimulation calms the animal and suppresses catecholamine and corticosteroid secretion. Catecholamines (noradrenaline and dopamine) are involved in imagination, as I have suggested. And corticosteroid fractions (ACTH 4–10) facilitate recall and block amnestic agents (Dunn & Rees, 1977). Neither imagination nor recall is active during slow wave sleep. Indeed, it may well be that their inhibition by slowing the conduction rate in the medial appraisal system may induce sleep. Methods of relaxation leading to sleep are often aimed at the inhibition of psychological activity; that is, of appraisal, memory, and imagination.

Slow Wave Sleep.   Serotonergic neurons are active during slow wave sleep. Any damage to these neurons in the rostral raphé, whether by lesions or drugs, results in insomnia. Sleep can be restored immediately by a small dose of tryptophan, the precursor of sertonin (Jouvet, 1974). As discussed before, serotonin seems to mediate pleasure and relaxation.

Destruction of the basal forebrain in cats has resulted in sleeplessness that sometimes led to death (Sterman, 1974; Madoz & Reinoso-Suarez, 1968). When for therapeutic reasons a small lesion was placed in this area of the human brain, the patients lost their ability to sleep (Hauri & Hawkins, 1972). Bremer (1970) showed that stimulation of the basal forebrain area produced inhibition of cellular activity in the midbrain reticular formation and suggested that sleep is produced by a process of reticular deactivation. Basal forebrain and reticular formation are relay stations in the action circuit, which mediates both motor activity and motor relaxation.

Slow wave sleep can perhaps best be compared with general muscular relaxation. When relaxation is deep enough, it may actually lead to sleep. In recent years, training in muscular relaxation has been achieved by an ingenious feedback arrangement. A contact on the subject's forehead indicates by a steady tone that the frontalis muscle is tense; the subject is instructed to stop the sound. After a few sessions, most people lower their frontalis electromyogram (EMG) level by 50% or more. When the tone stops, they have achieved such profound relaxation that sleep is not far off (Stoyva & Budzynski, 1974). As soon as such relaxation is achieved, most of the EMG tracing drops out and bursts of frontal cortical rhythms can be seen, particulary alpha (8–12 Hz) and theta (4–7 Hz). Ordinarily, EEG rhythms are not observable because the high-frequency muscle potentials from the frontalis muscle mask them.

Such relaxation training demonstrates that a person can arrest his muscular activity and produce EEG synchronization voluntarily. He can initiate alpha and theta waves over the usual route of appraisal (good to stop the tone), followed by an impulse to relax, to watch, thus slowing conduction over the action circuit—

which eventually results in EEG synchronization. The next step is drowsiness accompanied by alpha spindles, which finally merge into the slow waves of deep sleep. The hippocampus, which mediates the intention to relax on the basis of appraisal, sends relays via the fornix to the anterior hypothalamus and the ventromedial hypothalamic nucleus in the hypothalamic branch of the action circuit: and the anterior hypothalamus is the site Sterman (1974) found involved in slow wave sleep.

In contrast, bilateral lesions in the lateral part of the posterior hypothalamus produce sleep (Swett & Hobson, 1968). Such lesions seem to interfere with the action circuit or at least the fibers ascending to the ventral thalamus via the hypothalamus and striatum. The lateral hypothalamus seems to include fibers mediating the impulse to action, while the anterior hypothalamus together with the ventromedial hypothalamus seems to contain fibers mediating relaxation.

Velluti and Hernández-Peón (1963) produced sleep in cats by applying acetylcholine-like drugs either to the medial preoptic region in the anterior hypothalamus, or to the interpeduncular nucleus in the midbrain. These authors postulate a descending cholinergic pathway within the medial forebrain bundle which produces sleep. However, as Shute (1970) pointed out, the cholinergic fibers in the medial forebrain bundle are part of an ascending pathway. More likely, the direct application may have had inhibitory effects; direct application to the caudate, for instance, produces drowsiness and mimics low frequency stimulation. Such low frequency excitation depresses conduction in the medial appraisal system which, in turn, slows conduction in the action, memory, and imagination circuits.

Slow wave sleep depresses movement but also eliminates imagination and recall, and results in a synchronized EEG.

D Sleep.   D sleep is accompanied by muscle atony with occasional muscle twitches, desynchronized fast EEG, and rapid eye movements. Other signs are hippocampal theta rhythm and ponto-geniculo-occipital (PGO) waves that appear first in the pons and slightly later in the lateral geniculate nucleus and occipital cortex. These waves coincide with rapid eye movements. During D sleep, neurons in an area around the locus coeruleus and in the reticular magnocellular nucleus in the pons send relays via the tegmentoreticular tract to inhibitory neurons in the medullary reticular formation which hyperpolarize spinal motoneurons and so produce muscular atony. These inhibitory neurons seem to be cholinergic (Sakai, 1980).

Apparently, D sleep depends on structures in the pons. Jouvet (1962) has shown that cats that had all brain tissue removed in front of the pons still had periods of D sleep with PGO waves, rapid eye movements and muscle atony. Yet it would seem that D sleep could hardly be associated with dreaming if it can occur without the forebrain. But the alternation between slow wave and D sleep could well depend on the pons, yet the occurrence of PGO wave could bring about the activation of the imagination circuit which results in dreams.

Neurotransmitters and D Sleep.   Indeed, Steriade et al. (1980) consider that the gigantocellular tegmental field in the pons generates PGO waves and rapid eye movements but does not initiate EEG desynchronization in D sleep. They found that the midbrain reticular cholinergic fibers to thalamus and cortex increase their activity during waking and D sleep, and decrease it during slow wave sleep.

And Pompeiano (1980) reported that systemic injection of eserine (which prolongs the effect of acetylcholine) into decerebrate cats produced episodes of catalepsy with all the symptoms of D sleep. However, these episodes are short and alternate regularly, different from the alternation of slow wave sleep, D sleep, and waking, in intact animals.

Vivaldi et al. (1980) reported that introducing carbachol into the pontine reticular gigantocellular field of waking cats produced D sleep with all its symptoms within a few minutes, a state that lasted for several hours. The same results were obtained with propranolol, a beta-adrenergic blocking substance, except that the induced D sleep lasted for no more than twelve minutes. They insist that the drug-induced state is indistinguishable from normal D sleep.

Other investigators have sought to associate the PGO waves of D sleep with known changes in the activity of locus coeruleus and raphé cells over the sleep cycle. According to McCarley (1980) and others, the highest activity rates of these cells occur during waking, lower rates during slow wave sleep, and the lowest rates in D sleep. They suggest that locus coeruleus and raphé neurons completely inhibit the gigantocellular tegmental field in the pons during waking, and inhibit it partially during slow wave sleep. As the inhibition subsides, the released neurons produce PGO waves, rapid eye movements, and atony (McCarley, 1980; Vivaldi et al., 1980). On this view, blocking both locus coeruleus and raphé activity should induce sleep. But Jouvet (1974) reported that destruction of the dorsal noradrenaline pathway at the isthmus resulted in increased serotonin synthesis and turnover in the brain, and also in a large increase in D sleep; but damage to the rostral raphé produced insomnia. And in the studies of Vivaldi et al. (1980), application of a beta adrenergic blocker was sufficient to induce D sleep. It would seem, then, that the inactivation of the locus coeruleus rather than of the raphé is sufficient to induce D sleep, and that serotonin activity promotes slow wave sleep (cf. Jouvet, 1974).

The EEG in D Sleep.   According to Steriade et al. (1980), the firing rate of midbrain reticular neurons increased 2–8 seconds before waking and during D sleep, which seems to indicate that it is their activity that brings about both EEG arousal and waking. In contrast, the transition from waking to slow wave sleep is accompanied by a striking inhibition of transmission through the ventrolateral thalamic nuclei to the frontal cortex, although the input from the cerebellum may be unchanged. These authors also found that stimulation of the amygdala can still elicit EEG arousal in an animal after high precollicular transection, that is, after any activation via the midbrain reticular formation had been excluded.

Apparently, dreaming is primarily associated with the desynchronization of the EEG observed in D sleep, which may well be brought about by the excitation of cholinergic fibers belonging to the memory circuit. Since dopaminergic neurons are cholinoceptive, such excitation would also activate the imagination circuit.

Although the pontine reticular formation may originate the PGO waves of D sleep, the forebrain is necessary for imagination which results in EEG arousal and dreaming. The forebrain has considerable influence on the sleep-waking cycle. External stimuli alert the animal and result in increasing discharges in the locus coeruleus and raphé cells (McCarley, 1980). The waking individual continually appraises what he encounters as good/bad, familiar/unfamiliar, via noradrenergic and serotonergic pathways. When such appraisals drop out with lowered conduction in the appraisal system, he becomes indifferent, and can relax and sink into the unconsciousness of slow wave sleep.

D Sleep and Dreaming.   There is no doubt that D sleep in man and animal is accompanied by dreams. In human beings, the intensive research of the past decades has made that abundantly clear (see Sterman, 1974). But animals also dream. Cats with dorsolateral pontine lesions that destroy the relays to the inhibitory field in the medullary reticular formation, so lifting the motoneuron paralysis, have episodes of D sleep with motor activity suggesting flight, attack, and other organized actions. Apparently, the lesioned cats can act out their dreams, which intact animals cannot do because of the motor inhibition in D sleep. Human beings, particularly children, also walk in their sleep when, for whatever reason, the motor inhibition is temporarily lifted.

Dreams are imaginative action sequences. We are participants in the action, but we can do little to change it. As soon as the dream arouses too much emotion, the sleeper comes close to waking. During a nightmare, the dreamer often tries to run, without much success; but when at last he manages to break through the block and makes a movement, he finds himself awake.

Modality-specific recall or rather, the recognition that we are recalling a memory is not possible during sleep, probably because the affective memory circuit depends on relays from the midbrain appraisal system, which slows down during sleep. However, the imagination circuit, mediated via dopaminergic fibers which have their cell bodies in the substantia nigra, could be active during D sleep, excited by relays from the midbrain reticular system as it begins to be active. The dopaminergic neurons in the substantia nigra can be excited by cholinergic fibers (Glowinski et al., 1980).

D Sleep and Memory.   Sleep "stitches up the raveled sleeve of care"—but D sleep and its dreams do better than that. D sleep consolidates learning. Dreams give the sleeper an opportunity to imagine that he is performing the learned task and so preserves access to memory. Deprivation of D sleep immediately after learning impairs retention (Bloch et al., 1977; Pearlman & Becker, 1974). This deficit is most pronounced in complicated tasks (Greenberg & Pearlman, 1974). After learning trials, periods of D sleep lengthen. This has been confirmed with both positive and negative reinforcement in rats, with negative reinforcement in mice, and with positive reinforcement in cats (Bloch et al., 1977). Deprivation of D sleep in the mouse has extended the period during which learning could be disrupted by electroconvulsive shock (ECS), according to Fishbein et al. (1971).

Bloch et al. (1977) and Fishbein et al. (1974) found that D sleep was increased during the two hours following maze learning. The increase was greatest when learning had progressed well, and ceased when the task was learned. When the animal had to run the maze in a reversed pattern, D sleep was again increased. These authors found that sleep deprivation produces impairment of retention only when it occurs during the first three hours after learning, during the period when D sleep is increased in control animals. After that time, sleep deprivation has no effect. Weak stimulation of the reticular formation immediately after learning improved the performance of sleep-deprived animals. Hence the authors suggested that reticular stimulation arouses the animal so that it can process new information—but does D sleep also arouse the animal? Weak reticular stimulation immediately after learning almost totally suppressed the usual increase in D sleep, while no such increase occurred after reticular stimulation when learning was not involved. Hence weak reticular stimulation seems to substitute for D sleep. Bloch (1976) had suggested that either natural or artificial reticular stimulation seems necessary for storage; and D sleep implies brain activation. But in 1977, Bloch et al. admit the possibility that D sleep may not facilitate memory storage but may simply be a consequence of the memory process.

I would suggest that D sleep allows the animal to imagine performing the learned task. Motor imagination in dreams, like motor imagination in waking life, aids learning (see Arnold, 1946). Weak stimulation of the reticular formation seems to activate the dopaminergic imagination circuit and probably also the caudate, so rehearsing the motor patterns most recently practiced.

In summary, we may conclude that during sleep, conduction in the action circuit is slowed via the medial appraisal system (including the noradrenergic and serotonergic pathways), which results in motor inhibition via the ventrolateral thalamic nuclei, and depressed activity of the recall and imagination circuits during S sleep. D sleep occurs when the pontine gigantocellular tegmental field neurons are activated and (a) excite the dopaminergic imagination circuit, which results in EEG arousal; (b) produce PGO waves and rapid eye movements; and (c) inhibit spinal motoneurons and so produce atony.

27 The Action Circuit: Through the Hypothalamus

The human hypothalamus represents only three tenths of one per cent of the brain, yet it plays a fundamental role in the economy of the organism. Of its three zones, the periventricular and medial zones are rich in cell bodies while the lateral zone is dominated by longitudinal fiber systems, most of them in the medial forebrain bundle (Halász, 1978).

Halász remarks that "the reciprocal connections of the hypothalamus with the limbic forebrain structures and the mesencephalon are of such magnitude that it appears possible to interpret the hypothalamus . . . as a way station in both the ascending and descending limbs of a polysynaptic neural circuit which extends between the limbic forebrain on the one hand and the paramedian mesencephalic region on the other" (p.22). This agrees with my suggestion that the hypothalamus is a relay station in the descending as well as the ascending link of the action circuit (from fornix to midbrain and from midbrain to the frontal lobe). In addition, the dopamine pathway from the substantia nigra to the amygdala runs through the lateral hypothalamus, as do fibers of the noradrenergic and serotonergic systems.

The hypothalamus receives fibers from the frontal cortex, the olfactory lobe, striatum, amygdala, and the medial and anterior thalamic nuclei; also from the tectum and the spinal cord. The postcommissural fornix connects with the dorsal hypothalamic area and the lateral hypothalamus (in rodents, via the cortico-hypothalamic tract—Halász, 1978). The hypothalamus sends fibers to thalamus and epithalamus, striatum, amygdala, and septum, hence connects indirectly with the cortex; efferents also go to the tectum and spinal cord. The main tracts are the medial forebrain bundle and the dorsal longitudinal fasciculus, which carry both ascending and descending fibers.

The hypothalamus has developd from the basal plate. Its medial portion, part of the central gray, surrounds the lower region of the third ventricle. A small strip around the upper region of the ventricle, including the massa intemedia and other medial thalamic nuclei, is derived from the alar plate. Since the hypothalamus is derived mainly from the basal plate, it is primarily a motor system. It contains neurosecretory nuclei and cells that react to changes in the salt and glucose content of the blood and changes in body temperature. Its paraventricular and supraoptic nuclei synthesize oxytocin and vasopressin and transport these hormones in granules to the posterior pituitary gland. Anterior pituitary function is controlled by neurons in the median eminence. Hormone-releasing and hormone-inhibiting factors are synthesized by median eminence neurons and transported along their axons to portal capillaries that carry them to the anterior pituitary gland. Dopaminergic fibers with cell bodies in the hypothalamus conduct impulses to and from the median eminence and these fibers in turn are influenced by fibers of other transmitter systems (Fuxe et al., 1978).

Variations in the bodily state, detected by hypothalamic cells, induce degrees of pleasure or malaise via serotonergic and noradrenergic relays to the orbital limbic cortex. Increased salt content of the blood induces thirst, an impulse to drink, and also an image of water and where it is to be found. Cold is felt as unplesant (via noradrenergic fibers and limbic cortex), and induces an impulse to find a warm spot or put on more clothes.

The hypothalamus not only influences imagination and action, it can be influenced in turn, particularly by imagination and affective memory. A TV commercial in which people eat an appetizing snack or enjoy a glass of beer may arouse an impulse to do likewise. Sexual fantasies or pornographic material arouse sexual desire. Thus the hormonal state regulated by the hypothalamus can influence imagination but can in turn be influenced by it.

THE LATERAL HYPOTHALAMUS

Cells in the lateral hypothalamus can detect chemical compounds such as glucose, insulin and free fatty acids (Oomura, 1973; Oomura et al., 1974; Oomura et al., 1975). Cells in the anterior hypothalamus can detect the presence of various hormones. Oomura and Takigawa (1976) believe that hunger is initiated by free fatty acids in the blood which activate relays from the lateral hypothalamus to areas 6 and 10 in the frontal cortex. Since other hypothalamic neurons are activated by osmotic pressure, thirst and drinking might also be initiated by relays from those neurons to the frontal cortex.

According to Ono et al. (1979), the application of glucose, but also of morphine or enkephalin, inhibits the activity of glucose-sensitive neurons in the lateral hypothalamus. Ono et al. tested some neurons in the hypothalamus of monkeys with glucose and identified those inhibited by this substance. Then, they examined some of these neurons during bar-press feeding. All of them increased their activity ½–2 sec before the monkey pressed the bar, and increased their firing rate throughout bar-press feeding; in contrast, glucose-insensitive neurons decreased their firing during such bar presses. Motor cortex stimulation produced short-latency antidromic excitation in the glucose-sensitive neurons of the lateral hypothalamus, followed by inhibition, and by secondary long- or short-latency excitation. This did not happen in glucose-insensitive neurons.

Oomura et al. (1979) stimulated the lateral hypothalamus in urethane-anesthetized rats and found that cells in area 10 of the frontal cortex increased their firing rate. Apparently, this was a monosynaptic connection. Stimulation of area 10 in the frontal cortex produced excitatory postsynaptic potentials in the lateral hypothalamus. In both cases, inhibition followed the early excitation. Oomura suggested that the sensation of hunger is mediated by the projection from lateral hypothalamus to frontal cortex, which is the association area for sensations of hunger.

These two experiments certainly show that the lateral hypothalamus relays impulses to the frontal cortex that are experienced as hunger. But hunger is not primarily a sensation but a desire to eat. The sensation of "hunger pangs" is the secondary effect of stomach contractions that seem to be produced by excitation of the motor nerves to the stomach, occurring at the same time as the conduction of impulses to the frontal cortex. The desire to eat can be experienced even without hunger pangs.

However, the excitation of frontal neurons can at best produce a desire to eat; it is hardly sufficient to account for the widely differing actions necessary to forage for food or water. The animal must have some notion of what it wants to have and what it can do about it—an image of the goal and a plan of action. The felt impulse toward the imagined food must be appraised (via limbic cortex), must recall earlier experiences and actions (via modality-specific and affective memory circuits) and finally lead to action plans and action itself (via action circuit running through the lateral hypothalamus, connecting with the amygdala and the frontal cortex). It is conceivable, of course, that the simple impulse to eat, relayed from hypothalamus to frontal cortex, might be sufficient if food or water is in sight and can be appraised directly.

The impulse to instinctive action can be excited via hypothalamic neurons detecting the bodily state. But it can also be excited by sensory impressions. We may not be particularly hungry but on seeing something appetizing, may want and take it—hunger comes with eating. On the other hand, we may be so immersed in work or play that we forget to eat.

Lesion Effects

Bilateral lesions in the lateral hypothalamus have led to adipsia and aphagia, but also to hypokinesia, decreased exploration, sensory neglect, catalepsy, and lethargy (Balagura et al., 1969; Fonberg, 1969). Zeigler and Karten (1975) claimed that such lesions are likely to produce incidental damage to central trigeminal structures; and that the so-called lateral hypothalamic syndrome, particularly adipsia and aphagia, is the result of such damage. Trigeminal lesions alone produce aphagia, adipsia and sensory neglect, and so does damage to the trigeminal nerve and ganglion. According to these authors, the extent and presistence of aphagia can be reduced by giving the animals soft palatable food.

Striker et al. (1975) contested Zeigler and Karten's position and referred to reports that the effects of lateral hypothalamic lesions can be duplicated by extrahypothalamic lesions of ascending dopamine neurons which traverse the lateral hypothalamus. Chemical lesions by intracerebral injection of hydroxydopamine (6–OHDA), which leads to degeneration of dopamine terminals, also produce these symptoms. Both types of lesions result in catalepsy, akinesia, and sensory neglect. In their reply to Striker et al., Zeigler and Karten mentioned that rats made aphagic by 6–OHDA resume feeding despite an almost total depletion of striatal dopamine; they insisted that the symptoms of lateral hypothalamic lesions had to be the result of incidental damage to the sensory trigeminal lemniscus.

It is possible that lateral hypothalamic lesions damage the connection from olfactory tubercle to the nucleus interpolaris of the sensory trigeminal nuclear complex (Wold & Brodal, 1974; see chapter 17, p. 231). If so, it would block the reaction to anything smelled that is appraised as good to eat, via the vomeronasal system, and so prevent the animal from reacting to food. At the same time, severing this connection should not stop the animal from becoming hungry and wanting to feed. But if the lesion also interrupted the ascending dopamine axons in the lateral hypothalamus, as is likely, and perhaps the noradrenaline fibers as well, the desire for food would disappear together with the hunger that arouses it.

Ungerstedt (1977) pointed out that the "lateral hypothalamic syndrome" follows upon destruction of an area close to the crus cerebri. Since the ascending dopamine axons running through the lateral hypothalamus assemble into a dense bundle at the tip of the crus cerebri, surgical lesions at that point interrupt the dopamine pathway as effectively as an injection of 6–OHDA into the substantia nigra. According to Ungerstedt, bilateral interruption of the dopamine system by intercerebral injection of 6-OHDA into the bundle of dopamine axons at the point where it leaves the substantia nigra resulted in complete degeneration of both the limbic and the striatal dopamine system and produced cataleptic, akinetic, and rigid animals that refused to eat or drink and had to be tube-fed for weeks without ever regaining spontaneous eating or drinking.

Sensory Neglect.   Unilateral lesions of the lateral hypothalamus or unilateral destruction of the nigro-striatal dopamine pathway produced profound sensory neglect (Ungerstedt et al., 1977). The animals were unable to turn toward food or other things offered on the side contralateral to the lesion. Gradually, they recovered their ability to react to visual, auditory, and olfactory stimuli, but never regained their reaction to tactual stimuli. Ungerstedt et al. interpreted this sensory neglect as an "inability to perform the correct motor act in response to sensory stimuli"—which would be enough to prevent the animals from approaching food and drink or to perform a learned task.

Akinesia. But is doubtful that sensory neglect is the result of *inability* to perform such tasks. For instance, Ungerstedt (1977) found that rats with bilateral lesions of the dopamine path could learn an underwater Y-maze. The animals were submerged in a start box and had to swim to the choice point where they learned to select either a lighted or a dark arm to reach the surface. They learned to swim the maze despite the fact that they were seriously akinetic and were unable to learn ordinary tasks. This surely shows that the animals were able to make the correct motor responses. In the underwater maze, they were faced with an immediate threat of suffocation, hence tried to find the surface and learned the task. Since their motor memory was intact, they remembered the correct exit. Their lack of the dopamine system (involved in the imagination circuit, according to my theory) was little hindrance because no imagination was needed to aim for the surface where they could breathe.

Normally, dopamine fibers from the substantia nigra inhibit the striatum via the nigro-striatal pathway; and the striatum inhibits the ventrolateral thalamic nuclei which project to the motor cortex. The degeneration of the dopamine system after 6–OHDA disinhibits the striatum and causes increased firing in this structure. And the increased firing in the striatum inhibits the ventrolateral thalamic nuclei, so causing the severe akinetic symptoms.

However, the dopamine system innervates not only the striatum but also the amygdala (see Fig. 25.4B) although most investigators disregard this connection in their attempts to explain the lateral hypothalamic syndrome. According to Wepsic and Austin (1972), dopamine and noradrenaline excite some amygdala cells and inhibit others. We would expect that if the amygdala is the relay station in the imagination circuit. Normally, the revival of images would demand relays to some memory areas and none to others. After a complete degeneration of the dopamine system, as in Ungerstedt's experiments, imagination would be impossible because the dopamine relays to the amygdala are destroyed; and spontaneous behavior would be blocked because the absence of dopamine relays to the striatum would reduce conduction in the action circuit. Partial interruption of the dopamine pathway would make action difficult and imagination sluggish.

Effects on Feeding and Drinking. Mogenson (1976) showed that the amygdala is implicated in water intake. He found that stimulation of the lateral hypothalamus, which ordinarily induced drinking in rats, did not do so when a stimulation pulse to the bed nucleus of the stria terminalis preceded each pulse to the lateral hypothalamus by five milliseconds. Drinking was facilitated when the mediodorsal septum was stimulated five milliseconds before each pulse to the lateral hypothalamus. He further found that precommissural fornix fibers mediated the facilitatory response from the lateral hypothalamus, and stria terminalis fibers, the inhibitory effect. Apparently, the hippocampus is activated when the animal finds water or milk: The animal remembers that this was good to drink. Fornix fibers then relay this excitation to midbrain and lateral hypothalamus to connect with the action circuit. On the other hand, electrical stimulation of the stria terminalis, part of the imagination circuit, may excite all kinds of images, not only images of water. Such random images do not lead to drinking but inhibit it instead, via the stria terminalis fibers connecting with the frontal lobe and lateral hypothalamus. In addition, Mogenson reported that the firing rate of hypothalamic cells at a given time seemed to determine whether septal afferents excite or inhibit them. Thus it seems likely that both imagination and memory can influence the hypothalamus and so determine the actions that lead to eating or drinking.

When Grossman and Grossman (1973) made bilateral parasagittal cuts along the lateral border of the hypothalamus, interrupting most of the fibers entering or leaving laterally, they observed postoperative symptoms that were indistinguishable from those after lateral hypothalamic lesions. The rats neither ate nor drank for months, had to be tubefed and did not respond to changes in blood glucose like intact animals. Even those rats that eventually began to eat and drink again, did not increase their food intake after insulin like normal rats. These animals overreacted to changes in taste, which is not seen after lateral hypothalamic lesions.

According to the authors, the ascending fibers of the ventral amygdalofugal tract, which leave the hypothalamus laterally, were not responsible for these symptoms: A cut lateral to the lateral border of the hypothalamus produced no significant effect on food and water intake. Apparently, the majority of the fibers cut in the above experiment belong to a pathway interconnecting the striatum, zona incerta, subthalamus, substantia nigra, and the midbrain tegmentum.[1] The authors pointed out that lesions in the globus pallidus have produced long-term aphagia and adipsia, and so have lesions of the substantia nigra and its projections to the striatum. This agrees with my suggestion that the impulse to eat and drink is mediated by fibers of the action circuit from midbrain tegmentum via lateral hypothalamus to striatum, ventral thalamic nucleus, and cortex.

The lateral cuts made by the authors also seem to have disconnected the lateral hypothalamic cells that detect changes in blood glucose and fatty acids in the blood, from the action circuit. As a result, the animals would no longer be hungry and thirsty and so would have no impulse to eat or drink. The finicky eating

---

[1] It is possible that the fibers cut by Grossman and Grossman belong to the branch of the cholinergic pathway sketched by Shute (1970), which crosses the lateral hypothalamus on its way to the striatum (see Fig. 27.1)

in recovered animals resembles one of the symptoms found after lesions of the ventromedial hypothalamic nucleus (see p. 440f.), but seems to have a different root. Even without hunger, these animals might still be tempted by something tasty and eat; for them, feeding may depend on appetite rather than hunger, as Grossman and Grossman say.

Effect on the Action Circuit.   That the lateral hypothalamus is a link in the action circuit projecting to the frontal cortex is confirmed by several reports. Teitelbaum and Cytawa (1965) showed that the cortex is necessary for foraging and feeding. After animals had recovered from the effect of lateral hypothalamic lesions, the authors damaged the cortex by applying potassium chloride to it. This second insult required another three weeks' recovery time. The cortex is necessary because it contains the engrams on which the animal must draw when imagining food or planning action. Without the cortex, the animal may eat when food is set before it but is not able to forage for it.

Rice and Campbell (1973) implanted stimulating electrodes in the lateral hypothalamus of rats. When the current was turned on, the animals started to eat. This elicited feeding could be markedly reduced if large parts of the frontal lobes were removed. That means that the impulse to eat is mediated via the projection from lateral hypothalamus to the frontal lobe, which would support my theory. The animal is aware of an impulse to eat as soon as the nerve impulse has reached the frontal lobe (area 6) via striatum and ventrolateral thalamic nuclei. Since stimulation of the lateral hypothalamus elicits eating after a latency of 3–5 minutes (Leibowitz, 1977), it would seem that such stimulation excites first the imagination circuit (via amygdala), initiating images of food via various cortical association areas, as well as plans for action via the frontal cortex. (As Braun, 1975, has shown, cortical lesions in various areas can disrupt feeding.) Next, these images of food and feeding are appraised as good and initiate an action impulse via hippocampus and action circuit, which normally joins in the lateral hypothalamus with the hunger-induced impulse to eat. If the animals are not hungry, stimulation apparently must be continued for some time before feeding begins.

Hunger seems to be a reaction to the depleted state of the organism (lack of glucose or free fatty acid in the blood; see Oomura & Takigawa, 1976), detected by lateral hypothalamic cells which send relays to the frontal lobe.

Rewarding Brain Stimulation

Hunger facilitates bar pressing for brain stimulation when the stimulating electrode is in the lateral hypothalamus, but does not do so when it is in the septal area; high androgen levels favor brain stimulation when the stimulating electrode is in the medial septal area but not when it is in the lateral hypothalamus. Hence it has been suggested that brain stimulation may have the effect of a food reward in the lateral hypothalamus, and of a sexual reward in the medial septal area (Hoebel, 1969). Gallistel (1969) has investigated this problem by using two or three reward electrodes in each rat brain. One of these electrodes was used for "priming," the other for the experimental reward. Priming, that is, giving the rat a few trains of electrical brain stimulation before a trial, is necessary to induce running. Since the animals are not hungry or thirsty and don't have a high androgen level, there is no natural drive state to motivate running along a runway and press a lever at the end. The priming reminds them of what to expect at the end of the run. Gallistel found no qualitative difference in the rewards dispensed by the different electrodes. Rats ran as fast when the priming stimulation was given over the reward electrode as they did when it was given over a different electrode. Indeed, in many cases, they ran faster if the reward stimulation was given over a different electrode. In a T-maze, where the animals could choose the priming or the alternative electrode as reward, they showed no preference. Hence Gallistel concluded that there was no difference in the quality of reward between the different electrode sites.

Brain Stimulation versus Natural Drive.   Brain stimulation is different from a natural drive like hunger, thirst, or sexual desire. A natural drive is continuous and can be reduced only by its satisfaction. Hungry rats might prefer brain stimulation to food, but afterwards they would still be hungry. Priming may induce running and bar pressing but it is not a drive. It is a pleasurable experience that animals have learned to expect from a particular action. Unlike a natural drive, it does not continue during running: Only its affective memory remains and is sufficient for the rat to want to repeat the experience. That the pleasure from brain stimulation is different from the pleasure of satisfying a drive is shown by numerous reports that animals pressing a bar for brain stimulation extinguish quickly when they do not receive it, in contrast to hungry or thirsty animals pressing a bar for food or drink. However, when the rats are on short rations, hence are hungry when they press the bar for brain stimulation, they increase the rate of bar pressing during reward trials and extinguish very slowly during non-reward trials, just as do hungry or thirsty animals pressing the bar for food or water (Deutsch & DiCara, 1967). When the hunger drive is added to the affective memory of pleasurable brain stimulation, it adds urgency to the rat's performance.

The fact that the animals were motivated by brain stimulation at any reward site does not mean that all sites have the same reward quality. I would suggest that the pleasure from lateral hypothalamic stimulation is that of getting food and eating. For hungry rats, this is the only pleasure that can promise satiation. But for animals that are not hungry and only have had a pleasant experience from priming, any kind of pleasure will do—they might even appreciate variety.

Hunger and thirst are unpleasant, based on a negative appraisal; and such appraisals, according to my theory, are mediated by the noradrenaline system. Indeed, many reports connect noradrenaline with hunger. Myers (1974) found that the noradrenaline level in the hypothalamus is incresed in hungry animals. A perfusate collected from the perifornical area of a food-deprived monkey has induced eating when injected into the analogous site of a sated monkey. A microinjection of noradrenaline in the lateral and anterior hypothalamus of rhesus monkeys has induced eating. In aphagic animals with lateral hypothalamic lesions, the injection of noradrenaline has restored milk drinking (Berger et al., 1971). Grossman (1960) reported that eating could be elicited in rats by direct noradrenergic stimulation of the lateral hypothalamus, and blocked by adrenergic blocking agents. Drinking could be elicited in these animals by direct cholinergic stimulation and blocked by cholinergic blocking agents. Hence we can conclude that noradrenaline fibers mediate the impulse to eat, cholinergic fibers mediate the impulse to drink. The dopamine system also is involved because it can either facilitate or inhibit action via the striatum. In addition, the dopaminergic imagination circuit makes it possible to anticipate food and drink and plan how to obtain it.

Over and above the action impulses induced by the hypothalamus as a reaction to variations in the bodily state, action impulses induced by appraisals (via limbic cortex and hippocampus) are also carried over hypothalamic pathways. For instance, Lisander and Martner (1976) found that electrical stimulation of the cerebellar fastigial nucleus produced licking, chewing, predatory attack, and similar behavior patterns in cats. Such behavior patterns were also produced by stimulation of the hypothalamus. In the freely roaming animal, stimulation of the hypothalamus may induce looking, sniffing, exploring; often, the animal will lick from a water bottle, eat a food pellet, gnaw at a block of wood, drink water from a cup, or make a sexual or aggressive approach.

Stimulation Experiments

Hess (1956) found long ago that stimulating a region about 2 mm from the midline in the posterior hypothalamus can induce fear and flight in animals; attack and fight was induced by stimulating other hypothalamic sites. And Roberts (1958) reported that electrical stimulation of the posterior hypothalamus, just rostral to the mamillary bodies, produced a "flight reaction" in cats, with alerting, looking around, and attempted escape. The animals quickly learned to escape such stimulation by climbing through an opening. But they never learned to avoid stimulation on cue, unlike cats which were given an electric shock through the bottom of the cage, or whose somatosensory cortex was stimulated. This surely confirms my suggestion that a relay from cerebellum to motor cortex runs through the hypothalamus and initiates emotion and action. When some points along this cerebello-hypothalamic relay are stimulated, the animal experiences an impulse to flee (fear) and tries to run. Roberts' cats felt fear, an impulse to run, as soon as their hypothalamus was stimulated, hence they quickly learned to escape. Before such stimulation, they felt no fear, no impulse to escape, hence they could not learn to avoid stimulation by escaping in time. In contrast, when the somatosensory area was stimulated, they felt something unpleasant they wanted to avoid—hence they could escape on cue, so avoiding repeated stimulation.

Aggression also has been evoked by stimulation of the lateral hypothalamus, whether that stimulation was electrical or chemical (carbachol, see Bandler, 1971, Flynn, 1967). Apparently, the fibers involved in mediating aggressive impulses are cholinergic. Smith et al. (1970), showed that neostigmine, a cholinesterase inhibitor, evoked mouse-killing in rats, and methyl atropine blocked it. Aggression evoked by hypothalamic stimulation can be influenced by stimulating the amygdala (Egger & Flynn, 1963). An aggressive impulse can certainly be overridden or changed by intensive imaginative activity.

As mentioned before, behavior elicited by hypothalamic stimulation is different from similar behavior evoked by stimulation of various sites in the amygdala. For instance, attack elicited by hypothalamic stimulation is carried out immediately and stops as soon as the electrical stimulation stops. In contrast, amygdala stimulation leads to a gradual build-up of aggressive attack and gradually subsides after stimulation has stopped (King, quoted by Isaacson, 1974). Apparently, hypothalamic stimulation directly activates an impulse to action—as it should if the stimulation site is within the action circuit. Amygdala stimulation, however, seems to activate images of attacking an obstacle which gradually lead to attack.

Changes in Elicited Behavior.   Elicited behavior may change in a changing environment. For instance, if electrical stimulation has produced licking from a water bottle, the animal does not lick anything else when the water bottle is no longer available. If the animal is stimulated for some length of time, it might start gnawing wood or eating food just as readily as drinking from a dish. If the bottle is later replaced, the animal will not return to licking from the bottle but will continue with the habit it has formed after the bottle had been removed (Valenstein, 1969). Apparently, electrical stimulation had induced an impulse to mouth something. When the bottle was no longer available, this action impulse urged the animal to turn to something else that could be mouthed or eaten. Once it has experienced satisfaction, whether in eating or in drinking from a dish, it continues to do what has proved to be pleasant even when the bottle is returned.

Action impulses relayed in the action circuit seem to be specific for body or head movement (exploring versus sniffing). For instance, eating or drinking may be elicited from one site in the lateral hypothalamus, and general exploration from a neighboring site. On the other hand, consummatory activities that bring pleasure and are followed by satiety can apparently be substituted for each other, depending on what is available. So Gallistel (1969) found that a posterior hypothalamic electrode eliciting eating and a lateral hypothalamic electrode eliciting sexual behavior might later elicit either. Once the animal experiences pleasure when following the urge to action induced by brain stimulation, it may approach whatever promises satisfaction.

This means that despite the induced impulse to action, the animal still appraises what it encounters and can modify its action. For instance, stimulating certain points in the posterior hypothalamus of a cat elicits an attack on the experimenter but not on a rat. Stimulation at other points elicits an attack on a rat but not on the experimenter. The degree of rage evoked by the stimulation may determine whether the animal will attack something small (rat) or something large (experimenter), according to Isaacson (1974).

Elicited Behavior versus Self-stimulation.   Huston (1971) measured the current levels required to elicit eating, drinking, copulating, or to evoke the reappearance of a previously extinguished response, or the increase in response rates to a fixed-ratio schedule. In every case, the current level required for such elicited behavior was much lower than that required for self-stimulation. In elicited behavior, the action circuit itself is stimulated. The animal feels an impulse to action and all it has to do is to act as it feels urged to act. In contrast, self-stimulation via electrode activates the serotonin system and must do so sufficiently for the animal to experience pleasure and to want to repeat the action that will provide more pleasure. This requires a complicated sequence of appraisal, wanting, motor memory and motor imagination, and finally, an impulse to action and the overt movements to carry it out.

I have suggested that the action circuit is cholinergic and runs via the lateral hypothalamus to striatum and ventral thalamic nuclei to end in the frontal cortex. According to Shute (1970), an ascending cholinergic pathway from the reticular formation via the substantia nigra and lateral hypothalamus could be responsible for the rage and attack seen after stimulation of these regions. Shute thinks that the ascending cholinergic fibers in the lateral hypothalamus (Fig. 27.1) are part of the extrathalamic portion of the ascending reticular activating system. I have suggested that this system is part of the modality-specific memory circuit which is also cholinergic; but activating motor memory means evoking an impulse to action. Stimulation of the cerebellum can also induce rage (Sprague & Chambers, 1955). Both cerebellum and hypothalamus are relay stations in the action circuit, according to my theory.

The hypothalamus is primarily a motor system, activating secretary gland to produce various hormones but also sending impulses via various motor relay stations to the frontal cortex.

The Cholinergic Memory Circuit

Animals with bilateral lesions in the lateral hypothalamus are difficult to train because they have trouble initiating action. They often have to be forced to run, usually by applying foot shock, often repeatedly, to force them to complete the

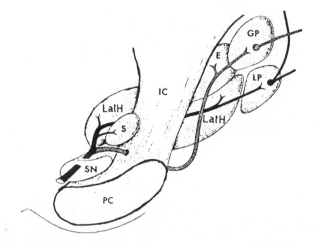

FIG. 27.1 Diagram illustrating the double route through the ventral diencephalon taken by the ascending cholinergic type of reticular fibers in the cat. Right side of brain seen from behind; lateral pathway stippled. Abbreviations: E, entopeduncular nucleus; GP, globus pallidus; IC, internal capsule; LatH lateral hypothalamus; LP, lateral preoptic area; PC, cerebral peduncle; S, subthalamic nucleus; SN, substantia nigra. From: C. C. D. Shute, 1970.

task. Thompson and Hawkins (1961) found that such lesions produced a deficit in active avoidance (jumping to grip the edge of a wall when a light announced an electric shock) and in learning a simultaneous discrimination between an upward and a downward sloping path; errors were punished by shock. The same impairment was revealed after lesions of the interpeduncular nucleus or the habenulo-interpeduncular tract. In all cases, the animals showed fear when they saw the light. The deficit in active avoidance is not surprising, considering the animal's reluctance to start any kind of action. The fact that they showed fear indicates that they remembered the shock and anticipated pain: The relays from limbic system to hippocompus and amygdala were intact.

There is considerable evidence that lateral hypothalamic stimulation facilitates learning over a cholinergic pathway. Sepinwall (1966) found that cholinergic excitation (application of carbachol to the lateral hypothalamus) enhanced active avoidance. According to Squire (1969), such excitation 15 minutes before a trial increased alternation rate in a T-maze; application of a cholinergic blocking agent (scopolamine) decreased it. Finally, Sepinwall (1969) reported that application of carbachol to the lateral hypothalamus of rats trained to avoid shock by turning a wheel greatly facilitated their performance while the application of atropine (cholinergic blocking agent) impaired it.

These results indicate that a cholinergic fiber system in the lateral hypothalamus facilitates motor learning. Since atropine and scopolamine blocked conduction, the circuit involved seems to be the motor memory circuit. As I have pointed out before (see Chapter 26), the motor memory circuit is closely allied with the action circuit. Motor memory is recalled as action is initiated and proceeds via the projection from anterior ventral (VA) thalamic nucleus to the prefrontal cortex.

Activation of this circuit seems to be pleasurable because the remembered action was pleasurable. According to Olds (1976), rats learned to press a lever to self-inject a cholinergic drug into the lateral hypothalamus. Such brain stimulation reward seems to excite the serotoninergic fibers in the medial forebrain bundle, that accompany the action and motor memory circuits.

THE VENTROMEDIAL HYPOTHALAMIC NUCLEUS

Lesion Effects

Bilateral lesions of this area have resulted in permanent overeating and obesity, both in animals (Epstein, 1960; Teitelbaum & Epstein, 1962) and in human beings (Killeffer & Stern, 1970). Animals with ventromedial hypothalamic lesions behave as if they were hungrier than intact animals, but they are finicky eaters. They turn away from food mixed with quinine or other unpalatable substances at concentrations willingly accepted by intact animals. If their food is mixed with cellulose, they do not eat enough to maintain their weight, while intact animals eat more than normally (Teitelbaum, 1955).

Hunger and Satiety. It had been assumed for many years that these lesions disrupt a satiety mechanism. But doubts were raised by reports that animals with ventromedial hypothalamic lesions did not press a lever for additional food when they were put on short rations (Miller et al., 1950). Indeed, if they have to press a lever for intragastric feeding so that they cannot taste the food, they refuse to feed themselves (McGinty et al., 1965). More recently, however, Kent and Peters (1973) have shown that animals with ventromedial hypothalamic lesions do take more food than intact animals. They run down a straight alley for a food reward more quickly than control animals; and they eat more in their home cages, whether they have little food or a great deal. The authors found, however, that leasioned hungry animals did not increase their response rates when they had to press a lever to receive food, but neither did they press more slowly when their rations were increased. Kent and Peters concluded that lesioned animals do take more food than intact animals when food is freely available, but they do not seem to adjust their response to the situation.

Apparently, the only satisfaction these animals can obtain in eating is from the taste of food. The usual satisfaction that comes from repletion and brings about muscular relaxation is no longer available. Since the ventromedial hypothalamic nucleus has a direct reciprocal connection with the amygdala, lesioned animals can no longer imagine what to do to achieve satisfaction. They press the lever at a steady rate, no matter how hungry they are. They "work" for palatable food but refuse to do so if the pleasure of taste is denied them.

Normal eating habits depend on an uninterrupted action circuit. When it is interrupted in any way, animals show symptoms of hyperphagia or aphagia, depending on the site of the lesions. For instance, Grossman and Grossman (1971) found that bilateral knife cuts separating the medial from the lateral hypothalamic areas resulted in mild hyperphagia if the animals could eat what they liked. But if the food was unpalatable, they stopped eating even when hungry. This period of mild hyperphagia followed a 2–3 week period of aphagia and adipsia. Apparently, the knife cuts resulted in edema, hence the lateral hypothalamic pathway was nonfunctional for a time and a transitory aphagia and adipsia was the result. As soon as the edema subsided, the animals began to overeat, probably because the cut interrupted the relays from ventromedial hypothalamic nuclei to the lateral hypothalamus, so releasing the action circuit from inhibition. It also seems that the ventromedial nucleus is excited by relays from the lateral hypothalamus; these relays also were cut and produced an inability to experience satiation.

Ellison and his coworkers (1970) have isolated the hypothalamus surgically from the rest of the brain in cats and rats and found that the animals would take neither food nor water although both were freely available. When they touched a leasioned animal's lips with an eyedropper of liquid, it would turn toward the dropper and grasp it with its teeth. When the liquid was then dropped in its mouth, the animal swallowed immediately. In such a procedure, the hypothalamic cells may detect the nutritional state of the body but cannot send relays to the frontal lobe. Hence the animal feels neither hunger nor thirst and has no impulse to eat or drink. The swallowing reflex is all that is left.

From these reports we can conclude that the ventromedial hypothalamus mediates the pleasure of repletion and relaxation. After ablation of the ventromedial hypothalamic nucleus, the animal can no longer experience such pleasure and only the pleasure of taste remains. When food is not palatable, either because it is contaminated by quinine or merely mixed with cellulose, such animals do not eat as readily as intact animals, even when put on short rations.

Transmitter Systems

Noradrenaline. Leibowitz has a different explanation for the hyperphagia after ventromedial hypothalamic lesions. She pointed out that noradrenergic neurons in the brain, as in the periphery, have two kinds of receptors, alpha and beta; and these have different effects on eating and drinking. A hungry rat can be stopped from eating by peripheral or central injection of an alpha receptor blocker, but injection of a beta blocker increases feeding (Slangen & Miller, 1969; Leibowitz, 1977). Hence feeding is stimulated by alpha receptor activity. In contrast, drinking is suppressed by alpha receptor activity but is stimulated by alpha plus beta excitation (Leibowitz, 1977). Eating can be induced in sated rats and monkeys by a hypothalamic injection of noradrenaline, which has a potent alpha action (Slangen & Miller, 1969; Myers, 1974); the injection of isoproterenol, which strongly excites beta receptors and has very little alpha activity, has no effect (Slangen & Miller, 1969; Leibowitz, 1977). Indeed, injection of this drug in hungry rats suppressed feeding for various periods, depending on the drug dosage. Leibowitz emphasized that normally both types of receptors are active. It depends on the proportion of alpha and beta activity whether eating and drinking will be increased or decreased.

The ventromedial hypothalamus is considerably more sensitive than the lateral hypothalamus to alpha receptor stimulation (which increases feeding and suppresses drinking) while the lateral hypothalamus is more sensitive to beta receptor excitation (which suppresses feeding). Leibowitz assumes that alpha substances inhibit ventromedial "satiety" neurons so that the animal starts or continues feeding, while beta substances inhibit lateral hypothalamic pathways so that feeding stops.

But that is not the end of the story. Ungerstedt et al. (1977) reported that noradrenaline pathways do not seem to initiate eating. He injected 6–OHDA directly into both ascending noradrenaline pathways, which caused degeneration of nordrenaline neurons without affecting the dopamine pathway. Such animals showed no signs of aphagia or adipsia. In fact, they seemed to be overeating. And Ahlskog et al. (1975) found that the destruction of the ventral noradrenaline pathway by midbrain injection with 6–OHDA, which reduced hypothalamic noradrenaline to 6% of normal, produced overeating in rats, but only at night. In comparison, ventromedial hypothalamic lesions induced overeating both by day and by night. In fact, the two procedures were additive: When ventromedial hypothalamic lesions were inflicted on rats after 6–OHDA lesions, the animals increased their food intake dramatically.

Destruction of the noradrenaline pathway by 6–OHDA would reduce the unpleasantness of hunger, but hunger as an impulse to eat would still remain and would be intensified by increased dopamine activity, producing food images: Since dopamine could no longer be converted to noradrenaline, the total dopamine obtained from Dopa would be available for imagination via amygdala, and for action via striatum. The end result would be increased feeding at night, which is the waking time for rats. When ventromedial hypothalamic lesions were added, the inhibition of repletion was lost so that the animals now would eat whenever food was available, during the day as well as during the night. If the action circuit is cholinergic, as I am suggesting, and produces inhibition via the ventromedial hypothalamic nucleus and excitation via the lateral hypothalamus, a ventromedial hypothalamic lesion would increase the urge to feed.

Acetylcholine   Indeed, Stark and Totty (1967) found that cholinergic excitation facilitates eating. They reported that systemic administration of physostigmine lowered the threshold for eating, elicited by stimulation via lateral hypothalamic electrodes. But Margules (1968) found that application of atropine to the ventromedial nucleus of sated rats did not elicit feeding. However, most of the lesioned animals became hyperactive, which contrasted sharply with the usual apathy and somnolence of sated controls. Indeed, the animals continued to press the lever for milk but did not drink it. Margules suggested that the ventromedial hypothalamic nucleus acts not only as satiety system but also as part of a punishment system via cholinergic excitatory synapses.

To call a system that suppresses punished responses a punishment system is rather misleading. Cholinergic drugs in the ventromedial hypothalamic nucleus decreased punished responding and atropine increased it; atropine also increased motor activity suppressed by satiation. Hence we can conclude that this nucleus contains cholinergic synapses that inhibit responses, probably by inhibiting the action circuit in the lateral hypothalamus. Eating does seem to be mediated by a cholinergic pathway; but inhibiting the inhibitory relays to the lateral hypothalamus (thus releasing the action circuit) would not arouse a specific urge to eat, merely increase general activity. Only when the impulse to action is joined to an impuse to eat, that is, when the animals are hungry, does an excitation of the action circuit initiate eating. Hence atropine, which released cholinergic relays, did not elicit eating.

Noradrenaline may not be necessary for the initiation of eating, but it does seem to contribute to the urge to look for food. Since hunger is unpleasant, we would expect increased noradrenaline production; indeed, the noradrenaline level in the hypothalamus is raised during hunger and lowered during feeding. It may well be that noradrenaline is responsible for the unpleasantness of hunger. Its alpha receptors may inhibit the ventromedial hypothalamic nucleus and so increase the animal's urge to find food and eat it, as Leibowitz says; and beta receptors may inhibit the lateral hypothalamus so that foraging and eating stops. That would imply that nordrenergic fibers can influence cholinergic conduction, i.e., that cholinergic neurons are monoaminoceptive just as monoaminergic fibers seem to be cholinoceptive.

Cholinergic stimulation of the ventromedial hypothalamic nucleus seems to induce not only eating but aggressive attack (in cats). Electrical stimulation has the same effect as a microinjection of acetylcholine or carbachol at the stimulation site. Nakao et al. (1979) found that raising the current intensity produced dilation of the pupils, ear flattening, hissing, and directed attack in cats, in that order. A microinjection of GABA lowered the effective current threshold; this decrease could be antagonized by picrotoxin. In contrast, a minute injection of glycine into the same site in the ventromedial hypothalamic nucleus raised the current threshold, an effect that could be antagonized by strychnine. Hence Nakao et al. suggest that glycine (but not GABA) normally inhibits the cholinergic conduction of relays that lead to aggressive action. At any rate, the ventromedial hypothalamic nucleus seems to mediate the impulse to relax or stop eating, either via inhibitory relays to the lateral hypothalamus, or by the inhibition of cholinergic fibers in the ventromedial hypothalamus itself.

Such inhibition, it seems, can also be initiated by imagination and affective memory via amygdala and hippocampus. This would explain why cuts made anterior or posterior to the ventromedial hypothalamic nuclei produce hyperphagia and hyperdipsia, effects that were noticed immediately after surgery (Grossman, 1971). Apparently, anterior cuts produced increased eating and drinking because repletion could no longer evoke images of resting and relaxing (via amygdala and frontal lobe). Posterior cuts may produce these symptoms because the ventromedial hypothalamic nucleus could no longer relay the impulse to stop eating and relax (via striatum, ventral thalamus to motor cortex).

Serotonin. The rest and relaxation accompanying satiety is pleasant. It seems to be mediated by cholinergic excitation of the ventral hypothalamic nucleus while the feeding of pleasure may be the result of serotonergic excitation of fibers accompanying the action circuit. The destruction of the ventromedial hypothalamic nuclei not only abolishes satiety, it produces savage and aggressive rats, cats, and monkeys (Eclancher & Karli, 1971). When animals can no longer relax, when they can no longer feel the pleasure of satiety and rest, every obstacle will arouse aggression.

The administration of morphine has resulted in excitation of ventromedial hypothalamic neurons and inhibition of neurons in the lateral hypothalamus. Naloxone or nalorphine, the morphine antagonists, have reversed these effects (Kerr et al., 1974). Morphine produces not only relaxation but pleasure, via the serotonin system (see Chapter 25). Morphine inhibits not only the lateral hypothalamus but also cells in the ventral tegmental area—another proof that this area is a relay station in the action circuit including not only cholinergic but serotonergic fibers.

Learning

Active Avoidance. Lesions of the ventromedial hypothalamic nucleus facilitated two-way active avoidance (Grossman, 1966a, 1972a), but transverse sections just behind this nucleus interfered with the acquisition of this task: The animals required more trials to begin making avoidance responses. If the cut was just ahead of the ventromedial nucleus, the animals remained unimpaired. Apparently, lesions of the ventromedial hypothalamus facilitated active avoidance because conduction in the action circuit was now unopposed; and greater activity meant quicker avoidance. In contrast, when the hypothalamus was cut behind the ventromedial hypothalamus, the relays from the ventral tegmentum to the lateral hypothalamus were interrupted before turning toward the lateral hypothalamus. Hence the animals had difficulty initiating action. A cut just ahead of the ventromedial hypothalamus would leave the lateral action circuit unimpaired.

Passive Avoidance. Bilateral lesions in the ventromedial hypothalamic nucleus resulted in a passive avoidance deficit. Rats learned less readily than normals to refrain from drinking water when this response had been punished by electric shock. Passive avoidance deficits after such lesions were also reported by McNew and Thompson (1966); Sclafani and Grossman (1971). Margules (1968) found that the application of the cholinergic antagonist atropine directly to the ventromedial hypothalamic nucleus resulted in a substantial passive avoidance deficit in a task in which punished and unpunished lever presses alternated. In the unpunished schedule, a lever press was rewarded with milk at infrequent intervals; in the punished schedule, every bar press was rewarded with milk but at the same time punished with shock to the paws. After atropine, the rate of unpunished and rewarded responses remained stable during the test, but the rate of punished and rewarded responses increased materially. In contrast, application of cholinergic drugs (physostigmine or neostigmine) produced a significant decrease in the rate of punished as well as unpunished responses. This suppression was not the result of any difficulty in moving.

The lesioned animals' advantage in active avoidance and impairment in passive avoidance seems to result from the loss of inhibition ordinarily exercised via the ventromedial hypothalamic nucleus. With the action circuit overactive, the animals would run faster than normal from a signal announcing shock, and would be unable to stop approaching the food cup although the cue indicated that approach will be punished by shock.

The Action Circuit and Motor Memory Circuit: From Midbrain to Frontal Lobe

In discussing the last link of the action and motor memory circuits I first outline the established connections from ventral midbrain and substantia nigra to the striatum and thalamus. Next, I discuss the transmitter systems involved in these pathways and the effect of damage to these systems. I hope to show that at least two systems are involved, one a branch of the action circuit, the other a branch of the motor memory circuit. Since the motor memory circuit is so closely allied to the action circuit, I discuss both in their transit from ventral tegmentum to striatum and thalamus, and try to show where they diverge. Both circuits seem to course closely linked through the substantia nigra and striatum but diverge from globus pallidus to the thalamus.

THE BASAL GANGLIA

These structures consist of a group of nuclei at the base of the fore- and midbrain. Usually, they are understood to include the caudate and putamen, the globus pallidus, subthalamic nucleus, and substantia nigra (Anderson, 1981).

The Substantia Nigra. In frontal sections, this nuclear mass appears as an oblique band within the cerebral peduncles. It consists of a ventral red zone and a dorsal black zone. Rostrally, the substantia nigra is continuous with the globus pallidus; caudally, it reaches the pontine nuclei. The black zone has a compact dorsal and a reticular ventral part. A strongly developed topically organized projection from the caudate and putamen travels via the globus pallidus to the reticular part of the substantia nigra. This pathway uses GABA as transmitter. The substantia nigra also receives fibers from the pallidum and subthalamus.

The major efferent pathway from the substantia nigra comes from the compact part, runs to the striatum and consists mainly but not exclusively of dopaminergic fibers. A substantial projection from the reticular part courses through field H of Forel and distributes to the magnocellular part of the ventral anterior, the medial part of the ventrolateral thalamic nuclei, and the dorsomedial thalamic nuclei. Its terminals overlap with fibers from the cerebellum. The transmitter in this pathway is unknown, but is not aminergic. A smaller branch runs in the lenticular fasciculus via the subthalamic nucleus to the thalamic reticular nucleus (Carpenter, 1973; Nieuwenhuys, 1977; Beckstedt et al., 1979; see Fig. 28.1). Many nigral neurons have two branches, one going toward the thalamus, the other toward the superior colliculus (Anderson, 1981).

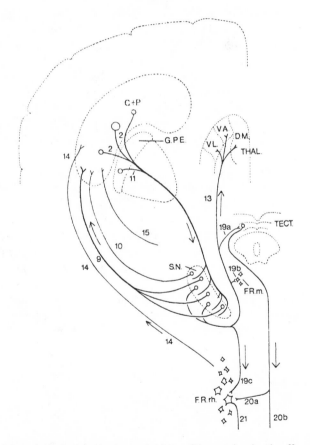

FIG. 28.1   Connections of substantia nigra and striatum. Diagram showing the afferent and efferent connections of the substantia nigra, the tectospinal tract, and some connections of the reticular formation. Abbreviations: D.M., nucleus dorsomedialis thalami; F.R.m., mesencephalic reticular formation; F.R.rh., rhombencephalic reticular formation; S.N., substantia nigra; TECT., tectum mesencephali. From R. Nieuwenhuys, 1977.

Most of the lesion experiments concerned with learning involve the connection of substantia nigra and striatum. I will discuss the effect of such lesions after discussing the striatal connections.

The Striatum.   This complex consists of the caudate nucleus and the putamen (neostriatum) and the globus pallidus (paleostriatum). The globus pallidus (pallidum) and putamen taken together have the shape of a lens, hence are often called the lenticular nucleus (Noback & Demarest, 1981). The caudate nucleus, head to tail, curves around the lenticular nucleus and is separated from it by the fibers of the internal capsule. These are ascending and descending projection fibers that connect the hemispheres with the brainstem. Because of these intervening fibers, caudate and putamen appear striped when cut, hence they are also called the corpus striatum. The neostriatum, phylogenetically more recent than the globus pallidus, receives projections from all areas of the neocortex, also from thalamus and substantia nigra. Each cortical area seems to send relays to a different region of the neostriatum, although there is some overlap. The prefrontal cortex projects to a much larger region of the neostriatum than do other cortical areas. Lesions of the neostriatal region, which receives its major input from the prefrontal cortex, duplicate the effects of prefrontal ablations. Hence Divac (1977) suggests that different parts of the neostriatum form functional units with anatomically related neocortical areas.

Both caudate and putamen project to the globus pallidus which serves as relay station for both. Stimulation of the caudate can either excite or inhibit pallidal and nigral neurons (Anderson, 1981). In the monkey, fibers from the pallidum run through the ansa lenticularis and the lenticular fasciculus to course dorsolaterally and rostrally to enter the ventral anterior and ventrolateral thalamic nuclei, also the centromedian and dorsomedial thalamic nuclei. Some fibers run as pallido-tegmental bundle to the caudal midbrain tegmentum. At the level of the inferior colliculus, these fibers sweep dorsally to spread around the pedunculopontine nucleus. This nucleus receives afferents from the red nucleus and sends relays to the globus pallidus (Anderson, 1981). Carpenter (1973) found no fibers from the pallidum descending in the brainstem caudal to the isthmus, and no pallidofugal fibers in the hypothalamus, zona incerta, red nucleus or inferior olive.

It is generally accepted that the basal ganglia regulate motor activity. Animals with lesions of the globus pallidus or the substantia nigra show great reluctance to move, as do Parkinson patients. Lesions of caudate and putamen produce hyperactivity and hyperreactivity in animals; in human beings, chorea and rigidity.

Striatum and substantia nigra contain several neurotransmitters. The dopamine level is higher than in any other part of the nervous system; the acetylcholine level also is high, especially in caudate and putamen. GABA and serotonin also serve as neurotransmitters in the basal ganglia. But the role played by these structures in coordinating movements or the mechanism by which such control is achieved is not known as yet (Anderson, 1981).

Lesions of the basal ganglia have produced not only motor impairment but also learning deficits. According to Scheibel and Scheibel (1966), the striatum projects to the anterior thalamic nuclei, which are relay stations in the affective memory circuit in my theory. This connection would make it possible to retrieve the memory of the "good" move during learning.

Learning Deficits. Caudate lesions consistently produced learning and retention deficits. Thompson and Mettler (1963) found that bilateral ablation of about 75% of the head of the caudate in cats produced a permanent deficit in active avoidance and food approach learning. Such lesions also impaired delayed alternation learning and extinction, as did septal lesions. Butters and Rosvold (1968a,b) believe that the ventrolateral sector of the caudate nucleus, the septal nuclei, and the orbital frontal cortex form part of a neural system regulating response tendencies. However, Green at al. (1967) reported impaired two-way active avoidance learning after caudate lesions of less than 20% in the caudate/putamen complex, while septal lesions facilitated such learning. Indeed, it is not likely that the septal area with its manifold connections is as closely associated with the caudate as Butters and Rosvold believe. It seems certain, however, that the caudate is necessary for motor learning and retention.

There are some contrary results. Winocur and Mills (1969a) found that rats with caudate lesions learned active avoidance within normal limits, and so did Fox et al. (1964), working with cats. Their lesions were aimed at the more anterior parts of the head of the caudate, and damaged mostly the anterodorsal regions. In contrast, Green et al. and Thompson and Mettler (1963) placed their lesions, which were large, in a more posteroventral area.

Lesions in the substantia nigra, which is reciprocally connected with the caudate, have practically the same effect. So Kirkby (1970) as well as Mitcham and Thomas (1972) reported that rats with small bilateral lesions in the anteroventral caudate nucleus or the rostral substantia nigra were significantly impaired in one-way active avoidance and later, in learning to approach the cue that before had triggered active avoidance. They were also impaired in a two-way shuttle box active avoidance task. Rats with nigral lesions learned one-way active avoidance much more slowly than animals with caudate lesions. Mitcham and Thomas suggested that lesions of the ventral caudate or lesions of the substantia nigra pars compacta damage the dopaminergic pathway from this nucleus to the caudate and so interfere with an "avoidance" circuit from neocortex to caudate and substantia nigra, which returns to the caudate and runs via ventrolateral and ventral anterior thalamic nuclei to the frontal neocortex, to initiate avoidance via the pyramidal and rubrospinal tracts.

Unilateral lesions also disrupt performance. Hansing et al. (1968) reported that rats with unilateral lesions of the caudate could not use the contralateral paw in pressing a bar (which was recessed and could not be seen) for a sucrose solution; but they could use the ipsilateral paw. When the other caudate was lesioned also, three of five animals did not respond with either paw; two (with smaller lesions) slowly began to respond with the paw contralateral to the second lesion. Apparently, during the interval between the two lesions, the animals had learned responding with that paw well enough so that they could use it now and then even after the second lesion. These animals used both paws in walking, climbing, or grooming, but did seem to have some muscular weakness. The lesioned animals seemed to be aware of the lever, and sometimes made abortive responses or explored in the area of the lever. Small unilateral lesions of the globus pallidus reproduced the same pattern of contralateral defects.[1]

Unilateral ablation of the somatomotor cortex did not prevent the rats from responding with the contralateral paw. These lesions produced heavy degeneration of the ipsilateral ventrolateral thalamus; but since they did not produce the same effect as the unilateral caudate or pallidal lesions, the authors concluded that the impairment did not stem from the interruption of the connection between striatum, ventrolateral thalamus, and cortex. Perhaps; but it is also possible that lesions of the motor cortex did not result in impairment because the animals could still plan their action via amygdala and prefrontal cortex and could initiate it over the connection from striatum and globus pallidus to substantia nigra, midbrain, and spinal cord. When Hansing et al. added unilateral caudate lesions on the same side as the earlier cortical lesions, the animals stopped responding with the contralateral paw but could be retrained, though slowly. Apparently, the practice they had in responding via substantia nigra and spinal cord now enabled them to relearn.

In another experiment, Hansing et al. trained rats with bilateral caudate lesions on a fixed interval schedule with the lever visible. In this task, the animals never ceased responding but actually increased lever pressing during the first part of the interval, when intact rats decreased it. Apparently, seeing the lever enabled the animals to compensate for their impaired motor memory. However, unilateral lesions in this experiment also resulted in reduced bar pressing with the contralateral paw.

A report from Hore et al. (1977) seems to confirm that vision can mask the impairment after striatal lesions. These authors cooled the globus pallidus of monkeys and found that the animals could no longer execute learned arm movements when they were blindfolded. Hore et al. pointed out that vision enables animals to compensate for the motor difficulties they experience after globus pallidus damage, so that they often seem unimpaired when observed in their cages.

---

[1]Unilateral lesions within the action circuit, interrupting either the relays from brachium pontis to cerebellum, or from cerebellum to striatum, have produced inattention (sensory neglect); see Fig. 17.3.

Stimulation Effects on Learning.   Electrical stimulation of the caudate inter-feres with learning in many tasks and in many animal species. Continuous low-level stimulation during learning a delayed alternation task interfered with per-formance in monkeys (Rosvold & Delgado, 1956). When the caudate was stimulated bilaterally after cats had learned a reversal task, their memory deficit increased with increases in current intensity, frequency, pulse duration, and stimulus train duration (Thompson, 1958). Wyers et al. (1968) investigated the effect of bilateral single-pulse brain stimulation after each trial of a passive avoidance task. Of all the brain structures investigated, only stimulation of the caudate and the ventromedial hippocampus resulted in a retention deficit.

Caudate stimulation has also interfered with food-rewarded maze learning in rats (Peeke & Herz, 1971). Whether stimulation followed each choice point in the maze or each trial, it resulted in a significant deficit. Multiple-pulse stimula-tion seems to be more disruptive than single-pulse stimulation. Caudate stimula-tion also interferes with the extinction of one-trial passive avoidance in mice (Zornetzer et al., 1977).

These results support my suggestion that the striatum is involved in the acqui-sition of the motor pattern required for a particular task. It seems to be a relay station in the motor memory circuit. When the caudate is stimulated during or immediately after a trial, the registration of this motor pattern is disrupted and the learned task is not retained.

This conclusion is confirmed by the results of Routtenberg and Kim (1978). They found that stimulation of the substantia nigra, compact part, during learn-ing always produced a deficit in retention but did not disturb the original learning (trials to criterion). Stimulation of the reticulate part had no effect. They pointed out that low-level electrical stimulation, as used in their study, did not affect ac-tivity in the open field, nor did it result in circling or any other deviation from normal motor activity.

Chemical stimulation of the caudate also affects motor memory. Brust-Carmona et al. (1974) trained cats to walk to a food box to receive meat as soon as a light flashed; and to refrain from approaching when clicks accompanied the flashing light. Microinjection of adrenaline or noradrenaline into the head of the caudate slightly depressed motor activity but did not disturb the cats' approach to food, although the cats did tend to hold back during clicks. In another experi-ment, cats were trained to press a bar for milk when a light appeared above the lever; and not to press it when the light was off. Microinjection of noradrenaline into the caudate reduced the rate of lever pressing, but only the reduction with the light off was significant. Noradrenaline depressed motor activity but did not ma-terially influence learning. According to my theory, the animals injected with noradrenaline would feel movement as slightly unpleasant, and would not move as willingly; but the attraction of the food easily overcame their reluctance.

Finally, the authors trained cats to press a lever at a steady rate. After microinjection of acetylcholine into the head of the caudate, this rate increased significantly, as compared to lever pressing after a microinjection of salt solution. Atropine neutralized the acetylcholine effect. Shute and Lewis (1975) pointed out that the striatum is cholinoceptive; it has a small population of intrinsic cholinergic neurons. Since acetylcholine facilitated lever pressing and atropine neutralized the improvement, we can conclude that cholinergic (muscarinic) excitation facilitates movement.

The Dopamine System.   As mentioned in chapter 26, both the mesolimbic and the nigrostriatal dopamine systems seem to be involved in motor functions. Excitation of the mesolimbic system seems to produce increased locomotor activity. Clozapine and sulpiride, drugs with high antipsychotic activity, block locomotion; these drugs do not affect the motor system. In contrast, excitation of the nigrostriatal dopamine system produces stereotyped behavior in animals (gnawing, sniffing, etc.). Haloperidol, a dopamine blocker with antipsychotic potency which affects motor behavior, blocks stereotypic behavior but does not reduce locomotor activity (Ungerstedt, 1977). The mesolimbic dopamine system projects to stria terminalis, amygdala, and frontal cortex, hence seems to be part of the motor imagination circuit in my theory. It may well be that the increased running is a result of the increased motor imagination. Intense activity in the imagination circuit may also account for the visual, auditory, and tactual hallucinations of schizophrenics: the amygdala projects not only to the frontal cortex but also to sensory memory areas.

Bilateral degeneration of the dopamine pathway produced by 6–OHDA results in severe akinesia, adipsia, and aphagia. The animals no longer act spontaneously and die if not tubefed (Ungerstedt, 1971b). This procedure seems to destroy both dopamine systems. When both memory and imagination circuits are unavailable, the animals can neither remember nor imagine what to do when they need food. Of course, it could be that the severe akinesia by itself accounts for their failure to drink, eat, or perform a learned task.

Despite the continuing interest in the nigrostriatal dopamine system, we still do not know how it affects the motor system or whether the same pathways also mediate reactivation of motor memory. The first question I propose to discuss is whether the nigrostriatal pathway is involved in learning and retention; the second, whether this pathway as well as the striatonigral path are responsible for both memory retrieval and motor regulation.

Many reports maintain that destruction of the nigrostriatal pathway impairs learning. Zis et al. (1974) found that the application of L-Dopa restored retention after such a lesion. Routtenberg and Kim (1978) reported that a posttrial injection of 6–OHDA into the substantia nigra dramatically disrupted retention of a passive avoidance step-down task 24 hours later. Retention was also impaired by electrical stimulation of the substantia nigra, pars compacta (the origin of the nigrostriatal tract). Stimulation of most of the pars reticulata had no effect. According to the authors, the excess dopamine either injected or produced by stimulation prevented conduction.

Fibiger and Phillips (1976), however, concluded on the basis of their own experiments that the substantia nigra and the nigrostriatal bundle are not critical in learning. They stimulated the substantia nigra pars compacta unilaterally in intact animals and found the usual passive avoidance deficit in a step-down task. A lesion of the nigrostriatal dopamine pathway by 6–OHDA on the side stimulated blocked the deficit and restored passive avoidance. However, unilateral or bilateral lesions of this pathway did not disrupt learning or retention of this task. Also, such lesions did not block the memory deficit produced by electrical stimulation of the striatum. They concluded that stimulation of the substantia nigra pars compacta and the nigrostriatal path results in excessive release of dopamine in the striatum which interferes with normal conduction. Later, Fibiger (1977) suggested that reported deficits in active avoidance after substantia nigra pars compacta lesions are not true memory deficits. Rather, the lesions seem to interfere with the animal's ability to react to the conditioned stimulus—a symptom of the akinesia found after such lesions.

Ungerstedt (1977) tried to overcome such objections. He argued that dopamine-denervated animals can learn and retain what amounts to a natural reaction but would not be able to learn a response that is opposed to their natural inclinations. He set up an experiment in which rats had to learn a brightness discrimination in an underwater T-maze. Intact animals, pushed under water, soon managed to find the open arm. Their natural preference was for the lighted arm, but they found their way even if the open arm was dark. The lesioned animals swam slowly and awkwardly but managed to find the bright arm; but they were unable to find their way out when the bright arm was closed and only the dark arm was open. Ungerstedt's point applies to one experiment Fibiger reported in which the lesioned animals learned to avoid shock by escaping into a dark shock-free alley: Escape into the dark is a natural response. But in Fibiger and Phillips' step-down task the rats had to refrain from stepping down from their perch: and stepping down is a natural response, yet lesioned animals showed no passive avoidance deficit. Of course, it could be argued that the difficulty in initiating a movement after a lesion of the nigrostriatal path would delay their reaction so that they showed no passive avoidance deficit. Hence the question of a memory or a motor deficit still remains open.

Whether the nigrostriatal dopamine system is involved in memory or not, the neostriatum certainly has a part in it. If it is a link in the motor memory circuit, as I believe, it should connect with the ventral thalamic motor nuclei and the frontal cortex. Indeed, Carpenter and Peter (1972) and Carpenter et al. (1976) demonstrated a projection from the substantia nigra pars reticulata, the receiving area of the striatonigral pathway, to the ventrolateral, ventral anterior and dorsomedial thalamic nuclei via field H of Forel. And Wright et al. (1977) suggested that this projection represents the motor output from the pars reticulata which affects the activity of the cerebello-thalamic pathway. Wright et al. lesioned the striatonigral bundle on one side while leaving the nigrostriatal projection intact. They found the same motor deficits as after unilateral lesions of the striatum. The animals turned toward the side of the lesion and did not react to anything on the opposite side, a clear sign that the connection with the action circuit had been interrupted unilaterally. If the lesion is on the left side, any movement must be initiated by the intact right side; the impulses from motor cortex cross over to the left pyramidal tract, so that the animal moves only with the left side of the body while the right side is practically stationary; the animal circles toward the right, lesioned side.

This experiment provides evidence that the motor effects of striatonigral lesions are the same as those of striate lesions. But there seems to be no direct evidence that this pathway is involved in motor memory. Routtenberg and Kim (1978) reported that a posttrial injection of picrotoxin (a GABA blocker) into the substantia nigra produced a retention deficit in a step-down task. However, the authors pointed out that this does not necessarily mean a blocking of the GABA-using striatonigral path. GABA terminals have synapses both on non-dopaminergic and dopaminergic neurons in the substantia nigra, so that the blockade may have affected the dopaminergic nigrostriatal pathway. The fact that intranigral picrotoxin alters neostriatal dopamine turnover, and that stimulation of the compact (but not the reticulate) zone of the substantia nigra produced a retention deficit, seems to confirm this possibility.

If the connection from the striatum via substantia nigra to ventral thalamic motor nuclei is not involved in memory retrieval, let us look for an alternative connection. There is a pathway from the striatum via globus pallidus and ansa lenticularis to the ventrolateral and ventral anterior thalamic nuclei (Carpenter, 1973), and there is some evidence that this pathway is involved in memory retrieval.

Caruthers (1968) found that cats with lesions of the ansa lenticularis had a significant active avoidance deficit in a two-way shuttle box with a flicker announcing shock. After a few trials, the onset of flicker produced crying, crouching, attack movements, and other autonomic signs of fear, but the cats were unable to run to the safe compartment and so avoid the shock. Apparently, the lesions had interrupted the motor memory circuit from globus pallidus via ansa lenticularis to ventral thalamus, so that the animals did not remember what to do to avoid the shock. The autonomic accompaniment of action, initiated by the appraisal that the flicker was "bad" was carried by the action circuit, hence intact. The animals were afraid, the more so as they could not remember what to do to eliminate the danger. Caruthers mentioned that only the avoidance response to flicker was abolished; lesioned cats could learn avoidance when the cue was a tone. Probably, the tone itself was appraised as dangerous and induced flight—motor memory was not needed.

Motter (1978) thinks that the pallido-thalamic pathway "contacts an indirect, polysynaptic cerebello-thalamic-cortical pathway, whereas the nigral pathway . . . contacts a direct monosynaptic cerebello-thalamic-cortical pathway" (p. 153). It is tempting to think that the former may affect the cerebello-rubro-thalamic projection while the latter may end on cells that receive the direct projection from cerebellum to ventral thalamus. The red nucleus, like the striatum, is involved in memory retrieval (see chapter 26). At any rate, it would appear that only the pallidothalamic pathway is a link in the motor memory circuit; the striatonigral bundle reaching the substantia nigra pars reticulata and its projection to the ventral thalamus seems to be a link in the action circuit, facilitating movement.

Finally, it seems important to discover whether the dopaminergic nigrostriatal projection is a dopaminergic link in the motor memory circuit, or whether the motor memory circuit, like the sensory memory circuit, is cholinergic in its course, but either influences or is influenced by the dopaminergic nigrostriatal system.

Cholinergic Connections.   It is a fact that a muscarinic cholinergic pathway adjoins dopaminergic fibers. Cholinergic fibers synapse in the substantia nigra and project to the striatum. Electrical stimulation or surgical lesions of the substantia nigra or the nigrostriatal pathway may affect cholinergic neurons. Morgane and Stern (1974) have suggested that even chemical (6–OHDA) lesions of the dopaminergic system might affect neighboring cholinergic fibers; 6–OHDA injections can abolish acetylcholine-esterase staining in the central nervous system. Also, the cholinergic and dopaminergic pathways interact at various points, both in the substantia nigra and the striatum. It seems a reasonable assumption that motor memory and hence motor learning is mediated by the cholinergic memory circuit while the motor effects of nigrostriatal lesions are the result of a dopamine deficiency.

There is a cholinergic pathway from midbrain ventral tegmentum coursing through the hypothalamus and the basal ganglia to all parts of the forebrain, which can affect dopaminergic neurons. According to Shute and Lewis (1975), the monoamine system in the brain in general seems to be cholinoceptive, particularly the cerebellum, red nucleus, and striatum. The ascending cholinergic system originates in the ventral tegmental area of the midbrain and the substantia nigra; in the midbrain, the cuneiform nucleus is the main site of origin. This ventral tegmental pathway has many synapses, unlike the monoaminergic paths. The direct projection from the midbrain nuclei may terminate either on cholinergic or noncholinergic neurons. One branch of this projection sends direct fibers to tectum, thalamus, and subthalamus which terminate on noncholinergic neurons. Other direct fibers go to the posterior and lateral hypothalamus and the lateral preoptic area, and synapse with fibers that form a striatal, an amygdaloid, and an olfactory radiation which disperse to various cortical areas, including limbic cortex and hippocampus (Shute & Lewis, 1967; see Fig. 24.3). This polysynaptic projection is assumed to be identical with the ascending reticular activating system (Noback & Demarest, 1981; see Ch. 17).

Phillis (1974) has shown that striatal and septal cholinergic fibers terminate on cortical neurons. The thalamus also sends cholinergic relays to the cortex. I have argued before that these connections are part of the sensory memory circuit; the connections via the striatum may be part of the motor memory circuit. The connection from striatum via the ventral motor nuclei of the thalamus ensures the influence of motor memory on the action about to be taken. According to Phillis, the ventral tegmental pathway mediates inhibition as well as excitation, both of which are antagonized by atropine, which means muscarinic rather than nicotinic transmission.

The Hypothalamic Branch of the Action Circuit.   A nicotinic cholinergic pathway has been reported by Butcher and Talbot (1978). Its fibers are arranged mediolaterally in the rostral midbrain, with medially and laterally arranged fibers coming from medial and lateral portions of the substantia nigra pars compacta. They course not in the medial forebrain bundle but dorsolaterally to it. Part of this path traverses the dorsolateral hypothalamus and field H of Forel through the medial globus pallidus to reach the lateral caudate and putamen. These fibers distribute many collaterals to the neostriatum. According to Butcher and Talbot, neurons in this pathway may interact with neurons in the dopaminergic pathway from substantia nigra to striatum. If this is the hypothalamic link of the action circuit, we would expect that its course from striatum to ventral thalamic motor nuclei would be via substantia nigra pars reticulata, since it is this pathway that seems to have pronounced motor effects.

Apparently, both the muscarinic and nicotinic cholinergic pathways interact with the dopaminergic projection from substantia nigra to striatum. In terms of my theory, the dopaminergic system would influence and be influenced by both the motor memory and the action circuits. The dopaminergic system does seem to play a role in both memory retrieval and motor activity. But until its exact functioning is better known, all we can do is admit the possibility of such a three-way interaction.

THE ACTION CIRCUIT: FROM VENTRAL THALAMUS TO FRONTAL CORTEX

Relays from the cerebellum run via cerebellar nuclei to the ventral thalamus. These relays, originating in the dentate, interpositus and fastigial nuclei, run in the brachium conjunctivum directly to the ventrolateral and ventral anterior thalamic nuclei; and these, in turn, project to the motor and premotor cortex. Relays from the cerebellar nuclei also go to the red nucleus, substantia nigra, hypothalamus, and striatum, both directly and via the reticular formation (Chan-Palay, 1977). Hence the cerebellum projects to the frontal lobe via a broad sheet of fibers. In my theory, this is the ascending link of the action circuit.

I have argued that the projection from cerebellum via ventral thalamus to frontal cortex serves the intention to act. In fact, this direct connection from cerebellum to thalamus seems to carry the sheer impetus to move body and limbs required for the intended action; while the cholinergic (nicotinic) branch of the action circuit that runs via hypothalamus and striatum to the ventral thalamus (via substantia nigra pars reticulata) seems to regulate this action pattern, facilitating or inhibiting body and limb movements.

Facilitation or inhibition of movement is possible not only via the striatum but via the medial thalamus. For instance, Purpura et al. (1966) have reported that low-frequency stimulation of either caudate or medial thalamus evokes short-latency excitatory post-synaptic potentials, followed by long-latency prolonged inhibitory potentials in the ventrolateral thalamic nucleus which lead to cortical EEG synchronization. These inhibitory potentials antagonize the excitation from cerebellar relays. High-frequency medial thalamic or pontine reticular stimulation blocks these inhibitory potentials and increases the excitation in ventrolateral thalamic nucleus cells relaying to the frontal cortex. Similarly, high-frequency caudate stimulation facilitates excitatory potentials evoked from cerebellar relays and eliminates the inhibition produced by low frequency medial thalamic stimulation.

In its course through the hypothalamus, the action circuit is joined by fibers from nuclei that detect various bodily states (lack of food or water, warmth or cold). These fibers seem to run in the action circuit to septal area and frontal cortex, mediating hunger and thirst, an impulse to look for a warm or a cold spot. From the septal area, relays go to the hippocampus and amygdala, inducing the animal to recall where it had found what it needs, and to imagine what it could do this time.

Associated with the action circuit is the cholinergic muscarinic motor memory circuit, coursing from hippocampus via cerebellum to red nucleus and ventral thalamus, and via substantia nigra, striatum, and pallidum to the ventral thalamic motor nuclei and frontal cortex. Planning for action seems to be mediated via the mesolimbic dopaminergic imagination circuit (via piriform cortex, amygdala, and dorsomedial thalamic nuclei to the prefrontal cortex). While such planning does not always lead to action, it does lead to the activation of the muscles needed for the planned or imagined activity (Jacobson, 1932).

There is some doubt as to the transmitter used by the direct projection from cerebellum to ventral thalamus. According to Davis (1966), application of acetylcholine or carbachol increased the spontaneous discharge of ventrolateral thalamic nuclei and facilitated their excitation by cerebellar relays. The application of atropine to the ventrolateral thalamic nuclei blocked the excitation by acetylcholine and by brachium conjunctivum fibers from the cerebellum. Smaller amounts, either of atropine (a muscarinic blocker) or dihydro-beta-erythroidine (a nicotinic blocker) cancelled the effects of acetylcholine but did not block transmission from the cerebellum. Davis concluded that the cerebellar relays to the ventral thalamus cannot be cholinergic. Marshall et al. (1980) came to the same conclusion concerning the cerebello-rubro-thalamic projection.

Ventrolateral and Ventral Anterior Thalamic Nuclei

These nuclei partially degenerate after prefrontal lobotomy, together with the anterior thalamic nuclei. The dorsomedial thalamic nuclei degenerate completely (Meyer & Beck, 1954). Prefrontal lobotomy results in a loss of alertness, general slowing, and inertia. The patients show little interest and lack spontaneity. They often sit motionless for long periods, doing nothing (Landis & Clausen, 1955). Loss of motor imagination (degeneration of dorsomedial thalamic nuclei) is combined with a decrease of action impulses (partial degeneration of ventral thalamic nuclei). The partial degeneration of the anterior thalamic nuclei seems to indicate a loss of affective motor memory, which would further reduce the patients' inclination to any kind of activity, because nothing they could do seems to be desirable.

The ventral anterior nucleus seems to send specific relays to the posterior and medial orbitofrontal cortex, and projects diffusely to wider cortical areas. The ventrolateral nucleus sends specific projections to the motor and premotor area and projects diffusely to other cortical regions (Carpenter, 1976).

Stimulation Effects. In recent years, attempts to alleviate some symptoms of Parkinsonism have led surgeons to make small lesions in the ventral thalamus of patients. Not only the lesions themselves but the exploratory stimulation of these nuclei before surgery have contributed to our knowledge of their function. Hassler (1966), for instance, asked his patients to move one hand back and forth. When he then stimulated the ventrolateral thalamic nucleus on the opposite side, the patients moved the hand faster and insisted that "it goes faster all by itself." Stimulating the neighboring ventroposterolateral (somatosensory) thalamic nucleus never produced this effect. Speech also was speeded up by stimulation of the ventrolateral thalamic nuclei. The patients explained that they felt urged to speak faster. One patient said: "There was such a pressure on me that I had to speak faster and faster." Sometimes they spoke so fast that they could no longer be understood. Finally, they could no longer go on. Stimulation of the pallidum usually slowed down movements or speech to the point of complete arrest. Apparently, the impulse to speak, like the impulse to skilled action, is mediated by the action circuit via hypothalamus, striatum, and ventral thalamus, and relays to the motor cortex.

Lesion Effects. While exploring sites for therapeutic stereotaxic lesions, Ojemann et al. (1971) found a significant deficit in verbal memory when they stimulated the ventrolateral thalamic nuclei. The patients were impaired in learning sentences or series of words whenever they were stimulated in the left (but not the right) ventrolateral thalamic nucleus. Stimulation in the left ventrolateral thalamus disturbed short-term recall of words and sentences. When the patients were stimulated during recall, recall errors increased in all patients with electrodes in the left thalamus; but patients with electrodes in the right thalamus showed no interference. Since the motor memory area for speech is in the left frontal lobe, that is not surprising. When the patients were stimulated while being shown the list of words or sentences, recall was intact. Also, stimulation during any part of the test did not affect recognition. According to my theory, stimulation during recall would produce impairment because it interfered with the impulse to pronounce the words. Stimulation during the presentation of the lists did not affect recall because the patients' visual memory circuit was not disturbed. Finally, recognition was not affected because the affective visual memory circuit also was functioning normally. Stimulation of the ventral thalamus only interfered with verbal recall, a motor performance.

To alleviate Parkinson tremor, points in the ventrolateral thalamic nuclei which had shown bursts at the tremor frequency, have often been coagulated by electrolysis, ultrasound, or chemicals. According to Hassler (1966), such lesions do not affect the speed of movements. Of course, these lesions were very small; six non-overlapping bilateral lesions accounted for less than 5% of thalamic tissue. For a week or two after surgery, the patients did not use the contralateral limbs and facial muscles. After that, they learned to use their muscles (which were now practically tremorfree) except for facial expression, which remained minimal. These lesions in the ventrolateral thalamic nuclei, or lesions in the pallidum, also abolished the rigid muscle tension of the Parkinson patient. This decreased muscle tension seems to be one reason why patients tend to fall to the side opposite the lesion.

According to Riklan and Levita (1969), unilateral therapeutic lesions of the ventrolateral thalamic nucleus may produce transient postoperative losses in the digit span, digit symbol, and arithmetic subtests of the Wechsler-Bellevue Intelligence Scale. There was no clear dominance effect, probably because the intact corpus callosum and anterior commissure provided intercommunication between the two hemispheres. After bilateral lesions, many patients had a relatively permanent lack of energy and initiative, were less responsive, found it difficult to talk, and suffered occasional loss of emotional control. Indeed, among one thousand consecutive patients with bilateral lesions of the ventrolateral thalamic nuclei, 13.1% of patients had difficulties in articulation. Slurring, stuttering, and reduced voice volume have also been reported, particularly after left thalamic and left globus pallidus lesions (Hermann et al., 1966). In a study of patients who had had bilateral ventrolateral thalamic nucleus lesions, Riklan and Levita (1969) found mild or moderate impairment in 96 of 99 Parkinson patients before the operation, and severe impairment in quality, volume, pitch, rate, rhythm, and articulation in 20% of the patients afterwards. No doubt the breaks in the action circuit proudced by several small lesions are sufficient to disturb the motor coordination of the speech msucles.

An interesting finding is the severe reduction in the number of responses on the Rorschach test, and the reduction in animal movement and good form responses found in the follow-up test of Parkinson patients after left or right side lesions in the ventrolateral thalamus or globus pallidus. Parkinson patients without therapeutic lesions, retested at the same 9-month interval, showed no changes (Riklan & Levita, 1969). Apparently, the lesions interfered with imagination, or at least with reporting what they imagined, even more than the disease. The ventrolateral thalamic nucleus is connected with the dorsomedial thalamic nucleus, and so can activate the imagination circuit. Whatever Rorschach responses indicate about personality structure, they do report what the patient imagines.

Vilkki (1978) has found a decided difference in performance of Parkinson patients if surgical lesions were made in the left ventrolateral thalamic nucleus rather than the right one. Right ventrolateral nucleus lesions impaired visual recognition but did not disturb verbal recall. Left lesions impaired verbal recall but did not seem to impair visual recognition directly; however, some patients showed pronounced perseveration in verbal recall which seemed to mislead them in their visual recognition. Vilkki concluded that such lesions produce "disorganization of active perceptual regulation and control of the memory performance" (p. 435). Verbal (speech) memories are registered in the left prefrontal cortex (Broca's area) while visual pattern memory seems to be confined to the right occipital association cortex. But both visual recognition and verbal recall have to be reported verbally, via the motor memory and action circuits. No wonder that lesions that interrupt the motor memory circuit to the speech area also disorganize the report of visual pattern recognition. Vilkki also found that lesions of the left pulvinar caused a decline in verbal recall, although not as severe as lesions in the left ventrolateral thalamic nucleus. I have suggested that the pulvinar is a relay station in the sensory imagination circuit. If memory and imagination work together, it is reasonable that blocking of part of the imagination circuit would impair recall. But a lesion in the ventrolateral thalamic nucleus, the last relay station of the motor memory circuit, would have much more severe effects.

The Center Median-Parafascicular Complex.

This structure is a nuclear complex within the thalamic intralaminar group. It receives relays from the cerebellum and globus pallidus and projects diffusely to the cortex (Noback & Demarest, 1981). Caudate stimulation usually inhibits this complex (Dalsass & Krauthamer, 1981). After small substantia nigra lesions, this complex, which is normally quiescent, exhibited spontaneous activity in about 70% of its cells; many of these neurons could no longer be inhibited by caudate stimulation. Some neurons that could be so inhibited broke through the inhibition during a conditioning test (Dalsass & Krauthamer, 1981). In other words, the motor reaction to sensory stimulation is normally affected by caudate excitation, but substantia nigra lesions weaken or destroy this effect. Since such interference occurred in a conditioning test, it is possible that the lesion blocked the motor memory circuit, at least partially.

Motor Relays. The center median-parafascicular complex as well as the globus pallidus are often called "polysensory" because they respond to sensory stimulation in all modalities. These polysensory reactions seem to be motor reactions to sensory stimulation. Motor reactions may be identical whatever the sensory experience that induces them. Hence stimuli in any modality can excite a given structure in the action or motor memory circuit. Indeed, the red nucleus, the substantia nigra, the nigrostriatal dopamine path, the striatum, and striatonigral path all respond with long-latency potentials to sensory stimulation (Hommer & Bunney, 1980; Anderson, 1981). These findings add weight to my suggestion that these are motor reactions to sensory experience in all modalities.

Projection to the Frontal Lobe

The projection from ventrolateral, ventral anterior, and ventromedial thalamic nuclei via the internal capsule is the last link of the action circuit, before reaching the frontal lobe. According to Sasaki (1979), these nuclei receive relays from cerebellar nuclei and project somatotopically to the frontal cortex. The dentate cerebellar nuclei are connected with superficial thalamocortical neurons in the lateral motor cortex (foreleg area), and premotor cortex, and with deep thalamo-cortical neurons in the frontal association area. The medial (fastigial) cerebellar nuclei are connected with the medial part of the motor cortex (hindleg area) and the parietal association cortex; and the interpositus nucleus innervates the intermediate part of the motor cortex (mainly the trunk area). The action impulses relayed from cerebellum to frontal cortex apparently mediate an urge to move (premotor area), activate pyramidal tract neurons in the motor cortex to initiate action, but also register relevant motor memories via the frontal association cortex. Short association fibers from the motor memory area to the premotor and motor areas could then influence the action in progress.

Buser (1966) reported an "ascending multisensory pathway" from the midbrain reticular formation via the ventrolateral thalamic nuclei to the motor cortex and pyramidal tract. This pathway also seems to be "multisensory" only by virtue of the fact that it responds to multimodal sensory stimulation. Such responses indicate that it is an ascending link in the action circuit, relaying motor intentions to the frontal lobe.

Looking back over our discussion of the ascending link of the action circuit, we find that there are three routes from cerebellum to the frontal lobe, each with its own function. The direct route via the ventral thalamic motor nuclei seems to provide the strength and limb-body coordination required for a given action; the route via the hypothalamus and septum seems to initiate the neural impulses to secrete the hormones and adjust the bodily state appropriate for such action. Finally, the route via the striatum and striatonigral path to the substantia nigra pars reticulata to ventral thalamus may provide the necessary motor control.

Receiving Areas of the Action Circuit.   In chapters 14 and 15, I discussed the frontal motor areas which are the receiving areas of projection fibers from the ventral thalamus and the dorsomedial thalamic nuclei, the last link in the action and imagination circuits. The ventrolateral thalamic nucleus seems to project to the motor, premotor, and motor meory areas; the ventral anterior nucleus, to the limbic motor areas in the frontal lobe as well as to the anterior insula, the limbic motor area for mouth and speech muscles (see Yakovlev et al., 1966).

In the foregoing chapters, I have also discussed the specific deficits that follow from lesions in the motor memory areas and the limbic appraisal and affective memory areas. In describing the course of the action circuit, I have tried to show which additional circuits (modality-specific memory, affective memory, motor memory, and imagination circuits) are involved in these deficits, so that the effect of lesions along these pathways can be compared with the deficits stemming from lesions of their receiving areas.

With the last link of the action circuit, the sequence from sensory experience to overt action has reached its end. Sensory experience, complemented by imagination and memory, begins the sequence; the appraisal of the situation, supported by affective sensory and motor memory, leads to an action impulse organized and integrated in hippocampus and cerebellum; via the action, motor imagination and motor memory circuits, this impulse finally is expressed in action. While it is neither possible nor desirable to predict the content of our thinking or the action we propose from brain function, it is possible to show that thinking and action are mediated by sequences of neural impulses that can be followed over identifiable pathways and structures.

References

Adams, J. A., 1967. *Human memory.* New York: McGraw-Hill.

Adey, W. R., 1966. Neurophysiological correlates of information transaction and storage of brain tissue. In E. Stellar & J. M. Sprague (Eds.), *Progress in physiological psychology, Vol. 1,* New York: Academic Press.

Adey, W. R., Dunlop, C., & Hendrix, C., 1960a. Hippocampal slow waves: Distribution and phase relationships during approach performance in the cat. *Archives of Neurology, 3,* 74–90.

Adey, W. R., Dunlop C., & Hendrix, C., 1960b. Hippocampal slow waves: distribution and phase relations in the course of approach learning. *Archives of Neurology, 3,* 96–112.

Adey, W. R., & Meyer, M., 1952. Hippocampal and hypothalamic connexions of the temporal lobe in the monkey. *Brain, 75,* 358–384.

Adey, W. R., Walter, D. O., & Hendrix, C. E., 1961. Computer techniques in correlation and spectral analyses of cerebral slow waves during discriminative behavior. *Experimental Neurology, 3,* 501–524.

Ahlskog, J. E., Randall, P. K., & Hoebel, B. G., 1975. Hypothalamic hyperphagia: Dissociation from hyperphagia following destruction of noradrenergic neurons. *Science, 190,* 399–401.

Akiskal, H. S., & McKinney, W. T., 1975. Overview of recent research in depression. *Archives of General Psychiatry, 32,* 285–305.

Allen, G. I., & Tsukahara, N., 1974. Cerebro-cerebellar communication systems. *Physiological Review, 54,* 957–1006.

Allen, W. F., 1940. Effect of ablating the frontal lobes, hippocampi, and occipitoparietal temporal (excepting pyriform areas) lobes on positive and negative olfactory conditioned reflexes. *American Journal of Physiology, 28,* 754–771.

Allen, W. F., 1941. Effect of ablating the pyriform-amygdaloid area and hippocampi on positive and negative olfactory conditioned reflexes and on conditioned differentiation. *American Journal of Physiology, 132,* 81–92.

Allport, D. A., 1979. Conscious and unconscious cognition: A computational metaphor for the mechanism of attention and integration. In: L.-G. Nilsson (Ed.) *Perspectives on memory research.* Hillsdale, N.J.: Lawrence Erlbaum Associates.

Altman, J., & Bayer, S., 1975. Postnatal development of the hippocampal dentate gyrus under normal and experimental conditions. In Isaacson, R. L. & Pribram, K. H., (Eds.), *The hippocampus, Vol. 1.* New York: Plenum Press.

Andén, N.-E., Carlson, A., & Haggendal, J., 1969. Adrenergic mechanisms. *Annual Review of Pharmacology, 9,* 119–134.

Andén, N. E., Corrodi, H., Fuxe, K., & Ungerstedt, U., 1971. Importance of nervous impulse flow for the neuroleptic induced increase in amine turnover in central dopamine neurons. *European Journal of Pharmacology, 15,* 193–199.

Andersen, P., 1975. Organization of hippocampal neurons and their interconnections. In R. L. Isaacson & K. H. Pribram (Eds.) *The hippocampus, Vol. 1.* New York: Plenum Press.

Anderson, J. R., & Bower, G. H., 1973. Human Associative Memory. Hemisphere Publishing Corporation, Washington, D. C. 2nd ed. 1974.

Anderson, M. E., 1981. The basal ganglia and movement. In A. L. Towe & E. S. Luschei (eds.) *Handbook of behavioral neurobiology, Vol. 5. Motor coordination.* New York: Plenum Press.

Andy, O. J., Peeler, D. F. Jr., & Foshee, D. P., 1967. Avoidance and discrimination learning following hippocampal ablation in the cat. *Journal of Comparative and Physiological Psychology, 64,* 516–519.

Angaut, P., 1979. The cerebello-thalamic projections in the cat. In J. Massion & K. Sasaki (Eds.) *Cerebro-cerebellar interactions.* Amsterdam: Elsevier/North Holland Biomedical Press.

Angevine, J. B. Jr., 1965. Time of neuron origin in the hippocampal region: An autoradiographic study in the mouse. *Experimental Neurology, Supplement 2,* 1–70.

Angevine, J. B., Jr., 1975. Development of the hippocampal region. In: R. L. Isaacson & K. H. Pribram (Eds.), *The hippocampus. Vol. 1* New York: Plenum Press.

Arnold, M. B., 1946. On the mechanism of suggestion and hypnosis. *Journal of Abnormal and Social Psychology, 41,* 107–128.

Arnold, M. B., 1960. *Emotion and personality.* Vol. 1, *Psychological aspects; vol. 2, Neurological and physiological aspects.* New York: Columbia University Press.

Arnold, M. B., 1962. *Story sequence analysis.* New York: Columbia University Press.

Arnold, M. B., 1967. Stress and emotion. In M. H. Appley & R. Trumbull (Eds.), *Psychological stress.* New York: Appleton-Century-Crofts.

Arnold, M. B. 1969. Emotion, motivation and the limbic system. In E. Tobach (Ed.), Experimental approaches to the study of emotional behavior. *Annals of the New York Academy of Sciences, 159,* 1041–1058.

Arnold, M. B., 1970. Brain function in emotion: A phenomenological analysis. In P. Black (Ed.), *Physiological correlates of emotion.* New York: Academic Press.

Arnold, M. B., & Gasson, J. A. (Eds.), 1954. *The human person.* New York: Ronald Press.

Atkinson, R. C., Brelsford, J. W., & Shiffrin, R. M., 1967. Multiprocess models for memory with applications to a continuous presentation task. *Journal of Mathematical Psychology, 4,* 277–300.

Atkinson, R. C. & Shiffrin, R. M., 1968. Human memory: A proposed system and its control processes. In: K. W. Spence and J. T. Spence (Eds.), *The psychology of learning and motivation: Advances in research and theory. Vol. 2.* New York: Academic Press.

Atkinson, R. C., & Wickens, T. D., 1971. Human memory and the concept of reinforcement. In: R. Glaser (Ed.), *The nature of reinforcement.* New York: Academic Press.

Averbach, E., & Sperling, G. 1960. Short-term storage of information in vision. In: E. O. Cherry (Ed.), *Fourth London symposium on information theory.* London, Butterworth.

Babich, F. R., Jacobson, A. L., Bubash, S., & Jacobson, A., 1965. Transfer of a response to naive rats by injection of ribonucleic acid extracted from trained rats. *Science, 149,* 656–657.

Baddeley, A. D., 1976. The psychology of memory. Basic Books: New York.

Bagshaw, M. H., & Benzies, S., 1968. Multiple measures of the orienting reaction and their dissociation after amygdalectomy in monkeys. *Experimental Neurology, 20,* 175–187.

Bagshaw, M. H., & Coppock, H. W., 1968. Galvanic skin response conditioning deficit in amygdalectomized monkeys. *Experimental Neurology, 20,* 188–196.

Bagshaw, M. H., & Pribram, K. H., 1953. Cortical organization in gustation (Macaca mulatta). *Journal of Neurophysiology, 16,* 499–508.

Bahrick, H. P., & Bahrick, P. O., 1964. A re-examination of the interrelations among measures of retention. *Quarterly Journal of Experimental Psychology, 16,* 318–324.

Bailey, P., 1965. Personal communication.

Baird, H. W., Guidetti, B., Reyes, V., Wycis, H. T., & Spiegel, E. A., 1952. Stimulation and elimination of the anterior thalamic nuclei in man and cat. *Pflüger's Archiv für die Gesamte Physiologie, 255,* 58–67.

Balagura, S., Wilcox, R. H., & Coscina, D. V., 1969. The effect of diencephalic lesions on food intake and motor activity. *Physiology and Behavior, 4,* 629–633.

Bandler, R. J., 1971. Chemical stimulation of the rat midbrain and aggressive behavior. *Nature, New Biology, 229,* 222–223.

Banks, A. & Russell, R. W., 1967. Effects of chronic reductions in acetylcholinesterase activity on serial problem-solving behavior. *Journal of Comparative and Physiological Psychology, 64,* 262–267.

Bard, P., & Mountcastle, V. B., 1947. Some forebrain mechanisms involved in expression of rage with special reference to suppression of angry behavior. *Research Publication, Association for Research in Nervous and Mental Disease, 27,* 362–404.

Bard, P., & Rioch, D. McK., 1937. Study of four cats deprived of neocortex and additional portions of forebrain. *Bulletin Johns Hopkins Hospital, 60,* 73–147.

Barker, D. J., 1967. Alteration in sequential behavior of rats following ablation of midline limbic cortex. *Journal of Comparative and Physiological Psychology, 64,* 453–460.

Barker, D. J., & Thomas, G. J., 1965. Ablation of cingulate cortex in rats impairs alternation learning and retention. *Journal of Comparative and Physiological Psychology, 60,* 353–359.

Barker, D. J., & Thomas, G. J., 1966. Effects of regional ablation of midline cortex on alternation learning in rats. *Physiology and Behavior, 1,* 313–317.

Barker, J. L. & Smith, T. G., 1979. Three modes of communication in the nervous system. In Y. H. Ehrlich, J. Volavka, L. G. Davis, & E. G. Brunngraber (Eds.), *Modulators, mediators, and specifiers in brain function.* New York: Plenum Press.

Bartlett, F. C., 1932. *Remembering.* Cambridge: Cambridge University Press.

Bastian, H. C., 1869. The physiology of thinking. *Fortnightly Review, 11,* 57.

Bates, J. A. V., & Ettlinger, G. 1960. Posterior biparietal ablations in the monkey. Changes to neurological and behavioral testing. *A.M.A. Archives of Neurology* (Chicago) *3,* 177–192.

Batini, C., Moruzzi, G., Palestini, M., Rossi, G. F., & Zanchetti, A., 1958. Persistent patterns of wakefulness in the pretrigeminal midpontine preparation. *Science, 128,* 30–31.

Battig, K., Rosvold, H. E., & Mishkin, M., 1960. Comparison of the effects of frontal and caudate lesions on delayed response and alternation in monkeys. *Journal of Comparative and Physiological Psychology, 53,* 400–404.

Baumgarten, R. von, Mollica, A., Moruzzi, G., 1954. Modulierung der Entladungsfrequenz einzelner Zellen der Substantia reticularis durch corticofugale und cerebelläre Impulse. *Pflüger's Archiv der gesamten Physiologie, 259,* 56–78.

Beattie, D. M., 1949. *The effect of imaginary practice on the acquisition of a motor skill.* Unpublished M. A. Thesis, University of Toronto, Canada.

Beckstedt, R. M., Domesick, V. B., & Nauta, W. J. H., 1979. Efferent connections of the substantia nigra and ventral tegmental area in the rat. *Brain Research, 175,* 191–217.

Belcher, G., & Ryall, R. W., 1978. Effects of opiates on spinal interneurones. In R. W. Ryall & J. S. Kelly (Eds.), *Iontophoresis and transmitter mechanisms in the mammalian central nervous system.* Amsterdam: Elsevier.

Belluzzi, J. D., & Stein, L., 1977. Enkephalin may mediate euphoria and drive-reduction reward. *Nature, 266,* 556–558.

Bender, M. B., 1952. *Disorders of perception.* Springfield, Ill.: Chas. C. Thomas.

Bennett, M. H., 1968. The role of the anterior limb of the anterior commissure in olfaction. *Physiology and Behavior, 3,* 507–515.

Bennett, T. L., 1969. Evidence against the theory that hippocampal theta is a correlate of voluntary movement. *Communications in Behavioral Biology, 4,* 165–169.

Bennett, T. L., 1975. The electrical activity of the hippocampus and processes of attention. In R. L. Isaacson & K. H. Pribram (Eds.), *The hippocampus, Vol. 2.* New York: Plenum Press.

Berger, B. D., Wise, C. D., & Stein, L., 1971. Norepinephrine: Reversal of anorexia in rats with lateral hypothalamic damage. *Science, 172,* 281–284.

Berger, T. W., Laham, R. L., & Thompson, R. F., 1980. Hippocampal unit-behavior correlations during classical conditioning. *Brain Research, 193,* 229–248.

Berger, T. W., & Thompson, R. F., 1978a. Neuronal plasticity in the limbic system during classical conditioning of the rabbit nictitating membrane response. II. Septum and mammillary bodies. *Brain Research, 156,* 293–314.

Berger, T. W., & Thompson, R. F., 1978b. Neuronal plasticitiy in the limbic system during classical conditioning of the rabbit nictitating membrane response. I. The hippocampus. *Brain Research, 145,* 323–346.

Berlyne, D. E., 1967. Arousal and reinforcement. *Nebraska Symposium on Motivation, 15,* 1–110.

Bernbach, H. A., 1967. Decision processes in memory. *Psychological Review, 74,* 462–480.

Bernbach, H. A., 1970. Replication processes in human memory and learning. In: J. T. Spence and G. H. Bower (Eds.), *The psychology of learning and motivation: Advances in research and theory. Vol. 3.* New York: Academic Press.

Betz, V. A., 1870. *Two centers in the cerebral cortex.* Anatomical and Histological Investigations. Moscow, Medgiz, 1950.

Bianchi, L., 1920. *La meccanica del cervello e la funzione dei lobi frontali.* Torino; Bocca.

Bierley, R. A., & Kesner, R. P., 1980. Short-term memory: The role of the midbrain reticular formation. *Journal of Comparative and Physiological Psychology, 94,* 519–529.

Birkmayer, W., Jellinger, K., and Riederer, P., 1977. Striatal and extrastriatal dopaminergic functions. In A. R. Cools, A. H. M. Lohman, & J. H. L. Van den Bercken (Eds.), *Psychobiology of the striatum.* Amsterdam: North Holland Publishing Co.

Birkmayer, W., 1977. Discussion on p. 240, in P. Kielholz (Ed.), *Beta-blockers and the central nervous system.* Baltimore: University Park Press.

Bishop, G. H., 1959. The relation between nerve fiber size and sensory modality. Phylogenetic implications of the afferent innervation of cortex. *Journal of Nervous and Mental Disease, 128,* 89–114.

Black, A. H., 1975. Hippocampal electrical activity and behavior. In R. L. Isaacson & K. H. Pribram, *The hippocampus, Vol. 2,* New York: Plenum Press.

Blanchard, R. J., & Fial, R. A., 1968. Effects of limbic lesions on passive avoidance and reactivity to shock. *Journal of Comparative and Physiological Psychology, 66,* 606–612.

Bloch, V., 1976. Brain activation and memory consolidation. In M. R. Rosenzweig and E. L. Bennett (Eds.), *Neural Mechanisms of Learning and Memory.* Cambridge, Mass.: MIT Press.

Bloch, V., Hennevin, E., & Leconte, P., 1977. Interaction between post-trial reticular stimulation and subsequent paradoxical sleep in memory consolidation processes. In R. R. Drucker-Colin & J. L. McGaugh (Eds.), *Neurobiology of sleep and memory.* New York: Academic Press.

Bloom, F. E., 1974. Cyclic AMP and the inhibition of cerebellar Purkinje cells by noradrenergic synapses. In R. D. Myers & R. R. Drucker-Colin (eds.), *Neurohumoral coding of brain function.* New York: Plenum Press.

Bloom, F. E., 1978. Modern concepts in electrophysiology for psychiatry. In E. Usdin & A. J. Mandell (Eds.), Biochemistry of Mental Disorders. New York: Marcel Dekker Inc.

Bocca, E., Calearo, C., Cassinari, V., & Migliavacca, F., 1955. Testing "cortical" hearing in temporal lobe tumors. *Acta otolaryngologica, 45,* 289–304.

Bogen, J. E., & Gazzaniga, M. S., 1965. Cerebral commissurotomy in man; minor hemisphere dominance for certain visuo-spatial functions. *Journal of Neurosurgery, 23,* 394–399.

Bonin, G. von, & Bailey, P., 1947. The neocortex of *Mucaca mulatta.* Urbana, Ill., University of Illinois Press.

Bouillaud, J., 1825. Recherches cliniques propres à démontrer que la perte de la parole correspond à la lésion des lobules antérieurs du cerveau. *Archives Génerales de Médecine, 8,* 25–45.

Bower, G. H., 1967. A descriptive theory of memory. In D. P. Kimble (Ed.) *The organization of recall. Vol. 2,* New York, New York Academy of Sciences.

Bower, G. H., 1970. Imagery as a relational organizer in associative learning. *Journal of Verbal Learning and Verbal Behavior, 9,* 529–533.

Bradley, P. B., & Elkes, J., 1957. The effects of some drugs on the electrical activity of the brain. *Brain, 80,* 77–117.

Brady, J. V., Schreiner, L., Geller, I., & Kling, A., 1954. Subcortical mechanisms in emotional behavior: The effect of rhinencephalic injury upon the acquisition and retention of a conditioned avoidance response in cats. *Journal of Comparative and Physiological Psychology, 47,* 179–186.

Braun, J. J., 1975. Neocortex and feeding behavior in the rat. *Journal of Comparative and Physiological Psychology, 89,* 507–522.

Brazier, M. A. B., 1972. The human amygdala: Electrophysiological studies. In B. E. Eleftheriou (Ed.), *The neurobiology of the amygdala.* New York: Plenum Press.

Bremer, F., 1970. Preoptic hypnogenic focus and mesencephalic reticular formation. *Brain Research, 21,* 132–134.

Bresnahan, E., & Routtenberg, A., 1972. Memory disruption by unilateral low level sub-seizure stimulation of the medial amygdaloid nucleus. *Physiology and Behavior, 9,* 513–525.

Broadbent, D. E., 1958. *Perception and communication.* Pergamon Press: New York.

Broadbent, D. E., 1967. Distinction among various types of memory. In: D. P. Kimble (Ed.), *The organization of recall.* New York, The New York Academy of Sciences.

Broadbent, D. E., 1967b. Word-frequency effect and response bias. *Psychological Review, 74,* 1–15.

Broadbent, D. E., 1971. *Decision and stress.* New York: Academic Press.

Broadbent, W. H., 1872. On the cerebral mechanism of speech and thought. *Transactions of the Medical and Chirurgical Faculty of Maryland, 55,* 145–194.

Broadbent, W. H., 1879. A case of peculiar affection of speech with commentary. *Brain, 1,* 484–503.

Broca, P., 1861. Perte de la parole. Ramollissement chronique et destruction partielle du lobe antérieur gauche du cerveau. *Bulletin de la Société d'Anthropologie, 2,* 235–238.

Brodal, P., 1978a. Corticopontine projection in the Rhesus monkey. *Brain, 101,* 251–283.

Brodal, P., 1978b. Principles of organization of the monkey corticopontine projection. *Brain Research, 148,* 214–218.

Brodmann, K., 1914. Physiologie des Gehirns. In Die allgemeine Chirurgie der Gehirnkrankheiten. *Neue Deutsche Chirurgie, Vol. 11,* Verlag Ferdinand Enke, Stuttgart.

Brooks, V. B., 1978. Control of intended limb movements by the lateral and intermediate cerebellum. In H. Asanuma & V. J. Wilson (Eds.), Tokyo: Igaku-Shoin.

Brown, G. E., and Remley, N. R., 1971. The effects of septal and olfactory bulb lesions in stimulus reactivity. *Physiology and Behavior, 6,* 497–501.

Brown, R., & McNeill, D., 1966. The "tip of the tongue" phenomenon. *Journal of Verbal Learning and Verbal Behavior, 5,* 325–337.

Brown, T. S., 1963. Olfactory and visual discrimination in the monkey after selective lesions of the temporal lobe. *Journal of Comparative and Physiological Psychology, 56,* 764–768.

Brown, T. S., Rosvold, H. E., & Mishkin, M., 1963. Olfactory discrimination after temporal lobe lesions in monkeys. *Journal of Comparative and Physiological Psychology, 56,* 190–195.

Brush, E. S., Mishkin, M., & Rosvold, H. E., 1961. Effects of object preferences and aversions on discrimination learning in monkeys with frontal lesions. *Journal of Comparative and Physiological Psychology, 54,* 319–325.

Brust-Carmona, H., Prado-Alcalà, R., Grinberg-Zylberbaum, J., Alvarez-Leefmans, J., & Coronado, I. Z., 1974. Modulatory effects of acetylcholine and catecholamines in the caudate nucleus during motor conditioning. In R. D. Myers & R. R. Drucker-Colin (Eds.), *Neurohumoral coding of brain function.* New York: Plenum Press.

Brutkowski, S., Mishkin, M., & Rosvold, H. E., 1963. Positive and inhibitory motor SRs in monkeys after ablation of orbital and dorsolateral surface of the frontal cortex. In E. Gutman (Ed.), *Central and peripheral mechanisms of motor functions.* Prague, Czechoslovak Academy of Sciences.

Buddington, R. W., King, F. A., & Roberts, L., 1967. Emotionality and conditioned avoidance responding in the squirrel monkey following septal injury. *Psychonomic Science, 8,* 195–196.

Bugelski, B. R., 1970. Words and things and images. *American Psychologist, 25,* 1002–1012.

Bunney, W. E. Jr., & Gulley, B. L., 1978. The current status of research in the catecholamine theories of affective disorders. In E. Usdin & A. J. Mandell (Eds.), *Biochemistry of mental disorders.* New York: Marcel Dekker.

Bureš, J., 1959. Reversible decortication and behavior. In: M. A. B. Brazier (Ed.), *The central nervous system and behavior. Transactions, Second Conference on the central nervous system and behavior,* New York: Josiah Macy, Jr. Foundation.

Bureš, J., Bohdanecky, Z., & Weiss, T., 1962. Physostigmine induced hippocampal theta activity and learning in rats. *Psychopharmacologia, 3,* 254–263.

Burkett, E. E. & Bunnell, B. N., 1966. Septal lesions and the retention of DRL performance in the rat. *Journal of Comparative and Physiological Psychology, 62,* 468–472.

Buser, P., 1966. Subcortical controls of pyramidal activity. In D. Purpura & M. D. Yahr (Eds.), *The thalamus.* New York: Columbia University Press.

Butcher, L. L., & Talbot, K., 1978. Acetylcholinesterase in rat nigro-neostriatal neurons: Experimental verification and evidence for cholinergic-dopaminergic interactions in the substantia nigra and caudate-putamen complex. In L. L. Butcher (Ed.), *Cholinergic-monoaminergic interactions in the brain.* New York: Academic Press.

Butcher, S. H., 1978. Effects of dopaminergic and serotonergic agonists and antagonists on acetylcholine levels and synthesis in the neostriatum. In L. L. Butcher (Ed.), *Cholinergic-monoaminergic interactions in the brain.* New York: Academic Press.

Butter, C. M., 1965. Effective stimuli for pattern discrimination in monkeys. *Psychonomic Science, 2,* 325–326.

Butter, C. M., 1968. The effect of discrimination training on pattern equivalence in monkeys with inferotemporal and lateral striate lesions. *Neuropsychologia, 6,* 27–40.

Butter, C. M., & Doehrman, S. R., 1968. Size discrimination and transposition in monkeys with striate and temporal lesions. *Cortex, 4,* 35–46.

Butter, C. M., & Gekoski, W. L., 1961. Alternations in pattern equivalence following inferotemporal and lateral striate lesions in rhesus monkeys. *Journal of Comparative and Physiological Psychology, 61,* 309–312.

Butter, C. M., Mishkin, M., & Rosvold, H. E., 1963. Conditioning and extinction of a food reward response after selective ablations of frontal cortex in rhesus monkeys. *Experimental Neurology, 7,* 65–75.

Butters, N., & Cermak, L., 1975. Some analyses of amnesic syndromes in brain-damaged patients. In: R. L. Isaacson & K. H. Pribram (Eds.), *The hippocampus. Vol. 2.* New York: Plenum Press.

Butters, N., & Rosvold, H. E., 1968a. Effect of caudate and septal nuclei lesions on resistance to extinction and delayed-alternation. *Journal of Comparative and Physiological Psychology, 65,* 397–403.

Butters, N., & Rosvold, H. E., 1968b. Effect of septal lesions on resistance to extinction and delayed alternation in monkeys. *Journal of Comparative and Physiological Psychology, 66,* 389–395.

Caldwell, J. R., 1958. *Olfactory discrimination in lobotomized patients.* Unpublished M. A. Thesis, Loyola University of Chicago.

Campbell, R. J., & Harlow, H. F., 1945. Problem solution by monkeys following bilateral removal of the prefrontal areas: V. Spatial delayed reactions. *Journal of Experimental Psychology, 35,* 110–126.

Carlson, N. R., 1970. Two-way avoidance behavior of mice with limbic lesions. *Journal of Comparative and Physiological Psychology, 70,* 73–78.

Carpenter, M. B., 1973. Comparisons of the efferent projections of the globus pallidus and the substantia nigra in the monkey. In J. D. Masser (Ed.), *Efferent organization and the integration of behavior*. New York: Academic Press.

Carpenter, M. B., 1976. *Human neuroanatomy, 7th ed.*, Baltimore; Williams & Wilkins.

Carpenter, M. B., Nakano, K., & Kim, R., 1976. Nigrothalamic projections in the monkey demonstrated by autoradiographic technics. *Journal of Comparative Neurology, 165*, 401–412.

Carpenter, M. B., & Peter, P., 1972. Nigrostriatal and nigrothalamic fibers in the Rhesus monkey. *Journal of Comparative Neurology, 144*, 93–110.

Carroll, J. B., 1971. Reinforcement: Is it a basic principle, and will it serve in the analysis of verbal behavior? In: R. Glaser (Ed.), *The nature of reinforcement*. New York: Academic Press.

Caruthers, R. P., 1968. Ansa lenticularis area tractotomy and shuttle avoidance learning. *Journal of Comparative and Physiological Psychology, 65*, 295–302.

Chan-Palay, V., 1977. *Cerebellar dentate nucleus*. Berlin: Springer Verlag.

Cherlow, D. G. & Serafetinides, E. A., 1976. Speech and memory assessment in psychomotor epileptics. *Cortex, 12*, 21–26.

Chorover, S. L., 1965. Discussion (p. 254) in D. P. Kimble (Ed.), *The anatomy of memory*. Palo Alto, Calif., Science and Behavior Books.

Chorover, S. L., 1976. An experimental critique of "consolidation studies" and an alternative "model-systems" approach to the biophysiology of memory. In: M. R. Rosenzweig & E. L. Bennett (Eds.), *Neural mechanisms of learning and memory*. Cambridge, Mass. MIT Press.

Chronister, R. B., Sikes, R. W., & White, L. E. Jr., 1976. The septo-hippocampal system: Significance of the subiculum. In J. F. DeFrance (Ed.), *The septal nuclei*. New York: Plenum Press.

Chronister, R. B., & White, L. E. Jr., 1975. Fiberarchitecture of the hippocampal formation: Anatomy, projections, and structural significance. In R. L. Isaacson & K. H. Pribram (Eds.), *The hippocampus, Vol. 1*. New York: Plenum Press.

Clara, M., 1959. *Das Nervensystem des Menschen*. Leipzig: Barth.

Clark, C. V. H. and Isaacson, R. L., 1965. Effect of bilateral hippocampal ablation on DRL performance. *Journal of Comparative and Physiological Psychology, 59*, 137–140.

Clark, R., Schuster, C. R., & Brady, J. V., 1961. Instrumental conditioning of jugular self-infusion in the rhesus monkey. *Science, 133*, 1829–1830.

Clody, D. E. & Carlton, P. L., 1969. Behavioral effects of lesions of the medial septum of rats. *Journal of Comparative and Physiological Psychology, 67*, 344–351.

Cohen, D., Chambers, W. W., & Sprague, J. M., 1958. Experimental study of the afferent projections from the cerebellar nuclei to the brainstem of the cat. *Journal of Comparative Neurology, 109*, 233–259.

Cohen, S. M., 1972. Electrical stimulation of cortical-caudate pairs during delayed successive visual discrimination in monkeys. *Acta Neurobiologica Experimentalis, 32*, 211–233.

Collier, B., & Mitchell, J. F., 1966. The central release of acetylcholine during stimulation of the visual pathway. *Journal of Physiology, 184*, 239–254.

Collier, B., & Mitchell, J. F., 1967. The central release of acetylcholine during consciousness and after brain lesions. *Journal of Physiology, 188*, 183–198.

Conneely, J. E., 1967. *The effect of bilateral lesions of the cingulum on the retention of five sensory modalities in the albino rat*. Unpublished M. A. Thesis, Loyola University of Chicago.

Corkin, S., 1965. Tactually-guided maze learning in man: Effects of unilateral cortical excisions and bilateral hippocampal lesions. *Neuropsychologia, 3*, 339–351.

Corkin, S., 1968. Acquisition of motor skill after bilateral medial temporal-lobe excision. *Neuropsychologia, 6*, 255–265.

Cornwell, P., 1966. Behavioral effects of orbital and proreal lesions in cats. *Journal of Comparative and Physiological Psychology, 61*, 50–58.

Correll, R. E. & Scoville, W. B., 1965. Effects of medial temporal lesions on visual discrimination performance. *Journal of Comparative and Physiological Psychology, 60*, 175–181.

Craik, F. I. M., & Jacoby, L. L., 1979. Elaboration and distinctiveness in episodic memory. In: L.-G. Nilsson (Ed.), *Perspectives on memory research.* Hillsdale, N.J.: Lawrence Erlbaum Associates.

Crosby, E. C., Humphrey, T., & Lauer, E. W., 1962. *Correlative anatomy of the nervous system.* New York: Macmillan.

Crowder, R. G., 1967. Short-term memory for words with a perceptual-motor interpolated activity. *Journal of Verbal Learning and Verbal Behavior, 6,* 753–761.

Crowder, R. G., 1976. *Principles of learning and memory.* Hillsdale, N.J.: Lawrence Erlbaum Associates.

Crowne, D. P., & Radcliffe, D. D., 1975. Some characteristics and functional relations of the electrical activity of the primate hippocampus and hypotheses of hippocampal function. In R. L. Isaacson & K. H. Pribram (Eds.), The *hippocampus, Vol. 2,* New York: Plenum Press.

Dahl, D., Ingram, W. R., & Knott, J. R., 1962. Diencephalic lesions and avoidance learning in cats. *Archives of Neurology, 7,* 314–319.

Dahlström, A., & Fuxe, K. A., 1964. A method for the demonstration of monoamine-containing nerve fibers in the central nervous system. *Acta Physiologica Scandinavica, 60,* 293–295.

Dalby, D. A., 1970. Effect of septal lesions on the acquisition of two types of active avoidance behavior in rats. *Journal of Comparative and Physiological Psychology, 73,* 278–283.

Dalsass, M., & G. G. Krauthamer, 1981. Behavioral alterations and loss of caudate modulation in the centrum medianum-parafascicular complex of the cat following electrolytic lesions of the substantia nigra. *Brain Research, 208,* 67–79.

Dalton, A., & Black, A. H., 1968. Hippocampal electrical activity during operant conditioning of movement and refraining from movement. *Communications in Behavioral Biology, 2,* 267–273.

Davis, R., 1966. Acetylcholine-sensitive neurons in ventrolateral thalamic nucleus. In D. P. Purpura & M. D. Yahr (Eds.), *The thalamus.* New York: Columbia University Press.

Davis, R., Sutherland, N. S., & Judd, B. R., 1961. Information content in recognition and recall. *Journal of Experimental Psychology, 61,* 422–29.

De Olmos, J. S., 1972. The amygdaloid projection field in the rat as studied with the cupric-silver method. In B. E. Eleftheriou (Ed.), *The neurobiology of the amygdala.* New York: Plenum Press.

De Renzi, E., 1967. Asimmetrie emisferiche nella rappresentatione di talune funzioni nervose superiori non verbali. Atti del XVI Congresso Nazionale de Neurologia, Rome, October 1, 371–430.

De Robertis, E. 1972. Molecular organization of synapses for chemical transmission in the nervous system. In A. G. Karczmar & J. C. Eccles (Eds.), *Brain and behavior.* New York: Springer.

DeRyck, M., Køhler, C., Ursin, H., & Levine, S., 1976. Plasma corticosterone levels during active avoidance learning in rats with septal lesions. In J. F. DeFrance (Ed.), The septal nuclei. New York, Plenum Press.

Deagle, J. H., & Lubar, J. F., 1971. Effect of septal lesions in two strains of rats on one-way and shuttle avoidance acquisition. *Journal of Comparative and Physiological Psychology, 77,* 277–281.

Deese, J., 1961. From the isolated verbal unit to connected discourse. In: C. N. Cofer, (Ed.), *Verbal learning and verbal behavior.* McGraw-Hill: New York.

Déjérine, J., 1891. Sur un cas de cécité verbale avec agraphie suivi d'autopsie. *Mémoires de la Société de Biologie, 3,* 197–201.

Deutsch, J. A., 1972. The cholinergic synapse and the site of memory. In J. McGaugh (Eds.), *Chemistry of mood, motivation and behavior.* New York: Plenum Press.

Deutsch, J. A., & DiCara, L., 1967. Hunger and extinction in intracranial self-stimulation. *Journal of Comparative and Physiological Psychology, 63,* 344–347.

Dillon, R. F., & Reid, L. S., 1969. Short-term memory as a function of information processing during the retention interval. *Journal of Experimental Psychology, 81,* 261–269.

Dimond, S. J. & Beaumont, J. G. (Eds.), 1974. *Hemisphere function in the human brain.* New York: Wiley.

Divac, I., 1977. Does the striatum operate as a functional entity? In: A. R. Cools, A. H. M. Lohman, & J. H. L. Van den Bercken (Eds.), *Psychobiology of the striatum*. Amsterdam: North-Holland Publishing Co.

Divac, I., Rosvold, H. E., & Szwarcbart, M. K., 1967. Behavioral effects of selective ablation of the caudate nucleus. *Journal of Comparative and Physiological Psychology, 63,* 184–190.

Donovick, P. J., 1968. Effects of localized septal lesions on hippocampal EEG activity in behavior in rats. *Journal of Comparative and Physiological Psychology, 66,* 569–578.

Dott, N. M., 1938. Surgical aspects of the hypothalamus. In: W. E. L., Clark, W. E. Beattie, G. Riddoch, and N. M. Dott (Eds.), *The hypothalamus: Morphological, functional, clinical and surgical aspects*. Edinburgh: Oliver and Boyd.

Doty, R. W., 1979. Neurons and memory: some clues. In M. A. B. Brazier (Ed.), *Brain mechanisms in memory and learning*. New York: Raven Press.

Doty, R. W., & Overman, W. H., 1977. Mnemonic role of forebrain commissures in macaques. In S. Harnad, R. W. Doty, J. Jaynes, L. Goldstein, & G. Krauthamer (Eds.), *Lateralization in the nervous system*. New York: Academic Press.

Douglas, R. J., 1966. Transposition, novelty, and limbic lesions. *Journal of Comparative and Physiological Psychology, 62,* 354–357.

Douglas, R. J., 1967. The hippocampus and behavior. *Psychological Bulletin, 67,* 416–442.

Douglas, R. J., 1975. The development of hippocampal function: Implications for theory and therapy. In R. L. Isaacson & K. H. Pribram (Eds.), *The hippocampus. Vol. 2*. New York: Plenum Press.

Douglas, R. J., & Pribram, K. H., 1966. Learning and limbic lesions. *Neuropsychologia, 4,* 197–220.

Douglas, R. J., & Pribram, K. H., 1969. Distraction and habituation in monkeys with limbic lesions. *Journal of Comparative and Physiological Psychology, 69,* 473–480.

Downer, J. L. C., 1958. Role of corpus callosum in transfer of training in Macaca mulatta. *Federation Proceedings, 17,* 37.

Downer, J. L. C., 1959. Changes in visually guided behaviour following midsagittal division of optic chiasm and corpus callosum in monkey (Macaca mulatta). *Brain, 82,* 251–259.

Drachman, D. A., 1977. Memory and the cholinergic system. In W. S. Fields (Ed.) *Neurotransmitter function*. New York: Stratton.

Drachman, D. A., & Arbit, J. A., 1966. Memory and the hippocampal complex. II. Is memory a multiple process? *A. M. A. Archives of Neurology, 15,* 52–61.

Drachman, D. A., & Ommaya, A. K., 1964. Memory and the hippocampal complex. *Archives of Neurology, 10,* 411–425.

Driessen, G., 1965. *The effect of bilateral lesions of the hippocampus on the learning and retention of auditory and visual discrimination in the albino rat*. Unpublished Ph.D. dissertation, Loyola University of Chicago.

Dufour, V. L., 1967. *The importance of hippocampal remnants in discrimination ability*. Unpublished Ph.D. dissertation, Loyola University of Chicago.

Duncan, P. M., & Duncan, N. C., 1971. Free-operant and T-maze avoidance performance by septal and hippocampal-damaged rats. *Physiology and Behavior, 7,* 687–693.

Dunn, A. J., & Rees, H. D. 1977. Brain RNA and protein synthesis during training: The interpretation of changes of precursor incorporation. In R. R. Drucker-Colin & J. L. McGaugh (Eds.), *Neurobiology of sleep and memory*. New York: Academic Press.

Dykes, R. W., 1978. The anatomy and physiology of the somatic sensory cortical regions. *Progress in Neurobiology, 10,* 33–88.

Eagle, M., & Leiter, E., 1964. Recall and recognition in intentional and incidental learning. *Journal of Experimental Psychology, 68,* 58–63.

Eccles, J. C., 1977. *The understanding of the brain*. 2nd ed. New York: McGraw-Hill.

Eccles, J. C., 1979. Introductory remarks. In J. Massion & K. Sasaki (Eds.), *Cerebrocerebellar interactions*. Amsterdam: Elsevier/North-Holland Biomedical Press.

Eclancher, F. S., & Karli, P., 1971. Comportement d'aggression interspécifique et comportement alimentaire du rat: Effets de lesions des noyeaux ventromédians de l'hypothalamus. *Brain Research, 26,* 71–79.

Economo, C. von, 1929. *The cytoarchitecture of the human cerebral cortex.* Translated by S. Parker. New York: Humphrey Milford.

Economo, C. von, & Koskinas, G., 1925. *Die Cytoarchitektonik der Hirnrinde des erwachsenen Menschen.* Berlin.

Edinger, H., & Siegel, A., 1976. Functional aspects of the hippocampal-septal axis. In J. F. DeFrance (Ed.), *The septal nuclei.* New York: Plenum Press.

Egan, J. P., Carterette, E. C., & Thwing, E. J., 1954. Some factors affecting multichannel listening. *Journal of the Acoustical Society of America, 26,* 774–782.

Egger, M. D. & Flynn, J. P., 1963. Effects of electrical stimulation of the amygdala upon hypothalamically elicited attack behavior in cats. *Journal of Neurophysiology, 26,* 705–720.

Ekkers, C. L., 1975. Catecholamine excretion, conscience function and aggressive behavior. *Biological Psychology, 3,* 15–30.

Ekstrand, B. R., 1967. Effect of sleep on memory. *Journal of Experimental Psychology, 75,* 64–72.

Ekstrand, B. R., Wallace, W. P., & Underwood, B. J., 1966. A frequency theory of verbal discrimination learning. *Psychological Review, 73,* 566–578.

Eleftheriou, B. E., Elias, M. T., & Norman, R. L., 1972. Effects of amygdaloid lesions on reversal learning in the deermouse. *Physiology and Behavior, 9,* 69–73.

Ellen, P., & Powell, E. W., 1962. Effects of septal lesions on behavior generated by positive reinforcement. *Experimental Neurology, 6,* 1–11.

Ellen, P., Wilson, A. S., & Powell, E. W., 1964. Septal inhibition and timing behavior in the rat. *Experimental Neurology, 10,* 120–132.

Ellison, G. D., Sorenson, C. A., & Jacobs, B. L., 1970. Two feeding syndromes following surgical isolation of the hypothalamus in rats. *Journal of Comparative and Physiological Psychology, 70* 173–188.

Emson, P. C., Kanazawa, I., Cuello, A. C., et al., 1977. Substance-P pathways in rat brain. *Biochemical Society Transactions, 5,* 187–189.

Epstein, A. N., 1960. Water intake without the act of drinking. *Science, 131,* 497–498.

Erickson, C. K., & Patel, J. B., 1969. Facilitation of avoidance learning by posttrial hippocampal electrical stimulation. *Journal of Comparative and Physiological Psychology 68,* 400–406.

Essman, W. B., 1973. Experimentally induced retrograde amnesia: Some neurochemical correlates. In W. B. Essman & S. Nakajima (Eds.), *Current biochemical approaches to learning and memory.* Flushing, N.Y.: Spectrum.

Estes, W. K., 1950. Toward a statistical theory of learning. *Psychological Review, 57,* 94–107.

Estes, W. K., 1960. Learning theory and the new "mental chemistry." *Psychological Review, 67,* 207–223.

Estes, W. K., 1971. Reward in human learning: Theoretical issues and strategic choice points. In R. Glaser (Ed.), *The nature of reinforcement.* New York: Academic Press.

Ettlinger, G., & Kalsbeck, J. E., 1962. Changes in tactile discrimination and in visual reaching after successive and simultaneous bilateral posterior parietal ablations in the monkey. *Journal of Neurology, Neurosurgery and Psychiatry, 25,* 256–268.

Ettlinger, G., & Wegener, J., 1958. Somesthetic alternation, discrimination and orientation after frontal and parietal lesions in monkeys. *Quarterly Journal of Experimental Psychology, 10,* 177–186.

Exner, S., 1881. *Untersuchungen über die Lokalisation der Funktionen in der Grosshirnrinde des Menschen.* Wien: Braumüller.

Fagot, J. H., 1962. *Effects of lesions in the hippocampal rudiment on conditioned olfactory discrimination in the albino rat.* Unpublished Ph.D. dissertation, Loyola University of Chicago.

Falck, B., 1962. Observations on the possibilities of the cellular localization of monoamines by a fluorescent method. *Acta Physiologica Scandinavica, 56 (Supplement 197),* 1–25.

Falk, J. L., 1961. Septal stimulation as a reenforcer of and an alternative to consummatory behavior. *Journal for the Experimental Analysis of Behavior, 4*, 213–217.

Fallon, D., & Donovick, P. J., 1970. Low resistance to extinction in rats with septal lesions under inappropriate appetitive motivation. *Journal of Comparative and Physiological Psychology, 73*, 150–156.

Faust, C., 1955. *Die zerebralen Herdstörungen bei Hinterhauptverletzungen und ihre Beurteilung.* Stuttgart, Thieme.

Fedio, P., & Ommaya, A. K., 1970. Bilateral cingulum lesions and stimulation in man with lateralized impairment in short-term verbal memory. *Experimental Neurology, 29*, 84–91.

Fibiger, H. C., 1977. On the role of the dopaminergic nigro-striatal projection in reinforcement, learning and memory. In A. R. Cools, A. H. M. Lohman, & J. H. L. Van den Bercken (Eds.), *Psychobiology of the striatum.* Amsterdam: North-Holland Publishing Co.

Fibiger, H. C., & Phillips, A. G., 1976. Retrograde amnesia after electrical stimulation of the substantia nigra: Mediation by the dopaminergic nigro-striatal bundle. *Brain Research, 116*, 23–33.

Fields, C., 1969. Visual stimuli and evoked responses in the rat. *Science, 165*, 1377–1379.

Fischman, M., & R. A. McCleary, 1966. A patterned perseveration deficit following fornicotomy in the cat. In E. Stellar & J. M. Sprague (Eds.), *Progress in Physiological Psychology, Vol. 1.*, New York: Academic Press.

Fischman, M. W., & Meikle, T. H., Jr., 1965. Visual intensity discrimination in cats after serial tectal and cortical lesions. Journal of Comparative and Physiological Psychology, 59, 193–201.

Fishbein, W., Kastaniotis, C., & Chattman, D., 1974. Paradoxial sleep: Prolonged augmentation following learning. *Brain Research, 79*, 61–75.

Fishbein, W., McGaugh, J. L., & Swarz, J. R., 1971. Retrograde amnesia: Electroconvulsive shock effects after termination of rapid eye movement sleep deprivation. *Science, 172*, 80–82.

Flechsig, P., 1876. *Die Leitungsbahnen im Gehirn und Rückenmark des Menschen.* Leipzig: Engelmann.

Flourens, M. J. P., 1842. Examen de phrénologie. Paris, Hachette.

Flynn, J., 1967. The neural basis of aggression in cats. In D. H. Glass (Ed.), *Neurophysiology and emotion.* New York: Rockefeller University Press.

Foerster, O., 1936. Symptomatologie der Erkrankungen des Gehirns. Motorische Felder und Bahnen. Sensible corticale Felder. In O. Bumke & O. Foerster (Eds.), *Handbuch der Neurologie, Vol. 6*, Berlin, Springer.

Fonberg, E., 1965. Effect of partial destruction of the amygdaloid complex on the emotional-defensive behaviour of dogs. *Bulletin of the Polish Academy of Science (Biology), 13*, 429–432.

Fonberg, E., 1968. The role of the amygdaloid nucleus in animal behaviour. *Progress in Brain Research, 22*, 273–281.

Fonberg, E., 1969. The role of the hypothalamus and amygdala in food intake, alimentary motivation and emotional reactions. *Acta Biologiae Experimentalis, 29*, 335–358.

Fonberg, E., 1981. Specific versus unspecific functions of the amygdala. In Y. Ben-Ari (Ed.), *The amygdaloid complex.* Amsterdam: Elsevier/North-Holland Biomedical Press.

Fonberg, E., & Delgado, J. M. R., 1961. Avoidance and alimentary reactions during amygdaloid stimulation. *Journal of Neurophysiology, 24*, 651–664.

Fox, C. A., 1949. Amygdalo-thalamic connections in macaca mulutta. *Anatomical Record, 103*, 537–538.

Fox, S. S., Kimble, D. P., & Lickey, M. E., 1964. Comparison of caudate nucleus and septal area lesion on two types of avoidance behavior. *Journal of Comparative and Physiological Psychology, 58*, 380–386.

Frank, B., Stein, D. G., & Rosen, J., 1970. Interanimal "memory" transfer. Results from brain and liver homogenates. *Science, 169*, 399–402.

Freeman, W., 1951. Psychosurgery. *American Journal of Psychiatry, 107*, 524–525.

Freeman, W., & Watts, J. W., 1942. *Psychosurgery.* Springfield, Ill.: Thomas.

French, J. D., Hernández-Peón, R., & Livingston, R. B., 1955. Projections from cortex to cephalic brainstem (reticular formation) in monkey. *Journal of Neurophysiology, 18,* 74–95.

French, J. D., Verzeano, M., & Magoun, W., 1953. An extralemniscal sensory system in the brain. *A.M.A. Archives of Neurology and Psychiatry, 69,* 505–518.

Fritsch, G., & Hitzig, E., 1870. Ueber die elektrische Erregbarkeit des Grosshirns. *Archiv für Anatomie, Physiologie und Wissenschaftliche Medizin, 37,* 300–332.

Fulton, J. F., Aring, C. D., & Wortis, S. B., (Eds.), 1948. *The frontal lobes.* Baltimore: Williams and Wilkins.

Fulton, J. F., 1949. *Physiology of the Nervous System.* 3rd ed. New York, Oxford University Press.

Fuster, J. M., 1973. Transient memory and neuronal activity in the thalamus. In K. H. Pribram & A. R. Luria (Eds.), *Physhophysiology of the frontal lobes.* New York: Academic Press.

Fuxe, K., 1965. Evidence for the existence of monoamine neurons in the central nervous system. IV. Distribution of monoamine nerve terminals in the central nervous system. *Acta Physiologica Scandinavica, Supplement 247, 64,* 37–85.

Fuxe, K., Ferland, L., Andersson, K., Eneroth, P., Gustafsson, J. A., & Skett, P., 1978. On the functional role of hypothalamic catecholamine neurons in control of the secretion of hormones from the anterior pituitary, particularly in the control of LH and prolactin secretion. In D. E. Scott, N.Y. Rochester, G. P. Kozlowski, & A. Weindl (Eds.), *Brain-endocrine interaction. III. Neural hormones and reproduction.* Basel: Karger.

Fuxe, K., & Hanson, L. C. F., 1967. Central catecholamine neurons and conditioned avoidance behavior. *Psychopharmacologia, 11,* 439–447.

Fuxe, K., & Jonsson, G., 1974. Further mapping of central 5-hydroxytryptamine neurons: studies with the neurotoxic dihydroxytryptamines. *Advances in Biochemical Psychopharmacology, 10,* 1–12.

Gaffan, D., 1978. Discussion, p. 396. In *Ciba Foundation Symposium 58. Function of the septo-hippocampal system.* Amsterdam: Elsevier.

Gall, F. J., 1825. *Sur les fonctions du cerveau et sur celles de chacune de ses parties.* 6 vols. Paris, Baillière.

Gallistel, C. R., 1969. Failure of pretrial stimulation to affect reward electrode preference. *Journal of Comparative and Physiological Psychology, 69,* 722–729.

Gallistel, C. R., 1973. Self-stimulation: The neurophysiology of reward and motivation. In J. A. Deutsch (Ed.), *The physiological basis of memory.* New York: Academic Press.

Garber, E. E., & Simmons, H. J., 1968. Facilitation of two-way avoidance performance by septal lesions in rats. *Journal of Comparative and Physiological Psychology, 66,* 559–562.

Garcia Bengochea, F., de la Torre, O., Esquival, O., Vieta, R., & Fernandez, C. 1954. The section of the fornix in the surgical treatment of certain epilepsies. *Transactions of the American Neurological Association, 79, 176–178.*

Gasson, J. A., 1954. Personality theory: A formulation of general principles. In M. B. Arnold & J. A. Gasson, *The human person.* New York: Ronald Press.

Gastaut, H., 1952. Corrélations entre le système nerveux vegétatif et le système de la vie de relation: Dans le rhinencéphale. *Journal de Physiologie, 44,* 431–470.

Gastaut, H., 1954. The brain stem and cerebral electrogenesis in relation to consciousness. In: J. F. Delafresnaye, (Ed.), *Brain mechanisms and consciousness.* Springfield, Ill.: Thomas.

Gastaut, H., & Lammers, H. J., 1961. *Anatomie du rhinencéphale.* Paris: Masson.

Gavin, H., 1963. *Effects of lesions in the hippocampal rudiment of T-maze single alternation in the albino rat.* Unpublished Ph. D. dissertation, Loyola University of Chicago.

Gazzaniga, M. S., 1970. *The bisected brain.* New York: Appleton-Century-Crofts.

Gazzaniga, M. S., 1972. One brain—two minds? *American Scientist, 60,* 311–317.

Gazzaniga, M. S., 1975. Brain mechanisms and behavior. In M. S. Gazzaniga & C. Blakemore (Eds.), *Handbook of psychobiology.* New York: Academic Press.

Gazzaniga, M. S., 1976. The biology of memory. In M. R. Rosenzweig & E. L. Bennett (Eds.), *Neural mechanisms of learning and memory.* Cambridge, Mass.: MIT Press.

Gerbrandt, L., 1965. The effects of anteromedial and dorsomedial thalamic lesions on passive avoidance and activity. *Psychonomic Science, 2,* 39–40.

German, D. C., & Bowden, D. M., 1974. Catecholamine systems as the neural substrate for intracranial self-stimulation: a hypothesis. *Brain Research, 73,* 381–419.

Geschwind, N., 1965. Disconnexion syndromes in animals and man. *Brain, 88,* 237–294; 585–644.

Geschwind, N., 1970. The organization of language and the brain. *Science, 170,* 940–944.

Geschwind, N., 1974. The anatomical basis of hemispheric differentiation. In S. J. Dimond & J. G. Beaumont (Eds.), *Hemisphere function in the human brain.* New York: Wiley.

Geyer, M. A., 1978. Heterogeneous function of discrete serotonergic pathways in the brain. In E. Usdin & A. J. Mandell (Eds.), *Biochemistry of mental disorders.* New York, Marcel Dekker.

Ghent, L., Mishkin, M., & Teuber, H. L., 1962. Short-term memory after frontal-lobe injury in man. *Journal of Comparative and Physiological Psychology, 55,* 705–709.

Gibson, A. R., Dimond, S. J., & Gazzaniga, M. S., 1972. Left field superiority for word matching. *Neuropsychologia, 10,* 463–466.

Gittelson, P. L., & Donovick, P. J., 1968. The effects of septal lesions on the learning and reversal of a kinesthetic discrimination. *Psychonomic Science, 13,* 137–138.

Glass, A. V., Gazzaniga, M. S., & Premack, D., 1973. Artificial language training in global aphasias. *Neuropsychologia, 11,* 95–103.

Glass, D. H., Ison, J. R., & Thomas, G. J., 1969. Anterior limbic cortex and partial reinforcement effects on acquisition and extinction of a runway response in rats. *Journal of Comparative and Physiological Psychology, 69,* 17–24.

Glees, P., Cole, J., Whitty, C. W. M., & Cairns, H., 1950. The effects of lesions in the cingular gyrus and adjacent areas in monkeys. *Journal of Neurology, Neurosurgery and Psychiatry, 13,* 178–190.

Glezer, I. I., 1955. New data on the development of the cortical nucleus of the motor analyzer in man. In *Proceedings of the Second Conference on Age; Morphology and Physiology.* Moscow: Izv.Akad. Ped. Nauk.RSFSR.

Glickstein, M., Arora, H., & Sperry, R. W., 1960. Delayed response performance of split-brain monkeys with unilateral prefrontal ablation and optic tract section. *Physiologist, 3,* 66.

Glickstein, M., Arora, H., & Sperry, R. W., 1963. Delayed-response performance following optic tract section, unilateral frontal lesion, and commissurotomy. *Journal of Comparative and Physiological Psychology, 56,* 11–18.

Gloning, L., Gloning, K., Haub, G., & Quatember, R., 1969. Comparison of verbal behavior in right-handed and non-right-handed patients with anatomically verified lesion of one hemisphere. *Cortex, 5,* 41–52.

Gloor, P., 1972. Temporal lobe epilepsy: Its possible contribution to the understanding of the functional significance of the amygdala and of its interaction with neocortical-temporal mechanisms. In B. E. Eleftheriou (Ed.), *The neurobiology of the amygdala.* New York: Plenum Press.

Gloor, P., Olivier, A., & Quesnay, L. F., 1981. The role of the amygdala in the expression of psychic phenomena in temporal lobe seizures. In Y. Ben-Ari (Ed.), *The amygdaloid complex.* Amsterdam: Elsevier/North Holland Biomedical Press.

Glowinski, J., Giorguieff, M. F., & Cheramy, A., 1980. Regulatory processes involved in the control of the activity of nigrostriatal dopaminergic neurons. In J. A. Hobson & M. A. B. Brazier (Eds.), The reticular formation revisited. New York: Raven Press.

Goddard, G. V., 1964a. Functions of the amygdala. *Psychological Bulletin, 62,* 89–109.

Goddard, G. V., 1964b. Amygdaloid stimulation and learning in the rat. *Journal of Comparative and Physiological Psychology, 58,* 23–30.

Goddard, G. V., 1972. Long term alteration following amygdaloid stimulation. In B. E. Eleftheriou (Ed.), *The neurobiology of the amygdala.* New York: Plenum Press.

Gold, P. E., Hankins, L. L., & Rose, R. P., 1977. Time-dependent post-trial changes in the localization of amnestic electrical stimulation sites within the amygdala in rats. *Behavioral Biology, 20,* 32–40.

Goldstein, K., 1949. Frontal lobotomy and impairment of abstract attitude. *Journal of Nervous and Mental Disease, 110*, 93–111.

Goltz, F., 1876–1884. Ueber die Verrichtungen des Grosshirns. *Pflüger's Archiv der Gesamten Physiologie, 13*, 1-44, *14*, 412-433, *20* 1-54, *26* 1-49.

Gorman, A. M., 1961. Recognition memory for nouns as a function of abstractness and frequency. *Journal of Experimental Psychology, 61*, 23–29.

Grant, L. D., Coscina, D. V., Grossman, S. P. et al., 1973. Muricide after serotonin depleting lesions of midbrain raphé nuclei. *Pharmacology, Biochemistry and Behavior.* 1, 77–80.

Grastyán, E., Lissák, K., Madarász, I., & Donhoffer, H., 1959. Hippocampal electrical activity during the development of conditioned reflexes. *Electroencephalography and Clinical Neurophysiology, 11*, 409–429.

Green, J. D., 1960. The hippocampus, In J. Field (Ed.), *Handbook of physiology, Section I. Neurophysiology, Vol. 2*. Washington, D. C., Physiology Section.

Green, J. D., & Arduini, A. A., 1954. Hippocampal electrical activity in arousal. *Journal of Neurophysiology, 17*, 533–557.

Green, J. D., Clemente, C. D., & De Groot, J., 1957. Rhinencephalic lesions and behavior in cats. *Journal of Comparative Neurology, 108*, 505–546.

Green, J. D. & Morin, F., 1953. Hypothalamic electrical activity and hypothalamocortical relationships. *American Journal of Physiology, 172*, 175–186.

Green, R. H., Beatty, W. W., & Schwartzbaum, J. S., 1967. Comparative effects of septohippocampal and caudate lesions on avoidance behavior in rats. *Journal of Comparative and Physiological Psychology, 64*, 444–452.

Green, R. H., & Schwartzbaum, J. S., 1968. Effects of unilateral septal lesions on avoidance behavior, discrimination reversal, and hippocampal EEG. *Journal of Comparative and Physiological Psychology, 65*, 388–396.

Greenberg, R., & Pearlman, C., 1974. Cutting the REM nerve: An approach to the adaptive role of REM sleep. *Perspectives in Biology and Medicine, 17*, 513–521.

Gromova, E. A., Semenova, T. P., & Vekshina, N. L., 1976. Functional interactions of the serotonin systems of the brain during conditioning. *Doklady Biol. Sci. 227*, 149–151. Translated from "Doklady Akademii Nauk SSSR."

Grossman, S. P., 1960. Eating or drinking elicited by direct adrenergic or cholinergic stimulation of hypothalamus. *Science, 132*, 301–302.

Grossman, S. P., 1964a. Behavioral effects of chemical stimulation of the ventral amygdala. *Journal of Comparative and Physiological Psychology, 57*, 29–36.

Grossman, S. P., 1964b. Effects of chemical stimulation of the septal area on motivation. *Journal of Comparative and Physiological Psychology, 58*, 194–200.

Grossman, S. P., 1966a. The VMH: A center for affective reactions, satiety or both. *Physiology and Behavior, 1*, 1–10.

Grossman, S. P., 1966b. Acquisition and performance of avoidance responses during chemical stimulation of the midbrain reticular formation. *Journal of Comparative and Physiological Psychology, 61*, 42–49.

Grossman, S. P., 1971. Changes in food and water intake associated with an interruption of the anterior or posterior fiber connections of the hypothalamus. *Journal of Comparative and Physiological Psychology, 75*, 23–31.

Grossman, S. P., 1972a. Aggression, avoidance and reaction to novel environments in female rats with ventromedial hypothalamic lesions. *Journal of Comparative and Physiological Psychology, 78*, 274–283.

Grossman, S. P., 1972b. Cholinergic synapses in the limbic system and behavioral inhibition. Neurotransmitters. *Research Publication, Association for Research in Nervous and Mental Disease, 50*, 315–326.

Grossman, S. P., 1972c. The role of the amygdala in escape-avoidance behaviors. In B. E. Eleftheriou (Ed.), *The neurobiology of the amygdala*. New York: Plenum Press.

Grossman, S. P., 1978a. An experimental dissection of the septal syndrome. In *Ciba Foundation Symposium 58, Function of the septo-hippocampal system*. Amsterdam: Elsevier.

Grossman, S. P., 1978b. *Discussion in Ciba Foundation Symposium 58 (new series) Function of the septo-hippocampal system*. Amsterdam, Elsevier.

Grossman, S. P., & Grossman, L., 1966. Effects of chemical stimulation of the midbrain reticular formation on appetitive behavior. *Journal of Comparative and Physiological Psychology, 61*, 333–338.

Grossman, S. P., & Grossman, L., 1971. Food and water intake in rats with parasagittal knife cuts medial or lateral to the lateral hypothalamus. *Journal of Comparative and Physiological Psychology, 74*, 148–156.

Grossman, S. P., & Grossman, L., 1973. Persisting deficits in rats "recovered" from transections of fibers which enter or leave hypothalamus laterally. *Journal of Comparative and Physiological Psychology, 85*, 515–527.

Grossman, S. P., Peters, R. H., Freedman, P. E., & Willer, H. I., 1965. Behavioral effects of cholinergic stimulation of the thalamic reticular formation. *Journal of Comparative and Physiological Psychology, 59*, 57–65.

Grueninger, W., & Grueninger, J., 1973. The primate frontal cortex and allassostasis. In K. H. Pribram & A. R. Luria, (Eds.), *Psychophysiology of the frontal lobes*. New York: Academic Press.

Grünthal, E., 1947. Ueber das klinische Bild nach umschriebenem beiderseitigem Ausfall der Ammonshornrinde. *Monatschrift für Psychiatrie und Neurologie, 113*, 1–16.

Guthrie, E. R., 1959. Association by contiguity. In: S. Koch (Ed.), *Psychology: A study of a science, Vol. 2*. New York: McGraw-Hill.

Guttman, N., & Julesz, B., 1963. Lower limits of auditory periodicity analysis. *Journal of the Acoustical Society of America, 35*, 610.

Haber, B., Gabay, S., Issidorides, M. R., & Alivisatos, S. G. A. (Eds.), 1981. *Serotonin: Current aspects of neurochemistry and function*. New York: Plenum Press.

Hagino, N., & Yamaoka, S., 1976. A neuroendocrinological approach to the investigation of septum. In J. F. DeFrance (Ed.), *The septal nuclei*. New York: Plenum Press.

Haigler, H. G., 1978. Morphine: Effects on brainstem raphé neurons. In R. W. Ryall & J. S. Kelly (Eds.), *Iontophoresis and transmitter mechanisms in the mammalian central nervous system*. Amsterdam: Elsevier.

Halász, B., 1978. Functional anatomy of the hypothalamus. In B. Cox, I. D. Morris, & A. H. Weston (Eds.), *Pharmacology of the hypothalamus*. Baltimore: University Park Press.

Halgren, E., 1981. The amygdala contribution to emotion and memory: Current studies in humans. In Y. Ben-Ari (Ed.), *The amygdaloid complex*. Amsterdam: Elsevier/North Holland Biomedical Press.

Hall, W. C., & Diamond, I. T., 1968. Organization and function of the visual cortex in hedgehog: II. An ablation study of pattern discrimination. *Brain, Behavior and Evolution, 1*, 215–243.

Halpern, M., & Frumin, N., 1979. Roles of the vomeronasal and olfactory systems in prey attack and feeding in adult garter snakes. *Physiology and Behavior, 22*, 1183–1189.

Hamilton, L. W., 1969. Active avoidance impairment following septal lesions in cats. *Journal of Comparative and Physiological Psychology, 67*, 420–431.

Hamilton, L. W., 1976. *Basic limbic system anatomy of the rat*. New York: Plenum Press.

Hampson, J. L., Harrison, C. R., & Woolsey, C. N., 1946. Somatotopic localization in the cerebellum. *Federation Proceedings, 5*, 41.

Hampson, J. L., Harrison, C. R., & Woolsey, C. N., 1952. Cerebro-cerebellar projections and the somatotopic localization of motor function in the cerebellum. In P. Bard (Ed.), *Patterns of organization in the central nervous system*. Baltimore: Williams & Wilkins.

Hansing, R. A., Schwartzbaum, J. S., & Thompson, J. B., 1968. Operant behavior following unilateral and bilateral caudate lesions in the rat. *Journal of Comparative and Physiological Psychology, 66*, 378–388.

Harlow, H. F., 1952. Functional organization of the brain in relation to mentation and behavior. In *Milbank Memorial Fund, the biology of mental health and disease*. New York: Hoeber.

Harvey, J., & Hunt, H. F., 1965. Effect of septal lesions on thirst in the rat as indicated by water consumption and operant responding for water reward. *Journal of Comparative and Physiological Psychology, 59,* 49–56.

Harvey, J. A., Lints, C. E., Jacobson, L. E., & Hunt, H. F., 1965. Effects of lesions in the septal area on conditioned fear and discriminated instrumental punishment in the albino rat. *Journal of Comparative and Physiological Psychology, 59,* 37–48.

Hassler, R., 1956. Die zentralen Apparate der Wendebewegungen. *Archiv für Psychiatrie und Nervenkrankheiten, 194,*481–516.

Hassler, R. 1961. Motorische and sensible Effekte umschriebener Reizungen und Ausschaltungen im menschlichen Zwischenhirn. *Deutsche Zeitschrift für Nervenheilkunde, 183,* 148–171.

Hassler, R., 1966. Thalamic regulation of muscle tone and the speed of movements. In D. Purpura & M. D. Yahr (Eds.), *The thalamus*. New York: Columbia University Press.

Hauri, P., & Hawkins, D. R., 1972. Human sleep after leucotomy. *Archives of General Psychiatry, 26,* 469–473.

Hebb, D. O., 1950. Animal and physiological psychology. *Annual Review of Psychology, 1,* 173–188.

Hebb, D. O., 1961. Distinctive features of learning in the higher animal. In J. F. Delafresnaye (Ed.), Brain mechanisms and learning. Springfield, Ill., C. C. Thomas.

Hécaen, H., 1979. Aphasia. In M. S. Gazzaniga (Ed.), *Handbook of behavioral neurobiology. Vol. 2, Neuropsychology*. New York: Plenum Press.

Hécaen, H., & Marcie, P., 1974. Disorders of written language following right hemisphere lesions: Spatial disgraphia. In S. J. Dimond & J. G. Beaumont (Eds.), *Hemisphere functions in the human brain*. New York: Wiley.

Heimer, L., 1981. Chairman's comments. In Y. Ben-Ari (Ed.) *The amygdaloid complex*. Amsterdam: Elsevier/North Holland Biomedical Press.

Heller, A., 1972. Neuronal control of brain serotonin. *Federation Proceedings, 31,* 81–90.

Hemsworth, B. A., & Mitchell, J. F., 1969. The characteristics of acetylcholine release mechanisms in the auditory cortex. *British Journal of Pharmacology, 36,* 161–170.

Henneman, E., 1974. Organization of the motor system—a preview. In: V. B. Mountcastle & C. C. Mosby (Eds.), *Medical physiology, Vol. 1,* 13th ed.

Henneman, E., Cooke, P. M., & Snider, R. S., 1952. Cerebellar projections to the cerebral cortex. In P. Bard (Ed.), *Patterns of organization in the central nervous system*. Baltimore: Williams and Wilkins.

Hermann, K., Turner, J. W., Gillingham, F. J., & Gaze, R. M., 1966. The effects of destructive lesions and stimulation of the basal ganglia on speech mechanisms. *Confinia Neurologica, 27,* 197–207.

Hernández-Peón, R., 1961. Reticular mechanisms of sensory control. In W. A. Rosenblith (Ed.), *Sensory communication*. Cambridge, Mass.: M.I.T. Press.

Hernández-Peón, R., 1966. Physiological mechanisms in attention. In. R. W. Russell (Ed.), *Frontiers in physiological psychology*. New York: Academic Press.

Hernández-Peón, R., and Brust-Carmona, H., 1961. Inhibition of tactile and nociceptive evoked potentials in the cat during distraction. *Acta Neurologica Latinoamericana, 7,* 289–298.

Hernández-Peón, R., Brust-Carmona, H., Eckhaus, E., Lopez-Mendoza, E., & Alcoler-Cuaron, C., 1956. Functional role of brainstem reticular system in salivary conditioned response. *Federation Proceedings, 15,* 91.

Hernández-Peón, R., O'Flaherty, J. J., & Mazzuchelli-O'Flaherty, A. L., 1967. Sleep and other behavioral effects induced by acetylcholinic stimulation of basal temporal cortex and striate structures. *Brain Research, 4,* 243–267.

Herz, A., & Nacimiento, A., 1965. Ueber die Wirkung von Pharmaka auf Neurone des Hippocampus nach mikroelektrophoretischer Verabfolgung. *Archiv für experimentelle Pathologie und Pharmakologie, 250,* 258–259.

Hess, W. R., 1943. Symptomatik des durch elektrischen Reiz ausgelösten Schlafes und die Topographie des Schlafzentrums. *Helvetische Physiologie, 1,* C 61.

Hess, W. R., 1956. Beziehungen zwischen psychischen Vorgängen und Organisation des Gehirns. (I. Teil) *Studium Generale, 9,* 467–479.

Hill, R. G., & Pepper, C. M., 1978. Studies on the pharmacology of nociceptive neurones in the rat thalamus. In R. W. Ryall & J. S. Kelly (Eds.), *Iontophoresis and transmitter mechanisms in the mammalian central nervous system.* Amsterdam:Elsevier.

Himwich, H. E., & Narasimhachari, N., 1974. Comparative biochemical and behavioral studies of chronic schizophrenic patients and normals. In R. D. Myers & R. R. Drucker-Colin (Eds.). *Neurohumoral coding of brain function.* New York: Plenum Press.

Hines, M., 1922. Studies in the growth and differentiation of the telencephalon in man. The fissura hippocampi. *Journal of Comparative Neurology, 34,* 73–171.

Hoebel, B. G., 1969. Feeding and self-stimulation. *Annals of the New York Adademy of Sciences, 157,* 758–777.

Hoff, H., & Pötzl, O., 1930. Ueber die Grosshirnprojektion der Mitte und der Aussengrenzen des Gesichtsfeldes. *Jahrbuch der Psychiatrie, 52.*

Hollingworth, H. C., 1913. Characteristic differences between recall and recognition. *American Journal of Psychology, 24,* 532–544.

Holmes, G., 1922. Clinical symptoms of cerebellar disease, and their interpretations. *Lancet, 1,* 1177–1182, 1231–1237; *2,* 59–65, 111–115.

Hommer, D. W., & Bunney, B. S. 1980. Effect of sensory stimuli on the activity of dopaminergic neurons: involvement of non-dopaminergic nigral neurons and striato-nigral pathways. *Life Sciences, 27,* 377–386.

Hore, J., Meyer-Lohmann, J., & Brooks, V. B., 1977. Basal ganglia cooling disables learned arm movements of monkeys in the absence of visual guidance. *Science, 195,* 584–586.

Horel, J. A., 1968a. Effects of subcortical lesions on brightness discrimination acquired by rats without visual cortex. *Journal of Comparative and Physiological Psychology, 65,* 103–109.

Horel, J. A., 1968b. A visual function for the ventral nucleus of the lateral geniculate body. *Anatomical Record, 160,* 367–368.

Horel, J. A., Bettinger, L. A., Royce, G. J., & Meyer, D. R., 1966. Role of neocortex in the learning and relearning of two visual habits by the rat. *Journal of Comparative and Physiological Psychology, 61,* 66–78.

Horvath, F. E., 1963. Effects of basolateral amygdalectomy on three types of avoidance behavior in cats. *Journal of Comparative and Physiological Psychology, 56,* 380–389.

Hostetter, G., & Thomas, G. J., 1967. Evaluation of enhanced thigmotaxis as a condition of impaired maze learning by rats with hippocampal lesions. *Journal of Comparative and Physiological Psychology, 63,* 105–110.

Hubel, D. H., 1963. The visual cortex of the brain. *Scientific American, 168,* 2–10.

Hubel, D. H., & Wiesel, T. N., 1962. Receptive fields, binocular interaction and functional architecture in the cat's visual cortex. *Journal of Physiology* (London), *160,* 106–154.

Hubel, D. H. & Wiesel, T. N., 1963. Shape and arrangements of columns in cat's striate cortex. *Journal of Physiology* (London), *165,* 559–568.

Hubel, D. H. & Wiesel, T. N., 1965. Receptive fields and functional architecture in two nonstriate visual areas (18 and 19) of the cat. *Journal of Neurophysiology, 28,* 229–289.

Hubel, D. H., & Wiesel, T. N., 1968. Receptive fields and functional architecture of monkey striate cortex. *Journal of Physiology* (London), *195,* 215–243.

Humphrey, T., 1972. The development of the human amygdaloid complex. In B. E. Eleftheriou (Ed.), *The neurobiology of the amygdala.* New York: Plenum Press.

Hunsperger, R. W., & Bucher, V. M., 1967. Affective behavior produced by electrical stimulation in the forebrain and brain stem of the cat. In W. R. Adey & T. Tokizane (Eds.), Structure and function of the limbic system. *Progress in Brain Research, 27,* 103–127.

Huston, J. P., 1971. Relationship between motivating and rewarding stimulation of the lateral hypothalamus. *Physiology and Behavior, 6,* 711–716.

Hyde, T. S., & Jenkins, J. J., 1969. Differential effects of incidental tasks on the organization of recall of a list of highly associated words. *Journal of Experimental Psychology, 82,* 472–481.

Hyyppä, M., Lehtinen, P., & Rinne, U. K., 1973. L-dopa; its action on sexual behaviour and brain monoamines of the rat. In K. Lissák (Ed.), *Hormones and brain function. New York: Plenum Press.*

Igic, R., Stern, P., & Basagic, E., 1970. Changes in emotional behavior after application of cholinersterase inhibitor in the septal and amygdala region. *Neuropharmacology, 9,* 73–75.

Ilyutchenok, R. U., Gilinsky, M. A., & Abuladze, G. V., 1973. Cholinergic mechanisms in the regulation of learning and memory. In W. B. Essman, S. Nakajima (Eds.), Current *Biochemical approaches to learning and memory.* Flushing, N.J.: Spectrum.

Irvine, D. R. F., 1980. Acoustic input to neurons in feline red nucleus. *Brain Research, 200,* 169–173.

Isaacson, R. L., 1974. *The limbic system.* New York: Plenum Press.

Isaacson, R. L., Douglas, R. J., & Moore, R. Y., 1961. The effect of radical hippocampal ablation on acquisition of avoidance response. *Journal of Comparative and Physiological Psychology, 54,* 625–628.

Isaacson, R. L., and Pribram, K. H., (Eds.), 1975. *The hippocampus.* 2 vols. New York: Plenum Press.

Isaacson, R. L., & Wickelgren, W. O., 1962. Hippocampal ablation and passive avoidance. *Science, 138,* 1104–1106.

Ito, M., 1972. Excitability of medial forebrain bundle neurons during self-stimulating behavior. *Journal of Neurophysiology, 35,* 652–664.

Ito, M., & Miyashita, Y., 1975. The effects of chronic destruction of the inferior olive upon visual modification of the horizontal vestibulo-ocular reflex of rabbits. *Proceedings of the Japanese Academy, 51,* 716–720.

Iversen, L. L., 1979. The chemistry of the brain. *Scientific American, 241/3,* 134–149.

Iversen, S. D., 1977. Striatal function and stereotyped behaviour. In A. R. Cools, A. H. M. Lohman, & J. H. L. Van den Bercken (Eds.), *Psychobiology of the striatum.* Amsterdam: North-Holland Publishing Co.

Iversen, S. D., & Iversen, L. L., 1975a. Chemical pathways in the brain. In M. S. Gazzaniga & C. Blakemore (Eds.), *Handbook of psychobiology.* New York: Academic Press.

Iversen, S. D., & Iversen, L. L., 1975b. Central neurotransmitters and the regulation of behavior. In M. S. Gazzaniga & C. Blakemore (Eds.), *Handbook of psychobiology.* New York: Academic Press.

Iwai, E., Yamaguchi, K., & Kido, S., 1979. Transient behavioral blindness following inferior parietal cortex lesion in monkey. In M. Ito, K. Kubota, N. Tsukahara, & K. Yagi (Eds.), *Integrative control functions of the brain, Vol. 2.* Tokyo: Kodansha Ltd.

Jackson, J. H., 1884. *Evolution and dissolution of the nervous system: Selected papers,* 2 vols. New York: Basic Books, 1958.

Jacobs, B. L., Mosko, S. S., & Trulson, M. E., 1977. The investigation of the role of serotonin in mammalian behavior. In R. R. Drucker-Colin & J. L. McGaugh (Eds.), *Neurobiology of sleep and memory.* New York: Academic Press.

Jacobs, B. L., Trimbach, C., Eubanks, G. E., & Trulson, M., 1975. Hippocampal mediation of raphé lesion and PCPA-induced hyperactivity in the rat. *Brain Research, 94,* 253–261.

Jacobs, B. L., & Trulson, M. E., 1979. Mechanisms of action of LSD. *American Scientist, 67,* 396–404.

Jacobs, B. L., Trulson, M. E., & Stern, W. C., 1976. An animal behavior model for studying the actions of LSD and related hallucinogens. *Science, 194,* 741–743.

Jacobs, J., 1887. Experiments on "prehension." *Mind, 12,* 75–79.

Jacobsen, C. F., 1935. The functions of the frontal association areas in primates. *Archives of Neurology and Psychiatry, 33,* 558–569.

Jacobsen, C. F., 1936. Functions of the frontal association areas in monkeys. *Comparative Psychology Monographs, 13,* 1–60.

Jacobson, E., 1932. Electrophysiology of mental activities. *American Journal of Physiology, 44,* 677–694.

Jacobson, E., 1934. Electrical measurement of activities in nerve and muscle. In M. Bentley & E. V. Cowdry (Eds.), *The problem of mental disorder.* New York: McGraw-Hill.

James, W. 1890. *Principles of psychology.* Vol. 1. New York: Holt.

James, W., 1892. *Psychology.* New York, Holt.

Jasper, H. H., & Bertrand, G., 1966. Thalamic units involved in somatic sensation and voluntary and involuntary movements in man. In D. P. Purpura & M. D. Yahr (Eds.), *The thalamus.* New York: Columbia University Press.

Johansson, G., 1979. Memory functions in visual event perception. In L.-G. Nilsson (Ed.), *Perspectives on memory research.* Hillsdale, N.J.: Lawrence Erlbaum Associates.

John, E. R., 1966. Neural processes during learning. In R. W. Russell (Ed.), *Frontiers in physiological psychology.* New York: Academic press.

John, E. R., 1967. *Mechanisms of memory.* New York: Academic Press.

Johnson, D. A., & Thatcher, K., 1972. Differential effects of food deprivation on the fixed ratio behavior of normal rats and rats with septal lesions. *Psychonomic Science, 26,* 45–46.

Jordan, L. M., Kenshalo, D. R. Jr., Martin, F. R., Haber, L. H., & Willis, W. D., 1978. The effect of iontophoretically applied serotonin on primate spinothalamic tract neurons. In R. W. Ryall & J. S. Kelly (Eds.), *Iontophoresis and transmitter mechanisms in the mammalian central nervous system.* Amsterdam: Elsevier.

Jouvet, M., 1962. Recherches sur les structures nerveuses et méchanismes responsible des différent phases du sommeil physiologique. *Archives Italiennes de Biologie, 100,* 125–206.

Jouvet, M., 1974. Monoaminergic regulation of the sleep-waking cycle in the cat. In F. O. Schmitt & F. G. Worden (Eds.), *The neurosciences.* Third Study Program, Cambridge, Mass.: MIT Press.

Kaada, B. R., 1951. Somato-motor, autonomic and electrocorticographic responses to electrical stimulation of ''rhinencephalic'' and other forebrain structures in primates, cat and dog. *Acta physiologica Scandinavica (Supplement 83), 24,* 1–285.

Kaada, B. R., 1972. Stimulation and regional ablation of the amygdaloid complex with reference to functional representations. In B. E. Eleftheriou (Ed.), *The neurobiology of the amygdala.* New York: Plenum Press.

Kaada, B. R., Rasmussen, E. W., & Kveim, O., 1962. Impaired acquisition of passive avoidance behavior by subcallosal, septal, hypothalamic, and insular lesions in rats. *Journal of Comparative and Physiological Psychology, 55,* 661–670.

Kaas, J., Hall, W. C., & Diamond, I. T., 1970. Cortical visual areas I and II in the hedgehog: Relations between evoked potential maps and architectonic subdivisions. *Journal of Neurophysiology, 34,* 595–615.

Kahneman, D., 1973. *Attention and effort.* Englewood Cliffs, N.J.: Prentice-Hall.

Kalinowsky, L. B., & Hoch, P. H. (Eds.), 1952. *Shock treatments, psychosurgery and other somatic treatments in psychiatry.* (Second ed.) New York: Grune & Stratton.

Kalra, S. P., & Sawyer, C. H., 1970. Blockade of copulation-induced ovulation in the rat by anterior hypothalamic deafferentation. *Endocrinology, 87,* 1124–1128.

Karli, P., Vergnes, M., Eclancher, F., Schmitt, P., & Chaurand, J. P., 1972. Role of the amygdala in the control of ''mouse-killing'' behavior in the rat. In B. E. Eleftheriou (Ed.), *The neurobiology of the amygdala.* New York: Plenum Press.

Kelsey, J. E., & Grossman, S. P., 1969. Cholinergic blockade and lesions in the ventro-medial septum of the rat. *Psychology and Behavior, 4,* 837–845.

Kelsey, J. E., & Grossman, S. P., 1971. Nonperseverative disruption of behavioral inhibition following septal lesions in rats. *Journal of Comparative and Physiological Psychology, 75,* 302–311.

Kemble, E. D., & Beckman, G. J., 1970. Vicarious trial and error following amygdaloid lesions in rats. *Neuropsychologia, 8,* 161–169.

Kent, M. A., & Peters, R. H., 1973. Effects of ventromedial hypothalamic lesions on hunger-motivated behavior in rats. *Journal of Comparative and Physiological Psychology, 83,* 92–97.

Kenyon, J., & Krieckhaus, E., 1965. Enhanced avoidance behavior following septal lesions in the rat as a function of lesion size and spontaneous activity. *Journal of Comparative and Physiological Psychology, 59,* 466–468.

Kerr, F. W. L., Triplett, J. N. Jr., & Beeler, G. W., 1974. Reciprocal (push-pull) effects of morphine on single units in the ventromedial and lateral hypothalamus and influences on other nuclei: with a comment on methadone effects during withdrawal from morphine. *Brain Research, 74,* 81–103.

Kesner, R. P., 1977. A neural system approach to the study of memory storage and retrieval. In R. R. Drucker-Colin & J. L. McGaugh (Eds.), *Neurobiology of sleep and memory.* New York: Academic Press.

Kesner, R. P., Fiedler, P., & Thomas, G. J., 1967. Function of the midbrain reticular formation in regulating level of activity and learning in rats. *Journal of Comparative and Physiological Psychology, 63,* 452–457.

Kety, S. S., 1976. Biological concomitants of affective states and their possible role in memory processes. In M. R. Rosenzweig & E. L. Bennett (Eds.), *Neural mechanisms of learning and memory.* Cambridge, Mass.: MIT Press.

Killeffer, F. A., & Stern, W. E., 1970. Chronic effects of hypothalamic injury—Report of a case of near total hypothalamic destruction resulting from removal of a craniopharyngioma. *Archives of Neurology, 22,* 419–429.

Kimble, D. P., 1963. The effects of bilateral hippocampal lesions in rats. *Journal of Comparative and Physiological Psychology, 56,* 273–283.

Kimble, D. P., 1975. Choice behavior in rats with hippocampal lesions. In R. L. Isaacson & K. H. Pribram (Eds.), *The hippocampus, Vol. 2,* New York: Plenum Press.

Kimble, D. P., & Gostnell, D., 1968. Role of cingulate cortex in shock avoidance behavior of rats. *Journal of Comparative and Physiological Psychology, 65,* 290–294.

Kimble, D. P., Kirkby, R. J., & Stein, D. G., 1966. Response perseveration interpretation of passive avoidance deficits in hippocampectomized rats. *Journal of Comparative and Physiological Psychology, 61,* 141–143.

Kimble, D. P., & Pribram, K. H., 1963. Hippocampectomy and behavior sequences. *Science, 139,* 824–825.

Kimura, D., 1963. Right temporal lobe damage: Perception of unfamiliar stimuli after damage. *A.M.A. Archives of Neurology* (Chicago), *8,* 264–271.

King, F. A., 1958. Effects of septal and amygdala lesions on emotional behavior and conditioned avoidance responses in the rat. *Journal of Nervous and Mental Disease, 126,* 57–63.

Kinsbourne, M., & George, J., 1974. The mechanism of the word-frequency effect on recognition memory. *Journal of Verbal Learning and Verbal Behavior, 13,* 63–69.

Kinsbourne, M., and Warrington, E. K., 1962. A disorder of simultaneous form perception. *Brain, 85,* 461–486.

Kintsch, W., 1970a. Models for free recall and recognition. In D. A. Norman (Ed.), *Models of human memory.* New York: Academic Press.

Kintsch, W., 1970b. *Learning, memory, and conceptual processes.* New York: Wiley.

Kirkby, R. J., 1970. The caudate nucleus and active avoidance: A comment on the report of Winocur and Mills. *Psychonomic Science, 18,* 269.

Kish, G. B., 1966. Studies of sensory reinforcement. In W. K. Honig (Ed.), *Operant behavior.* New York: Appleton.

Kleist, K., 1934. *Gehirnpathologie.* Leipzig: Barth.

Kling, A., 1966. Ontogenetic and phylogenetic studies on the amygdaloid nuclei. *Psychosomatic Medicine, 28,* 155–161.

Kling, A., 1972. Effects of amygdalectomy on social-affective behavior in nonhuman primates. In B. E. Eleftheriou (Ed.), *The neurobiology of the amygdala*. New York: Plenum Press.

Kling, A. J., Orbach, J., Schwarz, N., & Towne, J., 1960. Injury to the limbic system and associated structures in cats. *Archives of General Psychiatry, 3,* 391–420.

Klüver, H., & Bucy, P. C., 1939. Preliminary analysis of functions of the temporal lobes in monkeys. *Archives of Neurology and Psychiatry, 42,* 979–1000.

Knapp, H. D., Taub, E., & Berman, A. J., 1958. Effect of deafferentation on a conditioned avoidance response. *Science, 128,* 842–843.

Knapp, H. D., Taub, E., & Berman, A. J., 1963. Movements in monkeys with deafferented forelimbs. *Experimental Neurology, 7,* 305–315.

Kobayashi, R., Palkovits, M., Miller, R., Chang, K.-J., & Cuatrecasas, P., 1977. Brain enkephalin distribution is unaltered by hypophysectomy. *Life Sciences, 22,* 527–530.

Koella, W. P., 1977. Anatomical, physiological, and pharmacological findings relevant to the central nervous effects of beta blockers. In P. Kielholz, (Ed.), *Beta-blockers and the central nervous system*. Baltimore: University Park Press.

Koikegami, H., 1963. Amygdala and other related limbic structures—experimental studies on the anatomy and function. I. Anatomical researches with some neurophysiological obsevations. *Acta Medica et Biologica, 10,* 161–277.

Kononova, E. P., 1935. Studies of the structural variability of the cerebral cortex. The inferior frontal gyrus in the adult. *Contributions of the Brain Institute, 1,* 48–118. Moscow, USSR (in Russian).

Konorski, J., 1973. The role of prefrontal control in the programming of motor behavior. In J. D. Maser (Ed.), *Efferent organization and the integration of behavior*. New York: Academic Press.

Kreindler, A., & Steriade, M., 1964. EEG pattern of arousal and sleep induced by stimulating various amygdaloid levels in the cat. *Archivo Italiano di Biologia, 102,* 576–586.

Krettek, J. E., & Price, J. L., 1977. Projections from the amygdaloid complex to the cerebral cortex and thalamus in the rat and cat. *Journal of Comparative Neurology, 172,* 687–722.

Krieckhaus, E. E., 1964. Decrements in avoidance behavior following mammillothalamic tractotomy in cats. *Journal of Neurophysiology, 27,* 753–767.

Krieckhaus, E. E., & Lorenz, R., 1968. Retention and relearning of lever-press avoidance following mammillothalamic tractotomy. *Physiology and Behavior, 3,* 433–438.

Krieckhaus, E. E., & Randall, D., 1968. Lesions of mammillothalamic tract in rat produce no decrements in recent memory. *Brain, 91,* 369–378.

Krieg, W. J. S., 1942. *Functional neuroanatomy*. Philadelphia: Blakiston.

Krieg, W. J. S., 1946. Connections of the cerebral cortex. I. The albino rat: A topography of the cortical area. *Journal of Comparative Neurology, 84,* 221–275.

Krieg, W. J. S., 1954. *Connections of the frontal cortex of the monkey*. Springfield, Ill.: Thomas.

Krieg, W. J. S., 1957. *Brain mechanisms in diachrome*. Second ed., Evanston, Ill.: Brain Books.

Kuhar, M. J., 1975. Cholinergic neurons: Septal-hippocampal relationships. In R. L. Isaacson & K. H. Pribram (Eds.), *The hippocampus, Vol. 1*. New York: Plenum Press.

Kuypers, H., & Haaxma, R., 1975. Occipito-frontal connections, a possible sensory-motor link for visually guided hand and finger movements. In K. J. Zülch, O. Creutzfeldt & G. C. Galbraith (Eds.), *Cerebral localization*. New York: Springer-Verlag.

Kveim, O., Setekleiv, J., & Kaada, B. R., 1964. Differential effects of hippocampal lesions on maze and passive avoidance learning in rats. *Experimental Neurology, 9,* 59–72.

La Vaque, T. J., 1966. Conditioned avoidance response perseveration in septal rats during massed extinction trials. *Psychonomic Science, 5,* 409–410.

Lammers, H. J., 1972. The neural connections of the amygdaloid complex in mammals. In B. E. Eleftheriou (Ed.), *The neurobiology of the amygdala*. New York: Plenum Press.

Landau, W. M., 1953. Autonomic responses mediated via the corticospinal tract. *Journal of Neurophysiology, 16,* 299–311.

Landis, C., & Clausen, J., 1955. Changes in sensory and motor performances induced by active psychiatric treatment. *Journal of Psychology, 40,* 275–305.

Lapin, I. P., & Oxenkrug, G. F., 1969. Intensification of the central serotonergic processes as a possible determinant of the thymoleptic effect. *Lancet, 1,* 132–136.

Larsen, K. D., & Yumiya, 1980. Motor cortical modulation of feline red nucleus output: corticorubral and cerebellar-mediated responses. *Experimental Brain Research, 38,* 321–331.

Lashley, K. S., 1929. *Brain mechanisms and intelligence.* Chicago: University of Chicago Press.

Lashley, K. S., 1942. The mechanism of vision. XVII. Autonomy of the visual cortex. *Journal of Genetic Psychology, 60,* 197–221.

Lashley, K. S., 1952. Discussion. A. M. A. *Archives of Neurology and Psychiatry, 67,* p. 195.

Le Bars, D., Rivot, J. P., Menetrey, D., Guilbaud, G., & Besson, J. M., 1978. Effects of morphine upon dorsal horn cell responses induced by C fibre stimulation in the spinal rat pretreated or not with pCP. In R. W. Ryall & J. S. Kelly (Eds.), *Iontophoresis and transmitter mechanisms in the mammalian central nervous system.* Amsterdam: Elsevier.

LeBeau, J., 1954. *Psycho-chirurgie et fonctions mentales; technique, resultats, applications physiologiques.* Paris: Masson.

Leibowitz, S. F., 1977. Adrenergic receptor mechanisms in eating and drinking. In S. H. Snyder (Ed.), *Biochemistry and behavior.* Cambridge, Mass.: MIT Press.

Lennox, M. A., & Robinson, F., 1951. Cingulate-cerebellar mechanisms in the physiological pathogenesis of epilepsy. Electroencephalography and Clinical Neurophysiology, 3, 197–205.

Lesse, H., Heath, R. G., Mickle, W. A., Monroe, R. R., & Miller, W., 1955. Rhinencephalic activity during thought. *Journal of Nervous and Mental Disease, 122,* 433–440.

Levy, J., 1974. Psychobiological implications of bilateral asymmetry. In S. J. Dimond & J. G. Beaumont (Eds.), *Hemisphere function in the human brain.* New York: Wiley.

Lewinska, M. K., 1967. Changes in eating and drinking produced by partial amygdalar lesions in cat. *Bulletin of the Polish Academy of Science (Biology), 15,* 301–305.

Lewis, N., 1946. Personal communication.

Lewis, P. R., & Shute, C. C. D., 1967. The cholinergic limbic system: Projection to hippocampal formation, medial cortex, nuclei of the ascending cholinergic reticular system, and the subfornical organ and supraoptic crest. *Brain, 90,* 521–540.

Lindvåll, O., Björklund, A., & Divac, I., 1977. Subcortical afferents to the prefrontal cortex: Organization of mesencephalic dopaminergic and mediodorsal thalamic projections. *Acta Physiologica Scandinavica, Supplement 452,* 35–38.

Linke, D., 1977. Motor programming. 11th World Congress on Neurology, International Congress Series No. 427, Excerpta Medica 97 (A 34), p. 33.

Lints, C. E., & Harvey, J. A., 1969. Altered sensitivity to footshock and decreased brain content of serotonin following brain lesions in the rat. *Journal of Comparative and Physiological Psychology, 67,* 23–31.

Lisander, B., & Martner, J., 1976. Induction of oral behaviour and defence-like reactions by fastigial stimulation in chronically decerebrate cats. *Acta Physiologica Scandinavica, 60,* Supplement 440.

Liss, P., 1968. Avoidance and freezing behavior following damage to the hippocampus or fornix. *Journal of Comparative and Physiological Psychology, 66,* 193–197.

Lissák, K., & Endröczi, E., 1967. Involvement of limbic structures in conditioning, motivation and recent memory. In W. R. Adey, and T. Tokizane (Eds.), *Structure and function of the limbic system.* Amsterdam: Elsevier.

Livesey, P. J., 1975. Fractionation of hippocampal function in learning. In R. L. Isaacson, K. H. Pribram (Eds.), *The hippocampus, Vol. 2.* New York: Plenum Press.

Livingston, K. E., 1976. The experimental-clinical interface: Kindling as a dynamic model of induced limbic system dysfunction. In K. E. Livingston & O. Hornykiewicz (Eds.), *Limbic mechanisms: The continuing evolution of the limbic system concept.* New York: Plenum Press.

Llinas, R., Walton, K., and Hillman, D. E., 1975. Inferior olive: Its role in motor learning. *Science, 190,* 1230–1231.

Loftus, E. F., & Loftus, G. R., 1980. On the permanence of stored information in the human brain. *American Psychologist, 35,* 409–420.

Lohman, A. H. M., & Mentink, G. M., 1969. The lateral olfactory tract, the anterior commissure and the cells of the olfactory bulb. *Brain Research, 12,* 396–413.

Lohman, A. H. M., & Russchen, F. T., 1981. Cortical projections to the amygdaloid complex in the cat. In Y. Ben-Ari (Ed.), *The amygdaloid complex.* Amsterdam: Elsevier/North Holland Biomedical Press.

Loisette, A., 1896. *Assimilative memory or how to attend and never forget.* New York: Funk and Wagnalls.

Lømo, T., 1971. Patterns of activation in a monosynaptic cortical pathway: The perforant path input to the dentate area of the hippocampal formation. *Experimental Brain Research, 12,* 18–45.

Lorens, S. A., & Kondo, C. Y., 1969. Effects of septal lesions on food and water intake and operant responding for food. *Physiology and Behavior, 4,* 729–732.

Lorenz, K. Z., 1969. Innate bases of learning. In K. H. Pribram (Ed.), *On the biology of learning.* New York: Harcourt, Brace.

Lown, B. A., Hayes, W. N., & Schaub, R. E., 1969. The effects of bilateral septal lesions on two-way active avoidance in the guniea pig. *Psychonomic Science, 16,* 13–14.

Lubar, J. F., 1964. Effect of medial cortical lesions on the avoidance behavior of the cat. *Journal of Comparative and Physiological Psychology, 58,* 38–46.

Lubar, J. F., & Perachio, A. A., 1965. One-way and two-way learning and transfer of an active avoidance response in normal and cingulectomized cats. *Journal of Comparative and Physiological Psychology, 60,* 46–52.

Lubar, J. F., Perachio, A. A., & Kavanagh, A. J., 1966. Deficits in active avoidance behavior following lesions of the lateral and posterolateral gyrus of the cat. *Journal of Comparative and Physiological Psychology, 62,* 263–269.

Luh, C. W., 1922. The conditions of retention. *Psychological Monograph, 31,* 142.

Luria, A. R., 1943. *Psychological analysis of the premotor syndrome.* Unpublished investigation. Quoted in Luria, 1966a.

Luria, A. R., 1966a. *Higher cortical functions in man.* Translated by Basil Haigh. First ed., New York: Basic Books.

Luria, A. R., 1966b. *Human Brain and psychological processes.* Translated by B. Haigh, New York: Harper & Row.

Luria, A. R., 1968. *Mind of a mnemonist.* Translated by L. Solotaroff. New York, Basic Books.

Luria, A. R., 1970. *Traumatic aphasia: Its syndromes, psychology, and treatment.* Translated by M. Critchley. The Hague, Netherlands: Mouton.

Luria, A. R., 1973a. *The working brain.* Translated by B. Haigh, New York: Basic Books.

Luria, A. R., 1973b. The frontal lobe and the regulation of behavior. In K. H. Pribram & A. R. Luria (Eds.), *Psychophysiology of the frontal lobes.* New York: Academic Press.

Luria, A. R., Sokolov, E. N., & Klimkowski, M., 1967. Towards a neurodynamic analysis of memory disturbances with lesions of the left temporal lobe. *Neuropsychologia, 5,* 1–11.

Luttges, M., Johnson, T., Buck, C., Holland, V., & McGaugh, V., 1966. An examination of "transfer of learning" by nucleic acid. *Science, 151,* 834–837.

MacDougall, J. M., Van Hoesen, G. W., & Mitchell, J. C., 1969. Development of post S^r and post non S^r DRL performance and its retention following septal lesions in rats. *Psychonomic Science, 16,* 45–46.

MacLean, P. D., 1954a. The limbic system and its hippocampal formation. *Journal of Neurosurgery, 11,* 29–44.

MacLean, P. D., 1954b. The limbic system and its hippocampal formation: Studies in animals and their possible application in man. *Journal of Neurosurgery, 11,* 29–44.

MacLean, P. D., 1958. Contrasting functions of limbic and neocortical systems of the brain and their relevance to psycho-physiological aspects of medicine. *American Journal of Medicine, 25,* 611–626.

MacLean, P. D., 1967. The brain in relation to empathy and medical education. *Journal of Nervous and Mental Disease, 144,* 374–382.

MacLean, P. D., 1970. The limbic brain in relation to the psychoses. In P. Black (ed.), *Physiological correlates of emotion.* New York: Academic Press.

MacLean, P. D., 1975. An ongoing analysis of hippocampal inputs and outputs: Microelectrode and neuroanatomical findings in squirrel monkeys. In R. L. Isaacson & K. H. Pribram (Eds.), *The hippocampus, Vol. 1.* New York: Plenum Press.

MacLeod, P. 1971. Structure and function of higher olfactory centers. In L. M. Beidler (Ed.), Olfaction. *Handbook of Sensory Physiology, Vol. IV.* New York, Springer-Verlag.

McCarley, R. W., 1980. Mechanisms and models of behavioral state control. In J. A. Hobson & M. A. B. Brazier (eds.), *The reticular system revisited.* New York: Raven Press.

McCleary, R. A., 1961. Response specificity in the behavioral effects of limbic system lesions in the cat. *Journal of Comparative and Physiological Psychology, 54,* 605–613.

McGaugh, J. L., 1965. Facilitation and impairment of memory storage processes. In: D. P. Kimble (Ed.), The anatomy of memory. Palo Alto, Calif.: Science and Behavior Books.

McGaugh, J. L., & Gold, P. E., 1974. The effects of drug and electrical stimulation of the brain on memory storage processes. In R. D. Myers & R. R. Drucker-Colin (Eds.), *Neurohumoral coding of brain functions.* New York: Plenum Press.

McGaugh, J. L., & Gold, P. E., 1976. Modulation of memory by electrical stimulation of the brain. In M. R. Rosenzweig and E. L. Bennett (Eds.), *Neural mechanisms of learning and memory.* Cambridge, Mass.: MIT Press.

McGaugh, J. L., & Herz, M., 1972. Memory consolidation. San Francisco: Albion.

McGeoch, J. A., 1942. *The psychology of human learning.* New York: Longmans, Green.

McGinty, D., Epstein, A. N., & Teitelbaum, P., 1965. The contribution of oropharyngeal sensations to hypothalamic hyperphagia. *Animal Behavior, 13,* 413–418.

McGinty, D. J., Fairbanks, M. K., & Harper, R. M., 1973. 5-HT-containing neurons: Unit activity in behaving cats. In J. Barchas & E. Usdin (Eds.), *Serotonin and behavior.* New York: Academic Press.

McIntyre, D. C., 1970. Differential amnestic effect of cortical vs. amygdaloid elicited convulsions in rats. *Physiology and Behavior, 5,* 747–753.

McKellar, P., 1965. The investigation of mental images. In S. A. Barnett & A. McLaren (Eds.), *Penguin science survey.* Harmondsworth, England: Penguin Books.

McNew, J. J., 1968. Role of the red nucleus in visually guided behavior in the rat. *Journal of Comparative and Physiological Psychology, 65,* 282–289.

McNew, J. J., & Thompson, R., 1966. Role of the limbic system in active and passive avoidance conditioning in the rat. *Journal of Comparative and Physiological Psychology, 61,* 173–180.

Mabry, P. D., & Campbell, B. A., 1978. Cholinergic-monoaminergic interactions during ontogensis. In L. L. Butcher (Ed.), *Cholinergic-monoaminergic interactions in the brain.* New York: Academic Press.

Madoz, P., & Reinoso-Suarez, F., 1968. Influence of lesions in preoptic region on the states of sleep and wakefulness. *Proceedings of the International Union of Physiological Sciences, 7,* 276.

Magnusson, T., Carlsson A., Fisher, G. H. et al., 1976. Effect of synthetic substance P on monoaminergic mechanisms in brain. *Journal of Neural Transmission, 38,* 89–93.

Magoun, H. W., 1952. An ascending reticular activating system in the brain stem. *Archives of Neurology and Psychiatry, 67,* 145–154.

Magoun, H., W., & Rhines, R., 1946. An inhibitory mechanism in the bulbar reticular formation. *Journal of Neurophysiology, 9,* 165–171.

Malmo, R. B., 1942. Interference factors in delayed response in monkey after removal of frontal lobes. *Journal of Neurophysiology, 5,* 295–308.

Mandler, G., 1979. Organization and repetition: Organizational principles with special reference to rote learning. In: L. G. Nilsson (Ed.), *Perspectives on memory research.* Hillsdale, N. J.: Lawrence Erlbaum Associates.

Marg, E., 1973. Neurophysiology of the accessory optic system. In R. Jung (Ed.), *Visual centers in the brain. Vol. VII/3 Handbook of sensory physiology,* New York: Springer-Verlag.

Margules, D. L., 1968. Noradrenergic basis of inhibition between reward and punishment in amygdala. *Journal of Comparative and Physiological Psychology, 66,* 320–334.

Markowitch, H. J., & Irle, E., 1981. Widespread cortical projections of the ventral tegmental area and of other brain stem structures in the cat. *Experimental Brain Research, 41,* 233–246.

Marshall, K. C., Flumerfelt, B. A., & Gwyn, D. G., 1980. Acetylcholinesterase activity and acetylcholine effects in the cerebello-rubro-thalamic pathway of the cat. *Brain Research, 190,* 493–504.

Maser, J. D., 1973. Efferent response processes: Relationships among stimuli, movement and reinforcement. In: J. D. Maser (Ed.), *Efferent organization and the integration of behavior.* New York, Academic Press.

Massion, J., & Sasaki, K. (Eds.), 1979. *Cerebro-cerebellar interactions.* Amsterdam: Elsevier/North-Holland Biomedical Press.

Mead, B., 1969. *The effect of lesions of the cingulum on the retention of visual and olfactory discrimination and active and passive avoidance responses in the albino rat.* Unpublished Ph. D. Dissertation, Loyola University of Chicago.

Meek, J. L., & Neff, N. H., 1972. Tryptophan-5-hydroxylase: approximation of half-life and rate of axonal transport. *Journal of Neurochemistry, 19,* 1519–1525.

Mehler, W. R., Pretorius, J. K., Phelan, K. D., & Mantyh, P. W., 1981. Diencephalic afferent connections of the amygdala in the squirrel monkey with observations and comments on the cat and rat. In: Y. Ben-Air (Ed.) *The amygdaloid complex.* Amsterdam, Elsevier/North Holland Biomedical Press.

Melton, A. W., 1963. Implications of short-term memory for a general theory of memory. *Journal of Verbal Learning and Verbal Behavior, 2,* 1–21.

Melton, A. W., 1967. Discussion in D. P. Kimble (Ed.), *The organization of recall.* New York, New York Academy of Sciences.

Melton, A. W., & Martin, E., 1972. *Coding processes in human memory.* New York: Wiley.

Mettler, F. A. (Ed.), 1949. *Selective partial ablation of the frontal cortex.* New York: Hoeber.

Mettler, F. A., & Orioli, F., 1957. Ataxia and the rubrospinal tract. *Federation Proceedings, 16,* 88.

Meyer, A., & Beck, E., 1954. *Prefrontal leucotomy and related operations. Anatomical aspects of success and failure.* London: Oliver & Boyd.

Meyer, P. M., 1963. Analysis of visual behavior in cats with extensive neocortical ablations. *Journal of Comparative and Physiological Psychology, 56,* 397–401.

Meyer-Lohmann, J., Conrad, B., Matsunami, K., & Brooks, V. B., 1975. Effects of dentate cooling on precentral unit activity following torque pulse injections into elbow movements. *Brain Research, 94,* 237–251.

Meynert, T., 1868. Der Bau der Grosshirnrinde und seine örtlichen Verschiedenheiten nebst einem pathologisch-anatomischen Corollarium. Leipzig: Engelmann.

Migler, B. M., 1961. The effect of fornix lesions on emotional and timing behavior in the Rhesus monkey. *Dissertation Abstracts, 925.*

Miller, G. A., 1956. The magical number seven, plus or minus two: Some limits on our capacity for processing information. *Psychological Review, 63,* 81–97.

Miller, G. A., Galanter, E., & Pribram, K. H., 1960. Plans and the structure of behavior. New York: Holt.

Miller, N. E., Bailey, C. J., & Stevenson, J. A. F., 1950. Decreased ''hunger'' but increased food intake resulting from hypothalamic lesions. *Science, 112,* 256–259.

Miller, N. E., & Kessen, M. L., 1952. Reward effects of food via stomach fistula compared with those of food via mouth. *Journal of Comparative and Physiological Psychology, 45,* 550–564.

Milliser, S. C., 1972. *The role of peristriate cortex in visually guided behavior in the rat.* Unpublished Ph. D. Dissertation, Loyola University of Chicago.

Milner, B., 1958. Psychological defects produced by temporal lobe excision. *Research Publications of the Association for Research in Nervous and Mental Disease, 36,* 244–257.

Milner, B., 1959. The memory defect in bilateral hippocampal lesions. In D. E. Cameron & M. Greenblatt (Eds.), *Recent Advances in Neuro-Physiological Research. Psychiatric Research Reports, 11,* 43–52.

Milner, B., 1964. Some effects of frontal lobectomy in man. In J. M. Warren & K. Akert (Eds.), *The frontal granular cortex and behavior.* New York, McGraw-Hill

Milner, B., 1965. Visually-guided maze learning in man: Effects of bilateral hippocampal, bilateral frontal, and unilateral cerebral lesions. *Neuropsychologia, 3,* 317–338.

Milner, B., 1966. Amnesia following operation on the temporal lobes. In C. W. M. Whitty & O. L. Zangwill (Eds.), *Amnesia.* London, Butterworth.

Milner, B., 1967. Brain mechanisms suggested by studies of temporal lobes. In F. L. Darley & C. H. Millikan (Eds.), *Brain mechanisms underlying speech and language.* New York: Grune & Stratton.

Milner, B., 1968a. Visual recognition and recall after right temporal lobe excision in man. *Neuropsychologia, 6,* 191–209.

Milner, B., 1968b. Neuropsychological evidence for differing memory processes. Abstract for the Symposium on short-term and long-term memory. *Proceedings of the 18th International Congress of Psychology,* Moscow, 1966. Amsterdam: North-Holland Publishing Company.

Milner, B., 1970. Memory and the medial temporal regions of the brain. In K. H. Pribram & D. E. Broadbent (Eds.), *Biology of memory.* New York: Academic Press.

Milner, B., Corkin, S., & Teuber, H. L., 1968. Further analysis of the hippocampal amnesic syndrome: 14 year follow-up study of H. M. *Neuropsychologia, 6,* 215–234.

Mishkin, M., 1964. Perseveration of central sets after frontal lesions in monkeys. In J. M. Warren & K. Akert (Eds.), *The frontal granular cortex and behavior.* New York, McGraw-Hill.

Mishkin, M., 1966. Visual mechanisms beyond the striate cortex. In: R. Russell (Ed.), *Frontiers in physiological psychology.* New York: Academic Press.

Mishkin, M., 1972. Cortical visual areas and their interaction. In: A. G. Karczmar & J. C. Eccles (Eds.), *Brain and human behavior.* New York: Springer.

Mishkin, M., 1979. Analogous neural models for tactual and visual learning. *Neuropsychologia, 17,* 139–151.

Mishkin, M., & Hall., M., 1955. Discrimination along a size continuum following ablation of the inferior temporal convexity in monkeys. *Journal of Comparative and Physiological Psychology, 48,* 97–101.

Mishkin, M., & Pribram, K. H., 1955. Analysis of the effects of frontal lesions in monkeys. I. Variations of delayed alternation. *Journal of Comparative and Physiological Psychology, 48,* 492–495.

Mishkin, M., & Pribram, K. H., 1956a. II. Variations of delayed response. Journal of Comparative and Physiological Psychology, *49,* 36–40.

Mishkin, M., & Pribram, K. H., 1956b. The effects of frontal lesions in monkeys. C. Object alternation. *Journal of Comparative and Physiological Psychology, 49,* 41–45.

Mishkin, M., & Weiskrantz, L., 1958. Effects of delaying reward on visual-discrimination performance in monkeys with frontal lesions. *Journal of Comparative and Physiological Psychology, 51,* 276–281.

Mitcham, J. C., & Thomas, R. K. Jr., 1972. Effects of substantia nigra and caudate nucleus lesions on avoidance learning in rats. *Journal of Comparative and Physiological Psychology, 81,* 101–107.

Mogenson, G., 1976. Septal-hypothalamic relationships. In J. F. DeFrance (Ed.), *The septal nuclei.* New York: Plenum Press.

Monnier, M., Kalberer, M., & Krupp, P., 1960. Functional antagonism between diffuse reticular and intralaminary recruiting projections in the medial thalamus. *Experimental Neurology, 2,* 271–289.

Moore, R. Y., 1964. Effects of some rhinencephalic lesions on retention of conditioned avoidance behavior in cats. *Journal of Comparative and Physiological Psychology, 57,* 65–71.

Moore, R. Y., 1975. Monoamine neurons innervating the hippocampal formation and septum: Organization and response to injury. In R. L. Isaacson & K. H. Pribram (Eds.), *The hippocampus, Vol. 1.* New York: Plenum Press.

Moray, N., 1959. Attention in dichotic listening: Affective cues and the influence of instruction. *Quarterly Journal of Experimental Psychology, 11,* 55–60.

Morgan, J. M., & Mitchell, J. C., 1969. Septal lesions enhance delay of responding on a free operant avoidance schedule. *Psychonomic Science, 16,* 10–11.

Morgane, P. J., & Stern, W. C., 1974. Interaction of amine systems in the central nervous system in the regulation of states of vigilance. In R. D. Myers & R. R. Drucker-Colin (Eds.), *Neurohumoral coding of brain function.* New York: Plenum Press.

Morin, R. E., DeRosa, D. V., & Stulz, V., 1967. Recognition, memory, and reaction time. *Acta Psychologica, 27,* 298–305.

Morrell, F., 1960. Microelectrode and steady potential studies suggesting a dendritic locus of closure. *Electroencephalography and Clinical Neurophysiology, 12,* Supplement No. 13.

Morrell, F., 1961. Electrophysiological contributions to the neural basis of learning. *Physiological Review, 41,* 443–494.

Morrow, L., 1981. *Time,* April 13, 1981.

Moruzzi, G., 1954. The physiological properties of the brain stem reticular system. In J. F. Delafresnaye (Ed.), *Brain mechanisms and consciousness.* Springfield, Ill.: Thomas.

Moruzzi, G., & Magoun, H. W., 1949. Brain stem reticular formation and activation of the EEG. *Electroencephalography and Clinical Neurophysiology, 1,* 455–473.

Moscovitch, M., 1973. Language and the cerebral hemispheres: Reaction time studies and their implications for models of cerebral dominance. In P. Pliner, L. Krames, & T. Alloway (Eds.), *Communication and affect.* New York: Academic Press.

Mott, F. W., & Sherrington, C. S., 1895. Experiments upon the influences of sensory nerves upon movement and nutrition of the limbs. *Proceedings of the Royal Society,* London, *57,* 481–488.

Motter, B. C., 1978. Caudato-thalamic pathway interactions. In L. L. Butcher (Ed.), *Cholinergic monoaminergic interactions in the brain.* New York: Academic Press.

Müller, G. E., & Pilzecker, A., 1900. Experimentelle Beiträge zur Lehre vom Gedächtnis. *Zeitschrift für Psychologie, 1,* 1–300.

Murdock, B. B., Jr., 1974. *Human memory: Theory and data.* Potomac, Md.: Lawrence Erlbaum Associates.

Murdock, B. B., Jr., 1979. Convolution and correlation in perception and memory. In L. -G. Nilsson (Ed.), *Perspectives on memory research.* Hillsdale, N. J.: Lawrence Erlbaum Associates.

Musty, R. E., 1966. *Hippocampal function in externally and internally cued avoidance behavior.* Paper given at Eastern Psychological Association 37th Meeting, New York.

Myers, R. D., 1974. Neurochemical mechanisms of temperature regulation and food ingestion. In R. D. Myers & R. R. Drucker-Colin (Eds.), *Neurohumoral coding of brain function.* New York: Plenum Press.

Myers, R. E., 1955. Interocular transfer of pattern discrimination in cats following section of crossed optic fibers. *Journal of Comparative and Physiological Psychology, 48,* 470–473.

Myers, R. E., 1956. Function of corpus callosum in interocular transfer. *Brain, 79,* 358–363.

Myers, R. E., & Sperry, R. W., 1958. Interhemispheric communication through the corpus callosum: Mnemonic carryover between the hemispheres. *A. M. A. Archives of Neurology and Psychiatry, 80,* 298–303.

Nadel, L., 1968. Dorsal and ventral hippocampal lesions and behavior. *Physiology and Behavior, 3,* 891–900.

Nakao, H., Tashiro, N., Kono, R., & Araki, R., 1979. Effects of GABA and glycine on aggressive-defense reaction produced by electrical stimulation of the ventromedial hypothalamus in cats. In

M. Ito, K. Kubota, N. Tsukahara, & K. Yagi (Eds.), *Intergrative control functions of the brain. Vol. 2*, Tokyo, Kodansha.

Narabayashi, H., 1972. Stereotaxic amygdalectomy. In B. E. Eleftheriou (Ed.), *The neurobiology of the amygdala*. New York: Plenum Press.

Natadze, R., 1960. Emergence of set on the basis of imaginal situations. *British Journal of Psychology, 51*, 237–246.

Neisser, U., 1967. *Cognitive Psychology*. New York: Appleton-Century-Crofts.

Nielsen, J. M., 1941. *A textbook of clinical neurology*. 4th printing. New York: Hoeber.

Nielsen, J. M., 1943. *Agnosia, apraxia, aphasia. Their value in cerebral localization*. Second ed., 1946. New York, Hoeber.

Nielsen, J. M., 1956. Studies in memory and amnesia. Transactions of the American Neurological Association, 81st Meeting, p. 1–7.

Nieuwenhuys, R., 1977. Aspects of the morphology of the striatum. In A. R. Cools, A. H. M. Lohman, & J. H. L. Van den Bercken (Eds.), *Psychobiology of the striatum*. Amsterdam: North-Holland Publishing Co.

Niki, H., 1962. The effects of hippocampal ablation on the behavior of the rat. *Japanese Psychological Research, 4*, 139–153.

Niki, H., 1979. Cingulate unit activity after reinforcement omission. In: M. Ito, K. Kubota, N. Tsukahara, & K. Yagi (Eds.), *Integrative control functions of the brain. Vol. 2*, Tokyo, Kodansha.

Nilsson, L.-G., (Ed.), 1979. *Perspectives on Memory Research*. Hillsdale, N.J., Erlbaum Associates.

Noback, C. R., & Demarest, R. J., 1981. *The human nervous system: Basic principles of neurobiology*. 3rd Ed. New York: McGraw-Hill.

Noble, C. E., 1953. The meaning-familiarity relationship. *Psychological Review, 60*, 89–98.

Noble, C. E., 1954. The familiarity-frequency relationship. *Journal of Experimental Psychology, 47*, 13–16.

Norman, D. A., 1968. Toward a theory of memory and attention. *Psychological Review, 75*, 522–536.

Norman, D. A., 1969. Memory and Attention. *An introduction to human information processing*. New York: Wiley.

Norman, D. A. (Ed.), 1970. Models of human memory. New York, Academic Press.

Norman, D. A., 1979. Perception, memory, and mental processes. In: L.-G. Nilsson (Ed.), *Perspectives on memory research*. Hillsdale, N.J.: Lawrence Erlbaum Associates.

Norman, D. A., and Rumelhart, D. E., 1970. A system for perception and memory. In D. A. Norman (Ed.), Models of human memory. New York: Academic Press.

Ojemann, G. A., Blick, K. I., & Ward, A. A. Jr., 1971. Improvement and disturbance of short-term verbal memory with human ventrolateral thalamic stimulation. *Brain, 94*, 225–240.

O'Keefe, J., & Black, A. H., 1978. Single unit and lesion experiments on the sensory inputs to the hippocampal cognitive map. In *Functions of the septo-hippocampal system*. Ciba Foundation Symposium # 58 (new series). Amsterdam: Elsevier.

O'Keefe, J., & Conway, D. H., 1978. Hippocampal place units in the freely moving rat: Why they fire when they fire. *Experimental Brain Research, 31*, 573–90.

Olds, J., 1956. A preliminary mapping of electrical reinforcing effects in the rat brain. *Journal of Comparative and Physiological Psychology, 49*, 281–285.

Olds, J., 1960. Approach-avoidance dissociations in rat brain. *American Journal of Physiology, 199*, 965–968.

Olds, J., 1976. Behavioral studies of hypothalamic functions: Drives and reinforcements. In R. G. Grenell & S. Gabay (Eds.), *Biological foundations of psychiatry*. New York: Raven Press.

Olds, J., 1977. *Drives and reinforcements: Behavioral studies of hypothalamic functions*. New York: Raven Press.

Olds, J., & Milner, P., 1954. Positive reinforcement produced by electrical stimulation of septal area and other regions of rat brain. *Journal of Comparative and Physiological Psychology, 47,* 419–427.

Olson, L., & Fuxe, K., 1972. Further mapping out of central noradrenaline neuron systems: Projections of the subcoerulear area. *Brain Research, 43,* 289–295.

Olson, L., Leary, R. W., & Thompson, R. F., 1967. Size-discrimination deficit in primates with inferotemporal lesions. *Psychonomic Science, 9,* 511–512.

Olton, D. S., 1973. Shock-motivated avoidance and the analysis of behavior. *Psychological Bulletin, 79,* 243–251.

Olton, D. S., & Gage, F. H., 1976. Behavioral, anatomical and biochemical aspects of septal hyperreactivity. In J. F. DeFrance (Ed.), *The septal nuclei.* New York: Plenum Press.

Ombredane, A., 1951. *L'aphasie et l'élaboration de la pensée explicite.* Paris: Presse Universitaire.

Ono, T. Nishino, H., Sasaki, K., Muramoto, K., & Oomura, Y., 1979. Feeding and motor cortex effects on monkey hypothalamic glucose-sensitive neurons. In M. Ito, K. Kubota, N. Tsukahara, & K. Yagi, (Eds.), *Integrative control functions of the brain, Vol. 2.* Tokyo: Kodansha.

Oomura, Y., 1973. Central mechanism of feeding. In M. Kotani (Ed.), *Advances in biophysics, Vol. 5.* Tokyo: Tokyo University Press.

Oomura, Y., Kita, H., Shimizu, N., Ishizuka, S., & Kato, M., 1979. Functional interconnections between the frontal cortex and the lateral hypothalamus. In M. Ito, K. Kubota, N. Tsukahara, & K. Yagi (Eds.) *Integrative control functions of the brain, Vol. 2,* Tokyo, Kodansha.

Oomura, Y., Nakamura, T., Sugimori, M., & Yamada, Y., 1975. Effects of free fatty acid on the rat lateral hypothalamic neurons. *Physiology and Behavior, 14,* 483–486.

Oomura, Y., Sugimori, M. Nakamura, T., & Yamada, Y., 1974. Glucose inhibition on the glucose-sensitive neurone in the rat lateral hypothalamus. *Nature* (London), *247,* 284–286.

Oomura, Y., & Takigawa, M., 1976. Input-output organization between the frontal cortex and the lateral hypothalamus. In T. Desiraju (Ed.), *Mechanisms in transmission of signals for conscious behavior.* Amsterdam: Elsevier.

Ottersen, O. P., 1981. The afferent connections of the amygdala of the rat as studied with retrograde transport of horseradish peroxidase. In Y. Ben-Ari (Ed.), *The amygdaloid complex.* Amsterdam: Elsevier/North Holland Biomedical Press.

Overman, W. H., & Doty, R. W., 1979. Disturbance of delayed match-to-sample in macaques by tetanization of anterior commissure versus limbic system or basal ganglia. *Experimental Brain Research, 37,* 511–524.

Paivio, A., 1969. Mental imagery in associative learning and memory. *Psychological Review, 76,* 241–263.

Paivio, A., 1971. Imagery and verbal processes. Hillsdale N.J.: Lawrence Erlbaum Associates.

Papez, J. W. 1956. Central reticular path to intralaminar and reticular nuclei of thalamus for activating EEG related to consciousness. *Electroencephalography and Clinical Neurophysiology, 8,* 117–128.

Patton, H. D., Ruch, T. C., & Walker, A. E., 1944. Experimental hypogeusia from Horsley-Clark lesions of the thalamus in Macaca mulatta. *Journal of Neurophysiology, 7,* 171–184.

Pearlman, C. A., & Becker, M., 1974. REM sleep deprivation impairs bar-press acquisition in rats. *Physiology and Behavior, 13,* 813–817.

Pearlman, C. A., Sharpless, S. K., & Jarvik, M. E., 1961. Retrograde amnesia produced by anesthetic and convulsant agents. *Journal of Comparative and Physiological Psychology, 54,* 109–112.

Peeke, H. V. S., & Herz, M. J., 1971. Caudate nucleus stimulation retroactively impairs complex maze learning in the rat. *Science, 173,* 80–82.

Peele, T. L., 1954. *The neuroanatomical basis for clinical neurology.* New York: McGraw-Hill.

Peixotto, H. E., 1947. Proactive inhibition in the recognition of nonsense syllables. *Journal of Experimental Psychology, 37,* 81–91.

Pellegrino, L., 1968. Amygdaloid lesions and behavioral inhibition in the rat. *Journal of Comparative and Physiological Psychology, 65,* 483–491.

Penfield, W., 1952. Memory mechanisms. *A. M. A. Archives of Neurology and Psychiatry, 67,* 178–198.

Penfield, W., 1954. Studies of the cerebral cortex of Man—A review and an interpretation. In: J. F. Delafresnaye (Ed.), *Brain mechanisms and consciousness.* Springfield, Ill.: Thomas.

Penfield, W., 1969. Consciousness, memory, and man's conditioned reflexes. In: K. Pribram (Ed.), *On the biology of learning.* New York: Harcourt, Brace and World.

Penfield, W., & Milner, B., 1958. Memory deficit produced by bilateral lesions in the hippocampal zone. *A. M. A. Archives of Neurology and Psychiatry, 79,* 475–497.

Penfield, W., & Rasmussen, T., 1950. *The cerebral cortex of man.* New York: Macmillan.

Penfield, W., & Roberts, L., 1959. *Speech and brain-mechanisms.* Princeton, N.J.: Princeton University Press.

Peretz, E., 1960. The effects of lesions of the anterior cingulate cortex on the behavior of the rat. *Journal of Comparative and Physiological Psychology, 53,* 540–548.

Peterson, L. R., & Peterson, M. J., 1959. Short-term retention of individual verbal items. *Journal of Experimental Psychology, 58,* 193–198.

Petsche, H., Gogolák, G., & van Zwieten, P. A., 1965. Rhythmicity of septal cell discharges at various levels of reticular excitation. *Electroencephalography and Clinical Neurophysiology, 19,* 25–33.

Phillips, A. G., & Lieblich, I., 1972. Developmental and hormonal aspects of hyperemotionality produced by septal lesions in male rats. *Physiology and Behavior, 9,* 237–242.

Phillips, L. W., 1958. Mediated verbal similarity as a determinant of the generalization of a conditioned GSR. *Journal of Experimental Psychology, 55,* 56–62.

Phillis, J. W., 1974. Evidence for cholinergic transmission in the cerebral cortex. In R. D. Myers & R. R. Drucker-Colin (Eds.), *Neurohumoral coding of brain function.* New York: Plenum Press.

Pijnenburg, A. J. J., Honig, W. M. M., & Van Rossum, J. M., 1975. Inhibition of D-amphetamine-induced locomotor activity by injection of haloperidol into the nucleus accumbens of the rat. *Psychopharmacologia* (Berlin), *41,* 87–95.

Pinto-Hamuy, T., Santibanez, G., Gonzales, C., & Vicencio, E., 1957. Changes in behavior and visual discrimination performances after selective ablations of the temporal cortex. *Journal of Comparative and Physiological Psychology, 50,* 379–385.

Planek, T. W., 1965. *Effect of lesions in the hippocampal rudiment on tactual and visual learning and retention.* Unpublished Ph. D. Dissertation, Loyola University of Chicago.

Ploog, D., 1981. Neurobiology of primate audio-vocal behavior. *Brain Research Reviews, 3,* 35–61.

Ploog, D. W., & MacLean, P. D., 1963. On functions of the mamillary bodies in the squirrel monkey. *Experimental Neurology, 7,* 76–85.

Pollin, W., Cardon, P. V. Jr., & Kety, S. S., 1961. Effects of amino acid feedings in schizophrenic patients treated with iproniazid. *Science, 133,* 104.

Pompeiano, O., 1980. Cholinergic activation of reticular and vestibular mechanisms controlling posture and eye movement. In J. A. Hobson & M. A. B. Brazier (Eds.), *The reticular system revisited.* New York: Raven Press.

Poschel, B. P. H., & Ninteman, F. W., 1971. Intracranial reward and the forebrain's serotonergic mechanism: Studies employing para-chlorophenylalanine and para-chloroamphetamine. *Physiology and Behavior, 7,* 39–46.

Posner, M., 1973. Coordination of internal codes. In W. Chase (Ed.), *Visual information processing.* New York: Academic Press.

Posner, M. I., Boies, S. J., Eichelman, W. H., & Taylor, R. L., 1969. Retention of visual and name code of single letters. *Journal of Experimental Psychology Monograph, 79,* No. 1, 1–16.

Posner, M. I., & Rossman, E., 1965. Effect of size and location of informational transforms upon short-term retention. *Journal of Experimental Psychology, 70,* 496–505.

Postman, L., 1950. Choice behavior and the process of recognition. *American Journal of Psychology, 63,* 576–583.

Postman, L., 1964. Short-term memory and incidental learning. In: A. W. Melton (Ed.), *Categories of human learning.* New York: Academic Press.

Postman, L., & Rau, L., 1957. Retention as a function of the method of measurement. Berkeley, Calif.: *University of California Publications in Psychology, 8,* 217–270.

Powell, E. W., & Hines, G., 1975. Septohippocampal interface. In R. L. Isaacson & K. M. Pribram (Eds.), *The hippocampus. Vol. 1. Plenum Press: New York.*

Powers, J. B., Fields, R. B., & Winans, S. A., 1979. Olfactory and vomeronasal system participation in male hamsters' attraction to female vaginal secretions. *Physiology and Behavior, 22,* 77–84.

Praag, H. M. van, 1977. The significance of dopamine for the mode of action of neuroleptics and the pathogenesis of schizophrenia. In A. R. Cools, A. H. M. Lohman, & J. H. L. Van den Bercken (Eds.), *Psychobiology of the striatum.* Amsterdam: North-Holland Publishing Co.

Prange, A., 1973. The use of drugs in depression: Its theoretical and practical basis. *Psychiatric Annals, 3,* 55–75.

Prange, A. J. Jr., Wilson, I. C., Lynn, C. W., Alltop, L. B., & Stikeleather, R. A., 1974. L-Tryptophan in mania: Contribution to a permissive hypothesis of affective disorders. *Archives of General Psychiatry, 30,* 56–62.

Pribram, H. B., & Barry, J., 1956. Further behavioral analysis of the parieto-temporo-preoccipital cortex. *Journal of Neurophysiology, 19,* 99–106.

Pribram, K. H., 1950. Some physical and pharmacological factors affecting delayed response performance of baboons following frontal lobotomy. *Journal of Neurophysiology, 13,* 373–382.

Pribram, K. H., 1961. A further experimental analysis of the behavioral deficit that follows injury to the primate frontal cortex. *Experimental Neurology, 3,* 432–466.

Pribram, K. H., 1967. Neurophysiology and learning. I. Memory and the organization of attention. In D. B. Lindsley & A. A. Lumsdaine (Eds.), *Brain function and learning.* Vol. 4 of Brain Function. Berkeley, Calif.: University of California Press.

Pribram, K. H., 1969. The neurophysiology of remembering. *Scientific American, 220,* 73–87.

Pribram, K. H., 1973. The primate frontal cortex. In K. H. Pribram & A. R. Luria, (Eds.), *Psychophysiology of the frontal lobes.* New York: Academic Press.

Pribram, K. H., Lennox, M. A., & Dunsmore, R. H., 1950. Some connections of the orbito-frontotemporal, limbic and hippocampal areas of Macaca mulatta. *Journal of Neurophysiology, 13,* 127–135.

Pribram, K. H., & Luria, A. R. (Eds.), 1973. *Psychophysiology of the frontal lobes.* New York: Academic Press.

Pribram, K. H., & MacLean, P. D., 1953. Neuronographic analysis of medial and basal cerebral cortex. II. Monkey. *Journal of Neurophysiology, 16,* 324–340.

Pribram, K. H., & Mishkin, M., 1956. Analysis of the effect of frontal lesions in monkey. III. Object alternation. Journal of Comparative and Physiological Psychology, 49, 41–45.

Pribram, K. H., Mishkin, M., Rosvold, H. E., & Kaplan, S. J., 1952. Effects on delayed response performance of lesions of the dorsolateral and ventromedial frontal cortex of baboons. *Journal of Comparative and Physiological Psychology, 45,* 565–575.

Pribram, K. H., & Tubbs, W. E., 1967. Short-term memory, parsing, and the primate frontal cortex. *Science, 156,* 1765–1767.

Pribram, K. H., Wilson, W. A. Jr., & Connors, J., 1962. Effects of lesions of the medial forebrain on alternation behavior of Rhesus monkeys. *Experimental Neurology, 6,* 36–47.

Prisko, L., 1963. *Short-term memory in focal cerebral damage.* Unpublished Ph. D. Dissertation, McGill University, Montreal.

Purpura, D. P., Frigyesi, T. L., McMurtry, J. G., & Scarff, T., 1966. Synaptic mechanisms in thalamic regulation of cerebello-cortical projection activity. In D. P. Purpura & M. D. Yahr (Eds.), *The thalamus*. New York: Columbia University Press.

Putnam, B., 1979. Hypnosis and distortions in eyewitness memory. *International Journal of Clinical and Experimental Hypnosis, 27,* 437–448.

Raeburn, V. P., 1974. Priorities in item recognition. *Memory and Cognition, 2,* 663–669.

Raisman, G., 1966. The connexions of the septum. *Brain, 89,* 317–348.

Ranck, J. B. Jr., 1975. Behavioral correlates and firing repertoires of neurons in the dorsal hippocampal formation and septum of unrestrained rats. In R. L. Isaacson & K. H. Pribram (Eds.), *The hippocampus, Vol. 2*. New York: Plenum Press.

Ranje, C., & Ungerstedt, U., 1976. Characterization of the behavioural deficits following the interruption of central dopamine neurotransmission. *Acta Physiologica Scandinavica, Supplement 440,* No. 59.

Rasmussen, T., 1975. Discussion after O. Zangwill: Excision of Broca's area without persistent aphasia. In: K. J. Zülch, O. Creutzfeldt, & G. C. Galbraith (Eds.), *Cerebral localization*. New York: Springer-Verlag.

Rasmussen, T., & Milner, B., 1975. Clinical and surgical studies of the cerebral speech areas in man. In K. J. Zülch, O. Creutzfeldt, & G. C. Galbraith (Eds.), *Cerebral localization*. New York: Springer-Verlag.

Ray, O. S., Hine, B., & Bivens, L. W., 1968. Stability of self-stimulation responding during long test sessions. *Physiology and Behavior, 3,* 161–164.

Reis, D. J. 1974. The chemical coding of aggression in brain. In: R. D. Myers & R. R. Drucker-Colin (Eds.), *Neurohumoral coding of brain function*. New York: Plenum Press.

Reitan, R. M., 1966. Problems and prospects in studying the psychological correlates of brain lesions. *Cortex, 2,* 127–154.

Reitman, W. R., 1970. What does it take to remember? In D. A. Norman (Ed.), *Models of human memory*. New York: Academic Press.

Rice, R. W., & Campbell, J. F., 1973. Effects of neocortical ablations on eating elicited by hypothalamic stimulation. *Experimental Neurology, 39,* 359–371.

Richardson, A., 1963. Mental practice: A review and discussion. *Bulletin of the British Psychological Society, 16,* No. 51.

Riklan, M., & Levita, E., 1969. Subcortical correlates of human behavior. Baltimore: Williams and Wilkins.

Riss, W., Halpern, M., & Scalia, F., 1969. Anatomical aspects of the evolution of the limbic and olfactory systems and their potential significance for behavior. In E. Tobach (Ed.), Experimental approaches to the study of emotional behavior. *Annals of the New York Academy of Sciences, 159,* 1096–1111.

Roberts, D. C. S., Zis, A. P., & Fibiger, H. C., 1975. Ascending catecholamine pathways and amphetamine-induced locomotor activity: Importance of dopamine and apparent non-involvement of norepinephrine. *Brain Research, 93,* 441–454.

Roberts, W. W., 1958. Rapid escape learning without avoidance learning motivated by hypothalamic stimulation in cats. *Journal of Comparative and Physiological Psychology, 51,* 391–399.

Robertson, R. T., & Kaitz, S. S., 1981. Thalamic connections with limbic cortex. I. Thalamocortical projections. *Journal of Comparative Neurology, 195,* 501–525.

Robinson, E., 1963. Effect of amygdalectomy on fear-motivated behavior in rats. *Journal of Comparative and Physiological Psychology, 56,* 814–820.

Rocha, A. F. da, 1980. Temporal influences of the reticular formation on sensory processing. In J. A. Hobson & M. A. B. Brazier (Eds.), *The reticular formation revisited*. New York: Raven Press.

Rolls, E. T., 1975. The brain and reward. New York: Pergamon Press.

Rose, A. M., Hattori, T., & Fibiger, H. C., 1976. Analysis of the septo-hippocampal pathway by light and electron microscopic autoradiography. *Brain Research, 108,* 170–174.

Rosenzweig, M. R., 1976. Summary. In M. R. Rosenzweig & E. L. Bennett (Eds.), *Neural mechanisms of learning and memory.* Cambridge, Mass.: MIT Press.

Rosvold, H. E., & Delgado, J. M. R., 1956. The effect on delayed-alternation test performance of stimulating or destroying electrical structures within the frontal lobes of the monkey's brain. *Journal of Comparative and Physiological Psychology, 49,* 365–372.

Rosvold, H. E., & Mishkin, M., 1961. Non-sensory effects of frontal lesions on discrimination learning and performance. In J. F. Delafresnaye (Ed.), *Brain mechanisms and learning.* Oxford: Blackwell.

Rosvold, H. E., Szwarcbart, M. K., Mirsky, A. F., & Mishkin, M., 1961. The effect of frontal-lobe damage on delayed-response performance in chimpanzees. *Journal of Comparative and Physiological Psychology, 54,* 368–374.

Routtenberg, A., 1978. The reward system of the brain. *Scientific American, 239/5,* 154–164.

Routtenberg, A., & Kim, H.-J., 1978. The substantia nigra and neostriatum: Substrate for memory consolidation. In L. L. Butcher (Ed.), *Cholinergic-monoaminergic interactions in the brain.* New York: Academic Press.

Routtenberg, A., & Santos-Anderson, R., 1977. The role of prefrontal cortex in intracranial self-stimulation. In L. L. Iversen, S. D. Iversen, & S. H. Snyder (Eds.), *Drugs, neurotransmitters and behavior. Vol. 8 in Handbook of psychopharmacology,* New York: Plenum Press.

Russell, B., 1927. Philosophy. New York: Norton.

Russell, I. S., & Ochs, S., 1965. Localization of a memory trace in one cortical hemisphere and transfer to the other hemisphere. In P. Milner & S. Glickman (Eds.), *Cognitive processes and the brain.* New York: Van Nostrand.

Russell, R. W., 1969. Behavioural aspect of cholinergic transmission. *Federation Proceedings, 28,* 121–131.

Russell, W. R., 1958. The physiology of memory. *Proceedings of the Royal Society of Medicine, 51,* 9–15.

Sabelli, H. C., Mosnaim, A. D., & Vazquez, A. J., 1974. Phenylethylamine: Possible role in depression and antidepressive drug action. In R. D. Myers & R. R. Drucker-Colin (Eds.), **Neurohumoral coding of brain function.** New York: Plenum Press.

Sachs, E. Jr., and Brendler, S. J., 1948. Some effects of stimulation of the orbital surface of the frontal lobe in the dog and monkey. *Federation Proceedings, 7,* 107.

Saint-Cyr, J. A., & Woodward, D. J., 1980. A topographic analysis of limbic and somatic inputs to the cerebellar cortex in the rat. *Experimental Brain Research, 40,* 13–22.

Sakai, K., 1980. Some anatomical and physiological properties of ponto-mesencephalic tegmental neurons with special reference to the PGO waves and postural atonia during paradoxical sleep in the cat. In J. A. Hobson & M. A. B. Brazier (Eds.), *The reticular formation revisited.* New York: Raven Press.

Sasaki, K., 1979. Cerebro-cerebellar interconnections in cats and monkeys. In J. Massion & K. Sasaki (Eds.), *Cerebro-cerebellar interactions.* Amsterdam: Elsevier/North-Holland Biomedical Press.

Sauerland, E. K., & Clemente, C. D., 1973. The role of the brain stem in orbital cortex induced inhibition of somatic reflexes. In K. H. Pribram & A. R. Luria (Eds.), *Psychophysiology of the frontal lobes.* New York: Academic Press.

Scalia, F., 1966. Some olfactory pathways in the rabbit brain. *Journal of Comparative Neurology, 126,* 285–310.

Scheibel, A. B., 1980. Anatomical and physiological substrates of arousal. In: J. A. Hobson & M. A. B. Brazier (Eds.), *The reticular formation revisited.* New York: Raven Press.

Scheibel, M. E., & Scheibel, A. B., 1966. Patterns of organization in specific and nonspecific thalamic fields. In D. P. Purpura & M. D. Yahr (Eds.), *The thalamus*. New York: Columbia University Press.

Schiff, B. B., 1964. The effects of tegmental lesions on the reward properties of septal stimulation. *Psychonomic Science, 1,* 397–398.

Schiff, B. B., 1967. Effects of tegmental lesions on the rewarding properties of stimulation. *Journal of Comparative and Psychological Psychology, 64,* 16–21.

Schilder, P., 1950. *The image and appearance of the human body.* New York: International Universities Press.

Schmaltz, L. W., & Isaacson, R. L., 1966. The effects of preliminary training conditions upon DRL performance in the hippocampectomized rat. *Physiology and Behavior, 1,* 175–182.

Schneider, R. C., Crosby, E. C., & Kahn, E. A., 1963. Certain afferent cortical connections of the rhinencephalon. In W. Bargmann & J. P. Schade (Eds.), *Progress in Brain Research, 3,* 191–217.

Schneider, W., & Shiffrin, R. M., 1977. Controlled and automatic human information processing: I. Detection, search and attention. *Psychological Review, 84,* 1–66.

Schreiner, L., Kling, A., & Galambos, R., 1952. Central nervous system lesions and aggressive behavior in cats. *Federation Proceedings, 11,* 142.

Schwartz, H. G., 1937. Effect of experimental lesions of the cortex on the "psychogalvanic reflex" in the cat. *Archives of Neurology and Psychiatry* (Chicago), *38,* 308–320.

Schwartzbaum, J. S., 1964. Visually reinforced behavior following ablation of the amygdaloid complex in monkeys. *Journal of Comparative and Physiological Psychology, 57,* 340–347.

Schwartzbaum, J. S., & Gay, P. E., 1966. Interacting behavioral effects of septal and amygdaloid lesions in the rat. *Journal of Comparative and Physiological Psychology, 61,* 59–65.

Schwartzbaum, J. S., Kellicut, M. H., Spieth, L. M., & Thompson, J. D., 1964. Effects of septal lesions in rats on response inhibition associated with food reinforced behavior. *Journal of Comparative and Physiological Psychology, 58,* 217–224.

Sclafani, A., & Grossman, S. P., 1971. Reactivity of hyperphagic and normal rats to quinine and electric shock. *Journal of Comparative and Physiological Psychology, 74,* 157–166.

Scoville, W. B., & Milner, B., 1957. Loss of recent memory after bilateral hippocampal lesions. *Journal of Neurology, Neurosurgery and Psychiatry, 20,* 11–21.

Segal, D. S., & Mandell, A. J., 1970. Behavioral activation of rats during intraventricular infusion of norepinephrine. *Proceedings of the National Academy of Sciences of the United States of America, 66,* 289–293.

Segal, M., 1975. Physiological and pharmacological evidence for a serotonergic projection to the hippocampus. *Brain Research 94,* 115–131.

Segal, M., 1978. Nicotinic transmission in the hippocampus. In *Functions of the septohippocampal system. Ciba Foundation Symposium 58 (new series).* Amsterdam: Elsevier.

Segal, M., & Olds, J., 1972. Behavior of units in hippocampal circuit of the rat during learning. *Journal of Neurophysiology, 35,* 680–690.

Seiden, L. S., & Dykstra, L. A., 1977. *Psychopharmacology: A biochemical and behavioral approach.* New York: Van Nostrand Reinhold.

Senden, M. von, 1932. *Raum- -und Gestaltauffassung bei operierten Blindgeborenen vor und nach der Operation.* Leipzig, Barth.

Sepinwall, J., 1966. Cholinergic stimulation of the brain and avoidance behavior. Psychonomic Science, *5,* 93–94.

Sepinwall, J., 1969. Enhancement and impairment of avoidance behavior by chemical stimulation of the hypothalamus. *Journal of Comparative and Physiological Psychology, 68,* 393–399.

Serafetinides, E. A., Walter, R. D., & Cherlow, D. G., 1975. Amnestic confusional phenomena, hippocampal stimulation, and laterality factors. In R. L. Isaacson & K. H. Pribram (Eds.), *The hippocampus, Vol. 2.* New York: Plenum Press.

Sessions, G. R., Kant, G. J., & Koob, G. F., 1976. Locus coeruleus lesions and learning in the rat. *Phyiology and Behavior, 17,* 853–859.

Sheffield, F. D., 1966a. A drive-inductive theory of reinforcement. In R. N. Haber (Ed.), *Current research in motivation.* New York: Holt.

Sheffield, F. D., 1966b. New evidence on the drive-induction theory of reinforcement. In R. N. Haber (Ed.), *Current research in motivation.* New York: Holt.

Shepard, R. N., 1967. Recognition memory for words, sentences, and pictures. *Journal of Verbal Learning and Verbal Behavior, 6,* 156–163.

Sherrington, C. S., 1934. The brain and its mechanisms. London: Cambridge University Press.

Sheu, Y. S., Nelson, J. P., & Bloom, F. E., 1974. Discharge patterns of cat raphé neurons during sleep and waking. *Brain Research, 73,* 263–276.

Shevrin, H., & Dickman, S., 1980. The psychological unconscious: A necessary assumption for all psychological theory? *American Psychologist, 35,* 421–434.

Shibasaki, H., Shima, F., & Kuroiwa, Y., 1978. Clinical studies of the movement-related cortical potential (MP) and the relationship between the dentatorubrothalamic pathway and readiness potential (RP). *Journal of Neurology, 219,* 15–25.

Shiffrin, R. M., 1977. Commentary on "Human memory: A proposed system and its control processes." In G. Bower (Ed.), *Human memory: Basic processes.* New York: Academic Press.

Shopsin, B., Gershon, S., Goldstein, M., et al., 1975. Use of synthesis inhibitors in defining a role for biogenic amines during imipramine treatment in depressed patients. *Psychopharmacology Communications, 1,* 239–249.

Shopsin, B., Wilk, S., Sathananthan, G., Gershon, S., & Davis, K., 1974. Catecholamines and affective disorders revised: A critical assessment. *Journal of Nervous and Mental Disease, 158,* 369–383.

Showers, M. J. C., & Crosby, E. C., 1958. Somatic and visceral responses from the cingulate gyrus. *Neurology, 8,* 561–565.

Shute, C. C. D., 1970. Distribution of cholinesterase and cholinergic pathways. In L. Martini, M. Motta, & F. Fraschini (Eds.), *The hypothalamus,* New York: Academic Press.

Shute, C. C. D., & Lewis, P. R., 1967. The ascending cholinergic reticular system: Neocortical olfactory and subcortical projections. *Brain, 90,* 497–520.

Shute, C. C. D., & Lewis, P. R., 1975. Cholinergic pathways. *Pharmacological Therapeutics, Series B, 1,* 79–87.

Sidman, M., 1966. Avoidance behavior. In W. K. Honig (Ed.), Operant behavior: Areas of research and application. New York: Appleton-Century-Crofts.

Sidman, M., Stoddard, L. T., & Mohr, J. P., 1968. Some additional quantitative observations of immediate memory in a patient with bilateral hippocampal lesions. *Neuropsychologia, 6,* 245–254.

Siegel, A., & Tassoni, J. P., 1971a. Differential efferent projections from the ventral and dorsal hippocampus of the cat. *Brain, Behavior and Evolution, 4,* 185–200.

Siegel, A., & Tassoni, J. P., 1971b. Differential efferent projections of the lateral and medial septal nuclei to the hippocampus in the cat. *Brain, Behavior and Evolution, 4,* 201–219.

Siggins, G., Nicoll, R., Bloom, F., & Ling, N., 1978. Reactional actions of endorphins, enkephalins and nor-morphine in rat brain. In R. W. Ryall & J. S. Kelly (Eds.), *Iontophoresis and transmitter mechanisms in the mammalian central nervous system.* Amsterdam: Elsevier.

Simma, K., 1955. Die psychischen Störungen bei Läsionen des Temporallappens und ihre Behandlung. *Monatschrift für Psychiatrie und Neurologie, 130,* 120–160.

Simon, H. A., 1976. The information-storage system called "Human memory." In M. R. Rosenzweig & E. L. Bennett (Eds.), *Neural mechanisms of learning and memory.* Cambridge, Mass.: MIT Press.

Sittig, O., 1931. *Apraxie.* Berlin: Karger.

Skinner, J. E., & Lindsley, D. B., 1973. The nonspecific mediothalamic-frontocortical system: its influence on electrocortical activity and behavior. In: K. H. Pribram & A. R. Luria (Eds.), *Psychophysiology of the frontal lobes*. New York: Academic Press.

Slangen, J. L., & Miller, N. E., 1969. Pharmacological tests for the function of hypothalamic norepinephrine in eating behavior. *Physiology and Behavior, 4,* 543–552.

Sloan, N., & Jasper, H , 1950. Studies of the regulatory functions of the anterior limbic cortex. *Electroencephalography and Clinical Neurophysiology, 2,* 317–328.

Slotnick, B. M., 1967. Disturbance of maternal behavior in the rat following lesions in the cingulate cortex. *Behaviour, 29,* 204–236.

Slotnick, B. M., & McMullen, M. F., 1972. Intraspecific fighting in albino mice with septal forebrain lesions. *Physiology and Behavior, 8,* 333–337.

Smith, C. M., 1972. The release of acetylcholine from rabbit hippocampus. *British Journal of Pharmacology, 45,* 172P.

Smith, C. M., 1974. Direct evidence for the existence of a cholinergic septo-hippocampal pattern. *Life Sciences, 14,* 2159–2166.

Smith, D. E., Krieg, & M. B., & Hoebel, B. G., 1970. Lateral hypothalamic control of killing: Evidence of a cholinoceptive mechanism. *Science, 167,* 900–901.

Smith, S., 1954. Experiment reported before the Eastern Psychological Association Annual Meeting.

Snider, R. S., 1950. Recent contributions to the anatomy and physiology of the cerebellum. *Archives of Neurology and Psychiatry* (Chicago) 64, 196–219.

Snyder, D. R., & Isaacson, R. L., 1965. Effects of large and small bilateral hippocampal lesions on two types of passive avoidance responses. *Psychological Reports, 16,* 1277–1290.

Snyder, J. F., 1965. *The effect of bilateral fornix lesions upon the learning and retention of an olfactory and auditory discrimination in the albino rat.* Unpublished Ph.d. Dissertation, Loyola University of Chicago.

Sodetz, F. J., 1970. Septal ablation and free-operant avoidance behavior in the rat. *Physiology and Behavior, 5,* 773–777.

Sodetz, F. J., & Bunnell, B. N., 1970. Septal ablation and the social behavior of the golden hamster. *Physiology and Behavior, 6,s* 79–88.

Sokolov, E. N., (Ed.), 1959. *Orienting reflex and problems of the higher nervous activity.* Academy of Pedagogical Science, Moscow.

Somjen, G., 1978. Chairman's review: Nociceptive neurones, opiates and endogenous ligands of the opiate receptor. In R. W. Ryall & J. S. Kelly (Eds.), *Iontophoresis and transmitter mechanisms in the mammalian central nervous system*. Amsterdam: Elsevier.

Spehlmann, R., 1971. Acetylcholine and the synaptic transmission of non-specific impulses to the visual cortex. *Brain, 94,* 139–150.

Spence, J. T., & Bower, G. H. (Eds.), 1970. *The psychology of learning and motivation: Advances in research and theory. Vol. 3.* New York: Academic Press.

Spence, K. W., & Spence, J. T., (Eds.), 1967. *The psychology of learning and motivation: Advances in research and theory. Vol. 1.* New York: Academic Press.

Spence, K. W., & Spence, J. T. (Eds.), 1968. *The psychology of learning and motivation: Advances in research and theory. Vol. 2.* New York: Academic Press.

Sperling, G., 1960. The information available in brief visual presentations. *Psychological Monographs, 74,* No. 11.

Sperling, G., 1963. A model for visual memory tasks. *Human Factors, 5,* 19–31.

Sperry, R. W., 1961. Cerebral organization and behavior. *Science, 133,* 1749–57.

Sperry, R. W., 1970. Perception in the absence of the neocortical commissure. In *Perception and its disorders*. Research Publication # 48 of the Association for Research in Nervous and Mental Disease.

Spiegel, E. A., Wycis, H. T., Conger, R. B., & Fischer, H. K., 1950. Effects of lesions of human thalamus in the region of dorsomedial nuclei. *Federation Proceedings, 9,* 119.

Spiegler, B. J., & Mishkin, M., 1981. Evidence for the sequential participation of inferior temporal cortex and amygdala in the acquisition of stimulus-reward associations. *Behavioral Brain Research, 3,* 303–317.

Spies, G., 1965. Food versus intracranial self-stimulation reinforcement in food deprived rats. *Journal of Comparative and Physiological Psychology, 60,* 153–157.

Spieth, W., Curtis, J. F., & Webster, J. C., 1954. Responding to one of two simultaneous messages. *Journal of the Acoustical Society of America, 26,* 391–396.

Sprague, J. M., & Chambers, W. W., 1953. Regulation of posture in intact and decerebrate cat. I. Cerebellum, reticular formation, vestibular nuclei. *Journal of Neurophysiology, 16,* 451–463.

Sprague, J. M., & Chambers, W. W., 1955. Evidence for sensory function of the cerebellum in the cat. *Anatomical Record, 121,* 369–370.

Squire, L. R., 1969. Effects of pretrial and posttrial administration of cholinergic and anticholinergic drugs on spontaneous alternation. *Journal of Comparative and Physiological Psychology, 69,* 69–75.

Srebro, B., Mellgren, S. I., & Harkmark, W., 1975. Acetylcholinesterase histochemistry of the septal region in the rat. In J. F. DeFrance (Ed.), *The septal nuclei.* New York: Plenum Press.

Stamm, J. S., 1955. The function of the median cerebral cortex in maternal behavior of rats. *Journal of Comparative and Physiological Psychology, 48,* 347–356.

Stamm, J. S., 1969. Electrical stimulation of monkeys' prefrontal cortex during delayed-response performance. *Journal of Comparative and Physiological Psychology, 67,* 535–546.

Stamm, J. S., & Rosen, S. C., 1973. The locus and crucial time of implication of prefrontal cortex in the delayed response task. In: K. H. Pribram & A. R. Luria (Eds.), *Psychophysiology of the frontal lobes.* New York: Academic Press.

Stamm, J. S., & Sperry, R. W., 1957. Function of corpus callosum in contralateral transfer of somesthetic discrimination in cats. *Journal of Comparative and Physiological Psychology, 50,* 138–143.

Stark, P., & Totty, C. W., 1967. Effects of amphetamines on eating elicited by hypothalamic stimulation. *Journal of Pharmacology and Experimental Therapeutics, 158,* 272–278.

Start, K. B., & Richardson, A., 1965. Imagery and mental practice. *British Journal of Educational Psychology, 34,* 280–284.

Starzl, T. E., Taylor, C. W., & Magoun, H. W., 1951a. Ascending conduction in reticular activating system with special reference to the diencephalon. *Journal of Neurophysiology, 14,* 460–477.

Starzl, T. E., Taylor, C. W., & Magoun, H. W., 1951b. Collateral afferent excitation of reticular formation of brain stem. *Journal of Neurophysiology, 14,* 479–505.

Stefanis, C., 1964. Hippocampal neurons: Their responsiveness to micro-electrophoretically administered endogenous amines. *Pharmacologist, 6,* 171.

Stein, D. G., Rosen, J. J., Graziadei, J., Mishkin, D., & Brink, J. J., 1969. Central nervous system; recovery of function. *Science, 166,* 528–30.

Stein, L., 1968. Chemistry of reward and punishment. In: D. H. Efron (Ed.), *Psychopharmacology; A review of progress: 1957–1967.* Washington, D.C.: U.S. Government Printing Office.

Stein, L., & Wise, C. D., 1971. Possible etiology of schizophrenia: Progressive damage to the noradrenergic reward system by 6-hydroxydopamine. *Science, 171,* 1032–1036.

Stein, L., Wise, C. D., & Belluzzi, J. D., 1977. Neuropharmacology of reward and punishment. In L. L. Iversen, S. D. Iversen, & S. H. Snyder (Eds.), *Drugs, neurotransmitters, and behavior. Vol. 8, Handbook of Psychopharmacology,* New York: Plenum Press.

Stenevi, U., Emson, P., & Björklund, A., 1977. Development of dopamine-sensitive adenylate cyclase in hippocampus reinnervated by transplanted dopamine neurons: Evidence for new functional contacts. *Acta Physiologica Scandinavica, Supplement #452.*

Stepien, L. S., Cordeau, J. P., & Rasmussen, R., 1960. The effect of temporal lobe and hippocampal lesions on auditory and visual recent memory in monkeys. *Brain, 83,* 470–489.

Stepien, L., & Sierpinski, S., 1960. The effect of focal lesions of the brain upon auditory and visual recent memory in man. *Journal of Neurology, Neurosurgery and Psychiatry, 23,* 334–340.

Steriade, M., Ropert, M., Kitsikis, A., & Oakson, G., 1980. Ascending activating neuronal networks in midbrain reticular core and related rostral systems. In: J. A. Hobson & M. A. B. Brazier (Eds.), *The reticular formation revisited.* New York: Raven Press.

Sterman, M. B., 1974. Sleep. In L. V. DiCara (Ed.), *Limbic and autonomic nervous systems research.* New York: Plenum Press.

Stern, J. A., Ulett, G. A., & Sines, J. O., 1960. The electrocortical changes during conditioning. In J. Wartis (Ed.), *Recent advances in biological psychiatry.* New York: Grune and Stratton.

Sternberg, S., 1966. High-speed scanning in human memory. *Science, 153,* 652–654.

Sternberg, S., 1967. Two operations in character-recognition. Some evidence from reaction-time measurements. *Perception and Psychophysics, 2,* 45–53.

Sternberg, S., 1975. Memory scanning: New findings and current controversies. *Quarterly Journal of Experimental Psychology, 27,* 1–32.

Stevens, J., 1977. Striatal function and schizophrenias. In A. R. Cools, A. H. M. Lohman, & J. H. L. Van den Bercken (Eds.), *Psychobiology of the striatum.* Amsterdam: North-Holland Publishing Co.

Stone, H., Carregal, E. J. A., & Williams, B., 1966. The olfactory-trigeminal response to odorants. *Life Sciences, 5,* 2195–2201.

Storm-Mathisen, J., 1978. Localization of putative transmitters in the hippocampal formation (with a note on the connections to septum and hypothalamus). In *Ciba Foundation Symposium 58 (new series), Functions of the Septo-hippocampal system.* Amsterdam: Elsevier.

Stoyva, J., & Budzynski, T., 1974. Cultivated low arousal—an antistress response? In L. V. DiCara (Ed.), *Limbic and autonomic nervous systems research.* New York: Plenum Press.

Straughan, D. W., 1975. Neurotransmitters and the hippocampus. In R. L. Isaacson & K. H. Pribram (Eds.), *The hippocampus, Vol. 1.* New York: Plenum Press.

Strick, P. L., 1979. Control of peripheral input to the dentate nucleus by motor preparation. In: J. Massion & K. Sasaki (Eds.), *Cerebro-cerebellar interactions.* Amsterdam: Elsevier/North-Holland Biomedical Press.

Striker, E. M., Rowland, N., & Zigmond, M. J., 1975. Trigeminal lemniscal lesions and the lateral hypothalamic syndrome. *Science, 190,* 694–695.

Strominger, N. L., Oesterreich, R. E., & Neff, W. D., 1980. Sequential auditory and visual discrimination after temporal lobe ablation in the monkey. *Physiology and Behavior, 24,* 1149–1156.

Strong, E. K. Jr., 1913. The effect of time interval upon recognition memory. *Psychological Review, 20,* 339–372.

Swanson, L. W., 1978. The anatomical organization of septo-hippocampal projections. In *Ciba Foundation Symposium 58, Function of the Septo-Hippocampal System.* Amsterdam: Elsevier.

Swanson, L. W., & Cowan. W. M., 1975. Hippocampo-hypothalamic connections: Origin in subicular cortex, not Ammon's horn. *Science, 189,* 303–304.

Swanson, L. W., & Cowan, W. M., 1976. Autoradiographic studies of the development and connections of the septal area. In J. F. DeFrance (Ed.), *The septal nuclei.* New York: Plenum Press.

Swanson, L. W., & Cowan, W. M., 1977. An autoradiographic study of the organization of the efferent connections of the hippocampal formation in the rat. *Journal of Comparative Neurology, 172,* 49–84.

Swett, C. P., & Hobson, J. A., 1968. The effects of posterior hypothalamic lesions on behavioral and electrographic manifestations of sleep and waking in cats. *Archives Italiennes de Biologie, 106,* 283–293.

Takagi, S. F., 1979. Brain mechanism of olfaction. In M. Ito, K. Kubota, N. Tsukahara, & K. Yagi (Eds.), *Integrative control functions of the brain. Vol. 2.* Tokyo: Kodansha.

Talbot, S. A., 1940. Arrangement of visual area of cat's cortex. *American Journal of Physiology, 129,* 477–478P.

Talbot, S. A., 1942. A lateral localization in the cat's visual cortex. *Federation Proceedings, 1,* 84.

Talland, G., 1965. *Deranged memory.* New York: Academic Press.

Tanabe, T., Yarita, H., Iino, M., Ooshima, Y., & Takagi, S. F., 1975. Olfactory projection area in orbitofrontal cortex of monkey. *Journal of Neurophysiology, 38,* 1269–1283.

Tapia, R., 1974. The role of gamma-aminobutyric acid metabolism in the regulation of cerebral excitability. In R. D. Myers & R. R. Drucker-Colin (Eds.), *Neurohumoral coding of brain function.* New York: Plenum Press.

Tapp, J. T., 1969. Current status and future directions. In J. T. Tapp (Ed.), *Reinforcement and behavior.* New York: Academic Press.

Taub, E., & Berman, A. J., 1968. Movement and learning in the absence of sensory feedback. In S. J. Freedman (Ed.), *The neuropsychology of spatially oriented behavior.* Homewood, Ill.: Dorsey Press.

Teitelbaum, H., 1964. A comparison of effects of orbitofrontal and hippocampal lesions upon discrimination learning and reversal in the cat. *Experimental Neurology, 9,* 452–462.

Teitelbaum, H., & Milner, P. M., 1963. Activity changes following partial hippocampal lesions in rats. *Journal of Comparative and Physiological Psychology, 56,* 284–289.

Teitelbaum, P., 1955. Sensory control of hypothalamic hyperphagia. *Journal of Comparative and Physiological Psychology, 48,* 158–163.

Teitelbaum, P., & Cytawa, J., 1965. Spreading depression and recovery from lateral hypothalamic damage. *Science, 147,* 61–63.

Teitelbaum, P., & Epstein, A. N., 1962. The lateral hypothalamic syndrome: Recovery of feeding and drinking after lateral hypothalamic lesions. *Psychological Review, 69,* 74–90.

Telegdy, G., & Kovács, G. L., 1979. Role of monoamines in mediating the action of hormones on learning and memory. In M. A. B. Brazier (Ed.), *Brain mechanisms in memory and learning.* New York: Raven Press.

Terzian, H., & Dalle Ore, G., 1955. Syndrome of Klüver and Bucy reproduced in man by bilateral removal of the temporal lobes. *Neurology,* (Minneapolis), *5,* 373–380.

Teuber, H. L., 1959. Some alterations in behavior after cerebral lesions in man. In *Evolution of nervous control.* Washington, D.C.: American Association for the Advancement of Sciences.

Teuber, H. L., 1964. The riddle of frontal lobe function in man. In: J. M. Warren & K. Akert (Eds.), *The frontal granular cortex and behavior.* New York: McGraw-Hill.

Thierry, A. M., Javoy, F., Glowinski, J., & Kety, S. S., 1968. Effects of stress on the metabolism of norepinephrine, dopamine and serotonin in the central nervous system of the rat. I. Modifications of norepinephrine turnover. *Journal of Pharmacology and Experimental Therapeutics, 163,* 163–171.

Thomas, G. J., 1971. Maze retention by rats with hippocampal lesions and with fornicotomies. *Journal of Comparative and Physiological Psychology, 75,* 41–49.

Thomas, G. J., Fry, W. J., Fry, F. J., Slotnick, B. M., & Krieckhaus, E. E., 1963. Behavioral effects of mammillothalamic tractotomy in cats. *Journal of Neurophysiology, 26,* 857–876.

Thomas, G. J., & Slotnick, B. M., 1962. Effects of lesions in the cingulum on maze learning and avoidance conditioning in the rat. *Journal of Comparative and Physiological Psychology, 55,* 1085–1091.

Thomas, G. J., & Slotnick, B. M., 1963. Impairment of avoidance responding by lesions in cingulate cortex in rats depends on food drive. *Journal of Comparative and Physiological Psychology, 56,* 959–964.

Thompson, R., 1958. The effect of intracranial stimulation on memory in cats. *Journal of Comparative and Physiological Psychology, 51,* 421–426.

Thompson, R., 1969. Localization of the "visual memory system" in the white rat. *Journal of Comparative and Physiological Psychology Monograph 69,* No. 4, Pt. 2.

Thompson, R., 1980. Sparing of an olfactory discrimination habit following extensive neocortical removal in rats. *Brain Research, 25,* 405–408.

Thompson, R., & Dean, W., 1955. A further study on the retroactive effects of ECS. *Journal of Comparative and Physiological Psychology, 48,* 488–491.

Thompson, R., & Hawkins, W. F., 1961. Memory unaffected by mamillary body lesions in the rat. *Experimental Neurology, 3,* 189–196.

Thompson, R., & Langer, S. K., 1963. Deficits in position reversal learning, following lesions of the limbic system. *Journal of Comparative and Physiological Psychology, 56,* 987–995.

Thompson, R., Lukaszewska, I., Schweigert, A., & McNew, J. J., 1967. Retention of visual and kinesthetic discriminations in rats following pretecto-diencephalic and ventral mesencephalic damage. *Journal of Comparative and Physiological Psychology, 63,* 458–468.

Thompson, R., & Malin, C. F., 1961. The effect of neocortical lesions on retention of a successive brightness discrimination in rats. *Journal of Comparative and Physiological Psychology, 54,* 326–328.

Thompson, R., & Massopust, L. C. Jr., 1960. The effect of subcortical lesions on retention of a brightness discrimination in rats. *Journal of Comparative and Physiological Psychology, 53,* 488–496.

Thompson, R., Rich, I., & Langer, S. K., 1964. Lesion studies on the functional significance of the posterior thalamomesencephalic tract. *Journal of Comparative Neurology, 123,* 29–44.

Thompson, R. F., 1980. The search for the engram. In D. McFadden (Ed.), *Neural mechanisms in behavior.* New York: Springer-Verlag.

Thompson, R. L., & Mettler, F. A., 1963. Permanent learning deficit associated with lesions in the caudate nuclei. *American Journal of Mental Deficiency, 67,* 526–535.

Thorndike, E. L., 1931. Human learning. New York: Appleton-Century-Crofts.

Thorndike, E. L., & Lorge, I. 1944. *The Teacher's word book of 30,000 words.* New York: Teachers College, Columbia University Bureau of Publications.

Tissot, R., & Monnier, M., 1959. Dualité du système thalamique de projection diffuse. *Electroencephalography and Clinical Neurophysiology, 11,* 675–686.

Tow, P. M., & Whitty, C. W., 1953. Personality changes after operations on the cingulate gyrus in man. *Journal of Neurology, Neurosurgery and Psychiatry, 16,* 186–193.

Towe, A. L., 1973. Motor cortex and the pyramidal system. In J. D. Maser (Ed.), *Efferent organization and the integration of behavior.* New York: Academic Press.

Trafton, C. L., Fibley, R. A., & Johnson, R. W., 1969. Avoidance behavior in rats as a function of the size and location of anterior cingulate cortex lesions. *Psychonomic Science, 14,* 100–102.

Treisman, A. M., 1960. Contextual cues in selective listening. *Quarterly Journal of Experimental Psychology, 12,* 242–248.

Treisman, A. M., 1964a. Monitoring and storage of irrelevant messages in selective attention. *Journal of Verbal Learning and Verbal Behavior, 3,* 449–459.

Treisman, A. M., 1964b. Selective attention in man. *British Medical Bulletin, 20,* 12–16.

Tucker, D., 1971. Nonolfactory responses from the nasal cavity: Jacobson's organ and the trigeminal system. In: L. M. Beidler (Ed.), *Olfaction. Vol IV, Handbook of sensory physiology.* New York: Springer-Verlag.

Tulving, E., 1968. When is recall higher than recognition? *Psychonomic Science, 10,* 53–54.

Tulving, E., 1975. Ecphoric processes in recall and recognition. In: J. Brown (Ed.), Recall and Recognition. London: Wiley.

Tulving, E., 1979. Memory research: What kind of progress? In L.-G. Nilsson (Ed.), *Perspectives on memory research.* Hillsdale, N.J., Lawrence Erlbaum Associates.

Tulving, E., & Pearlstone, Z. 1966. Availability versus accessibility of information in memory for words. *Journal of Verbal Learning and Verbal Behavior, 5,* 381–391.

Tulving, E., & Thomson, D. M., 1973. Encoding specificity and retrieval processes in episodic memory. *Psychological Review, 80,* 352–373.

Tunturi, A. R., 1945. Further afferent connections of the acoustic cortex of the dog. *American Journal of Physiology, 144,* 389–394.

Turner, B. H., 1973. Sensorimotor syndrome produced by lesions of the amygdala and lateral hypothalamus. *Journal of Comparative and Physiological Psychology, 82,* 37–47.

Turner, B. H., 1981. The cortical sequence and terminal distribution of sensory related afferents to the amygdaloid complex of the rat and monkey. In Y. Ben-Ari (Ed.), *The amygdaloid complex.* Amsterdam: Elsevier/North Holland Biomedical Press.

Turner, B. H., Mishkin, M., & Knapp, M., 1980. Organization of the amygdalopetal projections from modality-specific cortical association areas in the monkey. *Journal of Comparative Neurology, 191,* 515–543.

Turvey, M. T., & Shaw, R., 1979. The primacy of perceiving: An ecological reformulation of perception for understanding memory. In: L.-G. Nilsson (Ed.), *Perspectives on memory research.* Hillsdale, N.J., Lawrence Erlbaum Associates.

Ule, G., 1951. Korsakoff-Psychose nach doppelseitiger Ammonshornzerstörung mit transneuraler Degeneration der corpora mammillaria. *Deutsche Zeitschrift für Nervenheilkunde, 165,* 446–456.

Underwood, B. J., 1969. Attributes of memory. *Psychological Review, 76,* 559–573.

Underwood, B. J., & Freund, J. S., 1968. Two tests of a theory of verbal discrimination learning. *Canadian Journal of Psychology, 22,* 96–104.

Ungerstedt, U., 1971a. Stereotaxic mapping of the monoamine pathways in the rat brain. *Acta Physiologica Scandinavica, 82, Supplement 367,* 1–48.

Ungerstedt, U., 1971b. Adipsia and aphagia after 6-hydroxydopamine induced degeneration of the nigro-striatal dopamine system in the brain. *Acta Physiologica Scandinavica, 82, Supplement 367,* 95–122.

Ungerstedt, U., 1977. Brain dopamine neurons and behavior. In S. H. Snyder (Eds.), *Biochemistry and behavior.* Cambridge, Mass.: MIT Press.

Ungerstedt, U., Ljungberg, T., & Ranje, C., 1977. Dopamine neurotransmission and the control of behaviour. In A. R. Cools, A. H. M. Lohman & J. H. L. van den Bercken (Eds.), *Psychobiology of the striatum.* Amsterdam: North-Holland Publishing Co.

Uretsky, N. J., & Iversen, L. L., 1969. Effects of 6-hydroxydopamine on noradrenaline-containing neurones in the rat brain. *Nature, 221,* 557–559.

Ursin, H., 1971. Limbic control of emotional behavior. In E. R. Hitchcock & K. Varnet (Eds.), *Proceedings, Second international conference on psychosurgery in Copenhagen.* Springfield, Ill.: Thomas.

Ursin, H., & Kaada, B. R., 1960. Subcortical structures mediating the attention response induced by amygdala stimulation. *Experimental Neurology, 2,* 109–122.

Ursin, H., Linck, P., & McCleary, R. A., 1969. Septal differentiation of avoidance deficit following septal and cingulate lesions. *Journal of Comparative and Physiological Psychology, 68,* 74–79.

Valenstein, E. S., 1969. Behavior elicited by hypothalamic stimulation. A prepotency hypothesis. *Brain, Behavior and Evolution, 2,* 295–316.

Valenstein, E. S., & Beer, B., 1964. Continuous opportunity for reinforcing brain stimulation. *Journal for the Experimental Analysis of Behavior, 7,* 183–184.

Valenstein, E. S., Cox, J. C., & Kakolewski, J. W., 1967. Sex differences in taste preferences for glucose and saccharine solutions. *Science, 156,* 942–943.

Van Alphen, H. A. M., 1969. The anterior commissure of the rabbit. *Acta Anatomica, Supplement 57, 74,* 1–112.

Van Hoesen, G. W., 1981. The differential distribution, diversity and sprouting of cortical projections to the amygdala in the rhesus monkey. In Y. Ben-Ari (Ed.), *The amygdaloid complex.* Amsterdam: Elsevier/North Holland Biomedical Press.

Van Hoesen, G. W., MacDougall, J. M., & Mitchell, J. C., 1969. Anatomical specificity of septal projections in active and passive avoidance behavior in rats. *Journal of Comparative and Physiological psychology, 68,* 80–89.

Van Hoesen, G. W., Mesulam, M. M., & Haaxma, R., 1976. Temporal cortical projections to the olfactory tubercle in the rhesus monkey. *Brain Research, 109,* 375–381.

Van Hoesen, G. W., Pandya, D. N., & Butters, N., 1972. Cortical afferents to the entorhinal cortex of the rhesus monkey. *Science, 175,* 1471–1473.

Vanderwolf, C. H., 1964. Effect of combined medial thalamic and septal lesions on active avoidance behavior. *Journal of Comparative and Physiological Psychology, 58,* 31–37.

Vanderwolf, C. H., Kramis, R., Gillespie, L. A., & Bland, B. H., 1975. Hippocampal rhythmic slow activity and neocortical low-voltage fast activity: Relations to behavior. In R. L. Isaacson & K. H. Pribram (Eds.), *The hippocampus, Vol. 2.* New York: Plenum Press.

Vanderwolf, C. H., Kramis, R., & Robinson, T. E., 1978. Hippocampal electrical activity during waking behavior and sleep: Analyses using centrally acting drugs. In *Functions of the septo-hippocampal system. Ciba Foundation Symposium 58 (new series).* Amsterdam: Elsevier.

Velasco, M. E., & Taleisnik, S., 1969. Release of gonadotropins induced by amygdaloid stimulation in the rat. *Endocrinolgy, 84,* 132.

Velluti, R., & Hernández-Peón R., 1963. Atropine blockade within a cholinergic hypnogenic circuit. *Experimental Neurology, 8,* 20.

Vergnes, M., & Karli, P., 1965. Etude des voies nerveuses d'une influence inhibitrice s'exercant sur l'agressivité interspécifique du Rat. *Comptes Rendues des Séances de la Société de Biologie, 159,* 972.

Victor, M., Adams, R. D., & Collins, G. H., 1971. The Wernicke-Korsakoff Syndrome. Philadelphia: F. A. Davis.

Vilkki, J., 1978. Effects of thalamic lesions on complex perception and memory. *Neuropsychologia, 16,* 427–437.

Vinogradova, O. S., 1975. Functional organization of the limbic system in the process of registration of information: Facts and hypotheses. In R. L. Isaacson & K. H. Pribram (Eds.), *The hippocampus, Vol. 2.* New York: Plenum Press.

Vivaldi, E., McCarley, R. W., & Hobson, J. A., 1980. Evocation of desynchronized sleep signs by chemical microstimulation of the pontine brain stem. In J. A. Hobson & M. A. B. Brazier (Eds.), *The reticular system revisited.* New York: Raven Press.

Vogt, O., 1951. Die anatomische Vertiefung der menschlichen Hirnlocalisation. *Klinische Wochenschrift, 29,* 7–8.

Voneida, T. J., & Royce, G. J., 1974. Ipsilateral connections of the gyrus proreus in the cat. *Brain Research, 76,* 393–400.

Voss, J. F., 1971. Are reinforcement concepts able to provide reinforcement for theorizing in human learning? In R. Glaser (Ed.), *The nature of reinforcement.* New York: Academic Press.

Wålinder, J., 1976. Monoamines and psyche. *Acta Physiologica Scandinavica, Supplement 440,* Abstract 39.

Wålinder, J., Skott, A., & Carlsson, A., 1976. Potentiation of the antidepressant action of clomipramine by tryptophan. *Archives of General Psychiatry, 33,* 1384–1389.

Walter, W. G., 1973. Human frontal lobe function in sensory-motor association. In K. H. Pribram & A. R. Luria (Eds.), *Psychophysiology of the frontal lobes.* New York, Academic Press.

Wang, G. H., & Lu, T. W., 1930. Galvanic skin reflex induced in the cat by stimulation of the motor area of the cerebral cortex. *Chinese Journal of Physiology, 4,* 303–326.

Warburton, D. M., 1972. The cholinergic control of internal inhibition. In R. Boakes & M. S. Halliday (Eds.), *Inhibition and learning.* London: Academic Press.

Ward, A. A., Jr., 1947. Decerebrate rigidity. *Journal of Neurophysiology, 10,* 89–103.

Ward, A. A. Jr., 1948. The anterior cingular gyrus and personality. *Research Publications of the Association for Research in Nervous and Mental Disease, 27,* 438–445.

Ward, J. W., 1952. Motor phenomena elicited in the unanesthetized animal by electrical stimulation of the cerebral cortex. *Research Publications of the Association for Research in Nervous and Mental Disease, 30,* 223–237.

Warrington, E. K., & Shallice, T., 1972. Neuropsychological evidence of visual storage in short-term memory tasks. *Quarterly Journal of Experimental Psychology, 24,* 30–40.

Warrington, E. K., & Weiskrantz, L., 1973. An analysis of short-term and long-term memory defects in man. In: J. A. Deutsch (Ed.), *The physiological basis of memory*. New York: Academic Press.

Watkins, M. J., & Tulving, E. 1975. Episodic memory: When recognition fails. *Journal of Experimental Psychology: General, 1*, 5–29.

Webster, D. B., & Voneida, T. J., 1964. Learning deficits following hippocampal lesions in split-brain cats. *Experimental Neurology, 10*, 170–182.

Wegner, J. G., 1968. The effect of cortical lesions on auditory and visual discrimination behavior in monkeys. *Cortex, 4*, 203–232.

Weinland, J. W., 1957. *How to improve your memory*. New York: Barnes and Noble.

Weiskrantz, L., 1978. A comparison of hippocampal pathology in man and other animals. In *Ciba Foundation Symposium 58, Function of the septo-hippocampal system*. Amsterdam: Elsevier.

Weiskrantz, L., & Mishkin, M., 1958. Effects of temporal and frontal cortical lesions on auditory discrimination in monkey. *Brain, 81*, 406–414.

Weiskrantz, L., & Warrington, E. K., 1975. The problem of the amnesic syndrome in man and animals. In R. L. Isaacson & K. H. Pribram, *The hippocampus, Vol. 2*. New York: Plenum Press.

Wepsic, J. G., & Austin, G. M., 1972. The neurophysiological effects of amphetamine upon the cat amygdala. In B. E. Eleftheriou (Ed.), *The neurobiology of the amygdala*. New York: Plenum Press.

Wernicke, C., 1874. Der aphasische Symptomenkomplex. Eine psychologische Studie auf anatomischer Basis. Breslau: Cohn & Weigert.

Wetzel, A. B., 1969. Visual cortical lesions in the cat: A study of depth and pattern discrimination. *Journal of Comparative and Physiological Psychology, 68*, 580–588.

White, L. E., Jr., 1959. Ipsilateral afferents to the hippocampal formation in the rat.I. Cingulum projections. *Journal of Comparative Neurology, 113*, 1–41.

Wickelgren, W. A., 1970. Multitrace strength theory. In D. A. Norman (Ed.), *Models of human memory*. New York: Academic Press.

Wickelgren, W. A., & Norman, D. A., 1966. Strength models and serial position in short-term recognition memory. *Journal of Mathematical Psychology, 3*, 316–347.

Wickelgren, W. O., and Isaacson, R. L., 1963. Effect of the introduction of an irrelevant stimulus in runway performance of the hippocampectomized rat. *Nature, 200*, 48–50.

Wiener, N., 1961. *Cybernetics*. Second edition. Cambridge, Mass.: MIT Press.

Wiesendanger, M., Rüegg, D. G., & Wiesendanger, R., 1979. The corticopontine system in primates: Anatomical and functional considerations. In J. Massion & K. Sasaki (Eds.), *Cerebro-cerebellar interactions*. Amsterdam: Elsevier/North-Holland Biomedical Press.

Williams, M., & Pennybacker, J., 1954. Memory disturbances in third ventricle tumors. *Journal of Neurology, Neurosurgery and Psychiatry, 17*, 115–123.

Wilson, J. R., Mitchell, J. C., & Van Hoesen, G. W., 1972. Epithalamic and ventral tegmental contributions to avoidance behavior in rats. *Journal of Comparative and Physiological Psychology, 78*, 442–449·

Wilson, W. A. Jr., 1962. Alternation in normal and frontal monkeys as a function of response and outcome of the previous trial. *Journal of Comparative and Physiological Psychology, 55*, 701–704.

Wilson, W. A. Jr., Oscar, M., & Gleitman, H., 1963. The effect of frontal lesions in monkeys upon widely spaced delayed-response trials. *Journal of Comparative and Physiological Psychology, 56*, 237–240.

Wilsoncroft, W. A., 1963. Effects of medial cortex lesions on the maternal behavior of the rat. *Psychological Reports, 13*, 835–838.

Winans, S. S., & Scalia, F., 1970. Amygdaloid nucleus: New afferent input from the vomeronasal organ. *Science, 170*, 330–332.

Winocur, G., & Mills, J. A., 1969a. Effects of caudate lesions on avoidance behavior in rats. *Journal of Comparative and Physiological Psychology, 68,* 551–557.

Winocur, G., & Mills, J. A., 1969b. Hippocampus and septum in response inhibition. *Journal of Comparative and Physiological Psychology, 67,* 352–357.

Winson, J., 1975. The θ–mode of hippocampal function. In R. L. Isaacson & K. H. Pribram (Eds.), *The hippocampus, Vol. 2.* New York: Plenum Press.

Wise, C. D., & Stein, L., 1973. Dopamine-beta-hydroxylase deficits in the brains of schizophrenic patients. *Science, 181,* 344–347.

Wiseman, G., & Neisser, U., 1971. *Perceptual organization as a determinant of visual recognition memory.* Paper given at the Eastern Psychological Association Meeting, Spring 1971.

Wold, J. E., & Brodal, A., 1974. The cortical projection of the orbital and proreate gyri to the sensory trigeminal nuclei in the cat. An experimental anatomical study. *Brain Research, 65,* 381–395.

Wolstencroft, J. H., West, D. C., & Gent, J. P., 1978. Actions of morphine and opioid peptides on neurones in the reticular formation, raphé nuclei and the periaqueductal gray. In R. W. Ryall & J. S. Kelly (Eds.), *Iontophoresis and transmitter mechanisms in the mammalian central nervous system.* Amsterdam: Elsevier.

Woolsey, C. N., 1961. Organization of cortical auditory system. In W. A. Rosenblith (Ed.), *Sensory communication.* Cambridge, Mass.: MIT Press.

Wright, A. K., Arbuthnot, G. W., Tulloch, I. F., Garcia-Munoz, M., & Nicolaou, N. M., 1977. Are the striatonigral fibres the feedback pathway? In A. R. Cools, A. H. M. Lohman, & J. H. L. Van den Bercken (Eds.), *Psychobiology of the striatum.* Amsterdam: North-Holland Publishing Co.

Wyers, E. J., Peeke, H. V. S., Williston, J. S., & Herz, M. J., 1968. Retroactive impairment of passive avoidance learning by stimulation of the caudate nucleus. *Experimental Neurology, 22,* 350–366.

Wyss, O. A. M., & Obrador, A. S., 1937. Adequate shape and rate of stimuli in electrical stimulation of cerebral motor cortex. *American Journal of Physiology, 120,* 42–51.

Yakovlev, P. I., 1975. Discussion after: O. L. Zangwill, Excision of Broca's area without persistent aphasia. In: K. J. Zülch, O. Creutzfeldt, & G. C. Galbraith (Eds.), *Cerebral localization.* New York: Springer-Verlag.

Yakovlev, P. I., Hamlin, H., & Sweet, W. H., 1950. Frontal lobotomy: Neuroanatomical observations. *Journal of Neuropathology and Experimental Neurology, 9,* 250–285.

Yakovlev, P. I., & Locke, S., 1961. Limbic nuclei of thalamus and connections of limbic cortex. III. Corticocortical connections of the anterior cingulate gyrus, the cingulum, and the subcallosal bundle in monkey. *Archives of Neurology, 5,* 364–400.

Yakovlev, P. I., Locke, S., & Angevine, J. B. Jr., 1966. The limbus of the cerebral hemisphere, limbic nuclei of the thalamus and the cingulum bundle. In D. P. Purpura & M. D. Yahr (Eds.), *The thalamus.* New York: Columbia University Press.

Yakovlev, P. I., Locke, S., Koskoff, D. Y., & Patton, R. A., 1960. Limbic nuclei of thalamus and connections of limbic cortex. *Archives of Neurology, 3,* 620–641.

Yarita, H., & Takagi, S. F., 1978. An olfactory pathway to the orbitofrontal cortex through the thalamus. *Proceedings of the Japan Academy,* Series B, 54, 30–34.

Yntema, D. B., & Trask, F. P., 1963. Recall as a search process. *Journal of Verbal Learning and Verbal Behavior, 2,* 65–74.

Yunger, L. M., & Harvey, J. A., 1973. Effect of lesions in the medial forebrain bundle on three measures of pain sensitivity and noise-elicited startle. *Journal of Comparative and Physiological Psychology, 83,* 173–183.

Yuwiler, A., 1978. Discussion. In E. Usdin & A. J. Mandell (Eds.), *Biochemistry of mental disorders.* New York: Dekker.

Zangwill, O. L., 1975. Excision of Broca's area without persistent aphasia. In K. J. Zülch, O. Creutzfeldt, & G. C. Galbraith (Eds.), *Cerebral localization.* New York: Springer-Verlag.

Zbrozyna, A. W., 1972. The organization of the defense reaction elicited from amygdala and its connections. In B. E. Eleftheriou (Ed.), *The neurobiology of the amygdala.* New York: Plenum Press.

Zeigler, H. P., & Karten, H. J., 1975. Comment to Striker et al.: Trigeminal lemniscal lesions and the lateral hypothalamic syndrome. *Science, 190,* 695–696.

Zeman, W., & Innes, J., 1963. Craigie's *neuroanatomy of the rat.* New York: Academic Press.

Zis, A. P., Fibiger, H. C., & Phillips, A. G., 1974. Reversal by L-DOPA of impaired learning due to destruction of the dopaminergic nigro-neostriatal projection. *Science, 185,* 960–962.

Zornetzer, S. F., Gold, M. S., & Boast, C. A., 1977. Neuroanatomic localization and the neurobiology of sleep and memory. In R. R. Drucker-Colin & J. L. McGaugh (Eds.), *Neurobiology of sleep and* memory. New York: Academic Press.

Zucker, I., 1965. Effect of lesions of the septal-limbic area on the behavior of cats. *Journal of Comparative and Physiological Psychology, 60,* 344–352.

Zucker, I., & McCleary, R. A., 1964. Perseveration in septal cats. *Psychonomic Science, 1,* 387–388.

Author Index

Numbers in *italics* denote pages with complete bibliographic information.

Subject Index